# THE FARHUD

# The Books of Edwin Black

www.edwinblack.com

**Financing the Flames**
*How Tax-Exempt and Public Money
Fuel a Culture of Confrontation
and Terrorism in Israel*
www.financingtheflames.com
2013

**British Petroleum and the
Redline Agreement**
*The West's Secret Pact to Get
Mideast Oil*
www.redlineagreement.com
2011

**The Farhud**
*Roots of the Arab-Nazi Alliance in
the Holocaust*
www.farhudbook.com
2010

**Nazi Nexus**
*America's Corporate Connections
To Hitler's Holocaust*
www.nazinexus.com
2009

**The Plan**
*How to Rescue Society When
the Oil Stops*
www.planforoilcrisis.com
2008

**Internal Combustion**
*How Corporations and
Governments Addicted the World to
Oil and Derailed the Alternatives*
www.internalcombustionbook.com
2006

**Banking on Baghdad**
*Inside Iraq's 7,000 Year History of
War, Profit, and Conflict*
www.bankingonbaghdad.com
2004

**War Against the Weak**
*Eugenics and America's Campaign
to Create a Master Race*
www.waragainsttheweak.com
2003 and 2012

**IBM and the Holocaust**
*The Strategic Alliance Between
Nazi Germany and America's Most
Powerful Corporation*
www.ibmandtheholocaust.com
2001 and 2012

**The Transfer Agreement**
*The Dramatic Story of the Pact
Between the Third Reich
and Jewish Palestine*
www.transferagreement.com.
1984, 2001, and 2009

**Format C:**
*A Novel*
www.formatnovel.com
1999

# THE FARHUD

## Roots of the
## Arab-Nazi Alliance
## in the Holocaust

\* \* \* \*

## Edwin Black

Dialog Press

WASHINGTON, DC

*To All Those Who Will Use a Legacy of Hate*
*to Create a Future of Peace*

This book is printed on acid-free paper.

ISBN 978-0914153146

Printed in the United States of America

14 13 12 11 10    5 4 3 2 1

Cover designed by Tallgrass Studio

Modern book text is produced using a variety of collaborative software, including spell-checkers and text revision tools. It is possible for such software to create typographical errors or other textual changes beyond the control of the author, editors, or publisher. Any changes, corrections, or additions to this book should be reported to, and/or can be found at http://www.farhudbook.com. \ Web site addresses (URLs) were accurate as of press time. Neither the author nor the publisher is responsible for URLs that have expired or moved since the manuscript was prepared.

# CONTENTS

# ACKNOWLEDGMENTS

Some of my researchers may be among the most skilled, informed, and experienced anywhere in the world. I have worked with many of them for years through several book projects. Their job is to argumentatively split hairs, cross-examine every fragment of every detail, and create the physical, printed documentary record that will ultimately reside in thousands of physical footnote folders in my office for instant access at a later time. This involved a team of people retracing my academic, intellectual, and journalistic steps to re-create that knowledge base in thousands of endnote entries.

Chief among my researchers is team leader Eve Jones in New York, probably one of the most intellectually-driven people on the planet. I have been blessed to work with Eve on numerous books. In many cases, all the other fact-checkers passed their information up the chain of command to her before it came to me. Her impeccably high standards gleam on every page. In London, Nick Charles, a man immersed in the undercurrents of the most complex historical questions, yielded enormous skill both in the archives of London and during electronic searches. He also led the international indexing team. Nick's fire to discover more never stops burning. Carol DiSalvo must be thanked for her enormous help in all aspects of the book and her efforts can be seen in every chapter.

Among the many others who labored long and hard was the passionate and devoted Martin Barillas in Michigan, the astute historical investigator Paul Dwyer in Virginia, and dedicated researcher Juda Engelmayer in New York. Kenneth Bobu in California gave us great German language skills and technical support. Our bibliography is in large measure the result of long labors by Annie Steinmetz in Arizona. Elizabeth Black in Kansas gave key editorial help at the vital moments. Marie Salerno was among a team that helped us manage manuscript formatting issues. These names are augmented by many more too numerous to mention, located in five countries.

We also received significant technical support—often at a moment's notice—from Benjamin Ratner in New York and our supremely talented German webmaster Uwe Junge who has labored so intensely to bring our work to the wider Internet world. Additional technological power came from Jon Watrous who hand-built the powerful state-of-the-art computer I used for the project. Alan Hall and Michael Feigenson of Washington, D.C. labored so hard to make sure my network of computers, our Toshiba scanner, and five high-speed printers were functioning.

Prior to publication, every chapter was reviewed and vetted in painstaking detail by a consortium of top historians and scholars. I do this on every project. Leading the list of reviewers is top Iraqi Jewry expert Shmuel Moreh in Israel, as well as the noted Iraqi Jewry authority Moshe Gat in Israel, plus Mideast and Holocaust scholar Samuel Edelman in California, and Haim Shaked and Mitchil Dabach in Miami. Other experts who assisted by either close consultation, manuscript review, or informational assists include Sir Martin Gilbert, Malcolm Hoenlein, Walid Phares, Lawrence Schiffman, Yitz Santis, Shelomo Alfassa, Stan Urman, and a long list of others.

Numerous archivists and librarians around the world graciously helped us every day. At the top of the list stands Gerhard Keiper of Auswärtiges Amt Archiv in Berlin, who I have worked with on earlier projects. Many years ago, getting a document from his archive required an airplane ticket to Germany, days of research, and a one-week advance request to the in-house photocopy service. Today, these requests can be searched, and transmitted as PDFs in a matter of moments via email. I also thank the eminent Robert Wolfe, former chief of Nazi documentation for the National Archives in Washington, D.C. for his time, effort, and guidance. Wolfe knows where the Nazi documents are and, in many cases, personally processed them. From time to time, I spoke to other esteemed scholars about their work, and among them were Norman Stillman and Wolfgang Schwanitz—two of the best and brightest.

Heading the library list is New York Public Library's General Research Division, and NYPL's Dorot Jewish Division, in particular, Anne Marie Belinfante and Eleanor Yadin, both of whom helped enormously. Special praise is also tendered to the Coventry, England-based staff of the corporate archives of British Petroleum, Turkish Petroleum and other oil companies, especially Peter Housego, who worked tirelessly, energetically, and graciously to provide me with thousands of pages of corporate history.

Also assisting with high-velocity support in finding and transmitting obscure materials: the Asher Library of Spertus Jewish Institute in Chicago, the Klau Library of Hebrew Union College and the American Jewish Archives library in Cincinnati, the Leo Baeck Institute library in New York, the Ostrow Library of American Jewish University in Los Angeles, Monterey Institute of International Studies in Monterey, the Montgomery County Libraries in suburban Washington, D.C. which expedited inter-library loan requests, and many other fine institutions. Sadly, the collegiate library closest to my home,

Montgomery College Library, found itself too disorganized and embattled with its own fractured management processes to assist, even though its dedicated staff wanted to.

Towering above all the libraries and librarians that assisted is the Alvin Sherman Library of Nova Southeastern University in Ft. Lauderdale which provided remote access to its indispensible database gateways. These precious resources were utilized almost every hour of every day by me or someone on my team. The Alvin Sherman Library has long exemplified the best traditions of a university library, gladly opening its impressive resources to those in its immediate community and to leading recognized scholars. This book, in its present form, simply would not have been possible without the university's assistance. Therefore, thanks are also in order for longtime friends NSU president Ray Ferrero, as well as executive director of university relations David Dawson, chief librarian Lydia Acosta, Circle of Friends President Anita Paoli, librarian Elaine Blatner and many more at that exemplar institution and its library.

Regretfully, the only institution in the world that refused to assist, and actually obstructed my work, was the United States Holocaust Memorial Museum which has been under fire for years by a diverse coalition of Jewish groups, congressmen, communal leaders, Holocaust survivors, children of Holocaust survivors, historians, academics, and even devoted museum supporters due to the institution's resistance to include information about the Farhud and the Mufti of Jerusalem. Because of this, the Sephardic Leadership Council launched a formal written complaint against the Museum's historian, Peter Black. New York Rep. Eliot Engel was among a number of speakers who came to a Washington, D.C. synagogue to protest the Museum's continued silence on the topic. When, in 2005, I and a coalition of scholars and Jewish groups first proposed that the Farhud be recognized, USHMM refused to cooperate and actually sent emails encouraging other Holocaust museums and institutions to do the same. An internal USHMM investigation obligated numerous staffers to delete emails they had expropriated in an effort to undermine the Sephardic community's efforts to recognize its own tragedy. After years of community pressure, including more formal complaints, web protests, and community gatherings, the Museum has yielded and offered some token recognition of these topics, although in many ways inaccurate. At press time, the USHMM continues to obscure the real role of the Mufti. More than that, during the research for this book, Museum spokesman Andrew Hollinger, specifically and in writing, blocked my request to ask a single question of its Yugoslavia expert, Emil Kerenji. I encouraged Kerenji to disobey Hollinger. But at press time, Kerenji has not done that. Kerenji answers to history not Hollinger. That said, slow progress is being made at the USHMM as it adds token content on these topics. USHMM is a precious resource for what it does well. Perhaps the documentation in this book will help them acknowledge further that, of the millions of Jews murdered in the Holocaust, the ones who lived in Arab countries should not be forgotten. History must never be political, even in a political city.

My production team deserves special honors. Here I mean the supremely skilled Richard Farkas, our cover design team of Carey Treanor and Nancy Percich, plus Carol Cardello and Christine Sanders. Similarly, this book is available worldwide solely because of the confidence and support shown by the publishing team at NBN, including Jeff Harris and also Jed Lyons, Jeanne Kramer, Spencer Gale, my agent Lynne Rabinoff, and many others who waited patiently despite delay after delay as *The Farhud* tripled in size and telescoped in content.

Likewise, I salute my post-publication legal team, now in place worldwide, to ensure that the book's contents are not misused or misquoted. This book has been created to promote understanding, not confuse it.

Creative inspiration was continually derived from the soundtracks of Hans Zimmer, Danny Elfman, James Newton Howard, John Powell, James Horner, and BT. I drew strength from key cues in *Inception*, *Tears of the Sun*, *Avatar*, *King Arthur*, and *The Green Zone*, among many that others that played loudly every day as I transduced the madness of the Holocaust into a cohesive and dramatic saga. I also salute the music of the best singer I know—my daughter, Rachel Black. I was fortified by her songs, especially *Always* and her rendition of Kol Nidre.

I complete my Acknowledgements by thanking the most important members of the project—the readers, who I hope will work hard to ensure that the dark times of prior decades do not revisit us in the future. The furnace of history always burns, and will incinerate us once again unless we use our knowledge to firmly shut the door, and keep it latched.

FOREWORD

# APPROACHING
# THE FARHUD

## by Sir Martin Gilbert

**E**dwin Black has given us, once again, copious documentation, impressive
detective work, and a hard-hitting narrative. In these pages, the life and
fate of the age-old Jewish community of Iraq comes under his eagle eye.
Its climax, the Farhud of 1941, is a moment of tragedy following many years
of achievement; a moment of savage violence that foreshadowed the end of a
vibrant 2,600-year-old Jewish community.

Britain had its part to play in this story. British rule after 1918 was often
far from benign. A senior British Royal Air Force officer resigned in disgust
after seeing the mangled bodies of Iraqi civilians killed by British bombs. In
1920 the *London Sunday Times* published a letter from T.E. Lawrence ("Lawrence of Arabia") calling the British administration "more bloody and inefficient than the public knows. It is a disgrace to our imperial record, and may soon
be too inflamed for any ordinary cure. We are today not far from a disaster."
Churchill agreed, warning his colleagues in the British cabinet: "There is something very sinister to my mind in this Mesopotamian entanglement … It seems
to me so gratuitous that after all the struggles of the war, just when we want to
get together our slender military resources and reestablish our finances and have
a little on hand in case of danger here or there, we should be compelled to go on
pouring armies and treasure into these thankless deserts."

Iraq became independent in 1932. Nazi intrigue followed within a year. The Christian-owned daily newspaper *al-Alam al-Arabi* (*The Arab World*) published daily extracts from the Arabic edition of *Mein Kampf*, with its virulent anti-Jewish propaganda. Deleted from this edition was Hitler's "racial ladder," in which the Arabs came almost as low down as the Jews.

In 1935, as German influence grew, a pro-Nazi society, *al-Muthanna*, was established in Baghdad, with branches in Basra and Mosul, headed by a well-known enemy of the Jews, Dr. Saib Shawkat, director of the Royal Hospital in Baghdad, whose brother Sami Shawkat, a fellow-physician, founded the *al-Futuwwa* ("Chivalry") youth brigades, which disseminated anti-British and anti-Jewish leaflets.

The Iraqi government, encouraged by Hitler's emissary Fritz Grobba, closed its borders to Jewish refugees. Between 1933 and 1935, only six German Jewish doctors were granted admission. Hitler's malign influence had penetrated to the heart of a proud Muslim land in which Jews had made substantial contributions to its administration and well-being, remarkably so between 1920 and 1939 in health, education and good governance.

A central and malign figure in Edwin Black's masterful narrative is the Mufti of Jerusalem, Haj Amin al-Husseini, who, having escaped in 1936 from Palestine where he was wanted by the British for murder—as the fomenter of Arab riots that had resulted in many British and Jewish deaths—arrived in Iraq and took up residence in Baghdad. There he spread anti-British as well as anti-Jewish animus. In February 1941, the Mufti wrote to Hitler (the two men are pictured together on the cover of this book), seeking "recognition of the right of the Arabs to solve the Jewish question in accordance with Arab nationalist aspirations and in the same manner as in the Axis countries."

Then came the Farhud, and after it, the steady elimination of Jewish influence in Iraq, and mass emigration. No one is better qualified than Edwin Black, or more determined than he, to tell this story with precision.

*Sir Martin Gilbert*
*October 3, 2010*
*London*

*SIR MARTIN GILBERT is the author of 82 books, including his latest* In Ishmael's House: A History of Jews in Muslim Lands. *He is Winston Churchill's official biographer and a leading historian of the modern world. In 2009, he served as a member of the British Government's Iraq War Inquiry. Find him at http://www.martingilbert.com*

# INTRODUCTION

This book is a nightmare. I regret anyone must read it. I regret it was necessary to write. I regret that I was the one who had to write it. I hope it never becomes necessary to write another like this one. Perhaps that is why I labored ten hours per day for more than a year to document the Farhud and the roots of the Arab-Nazi alliance in the Holocaust—that is, the truth about what happened and why.

Readers will see the word *Farhud*—the violent dispossession of the Jews of Baghdad—writ large upon the cover of this book. Yet, this work is about much more than one pogrom—a senseless orgy of violence on June 1–2, 1941, when Arab-Nazis murdered, raped, and pillaged the Jewish community who had dwelled there for 2,600 years. The *Farhud* is but a symbol of a vastly larger story that unfolds in this book. On the cover, readers will see the famous, iconic picture of the Grand Mufti of Jerusalem talking to Hitler. But the Mufti is merely the glittering tip of the curved sword. The saga within these pages is not about a Mufti, nor any one man, as much as a repetitive mass movement for mass murder, erupting decade after decade, until it became volcanic during the Holocaust. As you will see, the principal figures explain why and how this was done—in their own words.

Excavating hidden Holocaust histories is in my DNA, being the son of Polish Holocaust survivors. My mother escaped from a train, my father from a shooting squad. *Why* became the imprinted fire of my existence.

In my first book, *The Transfer Agreement*, I chronicled the dramatic and seemingly impossible Zionist entanglements with the Third Reich during the painful negotiations to achieve the release of Jews and their property from Germany into Palestine. Then, in *IBM and the Holocaust*, I exposed the sordid story of IBM's conscious co-planning with the Hitler regime of all six phases of the Holocaust; that is, identification, exclusion, confiscation, ghettoization, deportation, and physical extermination—all because "business" was the company's middle name. Then, in *War Against the Weak*, I uncovered the extraordinary history of the American eugenics movement, its early twentieth century quest for a master race—decades before the Hitler regime, and how the Carnegie Institution and the Rockefeller Foundation spent millions in philanthropic donations to transfer their racist platform into Nazi Germany— even to the point of funding the program that ultimately sent Mengele into Auschwitz.

It was in my third book, *Banking on Baghdad*, in 2005, futilely hoping to move into another realm of research, oil and the history of Iraq, that I first encountered the details of the Farhud riot and the impact of oil on the lives of the Jews and Arabs of the Middle East. My fourth book, *Internal Combustion*, on the history of fuel and energy, once again brought me to this same precipice as I discovered the odious intersection of General Motors and its mass production of trucks, tanks, bombers, and other weaponry for the Nazi military machine. Without that sudden motorization, the world might well have seen a profoundly less mobile Holocaust, and one that did not hinge on petroleum. Those issues were recurring themes in my fifth volume, *The Plan*, and my sixth book, *Nazi Nexus*—which tied it all together in a single, dark fabric.

For me, the voyage of history has always been one of circumnavigation. No matter how far I travel, I end up where I started.

Hence, I was more than prepared to tie together the last great thread of my mission—the role of the Arabs and Islam in the extermination of more than six million Jews and other "ethnic enemies"—during the Holocaust. I first began researching and writing about the Mufti of Jerusalem in the late 1970s on *The Transfer Agreement*. To me, the Mufti was nothing more than a hatemonger, an inexplicably aberrant Arab leader aligned with the Third Reich. But how could this happen and why did it happen? Discovering the tragedy of the Farhud led me to also ask how it was possible that a large community of Jews, which had dwelled in Iraq for 2,600 years, a millennium before the advent of Islam, could become alien in their own land and the object of planned extermination in their cities.

That required a personal voyage, one the reader will share. It was not enough to document the blood and blades of the two-day *Farhud* pogrom. That would have been too easy.

The real questions were these. Who were the Jews? That took me all the way to that ancient Mesopotamian, Abraham, and then to the Romans in Jerusalem two thousand years ago. Who were the Muslims? That took me back to Muhammad in seventh century Arabia. Who indeed were the people of Iraq or Mesopotamia? That took me back to the beginning of recorded time, some 5,000 years ago, when the so-called "cradle of civilization" first began to tremble. How did the West, from Great Britain to Germany, come to be so involved in Iraq? That last question took me into the hidden annals of the 160-year history of commercial oil, its discovery, the lust for its black magic, and the fact that Iraq had it—and the West wanted it. What orogenous factors of history brought these tectonic forces together? Only by illuminating the dark and often inaccessible crevices of all these stories can we understand the vast, international Arab-Nazi alliance during the Holocaust, the many tens of thousands of ordinary Arabs and Muslims, prompted by audacious leaders, who crusaded against their Jewish cousins.

When we speak of German Jew-hatred resulting in the Holocaust, we can never mean all Germans, a corrupt idea. Today, Mercedes-Benz is among the vehicles of choice in Israel; Germany sells the Jewish State her submarines. German volunteers have always been the mainstay of my projects. When we speak of the Turks mass-murdering the Armenians, it would be corrupt to generalize to include all Turks, as many refused to participate and have their own noble culture of peace with their neighbors. When we speak of the extermination of the Native Americans by the white man in America, or the slavery inflicted against Africans, those despicable stories are defined as much for their racist transgression as by the many European Americans who fought against those horrors, often giving their lives to undo these crimes.

While this volume chronicles in great detail the horrible acts of Muslims against Jews, going back centuries, that bear a direct impact on the Holocaust, using the precise Holocaust-era and post-World War I words of the original actors, no monolithic generalization against Muslims or Arabs can be made. That, too, would be a corruption of my work. In this volume, you will learn that when Catholic Spain expelled the Jews during the Inquisition, it was the Muslim world that took them in for the sole purpose of sponsoring their thriving existence. Readers will learn sadly that going back more than a century, there never was a day of peace between the Arabs and the Jews in Palestine. Make no mistake—Palestine functioned as the inextricable fulcrum between Iraq and Nazi Germany. Yet, history records that at all times, many Arabs in Palestine tried to stand tall for peace with their Jewish neighbors, risking extreme political and communal consequences. You will learn the names of those Arabs in Palestine who tried and lost the quest for peace. You will discover that in the darkest hour for Jews in the Muslim world suffering in the Holocaust, many Jews are alive today in many countries for only one reason: their Muslim neighbors refused to allow them to perish and gave them a hand to safety when Jewish victims barely had the strength to take it.

In all of my books, I have established an explicit contract with my readers based on the complete storyline that unfolds. That contract holds as follows. If you cannot read the entire book without skipping around, do not buy it. Close the cover, and walk away. That injunction holds supremely true for this volume. I do not seek partial readers. Partial understanding is why this book, *The Farhud*, was necessary. That said, when one tackles a topic of such enormity, going back to the beginning of recorded time, sweeping across millennia, continents, a world raging in war, and corporations contending to prosper in the process, the writer must omit 99.9 percent of everything. Indeed, every chapter is a mere invitation to read a bookshelf of other excellent works about the subject of that chapter.

Another caution is required. *The Farhud: Roots of the Arab-Nazi Alliance in the Holocaust* is a story of the twentieth-century—decades ago. It is being published in the twenty-first century in an era of polemics, politicization, and polarization on the core issues of the history. This book and this author will not participate. Do not use this book to contrive a feeling against any of our neighbors, as the pendulum of bigotry is a perpetual motion machine that finds all who approach it. Do not fear history, as facing it is the only means by which we can emerge from the dark past, switch on the lights of our future path, and achieve equality and peace between peoples. Only by facing the stark realities of yesterday can we hope to create an honest tomorrow of harmony. This has been the experience worldwide where peoples have emerged from conflict.

I want this Holocaust history to prove any point other than the one I made the week before this book was published, when I lectured on the topic to an auditorium of high school students in North Carolina. After the presentation, I went to each table and reminded them: use a legacy of hate to create a future of peace. Can it be done? Yes, it has been done and can yet be done again in the Middle East. I keep hearing the song Holocaust survivors sang as they sailed from the charnel house of Europe to Israel. The song is named "Hatikva." It became the national anthem of the Jewish people and the State of Israel. In Hebrew, *hatikva* means "hope."

*Edwin Black*
*October 23, 2010*
*Washington, D.C.*

# PART ONE

# BEFORE HITLER

CHAPTER

1

# BAGHDAD BURNING

A s thick swirls of black smoke wafted across the Baghdad sky, as orange tongues of flames leapt through stone-framed doors and windows, as the stinging smell of torched Jewish households and shops filled the air, the irrepressible screams continued. Cheers and jeers from the rioting Arab crowds competed with cries of horror and anguish as family after family were pulled from their vehicles or chased down the street. The Jews of Baghdad were captured by the nightmare that raced through the city that June 1 and 2, 1941. It was bloody. It was beastly.

Infants were viciously bashed to death against the pavement and then thrown lifeless into the Tigris. Jewish women—hundreds of them—were mercilessly and openly raped in front of their husbands, in front of their parents, in front of their children, and in front of the wild Muslim mobs. If the woman was pregnant, sometimes she was first raped, and then sliced open to destroy the unborn baby; only then was she killed. Men who defended their women and children were killed and their homes plundered. Commonly, after murdering the defenseless Jewish men and women with hatchets, axes, and swords, the chanting throngs hacked their inanimate bodies to pieces, thus further defiling the infidels and—temporarily—sating the mob's blood lust.

Rooftops became escape routes. Not a few children escaped when their parents threw them off rooftops into waiting arms and outstretched blankets in the backyards. Older children were told to jump from rooftop to rooftop. Often their escape was just moments before howling invaders squeezed past barricaded entrances and raced up the stairs to commit mayhem. Some Jews escaped with their battered and shattered lives only because the murderous mobs were distracted by the frantic race to loot the invaded homes and shops before the next man could.

Baghdad was a burning madhouse. It burned not just with ethnic hatred but with cries to murder and destroy the Jewish community who had lived peaceably in the country for 2,600 years, since a millennium before the advent of Islam. The rampage would be forever seared upon the collective Iraqi Jewish consciousness as the Farhud. In Arabized Kurdish, *farhud* means something beyond mere chaos, something more than just a riot. Perhaps farhud is best translated as "violent dispossession." Some translate it as "mass rape and killing."

But the events of June 1 and 2, 1941 were not just the sudden frenzied carnage of local Arab hooligans against their neighbors. This was a well-planned Holocaust-era pogrom, organized by Arab Nazis in sympathy with, and under the direction of the Third Reich's surrogates in Iraq, the Arab and Islamic world, as the ignition switch for an international Arab-Nazi alliance. This alliance, embraced by many ordinary Arabs, was led by Hajj Muhammad Amin al-Husseini, the Mufti of Jerusalem. The Mufti was acknowledged by Hitler himself as Berlin's most important leader in the Arab nation. The Mufti, in coordination with his handlers in Germany, worked passionately to inflame Arabs across the Middle East into a broad wartime axis with the Reich. This axis fervently hoped to help the Nazis and fascism conquer Europe, defeat Britain, and mass-murder every living Jew. The Arab national movement, in fact, became the hand of the Holocaust in the Islamic world as well as an integral member of Germany's hour-to-hour military machine both in Europe and the Middle East.

What was behind this unlikely coalition of racial enemies—Arab Semites and Aryan Nazis? What caused Arabs to actively join Hitler's war against humanity and his war against the Jews? What caused the Arabs to fight shoulder to shoulder with the Nazis on the battlefield and agitate for more death camps to mass murder Jews with greater efficiency? Was it mere ethnic, class, and religious hatred? That would be the easy answer—too easy.

In truth, the Arab-Nazi alliance was a complicated mixture of political ingredients that had been stewing for decades. Swirling in this soup were the changing Jewish demographic nature of Palestine during the Hitler regime, the yoke of British imperialism, and Berlin's changing strategy for world domination. But binding it all despite the incessant stirring was one precious substance. At the bottom of the pot was oil.

# 2,600 YEARS OF IRAQI JEWRY

Iraq has been integral to Judaism since the culture's earliest centuries. In about 2000 BCE, according to tradition, Abraham traveled to Canaan from the Sumerian port city of Ur on the Euphrates. Within a millennium, his Hebrew descendants had established themselves in Israel. Over a period of centuries, beginning in 722 BCE, Babylonian kings conquered the Israelites. Those taken into Babylonia included prophets, sages and the best artisans. First, 27,290 persons were taken in 722 BCE, according to the record. Later, beginning in 586 BCE, some 50,000 souls were abducted. These events constituted the longest exile in history. The saga of Jewish existence in Iraq would stretch across the centuries. But it would culminate in the 1941 massacre known as the *Farhud* and its aftermath.

The rise of Iraqi Jewish culture gained impetus in approximately 537 BCE after the Persian king, Cyrus the Great, ended the captivity of the Israelites in Babylon. What was then Babylon approximates the land known through much of history as Mesopotamia and today as Iraq. After emancipation, many liberated Israelites just stayed where they were and flourished, raising a great Jewish culture rich in learning and art. Babylonian Jewish institutions continued to prosper and became pivotal to Judaism worldwide, particularly after the Romans destroyed the Jewish Temple in 70 CE; and after razing Jerusalem in 135 CE, Caesar formally renamed Israel as *Syria Palestina.*[1]

Ancient Mesopotamia, that is "the land between the two rivers," territorially constituted the land that many centuries later would be renamed Iraq, so named for its ancient toponym. During the first centuries of the Common Era, Mesopotamia also maintained a substantial Christian character. As such, Judaism and Judeo-Christian derivatives flowered in Mesopotamia for hundreds of years before the advent of Islam in the seventh century.[2]

Islam's confrontation with Jews began in the early seventh century—but not in Iraq. Amid his efforts to establish his new religion after his flight from Mecca to Medina in 622, the prophet Mohammed found Jews settled throughout the Arabian Desert world that he would ultimately rule. Indeed, Jews had been well established in Arabia for centuries.

Following the destruction of the Second Temple and the Roman suppression of the Jewish revolt around 135 CE, the Jewish refugee presence in the Arabian Peninsula became more pronounced. During those first Common Era centuries, Jews occupied major niches in the Arabia-to-Syria caravan trade. They were among the most successful date growers and artisans. Jews comprised much of the merchant class in such Arabian towns as Mecca and Medina. In the fourth and fifth centuries, several rulers of the Yemenite Himyar kingdom converted to Judaism. The language of the Arabian Jews was a Hebraic Arab dialect, and more than a few Hebrew words migrated into common Arabic parlance. The ancient Arabian oasis, Yathrib, became a magnet for Jewish refugees from the Roman wars. Indeed, only later was Yathrib renamed al-Madinat—or Medina. Many etymologists trace this name from the original Aramaic word *medinta*, which is equivalent to the Hebrew word for "the district" or "jurisdiction" or "the state." Later, around the fifth century, two major Arab tribes, the Aws and the Khazrajs, migrated to the town, joining the Jews.[3]

No longer connected to their sacred Temple in Jerusalem, Jews took their monotheism with them wherever they traveled, including the by-ways and encampments of the dune-wrinkled Arabian Desert. The Jews not only observed their own faith, they promulgated their beliefs to the polytheist Arab pagans of the area. Mohammad himself first discovered his own sense of "one God" from the Jewish caravan figures he encountered as well as the highly established Jewish communities residing in cities, towns, and villages. He also came to know the Judeo-Christian sects and pure Christian communities that dwelled peaceably in the desert. These Judeo-Christians also exemplified a belief in "one God," the same "one God" worshipped by the Jews.[4]

In the year 610, within the cloistered confines of a mountain cave near his home in Mecca, Mohammad experienced his first divine revelation, this from the angel Gabriel, according to tradition. It was the monotheistic message imparted to many Holy Land prophets, from Noah to Moses to Jesus. But Mohammad's revelation was different. His was not in Aramaic or Hebrew and not aimed at the Jews and Christians who previously inhabited Israel.

Mohammad's revelation was in Arabic and aimed at the Arabs, that is, the fractious tribes that inhabited the Arabian Peninsula. Moreover, the almighty God of Mohammad's vision was not known as Jehovah or Yahweh. He was called Allah.[5]

Political undercurrents attached to the Jews who were associated with the Judaic centers of Babylonia and to the Christians who by this time were connected to Byzantium. But beyond the geopolitical subscript of their religion, the monotheists resembled their Arab neighbors and, as accomplished merchants, goldsmiths and sword makers, were prominent members of local society.[6]

At the time, the Arabs of the region were polytheistic pagans, many of whom worshipped idols. Many holy men preaching divine messages circulated among the Arabs of the day. But Mohammad would become the prevailing and reigning prophet, bringing the Arabs to the "one God," the same God revered by the Jews and Christians—those he called "the People of the Book." Mohammad's revelations would be the last from Allah, he declared, ruling there would be no other prophets after him.[7]

Sun-seared spiritualism swells swiftly, and soon Mohammad was preaching his new ideas to any who would listen—and, indeed, to many who would not.

The Jews were exclusionary. The Christians were inclusionary. But Mohammad's version of monotheism sprang forth as a religion of imperial conquest. Islam—surrender to the one God, under the precepts Mohammad enunciated, was the way. Indeed, Mohammad's way would be the only way permitted. At first, Mohammad made alliances with the Jews of Mecca. Muslim converts were instructed to pray facing Jerusalem. But Jewish communities and Christian sects quickly became Mohammad's chief adversaries as he sought to reinvent the "one God's teachings" into his new and uniquely Arab spiritualism, based not on tolerance, but destruction or subjugation of any who would not submit to Islam and Allah. Mohammad and his theism were rejected, mocked, and his followers oppressed. Jews and Christians, in Muslim eyes, became corrupters of God's word, they became the enemy, and Muslims were instructed to revise the direction of prayer from Jerusalem to Mecca.[8]

What was Islam? Islam, according to Mohammed, was eventually built on five pillars: faith in one God ("there is no God but Allah"); prayer five times daily; charity equaling 2.5 percent of one's income; pilgrimage to Mecca—the Hajj—at least once in a lifetime; and fasting.[9]

In his soon-to-be Holy City of Medina, Mohammad found about 20 Jewish clans, constituting three large, well-entrenched Jewish tribes, the Banu Qaynuqa, the Banu Nadir, and the Banu Qurayza. The Aws and the Khazraj were the two main Arab tribes who had settled there later. By Mohammad's day, these two late-arriving Arab tribes probably had grown into the city's majority. Like most desert tribes, they constantly warred and feuded with each other. Tribal alliances were the custom as well as a necessity in desert realms. The three neighboring Jewish tribes in Medina formed protective alliances with either of the two Arab sides. The Jewish clans even fought amongst themselves as they allied with the two Arab rivals. By now, Medina had become a collection of nearby forts as opposed to a compact city.[10]

Beginning in 622, when Mohammad arrived in Medina as a peacemaker invited by the warring factions, he began converting dozens of Arab pagans to his new monotheism. But the Jews of Medina, like the Jews of Mecca, a central target for conversion because of their inherent dominance in the area and preexisting belief in the one God, continued to completely refuse Mohammad's overtures. The Jews had fought the Romans for their Judaism, lost their Temple for their Judaism, and been expelled from their country for their Judaism. The mainstream Jews fiercely rejected the prophet Jesus and the tripartite deism of Christianity. There was no chance the Jews would convert to Islam *en masse,* and there was every chance they would fight to preserve their religion as it was, and as it had been for millennia.[11]

Mohammad was a great warrior who led eager bands of warring followers, many skilled horsemen. After conquering clans in his hometown of Mecca in 624, he turned his newfound strength toward Medina and its Jews. The first to fall was the Jewish artisan clan of the Banu Qaynuqa. They surrendered after only a brief siege and were allowed to leave for the north of the Peninsula with some of their possessions.[12]

The landed and wealthy Banu Nadir Jews were the next to fall. Haughty and even mocking Muhammad's Allah, unyielding in their refusal to submit to money demands, the Banu Nadir Jews falsely believed their former alliances with Arab neighbors would save them from the onslaught. It did not. Claiming the Jews were out to kill him, Mohammad waged war against them. This second Jewish clan was also expelled from Medina, and the spectacle of their departure was a sight for all. A procession of some 600 camels laden with possessions and finery left the city in a well-orchestrated defeat. The Jewish lands were seized and divided among Mohammad's believers.[13]

The Banu Qurayza Jews of Medina were the last holdouts. In 627, Mohammad turned on them. They surrendered after more than three weeks of siege. Certainly, Banu Qurayza Jews hoped for some sort of merciful exit, just as the two other Jewish clans had secured. But Mohammad gave no quarter. He assembled from 600 to 900 of them in Medina's marketplace. Group after group, one by one, Mohammad had them beheaded and their lifeless bodies thrown into great public trenches dug for the occasion, it is recorded. The Jewish women were taken as slaves.[14]

Finally, the leader of the Banu Qurayza Jews, Huyayy b. Akhtab, was brought out— not in a group but alone. His hands were bound around his neck. Huyayy b. Akhtab had torn his tunic to avoid it becoming spoils. He had already refused an offer to forsake the Torah and convert. In his last words, as one of "the People of the Book," he is reported to have declared to Mohammad, "By God, I do not blame myself for opposing you ... He who forsakes God will be forsaken. God has ordained a book, a decree ... and," he concluded, "slaughter for the Children of Israel." Then Huyayy b. Akhtab sat down. A moment later his head was sliced off.[15]

In 628, about ten years after their exile from Medina, the exiled Banu Nadir Jews were hunted down in the nearby oasis at Khaybar where they had settled. Knowing of Mohammad's victories against other Jewish clans, the Banu Nadir Jews, this time, organized to fight back from seemingly safe forts. They paid Bedouin soldiers and horsemen from other clans to help. All their efforts failed miserably. Eventually, most were killed or expelled, although some Banu Nadir were allowed to stay at Khaybar on condition that they pay half their annual wealth in tribute. Mohammad's dramatic victories over the Jews, including the mass murder of resisters, the seizure of their property and the forced tribute for those who survived, made Islam's prophet a feared force throughout Arabia. Quickly, other tribes volunteered to convert, submit to become an underclass, or pay tribute that is, a poll tax. Islam ruled the desert and Mohammad was the ruler of Islam.[16]

Unquestionably, mass beheadings, conquest and booty, the seizure of women as slaves, and exacting tribute were the common ways of the ancient world that saw the rise of Islam. From Persia to Rome and beyond in every direction, the custom of victorious armies everywhere was unbridled extermination, heinous torture, group decimation, local subjugation, religious vandalism, and expropriation. Pyramids piled high with corpses and pikes topped with decapitated heads, cities in grey-black smolder, highways lined with thousands of crucified men, women carted off wholesale in wagons or on the back of saddles, children kidnapped as custom, legions of slaves, and other gruesome acts of inhumanity—these were the awful inescapable realities of the ancient world of kingdoms and conquerors.[17]

But unspeakable violence was not the way of the evolved monotheists of the first Common Era centuries. Their teachings sought to achieve a moral ascent and equilibrium with others. Tolerance became a manifesto. For the Jews, that approximated a standoffish *live and let live* ethos while observing strict, worshipful adherence to the word of the one God. Christians sought to reform Judaism by opening the word of God up to all, regardless of diet, tradition, worship day, or ethnic origin—while embracing the concept of "turning the other cheek." Mohammad termed Jews and Christians "People of the Book," referring to their Holy Bibles.

The new Arab iteration of monotheism that created the Koran and related sacred writings adopted or perhaps re-adopted the brutal concept of conquest and domination that had thrived among those earlier ancient victors who worshipped warrior gods. Whereas Jewish and Christian religious order arose from a state of mind, Muslim religious order arose from a territorial state created wherever Muslims lived and ruled. Where Muslims were, their rules prevailed, *ipso facto*. Inner peace, devotion to God, and love and compassion were commandments and poetic aspirations for all Muslims. But those who declined to follow the new path to this new Islamic sanctity and surrender to Allah were not tolerated as equals—even if they believed in the same God. Rather, they were reviled as unclean and untouchable inferiors, held in a permanent caste of humiliation.

The Koran's 141 chapters, or *suras,* include some of passion and enlightenment toward Jews. But the Koran is also replete with derogatory references to the Jews. More than forty such references can be found. Translations of these *suras* differ significantly, as do commentaries by recognized Islamic sages. But in many verses, the quality of revulsion is clear.[18]

*2:61 Wretchedness and baseness were stamped upon them* [that is, the Jews], *and they were visited with wrath from Allah. That was because they disbelieved in Allah's revelations and slew the prophets wrongfully. That was for their disobedience and transgression.*[19]

*4:46 Of those who are Jews [there are those who] alter words from their places ... distorting (the word) with their tongues and taunting about religion ... Allah has cursed them on account of their unbelief.*[20]

*4:160 Wherefore for the iniquity of those who are Jews did we disallow to them the good things which had been made lawful for them and for their hindering many (people) from Allah's way?*[21]

*5:51 O you who believe! Do not take the Jews and the Christians for friends; they are friends of each other; and whoever amongst you takes them for a friend, then surely he is one of them; surely Allah does not guide the unjust people.*[22]

*9:30 And the Jews say: Uzair [Ezra] is the son of Allah; and the Christians say: The Messiah is the son of Allah; these are the words of their mouths; they imitate the saying of those who disbelieved before; may Allah destroy them; how they are turned away!*[23]

In the Hadith, that is, the holy book of narrated clarifications and interpretations of the Koran and what is said to be Mohammad's very words, the Jews are often referred to as objects of hatred and opponents to be murdered.

***Book 041, Number 6983*** Abdullah b. 'Umar reported Allah's Messenger as saying: You and the Jews would fight against one another until a stone would say: Muslim, here is a Jew behind me; come and kill him.[24]

***Book 041, Number 6984:*** Abdullah b. 'Umar reported that Allah's Messenger said: The Jews will fight against you and you will gain victory over them.[25]

***Book 041, Number 6985:*** Abu Huraira reported Allah's Messenger as saying: The last hour would not come unless the Muslims will fight against the Jews and the Muslims would kill them until the Jews would hide themselves behind a stone or a tree and a stone or a tree would say: Muslim, or the servant of Allah, there is a Jew behind me; come and kill him.[26]

In other suras of the Koran and passages of the Hadith, lyrical ambiguity gave way to institutionalized—and often codified—maltreatment. In many ways, it was not the words that mattered as much as the interpretations and actions they inspired.

Mohammad returned to Mecca with a conquering army. The rapidly spreading Islamic conquest subsumed much of the Arabian Peninsula. The Prophet died on June 8, 632 CE, in Medina, ten years after his arrival. Shortly thereafter, his best generals finished the conquest and forced conversion of Arabia. They then turned their sights on the Middle East and beyond. The northeastern coast of Arabia constituted the fringe of the mighty Persian Sassanid Empire which at that time encompassed ancient Iraq.[27]

In 633 CE, Mohammad's administrative successor, Abu Bakr, the first caliph of Islam, launched hordes of Arab tribesmen, paid fighters and fiery idealists in a mighty imperialist *jihad* or holy war. Their goal: to conquer as much territory as they could. Where Arabs occupied the land, Islam would become the enforced religion. The Arab conquest began in earnest with a push north toward the Euphrates delta, gateway to Persia. Ancient Iraq and Ancient Persia, because of their adjacency, were often ruled by one dynasty.[28]

Stretching for miles were armies of as many as 18,000 fierce Arab horsemen, swift camel warriors, and cunning siege experts—a terrifying sight as they approached. They were even more terrible in battle. These *jihadi* hordes were led by the brilliant military strategist, General Khalid ibn al Walid, a battle genius who was known and feared as *The Drawn Sword of Allah*.[29]

In April 633 CE, the first major confrontation for Mesopotamia pitted Khalid's Islamic forces against a vastly greater occupying Persian power. But those Persian troops were physically exhausted from endless combat with Byzantines and other enemies. The Arabs attacked the Persian armies at their weakest moment. Never falling back, always pressing on, Arabian fighters overwhelmed the Persian defenders. The bloody contest became known as the "Battle of the Chains," so named because Persian soldiers were supposedly chained to each other, thus insuring that none could run away in the face of ceaseless attack. The Muslim armies, disregarding the prospect of certain death and defeat, ultimately prevailed in that contest. Throughout April and May of 633, the Arab hordes launched additional attacks. In the third week of April 633, it was the Battle of River; days later in May 633, it was the Battle of Walaja; followed by the Battle of Ullais in the middle of that month.[30]

General Khalid offered the inhabitants of Mesopotamia and the Persian armies the usual ultimatum: "Accept the faith and you are safe; otherwise pay tribute. If you refuse to do either, you have only yourself to blame. A people is already upon you, loving death as you love life."[31]

The battles of April and May, 633 CE, conquering the south of Mesopotamia, were the first tremendous battles in the campaign—but not the last. After a bloody three-phase, fall back-and-resurge, month-to-month campaign, lasting some four years, the Persian Sassanid Empire in Iraq was finally toppled in 636 by Muslim armies battling at al-Qadisyah. Region by region, Persian-dominated Iraq surrendered to the superior forces of Islam.[32] The word *Islam* means "surrender to God."

Surrenders were relished. "O men, do you not see how Persia has been ruined and its inhabitants humiliated," an Arab poet glorified, adding, "They have become slaves who pasture your sheep ... God gave us victory over them, allowing us to take their countries and settle in their lands, their homes and their property."[33]

General Khalid was given no rest after his victories and was sent on to fight the Byzantines in Syria. Islam became Mesopotamia's ruling religion. A harsh concept of subjugation would be quickly applied to communities that had dwelled there for many centuries, including Zoroastrians, Christians, Hindus, and especially Jews.[34] The Jews, for the last sixteen years during the rise of Mohammad, had been demonized as the great enemies of Allah. Soon much would change for Jews in Iraq.

*     *     *     *

What was Iraq and how did it become a pivotal region for humanity? Eventually, this land would become precious to the world as "the cradle of civilization." Of course, the very term *cradle of civilization* is imbued with the values of an advanced society determined to categorize primitive and ancient people in its own image. But what qualified ancient Iraq to be exalted as the *cradle of civilization* may speak volumes about its enduring relationship to the larger world.

When the last Ice Age receded, around ten thousand years ago, some peoples migrated to the marshy plain between the Tigris and the Euphrates. This territory, later known as Mesopotamia—or "the land between the two rivers"—evolved into modern Iraq. About 7,000 years ago, the so-called Halaf farming culture stretched across the northern tier of Mesopotamia, reaching the Anatolian coast in what is modern Turkey and modern western Iran. A swath of these small agrarian Halaf settlements thrived across the region. The Halaf were known for their archetypal domed mud or limestone buildings. They exchanged distinctive ornate pottery goods, amulets, and stamping seals, as well as ritualized figurines with exaggerated female sexual features.[35]

Despite a veritable nursery of cradle sites worldwide where civilized and complex social behavior emerged many millennia earlier, it is not until the simple Halaf village culture melded into the more complex Ubaid culture of alluvial Mesopotamia, around the late fifth millennium BCE, that the world could dub any realm the so-called cradle of civilization.[36]

No one is quite sure when the term was first coined. Perhaps one of the first to express it was Sir Henry Rawlinson on April 8, 1867, during a discussion at the Royal Geographical Society in London. Following a paper on Mesopotamia by surveyor J. B. Bewsher, the president of the society invited comment from other fellows. Rawlinson rose to declare enthusiastically, "The country to which Lt. Bewsher's paper referred was the cradle of civilization. In it were first cultivated ... the natural sciences and that study of art which afterwards spread through the world."[37] The notion and the cliché took root.

Certainly, during the fifth millennium BCE, numerous small villages in what is now modern Iraq had advanced into a set of more organized central societies.[38] Survival demanded it.

In the marshy realm between the Tigris and the Euphrates, the ancient Mesopotamian people were compelled to cooperate extensively between phases of ruinous havoc and hopeful cultivation. When the waters were tame enough to nourish agriculture and bestow plenty, society thrived. Canals and irrigation were required. The inhospitable marshlands of alluvial Mesopotamia offered an abundance of reeds but were devoid of stone, metals, and to some extent, the wood needed to create shelter, storage, and the infrastructure of an advanced society. Intense labor cooperation was vital to overcoming the harsh environment. Survival and prosperity accrued to those who could work together, store grain and commodities, trade, and plan between those unpredictable river cycles. Success, at some point, pushed beyond subsistence to surplus.[39] The surplus made all the difference to economic development.

Resilient and innovative, the Sumerians in about 3500 BCE invented the wheel, which led to the cart, which, in tandem with boats, could move heavy loads for added productivity and thus promote commerce. Later, people in the region developed the chariot for efficient transportation and for war.[40]

Around the same time, 3500 BCE, the region also yielded what many consider the first genuinely urbanized city, Uruk, located just northwest of modern Nasiriyah. Uruk developed into a complex, cohesive urban setting, rich in personal dwellings, public buildings, and structures, as well as a hierarchical administrative character and a highly developed temple-based economy. Sacred temples warehoused and dispensed the food and oversaw the labors. By 3000 to 2500 BCE, at least one of the temples was distributing rations of beer and bread.[41] Thus, from the beginning, true commerce and economics became a sanctified institution associated with the gods.

More villages and even greater cities followed throughout Mesopotamia. A pivotal quality in the development of Sumer's cities was an early sense of commerce. More than mere barter, trade, or plunder, it was the organization and regulation of transactions, trade, and surplus commodities that constituted true commerce.

Clay tokens were employed to record counts and, to a lesser extent, commodities. Rudimentary tokens to signify economic information had existed throughout the Near East from the ninth millennium BCE. As this system developed, tokens, both simple and complex, were inserted into hollow clay "envelopes," and later the contents were marked on the outsides of these envelopes, creating a more recognizable and readily accessible ledger-like record.[42] This was a major step towards a complex system of accounting. As the world sees it, the transition of simple tokens to complex tokens tracks the very history of man's ascent to civilization.

The shapes and markings of accounting tokens led to two-dimensional pictographs engraved on clay tablets and numerical systems to count them, which, in turn, evolved into the famous wedge-based script known as *cuneiform*. Sumerian culture progressed from token to script in a relatively short period of time—some suggest four hundred years. Originally, flanged reed implements were used to engrave signs. In the beginning, those cuneiform signs represented accounting shorthand, but they gradually developed into representations of spoken language and thence a stepping-stone en route to modern alphabets.[43] Hence, our very written language emerged not from the need to worship a god, sing praise, honor a family, immortalize sagas, or express love—but from the need for commercial accounting, that is, to certify who controlled, owned, and owed what.

But these writing systems vastly exceeded the mute imperative of mere numbers and measurements. Writing captured the verbal sounds of spoken language and conveyed them beyond one individual, and beyond one individual's lifetime, to unseen individuals and lifetimes. Surely, the immortality of the spoken word and thought, more than anything else, cross-pollinated and bequeathed the ideas and culture of one Mesopotamian generation to the next, and the next, and the next—as well as distant generations in adjacent lands. Millions of cuneiform tablets were created to record trades, labors, mortgages, slave sales, commands and decrees, stories and wisdoms, epics, maps, and histories, as well as academic instruction. More than 500,000 such tablets have already been unearthed.[44] Knowledge and communication were the most powerful forces arising from Mesopotamia. More than bronze swords and swift chariots, it was the careful cuts and grooves sequenced into clay that made Mesopotamia the powerhouse of humanity.

In the eighth century BCE, the exalted Hammurabi, the sixth king of the first Babylonian dynasty, proclaimed a collection of mainly commercial laws to "provide just ways for the people of the land ... establish truth and justice ... [and] enhance the well-being of the people." Carved onto a black, eight-foot stele, topped by an image of Hammurabi receiving encouragement from the enthroned and crowned deity, Shamash, the laws were prominently displayed to be a guiding light to his subjects. Copies likely were erected in other Babylonian cities.[45]

More urbanized centers arose in Mesopotamia. One of them, Babylon, about 50 miles south of modern Baghdad, grew to be a magnificent city-state and the capital of the region. Babylon's canals, statuary, thoroughfares, temples, and public buildings were nothing less than spectacular.

Thus ancient Mesopotamia leapt upon the consciousness of humanity. It was where commerce and civilization cohabitated to create a new world social order.

Great science and turning-point inventions sprang from the civilizations of Mesopotamia. Astronomy, cartography, medicine, metallurgy, and architecture all advanced into organized disciplines. The wheel, bronze, chariots, military tactics—all were either invented or flourished in the hands of those who dwelled in or ruled these lands.[46]

But it was not enough to try to master the material and intellectual world. Mesopotamians sought to touch the gods. They developed intricate belief systems to identify, define, and even lay hands upon the all-powerful. Religion became more than mere ritual; it was a way of living. From about 3500 BCE, great stepped ziggurat temples at Uruk and elsewhere ascended 70 feet and higher. Such ziggurats, boldly aspiring toward the sky, formed the basis for a later biblical story in which men, consumed with pride and arrogance, too eager to touch the heavens, erected a great tower; God foiled their lofty desires by confounding their language into *babble* so they could not communicate.[47]

Among all the bronzed, gilded, and engraved wonders Mesopotamia had to offer, Babylon emerged as its most magnificent treasure. *Babylon!* The name itself means *gateway to god*. It thrived as a mighty city-state for millennia.

By the eighteenth century BCE, Babylon emerged as the all-important capital of Hammurabi's empire that burgeoned north to Assyria, east toward Elam in southwest Persia, and west toward the Mediterranean. Soaring temples, ornate shrines and gateways, well-constructed boulevards and canals—all rose as part of a renowned, cosmopolitan center.[48]

During the centuries of greatness, decline, and resurgence, Babylon's influence stretched a thousand miles in either direction to the nations of Egypt, Persia, and Greece.[49] Babylon was feared and desired by its neighbors. In the late 600s BCE, the Assyrians utterly destroyed Babylon, piling corpses by the thousands high along the thoroughfares. Babylon's riches were looted and carried away to the far-off Assyrian capital, Nineveh. When the pendulum swung back, the next Assyrian king arduously rebuilt Babylon to its former splendor.[50]

Assyrian kings in the eighth to sixth centuries BCE razed about 90 cities and hundreds of villages, plundering thousands of horses, sheep, and oxen, and capturing more than 200,000 prisoners of various groups. Among these prisoners, according to the writings, became the first of the Israelites to dwell in ancient Babylon.[51]

Nebuchadnezzar II was installed as king of the neo-Babylonian dynasty of Chaldea. He fortified Babylon and transformed it into a majestic metropolis as never before, erecting magnificent palaces and public works. The crest of the city's grandiose outer wall was broad enough for chariots to patrol. The Hanging Gardens of Babylon, created by Nebuchadnezzar for his wife, were famed as one of the seven wonders of the ancient world. Nebuchadnezzar's cities were nothing less than fabulous. But Nebuchadnezzar also ruthlessly conquered other lands and displaced whole peoples. In the early sixth century BCE, for example, he sacked Jerusalem and deported an additional 10,000 Judeans to Babylonia.[52]

However, when the Persian king, Cyrus the Great, conquered Babylon in about 539 BCE, Mesopotamia finally entered a new era of civilization and enlightenment. Cyrus's armies liberated the inhabitants, restored exiled peoples to their homes, helped Babylonians and all others live in dignity, and established respect for all individuals as the law of his lands. He issued the first international human rights declaration, inscribed in cuneiform onto a large elliptical cylinder.[53]

On the day of his coronation, he announced to all, "I am Cyrus, king of the world, great king, mighty king, King of Babylon ... When I, well-disposed, entered Babylon, I established the seat of government in the royal palace amidst jubilation and rejoicing ... My numerous troops moved about undisturbed in the midst of Babylon. I did not allow any to terrorize the land ... I kept in view the needs of Babylon and all its sanctuaries to promote their well-being. [And for] the citizens of Babylon ... I lifted their unbecoming yoke. Their dilapidated dwellings I restored. I put an end to their misfortunes ... I gathered together all their inhabitants and restored to them their dwellings."[54]

As part of his human rights regime, Cyrus returned the Judeans to Jerusalem to rebuild their temple. The Old Testament records: "In the first year of Cyrus, King of Persia… the Lord moved the heart of Cyrus, King of Persia, to make a proclamation throughout his realm and to put in writing: … 'The Lord, the God of Heaven, has given me all the kingdoms of the earth and he has appointed me to build a temple for him at Jerusalem in Judah. Anyone of his people among you—may his God be with him, and let him go up to Jerusalem in Judah and build the temple of the Lord, the God of Israel, the God who is in Jerusalem. And the people of any place where survivors may now be living are to provide him with silver and gold, with goods and livestock, and with freewill offerings for the temple of God in Jerusalem.'"[55]

But Mesopotamia's peace did not last long. Persian successors to Cyrus did not rule benevolently. As a crossroads between the empires of southern Europe, Asia, and Asia Minor, Babylon was too opulent and prized for coexistence. For a thousand years after Cyrus, and well into the Common Era, Mesopotamia was incessantly catapulted to heights of splendor only to careen back to depths of slaughter as it passed from the alternating clutches of Alexander the Great of Greece, the Seleucid Greeks, the Parthian Empire, the Romans, and the Sassanid Persians.[56]

By the birth of Christ, Mesopotamia was millennia removed from any cradle of civilization. The cradle had been expropriated, subjugated, rehabilitated, and liberated so many times that Mesopotamia's history had become little more than an endless catalog of conflict between its competing conquerors.

Despite the rule of violent contending empires, various forms of monotheism survived in Mesopotamia and its surrounding region since Abraham is said to have left Ur around the year 2000 BCE. Originally known as Abram, the son of an idolater, he left the south of Mesopotamia, following a mystical revelation from an unidentified supernatural voice commanding, "Leave your country, your people, and your father's household, and go to the land I will show you … I will make you into a great nation."[57]

According to the writings, the Almighty later told Abram, "Look at the heavens and count the stars … so shall be your offspring." In a later covenant, the Almighty is said to have pledged, "You will be the father of many nations. No longer will you be called Abram; your name will be called Abraham, for I have made you a father of many nations." The name Abraham is thought to mean "father of many nations."[58]

Among the many descendants of Abraham, according to tradition, were the Jews begat by the generations of Abraham's son, Isaac, and the Arabs begat by the generations of Abraham's son, Ishmael.[59]

The Jews dwelled in Mesopotamia as monotheists for about a thousand years before the arrival of the Arabs and Islam. Whoever came to conquer, the

Jews learned to coexist, so long as their religious observances were unhampered. Cut off from their destroyed temple, their beliefs emerged as the quintessence of their surviving monotheism. During the Greek conquest of Babylon, and then the Parthian occupation, Jews were allowed to worship in relative freedom and prospered in their own way.[60]

In the several centuries before the Arab conquest, the Sassanid Persians ruled Mesopotamia. The Sassanids permitted religious groups such as the almost monotheist Zoroastrians, as well as the purely monotheist Assyrian Christians and Jews, to dwell almost as autonomous sanctioned corporations, chartered and authorized by the Sassanid state. As such, these religious communities flowered. They were allowed to create their own communal hierarchy, mimicking the same titles and administrative organization as the Sassanid state itself. Indeed, these religious corporations were limited to and identified with the actual boundaries of the Sassanid Empire, giving them a true national character. Jews, Assyrian Christians, and Zoroastrians accepted and lived within the Sassanid state as loyal subjects, commonly verbalizing their proud obedience to the empire's national defense needs, paying communal taxes, and even ritually praying for the health and success of Sassanid officialdom.[61]

Zoroastrianism was elevated to a semi-official religion because its polytheist dogma, which venerated a single supreme being, as well as its rituals, appealed to Persian rulers. Zoroastrian religious practices eventually became interwoven with the dynasty itself as a state religion. In many instances, Zoroastrians were exempt from the same poll tax imposed on other groups. Zoroastrianism, whose adherents were also known as Magians, became the most favored brand of monotheism in Mesopotamia.[62]

As for the Jewish and Assyrian Christian establishments, they exercised nearly complete communal authority over marriages and divorce procedures, birth and death customs, all things involving schooling, theological doctrine, the appointment of their own priests and rabbis, and the regulation of communal officials. Sassanid officials were occasionally called upon to recognize and even enforce Judaic and Assyrian Christian decrees within the communal structure. Jews commonly adopted Persian names and considered themselves loyal and protected fully-functioning citizens of the empire.[63]

For hundreds of years in the Common Era, monotheistic communities in Mesopotamia lived in a pluralistic setting, albeit one that stressed their uniqueness so thoroughly it mandated a towering separateness. That separateness only reinforced the religious social units. Intermarriage was rare. Ecumenical collaboration was uncommon except for state purposes. The Jews knew they were Babylonian Jews and thrived as such. The Assyrian Christians knew they were Christians and thrived as such.

For Jews, the Sassanid Persian period was a golden era when their precious

*Talmud* was written down and codified. Essentially, the *Talmud* replaced the Temple tradition. The *Talmud* brought together an assemblage of thoroughly debated laws to govern all aspects of Jewish behavior based on Torah. In Jerusalem, the Temple allowed oral teachings and debate. The *Talmud* and its constituent parts stand as the very definition of Jewish law and morality.[64]

Beyond the *Talmud*, the learned rabbis of Babylon established some of the first synagogues. Certainly, synagogues existed in Judea, Egypt, and elsewhere centuries before the Temple was destroyed in 70 CE. These standalone houses of prayer were needed where Israelite communities were located far from Jerusalem and its gleaming white Temple. The *Talmud* itself records that 394 synagogues existed in Israel at the time of the Temple's destruction. In Babylon, from the onset of exile in about 587 BCE, history sees some of the earliest synagogues. Many experts argue whether indeed the very first synagogue in the world was established by Jews exiled in Babylon. But whether the first or among the first, certainly the earliest Mesopotamian synagogues evolved the conceptual and architectural precedents that forged the modern synagogue found universally today.[65]

The exiled Jews who originated the Babylonian *Talmud* and a community of the earliest synagogues were led by a unique personage known as *the Exilarch*. The legendary Exilarch was revered as a direct descendent of the House of King David. Successive Persian regimes that governed Mesopotamia lionized this Jewish personality as nothing less than Jewish royalty. The many stories of Sassanid reverence for the Exilarch, legendary and real, invoke images of thrones, pomp, and procession through the streets, and even strategic marriage of Persian princesses into Exilarch families. In Sassanid society, the Exilarch was functionally a client king, welcome at court and endowed with communal authority. Exilarch personalities are recorded by tradition to have existed for many centuries before the exile. But the first Exilarch documented in authentic history was Nahum who ruled until 170 BCE. As a regal lineage, the scepter of Judaic monarchy passed generation to generation as it would in any dynasty.[66]

The Exilarchate continued for hundreds of years and eventually became a simply ceremonial office, in some cases merely tolerated as a communal vestige. Outside of ancient Mesopotamia, Exilarch authority did not exceed the theoretical. Even in Babylon, the office became a mere honorary monarchy without genuine communal authority. Not infrequently, those in the Exilarch were dubbed corrupt if not irrelevant. Certainly, the Exilarchs endured periods of persecution at the hands of rabidly supremacist state-authorized Zoroastrians who sometimes compelled child conversions and communal restrictions, as occurred in 233 CE. But for most of the first half millennium in Persian Iraq, the perseverance of the Exilarchate was an outward manifestation of Jewish religious liberty.[67]

As the robust Judaic society in Mesopotamia continued its intellectual and religious development under the Persians, great academies of Talmudic learning emerged. These academies were commonly known by their Hebrew name, *yeshiva,* or the plural *yeshivot.* Two such academies established primacy in the Jewish world. The first was Nehardea, tracing from the earliest exile era; the venerable institution was virtually synonymous with the seat of the Exilarchate located in the same town. Later, when the Exilarch family lost some its political prestige, the Nehardea *yeshiva* relocated to the town of Pumbedita, near the modern city of Fallujah. Pumbedita became famous for its elucidations of Torah and its endless hair-splitting debates. Those indefatigable intellectual Talmudic exercises led to the iconic phrase, "Are you from Pumbedita, where they make an elephant pass through the eye of a needle?" The second yeshiva was established in the third century CE at Sura, a mainly Jewish town known for its Torah study located west of the Euphrates in southern Babylon.[68]

The rabbinic leaders of these *yeshivot* were revered with grandiloquent titles such the "Head of the Academy, Pride of Jacob." These extended honorifics were shortened to "the pride" or *gaon* in Hebrew. The moniker *gaon* does not convey the idiomatic quality of the day; the term corresponds more closely to *His Excellency.* The *gaonim* were the chief expounders of Torah truth that created the Talmud. They never ceased interpreting the interpretations and parsing what had been interpreted. Their final pronouncements on most issues became supreme Jewish doctrine or *Halacha,* or settled Jewish law, that has governed Jewish behavior into modern times.[69]

The Jews enjoyed enough ethnic freedom to purvey their own reigning figure, the Exilarch, to the ruling Sassanids. They wielded enough control over their affairs to see splits, factions, internecine rivalries, and Judaic schisms. Eventually the *gaon,* wielding genuine Judaic wisdom and the authorized code of conduct, became the true powerhouses in Babylonian Jewish life, not the Exilarch and his extended family generations. Jewish intellect, morality, and religious discipline supplanted mere genealogy. Power shifted due to tectonic movement from within, not pressure from outside. Soon, the rabbis—not royalty—ruled.[70] This self-determination only underscored Jewish independence in Babylon.

Indeed, Christians also enjoyed enough autonomy to effervesce an often bitter schism among their own ranks. Nestorian Christians believed in Jesus's duality as both a human and a deity, while the Monophysites saw Jesus as a pure and indivisible divinity without a human incarnation. Both Christian groups were allowed to contend with each other in Persian Babylonia. Not infrequently, internecine Christian competitors could bribe the Sassanid authorities to help them succeed against the opposition sect.[71]

Once again, such developments only further attested to Christian independence in the land.

History records that the pendulum swung to and fro for Jews under Persian control. On more than one occasion, benign treatment was replaced by
violent persecution of the barbaric sort so apt to erupt in the ancient world.
But at the same time, the exiled Jewish community in Babylon achieved historic and permanent greatness during their centuries under Persian control that
was permissive and enlightened. In many ways, the global Jewish identity up
to modern days is hardly detachable from the *Talmud*, inextricably bound up
in the concept of synagogue as the central house of worship, still connected to
those revered academies of learning, or *yeshivot*, and guided by the rulings of
Jewish piety known as *Halacha*. They all arose as a by-product of the exiled
Jewish community in Babylon, caused by that exile and nurtured by the generally tolerant nature of that exile.[72]

In 634 CE, the Arab conquest came to Babylonia.

*       *       *       *

Once the Persians had surrendered or fled neighboring Mesopotamia—
lands they had occupied and ruled for centuries—the conquered region was
completely rewoven. During the decade from 634 to about 644 CE, Islam's
Caliph Umar permanently transformed Mesopotamia into an Arab Islamic
nation. Nomadic Arabs, accustomed to desert tents, now found themselves
reveling in the palatial riches and baths of Babylonia's fallen cities. Two new
garrison cities were built in the south, Kufa and Basra, to acquire control of a
port. Both were populated with waves of soldiers from Arabia who were continuously schooled in the tenets of an Islam on the march. Mesopotamians
freely intermarried with Arab Bedouins, creating a new people, a new nation,
and a new identity.[73]

The ancient language of Aramaic was almost obliterated, except for certain religious purposes. Initially, Christian, Jewish, Zoroastrian, and polytheistic communities were raided and looted, property was confiscated, monks
were killed, and slaves taken. Zoroastrian temples were converted to mosques.
Jews who worshipped the one God, Christians who worshipped the trinity,
Zoroastrians who worshipped a panel of deities led by a single supreme being,
Hindus who worshipped a multiplicity of gods and goddesses and a creator
deity, pagans who worshipped an array of idols—all of them, from heathens
to Hebrews—were reviled by the new Muslim overlords as merely different
hues of untouchable infidel.[74]

However, the increasingly successful Arab conquest created a numerical
problem for Muslim imperialism. The more land the Arabs conquered, the

thinner became their ranks. By 651 CE, Muslims sweeping out of Arabia had conquered vast lands spanning the entire extended Middle East, from Persia and Mesopotamia to Syria, from Egypt to Yemen. Moreover, a bloody religious schism had erupted between mainstream Muslims—the Sunnis—and the rejectionist Shia who bitterly challenged who would be crowned to succeed Mohammad. Open military warfare between the Sunnis and Shia resulted in many gruesome battles and the death of many thousands of Muslim coreligionists. Ultimately, the prevailing Sunnis had killed all but a Shia remnant. When the Caliphate split, only about 10 percent of all Muslims remained rejectionist Shia. Most of these Muslims were now defeated and congregated in Mesopotamia and Persia.[75]

Quite simply, the intercontinental Islamic empire, forged with so much blood and steel, could not be governed by the Arabs alone. They became a ruling minority in their own newly cobbled Caliphate.

Coexistence with the unclean became a colonial imperative, especially in Mesopotamia. The "People of the Book," that is Jews and Christians, could continue with their detested religion by paying the *jizya* protection tax and becoming an acknowledged non-Islamic, subordinated underclass known as *dhimmi*. This tax saw its precedent in Sassanid poll taxes, earlier Jewish tributes exacted by Mohammad in Arabia, and Islamic concepts of punitive assessments. The Jews paid it, and many thousands of them could then maintain an entrenched existence as *dhimmis*. It was during the seventh and eighth century that the outlines of *dhimmitude* and the *jizya* were propounded. The unelaborated dogma creating the *dhimmi* concept is found in the Koran itself.

**9:29** *Fight those who do not believe in Allah, nor in the latter day, nor do they prohibit what Allah and His Apostle have prohibited, nor follow the religion of truth, out of those who have been given the Book, until they pay the tax in acknowledgment of superiority and they are in a state of subjection.*[76]

Numerous translations of Sura 9:29, from vague to vindictive, contend for authenticity among the experts. But the generally accepted middle ground phrasing makes clear that Jews would not only pay the tax, they would remit the payment in a state of "humiliation" or "humbling."

Three other widely accepted translations:

Islamic scholar Abdullah Yusufali: "Fight those who believe not in Allah, nor the Last Day, nor hold that forbidden which hath been forbidden by Allah and His Messenger, nor acknowledge the religion of Truth, (even if they are) of the People of the Book, until they pay the *Jizya* with willing submission, and feel themselves subdued."[77]

Islamic scholar Mohammed Marmaduke Pickthall: "Fight against such of those who have been given the Scripture as believe not in Allah nor the Last Day, and forbid not that which Allah hath forbidden by His messenger, and follow not the Religion of Truth, until they pay the tribute readily, being brought low."[78]

Islamic scholar M. H Shakir: "Fight those who do not believe in Allah, nor in the latter day, nor do they prohibit what Allah and His Messenger have prohibited, nor follow the religion of truth, out of those who have been given the Book, until they pay the tax in acknowledgment of superiority and they are in a state of subjection."[79]

By whatever translation, Sura 9:29 meant that when Jews, Christians, and other non-Muslims who had not converted or been expelled were allowed to live within the Muslim midst, they were reduced to the status of second-class subjects who enjoyed the "protection" of the majority while in a constantly humiliated state that taxed both their incomes and their sensibilities. *Dhimmitude* and *dhimmi* subjugation was ordained by the so-called Pact of Umar, according to tradition. This so-called pact was reputedly propounded sometime between about 697 and 717 CE, between the Christians of Syria and the fervent, luxury-spurning Caliph Umar II. Much of the pact's exact text and origin has always been disputed both by historians and devotees. But for sure its reputed text has been adopted by Muslims in many countries as the basis for subjecting the People of the Book to subservience, humiliation, and revulsion as part and parcel of special taxation. Unquestionably, implementation of the *dhimmitude* varied completely from place to place and from Arab generation-to-generation as an evolving persecution.[80]

However, most frequently, *dhimmis* were not permitted to build a structure higher than a Muslim's, were forced to ride donkeys without saddles or with uncomfortable wooden ones, and were often compelled to wear distinctive garb advertising their inferior status—generally yellow-hued garments marked with distinctive yellow patches for good measure. *Dhimmis* were not allowed to teach the Koran. They could not build new houses of worship or repair existing ones, nor make any noise nor attract any attention in pursuit of their religion or in burying their dead. If required, a *dhimmi* dwelling or house of worship could be forfeited and converted into a mosque. Should a Muslim enter the room, the *dhimmi* would have to rise and, if need be, relinquish his seat. The tax, often called a poll tax or head tax—the *jizya*—was to be paid in a humbled and disgraced position, head bowed low and prone, while the tax collector grabbed the *dhimmi's* beard and ritually slapped him on the cheek below the ear, this for the open amusement of other attending Muslims.[81]

Because the mandated Muslim persecution of the Jews in *dhimmi* status was never consistent, it was never a historical monolith. Rather, this inferior status was a long, mottled landscape of summits, valleys, and level plains. At times, the Jews were beaten down by their Arab masters. At other times, they were allowed to resume their normal existence. Still, during other eras and in other places within the Islamic world, Jews were allowed to excel and rise to second-class grandeur within the larger society. Jews saw the full range of maltreatment in Mesopotamia—sometimes a terrifying cruelty, sometimes just a tedious technicality.

Within years of the Arabs taking over Babylonian lands, the reign of the Exilarch was reinstated, and with much of the same honor and ceremony. After all, King David was an exalted prophet, mentioned throughout the Koran including in Sura 21 entitled "The Prophets." Hence, direct Davidic descent—as the Exilarch families could demonstrate or at least persuasively argue—was a link to heavenly predecessors that held a special place in the Islamic establishment. The first Exilarch to be formally re-enthroned in Mesopotamia was Bostani, in the mid-seventh century. He was affirmed by the Caliphate authorities in Babylon in the midst of an internal Jewish struggle for power within the Exilarchate, allowing Arab rulers to take sides and, in essence, create their own alliance.[82]

The Jews, left to prosper, and encouraged by their Muslim masters, began to fulfill for the Caliphate a vital role in commerce and banking that the Arabs could not generally undertake on their own, especially in view of Koranic restraints. Relaxed travel restrictions allowed Mesopotamia's Jews to move freely throughout the Islamic Empire—from East to West. Mesopotamian Jews, under the Caliphate, created a unique merchant class. On these travels, they proliferated the Talmudic authority of Babylonian *gaonim* and other leading rabbis, and raised funds for as many as 28 synagogues and 10 Babylonian *yeshivot* from other Jewish communities throughout the intercontinental Islamic Empire. Soon the Babylonian Jewish merchant class was able to extend its influence over the rabbis of Mesopotamia whose *yeshivot* were increasingly dependent upon fundraising.[83]

Unquestionably, great Jewish societies arose throughout Europe and North Africa during the latter centuries of the first millennium. A few of the great Judaic centers included Morocco, France, and, in later centuries, Lithuania. But Babylonian Jewish influence consistently made itself known as special, even exalted, among the far-flung exiled Jewish communities of the international Diaspora and even over the remnant Palestinian Jews. Nor was this influence limited to coreligionists. Babylonian Jewish influence extended within the ranks of the Caliphate itself.[84]

A Jewish voucher system was created to facilitate trade and donations, and this evolved into a skeletal international banking or monetary system. By the seventh and eighth centuries, great Jewish banks arose in Baghdad with lending activities reaching from the Indian Ocean to the Western Mediterranean. Some prominent Baghdadi Jews had already shed their Judaic patronymics and adopted strictly cosmopolitan names. For example, one esteemed and elevated Baghdadi Jewish banker, known by the single name Netira, thrived as banker both to the wealthiest Jewish merchants as well as ranking members of the Caliphate.[85]

By no means did Jews achieve primacy in banking or most other commercial or industrial endeavors. Christians, of course, outnumbered them and could rely on vast coreligionist connections throughout Europe. Muslim merchants and moneychangers were taxed at half the rate of Jews and commonly given preference.[86] So a Jew was at a distinct disadvantage in much of commerce. But the fact Babylonian Jewry was allowed to compete so effectively demonstrates that the Jews of latter half of the first millennium Arab Mesopotamia were a persecuted but still pivotal minority—sometimes humiliated, sometimes honored.

In short, Jews in Arab Mesopotamia had learned they could go far, as long as they did not go too far. Periodically, the pendulum would swing and waves of Muslim extremists would ask why Jews were allowed to achieve levels of prominence and even the outward manifestations of equality such as ordinary clothing. From 854 to 859 CE, decrees resulted in the razing of synagogues in Mesopotamia. In many other Arab lands, outside of Mesopotamia, Jews were regularly targeted for looting, arson, forced conversion, and special humiliation. Because anti-Jewish measures were so regular and so brutal in so many countries, whether dominated by Arabs or non-Arabs, whether at the hands of Christians or Muslims, the paucity of such anti-Jewish campaigns in Mesopotamia was yet another distinction this Jewish community held above many others.[87]

One of the reasons Mesopotamian Jews could rise was because they were part of a larger Arab society that saw itself as divinely endowed and guided and unshakeable in its dynastic control. But one day, a high-and-mighty Caliph, too secure in his imperial arrogance, flung a special insult. This led to a protracted nightmare from which there was no recovery for greater Mesopotamia and indeed much of the Arab world.

It began in about 1218 in the Khwarazm Empire, which occupied the originally Persian territories now known as modern Uzbekistan. The land had been Islamic since the Arab conquest, but as the Muslim Empire became fragmented, the Khwarazm shah created his own empire and functioned as a self-appointed rival Caliph. He expanded his dominion eastward toward Persia and beyond. When a foreign trade mission of several hundred merchants laden with valuables reached the Khwarazm city of Otrar, the governor, Inaljuk, with the Caliph's sanction, humiliated them as spies, seized their wares, and executed them all.[88] In its day, such regal fiat must have seemed trifling.

But that trade mission personally represented Genghis Khan, the most feared man on earth, the head of a mighty empire of horsemen warriors—the

Mongols—that terrorized all of Eurasia. The Khan had sent those merchants to Otrar to establish mutual commercial relations. Instead, they were robbed and executed. Therefore, the Khan—the battle-tested instrument of the one pantheistic god—was spurned. The Khan, this man who in his recent past had literally ordered the killing of hundreds of thousands, who had caused so much hardship and inhumanity, was now uncharacteristically overcome with grief and insult. According to the writings, Genghis Khan withdrew to a mountaintop where he prostrated himself for some three days and beseeched the heavens for guidance.[89]

What followed was, quite simply, the wrath of Genghis Khan.

Who were the Mongols? The Mongols were a race of fierce warriors from the scrubby Asian steppe who employed revolutionary war tactics, clever espionage, and divisive politics to conquer all. At the time of the trade mission to Otrar, the Mongol Empire stretched from China to the frontier of the Crusade-weakened Islamic Empire. Whereas the mighty Eurasian armies before them had won or lost battles on their bravery and superior numbers, Mongols used trickery, feigned retreat, and small attack groups to confuse their adversaries, bait them into traps—and then annihilate them. The Mongols sometimes put women and boys on horseback or strapped dummies to spare horses to create the appearance of larger cavalries.[90] Mongol nomads lived on their horses and cherished the natural world. They despised walled cities. They also despised any who did not submit. Resistance was futile, they believed. The Mongols waged organized terror as a war tactic to inspire surrender. When they approached, they often did so in a great tumult. Sometimes they simply beat drums outside a walled city for days before an onslaught. Or they hurled incendiary missiles, or bombarded the city walls in a perfection of siege craft. Even as terrified inhabitants did not sleep, the Mongol warriors rested and dined on the stores they had carefully pre-positioned.[91]

Unlike other invaders, their goal was not conquest and domination but utter destruction. Typically, an overrun city would be completely vanquished and rendered useless. Every living thing had to die—men and women, children, even cats and dogs. Death to opponents was a cruel, painful exercise—the more gruesome the murder, the greater the Mongol vindication. The Mongol custom was to report body counts by chopping off the ears of their victims. Bag after bag was filled and delivered to ranking officers as proof. Mongol warfare amounted to more than plunder and subjugation, more than mere triumph—it was extermination.[92]

The end of Khwarazm began when the Khan couriered to the Shah a succinct message: Deliver for punishment the insolent governor Inaljuk, the man who had humiliated his trade mission. Naturally, the Shah refused.[93] So the Khan assaulted the Persian cities—one by one. They were all laid waste.

By April 1219, after months of siege against Otrar, the scene of the original insult, the walls were finally breached.[94] But Otrar's governor Inaljuk escaped to a distant fortress with a force of defenders. The Mongols pursued him and after a siege of two months, swarmed into the fortress, slaying hundreds of defenders. Finally, they broke into his heavily blockaded sanctum. His last two bodyguards were slain. But simple execution was to be denied Inaljuk. Instead, he was dragged back—struggling, kicking, and screaming for his life—to Genghis Khan's camp near Samarkand. As a lesson about proper commerce, the Khan reportedly ordered molten silver poured into Inaljuk's eyes and ears.[95]

But the Khan was not finished. He swore, "All [Persian] cities must be razed, so that the world may once again become a great steppe, in which Mongol mothers will suckle free and happy children."[96]

The Mongols rode from city to city, leveling the walls and ravaging the mosques and public buildings. The great mosque of Bukhara was gutted and converted to a stable. All the books were burned, except a chosen few relics, and the wealth looted. Finally, the invaders destroyed the nearby irrigation canals to flood the fields and erase the viability of the area. With equal thoroughness, they murdered nearly all the people. Their means of massacre was intensely calculated. Mongol emissaries would politely order all the inhabitants out of the city into the fields for what they called "a census." Once assembled, the selections began—to the left, to the right. Those who could provide usable craft skills or who were sexually desirable were removed into bondage and worked, often to death. The rest were brutally killed.[97]

At Nessa, 70,000 people were ordered to bind each other's hands behind their backs. Then each one was systematically slaughtered as the masses awaited their turn. At Herat, now in modern day Afghanistan, about 60,000 were killed.[98]

At Nishapur, in modern day Iran, everything was burned, crushed, and pillaged, and all who lived were savagely murdered. The city disappeared. It was leveled to rubble, reduced to a space—except for three pyramids. To prevent any survivors from hiding among the heaps of corpses, orders went out to decapitate everyone. Those heads were towered into three ghastly monuments of extermination: one pyramid of male heads, one female, and one comprised of children.[99] They stood as grotesque beacons and warnings.

After devastating the eastern flank of Islam, the Mongols paused, declining to enter Mesopotamia proper. Spread thin, they had other business far to the east in China. For nearly three decades, the Mongols were content to consolidate their domination, creating a vast empire that all Eurasia fearfully kowtowed to. Protection tribute was regularly and punctually paid. Silks, gold, silver, cattle, horses, ornate gifts, and everything else of value were showered upon the barbarians to keep them at bay and demonstrate awe. A far-flung administration and governance system was established to keep peace throughout the Mongol Empire. At its core was the Mongol imperative—no one rivals the Khan, and no one's god rivals the Khan's. All who approached and paid tribute, be they kings, popes, or caliphs, were tolerated as vassals.[100]

When the great Genghis Khan died, the Mongol Empire divided itself into four hordes—one for each of his sons—stretching from China to the Mideast. The remnant of those who had decimated Khwarazm buffeted up against the ill-defined Persian border and greater Mesopotamia. Likewise, that part of the Muslim world was now becoming increasingly fragmented and autonomous. The Baghdad Caliph and other Muslim potentates secretly promoted a constant guerrilla war against the Mongols. Roaming bands had fled to the mountains around Nishapur before the Mongol slaughters. Now these bands killed local fellow Muslims, especially Sunnis, who cooperated with the Mongol-occupying administration.[101]

A vanguard of the guerrilla insurrection was a years-old sect of Shia Muslims devoted to the art of swift, secret, political murder, generally by a sudden, fatal stab wound. Shia Muslims were a disaffected political and religious minority in Islam who became a majority in both Iran and the southern portion of Mesopotamia. They hated the age-old establishment of Sunni caliphs as much out of religious dogma as economic disadvantage and class conflict. Ensconced in formidable mountaintop castles, this particular Shia group indoctrinated young murderers-in-training with equal doses of Islam and rigorous political doctrine. It was rumored, probably wildly, that to heighten their fanaticism and make them tools of death, the order regularly smoked hashish. Hence, they were called the "Hashashin." They seized several castles and created their own defiant realm from Syria to Egypt to Persia. They became so dreaded a force that Sunni officials began wearing armor under their robes to blunt an unexpected knife attack. The sect of killers reached legendary proportions; in Europe, the traditional transliteration of Hashashin, changing the *sh* to a simple *s*, permanently created a new word: *assassin*.[102]

The Assassins, according to accounts, sent 400 of their best to kill the ruling Khan in the name of Islam. The Khan's many bodyguards and spies foiled the conspiracy and blamed the entire Islamic establishment. In 1251, Grand Khan Mongke made the decision. Baghdad was to be demolished.[103]

The assignment was given to Hulagu Khan, the grandson of Genghis. After two years of painstaking preparation, Hulagu launched his forces. The spies, the conspirators, the astrologers, the livestock, the cavalry horses, the routes, the siege machines, a thousand Chinese engineers, work gangs to construct bridges and clear roads, the pre-positioned resupply of wine and flour—all was made ready. In 1253, Hulagu left Mongolia and swarmed west.[104]

Hulagu did not hate Islam. He just refused to bow to it or any belief system other than his own. Himself a pagan, intrigued by Buddhist precepts, and married to a Christian princess, Hulagu found Islam an affront to monotheistic Mongol beliefs about an omnipotent god of nature that was present in all things. What's more, Hulagu believed that the Mongols were the designated overlords of the earth and its inhabitants. Therefore, any organized religion that attempted to portray itself as supreme, including Islam, was anathema.[105]

Ironically, Hulagu's resentment of preeminent religion did not prevent him from creating uneasy alliances with crusading Christian Europe, which was eager to roll back the hegemony of Islam and oust it from Jerusalem. Hulagu related to Christian Europe not so much as an army of Christ but merely as geopolitical entities. His army was gladly reinforced with Christian contingents.[106]

By early January 1256, the long-awaited invasion was ready. Hulagu drove toward Baghdad. From his forward encampment at nearby Hamadan, Hulagu couriered a letter to Caliph Mostassim offering a chance to surrender and promulgating the usual warning: Resistance is futile. "Strike not the point of an awl with your fist," wrote Hulagu, adding, "Mistake not the sun for the glowing wick of a flameless taper. Level the walls of Baghdad at once, fill its moats, leave government ... and come to us ... If we march against Baghdad, you will not escape us even if you hide in the deepest earth or rise to the highest heaven."[107]

Caliph Mostassim, secure in his opulent surroundings in mighty, well-defended Baghdad, provocatively sent back a snide letter. "Young man, seduced by ten days of favoring fortune, you see yourself as High Lord of the universe and think you command the decisions of destiny ... Know you that from the West to the East, all who worship God and hold the true faith are my servitors ... Walk in the ways of peace and return."[108]

Hulagu gave the Caliph's envoys a return message: "War is all that remains."[109]

Quickly, Mongol forces mustered at all the roads from Baghdad. Flank by flank, the Mongol hordes approached the suburbs and killed all in their path. On February 5, 1258, after a six-day siege, the eastern fortifications were won. Entourage after entourage tried to reason with Hulagu, who would not lift his siege or the invasion. Escape was impossible. The rivers were blocked; the roads choked off; the mountain passes occupied. Finally, the people of Baghdad obeyed an invitation to peaceably file out of the city gates. They were promised safe passage to Syria. Normally, Baghdad's population was hundreds of thousands, but with the swell of terrified refugees from the surrounding suburbs and villages, it may have exceeded a million. Soldiers, clerics, civilians, merchants, children grappled by their parents—the high and mighty of Baghdad, as well as the low and obedient—filed out to the field, defenseless, their weapons left behind as instructed.[110]

Then, one by one, family by family, thousand by thousand, the Mongols did what they always did. Only the Caliph was spared—and only for a time.[111]

For seven days, the barbarians burned every mosque, dismantled every major building, gutted every vestige of authority, and utterly brought Baghdad to destruction. "They swept through the city like hungry falcons," wrote a Persian historian, "or like raging wolves attacking sheep, with loose reins and shameless faces, murdering and spreading fear ... Beds and cushions made of gold and encrusted with jewels were cut to pieces with knives and torn to shreds. Those hidden veils of the great harem were dragged ... through the streets and alleys, each of them becoming a plaything in the hands of a Tatar [Mongol] master."[112]

The Caliph himself, spared only to be taunted in his own palace, was finally executed. The method is recorded variously, but the most reliable accounts indicate he was wrapped in a carpet or sack and trampled to death by stampeding horses.[113]

Shia conspirators were appointed to govern what little was left of Baghdad. The stench of rotting corpses was so strong, even the mighty Hulagu was driven from the city. As he left, he ordered those not killed to reopen the bazaars and dispose of the mountains of bodies.[114]

No one will ever know how many were slaughtered at Baghdad. An Arab historian wrote, "If anyone were to say that at no time since the creation of man by the great God had the world experienced anything like it, he would only be telling the truth ... It may well be that the world from now until its end ... will not experience the like again." It is thought that Hulagu himself later bragged to King Louis IX of France that more than 2 million were killed. A Persian historian of the period stated the number was closer to 800,000. Others have estimated many more. The city's normal bustling population of nearly a million had been swelled by multitudes of Muslims fleeing nearby settlements.[115] So the higher death tolls are probably more accurate.

Elsewhere in Mesopotamia, Hulagu continued his extirpation of the Islamic hierarchy, especially Sunnis. Shia strongholds at Basra and Najaf were left unharmed; in fact, a Mongol guard was left to protect the shrine of Ali, revered by all Shia Muslims. In the northern Jazirah province, in the former Christian town of Martyropolis, Mongol generals sought out the fanatic Sunni Muslim Kamil Muhammad for an unspeakable death. Previously, Kamil Muhammad had crucified a Jacobite priest from Syria who had been traveling under a Mongol passport. Georgian and Armenian Christians allied with the Mongols helped surround the city until the population had been starved into submission. Once Kamil Muhammad was seized, bits of flesh were sliced from his body and forced into his mouth.[116]

To drive home the message to Islam, Hulagu deliberately spared the Christian churches that had existed under Islamic subservience. Nor were any of the church's members harmed. Indeed, one of the Caliph's palaces was handed over to the Christian patriarch. The relieved Christian patriarch's chronicler penned these words: "During the time of Baghdad's supremacy, like an insatiable bloodsucker, she swallowed up the whole world. Now she has been punished for all the blood she has spilled and the evil she has wrought, the measure of her iniquity being filled."[117]

Jews, too, were spared in some instances precisely because, like the Christians, they constituted an underclass. Their elevation was only a further insult to Islam. Eventually, both Jews and Christians were allowed to become functionaries in the Mongol Empire. Some Jews rose to prominence and special advisory positions within the Mongol court. Undoubtedly, the most prominent Jewish advisor was Saad al-Dawla, who alternately served as both treasurer and personal physician to the Arghun Khan, a fervent Buddhist and the fourth ruler of the Mongol Khanate. Al-Dawla was so trusted by Arghun Khan, he was appointed *vizier* of Baghdad, that is, the Khan's grand advisor for the city. Nepotism was the order of the day, and many in al-Dawla's family rose within the Khanate.[118]

Eventually the reconstituted Muslim population of Baghdad seized their moment as Arghun Khan was dying in 1291. Mobs roamed the city, seizing al-Dawla. They murdered him and killed many of his coreligionists previously in authority. What began in Baghdad, quickly spread throughout the region. The weakened Mongols were evicted, and their Jewish and Christian allies were ignominiously massacred. Gleeful Arab insurrectionists reveled in their sudden reemergence. As for the Jews, popular sentiment was based on the Muslim tradition that Jews were, in fact, the human descendents of pigs and monkeys. One Arab satirist began a commentary based on a Koranic declaration of Jew-hatred: "We praise Him in whose name the heavens turn. Those Jewish apes have been destroyed."[119]

But much more had been destroyed during Mongol times.

Mesopotamia began as the cradle of civilization. It flowered greatly into a majestic and vibrant empire where unstoppable knowledge, passionate thought, urbane sophistication, and the noblest aspirations of humanity coexisted with the violence, inhumanity, and the bloodlust of all-corrupting theocratic power. Jews were a cohesive, even pivotal, part of that history.

But now, as the dust cleared from the ousted ruling Khans, it became clear what had happened. Thousands of years in the making, the fruit of dynasties and divinities, the struggle of entire peoples hewn from throughout the Middle

East, mighty Mesopotamia had been reduced to scorch and rubble by Mongol hordes. Public buildings were demolished. Its irrigation systems were undone, decimating agriculture. Books were turned to ash. An intricate political structure was dismantled.

Mesopotamia never recovered from the Mongols. Never. Its great civilization had been robbed for the last time. This time it was permanent.[120]

The pendulum has swung one way, and swung back. By 1295, Jews were returned to servile *dhimmitude*. During the post-Mongol years, Jews had been forced to return to distinctive badges and other identifying clothing.[121] That status would remain for the centuries to come.

*    *    *    *

Hulagu was hardly the last Mongol to sweep incalculable horror and scorch over Mesopotamia. The wrath of the Mongols was no mere fleeting campaign. Theirs was literally a recurring ruination—something handed down from generation to generation, almost as a Mongol birthright.

One fierce group of emerging fourteenth-century Mongols was made up of ancestral Turkics, a rugged brand of Central Asian steppe horsemen and raiders from the region now known as Turkmenistan. The man who rose to lead them was Timur the Lame. A pock-faced and scarred barbarian, Timur's high cheekbones tapered to a pointy beard, creating the visage of a craggy spear tip. Because he walked with a noticeable limp from an early battle wound, his epithet in Europe was "Tamer the Lame" or Tamerlane. Lame or not, he was an intrepid warrior who killed with complete dispassion and unparalleled sadism. In the hierarchy of Mongol savagery, Timur distinguished himself as more barbarous and bloodthirsty than all his predecessors.[122]

Timur assumed power among his own horde. To bolster his leadership, he claimed common ancestry with Genghis Khan. In the years after 1370, Timur, who was himself raised Muslim, ruled with legendary violence, often killing for nothing more than perceived insolence.[123]

As thinning Mongol administrative control broke down, persistent rebellions and attacks by Muslim fighters provoked Timur to action. In 1383, he marched on windswept Sistan, in southeastern Persia. To terrorize all in Sistan who opposed him, Timur encased 2,000 living people in a sand and water mix, which was then used to make construction blocks. Using these ghastly megaliths, he erected a tall tower of screaming souls. Then the irrigation and dam system, so indispensable to the area, was wrecked, undoing centuries of agricultural development. Sistan was permanently returned to a parched desert. Timur did not discriminate when mass murdering. Many Persian Jews were said to have perished along with the rest of the population, but most fled.[124]

In his drive to destroy all resistance, Timur turned toward Mesopotamia. He swarmed in from southern Persia with a murderous Turco-Mongolian horde described as "ants and locusts covering the whole countryside, plundering and ravaging." In 1393, Timur terrorized Baghdad with three months of pure spoliation and slaughter. Jews are said to have been represented amply among the victims, but again most fled, principally north to Kurdistan and parts of Syria.[125]

Timur continued his conquests in various directions, almost always dispensing with either hegemony or tribute, preferring instead the incessant delivery of unrestrained torment and death. Only select artisans survived, and these were returned to his camp at the majestic garden city at Samarkand in what is now Uzbekistan. There they constructed a magnificent city attesting to Timur's glory. However, those deemed useless were never spared. When he encountered Christian Armenians in the Anatolia region of modern Turkey, the garrison sent children out to sing a song of peace; Timur's cavalry simply galloped over them. Later, he buried the soldiers alive in the city's moat. In Damascus, he massacred the men relentlessly; mothers were abducted as slaves, leaving their infants to die unattended.[126]

At Isfahan, in Persia, he ordered the entire city depopulated. When the citizens fought back and massacred his garrison, Timur retaliated with awesome wrath. Unlike his predecessors, content to stack dozens of heads, or even hundreds, into frightful pyramids or minarets, Timur built soaring twin towers in Isfahan. He used 70,000 beheaded beings. So many decapitated heads littered hellish Isfahan that the excess not arrayed atop ramparts was simply piled in the streets.[127]

On July 1, 1401, Timur returned to Baghdad for his second and final sacking. He launched a six-week siege at the height of an intolerable Mesopotamian heat wave that broiled and suffocated men inside their armor. At noon, when the heat was its most intense, he stormed the ramparts, knowing its defenders would have pulled off their stifling helmets. Some said he slew twenty thousand. As many as half of those killed were probably Jews, according to Arab writings. Some said the dead were simply too numerous to count. This time, Baghdad was thoroughly vandalized and its complex irrigation system systematically wrecked. So complete was the devastation that its prior recoveries were utterly negated. Nearly four decades later, an Egyptian historian observed that Baghdad could no longer be recognized as a true city.[128] The Jews, like most others, were gone.

Yet in spite of the smoldering remnant, Jews who had scattered, returned when possible to their ancient dwellings. As the decimated cities of Baghdad, Basra, and Mosul were re-populated, among the horrified returnees were Jews from earlier times who had fled near and far.[129]

The next half millennium for Jews in Mesopotamia would be written not by Arabs, and not by Mongols, but by Turks.

*    *    *    *

Who were the Ottomans? Who are the Turks?

Originally, the Turks were not one homogeneous people or even practitioners of one religion. The first Turkic tribes of the Central Asian steppe were fierce, unwashed fighters and horsemen raiders. In the first millennium, most were pagan, but many gradually converted to Islam. One group of Turkics, the Seljuks, had captured Baghdad in 1055 and established a dynasty until the Mongol slaughters.[130]

Large groups of Turkic clans either assimilated into the Mongol hordes or fled west toward Anatolia, which is now in modern Turkey. The transplanted masses were broadly Eurasian, melding the physical features of the Chinese, steppe tribes, Persians, Mesopotamians, and Armenians among others. These clans became known as *ghazis*, that is, lionized attackers of the infidels. How these Turkish raiders coalesced into the Ottoman nation is a blend of ethnic fact and dynastic myth. But it is said that in the 1320s, the migrated Turks formed an Anatolian principality, almost completely pastoral, under their leader Osman. The followers of Osman were termed *Osmanlis*, that is, "associates or followers of Osman." From the Turkish Osmanli, a series of rough permutations and transliterations yielded the European appellation *Ottoman*.[131]

True, the Ottomans began as an Anatolian principality in a region crowded with such realms. However, from this small home territory, the Ottomans conquered one neighboring city, emirate, and kingdom after another, creating the borders of a new world power, the Ottoman Empire. Indeed, the early Ottomans waged almost perpetual war. For more than a century, the new empire pushed west into the Balkans, Greece, and elsewhere in Europe, as well as east into the Fertile Crescent and south into North Africa and Arabia, creating a truly Eurasian dominion for Islam. In fact, the Ottomans' sphere was geographically more European than Asian.[132]

In 1453, the Ottomans finally overwhelmed the fortifications of Constantinople, the seat of the Christian Byzantine Empire. Heroes in the Islamic world, the Ottomans now shifted their capitol to Constantinople, also known as Istanbul—which sat astride the Strait of Bosphorus, where Europe meets Asia, where East meets West.[133]

The Ottoman battles against European Christian territories were deemed Holy Wars against infidels. The battles against Muslim territories were also considered Holy Wars, even though these lands belonged to other Muslims.

In many instances, Jewish citizens fought loyally alongside their Turkish neighbors. To justify hegemony against fellow Muslims, the Ottoman Sultan obtained specious religious rulings, such as those against the Persian Shias, declaring waging war against them to be "more important than fighting the infidels."[134] Hence, the Ottomans could rely upon Jews as battlefield allies even in their internecine fight against Muslim coreligionists.

Indeed, during the late Middle Ages, especially after the Crusades, it became common for Catholic European regimes to stigmatize Jews and Muslims as two halves of one despised group of non-Christians. In 1492, the Jews of Spain—about 200,000—were expelled for their Judaism or refusing to convert to Christianity. They were given four months notice. Many fled aboard ocean-going vessels, after purchasing passage at unconscionable rates, only to be thrown overboard once out to sea. With almost no refuge available, many fled to the Ottoman Empire, taking with them their culture, especially in the realm of medicine, printing, cannon casting, and performing arts as well as their mercantile expertise. The Sultan welcomed them with outstretched arms. In fact, Sultan Bajazet sent emissaries throughout the empire instructing them to receive the Jews warmly and make no effort to impede them. The Sultan was known to mock the Spanish King for the Jewish Expulsion of 1492. "How can you call Ferdinand of Aragon a wise king," he declared, "the same Ferdinand who impoverished his own land and enriched ours?"[135]

Jews freely settled everywhere in the empire. A census from 1520–1530 registered 16,326 households in Istanbul of which ten percent were Jewish. In Salonika, Jewish households constituted about half the city. An Ottoman chief rabbinate, the *Hakham Bashi*, was created in 1453 to extend religious authority throughout the realm.[136]

Jews brought with them printing presses—among the first in the Islamic world. The Ottoman tradition did not include printed materials and relied instead upon scores of thousands of scribes. Jews could engage in limited printing so long as they avoided Arabic characters. So Latin script and Hebrew printing were introduced into the empire. Writing was born in Babylon. But printing was a largely Jewish import. In addition, much of the Turkish textile trade arose from Jewish factories and still-viable Jewish trade connections in England. Textile production in the empire essentially tripled once the Jews arrived. Ottoman military uniforms were commonly the responsibility of the Jewish community.[137]

Indeed, Jews were settled into newly conquered lands as soon as the Ottomans seized them. The Ottomans were fond of transplanting populations for commercial and political reasons. When the Ottomans conquered Rhodes in 1523 and Cyprus in 1571, the Sultan issued decrees to transfer Jews into those territories to help develop them and ensure the loyalty of more residents.

For example, in 1576, the Sultan ordered "1,000 rich and prosperous Jews" together with their families and property transferred into Cyprus. As the Ottomans conquered, the Jews went along.[138]

With so much conquest, the Ottomans were constantly annexing large regions as *provinces*. After the Sultan's military overran Mesopotamia, its three main regions routinely became three separate provinces of the empire. Beginning in 1535, those three provinces were named for their largest cities: Mosul in the north, Baghdad in the middle, and Basra in the south.[139]

But not all provinces were equal members of the Ottoman Empire. Most Ottoman provinces were highly organized and administered, whether they were central to the empire's existence or merely maintained as remote sources of taxes and tribute. For many years, the Sultan delegated his authority to governors-general, one for each province. The more important the province, the more prestigious and valued was the appointment.[140]

Commerce and wealth became of paramount important to the Ottomans, who fell into the expensive gluttony that often accompanies regal power. Jewish merchants and traders, as well as other non-Muslims, were welcomed and allowed to thrive as *dhimmis.* As long as Jews, Christians, and other infidels acknowledged the primacy of the Islamic state, they could prosper unmolested. In 1477, a census of Istanbul and the nearby commercial quarter of Galata listed 16,324 families, but only 9,486 were Muslim. Greek Orthodox Christians totaled 3,743 families and Jews made up 1,647 families, with the balance composed of Armenians, Gypsies, and others.[141]

Greater Istanbul became a true metropolis, thriving on and tolerant of diverse ethnic groups. By the late 1500s, some 40 percent of its citizens were non-Muslim. The city's population may have neared 800,000, ranking it the second largest in Europe. Commerce became the lifeblood, bread, and salt of the empire. By the late 1600s, some 2,000 ships docked annually at Istanbul, transiting everything from wine to livestock to all corners of the earth.[142]

Jews again became important to the realm for their contribution to trade.

By 1528, a third of the empire's income arose from just two wealthy provinces: Syria and Egypt. The chief value of Mesopotamia to the empire was not in heightening the sultan's tower of material wealth, but in creating a strategic, perhaps even desolate, Sunni buffer against the still-viable Shia threat residing in Safavid Persia. But to bolster the province's ability to pay taxes to Istanbul, the Ottoman rulers allowed Jews to return to Baghdad. Beginning in about 1534, Jews began reconstituting their community in Mesopotamia, especially in Baghdad. Over the next decades and into the seventeenth century, of about 25,000 homes in rebuilt Baghdad, 250 belonged to Jewish families.[143]

But Baghdad never saw much peace and was constantly conquered and reconquered as the Persian Safavid Shia dynasty warred with the Sunni

Ottomans. In 1623, the Persians prevailed once more and recaptured Bagh-dad. For the next fifteen years, resettled Jews were subjected to persecution and increased enforcement of humiliating *dhimmi* requirements. In 1638, Ottoman Sultan Murād IV drove the Persians out of Baghdad and the sur-rounding Mesopotamian cities for the last time. The bitterly repressed Jews enthusiastically supported the Sultan's drive to retake the city and then rescue a senior rabbi of Basra. The day of the conquest and rescue was declared *Yom ha-Nes*, that is, a day of miracle. From that point on, Jews in Mesopotamia thrived more or less unhindered.[144]

By the eighteenth century, the ostentatiously lavish lifestyle of the Otto-mans against a collapsing financial base began eroding the ability of the Sul-tans to govern their provinces. The Ottoman grip on Baghdad, and indeed on all of Mesopotamia, was by now so tenuous that Istanbul had relinquished genuine authority to its local rulers. In the case of Baghdad, the city com-mander's son-in-law was appointed governor. He was a Mamluk, that is, a member of the Turkish slave army. The Mamluks then ruled Baghdad for decades, into the early 1800s, without interference, weathering a variety of insurrections and declining to send more than token tribute to Istanbul.[145]

Under nominal Ottoman rule during the eighteenth and nineteenth centu-ries, Jews continued to thrive, becoming part of Mesopotamia's commercial and political ruling class. Like Armenians, the Jews could engage in neces-sary commercial activities, such as moneylending and banking, which were proscribed for Muslims under Islamic law. Jews functioned as state treasur-ers and economic advisors. In some families, these professional involvements were handed down from generation to generation.[146]

Through the centuries, as the Arab national character dominated the Mid-dle East, minorities became identified and hyphenated as "Arab-Christians" and "Arab-Jews," that is, Jews and Christians who dwelled in Arab lands. Hence, these groups saw themselves as Arab nationals practicing a non-Islamic religion, just as French, Germans, and Americans saw themselves as members of the state first, and adherents of a religion second.

Ottoman Jews encouraged their own assimilation process and insisted on equal treatment throughout the empire. By and large, they received it. In that vein, in 1840, Sultan Abdulmecit I investigated a resurgence of the medieval blood libel against Jews, that is, the legend that accused Jews of using the blood of Christian children to mix *matzo* crackers used in place of bread for Passover. The Sultan issued a royal edict against this libel, declaring: "An ancient prejudice prevailed against the Jews. The ignorant believed that the Jews were accustomed to sacrifice a human being to make use of the blood at their feast of the Passover ... For this reason ... we cannot permit the Jewish Nation (whose innocence of the crime alleged against them is evident) to be vexed and tormented upon accusations which have not the least foundation in truth ... [Therefore], the Jewish Nation shall possess the same advantages and enjoy the same privileges as are granted to the numerous other nations [*dhimmis* groups] that submit to our authority ... In all parts of our Empire, [the Jews] shall be perfectly protected as well as all other subjects of the Sublime Porte [the Ottoman court]."[147]

Like many Ottoman decrees, the ruling against the blood libel did not erase the Muslim prejudice against them as *infidels,* harbored throughout the empire. Indeed, subsequent Ottoman regimes targeted them for special restrictions. Even still, the Jews of Baghdad were relatively resilient to such repression. When the Young Turk movement arose in 1908, Turkification was easy for Mesopotamia's Jews. They, of course, thought of themselves as Turkish first, second, and third, just as assimilated Jews anywhere felt about their settled homes.

In World War I, Iraqi Jews fought for the Arab nationalist cause alongside Lawrence of Arabia. An Iraqi prime minister once recalled that in 1917, when he was an officer in Cairo, "My attention was attracted by the presence of one hundred volunteers of Iraqi Jews, headed by two Jewish officers. They came from the [Turkish] prisoner camps [maintained by the British] to fight under the banners of King Hussein. The British and French Commands tried to separate these volunteers from their other brethren and employ them in the Palestine front, but did not succeed, as they [the Jews] insisted on serving under the Arab flag in the Hejaz."[148]

In 1920, the Allies, together with the League of Nations, installed colonial "mandates" across the Middle East and in Mesopotamia—which was reinvented as Iraq. Jews and Christians greatly expanded their middle class and establishment niches in Iraq. Moreover, Jews stepped into the vacuum created by the genocide against hundreds of thousands of Armenians during the war. Because of their education, Jews were often given preference by European mandatory officials. Jewish professionals and clerical workers flocked to the new Allied-run bureaucracies. Jews served as lawyers, doctors, and judges. Jews dominated the cotton trade via their connections in Manchester, and were pivotal in other imports and exports. Wealthy Jews operated nearly all the banks, continued as indispensible economic advisors to the Iraqi government, and in general, functioned as the bedrock of Iraq's entire financial apparatus. Once Iraq became independent in 1932, the new monetary system was actually devised by Jewish financial experts. Jewish negotiators loyally extracted the highest possible royalties from Turkish Petroleum for Iraq's national treasury. Several distinguished members of the Jewish community served in the Iraqi Chamber of Deputies and the Senate. Jews also became well known in the arts, letters, and music of the nation.[149]

By no means were all Iraqi Jews cosmopolitan Baghdadis. For many centuries, the Jews of the north who lived among the Kurds remained simple farmers and herders, tending flocks and orchards and rejoicing at weddings with the same abundant food, dancing, and music as their neighbors. They lived in Mosul, Kirkuk, Arbil, and other Kurdish areas along with the other Islamic and non-Islamic ethnic groups that comprised the Kurdish culture. In dress and manner, Kurdish Jews resembled their neighbors, and they adopted the national identity of their fellow Kurdish peoples in the Kurdish struggle for independence. In Iraq's Shia south, especially Basra, Jews also blended in with their fellow citizens as simple peddlers and bazaar stall owners. They shared the same coffeehouses and were equally affected when British forces invaded in the Mesopotamian campaign of World War I.[150]

Various censuses measured the Jewish population of Iraq differently, depending on which disputed territories were included and the demographic ebb and flow of volatile Iraq. A 1906 Ottoman census counted 256,000 Jewish citizens. A Young Turk census in 1914 listed 187,000. As a result of emigration during the upheaval years after WWI, Jewish numbers dropped in the third decade of the twentieth century, with the official 1920 census counting only 87,488. Slightly more than half of those lived in Baghdad, with the remainder split between the Mosul north and the Basra south.[151]

For 26 centuries, the Jews of Iraq had survived a turbulent and sometimes triumphant history that withstood Muslims and Mongols, massacres and marauders, sultans and Safavids, and the tectonic upheavals of religious imperialism determined to make them an underclass. But they had also danced beneath the stars of the God they prayed to, sung in whirling moments, broke glass beneath their heels during weddings, cradled their next hope, erected great institutions devoted to spiritual debate, and bequeathed tractates of elucidated wisdom for all their coreligionists regardless of land or era. The darkest impulses and the bloodiest conquerors could not shake them from their lands.

But in the final century of their existence in Iraq, the Jews would encounter a force stronger than any that had arisen in the many seasons of their sojourn. This force would not thunder in the distance like a horde of invaders. It would not tower above them like a fortress. It would not race through the streets like a shrieking monster. But the force was unstoppable and irresistible. It was a mere substance, one that dwelled not on high in exquisite castles but deep in the earth and so simple it could be held in the cupped palm of one's hand.

The one thing the Jews could not survive was the one thing they barely understood. It was oil.

CHAPTER

# OIL LUST

In the stew of racial supremacy, religious hatred, political conflict, and war that came to engulf the Jews of Iraq and ferment the Arab-Nazi axis, one binding ingredient floats unseen just beneath the surface. What substance caused the Arabs throughout the Middle East—and especially in Palestine and Iraq—to see Britain, Jews, and Zionism as an enemy to eradicate at all costs? What motivated the Nazis to find common cause with the Arab peoples, an ethnic group the Reich so racially reviled? What ignited, lubricated, and nurtured the German-Arab alliance that erupted into the Farhud and then a spectrum of other shoulder-to-shoulder operations from the airwaves of the Mediterranean to the hilly battlefields of Bosnia?

It was oil.

Nothing would be easier than to see the Farhud itself as a mere pogrom not unlike so many that had preceded it in so many countries throughout so many centuries. Nor can true understanding emerge from simply reciting the body count and beastly details of the Nazi-Islamic joint venture of hate. Without comprehending the nature and dynamic of petroleum and its pivotal influence on people and events from London to Baghdad and from Constantinople to Jerusalem, the vital Nazi-Islamic nexus will remain submerged.

What exactly is oil and how did it become injected into the veins of the massive, international Nazi-Muslim enterprise in the Holocaust? In truth, the answer spans all recorded history from the ancient times to the underpinnings of the twentieth century.

\*   \*   \*   \*

Man knew oil long before man knew civilization.

Many millennia before Mesopotamia's first city, cavemen understood the usefulness of a thick black tar, later called *bitumen*. As far back as 60,000 years ago, bitumen had already become a magical substance for prehistoric society, used as an adherent on spear points and tool blades, a salve on wounds, a lubricant for heavy objects, a sealant for construction, and a decoration on surfaces. Eventually, its flammable qualities were discovered, providing heat and light for even the most primitive cave dwellers and nomads.[1]

Bitumen was easily obtainable because it oozed up from the rocks, hence its eventual name, *petroleum*, which means "rock oil." Petroleum's usefulness is amply documented throughout the inscriptions of the first civilizations, as well as the Bible and other ancient writings. Babylon's ziggurats and its tower of Babel were built of bricks coated with bitumen. According to tradition, two famous infants—both the Mesopotamian ruler Sargon the Great and Moses the Prince—were sent floating down the river in cradles sealed with bitumen.[2]

In the ancient Mesopotamian region, pressure beneath vast deposits of bitumen sometimes forced jets of the flammable substance high into the air. Broiling summer heat regularly ignited the spray into awesome flaming towers equal to any a dragon could exhale. No wonder angry fire gods inhabited the mind of ancient man.[3]

As civilization advanced, new and better industrial and medicinal uses were found for bitumen. The thick residue from evaporated bitumen, called *asphalt*, could be used to pave roads. Gaseous, liquefied, and distilled forms of petroleum, such as naphtha, could be set aflame to light the darkness and scorch the enemy. Cyrus the Great, in the sixth century BCE, planned to use such flammables to burn out street resistance during his famous invasion of Babylon. A thousand years later, terrifying flamethrowers from Byzantine warships at Constantinople sprayed an almost inextinguishable naphtha-based mixture called Greek Fire.[4]

In 1846, a Canadian geologist working in the United States created a new flammable he named *kerosene,* distilled from asphalt and other hydrocarbons. This wonderful new illuminant, kerosene, efficiently brought light into the shadows and darkness of city streets and their great buildings. Within a few years, thousands of gallons per day were being distilled for commercial use in major American cities. Everything changed when a safe, smokeless kerosene lamp with a glass chimney vent was invented, allowing kerosene to become a household staple—rural and urban—both in Europe and America.[5]

Most of the slow seepages and great sprays of "rock oil," from the Americas to Asia Minor, were never efficiently captured. Petroleum-gathering operations included wringing oil from soaked rags, hauling buckets of the slimy crude up from deep ditches, and simply siphoning the runoff into containers lashed to donkeys. Ultimately, oil gatherers could only watch most of their precious product simply flow away, blackening the nearby environment and constantly spurring commercial explorers to devise better technologies for oil conquest. Natural wells had been excavated, deep holes had been bored, and taps had been injected into the surface flows. But until the mid-nineteenth century, no one had yet drilled into the oil deposits hidden beneath strata of earth and then industrially mastered its contents.[6]

But it all changed in the 1850s. Medicinal oil entrepreneurs began drilling at Oil Creek in rural Pennsylvania, where petroleum was migrating into salt layers. Travelers had noted seepages in the area for more than a hundred years. Although the main drillers at Oil Creek sought a new source of medicinal oil, others craved an abundant supply of commercially exploitable illuminant. On the afternoon of August 29, 1859, in the woodlands of northwestern Pennsylvania, at Oil Creek, just south of tiny Titusville, at a depth of 69.5 feet, an exploratory drill finally struck oil. Oil Creek spawned Oil City, which overnight became one of several wild and rambunctious Pennsylvania drilling towns where fortunes were furiously made and lost as fast as oil could spill.[7]

Once struck, oil could be efficiently managed, that is, controlled with pumps and caps, stored in tanks or other holding areas, and then transported by truck, pipeline, and ship. An industry waiting to be born was finally brought to life. The oil business—like its product—became the most explosive undertaking on earth, both chemically and politically.

Industrializing oil operations was far more complicated than merely capturing endlessly gushing streams of black gold. Finding oil, determining its grade, selling it, relying on the source, transporting it, and profiting from the enterprise required a volatile and perilous chain of events. Supply and demand is the mischievous devil of commercial oil—as it is in all commerce.

At first, demand for oil soared. America's Civil War and the country's increasingly mechanized and industrialized society powered an immediate, monumental need for kerosene, lubricants, sealants, and numerous other petroleum products. Titusville and the surrounding so-called oil regions experienced a frantic "gold rush." Endless wood-encased drilling towers, waiting teams of mules and horses, wagon-clogged service roads, as well as the omnipresent pipes, barrels, tanks, and pumping gear transfigured Pennsylvania's pastoral northwestern woodlands into a grimy, black-soaked, industrial oilscape.[8]

In 1860, within a year of the Titusville strike, western Pennsylvania had produced 450,000 barrels of oil. Two years later, production had multiplied to seven times that level. The market gladly gulped every barrel. Oil barges and other hauling ships floated down the Allegheny River in packs of 150 to 200 at a time. Drilling and distribution ran around the clock.[9]

But quickly, demand, compared to uncoordinated supply, became erratic and maddening. In January 1860, a barrel of oil fetched $10. By June of that year, due to oversupply, the price had dropped to 50 cents per barrel, and at year's end, a barrel sold for a mere dime. A year later in 1861, once supply was controlled, the price zoomed back up to $4 per barrel, and during 1863, a barrel sold for as much as $7.25.[10]

Manipulating supply and stimulating demand emerged as the fulcrum of success in the wild world of oil. Creating strategic shortages to keep prices high and occasional oversupplies to drive out competition became the special craft of oil's robber barons. That challenge became all the more complicated as oil became a worldwide commodity. By 1878, oil production in Pennsylania and other states, such as Ohio and West Virginia, had reached 15.5 million barrels annually, of which about half was exported. The volume tripled by 1890. Indeed, by then, oil had become America's number one nonagricultural industrial export. Distribution became all-important. Crude had to be pumped, transported, and refined in a series of careful steps from oil wellhead to end user, whether in the neighboring county or across the oceans.[11]

Timing was everything. Nobody wanted to drown in unused oil—but rather float on its lucrative flow. Massive pipelines traversing hundreds of miles, as well as tanker trucks and oil-hauling ships, were constructed to bring the crude to refineries and the refined oil to users—from the subterranean depths of Pennsylvania to kitchen stoves, bedroom nightstands, and industrial cogwheels a world away. It was a logistical miracle.[12]

Moreover, the pool of oil beneath a wellhead was hardly perpetual. One Titusville-area boomtown, known as Pithole Creek, was just a lush tract of Allegheny forest when, on January 7, 1865, an oil speculator brought in a gusher. Within a few months, a nearby farm was transformed into bustling "Pithole City," roiling with 15,000 excited oil zealots. The overnight population attracted more than 50 hotels and boardinghouses. The Astor House hotel was built in a day. A daily newspaper sprang up. Telegraph lines were strung. The town's brand-new post office, processing some 10,000 letters and packages per day, ranked just behind those in Philadelphia and Pittsburgh. Pithole farmland rocketed in value. One parcel sold for $1.3 million during the summer of 1865, and by the time the financing closed in September, the cost was $2 million. Pithole was for millionaires—but only briefly. By January 1866, the tempestuous gusher had been pumped dry. Most people left as suddenly as they had rushed in. Vacant buildings were mercilessly dismantled for firewood. A typical tract of that $2 million farmland was snatched up for a mere $4.37. The Danforth House Hotel, which had cost $30,000 to build, was sold for firewood for just $16. Pithole, an instant urban success, just as instantly became an abandoned city.[13] That was the power of oil—from greatness to ghost town in the blink of a barrel.

In 1892, Ottoman Sultan Abdulhamid II, later known as "Abdul the Damned," enthusiastically received a geological survey suggesting that Mesopotamia might hold great oil deposits. The Sultan ruled with absolute power. Anticipating that his distant almost disregarded province—Mesopotamia— might possess petroleum riches, Abdulhamid had already begun quietly transferring masses of Mesopotamian land into his private treasury, that is, the *Civile Liste*, hoping to sell oil concessions to Western governments with the technology and money to devote to their growing appetite for oil. Beginning in early 1889, additional vast sections of Mesopotamian land were personally expropriated, some as large as "the whole province of Mosul."[14]

But the Turks were incapable of developing their own oil wealth.

The Industrial Revolution had completely missed the Ottoman Empire. Like their other efforts to join advancing societies, the Ottomans were quite late in approaching the potential of modern oil exploration. For a full generation before the Sultan began acquiring oil lands, the petroleum business had been thriving worldwide. Within years of the Titusville strike, modern industrial oil operations appeared from Sumatra to Holland, from Poland to Canada, from California to the Carpathian Mountains.[15]

The advent of Thomas Edison's electric lightbulb in the early 1880s did nothing to slow petroleum's expanding market. True, by 1886, nearly 200,000 incandescent light bulbs were in use worldwide, and millions more soon after. This certainly reduced the need for illumination kerosene. But at that very time, horseless carriages, which had operated on steam and electricity for decades, were being outfitted with exciting new German-designed internal combustion machines. Those engines required fuel: oil.[16]

By 1890, the oil business was indeed a worldwide phenomenon—but not in the Ottoman Empire. Oil was not needed in Middle East lands where land transportation was mainly accomplished by mule, horse, and camel—or on foot. What's more, standard business practices in the region just seemed a barrier too high for foreign developers to hurdle. Systemic corruption and graft meant that business suitors approaching the authorities were compelled to grease a long line of outstretched palms, from the lowliest doorman to the aides and assistants of key advisors, from ministers to the monarchs themselves. Moreover, the lack of roads, railroad tracks, and other modern conveniences made every industrial endeavor trebly more expensive and daunting.[17]

The inherent inability to industrialize Mesopotamia was a symptom of everything that was wrong with the corrupt, overspending, lavish, harem-obsessed, and under-developed feudal-style realm known as the Ottoman

Empire. A typical pasha's household could maintain its own Master of Ceremonies, Chief Chamberlain, and a coterie of kitchen functionaries, such as Officer of the Coffee, Officer of the Sweetmeats, and of a gamut of other edibles. Many noble staffs even included an Officer of the Drinking Water. Ottoman rulers commonly spent their early lives confined to harems until propelled into leadership by the reigning caliph. Fratricide, as a means of eliminating rival heirs, was a commonplace practice.[18]

Turkey had turned its back on both the Age of Enlightenment and the Industrial Revolution of the later 1700s. Reckless spending on extravagant decadence of epic proportions necessitated continuous borrowing from European capitals. In the final decades of the nineteenth century, its centuries-long process of self-inflicted ruin and incessant war expenditure and imposed reparations had wrought the expected result. By 1875, after 14 major foreign loans, Istanbul was compelled to declare bankruptcy. In national receivership, the Empire created a Public Debt Administration in 1881, employing some 5,000 revenue agents, who forwarded Turkish tax revenues directly to European creditors.[19] Consequently, there was little development in Mesopotamia—only the continued extraction of what value existed for tribute, tax, and to assuage foreign levy.

Yet, as the twentieth century approached, the Ottoman Empire continued to massacre its own citizens and exploit its provinces unabated. Turkish sultans, who doubled as the Caliphs—that is, the supreme religious authorities of the majority Muslim world—were eating, drinking, sexing, and splurging themselves and their empire into rapid decay and destruction. The only question was not *if*, but *when* the empire would break apart, either from internal disintegration or external conquest or both.

The empire's cycle of self-inflicted barbarism and religious warfare seemed incurable. The Ottoman Empire was sick and dying.

So weakened was the empire that European leaders from London to Moscow were already publicly debating the so-called "Eastern Question." This debate argued what the powers-to-be should do when Turkey toppled of its own bloated weight and internal chaos. Who would seize and control its many colonies across Europe and Asia, especially in the Mideast? Who would seize and control the Middle East's vast undeveloped oil that within the coming decades would be the new gold—black gold? Secret treaties, private assurances, clandestine alliances, and a Möbius pattern of counterchecking bubbled up everywhere as diplomats pondered the coming collapse—and who would pick up the pieces.[20]

During a brief, conspiratorial conversation about the "Eastern Question" between Czar Nicholas and British ambassador Hamilton Seymour, the Czar remarked, "Look, we have on our hands a sick man … it will be … a great misfortune if he escapes us one of these days before all the necessary arrangements are made."[21]

Seymour replied, "Your Majesty will deign to excuse me if I point out that it is the strong and generous man who spares the sick and weak man."[22]

In the days to follow, Seymour injected the "sick man" reference into more dispatches to London and pointedly repeated the epithet in further discussions with the Czar as they jointly pondered whether the Ottoman Empire should be dismantled territory by territory, resuscitated, or something in between. Once the catchphrase was leaked to the newspapers, it spread across Europe as the vogue expression of the day.[23]

Turkey became the "Sick Man of Europe" in the parlance of international affairs. The world not only had to answer the Eastern Question, now it had to minister to the "Sick Man." Endless wordplays were propounded: Who would give the Sick Man his pills without the patient knowing, and who would withhold them? Who would come to the Sick Man's rescue, and who would euthanize him prematurely?[24]

As the nineteenth century came to a close, the "Sick Man of Europe," straddling three continents, was the world's looming problem. By then, its frontier provinces in Mesopotamia were simply the Sick Man's precious overland shortcut to someplace else. Even the international commercial way station that Mesopotamia became was about to be outmoded by faster, ocean-going vessels. By 1869, the Mediterranean and the Red Sea were linked by the newly opened Suez Canal; from there, vessels could sail to the Indian Ocean.[25]

The disintegration and dismantling of the Ottoman Empire would eventually be triggered by a long fuse that burned from one century into the next. That fuse was soaked in oil. England would ignite it. It would never stop burning.

*     *     *     *

The Sick Man was on his deathbed. Throughout the last decades of the nineteenth century, the Ottoman Empire and its neighbors had been fighting one bloody war or insurrection after another, from Bulgaria and Greece to Armenia and Russia. Turkish finances were a mirage of mirrors. The Eastern Question—who would inherit, lead, profit from, or be damaged by the inevitable collapse of the Ottoman Empire—was being answered simultaneously by all the leading European powers. They all had plans—and plans to realize their plans.

Some European capitols wanted to incorporate the soon-to-be dismantled territories into their own spheres of interest. Some merely wanted to prevent others from doing so. A few wanted to see new, friendly nations emerge in the aftermath of Ottoman disintegration. Certainly, local populations throughout the empire—and indeed throughout Europe—were rising up, angry and demanding an end to their dynastic, ecclesiastic, and purely monarchial regimes. The seams of Europe were unraveling.

To keep them stitched, endless overlapping alliances, pacts, and secret agreements were sewn among friends and enemies both, as London, Paris, Berlin, Vienna, Moscow, and Istanbul tried to maintain the so-called "balance of power" in Europe. War was to be avoided because the mechanical, scientific, and industrial advances of recent decades had created a new style of modern warfare that could rapidly kill millions. But if war could not be avoided, steeled preparation was needed.

Turkish Mesopotamia, and for that matter the entire extended Middle East, suddenly catapulted in importance—especially to England. No longer were Turkey's three backwater provinces in Mesopotamia—Mosul in the north, Baghdad in the center, and Basra in the south—considered mere transit corridors and stepping-stones to India and Asia. Now Mosul, Baghdad, and Basra were coveted for their legendary but as yet unexploited oil.

Quite simply, as the twentieth century opened for business, the world needed much more oil. Petroleum was no longer just to illuminate lanterns, boil stew, and lubricate moving parts. Modern armies and navies demanded vast new supplies of fuel.

Among the first to recognize the need for fuel-burning vessels was Admiral John Fisher, a visionary British naval leader with a decidedly imperialistic outlook. He knew the future of England's Navy lay in a fleet of swift battleships that could maneuver sharply and fire torpedoes and long-range guns from a distance. Speed required oil-burning vessels that could be refueled quickly and cleanly—even at sea. These advanced ships would make obsolete the messy, coal-burning monstrosities that required throngs of sooty dockside laborers hefting coal baskets into holds and gangs of grimy engine-room stokers. Fisher's revolutionary new battleships would be called *dreadnoughts*, and they would be the anchor of a rapidly expanding, well-financed, modern armada of fast and deadly vessels. In the early twentieth century, Britain pursued a "two power" naval policy, that is, a fleet as large as the two next largest foreign fleets combined.[26] Only an oil-powered flotilla could achieve that.

Abdul the Damned well understood that his lands might hold fabulous reserves of oil. But no effort was made to organize a national drilling enterprise or a Turkish petroleum company for the good of his nation. Oil wealth was not something to develop as a national treasure, but to auction off to industrial others.

Employing the tactics of the bazaar, the Sultan patiently, almost excruciatingly, juggled the several foreign offers, maneuvering for the best price. Many came calling. The Germans were especially interested and stepped forward as part of an effort to create a sphere of interest in Turkey. Kaiser Wilhelm's state visit to Istanbul in 1898—his second—was a momentous occasion for the Sultan. Abdulhamid staged enormous banquets wherever in the empire the Kaiser traveled. The Sultan even removed a section of Jerusalem's Old City wall to make way for Kaiser Wilhelm to enter on his magnificent white stallion. The cost of these festivities—a staggering 1 million Turkish pounds—prompted Ottoman government officials to protest this gauche opulence, which stood in stark contrast to "civil and military officers [who] are literally starving."[27]

In 1888, the Deutsche Bank, working through its essentially captive Anatolia Railway Company, acquired a concession to build a short railroad line to Ankara in central Turkey. In 1902, this right was extended all the way through Mesopotamia to Baghdad and ultimately to Basra on the Persian Gulf. This railroad line was not seen by the European powers as a mere transportation upgrade for the region but as a profound German military threat and oil asset—a land check to England's naval supremacy.[28]

Influential German writer Paul Rohrbach explained in his well-read pamphlet, *Bagdadbahn (Baghdad Railway)*, later expanded into a book of the same name, that "England can be attacked and mortally wounded on land in Egypt." He continued with great specificity, "The loss of Egypt will mean to England, not only the loss of control over the Suez Canal and its connections with India and Asia, but probably the sacrifice of its possessions in Central and Eastern Africa as well. Moreover, an Islamic power like Turkey could exercise a dangerous influence over England's 60 million Islamic subjects in India, Afghanistan, and Persia, that is, if Turkey should conquer Egypt. However, Turkey can subjugate Egypt only if it possesses an extended system of railroads in Asia Minor and Syria, and if by an extension of the Anatolian Railway it is able to ward off an English attack upon Mesopotamia."[29]

With the Baghdad railroad concession came fabulous mineral and oil rights for 20 kilometers on either side of the track, especially in the petroliferous north. About the still undeveloped Kirkuk oil fields in northern Mesopotamia, Rohrbach wrote, "We ought to attach the greatest importance to the circumstance that the Baghdad Railway will pass close to the petroleum districts. The only thing to be feared is … foreign speculators securing a preferential right in the exploitation of Mesopotamian naphtha before any effective German initiative."[30]

Britain feared Germany's fleet of oil burning ships and now her designs on Mesopotamian oil.[31]

London followed every vicissitude of German expansion into the Ottoman

Empire and the wider Middle East region. London undertook strategic pre-cautions and counterchecks everywhere it could. For example, in late 1898 and early 1899, the Kaiser tried to assist Abdulhamid in reasserting control over Kuwait, a distant and only nominally Ottoman territory in the Gulf. To thwart that, on January 23, 1899, the British sealed a pact with the Kuwaiti sheikh. In exchange for a one-time British payment of 15,000 Indian rupees, the sheikh agreed not to transfer or lease any part of his territory without Lon-don's approval. As part of the pact, British India would send troops should the Turks attempt to invade. Kuwait became a British protectorate, and remained one for more than 60 years.[32]

Pacts and political promises were only part of the *realpolitik* of the day. The beginning of the twentieth century was so serpentine a period in Europe that the great powers found it expedient to project their power and interest via strictly commercial corporations. The Deutsche Bank had launched its Bagh-dad Railway project through the Anatolia Railway Company, and this enter-prise was seen as little more than a surrogate for imperial Germany. In fact, in 1903, the Anatolia Railway Company restated its corporate rights in an actual treaty, the 1903 Baghdad Railway Convention. Article 22 specified the min-eral rights. This then elevated the commercial agreement to an international covenant.[33]

However, as Germany was securing the vast oil resources of Mesopo-tamia, Britain's thirst for naval fuel magnified. In 1903, Admiral Fisher, increasingly known as the "oil maniac," headed up the Admiralty's Oil Fuel Committee. That body later declared it "inexpedient to depend in peace time upon resources which would probably fail in wartime." Moreover, when Fisher became First Sea Lord, he commissioned a number of oil-only destroy-ers and torpedo boats, again increasing England's strategic requirement for petroleum. But the source for all this oil was still unknown. Fisher's catch-phrase of the day was "oil don't grow in England."[34]

London began to use its leverage with Istanbul to connive, bully, bribe, and seduce oil rights away from their rightful owner, that is, Germany's Deutsche Bank and its allied companies. Britain projected its imperial power through its own seemingly private corporations, which did London's geo-political bidding while making handsome profits. These companies included the National Bank of Turkey—a purely British financial house, not a Turkish bank—and Anglo-Persian Oil Company, which was protected and guided by both Parliament and Whitehall. The aim of these corporations was to snag the oil for Great Brit-ain and block any other suitors. If the Sultan did not quietly cooperate, Lon-don could always use its power as an international creditor to block new and needed Turkish taxes, garnish Turkish state bank accounts, and even attach and liquidate Turkish infrastructure. At times, the threat was hardly subtle.[35]

Many surmised that Europe's next big war would be between Germany and an alliance led by England and France. Mesopotamia's oil must be at the disposal of Britain regardless of Turkey's growing axis with Germany and its preference to grant favor to Berlin.

London's strategy was summarized precisely in one key dispatch from the British embassy in Istanbul to British foreign secretary Edward Grey: "During the last few years," the embassy stated, "our policy, if I may call it so, in Turkey has been, and for some time to come will be, to attempt the impossible task of furthering our commercial interests while pursuing a course ... which the Sultan interprets as preeminently hostile in aim and tendency. These two lines are diametrically opposed and consequently incompatible with one another. In a highly centralized theocracy like the Sultanate and Caliphate combined, with its pre-economic conceptions, every big trade concession is regarded as an Imperial favor to be bestowed on the seemingly friendly, a category in which, needless to say, we are not included."[36]

During the first years of the twentieth century, Britain's quest for Mesopotamian oil was, in a sense, future-looking. No successful oil wells had yet been drilled in Mesopotamia.

At 4:00 a.m., May 26, 1908, everything changed in Britain's quest for the Sultan's oil wealth. A British oil exploration company in neighboring Persia—now modern Iran—pierced beyond 1,180 feet of desert strata. The bore unleashed a monster gusher rising 75 feet toward the sky, soaking everything with black gold. Several months later, additional wells came in, including a sudden, unexpected, and bounteous oil spout on September 18. Excitement on London's financial markets could barely be contained. All available shares of Anglo-Persian Oil Company were purchased within 30 minutes.[37] Britain owned the oil through a concession granted earlier by the Shah of Iran. At first, it seemed that London would be assured of abundant Mideast oil supplies.

But throughout 1908, the shadowy dynamics of regional oil played out. Did the Persian oil strike outmode the quest for Mesopotamian oil or merely increase the frenzy to find it? Some could have easily argued that Anglo-Persian's oil was the answer to Britain's needs. On the other hand, abundance in business rarely satiates—it only whets the appetite for more.

The promising Mosul and Baghdad fields in Mesopotamia were, after all, just miles from the lush Persian oil fonts. If the British did not control those Mesopotamian fields, who would? The Germans? The French? The Russians? If the British did control them, England would possess a monopoly on the enormously wealthy deposits across an entire region. Moreover, a pipeline could transit Persia directly to the Turkish ports on the Mediterranean, avoiding the perilous mountain route to the Gulf. Hence, Mesopotamia remained directly in London's sight line even as England sped toward a feared armed conflict with its rivals over the Eastern Question and any number of linked crises.

Throughout 1908 and early 1909, London carefully navigated, cajoled, enticed, and bribed its way through political undercurrents of insurrection and economic intrigues. The Young Turk revolutionary movement was determined to launch a coup to depose the Sultan and, in the process, retain the oil for Turkey's national destiny. Oil-hungry competitors were constantly appearing in the corridors, from the Deutsche Bank to a mysterious but pivotal start-up enterprise called Turkish Petroleum Company. Turkish Petroleum's mission was to garner enough arguable oil land rights to act as a spoiler if London did not satisfy its ever-escalating financial demands.[38]

Through an admixture of threatening sticks wielded by Whitehall against British businessmen working against the Crown's interest and clever financial carrots, culminating in the spring of 1909, London finally won out. The right royalties would be paid, the right palms would be greased, and the right deference would be extended. The Sultan agreed to terminate Germany's contractual rights to develop Turkish petroleum fields. Anglo-Persian and its British government sponsors would be awarded those oil rights.

On April 14, 1909, the minister of the *Civile Liste* and the grand vizier, that is, the Ottoman prime minister, assembled all the paperwork and scheduled an immediate visit to the Sultan's office to obtain his signature.[39]

The sultan was ready to sign. But riots broke out in the city early in the day and could not be contained. Thousands of soldiers loyal to the sultan stormed into the main square. The counterrevolutionary mob invaded parliament and killed two deputies. Young Turks moved against them in armed conflict. The palace was locked down. Nothing came in or out.[40]

Anglo-Persian's all-important oil documents were not signed.[41]

In the days that followed, Istanbul deteriorated into complete chaos as contending armies and political factions clashed, and the fate of the barricaded sultan changed hour- to-hour. Germany, France, and Great Britain dispatched warships to protect their interests and their citizens. Day after day dragged on, and Anglo-Persian's documents were still not signed. All parties tensely hoped to just wait out the crisis. At the time, Abdul the Damned was rumored to be hiding in the British embassy—no, the Russian embassy—now it was the French Embassy—no, actually on a warship steaming away from Turkey. In fact, he was cowering in the palace, where food and electrical supplies had been cut off by the plotters in an effort to starve the royal household into surrender.[42]

On April 27, 1909, after tense negotiations between the angry factions, revolutionaries finally broke into the beleaguered palace. There they found a trembling Abdul the Damned, surrounded by 20 black eunuchs, pathetically

pleading for his life. The Young Turks and their cohorts agreed not to execute the Sultan, who had himself executed so many thousands, nor even to
subject him to a divisive trial. Instead, Sultan Abdulhamid would simply be
dethroned and exiled with his several wives to a small villa in Salonika. His
harem would be dispersed. The chief eunuch would be hung from a local
bridge for all to see. Abdul the Damned's personal fortune—some guessed it
to be $25 million while others guessed $200 million—was reclaimed. "His
property, acquired illegally, will be confiscated by the state," the new Turkish
prime minister declared to reporters. Within days, the billion-dollar oil properties were transferred to the Ministry of Finance. Those properties included
the fabulously valuable oil lands in Mesopotamia.[43]

As feared, a flood of fresh offers and exhumed claims began pouring in
from Romania, America, England, and within the Ottoman Empire itself. A
gallery of individuals, syndicates, aristocrats, and corporations coveted the
oil.[44]

But in the dust that settled on the smoldering revolt of the Young Turks,
no one would be awarded the right to Mesopotamia's oil.

*     *     *     *

Winston Churchill's zeal for oil exceeded Admiral Fisher's.

Churchill had become intimately familiar with the commercial thickets
surrounding oil during his stint from 1908 to 1910 as president of the Britain's
Board of Trade. In late October 1911, he became First Lord of the Admiralty,
where he intensified the race to build more ships, all faster and more powerful, all of them oil guzzlers.[45]

When Churchill arrived at the Admiralty, he discovered that some 189
vessels, from torpedo boats to dreadnoughts, had been built or were under
construction, every one fueled by oil, not coal. Those ships—never mind the
new ones envisioned—would consume more than 200,000 tons of oil annually. Yet Britain possessed a mere four-month reserve.[46]

Anglo-Persian's oil venture was making progress in Persia. But it was
hardly a reliable source. True, eight British wells were pumping in Persian
fields. But a working refinery was still needed. Construction on the refinery
at Abadan on the Persian coast began in 1910. But would that refinery dis-
till kerosene for stoves, fuel oil for battle cruisers, or some of both? It all
depended on the market and contracts. A gargantuan, nearly 150-mile pipeline
was being constructed to link the distant oil wells with that new refinery. Sixty
miles of five-inch pipe and 80 miles of eight-inch pipe had been ordered and
these would be laid, 16- and 22-foot segments at time, by backbreaking labor
under heatstroke conditions. Erratic personnel, periodic worker rebellions,

management conflicts, engineering problems, construction mishaps, and an unexpectedly smelly and sulfurous crude oil unsuited for many commercial uses, not to mention gnats and dysentery, plagued the entire project, from wellhead to refinery. The oil business entailed more than just bringing in a gusher. Oil—Britain's Anglo-Persian had it. But now Anglo-Persian lacked the cash and investors to pump it, pipe it, refine it, and then ship it to market and siphon off a profit. The company was determined to secure lucrative government contracts from London—or any other capital in Europe.[47]

In December 1911, Churchill summoned a departmental oil committee to forecast the Navy's needs. Estimated 1912 consumption was fully 225 times that of a decade earlier. Moreover, the study committee concluded that at least a one-year reserve supply was needed to sustain fleet operations. But where was this fuel to come from? Churchill established a more sweeping Royal Commission on Fuel and Engines and appointed the recently retired oil maniac himself, Fisher, to locate that fuel.[48]

In June 1912, Churchill wrote, "My Dear Fisher … You have got to find the oil to show how it can be stored cheaply, how it can be purchased regularly and cheaply in peace and with absolute certainty in war."[49]

But now the international Shell conglomerate was purchasing Anglo-Persian's oil, diverting it to other markets. The first 15,000 barrels had already been loaded onto a Dutch tanker in May 1912. Moreover, cash-strapped Anglo-Persian was contemplating a complete buy-out offer from Shell—exactly what the Admiralty and Foreign Office did not want. Shell was not British-controlled, it was Dutch-controlled. When Churchill tried to confirm a supply of a million barrels per year, Shell's Dutch executive arrogantly answered, "Make that a half a million."[50]

It dawned on London officials that even though an oil company had been born British, wielded as a tool of British of imperialism, and was under the control of British subjects, that the company's oil product could be sold anywhere. The company could be sold to a foreign source, or become foreign-dominated by virtue of any number of commercial transactions from investment to strategic lending. Corporate avarice was an inexhaustible commodity in the business.

How long could any oil supply be relied upon if war broke out? No one knew. As war in Europe became a topic openly discussed, the sure supply of petroleum ascended to one of arch importance.

In 1913, the attitude of Anglo-Persian Oil Company itself also turned alarming as the firm began developing a preference for a global market, far beyond Britain. Anglo-Persian Oil Company executive, Charles Greenway, bluntly told the Foreign Office his company wanted more than diplomatic support and a willing customer in the Royal Navy. Unless Anglo-Persian received a large contract and a significant cash infusion from the British government, the company would sell its holding to Royal Dutch Shell.[51] That sounded like blackmail.

Undersecretary of State Louis Mallet wrote bitterly, "I do not like the attitude of the Anglo-Persian Oil Company who have hitherto posed as being ultra-imperialist. Mr. Greenway first comes to me and hints that if Shell obtains the Mesopotamian oilfields, it will be difficult for the Anglo-Persian Oil Company to resist coming to an agreement with them—unless the Admiralty can give them a contract. I did not at that time understand that an agreement meant more than an understanding as to the sale price of oil. Greenway now threatens complete absorption with the Shell unless the Admiralty gives him a contract."[52]

Shortly thereafter, Foreign Secretary Edward Grey sent Anglo-Persian a message in plain words: "The support which His Majesty's Government have given your company in the past, both in obtaining their concession in Persia, and in other ways, was given on the understanding that the enterprise would remain British and that it would be a matter of great surprise and regret if your company made any arrangement whereby a syndicate, predominantly foreign, got control of their interests in that country." If that occurred, the Foreign Office continued, "Your company could not of course hope to get from His Majesty's Government the same support as in the past."[53]

As the British government was being squeezed, astonished officials could only wonder what had caused such a turn of events. "It is clear," Undersecretary Mallet wrote in 1913, "The Shell group are aiming at the extinction" of Anglo-Persian "as a competitor—one of their objects being to control the price of liquid fuel for the British Navy."[54]

Greenway audaciously admitted as much to the Royal Commission for Fuel when he testified, "We know very well that if we join hands with the Shell Company, we shall probably make very large profits, and that it will result in their securing a practical monopoly of oil in the Eastern Hemisphere if not in the whole world."[55]

The concept of price gouging by a Shell-directed monopoly clearly became fixed in Churchill's mind. The price of fuel oil was skyrocketing, having more than doubled during the previous eighteen months, from thirty-seven shillings six pence per ton to seventy-seven shillings six pence per ton. "Daily, the prices of oil are rising," proclaimed a memo given to Churchill.[56]

Ironically, Royal Shell only worsened official apprehension when the company suggested it might cut its promise of oil supplies by 50 or even 80 percent. "It is entirely a question of price," a senior Shell executive coldly warned, driving home the fear of price gouging. "If the Admiralty pays [a premium rate] … you will always get supplies with no difficulty."[57]

In 1913, the British were so worried about the prospects for oil that White-hall policymakers debated whether they should return to the less militarily effective but more reliable realm of coal. Speed at sea would be sacrificed, but at least Britain possessed its own coal. Budget planners even calculated the cost of coal retro-conversion: £150,000 per ship.[58]

A new approach would be needed to avoid what Churchill termed, "being mercilessly fleeced at every purchase."[59]

High-powered British diplomacy went into action. First, a strategic border issue was settled. For centuries, the fuzzy frontier between Mesopotamia, Persia, and Russia had been contentious and disputed—often militarily. As part of the many efforts to forestall the expected chain-reaction war in Europe, a border commission had been established during the previous year, 1912, to permanently set a mutually recognized boundary. After eighteen sessions, the delegates finally fixed the international border. By no accident, some of the richest oil-producing lands of Persia were placed into Ottoman Mesopotamia. A treaty was drawn up to delineate the so-called Transferred Territories.[60]

Now Mesopotamia was an even more precious source of oil for petroleum-starved London. The region was clearly in Britain's sights.

*      *      *      *

Throughout April 1914, arcane historical facts of who had a right to Turkey's oil were debated back and forth between officials of Britain, Germany, and Turkey. The rules had been rewritten by revolution, redrawn international boundaries, commercial concessions granted but not signed into law, and all the other vagaries of mineral rights in an ancient land being thrust into a twentieth century. Every petition from London and Berlin that invoked conflicting privileges conveyed by the Sultan's *Civil Liste* was answered by the pashas now ruling the Empire with a reminder that those original early-century concessions predated the post-revolution mining law and its new anti-monopoly provisions. So many different legal theories were expounded that the juridical haze surrounding Turkish oil rights seemed impenetrable. One solution suggested in British diplomatic circles was to just cement a secret understanding with the Turks that while a monopoly would not be ordained in law, it would be granted to one suitor *de facto*. Hence, other syndicates could apply, but none would actually be approved—just endlessly delayed.[61]

As turmoil among negotiators whirled endlessly in Istanbul during early 1914, the British Treasury and the Admiralty, together with Anglo-Persian, on May 20, 1914, finally ended fiery negotiations with a three-page, fourteen-point contract to regulate any oil that might come under the company's control. Adorned at the top with the words "An Agreement" in large gothic script, the accord conveyed to the government 51 percent of the company's shares. Whitehall would henceforth control Anglo-Persian's board of directors and the firm's commercial destiny—all in exchange for a £2.2 million infusion of cash. That same day, a private letter from the government was issued to Anglo-Persian stating that the day-to-day commercial affairs of the company would be left to the management. No veto would be invoked unless any action affected naval contracts, sales to foreign entities, the geo-political impact of drilling, or corporate status.[62]

While the specifics of the oil contracts with Anglo-Persian would remain secret, like any other military supply contract, the £2.2 million funding itself was a public expenditure that required ratification by an act of Parliament. Rather than subject the measure to an elaborate and protracted parliamentary process, Churchill prepared for a single significant public presentation before legislators, with an up or down vote.

Meanwhile, in Istanbul, the Ottoman Council of State reviewed the various German and British suitors for its Mesopotamian concession and, indeed, the whole question of whether the Empire would grant a monopoly. The pashas ruled that no monopolistic concession could be granted—regardless of London's threats of a tax increase veto.[63] This refusal opened the door for influential and cash-flush competitors to continue peddling their influence and push for petroleum. Mesopotamia's concession was again spun round within the Turkish maze.

As Churchill prepared to conclude a deal with Anglo-Persian in Persia to the exclusion of Shell, Shell top executives went on the offensive. Shell's reluctant involvement in Turkish Petroleum Company was a project for the future. There was oil to be sold to the British Navy in the here and now. Therefore, at the end of May 1914, Shell's senior officials circulated a series of letters attacking the plan to acquire Anglo-Persian as governmental market rigging and injecting intolerable favoritism into the oil business. Churchill denounced those criticisms as nothing more than vile efforts by unscrupulous Shell to "keep prices up to the present blackmailing levels."[64]

Parliament debated the matter with loud protests about tying the Navy's fate to so far off and as lawless a territory as Mesopotamia. "Nobody denies that the properties are valuable," asserted George Lloyd, MP, "but … the whole of that country and the whole of your properties is surrounded by material which is far more flammable than the oil which you seek … I am absolutely in favor of our seeking an oil supply … in any part of the world, outside or inside the British Empire, where it can be found and properly controlled. I say, 'properly controlled,' which this cannot be."[65]

Lloyd emphasized, "Those places [in Persia] are situated in a country which has no central control whatever … in a country which is surrounded by war-like tribes … which is in the hands of turbulent tribesmen whose influence is proportionate locally for their capacity to terrorize and raid, and whose policy is directed by no respect for foreign undertakings or treaties."[66]

Another member declared, "It is as if he had stored his gunpowder near some furnace."[67]

Some members wondered how Britain could morally meddle in another nation's territory without regard for the inhabitants. "It is almost amusing," charged MP Arthur Ponsonby, "the way the great powers, when discussing a matter of this sort, consider that they are conferring an untold benefit on the country in question, and the interests of that country, so far as its population is concerned, are entirely disregarded … It has been the policy of the British Government too often to concentrate attention on the material development of a country without sufficient regard to the welfare and liberties of the inhabitants to whom that country belongs."[68]

At the end of the day, a tempestuous Parliamentary debate ended in ratification of a bill known as "Anglo-Persian Oil Company—Acquisition of Capital." The vote was not even close: 254 ayes against only 18 nays.[69]

In an editorial the next day, the *Times* warned, "We want the Navy to have oil. But we do not want to run the risk of fresh embroilment anywhere in the Middle East; and it is for this reason that we fear the country may come to regret an impetuous and careless undertaking."[70]

On June 18 and 19, with Parliament's vote still fresh and even as the headlines raged, identical coordinated telegrams were sent to the Turkish prime minister by the British and German governments applying maximum pressure in pursuit of the long-awaited and decade-delayed concession. These two communications only reinforced a barrage of telegrams earlier that month ominously reminding that Turkish tax increases were completely contingent on the concession.[71]

On June 28, 1914, London received the requested definitive and positive response to its demand for an oil concession. The Turkish reply was: "The Ministry of Finance, which has taken over from the *Civil Liste* matters concerning petroleum deposits already discovered or to be discovered in the *villayets* [provinces] of Mosul and Baghdad agrees to lease them to the Turkish Petroleum Company and reserves the right later on to fix its own share as well as the general terms of the agreement." The Turkish Petroleum Company was a patched together consortium of Shell and German interests working with independent Turkish financiers.[72]

The Foreign Office was about to mount yet another démarche on that June 28, when the world's attention was suddenly riveted on Sarajevo in the tiny realm of Bosnia. Bosnia was one of those tiny emerging post-Ottoman realms swirling at the heart of the Eastern Question and the Balkans Wars.

Archduke Francis Ferdinand, heir apparent to throne of the Austro-Hungarian Empire, and his wife were on an official state visit to mountain-cradled Sarajevo that June 28, 1914. About a month earlier, while sipping tea beneath a flickering gaslight at Belgrade's Café Zlatna Moruna, three fanatical Serbian nationalists from an organization called the "Black Hand" were making plans. One had read a short newspaper notice about the impending state visit. They immediately organized a conspiracy of some twenty-two individuals. A vanguard of three assassins slowly made their way to Sarajevo.[73]

June 28. Approximately 10:00 a.m. Driving in an open car as part of a six-vehicle motorcade, with a wealthy loyal supporter riding upright on the sideboard, the archduke's attention was drawn by a loud crack. It was a hand grenade, thrown by one the conspirators. The grenade bounced off the vehicle, exploding harmlessly away from the car. Archduke Ferdinand and his wife Sofia sped off to their destination, city hall, to complain to the mayor about an assassination attempt. Believing the attack to be over, and deciding to stand up to fanatics, the archduke and his wife sat patiently through the mayor's trite speech. They were en route to their next stop when the driver took a wrong turn, accidentally cruising right into the sight lines of the second conspirator Gavrilo Princip. Princip approached the car, aimed, and shot twice.[74]

Princip was wrestled to the ground by guards and placed in shackles. At first, it was uncertain how seriously injured the couple was. But as the vehicle drove on, blood spurted from the archduke's mouth. His pregnant wife slumped to the floor in pain. The Archduke, himself mortally wounded, turned to her and pleaded, "*Sterbe nicht! Bleibe am Leben für unsere Kinder!*" "Don't die! Stay alive for our children!" Shortly thereafter, she died. Then he died.[75]

Europe was thrown into chaos. Throughout a tumultuous and nerve-wracking July, Vienna charged Serbia with trying to start a war. The many alliances that had been revving darkly for decades began lining up on either side of the conflict. The Eastern Question was about to be answered—on a global scale.

One month after the murders, July 28, Austria-Hungary invaded Serbia. On August 1, as the Czar rushed to bolster his ally Serbia, Germany declared war on Russia and the next day on Russia's ally, France. Britain demanded that the Kaiser respect Belgium's neutrality, and when he invaded Belgium on August 4, London declared war on Germany. Within days, Japan, too, declared war on Germany. The conflict deployed great new modes of warfare: submarines, airplanes, massive trenches, tanks, long-range cannons, and many more devices and methods of terrible devastation. The Great War was on, and it would be fueled by oil.

On October 29, 1914, the Ottoman Empire entered the war on Germany's side. That was all London needed. Within a week, Britain was at war with Turkey as well. There was no need for further negotiations over Turkey's Mesopotamian oil concession. What could not be obtained through commercial ploys and pressures would now be seized as a spoil of war.

The captains of industry and the leaders of nations had walked through the intoxicating vapors of Middle East petroleum, some for country, some for avarice, many for both. But two gunshots in Sarajevo ignited a fuse that exploded into a monstrous conflict that killed millions. Thereafter, fuel and fuse would be inseparable throughout the world. One would beget the other for decades.

# 4

# BRITAIN AND THE TAKING OF MESOPOTAMIA

The saga of the Nazi-Islamic alliance that stretched from the Arabian Desert to the Balkan valleys is generally attributed to long-festering Arab hatred of Jews. That is only half true. The other half of this history is the pan-Arab hatred of Great Britain. It was infidel Britain that occupied Palestine under the League of Nations Mandate—and made it the Jewish national home. It was infidel Britain that occupied Iraq to exploit its oil. Britain was the nemesis of the Arabs in Palestine and in Iraq and indeed throughout the extended Islamic Middle East. Hence, the Arab combination with Germany during the Holocaust fused two hatreds.

But what brought Britain to Baghdad? Oil was the motive, but the Great War was the mechanism.

What exactly was World War I, and how did so monstrous and murderous a conflict in Europe find such a pivot in the Middle East? Few have ever understood World War I, least of all those who fought in its reeking trenches and died bleeding in reddened mud. But that "war to end all wars" was the tectonic confrontation between the European continent and the Middle East rectangle that opened the earth to allow Britain's triumphant entry into both Mesopotamia and Palestine. This earthshaking geopolitical upheaval, so detested by the Arab inhabitants, caused the Arab-Nazi axis to arise. But how exactly did that happen?

*    *    *    *

World War I: 8 million dead, 21 million wounded, 2 million missing in action, $180 billion spent.[1]

The Great War that many thought would be concluded within weeks dragged on mercilessly for nearly half a decade. In numbers that defy the darkest imagination, young men continually climbed out of muddy trenches to valiantly charge barbed wire, mines, and machine-gun fire. They were blown to bits, poisoned by toxic fumes, and starved *en masse* in the bloody conquest, loss, and bloody reconquest of mere meters of territory.

The disastrous 1915 Gallipoli campaign killed more than a half million men from both sides. During the Battle of the Somme in 1916, about a million men died from all countries—on the first day alone, there were 58,000 British casualties, a third of which were killed. At Verdun in 1916, the dead and missing were estimated to be nearly a million. At war's end, Russia lost more than any country, mobilizing 12 million and suffering 1.7 million fatalities, 5 million wounded, and 2.5 million missing or taken prisoner. Germany's numbers were almost as staggering.[2] The best explanation of why the nations of Europe went to war and sacrificed so many men was this: they just wanted to.

However, long before most of Europe's deadliest battles, the British invaded Mesopotamia with a special purpose. Britain declared war on Turkey on November 5, 1914. But weeks before, sealed orders had been sent to Bombay for Indian Expeditionary Force D to sail to the Persian Gulf. Not one barrel of commercial oil had been pumped in Mesopotamia, nor had a drill been sunk, or a concession even granted. But one day the oil was expected to flow, and that day was what Britain was waging war to capitalize on.[3]

On October 31, 1914, after the Ottoman Empire joined the war on Germany's side, but before war had even been officially proclaimed with Turkey, the Admiralty in London dispatched a coded telegram to the British colonial Indian naval forces laying in wait in the Persian Gulf near Abadan. The message: "Commence hostilities against Turkey."[4]

Pre-positioned Indian forces promptly secured Anglo-Persian's facilities on November 6—just 24 hours after Whitehall actually declared war. British and Indian forces then pressed on toward Basra, which they occupied on November 23. When the British arrived in Basra, thousands of Turks rapidly retreated. One senior officer recalled, "We found the lower-class Arabs busily employed in looting and burning the houses and murdering the occupants." Order was restored only after several agitators were hanged. Thereafter, Basra became the center of a British occupation that steadily penetrated north.[5]

Now came a confluence of economic, political, and military invasions that established Britain as the new power in Mesopotamia. Indeed, as millions of young men hurtled back and forth across the ghastly trenches of Europe's battlefields, so did diplomats, oil executives, and occupation officials jockey across Mesopotamia's commercial landscape. Millions died in Europe. But in far-off Mesopotamia, the military-industrial oil complex survived and eventually prospered beyond anyone's dreams.

As London prosecuted the war, Anglo-Persian's oil contributed a mere 20 percent of Britain's fuel needs. The remainder was imported, chiefly from the United States. Yet by January 1915, a full British division—some 10,000 men—had occupied Basra, and thousands of additional British, Indian, and other colonial units were stationed nearby along the Persian Gulf.[6] The massive expenditure of men, materiel, and fuel was vastly more than needed to protect the Anglo-Persian refinery at Abadan. Britain was locking down not the present strategic advantage, but the future of Mesopotamian oil and Gulf commercial routes.

By the fall of 1915, the way forward from Basra to Baghdad was clearly foreseen. A British official flippantly suggested to the British palace, "My little show in Mesopotamia is still going strong, and I hope that Baghdad will soon be comprised within the British Empire."[7]

However, making Mesopotamia a British satellite required more than just defeating the Turks. It meant allying with the tradition-infused and insular Arabs who lived there. That brought Britain face-to-face with the rising tetrahedron of Arab nationalism—a fractious jumble of tribal rivalries and alliances, kings without constituents, and constituents without kings, all churning across obscure landscapes of impenetrable political intrigue.[8]

With the Great War raging, the Arab national moment finally arrived.[9]

Nationalist yearnings, percolating for years, manifested most fiercely beginning with the newest iteration of the Ottoman Empire under the rule of the Young Turks. True enough, Turkey's revolution in 1908 and 1909 had brought administrative reform to the corrupt ways of the sultans. But soon thereafter, the Committee for the Union and Progress—that is, the Young Turks—had turned repressively chauvinistic about their country. The ruling pashas decided that all the diverse ethnic groups within the empire should become one people: Turkish. They should speak one language: Turkish. Live with one identity: Turkish. Those who would not change willingly would be changed forcibly. The much-resented Turkification campaign of Arab lands throughout the Middle East administratively and economically favored those Arabs who assimilated into the modern Turkish culture and bowed to Istanbul's authority. The campaign pointedly snubbed the Arabic language and customs.[10]

However, the whole bundle of Arab wartime resentment toward the Turks also tore at the fabric of Islamic sensibilities. To side with the British against the Turks meant siding with the Christian infidel against other Muslims and, indeed, the modern center of the Islamic world, Turkey. After all, the sultans, for all their moral decay, were still the caliphs of Islam—the supreme leaders of all Muslims. For better or worse, Istanbul was the seat of the caliphate.[11] Thus, all Arab alliances were uneasy. Like so many mirages and dust devils in the desert, one minute an alliance with the Arab potentates was visible and furious, the next it was gone, only to reappear a moment later.

In Mesopotamia, demographics played a key role. Mosul in the north was Kurdish; Baghdad was largely Sunni; the south was overwhelmingly Shia. Of the approximate 2.6 million people in Mesopotamia's three provinces, more than half were Shia. The Kurds constituted about 20 percent. An additional 8 percent throughout Mesopotamia hailed from non-Arab and/or non-Islamic groups, such as the Jews, Christians, Armenians, Turkomans, and the secretive Kurdish Yazidis, a tiny sect that abhorred lettuce and dark blue clothing. Although concentrated into a dense and commanding power base in south and central Mesopotamia, the Shia were still considered by the larger Arab world to be Islam's outcast 10 percent.[12] In turn, the alienation that Mesopotamian Shias felt for the larger Arab world's Sunni majority never subsided. Hence, the ancient Shia–Sunni rivalries and ingrained disregard for infidels held fast as nationalists considered Mesopotamia's place in their precious campaign.

For each of the rival groups in Mesopotamia, London offered a promise of nationalism or demographic ascent if they would only come to the assistance of Great Britain in her war with Turkey. The same was done with Arab contingents elsewhere in the Middle East, especially in the Hejaz, the most important western part of the Arabian Peninsula. Among the promises considered and proffered was an Arab national state in Syria. This was key in many strategic ways. Arab soldiers in the Turkish Army hailed from Mesopotamia, but were actually stationed in Syria. What's more, by virtue of the deployments to Syria and that country's intellectual base and connections with France, Damascus, the capital of Syria, had become the epicenter of the Arab national movement.[13]

In truth, because of the inherent conflicts in allying with the British infidel against Muslim Turkey, Arab leaders did not care whether the facilitator of their national hopes was Istanbul or London. Arab activists simultaneously offered the same fierce allegiance to both the British and the Turks. In some cases, they rallied against "European imperialism." In other instances, the enemy was "Turkish domination."[14]

In the first flammable months of 1914, as prewar contingencies and stratagems were being brokered with Britain, one family rose to prominence: that of Hussein ibn Ali, the Sharif of Mecca. Hussein, a short but striking and bearded figure, had been appointed by the Young Turks in 1908 to be the guardian of Mecca's holy sites. Hussein's Hashemite clan traced its lineage directly to the first Quraysh chieftains of Mecca, some five centuries before the Prophet Mohammed rose against the local establishment in 610. Thereafter, the Quraysh descendants of the Prophet's wife, Fatima, became the honored Sunni rulers of Mecca, later known as "the Hashemites." These were the ancestors of Hussein. Through the ages, the distinguished Sunni Hashemite clan became the hereditary defenders of Mecca and superintendents of the *Hajj* (pilgrimage) to Mecca, mandatory for all Muslims. Hussein's family was known throughout the entire Arab domain as a noble one. For London, despite many seething competitors and detractors, it was easy to anoint Hussein and his two sons, Abdullah and Faisal, as the chief applicants and negotiators of the Arab national movement.[15]

London's price for any Arab national reward was strategic revolt against the Turks. But could any Arab deliver? On February 5, 1914, Abdullah met with Lord Kitchener in Cairo. Kitchener was Britain's consul general in Egypt and a leading military star who would soon become Britain's war minister. Abdullah's message: The Turks were threatening to administratively terminate his father's honorary position in Mecca. In such a case, Hussein just might lead a local revolt against the Turks. Would the British support him against Istanbul?[16]

Several weeks later, in late March 1914, Louis Mallet, British ambassador in Istanbul, reported to Foreign Secretary Grey, "It is still impossible to say what real prospect there may be of any united Arab movement." But Mallet added an enticing thought, "If the Arabs are eventually successful in defeating the Ottoman armies, the loss of the Caliphate would probably follow, where, shorn of a further large portion of territory and of the religious leadership, Turkish rule as it exists today would presumably disappear." To that, he added a caution: "Europe might then be faced with the question of a partition of the Turkish Empire, which might easily produce complications of a serious nature."[17]

Since war had not yet broken out, and commercial relations with the Ottomans remained vibrant, Britain was determined not be dragged into any localized revolt in Mecca or even in Baghdad. But by late October 1914, with the war in Europe fully under way and the war in the Middle East just days away from ignition, Whitehall reversed itself. In July 1915, the British high commissioner in Egypt, Sir Henry McMahon, entered a back-and-forth written correspondence with Hussein that included some 10 confidential letters. The full written exchange was kept secret for 15 years until revealed by the press and parliamentary investigation.[18] Those 10 letters, later to become famous as "the Hussein-McMahon correspondence," offered ambiguous British promises of national recognition within an ambiguously defined territory in exchange for ambiguous Arab offers of revolt predicated upon calculated deceptions and implied threats by both sides.

Decades later, activists on all sides of the Arab national debate would point to the McMahon-Hussein correspondence as proof—or lack of it—of broken pledges and unfulfilled national obligations. Any arguer indeed could seize upon passages within any of the most prominent letters to validate any argument. But embedded within the full set of 10 letters—including some of the forgotten ones—are British demands and the Arab willingness to cede control to the British over one specified region in exchange for national rights elsewhere. The region the Arabs were willing to cede: Mesopotamia.[19]

The prelude to the historic 10-letter McMahon-Hussein correspondence was Kitchener's introductory note of October 31, 1914, which stated: "If the Sharif and Arabs in general assist Great Britain in this conflict that has been forced upon us by Turkey … Great Britain will guarantee the independence, rights, and privileges of the Sharifate against all external foreign aggressions, in particular that of the Ottomans." Referring to the notion of replacing Turkish religious supremacy with Hussein himself, Kitchener appended, "It may be that an Arab of true race will assume the Caliphate at Mecca or Medina, and so good may come by the help of God out of all the evil which is now occurring."[20]

Arab self-definition and mapping began in earnest in early 1915 in Damascus. In March and April, during a series of secret meetings, the two leading nationalist societies, *al-Fatat* and *al-Ahd*, joined forces with each other and with Emir Faisal, who was representing his father, Hussein. Together they drafted "the Damascus Protocol," which created a map for the envisioned Arab state. It resembled a dented rectangle, tilted left toward eleven o'clock, encompassing and extending the Arabian Peninsula to the shores of the Mediterranean. The proposed northern border coursed east from the Mersin-Adana railway in Turkey, just beyond Syria, along the railroad tracks and across the 37th parallel to the Persian frontier. The eastern border followed the Persian frontier down to the Persian Gulf and then continued to the bottom of the Arabian Peninsula. From there, the outline traveled north to the Mersin-Adana starting point in Turkey, thus completing the geopolitical box. Both Palestine and the three Mesopotamian provinces resided completely within that approximate rectangle. The Damascus Protocol specified that if Britain granted this proposed new state, the British Empire would become the new Arab nation's defense partner. In addition, the new Arab nation would extend "the grant of economic preference to Great Britain."[21]

Fearing Turkey's seemingly omnipresent spies, the Damascus Protocol was reduced to miniature script and then sewn into the boots of a member of Faisal's party. Faisal returned to Mecca, where he unveiled the plan to enlist his father's support for a so-called Arab Revolt. The suggested insurrection would begin during the winter of 1915 in Syria, where the troops were supposedly standing by. But Ottoman commanders detected the conspiracy and suddenly transferred most of the Arab divisions out of Syria, east to the Gallipoli front. That brought certain death, and Arab soldiers were promptly cut down as part of that battle's mass carnage. The Arabs in Syria did not revolt that winter.[22]

But as 1915 dragged on, and the British found themselves embroiled in the south of Mesopotamia, strategic written exchanges with Hussein and Faisal resumed. One such letter from Hussein deferentially wrote, "In order to reassure your Excellency, I can declare that the whole [Arab] country, together with those who you say are submitting themselves to Turco-German orders, are all waiting the result of these negotiations, which are dependent only on your refusal or acceptance of the question of the limits [borders]." In the best tradition of the Turkish bazaar, Hussein's next sentence asked exactly what Great Britain wanted in return for national support. "Whatever the illustrious Government of Great Britain finds conformable to its policy on this subject, communicate it to us, and specify to us the course we should follow."[23]

McMahon's reply: Britain wanted Mesopotamia.

On October 24, 1915, McMahon wrote back that the United Kingdom would "recognize and support the independence of the Arabs in all the regions within the limits demanded by the Sharif of Mecca,"— minus the Turkish portion, minus any other area in which Britain enjoyed an obligation with other chiefs, and minus any other area, namely Syria, that would conflict with the interest of France. Syria had long been a French sphere of influence. Most importantly, McMahon wrote, "With regard to the *vilayets* [provinces] of Baghdad and Basra, the Arabs will recognize that the established position and interests of Great Britain necessitate special administrative arrangements in order to secure these territories from foreign aggression, to promote the welfare of the local populations, and to safeguard our mutual economic interests."[24]

Hussein quickly replied on November 5, with a flurry of great defensive conviction on behalf of Mesopotamia. Using the region's historic cartographic name, *Iraq*, Hussein staunchly explained that Iraq was inseparable and sacred to all Arabs—and had been since time immemorial. "As the Iraqi *vilayets* [provinces] are parts of the pure Arab Kingdom," wrote Hussein, "and were in fact the seat of its Government in the time of Ali ibn Abu Talib, and in the time of all the Caliphs who succeeded him; and as in them began the civilization of the Arabs, and as their towns were the first towns built in Islam where the Arab power became so great; therefore they are greatly valued by all Arabs far and near, and their traditions cannot be forgotten by them. Consequently," he insisted, "we cannot satisfy the Arab nations or make them submit to give us such a title to nobility."[25]

The Arabs would not give up Mesopotamia. But Britain could rent it.

"In order to render an accord easy," continued Hussein, "we might agree to leave under the British administration for a short time those districts now occupied by the British troops, without the rights of either party being prejudiced thereby (especially those of the Arab nation; which interests are to it economic and vital), and against a suitable sum paid as compensation to the Arab Kingdom for the period of occupation, in order to meet the expenses which every new kingdom is bound to support; at the same time respecting your agreements with the Sheikhs of those districts, and especially those which are essential."[26] Britain was now persuaded by a key Arab officer in the Turkish army, Mohammed Faruki, a defector, who functioned with unspecified rebel authority. Faruki declared that it was worth securing a deal with the Arabs to stage a revolt if the right terms could be obtained. In early November 1915, Faruki on behalf of Hussein passed a message to the British Foreign Office that once the Turks were ousted, the Arabs would be willing to grant Great Britain governance over Baghdad and north Mesopotamia. Faruki also assured, as a British diplomat recorded it, "Arabs would agree to Basra town and all cultivated lands to the south being British territory."[27]

In fact, several opportunities for the Arabs to rise up against the Turks in Mesopotamia were not taken before or during the McMahon-Hussein correspondence. For example, when the suspicious Turks in 1915 transferred numerous Arab divisions from Syria to the bloody Gallipoli front, they also moved two divisions, the 35th and the 36th, to Mesopotamia. There were suggestions that two leading Arab nationalists be sent in from Syria to foment the population in Baghdad and Basra. The Foreign Office shied away from such an idea, since national agitation in Mesopotamia would not only inspire rebellion against the Turks, but against the new British occupiers as well. The balking Foreign Office concluded, we cannot "let loose revolutionaries whose actions may extend beyond our control." Others in the British government concurred: "Their [the two proposed agitators] political views are much too advanced to be safe pabula [baby food] for the communities of occupied territories, and their presence in any of the towns of Iraq," as the three provinces were now increasingly being called, "would be, in our opinion, undesirable and inconvenient."[28]

Hussein and some of his scattered Arab forces did ultimately join the military action against Turkey in the Hejaz, Palestine, Gaza, Syria, and elsewhere. A jihad was promulgated by Hussein to justify joining infidel Christians against fellow Muslims: "The defense of the Hejaz from this evil and aggression [the Turks], the observance of the Rites of Islam that Allah has commanded, and the guarding of the Arabs and the Arab countries from the danger to which the Ottoman Empire is doomed because of the misbehavior of this wicked society—all of this will be achieved only by full independence and the cutting of all ties with the bloodthirsty conquerors and robbers."[29]

But in large part, Hussein's Bedouin fighters were "show forces." Not infrequently, they were ceremoniously marched into a town for local applause after a battle was hard-won from the Turks by British units from Australia, India, or elsewhere. Britain certainly provided money and rifles for a campaign of camel riders and horsemen, led by such liaison officers as T. E. Lawrence, dubbed "Lawrence of Arabia." Lawrence's exploits were later romanticized in movies and novels. In reality, as submarine wolf packs hurled torpedoes through the waves, as airplane formations dropped bombs and strafed from the air, as tanks rumbled across the battlefield, as poison gas wafted over the trenches, and as those fighting in Europe gave their lives in a cataclysmic war that swept away 15 million, many considered the scant Arab uprisings to be merely cosmetic. Lawrence himself termed the Arab raids a "sideshow to a sideshow."[30]

The Arabs were unimportant in defeating the Turks. But more important, there was no Arab uprising in Mesopotamia when the British first entered Mesopotamia—that is, not when the British first entered.

\*     \*     \*     \*

The British drive for Baghdad really began in late November 1914 as the military occupied Basra and pointedly asked itself: What next?

Everyone was optimistic. The Turks were oppressive masters. London believed its troops would be greeted as liberators.

"Arab element is already friendly, and notables here volunteer opinion that we should be received in Baghdad with the same cordiality as we have been here [in Basra]," reported Britain's military's chief political officer Percy Cox. He continued, "Baghdad in all probability will fall into our hands very easily."[31]

Cox had served as the key political resident in Persia from the first days of Anglo-Persian's oil strike. He added, "I find it difficult to see how we can well avoid taking over Baghdad ... but once in occupation, we must remain." Oil advocates, such as Admiral Fisher, pressed Britain's Prime Minster in a letter, "I hope you are not losing any time annexing the Tigris and the Euphrates!"[32]

For years after, the generals would argue about exactly who had authorized the decision to drive north to Baghdad to take the city. No one would take credit for the campaign. But most concluded that orders originated with British officials in Bombay—perhaps because many of the mesmerized civil administrators in colonial India considered Baghdad "the glittering prize to which all eyes turned." Certainly, Indian viceroy Hardinge energetically encouraged the campaign. In a mid-January 1915 letter to the Foreign Office, he wrote, "It is, in my opinion, a matter of cardinal importance to India that Basra should be retained and that the predominance of England in the Persian Gulf should thus be assured. We may never get the chance again." His braggadocio constantly encouraged movement north.

Newly installed Mesopotamian commander in chief Sir John Nixon, who led the push to Baghdad, could explain only vaguely that when he visited Bombay, "I gathered we were to advance on Baghdad." In any event, the War Office, fully apprised of the campaign once it began in September 1915, authorized its progress north.[33]

But no one was ready for what happened. The short drive up the road to Baghdad took 18 months. And it cost tens of thousands of lives.

Unbeknownst to the British, seasoned Turks were waiting in long defensive trenches at Kut, 100 miles south of Baghdad. Then at Kut, the British were effectively surrounded by as many as 60,000 Turks. Moreover, local Arabs elements hostile to the British energetically joined the Ottoman jihad against the infidel invader.[34]

By mid-January 1916, beleaguered commanding general, Charles Townshend, wired, "I have twenty-two days food left, but by … eating up the horses, we can last out much longer." Wasting no time, Townshend ordered the immediate slaughter of 1,100 animals. By February, rations, including horsemeat and mule meat, were halved. Regardless, many Indian troops refused to eat such animals, so their hunger increased more quickly.[35]

Local Turkish commanders offered to let the starving British men retreat for a £1 million bribe, but the Ottoman War Minister Enver Pasha in Istanbul blocked it. London doubled the offer to £2 million. This, too, was refused. Enver Pasha, mastermind of the alliance with Germany, did not want money—he wanted British troops to surrender. Finally, on April 29, 1916, in a humiliating defeat, 13,309 British troops and noncombatant support elements destroyed their weapons and equipment and surrendered to the Turks.[36]

When the Turks reoccupied Kut, British officers, including the sick and dying among them, were subjected to the most savage violence. The beatings were incessant. Hostile Arabs and Turkish soldiers alike looted their few possessions, boots, and blankets, and pummeled those who resisted.[37]

Quickly, the Turks turned to any Arabs in the town of Kut who had cooperated with the British. These people, drawn from the Arab leadership, were tortured, mutilated, and frequently strangled. One British translator from town was seized. The Turks broke his legs, and then hung him upside down until the pain was so unbearable he desired death. That he achieved when in an unguarded moment he hurled himself off a roof.[38]

As for the British soldiers, although too emaciated from disease or starvation to walk normally, they were nonetheless mercilessly marched almost the entire 100 miles from Kut to Baghdad. Hundreds died of thirst, starvation, or beatings. Local Arabs along the way demanded boots or clothing for mere handfuls of dates or black bread. Uniformed Arab soldiers in the Turkish army accompanying the march forced the feeble men forward by merciless whipping and assaults with rifle butts.[39]

But eventually British reinforcements arrived. Kut was retaken. Then the advance to Baghdad was resumed. The British entered Baghdad triumphantly on March 11, 1917 in columns of weary Tommies and turbaned Indians, Lee-Enfield bolt-action rifles on their shoulders, a dust storm swirling around them.[40]

Baghdad was not taken for oil. It was not taken for commerce. It was taken for Kut and the memory of 13,000 captured, many of whom were propelled through a bleak nightmare gauntlet that one commander described as Dante's Inferno.[41]

Baghdad was not taken for oil. Baghdad was taken because, while the British could swallow the horror of hundreds of thousands of their best and brightest dying courageously if naively in the slimed trenches and muddied fields of battle, they could not stomach the eye-searing images of their men being beaten, tortured, and slowly starved into shuffling skeletons yearning to go home or die.

Baghdad was not taken for oil. But Basra was.

And soon, the memory of misery *en route* to Baghdad would yield to the original mission in Mesopotamia. It was the oil.

The following proclamation was read aloud in Baghdad by General Stanley Maude on March 18, 1918, one week after occupation by the British.

### TO THE PEOPLE OF BAGHDAD

In the name of my King, and in the name of the peoples over whom he rules, I address you as follows: our military operations have as their object the defeat of the enemy and the driving of him from these territories ... Our armies do not come into your cities and lands as conquerors or enemies, but as liberators.

Since the days of Hulagu, your city and your lands have been subject to the tyranny of strangers, your palaces have fallen into ruins, your gardens have sunk in desolation, and your forefathers and yourselves have groaned in bondage. Your sons have been carried off to wars not of your seeking, your wealth has been stripped from you by unjust men and squandered in distant places ...

O people of Baghdad, remember that for twenty-six generations you have suffered under strange tyrants who have ever endeavored to set one Arab House against another, in order that they might profit by your dissensions ... Therefore I am commanded to invite you ... to participate in the management of your own civil affairs in collaboration with the political representatives of Great Britain who accompany the British Army, so that you may be united with your kinsmen in the North, East, South, and West in realizing the aspirations of your Race.[42]

But that is not what happened.

CHAPTER

# RETURN TO ZION

**Z**ionism—the movement for Jewish nationalism—is one of the most misunderstood concepts on the international landscape. It began as a mere idealistic dream nurtured by wishful Jews envisioning a return to Zion, that is, the Holy Land, which became known as Palestine. The land was known as Israel until the Jews had been expelled centuries before by the Romans. The whole idea of Zionism never became a political, philosophical, or ethnic monolith but rather an accretion of loose precepts that, in its formative years, defied every attempt to achieve cohesion or identity. Was Zionism a religious quest, a sovereignty movement, an agrarian plan, an economic transformation, a rescue plan, an urban vision—or was it all those things? Which great power was to be its sponsor? That was argued for years. Was it Germany, France, the Ottoman Empire, or Great Britain? Even the territory that Jews hoped to establish as a homeland was fiercely debated. Was it Palestine? Was it Uganda? Was it North Africa? Was it Argentina?

During the glissando decades between the late nineteenth and early twentieth centuries the movement was galvanized by campaigns of extreme persecution and mass murder against Jews throughout Eastern Europe and the Middle East. Turbulent world events in confluence with rivers of Jewish blood, flowing from Russia and from the far corners of the Arab world, made Zionism an urgent Jewish necessity during those pivotal years. Hence, the hard specifics and velocity of Jewish nationalism were determined less by the movement's great thinkers and advocates than by the onslaught of anti-Semitic campaigns as well as the political intrigues and self-interest of European capitals.

As the twentieth century opened for business, Jewish nationalists

—Zionists—were hardly alone in their quest for self-determination. During the latter half of the nineteenth century, colonized, occupied, persecuted, and otherwise subjugated people rose up in nationalist movements worldwide to reject the monarchial, dynastic, imperialist, and ecclesiastic regimes that had so harshly dominated them. The nature of nationalistic movements varied from realm to realm, but most often emerged from popular group identification along linguistic, religious, political, geographic, or ethnic lines. Some people came together because they lived between the rivers, some because they spoke the same dialect, some because they believed in a new economic order, some because they wanted the freedom of worship, and some to achieve religious primacy. Self-determination generally manifested as a quest for an independent territory, either in the form of nationhood or autonomous confederation with the larger state. In some cases, the freedom sought was merely to self-manage or inaugurate a social renaissance. Once successful, nationalists believed they would live a life no less free than that achieved by France, England, or the United States—running their own affairs for the good of their own people in a land with borders that they controlled.

National movements could be found in abundance throughout the world during the late nineteenth and early twentieth centuries. In Africa, the Aborigines Rights Protection Society in British-dominated Ghana was just one of the African continent's indigenous groups seeking independence from Europe. In Asia, the Meiji Restoration discarded the Shoguns of Japan in favor of an emperor. South America saw an endless series of local national movements seeking to achieve social, political, and economic independence from their faraway masters in Spain and Portugal.[1]

But in the vast Ottoman Empire that spanned three continents, national movements—both militant and intellectual—arose everywhere. During the later nineteenth century, the long-festering national aspirations of the Greeks erupted in numerous armed clashes with Ottoman forces. Albanians also sought to throw off the yoke of the Sultans. The Armenian "national awakening" led to uprisings that eventually ignited a cruel Turkish mass murder of some 1.5 million men, women, and children. Bosnians, Bulgarians, Serbs, Kurds, Romanians, and many other groups dwelling in the far-flung Ottoman domain each bubbled up in cultural, military, or political insurrection seeking a land of their own, some with repatriation to their ancestral home.[2]

Likewise, the expansive Arab world, largely under Turkish control, led by its twentieth century intellectual elite, recalled the Islamic Conquest more than a millennium earlier, a conquest that had itself stretched across three continents. In its golden age, Muslim rule extended from Mecca north to the furthest reaches of the extended Middle East, and west to the Iberian Peninsula of Spain and Portugal, and beyond into parts of the Pyrenees and regions of what is now known as France. Pan-Arab nationalism found its real beginnings in about 1908 with the Young Turk movement. Made cohesive by enzymatic British agitation during World War I, the disparate threads of Arab nationalism sought some sort of recognized nationhood with recognizable borders, a recognized capital, and a social order that recognized Islamic law. The Arabs of those years did not expect to reconstitute their massive Caliphate that had stretched from the Atlantic Ocean to the Mediterranean Sea and from the Persian Gulf to the Indian Ocean. But the Muslims did expect a twentieth-century political accommodation in some land somewhere that would allow them to take their rightful place among the community of nations.[3]

Zionists stood in a long line of ethnic groups—Christian, Islamic, geographic, ethnic, and otherwise, each seeking to create a territorial home and seize control of their own destiny. For Jews, the homeland they sought most energetically was the land they had been deported from, once known as Israel, and renamed Palestine by the Romans.

How the Jews returned to Palestine in the twentieth century and the very fact that they were allowed to reclaim their heritage was a central actuator of the war against the Jews conducted throughout the Arab world. This war was brought to a scalding point in the Farhud in 1941. Only by understanding Zionism—how the movement fit into two twentieth-century wars, the great geo-political powers that were at play, and the intersection of the Jewish mindset, the Nazi mindset, and the Arab mindset—can one begin to comprehend how an alliance of hate and converging opportunities arose between Muslims and Germans. The goal of this alliance was to destroy their common enemy: the Jews.

*　　*　　*　　*

For more than a thousand years, the Jews undertook a slow, tedious march toward assimilation. Yes, most lived in ghettos, imposed but then found too comforting to leave, as old prisoners find it difficult to leave their cells. Yes, most wore a distinctive dress, frequently imposed upon them but eventually found too familiar to shed. Yes, they had been dispersed throughout the world by the Roman Expulsion, the French Expulsion, the Spanish Expulsion, and so many other local and countrywide expulsions in so many places that, for centuries, Jewish bags were said to always be packed, at least mentally. But Jews treasured their peace when it lasted.

But no matter how settled, Jews were permanent strangers in European lands and forever strange in every Middle Eastern and Islamic land. When Jews took root, they did so without soil. Land ownership was commonly prohibited. For centuries, denied lands, denied access to the professions, denied military rank, Jews were forced to deal with money, with trade, with bargains, with influence, with middlemanship, and with the portable professions. They had little choice as regimes across Europe often required Jews to wear garish costumes often emblazoned with special yellow badges, just as Muslim dhimmitude had demanded, but then also made *de rigueur* in the Christian world. In their adopted homes, Jews often could not vote and were cast legally as second-class citizens. They existed in relative safety where they were until some warlord or monarch or ruling council decided otherwise. That peril was periodic.[4]

Not until the nineteenth century did some European governments begin treating their Jewish citizens as equals. France in 1791 was the first. In September of that year, a parliamentarian sympathetic to the Jewish plight vociferously demanded from the rostrum of the National Assembly: "I believe that freedom of worship does not permit any distinction in the political rights of citizens on account of their creed … Still, the Turks, the Muslims, the men of all sects are admitted to enjoy political rights in France. I demand … that the Jews in France [also] enjoy the privileges of full citizens." By acclamation, the National Assembly then and there ratified the proposal. *Voilà*. Jews became legal equals in a nation that had reinvented itself two years earlier by storming the Bastille under the banner "Liberty, Equality, Fraternity."[5]

Napoleon went so far in 1806 as to create commemorative prints of his egalitarian gesture to his country's 40,000 Jews. He then invited Jewish leaders to re-establish their *Sanhedrin*—the ancient Council of Sages. That occurred in 1807 in the Hôtel de Ville in Paris at a festooned ceremony, triumphantly ushered in by a military tattoo and honor guard. Letters from Jews in the newspapers of the day hailed France as the new "Palestine" and the new "Zion."[6]

Other European countries followed. *Emancipation* came in Great Britain via a sequence of enabling laws during the 1830s and 1840s, in the Ottoman Empire in 1839, and Switzerland in 1874. One by one, the umbrella of legal equality was extended throughout much of Europe.[7]

Some of the Jews who emerged from ghetto and peasant life began to assimilate. Assimilation was the protective impulse to join the larger host society as a loyal minority, indistinguishable from the rest of their countrymen except for a quietly pursued if different religious practice. Not infrequently, the assimilated citizen's Judaism was itself pared down, modernized, or reformed to lessen the dissimilitude with neighbors. In Germany and then the United States, the Reform Judaism movement reshaped its practices and worship to edge closer to that of the Christian world around them. In some Jewish communities, many cast off their Judaic burden altogether, converting to Christianity for convenience and sometimes by social compulsion.[8]

Assimilation had been the key to survival for many Western and Central European Jewish communities. Anything that suggested that French Jews did not belong in France, that British Jews did not belong in Great Britain, that Italian Jews did not belong in Italy and so on, was anathema to the Jews who had fought so hard to claw open a niche of acceptance. Zionism, the campaign to bring Jews out their adopted countries into a far-off nation of their own, was therefore not a welcome idea to established Jews who had achieved some measure of comfort and a degree of hard-won social peace. Assimilated Jews increasingly saw themselves not as Jews first and foremost, but rather as productive, cosmopolitan members of a hyphenated citizenry. For them, Judaism was their footnote, not their headline.[9]

The Jews of nineteenth-century Western and Central Europe as well as America were only interested in bettering their lot among their neighbors, not resettling in distant Palestine to reclaim their former heritage. And who would be? Palestine in the nineteenth century was a forsaken Ottoman backwater, devoid of infrastructure, roads, and nighttime safety from omnipresent Bedouin brigands. Mosquitoes, insufferable heat and humidity, swampy tracts, lack of arable acreage, blistering deserts, and unhygienic surroundings competed with baksheesh at every turn along with confiscatory Turkish taxes at every opportunity for distinction as the most miserable aspect of Palestinian life.[10]

Palestine's total population at the year 1840 was about 400,000, which included only about 5,000 to 6,000 Jews. Those Jews dwelled in four spiritually important cities: mainly Jerusalem, but also Tiberias, Safed, and Hebron. Most were pious and devotional, keeping a Jewish presence alive in the land of the Torah. Around 1840, just a few dozen were engaged in any kind of productive revenue-generating work or craft, the remainder being immersed in full-time Judaic worship and scholarship, supported almost completely by charitable donations from Europe. In other words, most of the Jews of Palestine prayed all day every day—and little more.[11]

The year 1840 was a turning point in Palestine. It was then that the politically and financially weakened Ottoman Empire reinstated its long-suspended *Capitulations* to various European governments. The capitulation system was an extraterritorial grant to another state that would entitle that country's commercial entities and citizenry to enjoy foreign national status and protection on Turkish land. In some instances, this created a mini-colony within a Turkish colony such as Palestine, generally including the display of a foreign flag and even extensions of the foreign nation's postal service complete with special stamps in foreign currency. The first of these capitulations dates back to a sixteenth-century Ottoman concession to France. But in truth, the Byzantine Empire had used the system with foreign powers as far back as the tenth century.[12] The Turks, however, had elevated such anomalous bilateral relationships to a political fundamental.

As a result of Europe's resurrected ability in the 1840s to project influence into Turkish territories, the French, British, Germans, and Russians, among other foreign nationals, began flowing into Palestine. Often these transplanted European citizens were associated with Christian churches that had had a historic prominence in Palestine. In some instances, individuals in Palestine could purchase a document of capitulatory protection, and this abuse was increasingly common for merchants and clerics alike. Jews were among these foreign transplants, especially as many were forced out of Europe by persecution. By this mechanism, they found new lives in Palestine circumventing the consent of Turkish authorities.[13]

From 1840, the Jewish populace of Palestine began to increase. By 1850, the Jewish community in the Holy Land had approximately tripled to 17,000 total inhabitants and was edging closer to a Jewish majority. By 1881, the number had swelled to 25,000. These Jewish transplants—about half *Ashkenazi* or European, and half *Sephardic* or of Middle Eastern heritage—were all under the protection of a foreign power and in many ways exempted from certain Ottoman tariffs, taxes, and daily tribulations.[14]

Certainly, the Palestinian population was accustomed to the many migrants from far reaches of the Ottoman Empire and especially the extended Middle East who settled in the land. But the local Arab community harbored a special resentment, at one level or another, for all these new Jewish neighbors. They were, after all, Jews and, as such, second-class citizens beneath the Syrian Moslems, Lebanese Muslims, Egyptian Muslims, and Turks who freely came and went from Palestine.

The Sephardic Jews, both the established residents and those transplanted, spoke Arabic, knew Arab customs, and blended more with Arab ways. So while they were reviled, they were tolerated as traditional *dhimmis*. The European Jews, often covered by a foreign flag, were openly despised. Regardless of the umbrella of protective capitulation, Ashkenazim were commonly confined by pressure or sensible preference to ghettos. Life was tense for such Jews. They were spat upon while walking along the public street, periodically stoned on sight, and sometimes lynched in the public square. Even their Sephardim coreligionists found themselves unwilling to comingle with the Ashkenazim lest the stain of the European Jewish infidel rub off on them.[15]

Yet the Jews continued to come, not because Palestine was an attraction—it was not—but because resettling there became a fate better than death under the czars and other ruling anti-Semites that burned their way into Jewish history during the last two decades of the nineteenth century.

During those years, the word *pogrom* debuted in everyday Western parlance. In Russian, the word *pogrom* means "a riot of violent havoc and destruction." That is exactly what the pogroms became as they were typically inflicted against Jews. Villages would be raided by Cossack horsemen. Houses set on fire. Women raped wholesale in front of their families. Men, women, and children mass murdered by the sword, the bullet, or the rope during frenzied mob actions.[16]

It is hard to know when the era of the pogrom actually started in Jewish history. Violent anti-Jewish riots date back to Roman times. Armies of eleventh-century Crusaders pillaged and massacred Jewish villages in France and Germany as a recurring asterisk to their years-long campaign to reconquer the Holy Land. Throughout the later Middle Ages, especially during the contagion years of the Black Death, anti-Jewish riots spread across Europe almost as quickly as the disease. Plague-bewildered peasants commonly burned Jews alive at the stake or in mass immolation pits, bound and drowned them in the river, or brutally expelled them, lashing out at anyone they feared could be responsible for the infection.[17]

The first general use of the term *pogrom* occurred not after the first Odessa anti-Jewish riots of 1821, but after the 1859 outbreak of mayhem in the region. The idea was cemented after violence was again visited on the Jews of Odessa during a four-day terror spree in 1871. Then in 1881, after the assassination of Czar Alexander II, Jews were falsely blamed. Across Russia, Jews were slaughtered wholesale during an unprecedented level of violence. The so-called "May Laws" were enacted to further restrict Jews to the Pale of Settlement, wherein they were systematically subjected to pauperization, starvation, and murder. Jewish villages, known as *shtetls*, were regularly raided in a new wave of pogroms. The stated policy was to "cause one-third of the Jews to emigrate, one-third to accept baptism, and one-third to starve."[18] In other words, more than five to six million Russian Jews were to be rapidly and systematically subtracted.

Russian and other Eastern European massacres in the 1880s, together with a renewed surge of anti-Semitism throughout Western Europe caused Jews across the Continent, like never before, to see the need to create a territorial safe haven. Jewish emigration from Eastern Europe began to multiply. In the first years after the Russian May Laws and accompanying pogroms, some 5,000 new immigrants entered Palestine from Romania, Russia, and other locales in Eastern Europe, joined by hundreds of mostly agrarian Jews from Ottoman Yemen. Thousands more came each year throughout the 1880s and 1890s. During these last two decades of the nineteenth century, Jews began slowly establishing settlements and enclaves of their own in Palestine. The Turks tried to block land purchases, even for their own Yemeni citizens who were Jewish. Istanbul even sent diplomatic messages to Washington and other capitals declaring that they welcomed any immigrants—other than Jews.[19]

Jews, in need of housing, purchased land anyway, generally at vastly inflated prices, through thinly-veined intermediaries. Yet few of these new-comers to Palestine brought with them any economic self-worth and contin-ued to be dependent on foreign remittances. The need became clear to inject economic and industrial self-reliance into the Jewish community in Palestine. This emerging enterprising Jewish presence intersected the advent of mod-ern political Zionism in the late nineteenth century led by Austrian Jewish journalist Theodor Herzl.[20] Herzl startled the world—Jewish and non-Jew-ish—when, in 1896, he published a pamphlet entitled *Der Judenstaat*, which means *The Jewish State.* Herzl wrote that the cause of anti-Semitism was the very presence of Jews in Diaspora countries: "The Jewish question persists wherever Jews live in appreciable numbers. Wherever it does not exist, it is brought in together with Jewish immigrants. We are naturally drawn into those places where we are not persecuted, and our appearance there gives rise to persecution. This is the case, and will inevitably be so, everywhere, even in highly civilized countries—see, for instance, France—so long as the Jewish question is not solved on the political level. The unfortunate Jews are now car-rying the seeds of anti-Semitism into England; they have already introduced it into America."[21]

In other words, asserted Herzl, anti-Semitism existed *because* Jews dwelled in countries other than a homeland of their own. Herzl was a pure intellectual, a visionary of the sort who characterized so many nationalist thinkers of that era. His idea for a Jewish state was that first the impoverished, persecuted Jews with no choice would seek refuge in the Jewish homeland, preferably Palestine, financed by the wealthy Jews who would never consider dwelling in the malaria-infested miasma of the Holy Land, but who thought well of rescuing their coreligionists. Once there, through the charity of the wealthy Jews, Zionist refugees would begin building a modern state that would attract the second population wave, a middle class seeking to capitalize on the new emerging colony. Once the Zionist home lifted itself through this initial growth process, Herzl postulated, the remaining wealthy Jews would come in a gradual third wave.[22]

The proposition that many thousands of Jews would leave their safe coun-tries of assimilation—especially the United States, France, and England—played directly into the hands of the many anti-Semites who resented Jewish presence and regularly mumbled about expulsion. Zionism squarely posi-tioned Jewish "national rights" against Jewish "civil rights" as a competitive question. Most established Jewish leaders in New York, London, and Paris were divided between being firmly *anti-Zionist* and *non-Zionist*, or neutral.

These terms become obsolete after the State was born but at the time were very much in vogue. Indeed, Zionists found few allies among the mainstream Jewish establishment. London's Baron de Rothschild, who had established his own charitable Jewish settlements in Palestine devoid of any nationalist idea, utterly refused to cooperate in the venture. In a July 1896 meeting with Herzl, Rothschild irately refused to finance a wave of what he called *"schnorrers,"* the Yiddish term for bothersome beggars.[23]

But the continuing bloody destruction of East European Jewry cried louder than the conflicted voices of comfortable Western and Central European Jews. More than 5 million Russian Jews were trapped in immediate life-or-death peril. This injected another international dynamic. The settled and assimilated Jewish communities of Europe and the United States were not keen for their cities to be inundated with desperate refugees. But that is exactly what happened during the close of the nineteenth century. Hundreds of thousands of terrified Jews fled to safety in Western Europe and the American East Coast. In the decade of the May Laws alone, some 200,000 desperate Jews from Russia and Eastern Europe entered the United States, and many thousands more poured into the urban centers of Great Britain.[24]

In the 1880s, an estimated 260,000 Eastern European Jews poured into America, many penniless, many unkempt, unhygienic, and not equipped for the transition from *"shtetl* life" to New York City's Lower East Side and the other major East Coast metropolises of the United States. No one knows the real numbers because American migrant records at the time were based on only national origin, not religion. But in the decade of the 1890s, more than a half million more Jewish refugees entered, communal experts estimate. During that same two-decade period—that is, the 1880s and the 1890s, demographers suggest, some 70,000 to 150,000 Eastern European Jews fled to Great Britain, likewise settling in already congested urban quarters.[25] These massive influxes forever changed the ethnic fabric of the United States and Great Britain.

It became clear that either hundreds of thousands of fleeing Jews would be crowded into the slums of New York, London, and Paris, or they would be resettled into desolate far-off Palestine as Herzl and the Zionists suggested. In other words, for the Jewish middle and upper classes, the spoken and unspoken mindset was "better over there than over here."[26] Hence, wealthy Jews in the West could help finance the rescue and resettlement of Russian and Eastern European Jewry both because of the humanitarian disaster unfolding and the personal goal of not importing a roiling Jewish problem to their cities.

Zionism was conceived as a democratic movement that would bring together all the arguing idealistic Jewish nationalists under one umbrella group. This group later became known as the Zionist Organization. The ZO organized the international Zionist congresses, where delegates debated where exactly the Jewish state would be, how it would be, and by what means it would be. The first of these congresses was held in Basel in 1897. Using donations from various wealthy Jewish philanthropists who had shown an interest in a Jewish presence in the Holy Land, Herzl and the Zionists were able to create a financing bank called the Jewish Colonial Trust Co. This bank would transduce Jewish contributions into land purchases, immigration programs, retraining, and other state-building expenses.[27]

The Zionist ideal always insisted upon a legal migration, recognized under international law, legitimatized through aboveboard land acquisition, chartered by sovereign governments, and organized as an officially sanctioned process. The Jews had no army and had developed precious few military traditions during their Diaspora centuries. They could only do what the international community allowed. In other words, Zionism had to ask permission.

So, Herzl immediately set out to obtain permission, seeking the same kind of land "charter" commonly granted to colonizing efforts and development projects throughout the world. America and Canada had both been settled by British charters or land grants. The Ottoman Empire was an experienced purveyor of charters, such as that given to Germany to develop the Berlin-to-Baghdad railway, a 20-mile-wide corridor across much of Mesopotamia. So, Herzl first turned to the sovereign Turkish ruler of Palestine, Ottoman Sultan Abdul Hamid II.[28]

In 1896, Herzl intrigued enough European diplomatic intermediaries and paid enough bribes to string-pullers in imperial Turkish circles to schedule a meeting in Constantinople with the Sultan's grand vizier and the foreign minister. Herzl openly proposed a chartered Jewish colony in exchange for which the Zionists would call upon Jewish financiers in London and Paris to organize a monumental purchase and conversion of much of the 1881 Ottoman Public Debt. In *Judenstaat*, Herzl speculated that if "His Majesty the Sultan were to give us Palestine, we could in return undertake to regulate the whole finances of Turkey." The crippling Ottoman debt was, after all, more than £106 million, equivalent to trillions of dollars in twenty-first-century money. Foreign debt was one of the debilitating illnesses weakening "the Sick Man of Europe"—England and Russia's term for the dying Ottoman Empire—and a root cause of the resented but constant foreign intrusion in Turkish life.[29]

Despite the offers, neither the grand vizier nor the foreign minister was impressed with Herzl's idea, although they agreed to pass on the idea of an autonomous Jewish territory to the Sultan himself. But he was not interested either. The Ottoman realm was already wracked with vituperative national movements from East to West. Sultan Abdul Hamid was not willing to authorize yet another national effort to encourage similar fractures among the restive colonies under his rule. The Sultan's curt rejection, transmitted via the grand vizier was: "When my empire is divided, perhaps they will get Palestine for nothing. But," continued the Sick Man, "only our corpse can be divided. I will never consent to vivisection."[30]

Herzl would not give up. He tried every approach to secure Palestine. The Ottoman Empire was increasingly in the German sphere of influence. So, perhaps Berlin was the proper route to Istanbul. In 1898, Herzl met with German and Austrian go-betweens, such as the Grand Duke of Baden and Berlin's ambassador in Vienna, hoping to convince them to convince Kaiser Wilhelm to convince the Sultan to make a future Zionist Palestine a German protectorate. Much of the Zionist movement was itself German or Austrian, emphasized Herzl to his contacts. The official international language employed at Zionist conferences was German, and most Jews spoke the Germanic Yiddish dialect. Many of the movement's central leaders were German or Austrian. If the Kaiser would intercede with the Sultan, Zionist Palestine would create a German bulwark in the Mideast and fortify Berlin's growing projection of influence in the region. Hence, Jewish Palestine would have a German sponsor and German allegiance—and every Jew would remember it. After some preliminary recommendations, the Kaiser agreed to meet Herzl during a forthcoming state visit to the Ottoman Empire, which was, coincidentally, to include a triumphant tour of Palestine.[31]

Perfect. Herzl packed his trunk and hustled off to the Orient Express. Destination: Istanbul. After days of anxious waiting at the Royal Hotel, on October 18, 1898, Herzl was finally summoned to the Yildiz Kiosk, the Sultan's guest house, where the Kaiser and his foreign minister were in residence. Excited and paying attention to every detail, the always dapper, full-bearded Herzl, maneuvered through his wardrobe until he found just the perfect soft grey gloves to compliment his appearance. During the hour-long private conference, Herzl found what Zionists often found—a helpful partner, but helpful for all the wrong reasons.[32]

Fact: Zionism appealed to anti-Semites, especially those who saw Jews as unwanted citizens in their adopted countries. The prospect of an orderly exit was obviously appealing to the Germans. Wilhelm did not hide his feelings, stating, "There are among your people certain elements whom it would be a good thing to move to Palestine." Herzl let that remark and several similar denigrations pass and instead dove into the heart of what was requested: "a charter company under German protection." The Kaiser accepted the notion, replying, "Good, a chartered company," promising to recommend the project to the Sultan.[33]

Next stop—Jerusalem.

As his vessel approached the Jaffa shore on October 26, 1898, and as the coast came into focus, Herzl and his colleagues openly wept. They quietly muttered, "Our country, our mother Zion!" Two days later, as Wilhelm was riding his magnificent white horse past a crowd of well-wishers, the monarch was told Herzl would be waiting among them. When Wilhelm spied Herzl, he pivoted down from his saddle and shook Herzl's hand. On November 12, Herzl met with the Kaiser again, this time in the sovereign's Jerusalem tent, hoping to nail down specifics. But by now Wilhelm's attitude had chilled to total disinterest. Learning that the Sultan was repelled by the whole idea, the Kaiser abandoned his support. Newspaper commentators at the time explained the *volte face* by reminding all of the lucrative German-Turkish arms trade that the Kaiser would not want to endanger. "The Ottoman Empire receives its rifles from Mauser, its cannon from Krupp," one wrote.[34]

Dejected, Herzl continued to dream of a colony granted by the Turks. After all, in his defining 1896 pamphlet *Judenstaat*, Turkish Palestine was proffered as the best idea. The next year, during the Turco-Greek war over Crete, Zionists openly raised funds for the Turkish Red Crescent and provided a group of doctors—this to show friendship to the throne.[35]

But Herzl clung to his original idea: coax the Sultan by helping to erase the Empire's massive debt. A Jewish company and bank was formed through the Jewish Colonial Trust Co. For several years after the 1898 debacle, Herzl spent whatever funds he could to bribe, entice, and otherwise parley himself into position to renew negotiation with the Sultan. The baksheesh even included 40,000 francs to the Sultan's minister. During these years, two pivotal dynamics were rapidly accelerating.[36]

First, the plight of Russian and East European Jewry was becoming progressively worse. Many Jews confined to the Pale of Settlement were being systematically starved to death. Jewish communities worldwide were becoming even more desperate to rescue them. Second, the crushing international debt and internal fracture of the Ottoman Empire were weakening the Sick Man of Europe as never before, even as the throne was becoming more desperate to buy time or arrange financial succor.[37]

In May 1901, the door swung open again. The palace in Istanbul cabled that Herzl should return at once for a conference with the Sultan himself— and be prepared to present a plan for a grand program of financial relief, millions of pounds to be accessed quickly. Filled with hope and hesitation, Herzl rushed off to the same Royal Hotel he had visited five years earlier, hoping once more to interest the Turkish government in his vision.[38]

Herzl penned a long proposal to the Sultan—one of several—making crystal clear what the Zionists could offer. "I have the honor to place at the foot of the Throne of Your Imperial Majesty the result of my proceedings," Herzl wrote, adding, "Following the line which Your Imperial Majesty deigned to indicate to me, I believe it most urgent to procure before the month of October, a million and a half of Turkish pounds which would replace in a less onerous fashion the difficult if not impossible work of unification of the debt … The 1,500,000 pounds could be procured by the immediate creation of a new resource … My friends are disposed to create a company with a capital of five million pounds Turkish. This company would have for its purpose, the development of agriculture, of industry, and of commerce, in a word, of economic life in Asia Minor, Palestine, and Syria. All the necessary concessions being given by the kindness of Your Imperial Majesty, the company … could immediately make a loan amortizable in eighty-one years. This loan would therefore, so to say, cost nothing because the cost of the interest and of the redemption would be made by the company, which would hold all the bonds of the loan and dispose of them afterwards. The government would simply receive £1,500,000."[39]

In exchange for this, Herzl asked that a Jewish company be recognized for settlement in Palestine, it being "understood that the company must be an Ottoman corporation, and the Jewish immigrants should immediately become Ottoman subjects, accepting military service under the glorious flag of Your Imperial Majesty. With the £1,500,000 raised, there would be time for study, and to realize other resources." Herzl spoke hopefully of an industrial future for the Empire with further development loans "for the exploitation of petroleum sources, of the mines, and likewise for electricity. The propositions for these other projects will be planned and figured out as soon as Your Imperial Majesty shall require … I am convinced that in this way, the moment will soon come when it will be recognized that the interest of the Ottoman Empire is to attract the economic forces of the Jews and to protect our unfortunates. On the other hand, it is to the greatest interest of the Jews to see Turkey strong and flourishing. This is the idea of my life."[40]

Herzl added further enticements, using the language of revenue that worked so well in Istanbul. "The Ottoman Jewish Company," he wrote, "would have, outside of the advantage of giving a signal of hope to the entire Jewish people, this other advantage that the taxable resources—men and things—would increase in every province where the company would work. The company would pay more and more taxes with the growth of its business. Jewish capital would rush in from all sides to establish itself and to remain in the Empire."[41]

As a final appended benefit, Herzl offered to silence the acidic Young Turk Ahmed Riza, the Sultan's greatest editorial critic in Paris. "I have been informed," Herzl suggested, "that there is in Paris, a writer, Mr. Ahmed Riza, who is well known for his attacks on the Imperial Government. I have been told that there is a means of putting an end to these attacks ... I shall do nothing without order, I shall not even see this person without authorization. But if Your Imperial Majesty believes it useful, I shall take up the case and it goes without saying, put an end to the attacks."[42]

With his long proposal in hand, Herzl met with the Sultan on May 19, 1901, at a lavish Istanbul banquet. This meeting with the Sultan—Abdul the Damned—a half decade in the making, struck Herzl as anti-climactic from the first moment he was ushered into the palace. "The dishonesty and bribery which begin at the door of the palace," Herzl had penned in his diary, "wind[s] up only at the foot of the throne ... Every official is a thief."[43]

When it was time for his much-anticipated face-to-face with the sovereign, Herzl found an unimpressive Sultan, wracked by years of gluttony and sexual exploits, a decrepit emperor of what Herzl belittled as a "dying robber kingdom." Herzl diaried with denigration: "Small, shabby, with a badly dyed beard, which is probably dyed only once in a week ... the hook nose of a Punchinello, the long yellow teeth and the big gap in the upper jaw to the right ... the fez drawn down deep over his head, which is probably bald ... the protruding ears ... the strengthless hands in the big white gloves, and the ill-fitting, big, multicolored cuffs ... the bleating voice, the limitation in every word. And *this* rules!"[44]

Inglorious or not, the hard bargaining began at that moment. The Sultan wanted the money before he would grant a Jewish charter. Herzl insisted on the Jewish charter being announced first, with the money to quickly follow. Finally, the Sultan offered a bitter compromise—refuge for Jews throughout the Empire, as Ottoman citizens—but not in Palestine.[45]

Excluding Palestine! Dejected, Herzl left the inconclusive event like so many negotiators before him who could not fathom the inscrutable and unpredictable Ottoman royal. But, absorbing and shaking off his dismay, Herzl set about trying to show good faith anyway by promising to make an advance deposit in certain Turkish banks, as if that would help.[46] But none of it mattered.

Herzl soon learned the massively orchestrated bargaining session was a just a ruse to develop a Jewish offer on debt consolidation that could be used as a bargaining chip to entice an even better deal from a French syndicate. That French offer succeeded, ending the negotiation.[47] The saga was over. Herzl now realized the Sultan would never grant a charter to a Jewish company or permit organized Jewish settlement in Palestine.

What now?

Jewish deaths were multiplying, both from Cossack swords and strategic starvation in the Pale of Settlement. Thousands were being expelled from cities and villages across Russia. Mass induction into Christian schools and conscription into the army were accelerated to erase the Jewishness of an entire generation. Quotas for Jews systematically forced more and more professionals and artisans out of their occupations, making even a meager subsistence impossible. In The Ukraine, Galicia, Romania—across Eastern Europe—the eradication of Jewish life was under way.[48]

Jews needed a haven and they needed it now. The collapse of hope for official Turkish sponsorship led to a distinct change in Herzl's tactics. He no longer saw the wisdom of pleading his case through German intermediaries. He gave up trying to entice Ottoman approval with promises of money and loyalty. Herzl now switched to hard diplomatic dealing. Zionist idealism was in need of *realpolitik*. That meant an alliance with Great Britain, which at the time was emerging as a counterweight to German and Turkish power in the Middle East.

London was interested—on many levels and for several reasons.

First, turn-of-the-century Great Britain enjoyed an influential community of Christian millennialists or proto-Christian Zionists. These individuals wanted to see the biblical fulfillment of the Jewish return to Jerusalem as a prelude to the return of the Messiah. Imbued with the Christian ethic, they also sought to make amends for centuries of Jewish persecution still underway. Among the most vocal of these Christians was Lawrence Oliphant, a Scottish-born traveler, mystic, and a prominent member of Parliament. For years before the efforts of Herzl, Oliphant had used his position and prestige to argue with the Sultan for a Jewish colony in Palestine. Indeed, the idea was initially approved by the Ottoman cabinet, but at the last minute Abdul Hamid vetoed the plan. The pogroms of 1881 caused Oliphant to redouble his efforts to help the Jews find a refuge. As each new wave of bloodshed erupted, Oliphant gathered more like-minded Christians to lobby Westminster and other governments to find a solution to the continuing carnage.[49]

Second, London's city fathers, the country's trade unionists, and the British people in general began to strain under the influx of hundreds of thousands of East European Jewish refugees crowding into certain urban areas. Numbers are debated because of blurred national origins and lack of religious markings during immigration record keeping, but experts suggest that tens of thousands of Jews, probably more than 100,000, fled to Great Britain during the pogrom years. Once packed into congested urban districts, such as the East End of London, the refugee Jews created their own burgeoning pocket of poverty, crime, and, most troubling to policymakers, a cheap labor pool.[50]

In 1902, a Royal Commission on Alien Immigration was convened to debate restrictions on any further Jewish influx into England. The squalor in Jewish parts of the East End offered no hope of improvement. Even New Yorkers, who had absorbed a million East European Jews, were fond of quipping that more Jewish paupers were now streaming into London than to American shores. It was a time when Romanian persecution had also forced Jewish artisans and craftsmen from earning a living, an oppressive measure that evoked denunciations both from Whitehall and Parliament as well as from America's President Rutherford Hayes. One Commission member complained that England had become a "dumping ground" for refugees. Seeking a solution to this human tidal wave of misery, Herzl was invited to give expert testimony to the Commission.[51]

Baron Rothschild, long a staunch opponent of any grand Zionist plan for a Jewish Palestine, was among the Commission members. Worried what might be said, Rothschild tensely questioned Herzl beforehand over lunch, hoping to secure a narrow approach. Unyielding, Herzl was determined to ask for a full colonial charter. Rothschild interjected, "Don't say 'charter.' The word sounds badly just now." Herzl retorted, "Call it how you will. I want to found a Jewish colony in a British possession." Rothschild came back, "Take Uganda." Herzl wrote on a small slip of paper the acceptable locales: Sinai, Palestine, Cyprus, declaring of East Europe's Jews, "The people must die—or go!" Rothschild gave in and reluctantly agreed to support a mass resettlement.[52]

In July 1902, Herzl appeared before the Royal Commission on Alien Immigration with the counter-intuitive declaration that the best way to rescue Jews and give them a safe haven was not to open London's gates wider. "The Jewish Question," he declared, "exists wherever we live in perceptible numbers." In other words, the existence of Jews in foreign lands itself incubated anti-Semitism. The only solution was for Jews to have a territory of their own.[53]

But where?

When Herzl wrote *Judenstaat* proposing a Jewish Palestinian state in exchange for relieving Ottoman debt, he did so in a section headlined "Palestine or Argentina," where he speculated that the South American country might be an option. "Argentina is one of the most fertile countries in the world, extends over a vast area, [and] has a sparse population and a mild climate," Herzl wrote, adding, "The Argentine Republic would derive considerable profit from cession of a portion of its territory to us."[54]

From 1897, several leading voices in the Zionist movement advocated Cyprus since it was under British, not Turkish, control. Herzl himself brought up the island territory to the Sultan as a bargaining chip in a November 1899 letter to Turkish officials. When Turkish negotiations disintegrated, Herzl made serious plans for a possible home in Cyprus under British auspices and discussed it in detail with Rothschild.[55]

Other possible landing sites for a Jewish colony Herzl considered—even if briefly—included Mesopotamia, which the Sultan and others had raised.[56]

True, East End overcrowding, vastly cheapened labor, the criminal element that ordinarily accompanies intense immigrant poverty, and a sense of Christian justice were all significant undercurrents. But there was a more strategic factor at play. Zionist failure in Istanbul came at the very moment when the British feared a looming German-Turkish denouement over the Eastern Question—that is, the ultimate disposition of Ottoman lands, especially the Balkans. At the same time, Mideast oil for military fuel became a sought-after commodity. Hence, the most persuasive appeal to the British government in the fall of 1902 undoubtedly hinged on the projection of imperial English power in the region, especially as both a buffer that could protect the Suez Canal and promote London's quest for petroleum in Mesopotamia.[57]

Now everything shifted to Colonial Secretary Joseph Chamberlain, the man empowered to talk about chartered colonies. Chamberlain was an all-business official accustomed to projecting British imperial power though the use of ethnic populations. A proper British gentleman, sometimes monocled and always well-attired, Chamberlain intellectually believed in a racial hierarchy with Anglo-Saxons at the apex and Jews at the bottom. His view was enshrined in his famous remark, "I believe that the British race is the greatest of the governing races that the world has ever seen." But that mindset, *au courant* with the eugenic raceology of the early twentieth century, was able to co-exist with a personal sense of fairness that nonetheless disapproved of anti-Semitism. Chamberlain felt no animus for the Jews and deplored their persecution. Herzl could do business with such a man. Moving fast, Herzl hastily utilized all available connections and intermediaries to arrange a meeting with Chamberlain. When Chamberlain and Herzl finally met on October 22, 1902, the conference was all nuts and bolts. No tedious cascade of cigarettes or coffees as was the custom in Istanbul, but rather the terse exchange of geopolitical ideas.[58]

Chamberlain was certainly interested in Herzl's project. He offered Herzl cooperation if the Zionist could show him "a spot in the English possession where there were no white people as yet." Chamberlain was as blunt as that. Several locales were mentioned—East Africa, Uganda, the Sinai coast at El Arish, and Cyprus among them. Chamberlain then ruled out Cyprus because the dense local Greek and Muslim population would object once the news became public, and that would release a "storm." The Colonial Secretary offered Egypt, but Herzl quipped, "We have been there."[59]

Under British control, El Arish on the Sinai coast at the eastern extremity of Egypt was an isolated and essentially empty desert but quite close to Palestine and not far from Mt. Sinai. However, settlement at this near vacant stretch required special irrigation and added security to protect colonists from marauding Bedouins. Discussions on El Arish, direct and indirect, continued for several months. An exploratory expedition was even organized to the territory, complete with a caravan of camels, an encampment of tents, surveys, reports, and optimistic negotiations. But by about March of 1903 British officials in both London and Cairo had rejected the El Arish idea as impracticable or undesirable for one reason or another. The objections were mainly logistical, but many thought they were mainly political—and perhaps both assessments were correct.[60]

Now, extreme violence on two continents separated by thousands of miles would continue to shape the geographic quest of Zionism in London.

The first theater of conflict was in Southern Africa. During the final two decades of the nineteenth century and the opening years of the twentieth, Dutch Boer settlers and British Imperialists at the bottom of the African continent fought two terrible wars, the First and Second Boer wars. The Second Boer War, beginning in 1899, was particularly gruesome. Scrappy Boer farmers, armed with precision German guns, formed guerrilla groups that disrupted British supply routes and laid siege to their cities. In response, Britain brought out the latest long-range weapons in its own arsenal and mercilessly suppressed the uprisings. Britain's scorched-earth policy decimated any home, farm, livestock, or commercial entity that could conceivably be thought to support the guerillas. Moreover, the British military forced Boer and native African families wholesale into desolate concentration camps. Some 150,000 civilians were interned by the British in miserable conditions of systematic starvation and neglect. Photographs of malnourished children as living skeletons—often mere hips on sticks—and of piles of corpses posed for body counts ripped the veneer off the war for both world opinion and the British public. A civilian commission dispatched by London toured the concentration camps. Horrified at the human squalor, Chamberlain as Colonial Secretary was ordered to reduce the death rate and tamp down the inhumanity. This he did in November 1901.[61]

Within months, by late May of 1902, Boer resistance dwindled to an end and the war concluded. Some 75,000 had died on all sides, but British soldiers were the largest group. During the brutal conflict, 300,000 horses were either ridden to death—500 in just one day-long battle—or slaughtered for meat. From the ashes, and by virtue of an act of Parliament, the Union of South Africa would rise several years later as a loyal member of the British Empire. But Great Britain's victory in South Africa was condemned internationally as a triumph of villainous brutality.[62]

Chamberlain sought to repair the damage with a new diplomatic initiative. On November 25, 1902, a month after his October meetings with Herzl, Chamberlain embarked upon the long journey to South Africa, sailing through the Suez Canal and ending at Johannesburg. Amid pomp and circumstance, he bid 1902 farewell and began his 1903 with a 10-day ride north on the Uganda railway. In a special seat positioned for him behind the locomotive, Chamberlain coursed steadily north to Nairobi through a region known as British East Africa—later to be named Kenya after the area's highest mountain.[63]

Looking down from the uplands, Chamberlain's train could be seen like a thick snake slithering steadily through the hills. Looking up from the bush, the mighty locomotive swept past, panting and rumbling like an imperial beast. As the train chugged north, the topography slowly began to change and soon resembled the pastoral clime of East Sussex in his native country. Chamberlain began to think. Yes, he could envision a transplant of English civilization to this verdant African realm. His imperialistic creed was best espoused by the observation, "It is not enough to occupy great spaces of the world's surface unless you can make the best of them. It is the duty of a landlord to develop his estate." This notion, amidst the syncopation of his motion, fused with Chamberlain's theories of racial supremacy in which Africans were at the bottom and Jews only slightly above that. [64]

An idea exploded in his mind: The Jewish state could be British East Africa. In his December 21, 1902, diary entry, Chamberlain wrote, "If Dr. Herzl were at all inclined to transfer his efforts to East Africa, there would be no difficulty in finding suitable land for Jewish settlers, but I assume that this country is too far removed from Palestine."[65]

As of that moment, the fertile East Africa land seemed to him to be under-occupied—by Europeans, at least. Zionists, in Chamberlain's racially-laddered mind, could uplift the base Black Africans through comingling and admixture, and plant a thriving white outpost of British colonization into the backward bush. When Chamberlain's vessel steamed into Southampton in March 1903, with his much-regaled homecoming, the idea of East Africa as a Jewish colony was peaking in his mind. Somewhere between the train line named Uganda Railway and the land northwest of Nairobi called Uganda—a land that Chamberlain never actually reached—and somewhere in the discussion with Herzl, the lush Kenyan territory in question became wrongly referred to as "Uganda." [66]

Thus was born the "Uganda Project," a mistakenly identified territory mistakenly offered out of a mistaken sense of race science to downtrodden people who would never accept it. But within days of Chamberlain's return to London, this compound mistake would become a proposition so serious it would split the Zionist movement. What endowed this wrong idea with any traction at all was the desperation caused by another episode of extreme violence far away from Whitehall, this time against Jews.

Herzl and Chamberlain met once more, on April 23, 1903. The Zionist Herzl tried to press the Englishman Chamberlain to reconsider Cyprus or El

Arish. The Englishman Chamberlain was intent on pressing the Zionist Herzl to consider East Africa. Indeed, El Arish had been effectively ruled out during the very days Chamberlain was traversing the African continent, and nothing Herzl could say would resurrect the idea. The Zionist, for his part, rejected Kenya—or Uganda—saying that maybe token colonization could be undertaken at future date. But for now, the foundation of any Jewish state would require a "base in or near Palestine."[67]

During their discussion, neither Herzl nor Chamberlain was aware of what had happened in the hours and days before they sat down. Russian censors had kept the news from escaping. The Bessarabia region of western Russia was an industrial and commercial province that had, for many decades, bounced between Turkish, Moldavian, and Czarist control. In 1903 it was firmly Russian territory. Kishinev, capital seat of Bessarabia, hosted a population of about 100,000. Almost half were Jews. Through industry, bribery, influence, and the payment of extortion when needed, Kishinev's Jewish establishment had survived the vexing sunset of the nineteenth century and the repressive May Laws. During the dawning years of the twentieth century, they fought with equal trepidation against recurring newspaper and pamphleteer accusations of the medieval Jewish "Blood Libel." The Blood Libel, irrepressibly whispered for centuries, invoked the fraudulent accusation that Jews needed to kill a Christian child for blood as a ghoulish ingredient of Passover matzo. Year after year in this new century, Kishinev's Jews had denied this outrageous myth, or ignored it, and simply struggled to live on amid ignorance. In 1903, Kishinev's Jews lost that struggle.[68]

April 19, 1903. Noon. Easter Sunday, and also the seventh day of Passover. Church bells announced not only the traditional end of Easter mass but, that year in Kishinev, the onset of its infamous Easter massacre. The carnage began as hundreds of young students, many intoxicated, poured through the main square shooing Jews away and hurling insults. Many were Albanians and Moldavians who had arrived by train earlier in the day, ready for menace. Soon Orthodox seminarians and other students, armed with axes and iron bars, joined the frenzy. As the fracas moved to the Jewish quarter of Kishinev, the mob wantonly broke windows and hounded Jews off the streets. Christian houses had already been marked with crosses or ikons so they would not be molested. As the disturbance escalated, police blatantly nodded their approval. Some policemen even joined the mob. The police chief failed to instruct his officers to confront the rioters. The vice-governor himself had written inflammatory articles for the *Bessarabetz*, the ragingly anti-Semitic local newspaper. The governor failed to mobilize the local garrison of more than 5,000 soldiers to restore order. Instead, the soldiers sat by passively as the gruesome mayhem unfolded. Soon the world would see nothing less than another state-sponsored Russian pogrom. But this one would be far more ghastly than any that had preceded it.[69]

As the afternoon wore on, vandalism, looting, demolitions, and thievery in Kishinev turned into a veritable orgy of bloodshed. The streets ran red with Jewish blood even as the town shook with the cheers of rioters amid the piercing shrieks of victims. Hundreds of Jews were viciously set upon, many being brutally murdered and dismembered where they stood. A two-year-old Jewish boy was seized by the mob and his tongue cut out as a trophy before they killed him. The meek grocer Weismann, already blind in one eye, pleaded for mercy and offered the crowd his last sixty rubles. His money was accepted, and then his grocery was destroyed nonetheless—but not before his other eye was gouged from its socket by a hooligan who screamed, "You will never again look upon a Christian child."[70]

Mercilessly, the fevered Kishinev throng chopped men, women, and children in half. Some victims were mutilated with nails pounded through their nostrils, or sliced open so their stomachs could be ignominiously stuffed with feathers. Women were repeatedly gang-raped on the public streets as enthusiastic crowds egged the perpetrators on. For many, there was no escape. Down in their basements, up in their attics, where they were discovered hiding, women and girls were raped in front of their pleading husbands and terrified families. Rifka Schiff was brutally gang-raped in front of her family, one holding her down and one violating her, even as several knelt next to her bellowing jeers and taunts as they waited their turns. This crime was repeated again and again throughout the Jewish quarter. In some cases, members of the mob carved off breasts as personal mementos.[71]

The few feeble attempts to intervene were overwhelmed. Few neighbors offered succor or shelter. Jews attempting to mount a defense were dispersed by the police. The local postmaster reportedly refused to accept residents' telegrams requesting help. No moderation could be seen as the painful hours dragged on—just the mad mania of scourging gangs. The upper-crust citizens of Kishinev took the time to tour the death and destruction strewn throughout their city but displayed what a Russian newspaper at the time called "the utmost indifference." Nor did the religious authorities subdue their followers. Orthodox Bishop Iaku himself, driven ceremoniously through the town in a carriage, only waved his blessings to the crazed mob. Iaku had made it clear to all that he believed that some Jews did engage in ritual murder.[72]

Some 2,000 hooligans continued their butchery all the next day, April 20, and did not quit until the morning sun of April 21. It was then that Russian Interior Minister Vyacheslav Plehev, tacit sponsor and puppet master of the entire pogrom, finally authorized a cessation of blood-letting. Plehev had reputedly wired the local governor weeks earlier, on March 25, that a well-planned operation was being organized against the Jewish community of Kishinev. The military, Plehev reportedly instructed, was to permit the mob action to unfold without interference. Only on April 21, after an unprecedented level of bloodshed was reported, did Plehev direct Bessarabia's governor to deploy the military. Soldiers were finally given orders to act and confronted the crowds. Within minutes, the mobs dispersed. [73] It was over. But not before a singularly repulsive and blood-curdling massacre had been launched into the history books.

In the smoldering aftermath, 41 bodies were recovered, including two babies and a twelve-year-old girl. Some 495 Jews were wounded, eight later dying of their injuries. More than 2,000 had been made homeless and thousands more were said to have become refugees or suddenly destitute. Property damage estimates reached 2.5 million rubles, or more than $1.25 million.[74]

When word finally did leak out, just hours after the April 23 meeting of Chamberlain and Herzl, the world was shocked. *The New York Times* and several other papers across America, in their April 24 editions, ran with a small item, the first mentions in the American media, reporting the killing of 25 Jews and the vicious wounding of 275. But as reports continued, and as journalists traveled to the scene, the news became more grisly. This was the era of the new mass media. The reports were magnified with photographs and wire service reports. Kishinev became the first atrocity covered promptly by the world's newspapers. Within days of the original news, *The New York Times* had republished a Yiddish newspaper dispatch that riots were "worse than the censor will permit to publish." The dead and dying might reach a vastly higher number, the articles warned, and this mob action was clearly yet another semi-official, Czar-sanctioned massacre—but on a far more heinous scale.[75]

New York Jewry mobilized to form a relief committee and by May 4, 1903, Jews across America were contributing money as part of a national appeal, well-publicized by the Yiddish, Jewish, and mainstream newspapers. The newspapers of William Randolph Hearst by themselves collected some $50,000 for Kishinev victim relief—more than a million dollars in twenty-first century money. Musical performances organized by Jews, Chinese, and other ethnic groups rallied a broad coalition of outrage. Politicians rose to protest. In Chicago, boat tickets for 6,000 Kishinev Jews were arranged to bring the victims out of Russia and into the American Midwest for resettlement. The Salvation Army offered to resettle 1,000 Kishinev families in the American South. Angry mass rallies of support and protest were staged in France, Denmark, Italy, and Belgium. Plays, poems, and songs were written in memory of a new *cause célèbre*, the victims of Kishinev. Nearly 13,000 Americans signed a protest petition. The State Department tried to deliver the petition but the Czar's government refused to accept it—and declared that the residents of Kishinev were not in need of relief funds from abroad.[76]

British and Irish journalists were immediately dispatched to the scene of the crime for further in-depth reporting. Londoners were aghast at the reports and horrified at the grotesque photographs of dead and mutilated children staged for the lens by the proud perpetrators. Similar pogroms were threatened throughout Eastern Europe and across Czarist Russia. Indeed many more such organized atrocities were either averted or eventually inflicted upon helpless Jewish populations in Europe during that period. Now thousands of Russian and East European Jews were either victims, displaced persons, or cowering in fear of the next wild assault. Entire Jewish communities were preparing to immigrate *en masse* to France, the United States, Great Britain, and other safe havens. The Jews had to get out, and their only destinations could be the already overcrowded immigrant slums of such cities as New York, London, and Paris. They would be coming to those cities in large numbers precisely because no Jewish homeland existed.[77]

The Jews who stayed in Russia until they could escape or find political peace took up arms. Pitchforks, crowbars, watch crews, self-defense committees, guns, rifles, homemade bombs. The pogromists and politicians of Russia and East Europe were wrong and speaking anti-Semitic myths when they accused ordinary Jews in their *shtetls* and ghettos of sedition, of anti-government agitation, and of being prepared to do battle against the state. That was a lie—before the pogroms that began in 1881. After a generation of oppression, that accusation became true. A militant Jew arose in Russia. A militant Zionist arose in Russia—one that had no time for long, drawn-out permissions. A radicalized Jewish socialist arose in Russia, fist clenched and battle-ready. It was time to live—or die trying.

History records that whatever Zionism thought it was, or hoped it would become, the embryonic notion of Zionism came alive not in the gilded palaces of Istanbul, not in the marble-floored congress halls of Basel, not in the oak-lined corridors of London, but only on the blood-, sinew-, and feather-stained streets of Kishinev. Jewish nationalism and the yearning for a homeland of their own, the erupted mass demand to exit from a dismal Diaspora and return to their original land, this fierce drive was finally brute-hammered into reality. Zionism, after its protracted and writhing gestation, was finally born. And now with muscles. The cause was multiplied and furthered, not by diplomatic entreaties carried in satchels, not by logical position papers bound up in leather, not by financial propositions flavored with baksheesh. It was Jewish blood, now in the glare of the modern media powered by abundant newspapers and far-reaching telegraph agencies, all illuminated by the clarity

of a new century. Zionism was fire-forged out of a philosophy into self-pres-
ervation by the barbarism and carnage of Kishinev. The calls everywhere were
"Remember Kishinev" and "No More Kishinevs."

*       *       *       *

The outrage over Kishinev was soon juxtaposed with the comprehen-
sion that the crowded East End of London was about to become vastly more
crowded. The "Jewish Problem" was now an international crisis. Earlier testimony before the Royal Commission now resounded. The Commission was, in
part, tasked with "diverting of the stream of migration that is bound to go on
with increasing force from Eastern Europe. The Jews of Eastern Europe cannot stay where they are—where are they to go?" Finally, the ripples of Zionism had become a tsunami that could no longer be ignored.

On May 20, 1903, about a month after Kishinev, British Zionist and journalist Leopold Jacob Greenberg was designated to meet with Chamberlain to
find a solution to the crisis. Greenberg was well acquainted with Chamberlain
and other leading British politicians. A Jewish land was needed—and needed
now. Chamberlain agreed. In their meeting, Chamberlain himself brought up
the Russian emergency as "evidence" that an immediate solution could no
longer be delayed. But as the conversation between Greenberg and Chamberlain progressed, it was clear the refuge territory would not be Jerusalem,
controlled by the intransigent Sultan; nor Cyprus, where the fabric of the population made an organized ingress impossible; nor El Arish, where the water
supplies and political flow did not cooperate; nor Argentina, which was disin-
clined to negotiate; nor Mozambique, where the Portuguese government said
it had prior commercial commitments. It would be the Kenyan region, mis-
named for the discussion as Uganda.[78]

Where?

Africa. "High ground with fine climate," extolled Chamberlain, "and
every possibility for a great colony, which could support at least a million
souls … I do hope Dr. H will consider very seriously the suggestion." Chamberlain even spoke of Jewish self-governance as an inducement.[79]

Painful as the notion was, with all ports closed, and with more rampages,
atrocities, and mass murders against Jews threatened every day, Herzl decided
to step cautiously toward a compromise country. After anguishing through
the ceaseless pressures of the moment, Herzl would recommend Uganda to
the upcoming Zionist Congress in Basel on August 26, 1903. More than that,
Herzl embarked upon a radical new approach. He decided to confront the
Czar himself in Russia to get support for the Zionist program.[80]

Reaching out to the Czar would construct the controversial and dangerous precedent that Zionist leaders would revisit with other tyrants for decades to come. If regimes wanted the Jews out, instead of seeing them murdered, Zionism would take them. In other words, Zionist officials would "deal with the devil." They would go directly to the door of those who had killed and brutalized Jews to negotiate their orderly exodus, while working out financial arrangements for starting a new life. That page—a Jewish exit with a financial remnant—was first written by Moses, for even Moses demanded the goats and sheep go, thus creating the basis for survival. But it meant that Zionists had to operationally work with the worst Jew-hating despots—a tactic that would save lives and restart lives but would always smack of "collaboration." This sort of help would haunt the movement forever.

On July 8, 1903, Herzl contacted a friend of a friend, a Polish noblewoman who was welcome at the Russian court. He sought to arrange an audience between himself and Czar Nicholas. She tried. But the Czar would not hear of such a meeting. Nicholas had already adopted the Imperial adage that the best idea would be to simply drown all five to six million Russian Jews in the Black Sea. But since that mass extermination was not feasible, the Czar was interested in any other way to make his Jewish citizens disappear. So the Czar authorized someone else in his government to meet with Herzl. It was Russian Interior Minister Plehev himself—the presumptive mastermind behind the Kishinev pogrom. The basis for the meeting was a single concept, jointly accepted by Herzl and Plehev: "emigration without return."[81]

Upon learning of the permission, Herzl packed his trunk again, embarking on the long, arduous train ride to St. Petersburg. The two men finally met on August 8, 1903, in Plehev's office. Stout and sporting a dense white mustachio, Plehev was curt and cautious as he spoke to the supposed syndic of the very Jewish people he wanted to destroy. Speaking in French, Plehev made it clear, "I granted you this interview, Doctor, which you requested, in order to come to an understanding with you about the Zionist movement of which you are the leader." He added that the Imperial government was willing to establish relations with the Zionist movement—albeit not "friendly relations."[82]

Nor was Plehev delicate in describing his determination to solve the "Jewish Question" by making Jewish identity disappear—one way or another. As he was speaking, Herzl requested a piece of paper to take notes. With irritation, Plehev reached for a sheet of his own stationery, tearing off the Imperial letterhead at the top so his name could not be used on the notes. Continuing, Plehev stated his government was willing to tolerate Zionism as long as it advocated emigration to a Jewish colony in Palestine. In recent days, Plehev had issued a countrywide ban on all Zionist meetings and activities because the government felt the movement had become entrenched in philosophy of remaining in Russia and rebelliously strengthening their identity. But that ban could be rescinded, suggested Plehev, if Zionism would return to the idea of a pure exodus. Plehev displayed his familiarity with Zionist politics, mentioning organizational personalities by name even as he reached for a large brown leather, gold-embossed volume entitled "The Ministerial Report on Zionism."[83]

Hatred was palpable in that room. Herzl felt like he was standing on "a scaffold awaiting the axe," but he gathered his strength and continued with the operational details. If the Czar wanted the Jews gone, Zionism would take them, Herzl asserted—if it could be done in a systematic and humane fashion.[84]

Finances would be important, explained Herzl. Any orderly exodus would require a Russian government subsidy to be raised from Jewish taxes, he stated. This money would be used to buy land, pay for transit, and re-establish Jews in a new locale. Plehev provisionally agreed and produced a note for the Russian Finance Minister, Serge Witte, given to Herzl in an envelope—sealed. Herzl was to hand the missive to Count Witte. Moreover, the "where" was imperative, insisted Herzl. Revisiting the quest for Palestine, Herzl wanted the Czar to pressure or persuade the Sultan to, at long last, grant a Jewish colony in the Holy Land. As a further enticement to the Sultan, Herzl revived the offer of Jewish money for Ottoman debt alleviation. There was more. Russian Zionist organizations would need official sanction and their activities in Russia facilitated. The ban had to be to be lifted. Moreover, for those Jews who could not or would not emigrate, the Czar must expand the restricted lands they were permitted to live, thus improving the lot of those who remained.[85]

Plehev, who seemed receptive, took all Herzl's points under advisement.

After an additional round of meetings, Herzl left St. Petersburg for Russian Vilna, which held a substantial Jewish population. Once there, Herzl was exuberantly greeted by Jewish leaders, rabbinic and Zionist alike. Triumphantly received as part Messiah, part Moses, Herzl was hailed as the one man who could lead the oppressed out of their tightening death trap. At the train station, a throng surrounded him, a crowd so dense that, at first, no one could move off the platform. Cheers showered down on Herzl as he made his way off the train. Later, community elders presented with him a Torah scroll. Well into evening, visitors made pilgrimages to his hotel room to pay tribute.[86]

The next day, while Herzl was touring in the Jewish quarter, a small girl approached. She and her brother were the sole support for her destitute family; for her, it meant sixteen-hour days sewing until the girl's eyesight failed. Herzl was awed by all he saw and met in Vilna. His last words as he boarded his train, still remembering the image of the helpless girl, were "Do not let your spirits fall, brothers. Better days are coming. They must come."[87]

From Vilna, Herzl hastened back to St. Petersburg for his second meeting with Interior Minister Plehev, this one on August 13, 1903. Czar Nicholas had agreed to the entire Zionist program—if that was what it took to be rid of Russia's Jews. Plehev gave Herzl a letter to be read at the upcoming Sixth Zionist Congress in Basel, which was to convene ten days later on August 23, 1903. That letter, sternly anti-Jewish in tone, promised "moral and material support" for Zionism, "so long as the measures it took in practice served to reduce the Jewish population in Russia." The goal endorsed by the Czar was "to create an independent state in Palestine."[88]

An ironic and distasteful realism now dawned on many. Friends of the Jews and even Jews themselves were indecisive or unwilling to support a Jewish state in Palestine. But the enemies of the Jews, those with blood on their hands, were eager to endorse it—for all the wrong reasons.

\*     \*     \*     \*

As Herzl made his way to the biannual Zionist Congress in Basel, the notion collapsed that Russian diplomats could convince the Sultan to change his mind. This meant that with the Russian emigration emergency only one territory was available. It was a 40,000 square mile zone, 200 miles wide at it greatest perimeter, wrongly called Uganda, actually what is now Kenya. Herzl would advance the idea as a "temporary" refuge, but one that needed immediate acceptance.[89]

A record audience assembled at Sixth Zionist Congress, some 600 delegates from nations around the world but especially Russia. The Kishinev crisis had bone-spurred the growth of the movement. One delegate walked 42 days to the conference from Bulgaria. An estimated 2,000 spectators were also in attendance. The observers included many diplomats and officials of a variety of governments. Representatives of the Czar and the Sultan were also lurking. Among the accredited delegates, purely factional disputes competed with roiling anger and heart-pounding hope to connect an unpredictable surge in voltage to the crisis at hand.[90]

Herzl, heavy with news, began his presidential address with an immediate reference to Kishinev. At the very utterance of the word ... Kishinev ... the chattering masses from wall to wall simultaneously rose from their creaking seats to stand in unison and in silence. "The bloody days of days of the Bessarabian town," thundered Herzl, "shall not make us forget that there is many another Kishinev, even beyond the borders of Russia ... Let us save those that can still be saved!" Slowly, as his dramatic speech unfolded, as he warned of future massacres, as the roll-call of potential territories of settlement were declared unavailable, inaccessible, or impermissible, as the Russian declaration of financial and political cooperation was announced to great applause, a totally new concept was unexpectedly wedged into the captivating oratory. The salient salvation territory Herzl now advocated was the one just confirmed in a written offer by Britain. That letter, transported to the Congress floor and in part read aloud, would create "an autonomous Jewish settlement in ... East Africa."[91]

Where?

"It is true," he explained, "that it [East Africa] is not Zion and can never become Zion." But it would be "an emergency measure" that must be considered. The letter from the British described the venture as an "amelioration of the position of the Jewish race." The notion of a Jewish settlement in East Africa, howsoever transitory, simply ripped the Congress in two. An up or down vote was eventually called for, not on any actual settlement in "Uganda," as it was called, but simply to authorize a Zionist "expedition" to examine the land. The shock of it all brought a slight majority for the decision, after scores of wondering delegates abstained. As for the Russians, doctrinaire and adamant to reach Palestine, they bolted the hall in rage. Grown men, then and there, began to cry in dismay and disillusion, some hysterically. Delegates dropped to the floor weeping as though mourning a suddenly deceased father, one man remembered.[92]

The rejectionists were so alienated that they immediately began referring to themselves as "Zionist Zionists" to show their determination to reach Palestine itself—not just any patch of soil.[93]

After the Congress adjourned, Herzl descended into personal turmoil. The Zionist world fractured, convened rival congresses and conferences, and lamented the "Uganda Project." Russian pressure on the Sultan—if any was actually exerted—yielded no results. As the Zionist and Jewish world spiraled down into its own political maelstrom, Herzl's health deteriorated as well. By early 1904, the man was quite weakened. During mid-May 1904, he wrote of his own "shattered health." By July 1904, he had returned to his beloved Vienna where he became bedridden.[94]

At 5:00 p.m., July 3, 1904, bereft of breath, with a weakened heart, and battered by Zionism's international convulsions, Herzl heaved his last breath and passed into history. Zionism's founding titan died ... not in Palestine, but in the Diaspora.[95]

CHAPTER 6

# THE ZIONIST MOMENT

**H**erzl's movement was adrift and deeply wounded. Millions who could be helped now trembled before the swords of Russians, Poles, Romanians, and many others ready to continue the steady pace of horrific pogroms. Anti-Jewish incidents, now contagious, even stretched to Ireland, where in 1904, the Jews of Limerick were terrorized. Following a concerted boycott instigated by a local clergyman, the Jewish community was eventually driven from the city. Indeed, during the coming years, hundreds of additional pogroms would be unleashed across the Tsar's empire. The burnt pages of infamy include Odessa, Kiev, Ekaterinoslav, Romny, Simferopol, and scores of other eastern European villages, towns, and cities. In Odessa alone, at least 400 Jews were heinously slaughtered.[1]

The response to the continued death and destruction of Jews in Europe was a shift in Zionism's center of gravity to the Russian organizations. "Practical Zionism" emerged, heavily influenced by Russian Jews. It called for the gradual, step-by-step process of building Jewish Palestine by incrementally purchasing property, settling Jews, building schools, and otherwise establishing a legal presence using *ad hoc* legal means. This would have to suffice in the absence of an overt political land grant and an organized mass population transfer. At the 1905 Seventh Zionist Congress, "the Uganda Project" was formally voted into oblivion. At about that time, a Russian–born Zionist emerged who would inherit the mantle of Herzl and play a pivotal role in bringing Great Britain to its decisive role in establishing the Jewish State.[2] That man was Chaim Weizmann.

Born in 1874 in the *shtetl* of Motol near the Russian city of Pinsk in the restrictive Pale of Settlement, Weizmann was a child of the pogrom era. He became a Zionist dreamer early on. At age 11, after the pogroms began, a young Weizmann penned a note in Hebrew lamenting the helplessness of the Jews, yet believing "England will nevertheless have mercy upon us … Jews, to Zion let us go." Quickly, he became an intellectual activist, and every bit looked the part with his balding head, trimmed mustache, and goatee sharpened to a point.[3]

Unable to acquire proper schooling or employment in Russia—because he was a Jew and subject to academic and employment prohibitions, Weizmann sought higher education outside the country. He found it in Germany, where he excelled in chemistry. Weizmann moved on to various teaching positions in Switzerland. In 1904, he had become a senior lecturer at the University of Manchester in Great Britain, establishing credentials in advanced chemical research. Splitting his world between Zionism and chemistry, Weizmann rose both within his laboratory and within the ranks of Britain's pro-Zionist organizations. By the time the 1905 Zionist Congress rejected Uganda, the young Weizmann had risen to become a member of the Larger Actions Committee, later renamed the General Zionist Council. This committee was the international ruling body of the Zionist movement that governed all decisions between biannual Congresses.[4]

Weizmann's approach differed diametrically from Herzl's. The new Zionist leader declared, "Why should we look to the kings of Europe for compassion that they should take pity upon us and give us a resting place?"[5]

Begging from capital to capital—that was a thing of the past. Bribing the Sultan—that was over. Considering territorial leftovers in East Africa to serve some race-based colonial scheme—impossible. Setting down roots without water in a desolate Egyptian desert stretch at El Arish—finished. Madagascar, Argentina, and all alternative points in between—out of the question. The goal was now one place—*Zion*. The methods to be employed would be steeped in the *realpolitik* of the new century. As Great Britain and the other powers rushed toward a collision over the toppling body of the Sick Man of Europe and along with it, the Ottoman colonies, their natural resources, and strategic parallax, the Zionists would join the fray.

From a mind rich in molecular combinations came Weizmann's new approach, which was dubbed "Synthetic Zionism."[6] It merged two active elements, Practical Zionism and Political Zionism, into a new force designed to change facts on the ground in Palestine in tandem with changing attitudes within the corridors of European political power.

In 1906, Weizmann, by now visible and active and in Manchester circles, encountered a leading politician who had been active in the Uganda debate in Parliament, a man who knew well the Jewish dilemma. As the conversation pressed on, Weizmann was asked point blank why the Jews turned down the offer of East Africa. Weizmann countered with his own question: If offered the territory of Paris over London, would he take Paris? The politician replied, "No, but London is the capital of my country." Weizmann shot back, "Jerusalem was the capital of our country when London was still a marsh." The answer penetrated the psyche of that politician, a man who had just been voted out as Prime Minister, but was still influential in the government. His name was James Arthur Balfour.[7]

Balfour was always one of England's Christian believers in the tragedy of the Jewish people. He once declared passionately, "There is no parallel to it, there is nothing approaching a parallel to it, in any other branch of human history. Here you have a small race originally inhabiting a small country, I think about the size of Wales or Belgium, at any rate of comparable size to those two, at no time in its history wielding anything that can be described as material power, sometimes crushed in between great Oriental monarchies, its inhabitants deported, then scattered, then driven out of the country altogether into every part of the world, and yet maintaining a continuity of religious and racial tradition of which we have no parallel elsewhere."[8]

From the moment he met Weizmann in 1906, Balfour was converted to the notion of a Zionist return to Palestine as the historically correct remedy to the millennia of persecution Jews had been forced to endure after their eviction from Jerusalem. Balfour was not alone. Others in the British political hierarchy were of the same opinion.[9] But Christian Zionist sympathies and the efforts of Weizmann were only the foundation of the British decision on the Jewish return to Palestine. Upon that foundation would be erected a complex compound of interlocking, hardened political factors, large and small, that would coalesce to activate the historic pivot point. There was no "one reason" behind Britain's ultimate decision. There were not "a dozen" reasons, but rather dozens of reasons. Enough twists and turns coursed throughout the process to fill many books. But certain events, punctuated by collapses and swells, were among the salient ones.

In 1905, Russia underwent a major upheaval, the Russian Revolution. In that year, the country saw the culmination of actions by Nihilists, anarchists, socialists, and others who wanted to see the complete dismantling of the brutal Romanov dynasty. The Romanovs had ostentatiously prospered from serfdom and saw the denial of human rights as a hallmark of their authority. In the first years of the twentieth century, a series of peasant and socialist riots arose in reaction to the continued economic oppression, famine, and abject hunger suffered by the people in the face of brazen regal opulence. Jewel-encrusted Fabergé eggs were showcased at a time when people could hardly purchase eggs to eat. Pogrom-embittered Jewish militants were visible and active in the Social Democratic movement—just one group in a coalition of the oppressed that agitated to topple the Imperial house. Indeed, the "General Jewish Workers' Party of Lithuania, Poland and Russia," commonly referred to as "the Bund," was some 23,000 members strong, wielding three times the membership of Lenin's "All Russian Social Democratic Party."[10]

Trouble at home was magnified by trouble beyond Russia's borders. The 15-month war with Japan over Manchuria descended into disaster with a humiliating maritime defeat at Tsushimi Strait. Japanese naval forces, suddenly equipped, outmaneuvered and outgunned the Russian fleet, thanks in part to massive foreign loans to Tokyo. Where did the loans come from? From German-Jewish bankers, led by New York financier Jacob Schiff. Schiff and his circles were waging a bitter economic war against the Czar as a penalty for his unbridled anti-Jewish persecution and pogroms. To contain the spreading 1905 revolution, Czar Nicholas was compelled to institute certain democratic reforms, including the establishment of the Duma, a legislative body.[11]

Now the political status quo and balance of power in Europe began changing before London's eyes. Whitehall took note that Jews were a factor. Jews were capable of exercising a political dynamic and were slowly migrating from London's peripheral vision to the foreground.

During the next eight years, a desire for oil and mapmaking dominated the minds of British policymakers. They crafted their diplomacy as though they were players deftly moving chess pieces against King Petroleum while protecting Queen India and her Knight Suez Canal. As Leo Amery, a rising star in the British government, later wrote, "That great Southern half of the British Empire which lies in an irregular semi-circle round the Indian ocean, South Africa, East Africa, Egypt, India, Australia, New Zealand … to secure the safety of this region during the next generation, it is imperative that its seas should be kept clear of all hostile naval bases, that potential armies of invasion should be kept as far away as possible and that intercommunication by railway and by air, as well as by sea, between the different portions of the Empire which it comprises should be as fully developed as possible. The retention of German East Africa, of Palestine and Mesopotamia, and of the German Pacific colonies is the indispensable means of securing this end." Amery is the government official who ultimately authored the historic document that laid out Britain's policy on the Jewish return to Palestine.[12]

In 1908, the Young Turks overthrew the Sultan, reinventing the Ottoman Empire as a new nationalistic power uninterested in pacifying or accommodating local ethnic groups. Instead, they demanded total "Turkishness" and loyalties to the central government from all citizens regardless of regional heritage. The Young Turks also set about reversing the national economic and administrative infirmities of the Sick Man of Europe.[13] Once again, the balance of power shifted.

As the first decade of the twentieth century played out, Britain was more and more determined to outrace the Germans for control of Mesopotamian oil, resources controlled by the newly nationalistic Ottomans but still unexploited, undrilled, and untapped by any country or company. Indeed, oil was needed just to compete in the naval arms race to get the oil. In other words, a Möbius took hold: oil would be needed to win a war, so a war for oil would be needed to get it. War was a foregone conclusion for many European leaders of the day. A tangled thicket of secret alliances among Europe's powers anticipated a war every day as the twentieth century's second decade clanged in. Eventually, they got it.

Finally, the moment all had been dreading—and all had been preparing for—came on June 28, 1914, when Austrian Archduke Ferdinand was assassinated in Sarajevo, Serbia. One by one, the short-fused leaders of Europe threatened armed hostilities upon each other. Turkey eventually joined its best ally, the German Empire, as well as Bulgaria and the Austro-Hungarian Empire, in a sprawling war against the French, British, and Russians supported by other allies. By the first week of August 1914, Europe and the world had clearly and officially descended into World War I.[14]

The Continent mobilized to industrially kill its young men by jingo, by gum.

London believed victory against Turkey would be advanced by allying with the Arabs of the Hejaz, that is, the rag-tag tribes of the Western Arabian Peninsula, nominally led by the charismatic figure known as Hussein. The Arab tribes resented Turkish infringement on their traditional rights and customs of taxation and regulation of the Hajj to Islamic pilgrimage sites at Mecca and Medina. The London Foreign Office, acting with and through T. E. Lawrence, known commonly as Lawrence of Arabia, cultivated rebellion. The Arabs were needed to disrupt Turkish train lines and Ottoman forces. If that could be done, Hussein was promised when the peacemakers became mapmakers, the Arabs could achieve independent statehood.[15]

Several small libraries would be needed to chronicle the evolving agreements—real and perceived—that dominated the British-Arab strategic relationship. But among the most salient was the so-called "McMahon Correspondence" and the subsequent Sykes-Picot Agreement.

In July 1915, with the war fully under way, the British High Commissioner in Egypt, Sir Henry McMahon, initiated a back-and-forth written correspondence with Hussein that included some 10 confidential letters. The full written exchange was kept secret for 15 years until revealed by the press and parliamentary investigation.[16] Those 10 letters, later to become famous as "the Hussein-McMahon correspondence," offered ambiguous British promises of national recognition within an ambiguously defined territory in exchange for ambiguous Arab offers of revolt predicated upon calculated deceptions and implied threats by both sides.

Decades later, activists on all sides of the Arab national debate would point to the McMahon-Hussein correspondence as proof—or lack of it—of broken pledges and unfulfilled national obligations. Any arguer indeed could seize upon passages within any of the several most prominent letters to validate any argument. But embedded within the full set of 10 letters—including some of the forgotten ones—are British demands and the Arab willingness to cede control to the British over one specified region in exchange for national rights elsewhere. The region they demanded: Syria, a centuries old stronghold of Islam. The region the Arabs were willing to cede: Mesopotamia.[17]

The prelude to the historic 10-letter McMahon-Hussein correspondence was a introductory note of October 31, 1914 from the British military, which stated: "If the Sharif and Arabs in general assist Great Britain in this conflict that has been forced upon us by Turkey … Great Britain will guarantee the independence, rights and privileges of the Sharifate against all external foreign aggressions, in particular that of the Ottomans." Referring to the notion of replacing Turkish-ordained religious supremacy with Hussein himself, that note appended, "It may be that an Arab of true race will assume the Caliphate at Mecca or Medina, and so good may come by the help of God out of all the evil which is now occurring."[18]

Arab self-definition and territory mapping began in earnest in early 1915 in Damascus. In March and April, during a series of secret meetings, the two leading nationalist societies, *al-Fatat* and *al-Ahd*, joined forces with each other and with Emir Faisal, who was representing his father, Hussein. Together they drafted "the Damascus Protocol," which created a map for the envisioned Arab state. It resembled a dented rectangle tilted left toward eleven o'clock, encompassing and extending the Arabian Peninsula to the shores of the Mediterranean. The proposed northern border coursed east from the Mersin-Adana railway in Turkey, just beyond Syria, along the railroad tracks and across the 37th parallel to the Persian frontier; the eastern border followed the Persian frontier down to the Persian Gulf, and then continued to the bottom of the Arabian Peninsula; from there the outline traveled back north to the Mersin-Adana starting point in Turkey, thus completing the geopolitical box. Both Palestine and all three Mesopotamian provinces resided completely within that approximate rectangle. The Damascus Protocol specified that if Britain granted this proposed new state, the British Empire would become the new Arab nation's defense partner. In addition, the new Arab nation would extend "the grant of economic preference to Great Britain."[19] That "economic preference" meant the oil in Mesopotamia that London craved.

Fearing Turkey's seemingly omnipresent spies, the Damascus Protocol was reduced to a miniaturized script, and then sewn into the boots of a member of Faisal's party. Faisal returned to Mecca, where he unveiled the plan to enlist his father's support for a so-called "Arab Revolt." The suggested insurrection would begin during the winter of 1915 in Syria where the troops were supposedly standing by. But Ottoman commanders detected the conspiracy, and suddenly transferred most of the Arab divisions out of Syria east to the Gallipoli front. That brought certain death to the Arab soldiers who were promptly cut down as part of Gallipoli's mass carnage. The Arabs in Syria did not revolt that winter.[20]

In truth, no one knows how many hundreds or thousands of Arab troops were ever really ready to turn on their commanders. But the aborted Syrian uprising was characteristic of an Arab Revolt that was always being devised and revised, located and relocated, launched and postponed. Moreover, the Arab leaders constantly exaggerated their forces, their base of popular support, and their willingness to take action. These demerits the British understood well, which is why the British were cool and uncertain about forming reliable military alliances with Arab elements.[21]

To reassure London, Hussein on July 14, 1915, began the famous exchange with McMahon. The letter tendered the Damascus Protocol territorial outline almost word for word, asking for a straight yes or no within 30 days. "If this [30-day] period should lapse before they [the Arabs] receive an answer, they reserve to themselves complete freedom of action," the letter stated in a soon-familiar veiled threat to instead seek alliance with the Turks against Britain.[22]

Not anxious to respond to arbitrary 30-day deadlines, and disturbed over Arab contingents already fighting valiantly in Turkish units, McMahon replied not within a month but a full 45 days later. Mixing overblown effusiveness with snubbing hesitation, McMahon wrote, "We rejoice ... that your Highness and your people are of one opinion—that Arab interests are English interests and English [are] Arab ... With regard to the questions of limits and boundaries," he continued, "it would appear to be premature to consume our time in discussing such details in the heat of war ... especially as we have learned, with surprise and regret, that some of the Arabs ... far from assisting us, are neglecting this, their supreme opportunity, and are lending their arms to the German and the Turk, to the new despoiler and the old oppressor."[23]

A worried Hussein replied on September 9, 1915, with obsequious fawning: "To his Excellency the Most Exalted, the Most Eminent—the British High Commissioner in Egypt; may God grant him Success. With great cheerfulness and delight I received your letter dated August 30, 1915, and have given it great consideration and regard, in spite of the impression I received from it of ambiguity and its tone of coldness and hesitation with regard to our essential point ... Permit me to say clearly that the coolness and hesitation which you have displayed in the question of the limits and boundaries by saying that the discussion of these at present is of no use and a waste of time … [and] might be taken to infer an estrangement or something of the sort."[24] Hussein's reply continued deferentially and at one point referred to McMahon's "perfectness." He emphasized, "In order to reassure your Excellency, I can declare that the whole [Arab] country, together with those who you say are submitting themselves to Turco-German orders, are all waiting the result of these negotiations, which are dependent only on your refusal or acceptance of the question of the limits [borders]." In the best tradition of the Turkish bazaar, Hussein's next sentence asked exactly what Great Britain wanted in return for national support. "Whatever the illustrious Government of Great Britain finds conformable to its policy on this subject, communicate it to us and specify to us the course we should follow."[25]

McMahon's reply: Britain wanted Mesopotamia.

On October 24, 1915, McMahon wrote back that the United Kingdom would "recognize and support the independence of the Arabs in all the regions within the limits demanded by the Sharif of Mecca," but minus the Turkish portion, and minus any other area in which Britain enjoyed an obligation with other chiefs, and minus any other area, namely Syria, that would conflict with the interest of French or British economic goals.[26]

The ink was barely dry on McMahon correspondence when another agreement was hammered out between senior diplomats Mark Sykes of Britain, Georges Picot of France, and Russian foreign minister Sergei Sazonov, the so-called Sykes-Picot Agreement. That agreement outlined "French and British economic goals."

Sykes-Picot, negotiated in early 1916, was a secret collection of letters, complete with colored maps, agreeing to carve up the Mideast after the war. Baghdad and the Mesopotamian port city of Basra were decreed British spheres of influence, while oil-rich Mosul and Syria would be French, with Russia exercising a privilege over its frontiers with Persia. France was virtually devoid of reliable oil fields. Therefore, controlling Kurdish Mosul would one day yield France the petroleum the Great War proved was necessary in a modern world. In return for ceding Mosul, Britain would be assured that her oil and general commerce from Persia, lower Mesopotamia, and the Gulf could transit across French-held Syria without encumbrance. Therefore, the control and extension of the Berlin-to-Baghdad Railway into Syria was geographically split between Britain and France, with the French taking over from Mosul east. Sykes-Picot's terms would reward France for the immense losses she was suffering in the war, while preserving British and Russian interests.[27]

Relinquishing the still untested but much coveted oil deposits of Mosul was difficult for the British. But, "It is clear, that we shall have to make up our minds to the inclusion of Mosul in the French sphere," a diplomat in the India Office told the London Foreign Office on January 13, 1916, even as the agreement was being negotiated.[28]

Sykes-Picot was concluded just after the ambiguous McMahon promises to Hussein that would create an Arab national entity, but one that would exclude Mesopotamia. Under Sykes-Picot, that Arab entity would be a mere "confederation" under French and British economic and administrative control, which would function as geographically and legally separated colonies even while imbued with an amorphous "Arab identity." The India Office in London expressed the thinking succinctly in a telegram to Charles Hardinge, the British viceroy of India: "What we want is not a United Arabia: but a weak and disunited Arabia, split up into little principalities so far as possible under our suzerainty—but incapable of coordinated action against us, forming a buffer against the Powers in the West."[29]

As the details unfolded, British diplomat George Buchanan in Petrograd, Russia, cabled Sykes a coded "urgent, private, and secret message" warning that French actions in Syria and Mosul might incite "suicidal and foolish fanaticism" in the region. But French plans seemed to be moving toward acceptance. "I therefore suggest," stated Buchanan, "that in regard to Arabs, our policy should be let Arabs do what they can for themselves and … make such concessions, declarations and arrangements in Mesopotamia with regard to Arab theory of independence and participation in administration … [But] keep actual terms of provisional government from knowledge [of] Arab leaders."[30] Indeed, during the give-and-take of the Sykes-Picot negotiations among the French, British, and Russians, neither the Arab residents of the territories, nor their leaders, were ever consulted.

Sykes-Picot was formalized by the French and British foreign ministers on May 15, 1916, and almost immediately regretted by Whitehall. Like other documents, its ink had still not dried when oil advocates within the British government initiated a campaign to scrap the agreement. Weeks before, in early April, British government oil official Maurice de Bunsen had been asked by the prime minister to establish a "Committee on Asiatic Turkey" to better assess Britain's true interests in the Middle East. The committee saw Mosul's abundance of oil as simply too precious to surrender to France. Just weeks after Sykes-Picot was framed, de Bunsen's report concluded that Turkish Mosul must remain British and that British forces ought to continue their Mesopotamian campaign northward. "Oil again makes it commercially desirable for us," de Bunsen's report concluded, "to carry our control on to Mosul, in the vicinity of which place there are valuable wells, possession of which by another power [France] would be prejudicial to our interests."[31]

\*     \*     \*     \*

While Britain and the Allies vacillated in their tenuous alliance with unpredictable Arab forces, the story was very different with the Zionist movement. As the shifting fortunes of the war charged ahead, the Zionists darted in cadence between the elephant legs. Zionism fell in line with the policy goals of Washington, London, and Paris, rendering aid, assistance, and support in whatever ways it could—individually and as a movement—and making sure the leadership knew it. In Great Britain and abroad, the Zionists were organized, steadfast, and unmistakable in their allegiance to the Allies. Hence, even military strategists and diplomatic leaders who were not particularly in the Zionist camp and did not even care about Jewish history found themselves supporting the Jewish national enterprise in Palestine, if for no other reason than British self-interest and strategic goals. This growing synchrony was all the more stimulated by the British military thrust against Ottoman Palestine as part of the Allied campaign in the Middle East, and the Turkish counterattack.

Britain's invasion of Mesopotamia was promptly launched with pre-positioned British forces just days after Turkey joined the War as Germany's ally on October 31, 1914. But warfare in the Sinai did not commence until February, 1915 when Turkey attacked the Suez Canal. Vital to the entire Allied effort, the canal was well-fortified. Turkish forces were outnumbered and rebuffed by the Allies, not just once, but in a second later attack. However, it was increasingly clear to the Allies that the Suez Canal must be protected. That meant Palestine was to be controlled.[32]

By 1916, the British began to cross the Sinai toward Palestine in a series of battles with a combination of victory and defeat under the command of Field Marshal Edmund Allenby—considered by many to be "the soldier's soldier." The British made three assaults on Gaza in the spring of 1916 before overrunning Arab and Turkish defenders in November 1917. During the intense hostilities of this third attempt, the British suffered some 18,000 killed, wounded, and missing. Turkish casualties numbered around 25,000 dead, wounded, or taken prisoner. Fighting took Allenby along the length of the Gaza-Beersheba line and concentrated his forces at the road to Jerusalem.[33]

By the morning of December 9, 1917, despite three days of constant rain and daunting skirmishes up the rocky Judean Hills, Allenby had surrounded Jerusalem. By noon of that day, the Turks surrendered. Allenby made good on his promise to London to take the city by Christmas. His formal occupation was enunciated when he dismounted his horse to walk through the gates of the Old City. Allenby immediately secured the holy sites, including Muslim shrines and the Mosque of Omar, which were placed under strict Muslim control.[34]

As 1918 dawned, Jerusalem and the land to its south were in the hands of the Allies. But the whole of Palestine itself had yet to fall. For four years, the Zionists and their supporters from both the Jewish and Christian communities had been in wartime tempo leading up to this moment. That fusion was robust and multidimensional, enough to fill a bookshelf, but certain landmarks may be among the more salient in the process.

Among the first of those landmarks was one which occurred in late 1914, on the very day war was declared on Turkey. That day, longtime Liberal Party member Viscount Herbert Samuel, who had held several key ministerial positions, enthusiastically proposed a Jewish State in Palestine to cabinet member David Lloyd George. Lloyd George was Secretary for War and Minister for Munitions. Later, Samuel suggested the same idea to Foreign Minister Edward Grey. Both Lloyd George and Grey saw the sense of it. Samuel himself was Jewish, but not really considered practicing. More importantly, as an archetypical, assimilated establishment Jewish Briton, he had never revealed any Zionist inclinations and indeed was expected to harbor a rejectionist view. Yet he now stunned Zionist organizers by arguing that 3 million Jews could be and should be settled in Palestine. This, he argued, would rescue many persecuted Jews in East Europe and encourage wartime support for Britain from Jews around the world. The British government as a whole took his suggestion in earnest. Soon, a number of Cabinet members—including those completely detached from the Jewish Question—began to believe the Holy Land should be annexed by Britain or otherwise placed into protectorate status. Shortly after Samuel offered his proposal, Prime Minister Asquith noted in his diary that he was surprised to find such receptiveness to the idea from personalities like Lloyd George, who "does not care a damn for the Jews, or their past or their future."[35]

Samuel's sudden support brought him into contact with a startled Weizmann, who never thought the man was in the Zionist camp. Being prominent in Manchester circles, Weizmann was known to *Manchester Guardian* editor C.P. Scott, who introduced him and other key Zionist leaders to other Cabinet ministers to further the discussion of a Jewish Palestine. On December 12, 1914 a meeting was arranged with Balfour. This was, in fact, their second meeting. Balfour vividly remembered the encounter eight years earlier in 1906 during which Weizmann had quipped about the pre-eminence of Jerusalem. Indeed, when the Weizmann meeting was first proposed, Balfour accepted with a note, "I still remember our conversation in 1906." During the December 1914 meeting itself, Balfour told Weizmann, "I was thinking of that conversation of ours, and I believe when the guns stop firing, you may get your Jerusalem." Balfour added, "You may get your things done much more quickly after the war."[36]

Zionism became a quiet ally of the Allies. With Jews vulnerable in Turkish-controlled Palestine, care had to be taken so as not to stir collective retribution from the Turks. The case of the Turks' treatment of the Armenians was fresh and front in the world's eye. U.S. Ambassador to Turkey Henry Morgenthau recorded in his diary that among the Ottomans, Christians were commonly referred to as "dogs," and ranked less valuable than a camel or a horse. The concept of the "Terrible Turk," committing heinous atrocities, was popularized in the West. Ottoman hatred of infidels played out most brutally against Armenians, who were highly nationalistic and arguably the oldest Christian community in Europe. In the mid-1890s, a series of heinous raids against Armenian villages by Ottoman Kurds led to an uprising by Armenian militias in which they took their revenge on Kurdish towns and villages. In retaliation, Sultan Abdul Hamid sent in shock troops to murder, maim, and rape masses of Armenians in the Sasun highlands. For example, in the village of Semel, the local Armenian priest was encouraged by Turkish commanders to peaceably surrender the populace, which he did. But once in captivity, the priest's eyes were gouged out, he was bayoneted to death, and then all the women were raped as their husbands screamed nearby from their own tortures and executions. British and American diplomats gave ample documentation of these horrors in regular dispatches to their foreign ministries. Such organized atrocities against Armenians continued throughout the Turkish realm, not only in the far-off districts, but also on the streets of Istanbul, before the eyes of ambassadors who pleaded in vain for a pause. Ghastly pictures of mass graves published in British magazines revolted the soul of London.[37]

True, the Young Turks deposed Abdul the Damned in 1908. But as the entrenched Young Turks turned ultra-nationalist, demanding to Turkify the entire empire, the Ottomans returned to old habits. In 1909, bloody massacres were again inflicted upon the Armenian population, this time in Adana. Provocative photographs published in Western capitals showed brutalized children, their skin flayed off with cotton-chopping tools.[38]

Beginning in 1915, in the midst of the raging war, the Turks mounted a systematic extermination of the Armenians on a monumental scale that left the twentieth-century world aghast. First, the Armenians were commercially boycotted, then identified and rounded up for utter destruction. They were "deported" from all over Turkey to numerous killing centers, including several in and around the Mosul province of Mesopotamia, where Kurds joined in the process. Railroad boxcars, concentration camps, and death marches through numerous Arab towns became the gruesome hallmarks of the process. Along the way, stragglers were shot, hacked to death, or hung from bridges. Newborns were ripped from their mothers' clutches and smashed to a bloody death against trees. Hundreds of thousands were sadistically murdered in a cohesive state effort to once and for all exterminate the entire Armenian people.[39]

In England, Lord Bryce submitted an official government white paper and denunciation in October 1915, using the now-accepted term for this genocidal program. Bryce called it "extermination."[40]

The leading newspapers of the world ceaselessly headlined the inhuman campaign. In 1915 alone, *The New York Times* published approximately 145 articles detailing what was openly called "extermination" using the word in headlines, subheads and often in capital letters. October 4, 1915: TELL OF HORRORS DONE IN ARMENIA; Report of Eminent Americans Says They Are Unequaled in a Thousand Years; TURKISH RECORD OUTDONE; A Policy of Extermination Put in Effect Against a Helpless People; ENTIRE VILLAGES SCATTERED; Men and Boys Massacred, Women and Girls Sold As Slaves and Distributed Among Moslems ... October 7, 1915: 800,000 ARMENIANS COUNTED DESTROYED; 10,000 DROWNED AT ONCE; Peers Are Told How Entire Christian Population of Trebizond Was Wiped Out ... December 15, 1915: MILLION ARMENIANS KILLED OR IN EXILE; American Committee on Relief Says Victims of Turks Are Steadily Increasing; POLICY OF EXTERMINATION; More Atrocities Detailed In Support of Charge That Turkey Is Acting Deliberately.[41]

Jews in Palestine were constantly in fear for their lives, dreading similar retaliatory action by the Turks. Brutal repression was constantly threatened and in some cases carried out. Thousands of Palestinian Jews were deported; many were tortured and publicly hanged—as both a preemptive measure and a warning. But while Jewish Palestine superficially functioned as a loyal Turkish constituency, key Zionist elements were secretly working for the Allies. Among them were spy rings gathering intelligence about Turkish movements. One such network was known by the acronym "Nili," and some of its operatives, tortured and executed when caught, gave their life to the effort.[42]

Chief of British Military intelligence Major General George Macdonogh recalled the work of Jewish spies in Palestine with these words: "You will no doubt remember the great campaign of Lord Allenby in Palestine and perhaps you are surprised at the daring of his actions. Someone who is looking from the side lines, lacking knowledge about the situation, is likely to think that Allenby took unwarranted risks. That is not true. For Allenby knew with certainty from his intelligence (in Palestine) of all the preparations and all the movements of his enemy. All the cards of his enemy were revealed to him, and so he could play his hand with complete confidence. Under these conditions, victory was certain before he began." General Allenby's Deputy Military Secretary seconded the sentiment in 1924:

"It was largely the daring work of young spies, most of them natives of Palestine, which enabled the brilliant Field-Marshal to accomplish his undertaking so effectively."[43]

Zionist leaders contributed more than spies to the Allied war effort. They provided several other means of support, including munitions. Weizmann became revered in military circles for his chemical breakthroughs in acetone production. Acetone was a miscible solvent needed in the production of cordite, a smokeless propellant indispensible for naval guns and artillery. The British lacked enough acetone to assure the rapid mass production of cordite to keep their guns firing. As a research chemist, Weizmann had developed a unique fermentation process that could yield previously unexpected quantities of acetone—albeit never at the immense scope the War Office required.[44]

The Ministry of Munitions in 1915 admitted to Weizmann that unless his still unproven process could be swiftly perfected, British long range naval guns and artillery would have to be redesigned—stunting the entire war effort. In a single day, in just one battle, some 8,000 shells were spent. More shells were needed and faster. First Lord of the Admiralty Winston Churchill summoned Weizmann and put it to him bluntly: "Dr. Weizmann, we need 30,000 tons of acetone. Can you make it?" An awestruck Weizmann did not know if he could make even one ton, let alone 30,000 tons. But he set about the task. Working day and night with brewers at secret installations, he refined his method. Ultimately, Weizmann was able to supply the British War Office and the Allies with the key ingredient needed to unleash the sustained fiery naval bombardments that in many ways won the war. Weizmann's success brought him into constant celebrated contact with the War Cabinet and other government ministers. Using these connections, he was able to introduce to the highest echelons of the government other top European Zionist leaders in London such as Nahum Sokolov. When asked by Lloyd George, now the Prime Minister, what compensation he wanted for his miraculous achievement, Weizmann replied simply, "There is only one thing I want—national home for my people."[45]

Zionists fought with the Allies, not only behind the scenes in clandestine espionage capers and game-changing laboratory processes, but on the front lines in the muddy trenches. The Jewish combat story begins in Alexandria in British-controlled Egypt in early 1915. More than 10,000 Zionists had already been deported in an act of community terror perpetrated by Turkish pashas. The British were caring for the refugees in barracks, and neutral American warships were helping in the transport to Alexandria as a humanitarian gesture. Hundreds of additional seaborne refugees were streaming in every few days. One day, as the *USS Tennessee* was offloading nearly 1,000 Zionists expelled by the Turks from the Holy Land, two Zionist fighters came together:

Josef Trumpeldor, a one-armed veteran of the Czar's army, now a refugee expelled from Palestine, and Ze'ev Jabotinsky, a Russian Zionist militant who was in Egypt as a journalist. Both men along with other Zionist leaders met with British Colonel John Henry Patterson, who had just arrived in advance of a major assault against the mighty Turkish positions at Gallipoli. The Jews offered to fight to liberate Palestine. This Patterson and the War Office refused because, under British law, foreign soldiers could not serve. But they could volunteer to "assist."[46]

How? Patterson answered, not by fighting in combat units, but by becoming muleteers? Mules? Yes, the Gallipoli front—a bold plan to capture Istanbul by invading up the Dardanelles strait—was expected to be a frightful and deadly assault. During the assault, British troops in the 29th Division along the beachheads and in the trenches would need to be resupplied constantly with everything from rations to fresh clothing to ammo. The task would take the mules and their handlers over impossible terrain in brutal weather under fierce unremitting enemy fire—Machine guns, artillery, rifle fire—all of it.[47]

Trumpeldor, Jabotinsky and their cohorts wanted to fight the Turks to liberate Palestine with arms, not ferry miscellany in a "donkey battalion" somewhere in a distant theatre. But in the end, several hundred agreed to serve, suggesting that even through this action, their efforts would "lead to Zion." The volunteers proudly offered to call themselves the "Jewish Legion." That moniker was vetoed by Patterson. The unit would have to be called ... the "Zion Mule Corps."[48]

Zion *Mule* Corps?

Mules? We are "men," protested the angry and determined refugees. The image of mules hardly imparted the concept of Jews fighting for nationhood. Even the Yiddish translation was considered insulting. But after another fierce debate among the dispossessed Jews assembled in Alexandria that night, the unit appellation eventually settled on them as yet another necessary, almost irrelevant slight in this mad experience. What was important was to join the fight to defeat the Turks. More than 500 immediately voted to sign up for the unit. One concession to their heritage was condoned by Patterson. A Jewish Star—the Shield of David—sharp points at every side, would be emblazoned on their shoulder patches. Quickly, 750 mules and wooden saddle-style cargo carriers were purchased in Alexandria. After an ever-so-brief combat training stint, the men and their pack animals sailed for the war zone. As the ships plied the seas, the Zion Mule Corps could be heard singing the Zionist anthem *Hatikva*.[49] In Hebrew, it means "hope."

A year or two later, the Arabs would also fight in celebrated glory. But in 1915, it was the Jews who showed their mettle—without the cinematic legend to follow. In the annals of combat, it will be remembered that the Arabs in the Hejaz swept across the majestic desert atop their horses waving their sun-sparkled swords, their resplendent tunics flowing in the wind as they attacked the Turkish trains. The Zionists trudged up and down muddy hills and blood-stained beachfronts fearlessly leading their mules into the thickest of the battle as Turkish artillery shells blasted incessantly to their left and their right. The Arabs rode their mighty steeds and syncopating camels through the exhila-rating heat and across the dunes grabbing booty and rejoicing in victory. The Zionists scampered through piercing rain and heat, facing flies dense enough they filled the mouth if one tried to eat, all so British soldiers could fire back and last another hour.[50]

When the drums of war are sounded, it summons the muscles of the magnificent and the meek.

Surely, among the Zion Mule Corps, there were many acts of group bra-vado and individual heroism, much of it forgotten in the din of history. For example, on May 5, near Krithia, during relentless Turkish fire, a Jewish pri-vate stood fast to hold back a small herd of spooked mules from stampeding off with urgent supplies. In standing firm his arm outstretched and pulled by agitated pack animals, the private was shot in both arms. Yet he would not release the reins of his mules. Then despite buzzing bullets and exploding incoming shells, he staggered through the smoke and flame and hot shrapnel to deliver his assigned ammunition to trapped British soldiers pinned down in trenches. For his courage, Private M. Groushkousky was sought out by a Brit-ish General, decorated in the field and promoted to Corporal.[51]

The British were decimated at Gallipoli. Their assault was decisively repulsed. The beaches were littered with British, Australian, New Zealand, French, and British Indian boys cut-down like mowed grass. In total, the Allies suffered 44,000 dead and 99,000 wounded. But the 29th Division suf-fered fewer losses. Just months after the calamitous assault, Colonel Patterson proudly extolled the valor of his muleteers, telling the *Jewish Chronicle* in London, "These brave lads who had never seen shellfire before most compe-tently unloaded the boats and handled the mules whilst shells were bursting in close proximity to them … nor were they in any way discouraged when they had to plod their way … walking over dead bodies while the bullets flew around them … for two days and two nights we marched … thanks to the Zion Mules Corp (ZMC), the 29th Division did not meet with a sad fate, for the ZMC were the only Army Service Corps in that part of Gallipoli at that time."[52]

The Arab attacks would be forever glamorized and remembered in film and bestselling books. The Zion Mule Corps would become a footnote to a thanatopsis of WWI. But these hundreds, said Patterson, had proven for the first time since the Romans that in the fiercest of battles Jews could be triumphant.[53]

Even though many forgot this mud-splattered trial by fire, in the after-math of the guns of Gallipoli, in which so many young Tommies died, London did not forget who was willing to die with them.[54]

Indeed, London remembered the Zion Mule Corps as it remembered Weizmann's acetone, as it remembered its precarious exposure at the Suez Canal, as it remembered its need to protect the reaches of the British Empire. It was yet another turn in the decision-making warren that London traveled as it pondered the Zionist dream.

In autumn 1916, eager nationalists from the Armenians to the Arabs to Zionists began planning for territorial fulfillment—each in their own way. The corridors of power in London began humming with talk of a Jewish State in Palestine as a foreseeable and assured outcome of the War. By year's end, Lloyd George, a staunch believer in the Zionist cause, had become Prime Minister. During the first months of 1917, the Zionist movement established an official national office in London—separate from the English Zionist Federation. Called the London Zionist Political Committee, the new office was staffed by a group of young British Zionist activists. Weizmann had submitted their names to the Chief of Military Intelligence asking them to be exempted from military service so they could work in his office on the Palestine project. The request was immediately granted.[55]

In those first months of 1917, the war took sudden, spectacular turns.

On January 19, 1917, the Royal Navy's ultra-secret cryptography unit, known as "Room 40," headed by Reginald Hall, also a Zionist advocate for strictly strategic reasons, had intercepted and decoded the famous Zimmer-man Telegram. The secret cable from German Foreign Minister Arthur Zimmerman was wired to the German Ambassador in Washington, with a request to pass it to Mexico's ambassador. The coded message was dispatched via Washington cable lines through neutral Sweden precisely because Germany's direct cable lines to Mexico were cut by the Allies.[56]

Zimmerman's cable was a bombshell: "We intend to begin on the first of February unrestricted submarine warfare. We shall endeavor in spite of this to keep the United States of America neutral. In the event of this not succeeding, we make Mexico a proposal of alliance on the following basis: make war together, make peace together, generous financial support and an understanding on our part that Mexico is to reconquer the lost territory in Texas, New Mexico, and Arizona. The settlement in detail is left to you. You will inform the [Mexican] President of the above most secretly as soon as the outbreak of war with the United States of America is certain and add the suggestion that he should, on his own initiative, invite Japan to immediate adherence and at the same time mediate between Japan and ourselves. Please call the President's attention to the fact that the ruthless employment of our submarines now offers the prospect of compelling England in a few months to make peace. Signed, ZIMMERMANN."[57]

On February 19, 1917, Hall and Room 40 passed Zimmerman's telegram to U.S. Embassy officials in London. This had to be accomplished without disclosing to the Germans that Room 40 had broken their cipher. Later, that month, embassy officials authenticated the decrypted telegram and then rushed it on to American President Woodrow Wilson. By early March, the disclosure made headlines throughout the American media including the Hearst newspaper chain. This all ignited at the height of American outrage over the cross-border raids of Pancho Villa and the carnage wrought on American merchantmen and other ocean-going vessels by German U-Boats. Leaving no doubt as to the cable's authenticity, from February 1, U-2 torpedoes sank more ships as promised. Then the German Foreign Minister himself admitted he had dispatched the message.[58]

Throughout February 1917, chronic food and material shortages, and constant acts of peasant defiance and outright insurrection spurred the nascent Russian Revolution. After months of demands that he resign, Czar Nicholas finally abdicated on March 2. Russia, still very much in the war, became torn between two rival governments—that of the liberal Provisional Government and that of the Socialists. London and Paris immediately recognized the Provisional Government. But no one knew how long the Provisional Government and the alliance would hold.[59]

Nine days later, on March 11, British forces finally took Baghdad. Much of Mesopotamia was now under British control, including its ancient capital. Now Allied forces pushed north, targeting the supremely prized petroliferous zones around Mosul.[60]

Three weeks and a day later, on April 2, in an impassioned late night speech to a special session of the U.S. Congress, President Wilson asked for war powers. He decried Germany's unrestrained submarine attacks. "It is a war against all nations," railed Wilson. "American ships have been sunk, American lives taken, in ways which it has stirred us very deeply to learn of, but the ships and people of other neutral and friendly nations have been sunk and overwhelmed in the waters in the same way. There has been no discrimination. The challenge is to all mankind." Wilson added, "We shall fight for the things which we have always carried nearest our hearts—for democracy, for the right of those who submit to authority to have a voice in their own governments, for the rights and liberties of small nations, for a universal dominion of right by such a concert of free peoples as shall bring peace and safety to all nations and make the world itself at last free."[61] That meant self-determination and national rights.

Congress voted yes. Four days later on April 6, 1917, America ended its neutrality and joined the Allies, declaring war on Germany. Ten days later, Vladimir Lenin arrived back in Petrograd, vowing to halt his country's involvement in the war, even as the Provisional Government promised to fight on.[62]

On April 20, 1917, Balfour, now British Foreign Secretary, arrived in the United States to coordinate war goals. For Zionism, it was imperative to have Wilson and his concepts of non-annexation by the victors and national self-determination firmly behind the cause of a Jewish State in Palestine after the war. British annexation of Palestine would not be acceptable, but a protectorate would. Upon arriving in Washington, Balfour immediately met with U.S. Supreme Court Justice Louis Brandeis at a White House gathering. Brandeis was one of America's most ardent and active Zionist leaders. In the days before Balfour's arrival, Weizmann cabled Brandeis, "An expression of opinion from yourself ... in favor of a Jewish Palestine ... under a British protectorate would greatly strengthen our hands."[63]

On May 6, 1917, Brandeis met privately with President Wilson for 45 minutes on the question of Jewish Palestine. Shortly after the Brandeis meeting, Wilson stated that he "was entirely sympathetic to the aims of the Zionist Movement ... to establish a publicly assured, legally secured homeland for the Jewish people in Palestine ... under England's protectorate." But for numerous fluctuating reasons of international consensus among the Allies, and efforts to detach Turkey from Germany since America was not at war with the Ottoman Empire, Wilson delayed any public statement.[64]

Now came numberless conferences and appeals between leading Zionists and British officials in London, including London's War Cabinet. Throughout the second half of 1917 and the first half of 1918, draft after draft of Britain's proposed public declaration in support of Jewish Palestine was proffered and re-proffered by Zionist leaders, and then debated and re-debated by the War Cabinet and Balfour himself. Weizmann and company coordinated their efforts with Brandeis, sending him urgent cables to persuade Wilson to support a definitive text advocating a Jewish Palestine.[65]

At the same time, Russia plummeted into utter economic upheaval and mass antiwar sentiment. The Bolsheviks seized power in October 1917. The Communists took control, nationalized all banks and industries, and immediately sued for peace with the Germans. This came just as Allenby had captured Jerusalem. Now, a new consideration for London was how a declaration for Jewish Palestine would impact Jews in Russia, including those among the revolutionary movement. Many of those Jews completely rejected their Jewish identity and any notion of a Jewish Palestine. Others remained passionately in favor of the Jewish State. London strategists hoped any declaration would keep Russia in the war.[66]

Throughout October and the first days of November, Zionists in London, Washington and Paris peppered officials with their version of the proclamation they had sought so long. With Jerusalem in British hands, there was no longer any fear of Turkish pogroms. The advocacy was open and debated with exhilaration among Jews and Zionists everywhere. Should the announcement refer to the "Jewish Race" or the "Jewish people?" Should it speak of "*the* national home," that is, the one home or "*a* national home, that is, one of several?" How was the promulgation to be phrased, if it was to be phrased, to allow for pluralism over the existing Arab and Christian populations and without delegitimizing the establishment Jews of all nations that for one reason or another rejected Zionism? Should the Jewish national home be "established" or "re-established?" Should any announcement even be made? The battle of the participles was in full force. As the War Cabinet in London dissected and sewed together numerous permutations of the proposed language, prominent Jewish anti-Zionists railed again the move. [67]

October 9, 1917, Weizmann cabled Brandeis in Washington pleading with him to intercede with President Wilson. "Final discussion takes place in about a week," wired Weizmann. "It is essential to have not only President's approval of text, but his recommendation to grant this declaration without delay. Further your support and enthusiastic message to us from American Zionists and also prominent non-Zionists most desirable to us. Your support urgently needed. Everything strictly confidential."[68]

October 16, Edward M. House, Wilson's key foreign policy advisor in all matters involving the War and the forthcoming Peace Conference, wired the British government speaking for the President. Wilson supported the British announcement.[69]

November 2, 1917, the War Cabinet mulled its final text. Weizmann was waiting outside near the conference room doors. The document, when approved, would be in the form of a letter from Foreign Minister Lord Balfour, even though, in fact, the wording and precepts were reflective not of him as much as the deliberations of the entire War Cabinet. Earlier, Balfour had asked him to whom any such a letter should be addressed? Weizmann, presumably? No, said Weizmann, but to Lord Rothschild, head of the English Zionist Federation. Unlike other members of the Rothschild clan who abhorred the Zionism enterprise, Lionel Walter Rothschild, the second Baron Rothschild and scion of the wealthy international banking clan, was Weizmann's close friend and an ardent supporter of a Jewish national Palestine. The letter would go to him.[70]

A nervous Weizmann waited for the door to open. Suddenly, out came Sykes himself holding the document. Sykes handed it to Weizmann with the congratulation, "Dr. Weizmann, it's a boy!"[71] Israel had been effectively born.

Forever more, the letter would become known as the "Balfour Declaration," the letter which breathed life into the waiting lungs of the Jewish people.

Foreign Office
November 2nd, 1917
Dear Lord Rothschild,
   I have much pleasure in conveying to you, on behalf of His
Majesty's Government, the following declaration of sympathy
with Jewish Zionist aspirations which has been submitted to,
and approved by, the Cabinet. "His Majesty's Government view
with favor the establishment in Palestine of a national home for
the Jewish people, and will use their best endeavors to facilitate
the achievement of this object, it being clearly understood that
nothing shall be done which may prejudice the civil and religious
rights of existing non-Jewish communities in Palestine, or the
rights and political status enjoyed by Jews in any other country."
I should be grateful if you would bring this declaration to the
knowledge of the Zionist Federation.
   Yours sincerely, Arthur James Balfour.

Balfour signed large in a flourish across the bottom.[72]

\*        \*        \*        \*

In March 1918, despite all Allied efforts to the contrary, the newly Communist Soviet government in Russia signed a separate peace treaty with Germany. England, France, and America were left to press on without Russia.[73] Moreover, as the summer of 1918 approached, not all of Palestine was yet in Allied hands. Everything changed during the last September of the war during a climactic battle that would usher in the historic return of the Jews to Israel.

By September 1918, Turkish lines were stretched thin across Palestine above Jerusalem as the Ottoman Empire's last defense. Some 34,000 Ottoman troops—its Fourth, Seventh and Eighth Armies—were dug in from the Mediterranean coast to the Judean Hills, and right through the upper Jordan Valley and east to the reaches of the Hejaz Railway at the town of Deraa in Syria. Istanbul's fighters were led by German General Liman von Sanders, the tough tactician who had lead the defeat of British at Gallipoli.[74]

Against the Turks, Allenby commanded 69,000 men in Palestine, of which 12,000 were cavalry. Allenby was a cavalry man. He planned one of his main attack columns to drive up the Mediterranean coast precisely because the terrain was inviting for cavalry. Feinting in the opposite direction, Allenby visibly sent his scouts up east to the Jordan Valley. As expected, the Turks thought Allenby was going to disrupt their supply lines by attacking the railways. General von Sanders reinforced his artillery positions and troop strength far to the east. This left the coast corridor with thin defenses.[75]

On September 18–19, British warplanes rained down on a Turkish telephone communications center near Afula, midway between the coast and the Turkish rail lines at Deraa at the eastern edge of the line. Then Lawrence of Arabia, leading a camel-borne army of more than one thousand Arab rebels over the hills, their tunics flapping behind them, supported by aroused anti-Turkish Arab villagers in the rear, swept down on the Deraa railway bridges. This assault reinforced the impression that Allenby was going to attack at the eastern edge. Turkish airplanes immediately scrambled aloft to defend Deraa, bombing and strafing but causing little damage to the scattering Arabs. The battle dragged on, but it was all a show.[76]

September 19, far from Deraa, on the western edge of the Turkish front, there was no hint of hostilities. Not until precisely 4:30 AM, when the night was shattered by a thunderous barrage of artillery shells from 383 British guns, firing as many as 1,000 shells per minute. Cordite—the Brits had cordite—made in awesome quantities with acetone, to propel the 15-minute hailstorm of shells.[77]

Shell-shocked, 8,000 Turkish troops had been softened into near submission, when Allenby gave the order. Up the coastal positions, British advance units punched holes. At the assigned moment, 9,000 cavalrymen charged in, supported by 35,000 infantry.[78]

All throughout the September 18–21 period, Allenby's forces bombed, strafed, and overran the beleaguered Turk and German units, forcing thousands to retreat into the hills, leaving nearly 1,000 mangled vehicles on a Highway of Death. Prisoners were taken by the battalion—25,000 men in all. The climactic battle broke the back of the Turks, who then sued for peace. The doorway to Syria had been flung open, and Lawrence and his Arabs marched on to Damascus to seize the city as the capital of their hoped-for nation. Syria and Mesopotamia quickly fell. And Palestine was now fully under British control.[79]

Where was the final battle centered? It was a tiny town which had existed at the pivot point of history for thousands of years. It was Megiddo. Indeed, the entire battle became known as the "Battle of Megiddo." Allenby took as his honorific thereafter the title of First Viscount Allenby of Megiddo. The Christian Zionists of the War Cabinet, imbued with a millennial sense, of course recognized the name. In the Bible, Megiddo is also known as Armageddon. *Revelation 16:16* speaks of the final battle between good and evil:

"And he gathered them together into a place called in the Hebrew tongue Armageddon." The final battle of the Mideast in this war to end all wars had been fought and had been won triumphantly at Armageddon.

The Jews would be returned to Zion.

That return at the hands of the British would trigger more than two decades of intense Arab hatred against a triumphant infidel who had brought despised *dhimmis* back to the land of their forefathers to rule over them in what was now called Palestine. This hatred would fester and then explode into an international axis with the Nazis that would find its most violent episode in Baghdad in 1941 during the Farhud. That bloody episode would be only one centerpiece of the alliance.

# CHAPTER 7

# CREATING IRAQ

How the Jews returned to their home in Palestine created only half the fuse for the Farhud. The other half arose from Britain's petro-colonization and domination of Mesopotamia. These two halves metastasized into an all-encompassing hatred that drove the Arabs into the Nazi sphere, a sphere that stretched across continents but saw Iraq as a key center of gravity—lubricated by petroleum.

The story of how and why the British created the nation now known as "Iraq" is the preamble to the larger chronicle of alliance that was written during the Hitler regime. It is the second half of the explanation. The first word of this explanatory preamble is *chaos*. Undoubtedly, chaos was the last word as well.

*Chaos* is actually too elevated a term to describe the Allied wartime policy in the Mideast.

As men died by the thousands each week, a glissando of contradictory public declarations, private letters, formal treaties, *sub-rosa* agreements, and governmental pledges was enunciated to allies, neutrals, strategic corporations, nationalist organizations in Turkish provinces, and international bodies. The long list of assuring and assured parties included France, England, the United States, competing Arab nationalist factions, the Zionist Organization, and petroleum companies. Nor did any government act monolithically or even cohesively. Foreign offices, war ministries, commercial bureaus, and colonial officers often issued their own promises and commitments at cross-purposes, often without checking with—or even informing—their superiors or central national authorities.

Promises *du jour* were *de rigueur*. If some British or French official sensed a need, perceived a valuable alliance, or sniffed an opportunity, out went a signed pledge. Nearly all of these undertakings were completely contradictory. More than a few were disingenuous. Some were simply dishonored when expedient. Many such commitments spawned their own universes of international conflicts, disputes, and lasting bitterness. Indeed, for the contracting parties of World War I, *chaos* was a condition to aspire to—a step up from the diplomatic bedlam that initially ruled.

Several small libraries would be needed to explore the evolving agreements that greatly impacted the British as they occupied Baghdad and the rest of Mesopotamia, as well as the Arabs who lived there. But to a large extent, oil was the ingredient that fueled those agreements. It was frequently admitted in the corridors of power of both London and Paris that the Allies were frantically quarreling over the spoils of war even before the war had been won. Turkey's carcass was being divided before the beast had been conquered, it was commonly quipped. The central player in this frenzy was a single company: its name was Anglo-Persian Oil Company (APOC), later to become known as "British Petroleum."

In many ways, Iraq was created by and for the Anglo-Persian Oil Company. Years later, the nation of Persia would change its name to its ancient fabled identity, "Iran." But decades before twentieth century Persia became Iran, Anglo-Persian became Britain's official oil company. The British-backed oil exploration company first secured rights to Persia's oil in 1901 by payoffs and negotiations with the elder Shah. As war approached, APOC was officially designated by the British government to expand Britain's oil monopoly into Mesopotamia. More than a mere corporate preference, the British government actually owned a majority stake in APOC, and could decide on all things relating to war and foreign policy.[1] Both hinged on oil.

Even though Persian oil had been flowing since 1908, the first Mesopotamia gusher was years away. But London knew Mesopotamia's day of black gold would come. For this reason, all the international agreements between the British and everyone else as of 1916 foresaw Mesopotamia as merely an invisible Mercator-straddling extension of the priceless Persian oil fields that lay beneath the ground. Once the war was won, Britain intended to simply colonize Mesopotamia.[2]

APOC, however, could not wait that long.

In fact, although Anglo-Persian still possessed no formal petroleum concession rights in Mesopotamia, the company in 1916 used Britain's occupation of war-time Basra in the south to commence oil exploration far to the north, ostensibly under the auspices of the British Admiralty. In a confidential dispatch, APOC company chairman Charles Greenway informed the Foreign Office undersecretary, "Our geological staff has carried out extensive reconnaissance over an area 100 miles inland from the Shatt-el Arab River [in the Basra region] ... which reconnaissance shows that there are possibilities of finding oil." Greenway explained that APOC was "not putting in [a petroleum research] application for the area" with the local authorities in anticipation that his company would simply "be given the complete oil rights over any portion of the Turkish Empire which may come under British influence."[3] This presumption appealed to oil allies in British India. British India was a colony of such magnitude that by itself it was increasingly exercising influence over all things in Mesopotamia. The bluntness of Greenway's notice stunned the Foreign Office in London, which was mindful of existing commitments to share oil lands with its French allies. London and Paris had especially agreed that in the oil-rich lands of Turkish Mosul, beyond Mesopotamia's border, France would rule.

London's international wartime understanding was a mere obstacle in Anglo-Persian's path. By 1916, it was clear. No longer was Anglo-Persian Oil focused solely on the traditional Mesopotamian realm of the land between the Tigris and Euphrates, but on any Turkish territory awarded to Britain and the Allies after the war. This new approach could stretch APOC's commercial domain all the way to Istanbul and beyond into Eastern Europe. As APOC's jurisdiction expanded, so did British India's commercial sub-colonization of the Mideast. Unhappy with APOC's self-driven foreign and wartime policy, Foreign Secretary Edward Grey insisted that Greenway's suddenly expanded view be "at once controverted" by London's top oil government official Maurice de Bunsen. Among a thicket of government agreements parleyed in March 1914, just before war broke out, was one that granted Shell Oil 25 percent of any new larger Anglo-Persian activity. APOC's new unrestrained course prompted another Foreign Office functionary to add his own caution: "In case there is litigation hereafter, as I am positive there will be if we admit Greenway's claim," Shell would certainly claim it was "unfairly treated by His Majesty's Government if ... jostled out of that 25 percent."[4]

Nonetheless, Anglo-Persian organized more pressure to keep Mosul out of French hands. The campaign intensified as far back as the first days of April 1916, just as the Sykes-Picot bargain was becoming known to inner circles. Now British India and APOC were forming an almost rebellious binary, operating in spite of if not against London's wishes. On April 1, the India Office in London sent a letter reminding the Foreign Office, "It will be borne in mind that His Majesty's Government have supported the claim of [Anglo-Persian company founder] Mr. [William] D'Arcy to a concession of all oil deposits in the *vilayets* [provinces] of Mosul and Baghdad." If that were the case, the India Office questioned whether Anglo-Persian could still exercise its claim if Mosul fell under French control.[5]

But the French needed oil too. Their petroleum industry was a fiction. Mosul was to be their war prize. One pivotal oil financier at the time wrote, "The French oil groups ... were nothing else than a monopolistic association of grocers ... in a pitiful condition in spite of the fact that French refiners had accumulated enormous fortunes by price rigging, and dubious methods, such as bribing the press."[6]

The French government had granted refiners special economic protections and incentives to encourage development of a refinery infrastructure on French soil. But, in fact, there was no actual refining in France. Fully refined oil was simply purchased, sometimes from American firms and sometimes from Royal Dutch Shell. Then, at the port, prior to shipment, French petroleum companies deliberately laced the oil tanks with "chemical dirt" that could be easily removed. This simple removal process was passed off as genuine "refining" to maintain the charade and continue the flow of French tax exemptions.[7]

But once war was declared, imported refined oil became scarce and the French government learned the truth: its refining industry was fundamentally nonexistent. French officials became convinced that without any real oil sources, France would have to control Mosul. Thus, the sense of insecurity became palpable as French diplomats in London felt Britain's subtle change of heart. Even as the main Sykes-Picot letter was being signed on May 15, 1916, Sir Edward Grey asked the French ambassador in London for written assurances that when France took over Mosul, France would recognize Britain's preexisting commercial rights. These so-called "commercial rights" referred to whatever oil concessions had been actually gained or even preliminarily negotiated by Anglo-Persian during its inconclusive wheeling and dealing with local Turkish authorities in the days before the war erupted in 1914. Of course, such agreements and negotiations had been deemed null and void when war broke out. But Britain wanted to preserve those potential commercial rights, even if only theoretical. By May 17, 1916, France provided written assurances that it was "ready to confirm, in the regions which might be attributed to it ... the various British concessions bearing a date prior to the war."[8] In other words, Britain could still control oil rights in Mosul.

*     *     *     *

A centerpiece of the new Mesopotamian industrial dream was petroleum. As the British military maneuvered, attacked, and fortified their positions from Basra to Baghdad, so did the combative oilmen in London.

As the Great War staggered forward, with its heavy tolls and oppressive requirements for fuel, the British government tried to balance its future oil partnerships to ensure both a British character and a guaranteed supply. Anglo-Persian continually tried to shim itself into prominence as the one company for both needs.

But Anglo-Persian simply lacked the ability to supply with certainty the entire nation's needs—and the British government knew it. Moreover, quality and grade issues were coming to the fore. Persian oil was constantly being denigrated in naval reports for its viscosity, which caused it to thicken at low temperatures. British officials, desperate for higher quality, now eyed oil fields as far-flung as Java, Mexico, Venezuela, and Romania. That meant scrutinizing Shell Oil, the only company outside America already operating in all those far-flung realms. Shell had been born British, as an oil transportation company, but quickly merged into an international behemoth that was of both British and Dutch descent with allegiance to neither national ancestor. How could this international entity be recast into a tool of British oil imperialism in Mesopotamia? The answer for Whitehall seemed to be an elaborate effort, crafted over many months, to remake the Dutch-English hybrid Shell Oil as a company completely British "in character," even if not British in "control," and somehow fuse the remade Shell company with Anglo-Persian. In this scenario, Shell would plunge headstrong into Mesopotamia under British aegis and finally overrun the original Anglo-Persian corporate identity, which, of course, operated under British aegis.[9]

Two oil titans would then rule the land, wrestling to topple each other in their race to petro-primacy. London would rule them both. In this way, Britain could immediately import all the oil necessary to turn Mesopotamia into a prized industrialized oil state, and then control the vast resource once it finally gushered up from the ground. London called its flammable corporate combination a "fusion."

"The Royal Dutch Shell would probably consider no sacrifices too great to bring about this fusion," wrote a Treasury department official, and thereby "give them all that they have been aiming at for years past." Such a government sanctioned fusion would give Shell control of nearly all major oil outside the significant American and Eastern European deposits and deliver much more to the growing British market, including the Royal Navy. The "sacrifices" by Royal Dutch Shell would entail allowing the minority British side of the combine—that is, the English side of Shell—to incongruously predominate as the majority, ensuring that British subjects would function as board directors, and agreeing to grant the United Kingdom preference over its global supplies.[10]

However, when Anglo-Persian realized that British officials were slowly favoring a move toward Royal Dutch Shell, with its well-entrenched, worldwide distribution system, a network that extended right across Great Britain, APOC rushed to compete. More than being a mere driller, refiner, and supplier, APOC desperately needed to be a wellhead-to-consumer oil company like Shell or Standard Oil. Such a network would take years to construct. The company did not have years.

So Anglo-Persian purchased an existing network. The Europaische Petroleum Union (EPU) was an amalgam of continental oil distribution arms, mainly controlled by German concerns. EPU owned an operating subsidiary in Britain. This subsidiary controlled both an international oil shipping division, the Petroleum Steamship Company, and a domestic consumer sales agency, the Homelight Oil Company. Formed in London in 1906, the EPU subsidiary was profitable, reporting a 14 percent dividend in 1914. It was ripe for a takeover. The EPU subsidiary's name was "British Petroleum Company," with its first name descriptive only of its operating territory, not its true ownership, which was mainly German.[11]

When World War I erupted in 1914, the British authorities seized British Petroleum Company as "enemy property." During 1915 and 1916, APOC chairman Greenway petitioned the custodian of enemy property to purchase those seized—and hence government-controlled—oil company assets. The war was not over, the seized subsidiary's disposition was not resolved, but the petition was nonetheless granted. Anglo-Persian was still short of the funds needed for any acquisition. But in late 1917, the £2.7 million "sale" was finalized by virtue of a cashless, loanless "self-financing" miracle. Payments would be made to the custodian of enemy property over five years, commencing in 1918, a sum which could easily be generated by expected revenues. The purchase balance sheets made clear in an explanatory note: "The Anglo-Persian Company will have no difficulty in meeting the above annual payments, without raising fresh capital, as they will be reserving [repayment funds] out of profits each year." Indeed, both the income and transferred depreciation from British Petroleum and its two divisions immediately began generating hundreds of thousands of pounds annually for Anglo-Persian. Decades later, Anglo-Persian Oil Company would change its full name to British Petroleum.[12]

With Great Britain entrenched from Basra to Baghdad and beyond, a runaway Anglo-Persian continued to press ahead as though it actually owned the oil rights in Mesopotamia. Even after being told by Foreign Secretary Grey that APOC did not, the company was fond of sending confidential and carefully misleading memoranda to government and financial officials implying that it did. For example, one confidential memo circulated to the Treasury asserted, "The D'Arcy Exploration Company holds a prior claim to the concession for the petroliferous deposits in the vilayets of Baghdad, Mosul, and Basra."[13]

In mid-1918, when the British army in Mesopotamia needed more oil faster for its remaining military campaigns in the region. Anglo-Persian was temporarily authorized to drill at Hit, south of Baghdad, and other locations along the Euphrates. This was to be an emergency war measure. The Foreign Office concurred, but specified that APOC could function only as a subcontractor to the military, not as an independent commercial concern, this so "such action is not subsequently advanced by them as an additional ground for claiming preferential treatment of their interests in Mesopotamia."[14]

However, Anglo-Persian continued to pummel the Treasury with vexatious entreaties to forgo any further interest in Shell and quickly grant the company the true monopoly in Mesopotamia. One such memo by Greenway, dated August 2, 1918, warned that forming a partnership with Royal Dutch Shell would mean "the government's investment [in APOC] ... will be entirely lost and the Empire [will] again be at the mercy of monopolists for its whole requirements of Petroleum products!"[15]

Continuing in all capitals, with generous use of triple exclamation marks and underlining, Greenway added: "COLLECTIVELY, THE LOSS TO THE BRITISH EXCHEQUER... WOULD BE NOT LESS THAN £5,000,000 PER ANNUM FROM THE CONCLUSION OF THE WAR UP TO SAY 5/6 YEARS HENCE, AND THEREAFTER ON A GRADUALLY INCREASING SCALE, NOT LESS THAN £10,000,000 PER ANNUM UP TO 10/12 YEARS HENCE — THE WHOLE OF WHICH SACRIFICE WOULD BE MADE FOR THE BENEFIT OF COMPANIES WHICH ARE EITHER WHOLLY OR LARGELY FOREIGN OWNED!!!"[16]

In the meantime, key analysts within the military and Foreign Office continued to sound the alarm throughout the summer of 1918 that abundant oil was now a must for the United Kingdom. A key paper compiled by Admiral Edmund Slade, one of the government's Anglo-Persian board members, put it bluntly: "It is no exaggeration to say that our life as an empire is largely dependent upon our ability to maintain the control of bunker fuel." After examining oil resources worldwide, from Appalachia to Galicia, Slade stated that the United States would soon consume all the oil produced in America and Mexico, and, since the world was industrializing, the options elsewhere were meager. But, he emphasized, "In Persia and Mesopotamia lie the largest undeveloped resources at present known in the world ... more than the whole of the Romanian and Galician fields put together."[17]

Slade's conclusion, backed by maps, tables, and studies: "The Power that controls the oil lands of Persia and Mesopotamia will control the source of supply of the majority of the liquid fuel of the future."[18]

Slade's conclusions were enthusiastically endorsed. One secret memo to the War Cabinet from the chief of the Air Staff echoed Slade's points "with all possible emphasis." The memo insisted, "It is essential … to monopolize all possible supplies of petroleum" in Mesopotamia and Persia. Another secret memo, this one from the Cabinet Secretariat to the Admiralty, used Slade's memo and maps to assert, "The retention of the oil-bearing regions in Mesopotamia and Persia in British hands … would appear to be a first-class British war aim."[19]

By the fall of 1918, the exhausted armies of Europe and the Ottoman Empire were desperate to end their seemingly senseless struggle. In early October, a broken Turkey began unraveling. The Turkish cabinet resigned, leaving the empire in the hands of caretakers eager to end the war. By mid-October, British commander Charles Townshend, previously taken prisoner at Kut, was summoned to Constantinople to arrange a cessation of hostilities. At the Sublime Porte, Townshend met privately with Field Marshal and Prime Minister Izzet Pasha in one of those solemn, dignified moments when enemy generals become weary enough to admit they have killed enough. Tears welling up in his eyes, the defeated Izzet Pasha conceded his battered country was demoralized and unable to continue. "You are willing to help us?" he asked Townshend. The former prisoner, who had been well treated during captivity, replied, "With all my heart."[20] On October 30, 1918, the Sick Man of Europe finally died. Aboard a ship at the port of Mudros in the Aegean Sea, Turkey surrendered and agreed to an armistice. Under its terms, all hostilities were to cease at noon the next day. By dawn, October 31, a riverbank of white flags began unfurling across Turkish entrenchments along the Tigris. The British march north was halted in place 40 miles from Mosul. But from Baghdad, the dream of a new British Iraq, enriched by the oilfields of Mosul, was too much to resist. A note marked "Very Secret—Important," sent just weeks earlier by a Cabinet officer to the Prime Minister's office was typical in urging, "There may be reasons other than purely military for pushing on in Mesopotamia where the British have an enormous preponderance of force. Would it not be an advantage, before the end of the war, to secure the valuable oil wells in Mesopotamia?"[21]

Civil Administrator Arnold Wilson in Baghdad had regularly nagged Whitehall "as to the desirability of extending the scope of our war aims to the Mosul vilayet." Possession is nine-tenths of the law. "Whether it was ultimately to be in the French or the British 'sphere of interest' [under the Sykes-Picot Agreement]," recalled Wilson, "it was essential that it [Mosul] should be occupied by British troops before or from the moment that hostilities ceased … I contended vehemently that a bird in the military hand was worth many in the thorny thickets of diplomacy, and that in dealing with Turkey, a valid post-war title could be obtained by the Allies only by securing possession."[22]

The war with Germany continued in Europe and elsewhere, but for Turkey it was over on October 31, 1918. Clause 16 of the armistice specified the surrender of all Turkish garrisons in "Syria and Mesopotamia." Civil Administrator Wilson wrote, "From our local point of view, everything turned on the meaning of the word *Mesopotamia*, which was not in current official or diplomatic use in Turkey. Was it open to us, under the Armistice, to regard Mosul … as forming part of Mesopotamia?" Wilson preferred it both ways: Mosul was not in Mesopotamia for purposes of seizing it, but it was in Mesopotamia for purposes of mandatory surrender.[23]

Within 48 hours of the October 31 effective date of the armistice at Mudros, Mesopotamian commander-in-chief William Marshall gave the order to take Mosul—ceasefire or no ceasefire. Only 1,650 outnumbered Turkish riflemen and a battery of 32 artillery pieces defended the city. General Marshall instructed the surrounded Ottoman commander to evacuate the town, and indeed the entire Mosul province, or be vanquished. The commander objected that moving on Mosul violated the ceasefire.[24]

Marshall refused to wait for clarification from England. Quoting Clause 7 of the armistice, Marshall directed, "'Allies have the right to occupy any strategic points' and War Office have ordered the occupation of Mosul." The full Clause 7 of course read: "The Allies to have the right to occupy any strategic points in the event of a situation arising which threatens the security of the Allies." It was intended for exigent circumstances. Haggard Turkish troops at Mosul were observing the ceasefire and no longer threatening British troops.[25]

For several days the two sides bickered while waiting for instructions to filter back. Finally, on November 7, Marshall, willing to wait no longer, offered the local Turkish commander an ultimatum. The besieged Turks reluctantly evacuated Mosul. The British marched in. Their occupation of Mesopotamia was now complete, and included three provinces, first Basra, then Baghdad, and now Mosul. The third province, Mosul, was home to approximately 800,000 persons, about 20 percent Arab, but more than 60 percent Kurd, with the remaining fifth split between Jews, Christians, Turks, and mystic Yazidis. An uneasy new national outline had been cobbled together that was mainly Kurdish in the north, Sunni in the midsection, and Shia in the south.[26]

"Thanks to General Marshall," recalled Wilson, "we had established *de facto*, the principle that the Mosul vilayet is part of 'Iraq,' to use the geographical expression … and whether for the woe or weal of the inhabitants, it is too soon to say." He added that had General Marshall waited just an additional 24 hours for the restraining instructions from London to arrive, history would be otherwise. But, Wilson continued, Marshall did not wait, and so "laid the foundation stone of the future State of Iraq."[27]

Iraq had been created by British petro-imperialism as an oil state.

A few days later, at the eleventh hour of the eleventh day of the eleventh month of 1918, all guns fell silent. The Germans had surrendered as well. The shooting had stopped.

But the shouting would now begin.

# PEACE AND PETROLEUM

L ike most everything else in Mesopotamia, the legality of Britain's rights to Mosul and its oil fields was fuzzy and disputed. As 1918 concluded, the once-Persian land inhabited by the diverse people of Mosul, now nominally under the sovereignty of the Turks, had been promised to the French by London officials, who did not own it, and was now occupied mainly by British India, which had only recently seized it. British forces were certainly the occupiers under international law, except they had occupied under a bruised—many said *violated*—proviso of the armistice. Not a few in the international community demanded an immediate withdrawal and reinstatement of the *status quo ante* of Turkish authority.[1] But that would have meant relinquishing the oil prize.

Moreover, the ongoing scramble to control all three provinces of the new Mesopotamia, soon to be Iraq, continued to rivet the attention of France, England, and British India long before any international peace conference had even decided the ultimate disposition of the Turkish Middle East. "I must confess … we are rather in the position of the hunters who divided up the skin of the bear before they had killed it," famously quipped Brigadier General George Macdonough, even as the Sykes-Picot Agreement was being negotiated in early January 1916, nearly three years before the Turkish surrender.[2]

*Non-annexation* was a guiding principle of the Allies. So even though possession was nine-tenths of the law, true sovereignty over all of Mesopotamia would be decided at the Versailles Peace Conference in Paris convening in 1919. Strongly influencing that process would be several principles from

133

the famous Fourteen Points enunciated in 1918 by President Woodrow Wilson after America joined the war.

*Point Five:* "A free, open-minded, and absolutely impartial adjustment of all colonial claims, based upon a strict observance of the principle that, in determining all such questions of sovereignty, the interests of the populations concerned must have equal weight with the equitable claims of the government whose title is to be determined."[3] Translation: self-determination.

*Point Twelve:* "The Turkish portion of the present Ottoman Empire should be assured a secure sovereignty, but the other nationalities which are now under Turkish rule should be assured an undoubted security of life and an absolutely unmolested opportunity of autonomous development."[4] Translation: self-determination.

Self-determination. It was the unfurling banner of the day. What was it? Misguided as it was, antidemocratic as it was, the reformist compulsion to grant remedial self-determination to long-exploited nationalist movements became astral among the postwar mapmakers. But who was entitled to self-determination, and how would it be implemented? Self-determination could preferentially enfranchise one identified people over another within a region along a variety of criteria: ethnicity, religion, a common language, geographic continuity, all of it, or just some of it. The result at Paris was a patchwork of impassioned, often competing, national claims: Kurds, Ukrainians, Armenians, Japanese, Chinese, Jews, and Arabs among others, and not infrequently overlapping traditional territorial boundaries.[5] In the final analysis, the anointed legitimacy of any self-determination movement is not in the eyes of the beholder, but in the interest of the bestower.

Nonetheless, the provinces of Mesopotamia, by any measure, were clearly a candidate for self-determination and eventual nationhood. The Allies understood that. But not all among the Allies wanted to admit it. Britain's numerous official agencies remained sharply divided over Mesopotamia's future. Should the new Iraq be an Indian appendage, a British protectorate, or an independent Arab nation led by Faisal, son of Hussein, or perhaps some other potentate?

Many senior ranks in the Foreign Office were steeled by an overriding commitment to Woodrow Wilson's principles. However, many were still hypnotized by centuries of imperialist traditions. Adding to the debate were major personalities in the Admiralty, the War Office, and the India Office, as well as a maelstrom of voices in Parliament, the Board of Trade, and the British media.

But the life-and-breath decisions and the map marks that ruled British Mesopotamia on the ground were, in fact, not decided in London, Bombay, or Paris. Those decisions were made in Baghdad by one man, waiting for no one and determined to wring and shape history between his own two hands. That man was Acting Civil Commissioner Arnold Wilson.

Occupying Mesopotamia meant administering Mesopotamia. Under the Hague Conventions of 1899 and 1907, an occupying military power was obligated to efficiently and properly administer lands under its control and safeguard the civilian populations. Within a week of overrunning Basra in November 1914, the British inaugurated a civilian administration. As the British moved north, and after they eventually captured Baghdad, their occupying civil administration was extended into the new territory. That civil administration was constructed and controlled by officials in British India. Almost overnight, the occupied portion of Mesopotamia became not a national Arab state-in-waiting, not a prelude to any pan-Arab vision. Instead, Mesopotamia became India. Wilson was the man who made it so.[6]

Who was Arnold Wilson? Acting Civil Commissioner Arnold Wilson was brought in from his post in Persia to manage civilian affairs in Mesopotamia. An experienced Near East technocrat and diplomat, Wilson had just finished a stint on the Turco-Persian Frontier Commission and was in large measure responsible for transferring the oil fields of Persian Mosul into Turkish sovereignty in 1913. For generations before oil became significant, the Mosul region had been a disputed territory between Russia, Persia, and Turkey. To reduce the potential of a border-clash in the run-up to Word War I, the international Turco-Persian Frontier Commission adjudicated the competing rights and sovereignty claims of all contenders and finally awarded them to Turkey. Wilson ensured that Anglo-Persian's Persian oil concession was transferred right along with the land, thus giving the company a gray zone of exploitation in Mesopotamia.[7] Ten months later, Britain was at war with the Ottoman Empire. Mosul and its oil wealth could be taken.

Known for his bad manners and good organizational skills, Wilson openly proclaimed himself a "rank imperialist" and freely admitted "a strong personal leaning to radicalism."[8]

In fact, no sooner had Britain taken Basra in November 1914 than Wilson fired off a memo to his political officer proposing the repopulation of Mesopotamia with Indians for the good of imperial Britain. "I should like to see it announced," Wilson wrote, "that Mesopotamia was to be annexed to India as a colony for India and Indians, that the government of India would administer it, and gradually bring under cultivation its vast unpopulated desert plains, peopling them with martial races from the Punjab."[9]

Wilson subscribed to the wisdom of his friend and fellow theorist, Arthur Hirtzel, head of the India Office political department, who at the advent of the drive to Baghdad quipped that Arabs were "no more capable of administering severally or collectively than the Red Indians [of America]."[10] In

Mesopotamia, Wilson stayed true to his contentious self-image and his doctrine, creating a tinderbox.

In theory, Britain had invaded to help the Arabs achieve national expression. In that vein, the Foreign Office regularly demanded local Arabs be employed to run their own affairs and create the infrastructure of their country's rehabilitation. For example, just days after capturing Baghdad, the War Cabinet telegraphed instructions to allow preexisting laws and customs to remain in place with subtle but *de facto* protectorate status afforded by England—not India. But Wilson launched a personal bureaucratic crusade to do the opposite, importing and imposing Indian law, Indian workers, Indian institutions, Indian currency, and broad strata of Indian officials.[11]

Turkish paper money was banned by proclamation and replaced with Indian rupees, although valuable Turkish gold liras temporarily remained in circulation, especially in the bazaars. The Eastern Bank of India opened branches in key centers of conquered provinces, sometimes in the very facilities of Deutsche Bank, which was by now an enemy German financial institution. So many rupees were needed, that they were boxed and shipped from Bombay, hot from the mint. When the supply for rupees was outpaced by demand, the Anglo-Persian Oil Company was asked to help through its connections at the Imperial Bank of Persia; the company was only too happy to assist. Ottoman postage stamps were retained but overprinted with Indian imprimaturs for use by the troops, and these worked their way into common use. A Revenue Department was opened at Basra to accept taxes, ordinary administrative fees, and routine payments—all required in rupees of course. All government funds now wove into a local civil occupation fisc controlled from Calcutta. Financial officials in India were astonished when their efficient replacement of Turkish corruption yielded a £130,000 surplus for 1915.[12]

The former Turkish territories were now increasingly called by their historic regional name, "Iraq," and this identity slowly came into common usage to usher in a new governmental status. By virtue of India, Great Britain already controlled the largest Islamic population in the world, some 40 million Muslims. Hence, London felt comfortable in morphing Mesopotamia into what was being called "an Indian appendage."[13]

The Iraq Occupied Territories Code, replicating the civil and criminal laws of India, was unveiled in August 1915, complete with courts, judges, and magistrates, all from India and under the administration of the Indian political department. Section 8 of the code explicitly declared that the Iraqi territories were the equivalent of "a district ... of Bombay." Those Indian laws were not translated into either Arabic or Turkish, and it was more than a year before any court business could be conducted in Arabic.[14]

For the tribal areas not accustomed to urbanized law, Britain imported and renamed the Indian Frontier Crimes Regulations that empowered a political officer to convene a tribal *majlis*, or arbitration of elders. The political officer could veto any majlis adjudication. In many cases, Iraqi tribal customs, such as token money payments to resolve feud murders and death to women who strayed from arcane Bedouin morality codes, were set aside for British traditions of punishment. Under transplanted British Indian law, murderers were now sentenced to capital execution; women accused of violating desert mores were not.[15]

Indian policemen, headed by E. G. Gregson, a senior officer of the Indian Police Service, were imported to keep order. Several hundred men in uniform patrolled, ran the jails, and superintended night watchmen. They enforced order at government offices, the Basra docks, and Baghdad facilities.[16]

A huge Indian-run bureaucracy was erected. British and Indian health officials assumed the sensitive inspection of Persian and Indian Shia corpses for burial at the cemetery in the Shia holy city of Najaf, and they supervised the many pilgrims who visited other Shia shrines. Prostitutes, all 180 of them, while not officially registered, were routinely inspected by the civil medical authorities to reduce venereal disease. Passenger priorities for boatmen and carriage drivers, the sale of liquor, sanitary conditions for horse stables, the treatment of sick dogs, the rental of property, carrying of arms, and all aspects of foodstuffs were regulated by Indian bureaucrats according to an English model.[17]

Reconstruction and development plans abounded to restore the golden era of Mesopotamia, and bring its long-neglected provinces into the twentieth century. British economic analysts studied all aspects of Mesopotamian commerce. Trade and traffic were to be expanded throughout the provinces and then connected to the world at large. Plans were outlined to dramatically increase the new Iraq's export of cotton and dates, as well as its imports of the manpower and machinery needed to make Iraq bloom once more.[18]

Extensive irrigation and flood control, what British trade planners called "the scientific control of the rivers," would be constructed to significantly increase food yields. Baghdad's railway chugging north and south would become a strategic commercial as well as military linchpin of this grand national design. Medical facilities, schools, public works, bridges, roads to reach the northern oil regions—so much was needed.[19]

To engineer the transformation, the heavy machines of progress were required: fleets of Ford and Peerless lorries, Caterpillar tractors, mechanized irrigation pumps, great stores of building materials, and spare everything. The primitive port at Basra, which often could not even handle conventional steamships, was completely in need of modernization. Within weeks of the 1914 invasion, three river steamers were requisitioned. Later, three dredgers were brought in from India to deepen the Shatt-el-Arab waterway leading to Basra and improve the port area generally. Lucrative and monopolistic contracts were awarded to British steamship and transport lines. Transport itself would be a fabulous economic center.[20]

There was a nation to build. But greater Basra's entire population was estimated at just 80,000. Baghdad's was approximately 230,000, split between Arabs, Jews, Persians, Syrians, and others. Many, perhaps a majority, were still living a tribal or pastoral lifestyle. More manpower was needed to implement the rapid and sweeping infrastructure improvements experts had in mind to support both the occupying army and trade expansion. "All schemes for the agricultural development and commercial exploitation of the country," declared one key trade survey, "are, however, conditioned and limited by the capacity, temperament and character of the inhabitants. The two vilayets [provinces] of Baghdad and Basra are thinly populated, possessing an average of 9 inhabitants per square mile, which is inadequate."[21]

So British eyes turned to India, which possessed an abundance of population and which could send in tens of thousands of laborers, who themselves would constitute a viable and economy-stimulating population in need of goods and services. "Stress must be laid upon the organic connection which already exists between Mesopotamia and India," the key trade survey concluded.[22]

Not a few who favored an industrial revolution for Iraq envisioned a new, revitalized nation that would be situated at the fulcrum of east-west trade and also to a large extent converted to an extension of India. Indeed, Sir William Willcocks, the man who a few years earlier had designed the original Mesopotamian irrigation scheme for the Turkish government, admitted his ultimate plan was systematic repopulation. Willcocks wrote: "The Euphrates-Tigris delta will be reclaimed and settled by millions of natives of India, who will make it again the Garden of the East." Under this vision, Arabs would become a fringe minority in the provinces, subsumed by the biggest regional migration since the Arab conquest of Mesopotamian Eurasians more than 12 centuries before. These notions did not escape the local population. Indeed, during these years, the very concept of railroads and passenger shipping lines on both sides of the Atlantic was associated with mass international migration and settlement campaigns. From time to time, thousands in the provinces angrily rallied at their mosques to condemn the latest rumored British shipping and irrigation plans as "sinister intentions" to transfer in masses of Indian workers, some said 10,000 at a time, thus transmogrifying the nation.[23]

Wilson also abolished the elected municipal councils that even the Ottomans had permitted, replacing them with appointed Indian political officers. The provincial identities and ethnic fabrics of Mosul in the north, Baghdad in the center, and Basra in the south were profoundly different, and the prevailing instruction by the Foreign Office was to administer Baghdad and Basra separately, being careful to maintain merely a defensive military presence in Mosul. But Wilson decided on his own to unify the three into an administrative whole. He even issued passports to cover all inhabitants in Mesopotamia who dwelled from the Persian Gulf north to the foothills of Kurdistan. By governing the three provinces—Mosul to Basra—from Baghdad, Wilson in essence created a future Iraq not under international law or popular consensus, but by personal fiat.[24]

As an occupying power, Great Britain declared it had come to liberate Mesopotamia from the Turks. "Our armies do not come into your cities and lands as conquerors or enemies, but as liberators," proclaimed the generals upon entering Baghdad. Instead, Great Britain suddenly found itself almost at war with the local population. Once again, Wilson was the central character, wielding oppressive civil regulations. Under Wilson's direction, families were routinely evicted and their homes requisitioned by occupying forces and administrators, with the token rent often less than satisfying. Piped water was restricted to the burgeoning administrative and military sectors, depriving even established merchants of Basra and Baghdad of their established basics. Large numbers of ordinary residents were dragooned as minimally paid compulsory laborers for British work projects, often pulling them away from fields, flocks, or shops. Freedom of movement was greatly curtailed, purportedly to preempt Turkish spies, but this practice continued long after the Ottoman threat had been purged. The local population bitterly resented these intrusive measures, which redefined their very way of daily life.[25]

In addition, Wilson controlled the movement of all food. Some foodstuffs could not be sold unless the army's needs were filled first. More important, in some cases, Wilson decided who could eat and who would starve. Those among the nomadic tribes who cooperated with the British were fed. Those who did not were blockaded. By this selective method, Wilson declared, he "was feeding 100,000 Bedouin," while he could "prevent hostile tribes from obtaining more than a modicum of subsistence." Recalling his activities in 1918, Wilson wrote, "The shortage of foodstuffs was so great in Iraq that without our assistance most of these [tribesmen] must have died of starvation." In justification, he wrote, "If the migrants [Bedouin nomads fleeing across borders in the wake of war movements] did not give us any material military assistance, they were at least giving none to our opponents."[26]

The British found numerous sheikhs willing to be co-opted to prop up the unpopular occupation. These sheikhs were empowered to collect taxes in their area and to settle disputes with the force of law, not according to tribal traditions but based on an imported Indian code, which was adapted from English legal precepts. During the 12 months spanning 1916 and 1917, for instance, the local British political officer in the Suq district, H. R. P. Dickson, found in each of the 22 Suq tribes one sheikh willing to be elevated. However, in many cases, the newly elevated sheikh was not the traditional ancestral chief. Hence, the tribal hierarchies, inculcated over centuries, were rewritten by Wilson's policy.[27] Petty abuses and high-handedness by Wilson's new strongmen were common. Both the populace and British openly considered these new boss sheikhs to be little more than stooges. One prominent reform-minded British official of the Indian government who later joined the Baghdad administration readily explained in 1916, "Once a sheikh has to rely on [the] government for support, he has lost the sympathy of his tribesmen." Refeudalizing Mesopotamia effectively restored the corrupt ways of the Sultan that had prevailed prior to the Young Turk reforms. But the occupation could count upon approbation from these new faces, on cue, in any controversy.[28]

Only the cash influx from British rentals, purchases, wages, and political subsidies, plus strict noninterference with religious activities, softened the blow of the occupation. But at times, when the power of the purse retreated, seething outrage erupted. For example, on January 28, 1918, Captain W. M. Marshall was installed as the new governor of the Iraqi city of Najaf, one of two Iraqi cities holy to Shi'a. During preceding months, Najaf had been mutinous. British patrols had been shot at, an airplane was almost downed by gunfire, and government offices were attacked. Intent on maintaining order, the newly installed Captain Marshall ordered all stipends and financial supports for local sheikhs terminated, demanded all rifles be turned in at once, and then fired the entire Najaf police force, replacing them with hand-selected officers from Kut.[29]

Local agitators, deprived of emoluments that had eased the pain of occupation, immediately decided to eliminate Captain Marshall. On March 19, timed with the Moslem Nawruz festivities, assassins dressed as policemen entered Marshall's home and killed him. Punjabi guards were summoned to hunt down the assailants, but insurgents fought them as well. When the real killers could not be found, the British blockaded Shia Najaf—nothing in, nothing out. Wilson and the military demanded the surrender of the murderers, plus a fine of 50,000 rupees, plus 1,000 rifles, plus deportation to India of 100 prisoners. Until those conditions were satisfied, Wilson ruled, the residents would suffer a total "food-and-water supply cut off." Any number of Shia intermediaries from both Persia and Mesopotamia entreated Wilson to accept "an amicable settlement" to help their holy city. Perhaps just the women and children could be evacuated, they pleaded.[30]

Wilson would not yield. He wanted the killers—or everyone could just starve. With food and water dwindling, many local sheikhs and ordinary citizens joined the rebellion, or strongly considered it, out of a sheer instinct for survival. Wilson remained impervious to telegrams from London and Calcutta seeking moderation. He controlled the facts on the ground regardless of instruction or protestation. After weeks of siege, dwindling food supplies could still be found, but the water was almost gone—this while approaching a summer that would reach 112 degrees. Finally, by May 4, 1918, quarter by quarter, the town had been starved into submission. Najaf surrendered the culprits.[31]

A British military tribunal at the second Shia holy city of Kufa speedily convicted 11 men of murder, sentencing them to death. Nine more were sentenced to jail time for complicity. Islamic notables appealed to Wilson not to execute all the ringleaders, only the two men who actually commited the murder. Wilson refused any clemency on these—or any other—grounds. On May 25, 1918, just a few weeks after Najaf's submission, all 11 were publicly hanged in Kufa. Just hours after the execution, Wilson perceived validation when he received an invitation to a feast at the home of the caretaker of one of Najaf's shrines.[32]

In recalling the episode, Wilson wrote these words: "Najaf has never again been a source of serious anxiety to the government of the country."[33]

Hence, as the British occupation expanded, the Arabs of Iraq, whom callous Ottoman Turkification had embittered, now wondered how they would resist British Indianization. To the Arabs, the threat to their identity was the same. Only the accents and garments differed.

*     *     *     *

While Wilson was busy creating and restoring order on the ground, a chorus of hopefuls claimed Iraq's still undrilled oil. The three-way tug-of-war between Royal Shell Oil, Anglo-Persian, and a small but feisty spoiler company named Turkish Petroleum was itself subject to pushes and pulls by the two European Allied victors: Great Britain and France. In fact, the future oil industry of the future Iraq became the pivot between the victors competing for territorial control of the ancient Mesopotamian provinces. Once the shooting stopped, the commercial contenders and their governmental sponsors generated yet another long cascade of overlapping and contradictory agreements, assertions, and revocations, completely consistent with the standard of confusion that characterized everything about the promise of Mesopotamia's oil.

Within a week of the war's end on November 11, 1918, French petroleum plenipotentiary Senator Henri Bérenger arrived in London to meet with his counterpart, Walter Long, Britain's Secretary of State for the Colonies and the newly appointed head of the evolving committee that became known as the

"Petroleum Executive." France wanted Mosul and its oil. Britain also wanted Mosul and its oil. On December 1, the British and French heads of state, Prime Minister David Lloyd George and President Georges Clemenceau, met in London to discuss a broad range of issues, including petroleum. In a secret exchange that even their senior ministers did not fully understand, the two leaders adopted a hazy *quid pro quo*. France would relinquish its claim on the Mosul territory on condition it retained all of Syria as promised in the Sykes-Picot Agreement—and so long as France received what it wanted all along, a significant share in Mosul's oil regardless of the territorial control issues. Britain agreed.[34]

Quickly, French and British negotiators began making progress on yet another deal. The men turned their attention to Turkish Petroleum which was 25 percent owned by Deutsche Bank, based on an oil concession granted to the Berlin-to-Baghdad Railway in 1898. Tiny Turkish Petroleum, based on its clever legal manipulation of assigned oil rights from Germany, the Deutsche Bank and the Baghdad Railway, was the only oil company with actual paperwork proving it owned an oil concession. Anyone drilling on Turkish Petroleum controlled fields without its consent would have to turn over the profits to Turkish Petroleum. The company had already retained enough expensive British lawyers to prove they meant business about retaining the company's rights.[35] All eyes riveted on the juridical key to Iraq's oil prize—Turkish Petroleum.

Capturing Deutsche Bank's stock seemed the soundest legal tactic to securing Mesopotamian oil rights in a way that would withstand legal scrutiny. But who really owned the Deutsche Bank's concession? A nervous Anglo-Persian, worried it would be cut out of any deal, claimed in a far-fetched rationale that Anglo-Persian did. On November 12, 1918, just one day after the war officially ended, Anglo-Persian delivered a four-page brief arguing that it had never finalized its intent to acquire half of Turkish Petroleum solely because of the war and due to explicit restraining instructions from the Foreign Office. The Foreign Office saw no reason to pay for a company it could simply take as enemy property. Underlining words for emphasis in the company's memo, Anglo-Persian executives pleaded for a *status quo ante* wherein their 50 percent intended ownership of Turkish Petroleum would be finally consummated or, in the alternative, a full, internationally binding cancellation of any Baghdad Railway rights by a formal Allied decision at the coming Paris Peace Conference.[36]

Possession is nine-tenths of the law. British government petroleum officials, aware of the coming clash over Deutsche Bank's minority ownership of Turkish Petroleum, based on its railway rights, decided to preempt. In early December 1918, they began seizing Deutsche Bank's shares wholesale as enemy property, "before the Peace Conference, not only on account of the French claims ... but in order to obviate any possibility, however remote, of the share reverting to Germany." Moreover, a Treasury official wrote on December 13, by seizing the ownership for itself, the British government ensured the shares would not "be sold to either of the rival oil groups, since this would ... complicate the [upcoming] delicate negotiations."[37]

Treasury convinced a trusted personality, Sir Lancelot Smith, to function as what officials termed "a neutral purchaser." Smith would be asked to expend only £21,000 of his own money to acquire the liquidated Deutsche Bank holdings in Turkish Petroleum—and even that expenditure might be backed by a parliamentary appropriation. Officials were at first hesitant about using public money for what was ostensibly a private sell-off, but they were convinced that "the rights to oil mining in Mesopotamia remains, and will undoubtedly be, a very burning one in our negotiations with the French."[38]

Indeed, the British wanted to seize control of German ownership in Turkish Petroleum before the French did so at the Paris Peace Conference. "The existence of shares in the Turkish Petroleum Company," explained the late December, 1918 Treasury memo, "which belong to an enemy, will give the French an opportunity of putting in a claim to such a share, and we shall be in a far stronger position to resist it if in fact these enemy-owned shares have [already] been disposed of." The strategy was to dispose of the shares through the contrived sale to "neutral purchaser" Sir Lancelot Smith. But he was hardly neutral. Sir Lancelot Smith was in fact a Board of Trade representative at that very time, sitting on one of the interministerial oil committees. Under the ruse, Smith would own the shares in his own name as a private individual, but would in fact function as a government nominee under government control.[39] It was all a façade of self-dealing to mask the British government's outright takeover of oil rights.

By mid-December, while Treasury officials were making arrangements to sell off Deutsche Bank's 25 percent of Turkish Petroleum to their straw man, other British and French petroleum negotiators acted at cross-purposes by agreeing to sell Deutsche Bank's ownership to a Shell subsidiary which would then discreetly transfer the stock to the French. Indeed, shortly thereafter, a rival Anglo-French agreement to sell Deutsche Bank's ownership to Shell was confirmed in a letter by the French *chargé d'affaires* in London to the British foreign secretary.[40] As 1919 opened for business, the jockeying only intensified.

Paris, in January 1919, became a monumental turning point in the modern history of the world. The Paris Peace Conference brought together President Woodrow Wilson, Prime Minister David Lloyd George, and President Georges Clemenceau, each with their great delegations in tow and their lofty agendas preceding them. As the top-hatted peacemakers bickered, postured, and rewrote maps and ethnic destinies, righted historical wrongs and created new ones, some empires were dismantled and some bolstered, new nations were created and old ones reincarnated. Millions was the *de facto* official unit of measure: millions dead, millions wounded, millions demobilized, millions massacred, millions in war cost, millions in reparations. But just behind the proprietors of peace were the captains of commerce who spoke of their own millions—and these millions were attached to francs, pounds, dollars and not infrequently barrels of oil.

By the end of January, 1919, Clemenceau remarked, "The petroleum question seems to be one of the most important economic questions at the Peace Conference." He added, "It crucially affects the future of our national defense as well as her general prosperity."[41]

Ironically, even at the Paris Peace Conference, as the world was being reshaped with pens, the legal gateway to Iraqi oil remained the Turkish Petroleum Company and Deutsche Bank's 25 percent ownership in it. The two mutually exclusive international efforts to acquire that ownership raced ahead. While one Anglo-French team of negotiators, led by Lord Long for England and Senator Bérenger of France, planned to transfer the shares to France, either directly or through Shell, the British Treasury was creating a fait accompli by preemptively seizing the company through a "sale" to its "neutral purchaser."[42]

Numerous plans and permutations unfolded between Long and Bérenger at Paris. For example, on February 3, 1919, British delegates proffered the notion of a 20 percent interest in Turkish Petroleum in exchange for a recip-rocal share in French Algerian oil resources, as well as transit guarantees for the planned British pipeline across Syria. That was not enough. On February 12, President Clemenceau interceded, writing Prime Minister Lloyd George to insist on "strict equality in the exploitation of petroleum in Mesopotamia," adding that London and Paris must not only enjoy parity as military victors, but also as commercial victors. "An agreement must be clearly manifested," wrote Clemenceau, "in the industrial as well as in other spheres."[43]

But so many legal vagaries attached to every aspect of the Sultan's origi-nal concessions to various competing oil suitors and indeed Turkish Petroleum Company itself. Negotiators decided that they would submit any final deal to Britain's attorney general for review. They suggested that any legally doubt-ful clauses could be "righted" by a subsequent friendly treaty with whatever national or administrative national entity arose in Iraq. Moreover, an idea was floated to grant the new national governmental authority in Iraq an unspeci-fied interest in the oil company, perhaps as much as 20 percent. This would certainly be an incentive for any Iraqi national authority. Even still, there was no assertion whether this minority holding would be a mere token voting presence or whether it would include any genuine beneficial rights or decision-making power. Moreover, it was assumed that Britain would control any such local government. Upping the ante, negotiators tacked on promises for France to approve not one but two British oil pipelines to the Mediterranean, one through Syria and a second via Haifa in Palestine, which Britain also hoped to administer.[44] Now Iraq would be linked to Palestine not only by history, culture, religious continuity and a legacy of strife, but now an oil pipeline as well.

Even as Long and Bérenger pondered the geographic and economic variables, the Foreign Office wondered just how real these far-reaching discussions about giving France a share of Turkish Petroleum actually were. In mid-March, 1919, the Foreign Office cautioned that talks could continue as wholly preliminary, as long as British representatives "made it clear to M. Bérenger that we were ready to admit French participation in the Turkish Petroleum Company." But the office added that in any event, nothing could be decided "until the ultimate nature of the territorial settlement is more clearly indicated."[45]

The more detailed and advanced the conversations between Long and Bérenger became, the more they seemed to rile the Foreign Office, which had to deal with all the Allies about all the territorial issues. In doing so, the Foreign Office would have to embrace Woodrow Wilson's insistence on self-determined rights. This would include the local population's right to control its own national economic resources. At one point, Foreign Secretary George Curzon dismissively remarked that Turkish Petroleum was being traded for "a promise of facilities for two pipelines which we may never be in a position to construct through a district in which the French may never be in a position to afford us the facilities promised."[46]

But the French were tenacious. What's more, they seemed to have a complete understanding of the ins and outs of Turkish Petroleum and the value of Mesopotamian oil fields. Senator Bérenger, the minister of industrial production, key personalities in the Ministry of Finance, and the leading magnates of French oil companies all maintained a close friendship with the key Istanbul-based personalities behind Turkish Petroleum.[47] The French were serious about retaining control—at least some control—of Mesopotamian oil.

Regardless, while the French edged forward on the control of Turkish Petroleum, the British were pulling back on those confiscated Deutsche Bank shares. On February 12, 1919, the custodian of enemy property petitioned the Chancery Division of the High Court to approve selling the precious enemy property to Sir Lancelot Smith—thus the shares would no longer exist as unclaimed enemy property. The court action set off a furious barrage of motions, arguments, and hearings from all parties, central and peripheral—including affidavits by Henri Deterding, the founding father of Royal Dutch Shell, who had engineered a merger with the British namesake company. Deterding was as worried as any of his competitors that his company would lose primacy over Mesopotamia's oil. All this juridical wrangling occurred concomitantly to the delicate negotiations in Paris on the subject of geo-political peace.[48]

Deterding and Royal Dutch Shell saw their own fortunes threatened by a British government takeover of Turkish Petroleum and from continued pressure plays by their quasi-governmental rival, Anglo-Persian. Royal Dutch Shell finally decided it was time to become a "British company" that would enjoy the benefits of official governmental favor and patronage—just like their rival. This corporate metamorphosis would not produce a company controlled by the British government, which was impossible due to its Dutch majority, but one "controlled" by British personalities and nominees who, in turn, could be controlled by British policies and preferences.[49] In other words, the Dutch firm would be re-invented as "British" while appearing to the world to be "Dutch."

How could this happen? Creative paperwork.

On March 6 and 7, 1919, Shell and British executives laboriously hammered out a complex eight-point protocol referred to as "Heads of Agreement of the Royal Dutch Shell and British Government." The document focused on Royal Dutch Shell's main British subsidiary, a company known as Anglo-Saxon Petroleum. For years, Anglo-Saxon Petroleum had operated profitably within the Ottoman Empire and was Royal Dutch Shell's official arm in its involvement with Turkish Petroleum Company. Under the agreement, "His Majesty's Government will be advised to use their best endeavors to secure, either by rearrangement of the capital in the Turkish Petroleum Company, or otherwise, that the Royal Dutch Shell by the medium of the Anglo-Saxon Persian Company...shall be admitted to equal participation [with Anglo-Persian Oil Company] in the exploitation of all oilfields in Asia Minor, including what is usually called Mesopotamia."[50]

Anglo-Saxon's operation would be completely reorganized and placed under British oversight. "Certain shares," the protocol stated, "with a special majority voting power in the company operating in Mesopotamia, shall be controlled by His Majesty's Government and the management shall be permanently British." The British government would receive 2 percent of Anglo-Saxon's shares. More importantly, the Turkish Petroleum voting percentages controlled by Royal Dutch's Anglo-Saxon, plus those of its rival Anglo-Persian, as well as the government, would all be replicated and twined into a special "Voting Trust," which controlled 70 percent of the voting rights of the new Mesopotamian subsidiary.[51]

Since both Royal Dutch Shell and the British government planned to lay pipelines across the Middle East to the Mediterranean, Shell also agreed not to "oppose or obstruct directly or indirectly the laying ... of a similar [pipe] line connecting the Anglo-Persian fields with that shore."[52]

Royal Dutch Shell's corporate parents were Royal Dutch in the Netherlands, controlling 60 percent, and Shell Transport in the United Kingdom, controlling 40 percent. As a further protection, the board of directors of Shell Transport was now mandated to be 75 percent "British born British subjects ... precluded from selling or disposing of their capital assets ... outside British control." Moreover, the current board of directors, all British, could not change "without the consent and approval of the Governor of the Bank of England, and/or some person of similar standing nominated by His Majesty's Government."[53]

As for Henri Deterding, the Dutchman whose nationality stood at the heart of Royal Dutch's "foreign" character, he changed as well. During the war, at the very beginning of the negotiations, he had become a naturalized British citizen. Shortly, he would become a knight of the British Empire, completing the transformation of his citizenship.[54]

By initialing the "Heads of Agreement" on March 7, 1919, a fiercely independent, highly competitive, unabashedly capitalist international oil combine carved out a major portion of its commercial empire only to become a government-controlled enterprise—not in name but in fact—not in dollar, but in deed. It was done not for love of country, but for the romance of Mesopotamia's oil fortunes.

The British now enjoyed overlapping and interlocking ownership, control, and competitive leverage in the oil of Mesopotamia, the oil that had been the subject of dreams and disputes since the previous century. Whitehall could empower or stall Shell, bury or resurrect Turkish Petroleum, favor or marginalize Anglo-Persian, govern all the oil, parcel a fraction to the French, or share a token with the local government. As the Paris peace negotiations proceeded, London could exercise some of those options, all of them, or none of them—as need or desire dictated. Oil became the lubricant of peace.

However, regardless of what contracts or court papers were being filed in London, Anglo-Persian Oil Company was actually functioning on the ground in Mesopotamia. With or without a concession, with or without further preferences from London, Anglo-Persian was cementing a real-world monopoly, partnering with both the invasion forces and the civil administration. Since 1918, the company had been actively drilling in the northwestern "transferred territories," that is, the oil-rich Naft Khana region—previously Persian but moved into Turkish Mesopotamia through a frontier treaty adjustment. Hence Persian oil lands became Turkish oil lands and those were now becoming

British oil lands—all engineered by a small cast of characters and one corporation. Most of the new Mosul-area drilling, under the original 1901 Persian
oil concession that transferred with the land, was proceeding under military
auspices with the full endorsement of Civil Commissioner Wilson. Enthusiastically, Wilson reported, "The Company takes so confident a view of the
potentialities of that field, that they have dismantled a refinery in New Zealand and have had the plant shipped to Basra for the purpose of dealing with
the Naft Khana output."[55]

What's more, Anglo-Persian managed and delivered all army needs
through the military's Inland Water Transport, a system of pump houses and
storage tank installations located in Amarah, Baghdad, Diwaniyah, Fallujah,
Kut, Ur Junction, and numerous other villages, as well as "advanced bases"
used by the troops. This network allowed Anglo-Persian to plan for future
retail distribution of both kerosene and petrol after military needs were satisfied. With this in mind, Anglo-Persian's chairman Greenway and Wilson
worked together to change the company's standing from a mere military vendor reporting to the army to a commercial distributor authorized by the civil
administration. Wilson liked the idea as long as the existing commercial mid-
dlemen were subtracted, thus moderating prices. Anglo-Persian approved, as
it was now ready to deal directly with consumers, and in a survey submitted
to the authorities, even calculated exactly how many gallons of kerosene it
could store at each of 14 locations. The total was 50,401 gallons. Naturally,
this would require a fleet of oil barges plying the Tigris and Euphrates. Both
Wilson and Anglo-Persian lobbied for these to be built and acquired.[56] The
future oil monopoly was taking shape.

Seeing Anglo-Persian's rapid entrenchment in Mesopotamia, Shell's
Deterding advised his associates to enter Mesopotamia at once and get a foothold somehow. Recalling one frank exchange, Deterding stated, "I told [him]
… go and get all the rights he could; as there is no government in Mesopotamia, [and] the only rights anybody can secure at present would be those of
possession."[57] Possession is nine-tenths of the law.

Back in Paris, on April 8, 1919, Anglo-French negotiators finally signed
an oil agreement, called simply the Long-Bérenger Agreement, which in some
parts read very much like the agreement signed just a month earlier with Shell.
As such, the new agreement could either contradict or comply with the earlier
agreement, as desired. This latest accord created yet another iteration of Turkish Petroleum, cutting the French in for 20 percent, but cognizant that everyone was indeed carving up a nation not yet acquired under the rules of victory,
and certainly not yet relinquished by the native population under the precepts
of self-determination.[58]

The Long-Bérenger Agreement declared: "In the event of His Majesty's

Government receiving the mandate in Mesopotamia, they undertake to make it their duty to secure from the Mesopotamian Government for the Turkish Petroleum Company, or the Company to be formed to acquire the interests of that Company, the rights acquired by the Turkish Petroleum Company in Mesopotamia, under arrangements made with the Turkish Government. The French Government [is] to have a share in the capital in the Company ... The Company shall be under permanent British control."[59]

France's payment for the shares, under Long-Bérenger, would be a mere token: "that paid by the British government to the public trustee for the shares belonging to the Deutsche Bank, plus 5 percent interest." It was now clear to the French that Whitehall was outright seizing those shares in court for a pittance or less. Ironically, France was agreeing to buy those shares before the court had even ruled they would available. Such a ruling was months away. Once the transaction was complete, however, the agreement stipulated, "The capital of the company shall be divided as follows: British interest 70 percent, French interest 20 percent, native [Mesopotamian] interest 10 percent," which would be divided between the two powers if the "native interest" declined. This last feature addressed the notion of "economic self-determination," albeit the terms of inclusion for any native interest were not set forth. For its part, the French agreed to facilitate two British pipelines plus storage depots and wharves on Syrian territory, once again emphasizing that the parties were not "implying that any territorial rights are in existence."[60]

Ten days later, the form and shape of the future Iraq and other liberated or occupied territories were becoming more apparent. In place of colonialism emerged a new concept, the mandate. Those populations identified for self-determination but not yet deemed capable of forming their own governments or national expression were to be mandated by the international community to "advanced nations" for "tutelage."

On April 28, 1919, the newly formed League of Nations finalized its noble covenant. Article 22 proclaimed: "To those colonies and territories which as a consequence of the late war have ceased to be under the sovereignty of the States which formerly governed them, and which are inhabited by peoples not yet able to stand by themselves under the strenuous conditions of the modern world, there should be applied the principle that the well-being and development of such peoples form a sacred trust of civilization and that securities for the performance of this trust should be embodied in this Covenant."[61]

The covenant continued, "The tutelage of such peoples should be entrusted to advanced nations who by reason of their resources, their experience or their geographical position can best undertake this responsibility ... as Mandatories on behalf of the League." Article 22 specifically referenced "certain communities formerly belonging to the Turkish Empire [which] have reached a stage of development where their existence as independent nations can be provisionally recognized subject to the rendering of administrative advice and assistance by a Mandatory until such time as they are able to stand alone."[62]

Hence, more than 7,000 years after Mesopotamia gave the world the gift of civilization, a concept of commercial fair play embodied in the Code of Hammurabi, and the written word itself, the great powers were convinced the battered, exploited region could not yet stand with the civilized nations and peoples of the world.

*    *    *    *

It was becoming crystal clear in Paris that Britain would receive the mandate for the new Iraq, including oil-rich Mosul, which Britain and Wilson occupied. France began to fear that perhaps it had conceded the greatest known oil field in the world too easily, for a mere percentage of a British-controlled commercial company. The Long-Bérenger Agreement was signed by the two men April 8, 1919, and sent on to Paris and London for formal adoption by their governments. The British, seeing the accord as the final and much-desired demise of Sykes-Picot, notified the French ambassador in London on May 16 that it had accepted. The French, however, refused to reciprocate. After continued delays, diplomatic nerves became frayed. In the midst of a fractious dispute regarding Syria, Prime Minister Lloyd George angrily denounced the entire arrangement.[63]

On June 17, 1919, the French government introduced a bill to establish a state oil monopoly to import refined oil. About a month later, with no progress on its reinstatement, Foreign Secretary Curzon of Britain formally annulled the Long-Bérenger Agreement. In the wake of this recession, both the French and the British exchanged notes that acknowledged the protracted and bitter end of Sykes-Picot.[64]

By the end of July 1919, the High Court ruled in favor of the British government's petition to liquidate Deutsche Bank's one-quarter holding in Turkish Petroleum, thereby enabling its sale to Sir Lancelot Smith.[65] The British government now controlled Turkish Petroleum directly through its acquisition of Deutsche Bank's 1898 oil concession and, even more substantially, albeit indirectly, through its March 1919 Heads of Agreement accord with Shell, which was an original 25 percent owner of Turkish Petroleum.

However, while the High Court did confirm the government's right to liquidate the enemy property, the judge also ruled that approving the government's right to liquidate was not the same as ruling on who actually owned Turkish Petroleum. That was anyone's guess.[66]

Efforts to revive the Anglo-French oil negotiations continued until the end of 1919. Long-Bérenger was reformulated and revised.[67] Other ideas were floated. But all discussions about just who owned the land and the oil of the still undeclared country of Iraq would soon be subordinated to events.

The jihad against Britain and its oil lust was coming.

CHAPTER 9

# JIHAD

In Paris, the Peace Conference began dismantling the Ottoman Empire in the Middle East. Nothing would be easier than to brand it all as a grand ploy for oil. But what empowered their avarice? What made it palatable and more than justifiable for the distinguished peace conferees to deprive Turkey of her provinces? It was the West's ingrained hatred of the Ottoman Empire, and despotic Turkish rule played a major role.

For centuries, despite its value as the commercial nexus between East and West, the Ottoman Empire had earned a dark place in the hearts of Europeans and Americans. The Ottomans were known to many Western minds as the "Terrible Turk" and the "Lustful Turk," caricatured as sexually perverted and bloodthirsty. Images of mass fratricides, palace murders, punishment by impalement, and severed heads presented to the Sultan on silver platters all created a whirlwind of disgust within polite modern society. Turkish royalty was commonly depicted in over-the-top Western illustrations as dripping in blood, consorting with skulls, or otherwise engaged in ghastly acts.[1]

Abdulhamid II, the sultan who reigned just before the Young Turks' revolution, became synonymous with the mass murder of Christians. That legacy persisted a generation later. For example, in the spring of 1876, a series of massacres collectively termed the "Bulgarian Horrors" or "Bulgarian Atrocities" was graphically reported by numerous eyewitnesses in the newspapers of the world, from New York and Washington to London, Paris, and St. Petersburg. In an attempt to suppress a Christian rebellion in the Balkans, Turkish troops and their militias raped the women and young girls in some 65

Bulgarian villages. In Kalifer, the women were herded into barns that were then set ablaze. In Karlovo, most of the homes were pillaged then burned, and many of the women ravished. In many cases, young girls were sold to other Moslems as sex slaves for five francs.[2]

In the wake of the Bulgarian outrages, former British liberal prime minister William Gladstone published his caustic pamphlet, "Bulgarian Horrors and the Question of the East," stigmatizing the Ottomans as bloodthirsty murderers. His tract became an immediate bestseller in London, selling 40,000 copies in a single week. A Russian-language version set a record, selling 10,000 copies in a month. In fact, it was Gladstone who coined the derogatory moniker "Abdul the Damned" that quickly gained worldwide acceptance.[3]

Turkey's brutal, systematic and highly individualized genocide of some 1.5 million Armenians, replete with mass torture and rape of helpless civilians during the war, was an enduring source of revulsion worldwide even after the shooting stopped. In the United States, the Armenian extermination became a *cause célèbre*. Families were jingoistically exhorted to "remember the starving Armenian children" dying in camps and on death marches. One day at the height of the killing, Talaat Pasha, one of the architects of the extermination, was so sure that all Armenians would perish that he summoned Ambassador Morgenthau to discuss their insurance policies. New York Life Insurance and Equitable Life of New York were both leading life insurers of the Armenian middle class. Talaat bragged that 75 percent of the million or more Armenians were already dead and the Turkish government would leave none living to take revenge. "I wish," Talaat then asked Morgenthau, "that you would get the American life insurance companies to send us a complete list of their Armenian policy holders. They are practically all dead now and have left no heirs to collect the money. It, of course, all escheats [legally defaults] to the State. The Government is the beneficiary now. Will you do so?" Morgenthau angrily refused in what became a public row.[4]

Talaat had previously challenged Morgenthau's protests over the Armenian extermination. "You are a Jew, these people are Christians ... Why can't you let us do with these Christians as we please?" Morgenthau replied that he was speaking as an American, not a Jew, and that made his protests "97 percent Christian." Adamant, Morgenthau assured Talaat that Americans "will always resent the wholesale destruction of Christians in Turkey." He also warned, "After this war is over you shall face a new situation ... You will have to meet public opinion everywhere, especially in the United States. Our people will never forget."[5]

In the Paris of 1919, all memories on all topics were still fresh. In fact, Armenia was one of the national groups identified for self-determination and nationhood, to be administered in mandate by the United States. The Armenian mandate was not pursued because the U.S. Congress never ratified America's entry into the League of Nations.[6]

Certainly, as the political vivisection of the Sick Man proceeded, the commercial captains circled, rubbed their hands and shifted into better positions buoyed by universal anti-Turkish animosity. But the Allied leaders, who tore the Ottoman Empire limb from limb, including Mesopotamia, thought of far more than oil and commercial primacy. Allied leaders also thought of 8 million soldiers dead, 21 million wounded, 2 million missing in action, whole populations uprooted, millions of civilians east and west massacred, and $180 billion spent. They also demanded war reparations of Germany, and an equivalent levy against Turkey in the form of oil resources. That's why Allied leaders felt completely justified in all they did in Mesopotamia. They even held the written consent of Hussein of Mecca—even if they never asked the Arabs who actually lived there.

*     *     *     *

Conflicting Allied declarations in the Middle East parted the sea for some fleeing persecution and drowned the hopes and aspirations of others chasing independence.

On November 2, 1917, the British foreign secretary issued a declaration to Zionist organizations worldwide that Britain had identified the displaced and long-persecuted Jews as one of the many groups qualified for self-determination. Specifically, it committed Britain to facilitate "the establishment in Palestine of a national home for the Jewish people ... it being clearly understood that nothing shall be done which may prejudice the civil and religious rights of existing non-Jewish communities in Palestine, or the rights and political status enjoyed by Jews in any other country."[7]

The intention of the Balfour Declaration, and its French equivalent, was to create two homelands, Arab and Jewish, living harmoniously side by side in the same fashion as other national groups.[8] The Jews would receive a homeland carved out of the larger territory of Palestine. But the Arabs despised the very idea of Zionism. Of course, Jews and many other religions groups had dwelled among the Arabs for centuries. But these Zionist Jews were seeking autonomy and self-determination. The Christians and Jews could live under Moslem authority as *dhimmis*, that is, "protected" second-class sub-citizens who acknowledged the sovereignty of Islam, paid special taxes, and observed special restrictive laws. But the idea of Jews establishing their own autonomous communities with international recognition was anathema.

Certainly, any number of other citizens of the Ottoman Empire, and indeed from elsewhere in the Eurasian region, had migrated into barren and sparsely settled Palestine during the preceding decades. Local Arabs, who constituted the majority in overall Palestine, especially outside Jerusalem, welcomed Moslem newcomers—but not the Jews. The Islamic tenet of honoring a guest was negated when the guest or newcomer was a Jew. Official protests and demands by Arab committees that the Sultan expel Jews date back to the earliest Russian pre-Zionist Jewish immigrants in the late 1880s. Long before Herzl's 1896 promulgation of Zionism, Turkish laws were enacted against Jews settling in or purchasing property in Palestine.[9]

When news of the Balfour Declaration reached the Arab masses, along with the explosive details of the Sykes-Picot Agreement, the Allies sought to reassure the restive and resentful Arabs that their national aspirations would not be supplanted. On November 7, 1918, just as the war was rapidly coming to a close, Paris and London issued the Anglo-French Declaration to the Arabs. The promulgation stressed one goal: "the complete and definite emancipation of the peoples so long oppressed by the Turks and the establishment of national governments and administrations deriving their authority from the initiative and free choice of the indigenous populations."[10]

The joint November 7 declaration guaranteed, "France and Great Britain are at one in encouraging and assisting the establishment of indigenous governments and administrations in Syria and Mesopotamia ... and recognizing these as soon as they are actually established." The declaration vowed that these "Governments and administrations [would be] freely chosen by the populations themselves."[11]

But as the Paris Peace Conference opened in January 1919, the Arabs, represented by Sharif Faisal, were snubbed by the French. Regardless of prior representations by the British, the French were completely uninterested in relinquishing their designs on greater Syria, especially since the Lebanon region was overwhelmingly Maronite Christian. Many French officials simply considered the Arabs a threat. Typical was a memo from the Quai D'Orsay that stated, "Damascus is a Moslem center which is very hostile to France, to tell the truth, the most hostile in all Islam. It is there that the fanatical Arabs of North Africa go who want to elude our control. It is there where all the plots against our authority in the Moslem countries are hatched, and it is there where the agitators come and preach rebellion ... Damascus [must] be placed under our control."[12]

Faisal, who now became the face of Arab nationalism to the Peace Conference, busily engaged in his own declaring and maneuvering. On January 1, 1919, he submitted a formal memorandum to the Supreme Council of the Peace Conference outlining his vision for Arab nationalism throughout the Mideast. It was not monolithic or pan-Arab. The Arab national movement was headquartered in Damascus and, plainly put, they wanted Syria, along with the region of the holy cities of Medina and Mecca.[13]

"The various provinces of Arab Asia—Syria, Iraq, Jezireh, Hejaz, Nejd, Yemen—are very different economically and socially," asserted Faisal's petition, "and it is impossible to constrain them into one frame of government." But, Faisal's petition was unyielding on Syria and the Hejaz, that is, the Arabian Peninsula encompassing Mecca. "Syria … thickly peopled with sedentary [settled] classes, is sufficiently advanced politically to manage her own internal affairs." He added proudly that while Syria would accept foreign advisors, it would do so only without paternalism. "We are willing to pay for this help in cash; [but] we cannot sacrifice for it any part of the freedom we have just won for ourselves."[14]

It was totally different for Mesopotamia. In keeping with his earlier promises in the McMahon-Hussein correspondence, Faisal reiterated that he was willing to relinquish Iraq to the British. Faisal readily acknowledged: "Jezireh [encompassing northeastern Syria and the Mosul provincial region] and Iraq are … made up of three civilized towns, divided by large wastes, thinly peopled by semi-nomadic tribes." He readily acknowledged Western petroleum designs, continuing, "The world wishes to exploit Mesopotamia rapidly, and we therefore believe that the system of government there will have to be buttressed by the men and material resources of a great foreign Power."[15]

Rather than seeking elections in Iraq, Faisal suggested a custodial government handpicked by London and patient British tutelage to bring the population into modern times. "We ask, however, that [while] the Government be Arab, in principle and spirit, the selective rather than the elective principle being necessarily followed in the neglected districts, until time makes the broader basis possible. The main duty of the Arab Government there would be to oversee the educational processes, which are to advance the tribes to the moral level of the towns."[16]

An Arab national state in Syria was of such major importance that Faisal was even willing to endorse both an Arab and a Zionist state in Palestine, existing side by side, under a British mandate, if that would smooth the way. Therefore, while Faisal's petition stipulated that "In Palestine, the enormous majority of the people are Arabs," he added in the next sentence, "The Jews are very close to the Arabs in blood, and there is no conflict of character between the races. In principles, we are absolutely at one." That said, he acknowledged that Palestine was important to many faiths and, therefore, the Arab national movement "would wish for the effective super-position of a great trustee, so long as a representative local administration commended itself by actively promoting the material prosperity of the country." That expression welcomed a British mandate over the envisioned two-canton Palestinian entity.[17]

Continuing his own political zigs and zags, Faisal then met in Paris with Zionist Organization president Chaim Weizmann. Following up on meetings the two leaders had held the previous year in Aqaba, Faisal signed an enlightened and tolerant nine-point agreement, endorsing the Balfour Declaration and inviting the Zionists to coexist in Palestine. "Article II: Immediately following the completion of the deliberations of the Peace Conference, the definite boundaries between the Arab State and Palestine shall be determined by a Commission to be agreed upon by the parties hereto. Article III: In the establishment of the Constitution and Administration of Palestine, all such measures shall be adopted as will afford the fullest guarantes for carrying into effect the British Government's [Balfour] Declaration of the 2nd of November 1917... Article IV: All necessary measures shall be taken to encourage and stimulate immigration of Jews into Palestine on a large scale, and as quickly as possible to settle Jewish immigrants upon the land through closer settlement and intensive cultivation of the soil. In taking such measures the Arab peasant and tenant farmers shall be protected in their rights and shall be assisted in forwarding their economic development."[18]

The entire agreement was typed in English in January 1919. But at the bottom, Faisal hand-penned in Arabic this stern warning: "Provided the Arabs obtain their independence as demanded in my [forthcoming] Memorandum dated the 4th of January, 1919, to the Foreign Office of the Government of Great Britain, I shall concur in the above articles. But if the slightest modification or departure were to be made [regarding our demands], I shall not be then bound by a single word of the present Agreement which shall be deemed void and of no account or validity, and I shall not be answerable in any way whatsoever." Directly beneath that inscription were the signatures of Weizmann and Faisal duly affixed.[19]

The Allies could have Palestine and Iraq, but Faisal and the Arab national movement demanded Syria.

In mid-April 1919, Faisal met with President Georges Clemenceau and was promised total Arab independence for Syria. A declaration was typed up on April 17. But the French offer of independence was a mere repackaging of European colonialism. As part of that "independence," the French army would occupy Damascus, and the new Arab nation would actually be a mere federation of local autonomous states in which all the government advisors, including the governors and heads of major government bureaus, as well as the judiciary, would be French and under Paris's control as they currently were in Lebanon, plus Faisal would be compelled to publicly declare the importance of France's historic relationship with the Maronite Christians.[20] Other than that, Syria would be completely independent.

Faisal quickly refused, encouraged by Lawrence of Arabia, who advised him to demand total independence "without conditions or reservations." Clemenceau, however, would not tolerate what he considered Arab impudence. Faisal summarily left Paris for Syria to claim his nation with or without French permission.[21]

Throughout later 1919, the multilateral negotiations dragged on with the usual permutations, frustrations, reversals, and "by the ways." Eventually, a disenchanted Faisal admitted he preferred that the mandate be given to any nation other than France. In July 1919, a joint promulgation by the General Syrian Congress, a representative assembly of Arab nationalists from many countries, formally rescinded any thought of any co-existence with Zionism, ruled out political sponsorship by France, and requested either the United States or Britain for a twenty-year government tutelage.[22] But France would not yield.

From the French point of view, it could not retreat from dominating Greater Syria, especially considering its extensive cultural roots in Lebanon. French troops, French religious groups, and French civilian organizations had undertaken an impressive economic and administrative reconstruction of the neglected Turkish Lebanese provinces. Courts were overhauled, new banks were installed with generous loans extended, emergency food was distributed, sewers laid, streets paved, and dozens of schools opened—all by the French. One leading French columnist and government advisor warned that if forced out of Syria and Lebanon, "World opinion would consider France 'a finished people.'" Using blunt language, an adamant Clemenceau made it clear if Faisal and the Arab nationalists did not have "absolute respect... [and] satisfy me," the entire region would be taken "through force."[23]

Finally, on January 6, 1920, Faisal and Clemenceau reached a provisional, if contentious agreement. Syria, under a Faisal regime, would include Lebanon and would be permitted a parliament that could enact laws and taxes; the national language would be Arabic, not French or Turkish; and the French army would not massively occupy the country. To help ensure that Faisal adhered to the January 6, 1920 accord, Clemenceau had already installed in Beirut a new high commissioner for Lebanon, General Henri Gouraud. Fiercely chauvinistic, pro-Christian and anti-Arab, Gouraud had been the commander at the Second Battle of the Marne and was still prepared to fight any enemy of France. Soon, Faisal found himself teetering atop a tightrope above two constituencies. Some virulently branded him a traitor to the infidel; others praised Faisal as the national hero who had negotiated Syria's independence.[24]

Moslem rejectionists had already been attacking the existing French troops in the region. Arab soldiers from the defeated Turkish army were now repatriated to Syria and ready to again take up arms. Rapidly, the situation deteriorated. Faisal now had to choose between the French and the possibility that their disingenuous promises might be kept, and the fervid and distrusting Arab nationalists who everywhere demanded instant independence. By late February 1920, Faisal had transformed himself again, this time insisting not only total on independence for Syria, but now demanding the British do the same for Palestine and Iraq.[25]

Nobody was keeping any promises. Pacts and promulgations were solemnly propounded, only to be breached, padded, and then reconstituted by all sides. Like the Great War that had just finished, political preemption led to political provocation, which led to further preemption. The vicious downward spiral was gaining velocity.

On March 7 and 8, 1920, the broadly representative Second General Syrian Congress raced ahead of any League of Nations decision. The Congress vehemently declared independence for a Greater Syria, to extend both into Lebanon and south into Palestine. The Congress elected Faisal king of Syria. Iraq was likewise declared independent and Faisal's brother, Abdullah, elected its king.[26] The Allies were outraged.

On March 11, the French premier insisted to Prime Minister Lloyd George that the Second General Syrian Congress was an illegitimate enterprise and its decisions of no value or import. The French were supporting the United Kingdom territorial desiderata on Iraq and Palestine; now Paris demanded Britain support French claims to Syria. Otherwise, the hard-fought rights gained in the Middle East would be lost to all the Allies. Lord Curzon, the British foreign secretary, angrily scolded the French ambassador in London, "The future of France and Great Britain in [the seized Turkish Mideast] was imperiled because of the way in which the French Government, in pursuance of traditional or historical aspirations, had insisted on forcing themselves into areas where the French were not welcomed by the inhabitants."[27]

The British, now also defensive, demanded that Faisal engineer the nullification of the Second General Syrian Congress's declaration of Iraqi independence. "The right of anybody at Damascus to decide the future of Mesopotamia or Mosul," insisted Lord Curzon in a letter to Faisal "is one that cannot be admitted in any circumstances."[28]

At stake was more than geography, more than prestige. There was oil in Iraq, and it had to be transported across Syria and Palestine, as well as south through Basra. The Allies needed the Mideast.

As the mapmaking denouement approached, the oil lust of the politicians was only buttressed by the political and moral animus still roiling against Turkey. The Ottoman Empire was deeply reviled by many twentieth-century Western leaders for creating the Eastern Question in the first place.

Typical was the combined opinion of three distinguished American envoys to the Sublime Porte, Ambassadors Henry Morgenthau, Oscar Straus, and Abram Elkis. In a major *Washington Post* essay, published March 21, 1920, and headlined "Former Envoys' Remedies for Evil of Turkish Rule," the three raised the question: "What is to become of those countries which constitute the Near East is a problem, which has always been of great interest to the whole world, and now of great and immediate interest to the American people. Today the great European powers are discussing what is to become of one of the great prizes of the war—the dominion of the Ottoman Empire... During the last two centuries ... every European war has had its origin or its cause in the Ottoman Empire."[29]

Beyond blame for the wars that were endured by nations, the Turk was particularly accursed for the wholesale slaughter of innocent civilians. "They had held in bondage many races, some of them Christian," exclaimed one April 1920 *Washington Post* editorial, "and had abominably mistreated them, so atrociously, in fact, that the very word 'Turk' conjured up in the minds of scores of millions the personification of all that was evil."[30] Indeed, decades before the word *genocide* was invented, the Turks systematically murdered whole populations, not once, not twice, but repeatedly. Frequently, these onslaughts were perpetrated against defenseless Christians, further inflaming Westerners.

On April 19, 1920, the Allies, working through their League of Nations, gathered at San Remo, Italy for a several-day conference to finally carve up Turkey. *Carving* was the word of the hour. The night before the conference, the *Washington Post* article about the conference was headlined "The Carving of Turkey." The *Post* presaged the conference's "far reaching importance" as "the allies try to arrange for satisfactory government of many races, some of them warlike and all of them backward" who had emerged from centuries of Turkish neglect. These included national groups in the Balkans, Azerbaijan, Greece, Hungary, Georgia, and across the many provinces of the Mideast. The delegates convened against the background of numerous bloody European conflicts still flaring. The Bolshevik revolution and its consequences were burning throughout Eastern Europe and Eurasia, including such countries as Latvia, Poland, and Bessarabia. Postwar Germany was in civil upheaval. Innocent civilians were being massacred regularly, as national groups contended for primacy.[31]

With the last dusk, political creation went forth from San Remo. The conferees granted France the mandate for both Syria and Lebanon—two new nations-in-waiting were created. The British received the mandate for Iraq—one new nation-in-waiting was created. Britain also received the mandate for Palestine, under a provision to create a Jewish homeland, therefore writing the Jewish nation's establishment into international law—one nation-in-waiting was recreated.[32]

The Zionists had cooperated with the British during the negotiations. The Jewish nation's major incubating governmental institutions were almost all British corporations based in London. Zionists understood that only desperate and persecuted Jews would relocate to Palestine's inhospitable terrain and, in so doing, bring it to life for later generations of middle-class Jews. Palestine would become a commercial engine in the region. Moreover, once established, a Jewish state in Palestine was sure to be a reliable Western ally and British foothold in the heart of the Middle East. All land gained was to be legally purchased under international law. The Jews were among several peoples selected for transfer. A million Greek Muslims were slated for transfer into Turkey, and a half million Turkish Christians were to migrate into Greece. All Jews going to Palestine were to transfer in under international auspices, just as decided for other national groups.[33]

True, many establishment Jews in the major cities of Europe and America, especially Jews of German origin, such as those associated with American Jewish Committee, still denounced the Zionist ethic as a threat to their precarious assimilated existence. But even as San Remo delegates met, helpless Jewish villagers were being murdered by the thousands in Poland as a mere sidelight to the latest Polish-Russian conflict. Masses of impoverished Jews, persecuted by European regimes, as well as Jews already dwelling throughout the Ottoman Empire, now waited to enter Palestine and escape persecution into a national homeland of their own.[34]

At San Remo, America did not receive the much-vaunted mandate for Armenia because Congress blocked U.S. admission into the League of Nations. America was not even a participant in the discussions. Consequently, France and Britain were both the grantors and the grantees of the mandates and the oil wealth that attached.[35]

On April 24, away from the main diplomacy of the San Remo Conference, Anglo-French petroleum negotiators concluded their own agreement. It was initialed by Frenchman M. Philippe Berthelot, director general of the commercial affairs section of the Foreign Ministry, and by John Cadman, Britain's latest oil czar. In many ways, the so-called Berthelot-Cadman Agreement resembled many of the previous accords negotiated and renegotiated by Anglo-French interlocutors. But Berthelot-Cadman was hardly an international treaty sanctioned by the League of Nations and subject to the elaborate peace process. This was a secret deal between France and Great Britain to divide up the oil of Europe, Asia Minor, North Africa, and Mesopotamia. The language made clear that this latest and seemingly final agreement was essentially a resurrection of previous oil contracts going back to prewar times.[36]

"By order of the two Governments of France and Great Britain," the document began, "the undersigned representatives have resumed, by mutual consent, the consideration of an agreement regarding petroleum. This agreement is based on the principles of cordial co-operation and reciprocity in those countries where the oil interest of the two nations can be usefully united." The memorandum listed Romania, Asia Minor, the former Czarist territories and Galicia, as well as the French and British colonies.

Clause 7 specified the previously acceptable language about the Turkish Petroleum Company: "Mesopotamia—The British Government undertake to grant to the French Government, or its nominee, 25 percent of the net output of crude oil at current market rates which His Majesty's Government may secure from the Mesopotamian oilfields, in the event of their being developed by Government action; or in the event of a private petroleum company being used to develop the Mesopotamian oilfields, the British Government will place at the disposal of the French Government a share of 25 percent in such company ... It is also understood that the said petroleum company shall be under permanent British control."[37]

Clause 8 committed both France and England to each offer a 10 percent participation of the private company to a Mesopotamian government if such a government emerged—this as a token to American concepts of self-determination. Nothing more about local participation was specified. Clause 9 assured that "the British Government agree to support arrangements by which the French Government may procure from the Anglo-Persian Company supplies of oil, which may be piped from Persia to the Mediterranean through any pipeline which may have been constructed within the French mandated territory and in regard to which France has given special facilities, up to the extent of 25 percent of the oil so piped, on such terms and conditions as may be mutually agreed between the French Government and the Anglo-Persian Company."[38]

The next day, April 25, 1920, the initialed Berthelot-Cadman agreement was confirmed and signed by the two heads of state, British Prime Minister David Lloyd George and newly elected French president Alexandre Millerand. The oil covenant remained secret, but the League of Nations mandates soon became public.[39] News of the mandates, denying Arab sovereignty in Syria while establishing a Jewish national home, quickly burned throughout the Arab world.

On May 8, an irked Faisal sent a formal protest to the Supreme Council of the Peace Conference that he "was much surprised to learn, through public channels, the decision taken at the Conference of San Remo on the Arab countries detached from Turkey ... The wishes of the inhabitants have not been taken into account in the assignment of these mandates." He cautioned grimly, "The Arabs, fully conscious of their rights and their duties, did not hesitate to take up arms against their coreligionists, and to sacrifice their noblest blood in defense of the Right, thereby rendering abortive the threatened Holy War [declared by the Ottoman Empire], which the Turks and Germans wished to exploit in their struggle with the Entente [the Allies]."[40]

Faisal reminded the League of Nations that the stated intent during the Arab uprisings against Turkey was "nothing less than their complete deliverance from a foreign yoke, and the establishment of a free and independent government, which would allow them [the Arabs] to resume their place in the concert of civilized nations." Ominously, Faisal added, "The decision of San Remo puts an end to this hope. The moderate elements in the young nation, who have endeavored, and are still endeavoring, to guide it towards a policy of sincere collaboration with the Allies, are now discouraged and rendered powerless by this decision."[41]

For more than a year, Arab and Kurdish resentment of the occupation, inflamed by Bolshevik agitation in the region and resurgent postwar Turkish nationalism everywhere, had yielded Christian massacres, assassinations of political officers, ambushes of British and Indian officers, and attacks on convoys throughout the three Iraqi provinces. As the fuse of San Remo burned, Arab militancy and violence across the occupied Mideast—in Palestine, Mesopotamia, and Syria—already a problem, now ratcheted up.[42]

On May 18, 1920, Britain's foreign secretary, fed up with the violence, washed his hands of Syrian Arabs, cabling Paris, "The French authorities must be the best judges of the military measures necessary to control the local situation, and … they have complete authority in taking such measures." Quickly, French president Millerand confirmed to General Gourand, "Action against Faisal is indispensable and urgent." General Gourand immediately prepared to invade Syria with several divisions backed by tanks, airplanes, and heavy artillery.[43]

General Gourand issued a 48-hour ultimatum to Faisal to desist and facilitate French efforts to restore order—or else. This ultimatum was calculated to be unanswerable because of the sheer difficulties of rapid communication across the region. Nonetheless, Faisal instantly agreed to General Gourand's demands, but his reply came one day late. Therefore, General Gourand's march on Damascus began in full force. Nonetheless, British and French diplomatic sources debated whether they could move against Syrian Arabs in view of Faisal's actual acceptance of the ultimatum—even though his reply had been one day late. An irate French president Millerand saw Faisal's promises as empty, a mere ploy for time. "So as not to fall back into the previous situation," demanded Millerand, "it is now necessary to continue to take—without lending yourself to the Sherifian's [Faisal's] game to gain time—all steps necessary for your safety and for the total execution of the mandate."[44]

On July 24, 1920, French forces continued their invasion toward

Damascus. The Arabs rallied to meet them at Maysalun, just west of the city. Charging with swords and bolt-action rifles, they were said to have displayed "strong resistance." But they were no match for the machines of modern warfare that had emerged over the recent years. French tanks, airplanes, machine guns, and overwhelming infantry force slaughtered the Arabs within eight hours. The French now occupied Damascus and successfully established their mandate.[45]

That same day, July 24, 1920, after persistent fragmentary leaks, the secret San Remo oil agreement became public after being submitted to the House of Commons.[46] Clearly, the French and British had divided up the Middle East for its oil.

That same day, July 24, 1920, the Zionist Conference concluded in London with a flourish for the future. Gathering in a large hall, bedecked with Jewish-star-emblazoned flags hanging vertically from the balconies and across the stained glass windows at the front, inspired before a great Union Jack with a Jewish star inset with a portrait of Herzl, the Jewish delegates were determined to end the tragic wandering, persecution, and decimation of their people. Their solution: a legal, internationally sanctioned return to the homeland from whence they had been exiled a millennium earlier. In many ways, the Zionist Conference functioned as a counterpart to the international Arab conclave at the Second General Syrian Congress in Damascus that voted to establish an Arab nation. The Zionist Conference did the same for Jewish Palestine. Its crowning resolution created the Keren Hayesod organization, £25 million to start, to support the Jewish National Fund with cash donations from Jews worldwide, to legally purchase lands for kibbutzim and finance the formation of new Jewish villages in Palestine. Just days earlier, Whitehall had appointed pivotal Zionist activist Sir Herbert Samuel as High Commissioner of Palestine, empowered to oversee the orderly immigration of Jews into Palestine. The Jewish homeland was being sanctioned, being purchased, being peopled, being slowly brought to life.[47]

On that same day, July 24, 1920, for the Arabs, it was over. The Jews had gained Palestine. The West had gained oil. The Arabs had lost Syria. This was to be *Am al-Nakba*—In Arabic, *Year of the Catastrophe.*

To the Arabs, it did not matter that during the war, Britain had deployed some 900,000 men against Turkey while only token platoons of Arabs had fought behind the lines; from the Arab perspective, Arabs did in fact fight and fight valiantly, upholding their end of the bargain. It did not matter that the Arabs had cruelly battled against the British in Mesopotamia alongside the Turks at Kut, at Baghdad, and elsewhere; from the Arab perspective, Mesopotamia was not part of the bargain anyway. It did not matter that within the pages of the serpentine McMahon-Hussein correspondence, nothing was firmly promised; from the Arab perspective, they sanctified the sentences most precious to them. What mattered most was that the West and the Jews had triumphed, and the domination of the Arabs would continue, but this time under a Christian mandate and now with autonomous Jews in their midst.

Three intertwined evils—the infidel European Allies, the infidel Zionists, and the black substance the West craved—became conflated in the Arab mind to create one Great Satan. Indeed, these three evils would galvanize the Arab consciousness for virtually the next century. For the first time in centuries, the Arabs stopped fighting each other. Sunni and Shi'a, tribal enemies, those of the desert and those of the city, the intellectual and the peasant could all unite under one Islamic banner, because this was *Am al-Nakba*. Forevermore, 1920 would be a black year in the collective Arabic consciousness.[48]

In Arabic, *Am al-Nakba* means "The Year of the Catastrophe."

Now, across the off-kilter Arab rectangle, a great jihad would be unleashed. Faisal had earlier warned the peace conference: "The unity of the Arabs in Asia has been made more easy of late years, since the development of railways, telegraphs, and air-roads. In old days the area was too huge, and in parts necessarily too thinly peopled, to communicate common ideas readily." Arab anger could now move quickly and with coordination. The Arabs would strike most fiercely where it would hurt most. They would strike in Mesopotamia, where Britain and France dreamed of the oil that had not yet been drilled and that had not yet flowed, but that the Allies could already taste. The Arabs wanted that taste to be bitter and bloody.

*    *    *    *

Ten perfect circles were drawn vertically on the paper along with the notations: "Speed = 75 MPH. Interval of Release = 2 Secs. Area: 2,000 feet long, half-mile wide, varying with wind."[49] The British had been preparing for more than a year.

War-weary and undermanned in Mesopotamia, poorly supplied and thinly deployed across the three provinces, Britain had concluded by early April 1919 that it could not police and control the Iraqi insurgency with ground troops. Air bombardment was the only answer. An Air Ministry survey of air squadrons in the Middle East and India revealed that less than two squadrons were available to bomb positions or provide reconnaissance in Iraq.[50]

But the insurgents in Iraq were too dispersed for concentrated bombardment, air service officers believed. Moreover, in the mountainous Mosul region, Kurdish rebels often hid in caves and hard-to-identify passes. A different weapon would be needed. Gas bombs were selected.

On April 29, 1919, the Royal Air Force in Cairo advised the Air Ministry in London, "Gas bombs are required by 31st Wing for use against recalcitrant Arabs as experiment, the suggestion being concurred in by the General Staff, Baghdad."[51]

Poison gas had been a staple of the Great War. The French were the first to use non-deadly irritant gas projectiles in August 1914, the first month of the war. The Germans responded with lethal gas. Although the German use of toxic gases was roundly condemned, eventually all the Allies joined in. In the last months of the War, President Woodrow Wilson also adopted the principle of poison gas warfare. On July 18, 1918, Wilson signed General Order #62, establishing the Chemical Warfare Service. The combatants deployed chlorine, phosgene, and mustard gases, generally in artillery shells, as the preferred killing agents. When the air had cleared after WWI, more than a million casualties had fallen, some 86,000 fatally. Russia sustained the most killed, some 56,000.[52]

But gas bombs had never been successfully deployed from the air. On May 2, a handwritten note was sent to the Flying Operations Directorate at the Air Board Office in London wondering about innocent casualties and the dangers posed to the troops: "1. Could you please give the War Office view concerning the employment of gas in any form against uncivilized tribes? 2. It should be pointed out that gas is dangerous both to those who employ it and, naturally, to those against whom it may be quite unwittingly used. The great difficulty of differentiation between innocent and guilty once more presents itself and is merely accentuated by this form of warfare. 3. Gas bombs are not available at present. The question of them being produced subsequently is under discussion. 4. [Air Vice Marshal] General [Geoffrey] Salmond is against the employment of gas in any form, is of the opinion that the necessary effect is quite satisfactorily obtained with bombs of the ordinary nature."[53]

A debate ensued about the morality of gas bombs. The matter was decided several days later on May 12, when Winston Churchill, then Secretary of State for War and Air, ruled in favor of tear gas and perhaps more. "I do not understand this squeamishness about the use of gas," he wrote. "We have definitely adopted the position at the Peace Conference of arguing in favor of the retention of gas as a permanent method of warfare. It is sheer affectation to lacerate a man with the poisonous fragment of a bursting shell and to boggle at making his eyes water by means of lachrymatory [tear] gas."[54]

He added with reservation, "I am strongly in favor of using poisoned gas against uncivilized tribes. The moral effect should be so good that the loss of life should be reduced to a minimum. It is not necessary to use only the most deadly gasses: gasses can be used which cause great inconvenience and would spread a lively terror and yet would leave no serious permanent effects on most of those affected."[55]

On May 19, 1919, the Deputy Chief of the Air Staff, R. M. Groves, confirmed in a note, "S of S [Secretary of State for War and Air Churchill] approves the policy of utilizing gas bombs—please see enclosure 5A. Will you therefore please take the necessary steps with DGSR [Director General of Science and Research] to obtain supplies?" Several days later, he also advised the Flying Operations Directorate, "I understand that the S of S ... has approved the general policy of using poisonous gas against uncivilized tribes. So far, although considerable time and trouble was expended on research during the war, we have not yet evolved suitable and practicable gas bombs for use from aircraft."[56]

Shortly thereafter, the Air Ministry's director of research Brigadier General Henry Robert Brooke-Popham dashed off a handwritten note. "I think," Brooke-Popham wrote, "the first thing is to obtain from the gas experts of the late trench warfare department an opinion of the best gas to use. A: For incapacitating the enemy without permanently injuring him. B: For killing or permanently incapacitating him. Also an opinion on the weight of gas or gas-producing material necessary to produce an effective concentration in a given area in average atmospheric conditions."[57]

On June 16, 1919, Brooke-Popham circulated a memo. "I sent Col. Ranken over to see the Chemical Warfare Department at the War Office to get accurate information regarding the position of gas bombs. The position is as follows – (a) the 9.45" Trench Mortar Shell has been converted into an aerial bomb. The design of this is completed and the shell has actually been tried in the air and found satisfactory. There are shells converted for use as aerial bombs available now and only require filling and exploders provided for them. I do not know the number. They could be filled with any of the following types of gas: (1) Lachrymatory; (2) Mustard Gas; (3) Chlorine; (4) Phosgene. It is estimated that it would take at least six weeks before any filled shells complete with all their exploders would be provided ... The Chemical Warfare Department have made up two sample 520 lb. Bombs with a modified case but these have never been tried or put up for approval. These cannot be considered a practical proposition at the present time and it would probably be months before this type could be issued as suitable."[58]

By the end of June, Brooke-Popham concluded, "The best gas to use appears to be as follows: A) Lachrymatory; B) Phosgene." He explained, "Mustard gas is likely to make a casualty of an affected person for some six months and will foul the ground for a long period so that people stepping on rocks or stone on which the bomb has burst will become casualties. I also understand that natives of India or Africa would be liable to be killed off by Mustard gas more than Europeans would be. I attach a chart showing the approximate area affected by ten 9.45 gas bombs dropped at 2 seconds intervals ... The chart assumes that the first bomb is dropped in approximately the correct position with reference to the objective and that the machine keeps on a straight course for 20 seconds during which the bombs are dropped in succession. I am having a calculation made ... The accuracy of bombing varies so enormously with the conditions on the ground and in the air."[59]

Attached was a chart. Ten perfect circles were drawn vertically on the paper, along with explanatory notations: "Speed = 75 MPH. Interval of Release = 2 Secs. Area: 2,000 feet long, half-mile wide, varying with wind."[60] Yes, it was possible, they concluded.

*     *     *     *

The jihad against Britain in Iraq did not have a precise starting date because insurgent violence, from simple sniper fire to massacres of Christians, had been ongoing in Mesopotamia since before the end of World War I. But a major precursor to the full-fledged revolt erupted at 3 a.m. on December 11, 1919. Hundreds, perhaps thousands, of tribesmen stormed Dair al-Zur, a town in the no-man's-land between Syria and Mosul. Invaders, joined by local residents, set fire to London's Political Office, forced open the safe and stole the money, then attacked the hospital, a church, and even a mosque. After that rampage, the gang broke into the prison, freeing all prisoners. Two hours later, the marauders raided the fuel depot, setting off explosions in the process which killed some 30 insurgents among them and injured dozens more. At first light, a British armored car sent out for patrol was repulsed by hostile gunfire. British machine guns, mounted on rooftops, took aim, but were also put out of commission by the rebels.[61]

Under fire, British soldiers and police retreated to the barracks on the outskirts of Dair al-Zur. But by mid-morning, the barracks was also under siege. Late in the morning, a momentary truce was declared, allowing the British commander to talk to the frenzied group. Just then, at 11:30 A.M., two airplanes from Mosul came into view. They carried no gas bombs, as such weapons were still months from completion. But the airborne machine guns let loose on the town, throwing the villagers into panic. A frantic second truce was called as the British bargained for the safe return of their hostages and the Arabs demanded a cessation of the air strike.[62]

On December 14, 1919, three days after the assault began, Churchill announced a greatly expanded air force. Since the war, the entire British air fleet worldwide had dwindled from 22,000 aircraft to a mere 200 planes in 28 thin squadrons. Churchill asked for the equivalent of $75 million annually to fund new aircraft. This included three squadrons for Iraq. However, those planes were months away. British forces could not hold Dair al-Zur on the ground. They were forced to withdraw, and the territory was later ceded to Syria.[63] Dair al-Zur, the British thought, would now be France's trouble.

But Dair al-Zur remained a British problem as well. Dair al-Zur was the closest contact point in Iraq to Damascus, and it became a new launch site for continuing insurrection. The revolt soon spread south. On March 31, 1920, some 4,000 tribal warriors met at Kaimakamjazir to plan a general uprising. Its first glimmer occurred within 48 hours, on April 2, as a British convoy was attacked 50 miles northeast of Mosul; 10 Indian soldiers were killed.[64]

On May 1, 1920, acting Commissioner Wilson received official confirmation of the San Remo decision. Several days later, he was instructed to publish news of the mandate over Iraq that was bestowed to England by the League of Nations. The gist of London's proclamation declared, "Iraq has now been rescued from Turkey by military conquests, and armies of the British Empire are in military occupation of the country." Using visionary language and uplifting justifications, Britain promised to establish an interim civilian authority to "prepare the way for the creation of an independent Arab State of Iraq." To that end, London also pledged to form "representative divisional and municipal councils in different parts of the country." Therefore, the British mandate, the announcement declared, was "in fulfillment of promises that have been made to Arab peoples" and to Faisal.[65]

Wilson was both resentful of the "independence" being promised and extremely nervous about the restive Iraqis. He urgently requested permission to announce within the coming days—certainly before the onset of Ramadan—that he planned to immediately implement a constitutional process. "Once this is done," he wrote," we shall be in a position to deal with extremists." In a separate memo, Wilson explained that in his view there were two types of extremists: "1) the sane extremists, who desire Arab independence under British control; and 2) the ultra-extremists, who desire to see the abolition of European control of all sorts throughout the East."[66]

Wilson's notion of Iraqi "independence" was colonial independence, or perhaps self-management. The notion of representative government for Mesopotamia's masses distressed him. The people of Iraq should be told, not asked. "I submit," he protested to London, "that it is for His Majesty's Government as Mandatory Power to prescribe what form of Government shall be set up in the immediate future. To refer the question afresh to divisional councils and to 'local opinion' can have but one result. The extremists who, following the example of their colleagues in Syria, are demanding absolute independence for Iraq—with or without [King] Abdullah [as their monarch]—will by threats and by appeals during the coming month of Ramadan to religious fanaticism win over moderate men who have hitherto looked to the Government for a scheme offering a reasonable chance of success... The moderates cannot afford to oppose extremists unless they know that Government is prepared to give them active support."[67]

On May 19, the Ramadan observances that so worried Wilson began at both Sunni and Shi'a mosques throughout the land. Apprehension became reality. After the religious services, combined audiences from the mutually antagonistic Shi'a and Sunni gathered in unison at the mosques to hear fiery nationalist rhetoric. In Baghdad, highly agitated throngs emerged from the mosques, rolling through the streets, chanting and demanding independence. Moreover, some mosques featured aspects of both Sunni and Shi'a traditions, and by inviting their coreligionists as special guests projected an open show of Islamic unity.[68] Unity worried Wilson.

It was what Wilson feared. He recalled, "The first symptom of a rapprochement had occurred in the summer of 1919, when on two occasions Sunnis attended religious meetings which were held in memory of... [a revered and recently] deceased Shi'a *mujtahid* [revivalist]." Wilson continued that it was not until Ramadan in May of 1920 "that the political significance of the reconciliation became apparent. We were well aware of the danger ... in March and April ... before the great fast began."[69]

Periodically, Arab deputations would try to communicate with Wilson. It was in vain. For example, when 15 delegates of the Baghdad community requested a meeting with Wilson to present their demands, he brusquely rebuffed them and denied they were genuine representatives of anyone. He instead chose to invite his own assembly of 40 handpicked representatives, all of whom he expected to support his agenda. The fact that one of these 40 was a Baghdadi Jew and two were local Christians further inflamed the populace, which only wanted a majority Islamic government.[70]

Secret meetings multiplied among the populace. A surreptitious network blossomed to help coordinate the coming revolt. Quietly, newly stitched national flags were circulated. Leaflets printed in Najaf and Karbala rallied tribe and townsman alike for a concerted uprising. Then Imam Shirazi, a spiritual leader of Najaf, issued a pivotal fatwa that declared, "None but Moslems have any right to rule over Moslems." Day and night, printing presses churned out copies of Shirazi's fatwa as activists disseminated them throughout the cities, villages, and tribal areas.[71]

The situation quickly deteriorated. In the early hours of June 4, 1920 in the village of Tel Afar, near Mosul, the commander of the gendarmes, Captain B. Stuart, was suddenly murdered in the street by his own Arab subordinate. Captain Stuart's two assistants tried to help, but a tossed bomb killed them in their bullet-riddled bunker. Another officer was taken captive; he managed to escape, but was chased down and murdered on the outskirts of town. Convoys on the nearby road were raided. Two armored cars were dispatched, but they were surrounded and overturned; their crews, totaling 14 men, were also killed.[72]

The British retaliated. The next day, June 5, 1920 troops marched out from Mosul to Tel Afar. En route, they burned crops needed to feed the vicinity. Once at the scene of the outrages, Wilson recounts, the troops, "chased the entire population of Tel Afar, innocent and guilty alike, into the desert." They destroyed suspect houses, but did not apprehend the killers.[73]

To reason with the most moderate militants, London tried to employ a more acceptable lexicon, parsing such concepts as *self-rule*, *autonomy*, *emerging democracy*, and other less-than-sovereign conditions—but all of it was nonetheless subject to the British "tutelage" prescribed by Article 22 of the League of Nations Covenant. Words, however, were worthless in this war. One rebellious newspaper from time to time typically verbalized the embittered feeling among the Arabs, belittling the Allied vocabulary: "We do not reject the mandate because of its name but because [of] its very meaning, which is destructive of independence… [Many] words … are used by the colonizers. But they all translate to 'mandate,' and are intended to deceive weak nations. Only the name is changed, just as when they talk of liberating humanity, [and] healing the weak."[74]

On June 6, 1920, nationalist pamphlets bearing the five-pointed emblem of resistance circulated everywhere, demanding the expulsion of the British. Ten days later, the new call to arms rallied defiance against the mandate decision in April at San Remo. Everywhere the movement proclaimed Faisal's brother, Abdullah, to be Iraq's king, as decided at the Second Syrian General Congress at Damascus several months earlier.[75]

On June 30, 1920, the revolt intensified dramatically. In the lower Euphrates river town of Rumaitha, an activist sheikh was gruffly rebuked for not paying his estimated agricultural tax and then arrested by the assistant political officer. Within hours, his followers descended on the local terra-cotta prison, freeing him. Emboldened, the rebels rampaged through the area, burning all the local bridges and cutting the railroad lines. Despite hard fighting and several attempts at reinforcement, the beleaguered garrison at Rumaitha was not relieved until July 20, and only then at a cost of 35 British soldiers killed and 150 wounded. A third of the garrison they came to rescue was dead. Their surviving comrades in hand, the British civil and military authorities promptly evacuated.[76]

Even as Rumaitha was overtaken, insurgents overran the village of Samawa. By mid-July, tribesmen asserted themselves in Abu Sukhair, Kufa was blockaded, and the Bani Hasan tribe rose up defiant. Revolutionary governments were set up in Najaf, Samawa, and in additional village after village as the undermanned British evacuated. Three companies of the Third

Manchesters, plus cavalry, artillery, and Sikh fighters, were deployed from Hilla to restore order, but only half survived the 118-degree heat and the onslaught of some 500 attackers who suddenly appeared on their flank. The British fought at close range with bayonets, but were overwhelmed with heavy losses: 180 killed, 60 wounded, 160 taken captive.[77]

Following the converging international events of July 24, 1920, crowned by the French victory over Damascus, nationalist Arabs concentrated their defiance in Iraq. Insurrection became all-out jihad once formal declarations from religious leaders were promulgated during the first week of August. National zeal escalated into religious fanaticism, as everywhere the Arabs attacked everything Western.[78]

Immediately, the whole country ignited. On August 9, the village of Baquba was ransacked, the rail line cut, and a nearby Armenian refugee camp attacked. On August 10, the British vessel *Greenfly* went aground on the lower Euphrates just outside Khizr; hostile Arabs surrounded the ship, prevented it from being towed, starved the crew into surrender, and then murdered them all. On August 11, extremists tried to assassinate a political officer in the midst of a truce negotiation; the tribesmen suddenly opened fire on his military escort. On August 12, a similar ambush occurred when a political officer tried to meet with an Arab leader at Arbil.[79]

Shortly thereafter, the supply ship "S9" ran aground in the low water of the Euphrates; it was captured, set afire, and the crew massacred. Trains fared little better. It did not matter whether the trains were armored. Once the track was blown, belligerents attacked and killed all the passengers. So much railroad line was blown up that the British were forced to erect a series of protective blockhouses mile by mile along the track, reminiscent of the Boer War. Even constructing these was often a fatal exercise, as work crews were constantly attacked. In the Hilla area alone, six waves of attacks were repulsed, with an estimated 200 dead among the rebels and 40 British casualties.[80]

Nor did it matter whether the victim was a soldier involved in combat or reconstruction. Colonel G. E. Leachman had spent much of his time dispensing liberal subsidies to Iraqis to win their hearts and minds. He spoke fluent Arabic and was popular among local farmers. On August 12, Leachman was summoned to a meeting with Sheikh Dhari at Fallujah to discuss crops and revenue. After arriving with a military escort, Leachman was abruptly informed of a highway robbery outside of town. Intuitively, the colonel dispatched his armed escorts to assist. That left Leachman unprotected. Sheikh Dhari then approached with two followers. Leachman knew Sheikh Dhari well, had assisted him in the past, and welcomed him. That's when Sheikh Dhari's followers shot Leachman at close range. Sheikh Dhari approached the dying man. Leachman looked up and asked why, as he had never offended anyone in Iraq. Without hesitation, Sheikh Dhari drew his sword, and mercilessly finished the job.[81]

Monstrous treatment at the hands of Arab captors was common. On occasion, British prisoners were marched from town to town in the summer heat, barefoot and nearly naked. Two captured pilots were set upon by angry crowds who murdered them, then cut off their ears to deliver them as prizes to the local mullah, knocked out all their teeth and sold these as trophies, and finally further mutilated the bodies for all to see.[82]

Nor it did matter if the British were Moslem Indians or Christian. Some 85 percent of Britain's civilian and military men were Indians—many of them Moslem; yet they were killed with equal fervor. Fallen Moslems were frequently denied an Islamic burial by the embittered religious authorities. Not infrequently, their wives were sought out and violated, and their children viciously beaten in the streets for their kinship with treasonous families.[83]

When jihadists who had been taken prisoner were interrogated, they were sometimes asked why they fought so fiercely. One report from Wilson gave this answer: "they tell me that … life or death is a matter of indifference."[84]

Britain was outnumbered and poorly situated. The new Mesopotamian commander, General Aylmer Haldane, semi-retired and physically unfit, had arrived just a few months earlier with Victorian flourish. Haldane himself recalled that he "disliked the idea of remaining in Baghdad throughout the hot weather" because he could only exercise "an hour or two in the late afternoon." What's more, he freely admitted, "I had no conception of the system on which we governed Mesopotamia, for it had not been possible to obtain much information regarding it."[85]

How many troops could Haldane deploy? Subtracting the sick and heat-stricken, as well as artillerymen, only 29,500 cavalry and infantry, 90 percent Indian, were available to restore civil order, guard 14,000 Turkish prisoners still unrepatriated from the war, and protect the substantial civil administration.[86]

Against Haldane's 29,500 poorly supported British soldiers were multitudes of Arab tribal warriors. From Basra to Baghdad along the Euphrates: 43,000 Muntafik, 11,500 Khazail, and 17,500 from smaller clans; and along the Tigris: 18,500 Bani Malich, 8,000 Albu Muhammad, plus 17,800 from lesser clans. From Fallujah to Ashur, some 27,000 Dulaim fighters were raiding. One military report estimated the total fighting strength in the Baghdad and Basra provinces as 160,000 warriors, plus 481,000 Kurdish fighters.[87] Everywhere and every day, the rebels sniped, murdered, pillaged, burned, kidnapped, robbed, laid siege, sabotaged, and unwove the very fabric of Britain's presence.

Only air power could save the British now, a reality that Churchill had accepted months earlier in late March 1920, when he announced to the House of Commons that the disturbances in Mesopotamia were too costly and challenging to control with ground troops alone. Air power would be used. Gas bombs were being rushed, but not yet ready. Trials and training were still under way.[88]

Throughout August and September of 1920, the Royal Air Force strafed and bombed enemy concentrations and sympathetic towns. August 21 at Baquba, the scene of numerous outrages: "today intense bombing raid carried out on rebel villages in neighborhood." August 23 at Baquba: "bombing raiders inflicted severe casualties on rebels—86 known killed in Baquba and [nearby] Shiftah." Kufa was bombed heavily, especially its mosque, which had become a center for political activities. On one day alone: At Samawa, "air bombing had good effect"; outside Baghdad, "aeroplanes retaliated by bombing"; seven miles northeast of Hilla at the village Munaihillalmarjan, "aeroplane today attacked."[89]

It was never enough. Haldane and Wilson continually asked for more airplanes to subdue the seemingly irrepressible insurrection. Additional planes did not exist. Once more, on September 28, gas was requested. London replied again they were not ready: "We have requested Air Ministry who are now carrying on trials to push on their experiments."[90]

The purpose of the airplanes was not just military, but to "shock and awe" the population, what the Air Ministry called "Morale Bombing." The chief advocate and developer of Morale Bombing was Chief of Staff Hugh Trenchard, who reported directly to Churchill. One Trenchard memo to Wilson, in June 1920, set forth the new philosophy of warfare. "Aircraft depend," the memo explained, "to a great extent on the morale effect that they create; this is at present considerable owing to ignorance in the native mind. If they are constantly used for petty operations which cause no great material damage and cannot, owing to the smallness of the unit, be long sustained, *respect will change to annoyance and contempt*. If this should ever come about, the re-inspiring of the natives with proper respect for the air arm will be a long and expensive task. It follows, therefore, that when air operations are resorted to, they should be carried out in a strength sufficient to inflict severe punishment and in numbers adequate to sustain the attack for as long a period as may be necessary. It will be realized then that aircraft...by their mere presence will often induce the natives to return to peaceful ways."[91]

A keen disciple of Trenchard's philosophy was Squadron Leader Arthur Harris, who relentlessly bombed Iraqi civilian areas. Harris would go on to earn the nickname "Bomber Harris." During the next major war with Germany, it would be Bomber Harris who advocated and oversaw the carpet bombing of the city of Dresden.[92]

What was not achieved in Iraq by bombing from the air was accomplished by torch on the ground as Britain intensified its retaliation. Village after village was set on fire. Gertrude Bell, a staunch Arabist ally of both T. E. Lawrence and Faisal, expressed the agonizing hopelessness of the campaign as the British found themselves in the schizophrenic position of reconstructing and democratizing the country while bombing and burning it into passivity. "We are hampered by the tribal uprising ... I think rightly ... the tribes must be made to submit to force. In no other way was it possible to make them surrender their arms, or teach them that you mustn't engage lightly in revolution, even when your holy men tell you to do so...Nevertheless, it's difficult to be burning villages at one end of the country by means of a British Army, and assuring people at the other end that we really have handed over responsibility to native ministers."[93]

By late October 1920, outside funding for the Iraqi fighters had dwindled to a trickle, their ammunition depleted. Karbala, a spiritual epicenter of the insurrection, was totally blockaded, and the canals cut to shut down the water supply; the village finally surrendered. Najaf notables were instructed to lay down their arms or the city would be bombed. To avoid plague and devastation to thousands of refugees, the elders complied. The submission of Karbala and Najaf was the beginning of the end of the revolution. Most of the fighters elsewhere simply retreated to their homes. Most—but not all—of the cities became quiet.[94] They were simply bombed and battered into submission.

Wilson was removed as acting civil commissioner. His replacement, Percy Cox, was brought in from Persia to oversee an immediate transition to a provisional government, which would include a general elective assembly and a constitutional process. Cox announced the provisional government on November 11, 1920. With that, two years after the Great War ended, the lingering conflict in Mesopotamia finally began to wind down. By spring 1921, the country was calm enough to bring in its new leader. It was not Abdullah, but Faisal. The British felt they could do business with him. The sharif of Mecca, who fought alongside Lawrence of Arabia, who became the elected leader of Damascus for just a few months, was now finally anointed by the British as the "King of Iraq." Faisal officially arrived in Iraq June 23, 1921, with all pomp and circumstance, and acceded to the throne August 23.[95] The nation of Iraq was finally born, kicking and screaming defiantly throughout the delivery.

The Iraq revolt of 1920 was costly: 426 British killed, 1,228 wounded, 615 missing or captured. Among the Arabs: some 8,450 casualties. British taxpayers spent some £40 million pounds. Iraq in many places was in cinders. The British public became dispirited over its losses in Mesopotamia. London's media regularly excoriated the government. One article in the *Daily Mail*, titled "The War Mongers," railed that "there is nothing in all our history to compare with our folly in Mesopotamia."[96]

Cox's replacement as high commissioner was Sir Henry Dobbs. Looking back, he wrote, "So now to raise up this Iraq we have squandered blood, treasure, and high ability. We have bound debts and taxes on the necks of generations of our descendants ... We have suffered the imputation that on the scene of their agony we living have betrayed the hopes of our dead. You ask: for all this shall we have our reward? I answer that I cannot say."[97]

George Buchanan, who had administered the waterways and dredging of Iraq in the Wilson administration, published his own retrospective years later. "And so the tragedy of Mesopotamia remains," Buchanan wrote, "a tragedy of heroism, suffering, wasted lives, and wasted effort, which began in 1914 when the Indian Expeditionary Force entered the Shatt-el-Arab River and which had not ended when military control ceased in 1921. The soldiers did their work, and by force of arms wrested the country from the Turks. The civilian administrators did their work and established law and order, peace and prosperity, throughout the land. The statesmen did their work and successfully annulled all that had been accomplished by the soldiers and administrators. Mesopotamia has been called the cradle of the human race, and was at one time the granary of the world. Will its former glories ever be revived and the enormous sacrifices made by Great Britain ultimately be justified by the evolution of a happy, prosperous, and free nation?"[98] Buchanan never answered his own question.

As for Wilson, the lifelong bureaucrat left government service for a new career. He went into industry. Wilson was immediately hired by Anglo-Persian Oil Company.[99]

*    *    *    *

Iraq was not quite a nation and Faisal was not quite a king when he and Great Britain signed a formal treaty of alliance on October 10, 1922. Although it was labeled a "treaty" as if between two governments and bore elaborate regal seals on its cover, the treaty was actually not with the nation of Iraq, but with the king as an individual. That is because the new Iraq was nominally an independent kingdom, yet under international law, it was still a mandated territory under the control and tutelage of the British. Moreover, King Faisal, although proclaimed a monarch, was required to take counsel and instructions from Britain's appointed resident, High Commissioner Sir Percy Cox.[100]

The 1922 treaty, in many ways, read like the 1899 protectorate contract with the Sheikh of Kuwait—protection in exchange for compliance. Except in this case, it was not the Iraqi nation being protected. After all, recalcitrant villages were still regularly being bombed by the RAF.[101] The real protectorates were British commercial interests—shipping, railroading, oil exploitation, and pipelines, and they were being protected against Iraq itself.

Article VIII of the 1922 treaty guaranteed that no Iraqi land would be ceded or leased to any power other than Britain. Article IV assured that Faisal "agrees to be guided by the advice of His Britannic Majesty tendered through the High Commissioner on all important matters affecting the international and financial obligations of His Britannic Majesty for the whole period of the treaty." Article XI included an all-important non-discrimination clause with a vital parenthetical: "There shall be no discrimination in Iraq against the nationals of any State" with whom England maintained diplomatic relations. The parenthetical added: "(including companies incorporated under the law of such State.)"[102] This last was in effect the key to the "Open Door."

What was the Open Door? This concept had manifested some three years earlier when Iraq's oil was handily split between England and France. The San Remo petroleum agreement granted Paris the 25 percent of the Turkish Petroleum Company once owned by Deutsche Bank. The French government then transferred that 25 percent to what later evolved into the Compagnie Française des Petroles, a combine of some scores of smaller oil concerns that created a new government-controlled oil monopoly.[103] By the authority invested in San Remo, and subject to a more stabilized Iraq, France and her petroplex now gained a reliable source of crude oil. At the same time, Great Britain would be able to drill deep into Iraq, continue its exploitation of Persian oil, and transport the black treasure across Syria to the Mediterranean. But France and Britain left out one great power, the newest of the great powers: the United States of America. Woodrow Wilson, the State Department, and even more important, Standard Oil of New Jersey demanded what they called "an Open Door Policy" to Iraq's oil.

By way of background, the first years of the twentieth century's oil development were completely different in America than in Europe. Rockefeller's Standard Oil had accrued too much commercial power too quickly and was stopped by the U.S. government with enormous antitrust prosecutions. But in Great Britain and Germany, the oil baronies were tools and extensions of the government itself—to a degree, even owned by the government. By the time the Great War ended in 1918, America's military-industrial self-conception had evolved, and no longer felt the pangs of containment. True, the Senate had refused to ratify Wilson's League of Nations and therefore America was the only victor excluded from the spoils. But who supplied 80 percent of Britain's oil? America. Who fielded great armies on land, sea, and air, shoulder-to-shoulder with the Allies? America. Who was now being left out of the oil riches of Mesopotamia? Once again, it was America.

Peace required equality, the Peace Conference ordained.

President Wilson demanded that equality in the great new world order as sketched by his Fourteen Points, specifically Point III: "The removal, so far as possible, of all economic barriers and the establishment of an equality of trade conditions among all the nations consenting to the peace." This point was buttressed by the league's own principle on mandates that the Mesopotamian territory was to be administered "to assure equal treatment to the commerce and to the citizens of all nations." What's more, Britain had secured international support for its mandate by pledging "that the natural resources of Mesopotamia are to be secured to the people of Mesopotamia and to the future Arab State to be established."[104] In other words, American oil interests were to have equality with those of France and Great Britain.

On March 14, 1925, after an intense back-and-forth, Faisal issued a new 75-year oil concession covering all of Iraq, even the territories such as Mosul which might still be in dispute. Three years later, culminating epic wrangling between European oil barons and the titans of Standard Oil Company representing a coterie of American oilmen, a secret covenant of monopoly was drawn up to rule over and divvy up Mideast oil. This included fabulous oil finds in Iraq that had finally gushered up to prove the precious worth of the property the West has spilled so much blood to siphon. That agreement, so mired in conflicting territorial names and claims, was finally demarcated with a thick, red line around a map of nearly the whole of the extended Middle East from Saudi Arabia to Istanbul. Pipelines from Iraq to Haifa in Palestine would create a new Kingdom, an oil empire. It was done all under diplomatic cover. The pact would remain a mere rumor for decades but such a secret agreement did exist, signed by the oil men and Iraqi authorities. It was called the "Red Line Agreement," named for the thick red line that carefully circumscribed the billions of barrels of oil beneath the map of the Arab World. That red line triggered a massive influx of occupying armies, corporations and commercial culture into Palestine which had no oil but which was destined for a pipeline, and Iraq which had the oil that needed to be piped.[105]

Infidel European Allies, dhimmi Jew Zionists, and the cursed oil that brought the West to their land indeed conflated within the Arab heart and mind to create one towering, inescapable Great Satan. Hate filled the hearts of the occupied. Hate seemed to flow the width and length of the occupied, newly populated Arab realms. Centuries of Arab and Islamic culture had produced a flammable new blend that burned resentment and anger in the average man and woman—from Palestine to Iraq and beyond. Many prayed for the day when they would be set free from the abomination that their world had become, take final vengeance on their enemies and restore the triumph of their earlier centuries. Palestine and Iraq would be free. Palestine and Iraq would be delivered.

Less than five years after the 1928 Red Line Agreement, a deliverer finally arose. He came not from the desert, the hills, the Casbah, nor the mosque, nor was he anyone from within their midst. Nor was this deliverer enrobed in white. Instead, he wore brown and arose in Berlin.

## PART TWO

# THE HITLER ERA

CHAPTER

# 10

# GERMANY AND THE MIDDLE EAST

Immediately after World War I, Germany became a pivotal supporter of the Zionist homeland in Palestine.

At first, the Arabs of mandatory Palestine either did not understand Berlin's relationship with Jewish Palestine or perhaps simply chose to overlook it. Instead, Arab leaders throughout the Mideast, and especially in Palestine, saw Germany as a sort of salvation from the abhorred Balfour Declaration and the prospect of Jewish settlement within their midst. Germany, they reasoned, had been the enemy of Great Britain during the just-ended war, was the traditional ally of the Ottoman Muslims, and was still a stalwart friend to the Arab people everywhere. But, as soon as World War I ended, that special relationship was over.

Nostalgically—perhaps self-deceptively—as the Balfour policy came to their doorstep, Arabs still exalted Germany. Why?

True, for decades, the Germans had been the Muslim world's non-Islamic bulwark against Europe. After the Ottomans were defeated by Russia in 1878, leading to the loss of major portions of European territory, the Sultan negotiated for two years with Berlin and Vienna for massively needed military reform. In the early 1880s, the Kaiser finally sent Germany's first military commission to Istanbul to help rebuild its corrupt, ill-equipped army. German officers, such as Lieutenant Colonel Colmar von der Goltz, revamped the Sultan's forces and were made revered generals in the Turkish army. German arms makers supplied most of the weaponry to re-equip the Turks. Krupp shipped its most advanced cannons. Mauser rifles became standard issue for the Sultan's troops. Eventually, Prussian officers commanded entire Turkish divisions. German armaments and German military men guarded the Turkish straits. For years, graduates of Baghdad's military academy were steeped in German military tactics and mutual friendship.[1]

In the last years of the nineteenth century, great Arab nationalist thinkers, such as Sati al-Husri, studied German and European philosophy to inculcate their own sense of Arab unity and identity. This included the German nationalistic notion of one people bound together by a common language. Hence, even without a territory to call their own, Arabs could become self-defined as a national group based on their common tongue, just as German thinkers advocated. Moreover, the concept of Aryan racial superiority, proclaimed by such European philosophers as Gobineau, percolated throughout Germany and Prussia in the last decades of the nineteenth century, and these supremacist precepts reached Arab intellectuals as well. Just as German national thinkers established the German tongue as a common denominator of a superior race, so too it would be for Arabs. German radicalist Johann Gottlieb Fichte and his concepts of inherent, non-rational, nationalistic rights were also studied. Islamic thinkers who studied these notions became the founders of the Young Turks and the bubbling wellspring of Arab racial superiority as well as the Arab national movement.[2]

The connection was also economic and industrial. The Deutsche Bank became a principal financier in Mesopotamia. The famed Berlin-to-Baghdad railway project, which Deutsche Bank owned largely through subsidiaries, was designed to forever unite the German and Ottoman empires across two continents in a grand alliance of commerce, transportation, and military union. Mesopotamia's first unexploited oil rights were bestowed upon Germany through fabulously valuable ten-mile right-of-ways on either side of the Berlin to Baghdad railway. The very idea of this grandiose project was viewed as enormously strategic by Berlin and enormously threatening by London. In fact, Germany's oil rights in Mesopotamia were a key obstruction to London's designs on Turkish oil and an integral spark for Britain's rush campaign to capture Mesopotamia.[3]

Moreover, German leadership enjoyed a personal bond with the average Arab common man. Arabs everywhere remembered the Kaiser's triumphant visit to Damascus in the fall of 1898. He paid homage at Saladin's tomb and declared his Empire a friend of all Muslims in their struggle against Russia, France, and England. Many considered that momentous speech a turning point in Germany's ascent to pre-eminence in the Islamic world.[4]

Likewise, in Palestine, ordinary Arabs remembered the Kaiser's triumphant visit to Jerusalem that same year. Riding through the Old City on his magnificent white steed through a special massive gate in the wall created for the moment, Kaiser waved to the throngs of Arabs on either side of his procession. Balcony flags fluttered everywhere in the cooler-than-normal October breeze, creating an enduring image. Arab well-wishers had come from across the Holy Land—Bedouins bedecked in checkered keffiyeh from Jordan, elders dressed in purple from Syria, and local shopkeepers enrobed in bleached white dishdashahs—all for a mere glimpse of the Emperor. Many had risen at four in the morning to make the journey that day. "Kaiser of the Germans," they cried ecstatically. The local population marveled at the electrical generator his entourage had brought from Germany, which dazzled onlookers with illumination during the night.[5]

Naturally, Britain followed every vicissitude of German expansion into the Ottoman Empire and the wider Middle East region. London undertook strategic precautions and counterchecks everywhere it could. For example, in late 1898 and early 1899, the Kaiser tried to assist the Sultan in reasserting control over Kuwait, a distant and only nominally Ottoman territory in the Gulf. To thwart that, on January 23, 1899, the British sealed a pact with the Kuwaiti Sheikh. In exchange for a one-time British payment of 15,000 Indian rupees, the Sheikh agreed not to transfer or lease any part of his territory without London's approval. As part of the pact, India would send troops should the Turks attempt to invade. Kuwait became a British protectorate, and remained one for more than 60 years. But Germany was remembered by the common man for its steadfast effort to keep Britain out.[6]

In the twentieth century, the Arabs undoubtedly recalled tough German General Liman von Sanders, the man who ruthlessly defeated the British at Gallipoli, and who valiantly commanded Turkish and allied forces in Palestine. Yes, the British ultimately prevailed in the Mideast. But Germany, under von Sanders, had fought shoulder-to-shoulder in the trenches and across the muddy fields with the Turks and their diverse Islamic troops. True, that entire alliance was with the oppressive Ottomans; but more importantly, it was against the greater enemy of the moment—Great Britain. When Turkey orchestrated the expulsion and extermination of more than a million Armenians, some of it through Mesopotamia, boxcars of the Berlin-to-Baghdad railway were utilized, while its railway tracks and sidings became deportation centers. German Lt. Col Böttrich, head of Railroad Department at the Ottoman General High Command, was widely reputed to have signed the deportation orders—even if reportedly against instructions from the German Foreign Office. When Lawrence of Arabia triumphantly entered Taif, he requested something other than Turkish music. But as the band played on, the only European serenades they knew were German, including "Deutschland Über Alles."[7]

So readily did Arabs admire Germans and Germany that they happily coexisted with a few thousand German Templar settlers who lived in Jerusalem, Haifa, and Tel Aviv. Templars—unrelated to the Crusades-era Knights Templar—were strict religious German Protestants, had successfully coexisted with Arabs for decades, and rarely, if ever, sided with Jews over Muslims.[8]

But the Arab phantasmagoria about Germany's continuing heartfelt friendship was just that—a desert mirage. Any outward signs of German solidarity with the Arab people were always merely strategic, so much *realpolitik* based on a now-finished compact with a now-dismantled Turkish empire. With World War I over, defeated Germany had little reason to embrace the Arabs. Instead, Germany wanted to embrace the Jewish people and the Zionist movement.

German government support for Zionism began in earnest even before the war ended, when Berlin seriously confronted the prospect of defeat. Billions in war reparations loomed, along with the loss of its colonies and the vanquishing of its foreign trade. Berlin decided that part of rejoining the postwar community of nations would include enhancing its relationship with the Jewish world, if for no other reason than to stay on par with London and the Entente Powers. Great Britain had reaped euphoric support from Jews worldwide as a result of the November 1917 Balfour Declaration. Not to be outdone, the Central Powers spurred on by Berlin followed suit.

Within two months of the Balfour Declaration, the German authorities persuaded Ottoman Grand Vizier Talaat Pasha to finally reverse twenty years of pernicious anti-Zionist policy. The Grand Vizier publicly declared on behalf of the Sultan that immigration restrictions in Palestine were being terminated and full Jewish settlement in Palestine was now welcomed. Days later, on January 5, 1918, Berlin ceremoniously issued its own Balfour-style declaration to a group of German Zionist leaders. The German pronouncement read: "With regards to the aspirations of Jewry, especially of the Zionists, towards Palestine, we welcome the recent statement of Talaat Pasha, the Grand Vizier, as well as the intentions of the Ottoman Government, made in accordance with its traditional friendship towards the Jews in general, to promote a flourishing Jewish settlement in Palestine, in particular by means of unrestricted immigration and settlement within the absorptive capacity of the country, local self-government in accordance with the country's laws, and the free development of their civilization."[9]

On November 11, 1918, Germany conceded a humiliating defeat and signed the armistice. The government quickly began reinventing itself. The Imperial German Empire was gone. The democratic Weimar Republic was established, so named for its announcement in the picturesque town of Weimar. Berlin now had every reason to become a supporter of all things arising from the League of Nations, all things British, and all things Zionist. Germany understood that her strategic interests included one that rested squarely in a Jewish national home in Palestine. Indeed, Berlin did all in her power to promote the growth and expansion of the Jewish presence in the Holy Land.

Just days after the November 1918 armistice, the German Foreign Office unveiled a new office, the "Jewish Affairs Department," evolved from a private predecessor organization, the German pro-Zionist "Committee for the East." The Jewish Affairs Department was dedicated to advancing Zionist settlement and expansion in Palestine, working proactively with other German Foreign Office sections and, indeed, with embassies and diplomatic organizations around the world. For example, at one point, the Jewish Affairs Department interceded with the Italian government in Rome and with the Vatican to counteract stiff papal opposition to Jewish Palestine. In a number of capitals, the Department secured visas for German Zionist Federation officials needing to travel across borders or into Palestine itself.[10]

Indeed, as an official section of the German Foreign Office, the Jewish Affairs Department was able to function on a worldwide basis, engaged in diplomatic Zionist advocacy with other governments and international entities everywhere as a sort of Zionist support agency within the Weimar government. It was highly visible. Jewish Affairs Department officials met with Zionist leaders in London. They attended Zionist international conferences, congresses, and exhibitions. It was not uncommon for the bureau to facilitate the travel of Zionist Organization leaders such as Chaim Weizmann and arrange top-level meetings with the highest echelon of government. When Weizmann visited Germany, he was treated as a veritable chief of state decades before any state had been declared.[11]

Conjunction with Great Britain in Jewish Palestine was also a priority for the Foreign Office. Almost all of the 2,000 German citizens, mostly Templars, residing in Palestine had been expelled to internment camps in Egypt as a wartime measure by the occupying British authorities. Their property had been confiscated by the British as enemy assets. London planned to expel some of them directly to Germany. Repatriating them to their homes in Palestine and restoring their assets in the Holy Land was a key goal of the Jewish Affairs Department by virtue of its Palestine portfolio.[12]

More than just the Zionist enterprise in Palestine, the Jewish Affairs Department also focused on the plight of East European Jews flooding out of Poland and Russia at a fantastic rate. This refugee phenomenon, of course, manifested its own Zionist dimension. Just as the dispossessed had poured into London and New York, Eastern European Jews also streamed into German cities, bringing with them their *shtetl* ways, their crime-ridden poverty, and their teeming urban congestion. No one knew the real immigrant numbers.

Some estimated the refugee population had reached as many as 50,000 during the war years and climbed to double that—more than 100,000—during the post-armistice period.[13]

In Germany, they were known as *Ostjuden* or "Eastern Jews." Their thorny place in German society was fraught with antagonism. Domestic strife in Germany over the *Ostjuden* would last for years to come. Their integration and non-integration was a constant irritant—these foreigners would not adapt into German society; these foreigners have now adapted too much into German society. In some regions of Germany, such as Upper Silesia and Bavaria, *Ostjuden* were actually expelled from the country. In 1920 and 1921, some Jews were even interned in what were commonly termed at the time, *Konzentrationslager* or "concentration camps." Such camps were established at Cottbus, Stagard, and several other locales. Pogroms broke out in various German cities, including Berlin. In all these cases, the Jewish Affairs Department, even though part of the Foreign Office, exercised an unusual domestic role. As in the London and New York migrations, the existence of a Jewish Palestine meant the masses of *Ostjuden* could be diverted there. Hence, the immigration issue came directly under the portfolio of the Jewish Affairs Department, as it tried to quell hateful, anti-Semitic domestic reactions to the influx, which earned Germany ill-repute worldwide. Simultaneously, the department tried to manage the diversion of many refugees to Palestine.[14]

In the 1920s, the uproar over the *Ostjuden* was seized upon by right wing, anti-Semitic German nationalists. The main group was the National Socialists—the Nazis—led by a rabid, race-baiting former corporal named Adolf Hitler. The Nazis marched, picketed, protested, and agitated in fractious post-War Germany, blaming Jews for the country's economic and social woes. Henry Ford's publications accused the Jews of using Zionism, capitalism, communism, and every other ism to enslave the world. After Ford mass-distributed copies of *The International Jew* and *The Protocols of the Elders of Zion* in Germany, Hitler's deeply ingrained anti-Jewish philosophy was elevated from simple out-group and religious hatred to an international political cause. *The Protocols of the Elders of Zion*, a forgery authored in part by the same anti-Jewish newspaper editor who played so pivotal a role in the 1903 Kishinev pogrom, was proffered to Ford as the genuine details of an ostensible international conspiracy whose timing matched the founding 1898 Zionist gathering in Basle.[15]

Hitler proclaimed that Ford was "my hero," and *der Führer* reprinted the auto magnate's screeds by the truckload with pictures of both himself and Ford on the covers. In *Mein Kampf*, Hitler wrote, "To what extent the whole existence of this people (Jewry) is based on a continuous lie is shown incomparably by *The Protocols of the Wise Men of Zion*." This was also a time of the dynamic growth of socialism, Russian-style Bolshevism, and anarchism in the United States and Europe, movements that militantly agitated to topple democratic governments in favor of communist rule or even no rule at all. Hence, fears of a communist takeover only magnified Nazi hate-mongering against Russian and Polish Jews in Germany.[16]

*Der Führer* also adopted the official American pseudoscience of eugenics, financed dogmatically by the Rockefeller and Carnegie foundations, which created an imaginary racial hierarchy among all mankind. Eugenics was a fake science based on faked evidence. As American eugenics functioned in Hitler's shattered-glass world view, race was everything and pre-determined all social, intellectual, cultural, and physical human attributes. Race was both history and destiny. More than just the philosophical postulations of Gobineau and Chamberlain, American eugenics seemed to provide the genuine rarefied science. America's quest for a master race of blond, blue-eyed, white Nordics was imported into Hitler's vision. It medicalized his bigotry. Out came the Nazi campaign for a master race, with the term *American Nordic* replaced by the pre-existing Nazi concept of *Aryan*. In this hand-molded, hate-heated, sham reality, Germans ruled as the dominant biological group at the top, and Jews parasitically dwelled at the bottom. Other Semitic groups, including the Arabs, inhabited the same reviled, lumpen racial caste as their cousins, the Jews.[17] Thus, Hitler detested them both—the Jew and the Arab.

Armed with Ford's phony political science and America's phony biological science, *der Führer* shouted from the rooftops and the beer gardens that Jews were of another nationality, not German. Nor could Jews ever be of the German race, regardless of intermarriage or the many generations they had dwelled peaceably in Germany. Jews were the cause of Germany's misfortune in every way and must be expelled, he vituperated. Expel the unassimilated. Expel the assimilated. Expulsion was the battle cry.

Expel them? But to where?

"To their own country, Jewish Palestine," was the reply. Thus, Nazism intersected Zionism in two powerful modalities. First, it leveled the charge that Zionism and Judaism were the binary world centers of all evil. Second, that Jews must be expelled and quarantined to their true nation, Palestine. As in the case of the Czar after Kishinev, the greatest Jew hater of the day—Adolf Hitler—became the greatest advocate for a Zionist state and for all the wrong reasons.[18]

Behold: the Nazis staunchly advocated the Zionist agenda.[19]

German Jews, highly assimilated for generations, now manifested their own anti-Zionist backlash. It was not enough that Russian Jewish coreligionistss were swarming onto German shores, causing ethnic discomfort for even the most assimilated German Jews. Now, Zionism was delegitimizing their very right to claim German nationality and continue living there. Germans considered themselves "German first" and "Jewish second." In fact, of approximately 550,000 Jews in Germany who were emancipated in 1871, by 1930, roughly 60,000 were either apostates, children raised without Jewish identity by a mixed marriage, or Jews who had drifted totally away. Even those consciously remaining within organized Jewish "communities" neglected their remnant Jewish identity. The mainly secularized Jews of twentieth-century Germany, like their Christian neighbors, embraced national identity far more than religious identity. In the minds of German Jewry, they were "101 percent" German, first and foremost. During World War I, about 100,000 Jews fought for Germany, 80,000 in the trenches. Some 12,000 died in service to their Fatherland.[20] Polish Jews spoke Yiddish, a bastardized and often offensive pidgin German. For every reason percolating up from the clash of cultures, economic class, internecine disparity, and national identity, the majority of establishment German Jews, often called *Hofjuden*, or courtly Jews, loudly opposed Zionism. Even the thought of a Jewish national home was anathema, hateful. At one point, the *Centralverein*, the main organization of German Jews, resolved to expel any member who professed Zionist national ideals. The "Jewish home," German Jews believed, was located on the manicured street where they lived in comfort with exquisite Oriental carpets and Tiffany lamps in security, not in the mosquito-infested climes of Palestine amid the dust and the dangers of the Zionist experiment.[21]

The German Foreign Office's Jewish Affairs Department navigated between its domestic upheavals over Zionism. It continued advocating with enlightenment for Jewish Palestine in spite and against the wishes of the majority of its own establishment Jews. In doing so, the Department genuinely, carefully, and publicly rejected the reasoning of both the impatience of ordinary Germans fed up with refugees and the militancy of the anti-Semitic Nazis that Zionism was a convenient channel for anti-Jewish expulsion.

Still, beyond the human tides of contending populations and international politics, an undeniable cultural bond existed between Germany and Zionism. Many Zionist leaders, from the Viennese Herzl onward, were known for their German or Austrian roots. For several years, beginning in 1905, the Zionist Organization itself was headquartered in Cologne, Germany. German or its pidgin variant, Yiddish, were common languages in Jewish Palestine and among Zionists worldwide. The Zionist movement had always been welcomed by the Kaiser in spite of his abortive attempt to enlist the Sultan. So the connection was undeniable in that sense as well. Indeed, three German Jews including the ranking bureaucrat of the Jewish Affairs Department, in his official capacity, sat on the board of trustees of Hebrew University.[22]

Berlin took an active role in the Palestine Mandate. However, Jewish

Palestine was not a colony or an independent nation but a League of Nations mandated territory. Thus, despite its efforts, Germany could not maintain a consulate there in the first Weimar years. The Spanish consulate oversaw its affairs in the Holy Land. However, once Germany was admitted to the League of Nations in 1926, Berlin assumed a seat on the Permanent Mandates Commission. That linked Berlin to Jerusalem in operational questions of governance.[23]

As a major overseer of Jewish Palestine, it was natural that the German Foreign Office encouraged the establishment of the *Pro-Palästina Komitee*, whose illustrious interfaith ranks included world famous physicist Albert Einstein, members of Catholic political organizations, and Count Johann von Bernstorff, then-recent pro-Zionist German ambassador to both the United States and the Ottoman Empire.[24]

Underpinning all the political dynamics, however, was the sheer financial prize of a Jewish Palestine. While as mandatory sponsor of the Jewish homeland Britain enjoyed a commercial windfall from importation of its goods, those goods were mainly consumer items. The more Jews that settled into Palestine, the more this overseas market expanded for Britain. But Germany was more concerned with exporting heavy industry and the infrastructure-related commerce that catered to the actual building blocks of Jewish Palestine. Experts had estimated that £20 million in expenditures would be needed in the near future. Pipes, steel, building materials, trucks, dredgers, excavators, irrigation pumps, and the grinding machinery of modern settlement construction created the sturdy rebar and mortar of the German-Zionist relationship. As Jewish Palestine expanded, so did the lucrative trade between Germany and the Zionist enterprise. The trade was two-way. Germany was increasingly becoming Jewish Palestine's number one market for its all-important orange crop, making the Jewish economy dependent upon export to Germany.[25]

In short, Germany was completely committed to the Jewish national homeland in Palestine. Yet the Arabs saw Germany as an ally and antidote.

The Arab population directed their protests and angers against the British, first and foremost. In March 1921, Winston Churchill, now Colonial Secretary, visited Palestine, motoring the length and breadth of the country, witnessing the transformative Jewish building projects already underway and discussing new ones. After four centuries of Turkish neglect, Jewish Palestine was engaged in rapid nation-building. Housing, cultivation, harbors, forestation, electrification, railways, roads, recovery of swamps, and other building blocks of modern statehood were being carved, squeezed, and planted into the territory. But the Arab residents did not want this modern world filled with alien Jews—hundreds of new ones every week—who spoke a different language, dressed a different way (especially the women), prayed from a different book, and lived in small congested housing. A protest memorandum, more than 30 pages long, was handed to Churchill, describing every conceivable reason to terminate the Jewish dream in Palestine, a dream that was becoming the Arab nightmare. Invoking the principles of Hitler, Ford, and *The Protocols of the Elders of Zion*, the Haifa Congress of Palestinian Arabs complained to Churchill: "The Jew is clannish and unneighborly and cannot mix with those who live about him. He will enjoy the privileges and benefits of a country and then lead its people, whom he has already impoverished, where he chooses. He encourages wars when self-interest dictates and thus uses the armies of the nations to do his bidding."[26]

The Arab protestors openly threatened Britain's entire standing in the Islamic world and suggested Germany could become the Arab ally once more. "Today the Arabs' belief in England is not what it was," the Haifa Arabs warned Churchill. "The Arab is noble and large-hearted; he is also vengeful and never forgets an ill-deed. If England does not take up the cause of the Arabs, other powers will. From India, Mesopotamia, the Hedjaz, and Palestine the cry goes up to England now. If she does not listen, then perhaps Russia will take up their call some day, or perhaps even Germany."[27]

But Arab remonstrations did not work on Churchill. Seeing twentieth-century progress and civilization everywhere he drove in Palestine, Churchill rejected the Arab protests. He firmly believed both peoples could live and prosper in peace as modernity set in. On March 28, 1921, Churchill replied with irritation to their demarches, "Your statements sound as if you overthrew the Turks; this is not so. Glance at the British war cemeteries; many British lives were sacrificed for Palestine." He went on to promise a bright future for both groups. "It is manifestly right," he stated, "that the Jews, who are scattered all over the world, should have a national center and a National Home where some of them may be reunited." Churchill continued, "And where else could that be but in this land of Palestine, with which for more than 3,000 years they have been intimately and profoundly associated? We think it will be good for the world, good for the Jews, and good for the British Empire. But we also think it will be good for the Arabs who dwell in Palestine, and we intend that it shall be good for them and that they shall not be sufferers or supplanted in the country in which they dwell or denied their share in all that makes for its progress and prosperity."[28]

Average Arabs, however, were not willing to tolerate modernity at the hands of the Jews. Everywhere, they attacked the Jewish presence. Armed gangs of Arabs incessantly assaulted Jewish townhouses and settlements throughout the land. Whenever Jews or Arabs gathered or could even be observed, the potential for a confrontation loomed. On March 1, 1920, Arabs attacked an outpost known as Tel Hai. Joseph Trumpeldor, the Russian-born one-armed fighter who had organized the Zion Mule Corps, was killed in the firefight.[29]

A particularly bloody outburst occurred in early April 1920 during the so-called Nabi Musa Festival. Held annually at Jerusalem's shrine to the Prophet Moses, the celebration was originally a religious holiday inaugurated by the Turks. But the Nabi Musa Festival had by now become a zealous outpouring of Arab nationalist fervor. During the 1920 observance, tens of thousands of Palestinian Arabs streamed toward the center of Jerusalem and the Old City. Many carried large posters of Faisal, who days earlier, in spite of the French, had been declared by the Syrian Congress to be King of Syria and, by extension, King of the Arab Nation. A celebrated rabble-rousing Arab editor on a horse, accompanying the procession, began exhorting the crowd with cries of "Independence! Independence!" and "Slaughter the Jews." It escalated. Soon in rhythmic cadence, the throng, in unison, began shouting a favorite refrain:

*Filastin Bladna wa-l-Yahud Klabna*
*Filastin Bladna wa-l-Yahud Klabna*
*Filastin Bladna wa-l-Yahud Klabna.*

The popular rhyme translates to "Palestine is our land, the Jew is our dog! Palestine is our land, the Jew is our dog! Palestine is our land, the Jew is our dog!" Accounts differ on what happened next. Many say a hostile encounter erupted between a single Jew and a Hebron Arab about a protest banner.[30]

Whatever ignited it this time, Arabs in frenzy began streaming through the alleys of the Old City, mercilessly savaging the Jews. Wherever the Jews sought refuge or tried to hide, they were seized and pummeled. The Jewish Quarter of Jerusalem—pillaged. Torah scrolls—vandalized and burned. In scenes reminiscent of the 1903 Kishinev pogrom, pillows were ripped open, wafting clouds of feathers into the air. Indeed, the Nabi Musa riots coincided with Easter, just as the Kishinev riots had. During this latest Old City riot, five Jews—including a young child—were killed, and about 160 Jews were wounded. As the police tried to subdue the violence, four Arabs died as well. Jewish leaders and British authorities called the riot what it was—a pogrom.[31]

The brutal incident at Nabi Musa, coming on the heels of the Tel Hai attack, hastened the advent of the Jewish defense forces known as the *Hagana*.[32] The British were seen as powerless to stop the constant attacks. From now on, the Jews would take charge of their own defense. With the Hagana and other self-defense efforts, there arose a militant, times-toughened Palestinian Jew—armed, politicized, highly nationalistic, and ready to spring into action.

But the Hagana could not be everywhere. Throughout 1921, attacks continued against Jews in many locales. On May 1, 1921, Communist Jews from Russia called for an abolition of British governance and a Jewish state. Boldly, and some said provocatively, the Zionists marched in neighborhoods where the British government conceded "Jews are not tolerated" by the Arabs. An Arab rampage broke out in Jaffa against nearby Jewish homes and their residents. Amid firing pistols, swinging swords, and pounding clubs, dozens of Jews were massacred, after which Arab women invaded to loot the premises. Soon, the violence spread to many other Jewish towns and settlements. The violence burned for days. A government report concluded, "The killing was accompanied and followed by an orgy of pillage, which was a disgrace to a civilized community." Any Jew within reach, including children, was repeatedly stabbed and in many cases, the skull cracked wide open. The chief medical examiner reported, "I was struck most with the number of wounds on each body and the ferocity of the wounds. I am speaking particularly of broken skulls. Some of the victims had dozens of wounds." Martial law was declared, and the British Navy was sent in to restore order. In all, 47 Jews were murdered and 147 wounded by Arab marauders. In every such event, scores of Arabs were also killed by police and military authorities trying to subdue the rioters. In this case, 48 Arabs died, and at least 73 were wounded.[33]

On another typical occasion in 1921, an angry group of Arabs from Hebron encountered Russian émigrés, and that visual encounter alone incited yet another sudden riot against the Jews. This one raged through Jerusalem for three days.[34]

Violence against Jews was the order of the day. Sometimes it was organized, sometimes spontaneous, sometimes it enveloped an entire city or a neighborhood, and sometimes it was a random knifing in a blink of an eye in the doorway of one family's residence. From under the robe, out came the blade, and in it deftly went. Sometimes the Jews fought back as the centrifugal cycle of assault and armed counter-defense took hold of the region. There was no peace in the Holy Land.

More than just violence, the Arabs of Palestine also organized an international political effort to combat what they saw as an international political hegemony against their world. Shortly after receiving Churchill's March 1921 rejection, a delegation of Arab notables visited the Vatican in Rome, this in conjunction with Pope Benedict's loudly stated opposition to Jewish settlement in Palestine. During an hour-long audience, the Pope confirmed to the Arabs that he opposed Jewish increase in Palestine. Going further, Benedict confided to Christian Arab Shibley Jamal, thinking that he was Catholic, the intensity of papal opposition not only to Jews but also to Protestants in the Holy Land. Jamal, however, was actually a Protestant, not a Catholic. Even still, Jamal did not correct the pontiff.[35]

With support from the Vatican in hand, the Palestinian delegation proceeded from Rome to London for another round of protest meetings with

Churchill. In August 1921, during a series of meetings hosted by the Colonial Office, the Arabs asserted they did not object to British control—just the concept of Jewish sovereignty in their midst. Churchill continued to rebuff their rejectionism with optimistic visions of the two peoples living in peace. The Arab delegation rejected any peace with the Jews and asserted that they were willing to remain in London for months to continue protesting. In the process, they rallied support from British opposition parties opposing the idea of a Jewish homeland and Churchill's policies. The Arabs also met with local British anti-Semitic circles to engender their backing. Just as important, British Muslims from London's substantial Indian community staged a massive banquet in honor of the Palestinians, and the evening was punctuated by inflammatory speeches stirring antipathy against Britain's policies toward the Turks, in India as well as Palestine.[36]

The Arabs also visited the German embassy in London to brief Ambassador Friedrich Stahmer and express their solidarity with everything German in Palestine, from its settlers to its exports. They "declared that the Arabs welcomed the return [to Palestine] of the German [Templar] settlers with satisfaction," according to a dispatch by Ambassador Stahmer to the German Foreign Office. Jews were not welcome. But Germans were. Indeed, the Arabs made it clear that "they had previously always gotten along with Germans and were pleased that the path was reopened to commence re-importation of necessary German goods not otherwise capable of being procured," the ambassador's report continued. Stahmer added the Arab delegation's assurance that "they had never expressed feelings of animosity for Germany. Rather, they trusted Germany more than any other world power because while pursuing her goals, Germany had never made the impression of being purely egotistical, instead having always also considered the interests of the indigenous populace." Jamal and his colleagues predicted the ambassador would see also Arab tumult rise up against Britain's rule in Egypt, assuring the British would be booted out within "a few years at most."[37]

While most of the Arab delegation extended their anti-British activities in London, two of their group left for Geneva for meetings at the League of Nations. The remainder stayed to press their demands with Whitehall. Their final message to Churchill: there would never be peace with Jews in Palestine. Never. They warned sternly that if they left London without a change in policy, a much bigger pogrom against the Jews could break out in Palestine.[38]

There were other efforts by Arab contingents to enlist German support. Earlier, in 1921, Syrian Christian Arabs had visited Germany and beseeched the government to become involved against the French in Damascus. Such approaches by Arabs for German intervention in Syria were repeated over the coming years.[39]

In truth, Berlin was a good listener. But Weimar Germany wanted no part of the Arab conflict with either the French or British mandates.

In December 1921, after the first Syrian Arab approach, the German Foreign Office circulated an instruction to its diplomats in Tehran and elsewhere in the Middle East that made clear Berlin's hands-off, no-comment policy. "The political situation in Europe," read the instruction, "obliges us to avoid any statement or action that could bring us into conflict with the western powers. This holds not only for Europe, but also especially for Persia and the lands of the Orient in general, where England, considering the movement and behavior of the Islamic peoples and the meddling of certain other powers, is very watchful, and continues to harbor a mistrust toward us that lingers from the war."[40]

Despite the violence in the Holy Land, with the help of the British, French, and German governments, and fortified by a growing Zionist national character, Jews continued to stream into Palestine. By necessity and by choice, they clustered in their own communities, created their own separate existence supported by a separate Jewish economy, a separate Jewish work force where possible, and a separate approach to modernity. Jews had assimilated in host countries for centuries, but not in their own country, not in Palestine. Now Jews would choose their own identity, modernity, and national destiny. It would not be a dhimmi status as it had been for centuries, not in the twentieth century, when people, including Jews, could chose for themselves.

Arabs in Palestine had seen migrations come and go for centuries. "They had been subjugated, integrated, and manipulated, and at times they had dominated, but for the past thousand years—except during two centuries of despised Crusader rule and some other brief but equally detested European interregnums—always as a cog in an Islamic empire in an Islamic world.

True, under Ottoman control over the prior several centuries, Palestine had been shunted into the backwater of the empire and wedged into the footnotes of history and world events. Palestine's amorphous geopolitical integrity had been diced, relabeled, and glued onto other territories by a cascade of Islamic rulers, recasting the region as a province of Syria, as a district of "Damascus-Syria," or some variation thereof. But now, the Arabs of Palestine would choose their own identity, modernity, and national destiny. It would not be a dhimmi status alongside the dhimmi Jews, not in the twentieth century, when people, including Arabs, could chose for themselves.

Centuries were colliding from every direction, the old creaking ones and the newly born flexing one, struggling against subduction. Tectonic ground zero was the city on the hill, Jerusalem, the fractious convergence of three great religions. Irresistible forces were coming to the immoveable object.

*     *     *     *

Population statistics in Mandate Palestine will forever be disputed by all sides of history. Flawed, politicized, and incomplete, the numbers were always manipulated by all sides, each for its own special reasons. That said, one measure has been the exhaustive, three-volume Survey of Palestine assembled in 1947 for the Anglo-American Commission of Inquiry as it assessed the Mandate in all its dimensions.

During the early mandate year of 1920, Jewish immigration into Palestine proceeded rapidly at the rate of hundreds of people per week. In that year, the total estimated Jewish influx was more than 5,500. In 1921, according to the survey, the estimated number almost doubled to more than 9,300. A slight dip in immigration followed increased violence, but with the advent of Zionist self-defense units such as the Hagana, the estimated flow continued strong, surpassing 7,800 in 1922 and 7,400 in 1923. As the Jewish Palestinian economy expanded, so too did immigration. The estimated Jewish ingathering jumped to more than an estimated 12,800 persons in 1924, about a third coming from Poland. Warsaw recorded that of 48,647 who left the country that year, 5,724 immigrated to Palestine—more than any other destination, including the United States.[41]

Official estimates almost tripled the next year, 1925, when Jewish immigration to Palestine from all sources reached an estimated level of almost 34,000. Some argued that the true numbers were even higher. [42]

Arabs also encouraged immigration into Palestine from other Arab communities across the Middle East to balance out the numbers. However, their totals were measured not in thousands per year, but in hundreds per year. Soon the Jews were exceeding 10 percent of Palestine's overall population.[43]

More important to the true demographic picture was not the Jewish percentage of overall Palestine, but that Jews constituted nearly 100 percent of the Zionist enclaves. Hence, two entrenched and physically separate communities dug in, one completely Jewish and one completely Arab, one old and one mainly new, with few exceptions to the rule.[44]

Concomitant to the immigration was the purchase of vast tracts of land across Palestine, from the desert to north of the Galilee, that made the separation physical not just ethnic. High fees, often enhanced with exorbitant baksheesh, were paid to the Arab or Turkish landowners. During the 1920s, Zionist institutions such as the Anglo-Palestine Bank estimated that a quarter billion dollars had been pumped into the local economy, most of that paid to Arab landlords and landowners demanding high rents and fees. Selling property to Jews was considered a mandatory death sentence in the Arab community, so transactions were often consummated through clandestine intermediaries.

Regardless of the names on the paper, the ultimate Zionist purchasers were rarely individuals, but international Jewish colonization and settlement funds, such as the Jewish National Fund. A government survey guesstimated total Jewish land ownership to be 650,000 *dunams* prior to 1920. One Turkish dunam roughly equaled 1000 square meters, or slightly less than one-quarter acre. Jewish land acquisition generally proceeded by thousands of dunams per sale. The pre-1920 estimate of 650,000 dunams in Zionist hands mushroomed by an additional estimated approximate of 193,000 dunams by 1924. During the next year, 1925, the peak immigration year, a further estimated 176,000 dunams were acquired, creating a Jewish land mass of more than a million dunams.[45]

Palestine's borders were not hard and fast and were estimated with great variance. On May 20, 1925, Lord Stanhope declared in the House of Lords that the total area of Palestine was approximately 27,000,000 Turkish dunams or about 8,528 square miles—this number was commonly quoted. Other official British statements surmised the area to be 10 percent greater. But by any measure, the Jews' possession of a million dunams constituted just a few percent of the entire region.[46]

Once purchased, Jewish land became part of the Zionist sovereign land trust, land that could never be resold. It was accreted into the future Jewish state in waiting. Hence, the Arabs saw not just an increase in Jewish newcomers, but an accompanying increase in Jewish acreage. Every additional Jewish dunam only further cemented the Arab collective rejection of all compromise, all binational thought, and any effort to achieve coexistence.

Violence became a useful commodity with a known utility. Functionally, British policy rewarded Arab violence with an almost predictable reaction from Whitehall and Parliament. After major riots, the British took political action intended to mollify the Arabs. Sometimes London appointed a commission of inquiry to produce a "white paper" to see if a pathway to peace could be found. But such efforts never caused a genuine pause in the hatred or the agitation.

The bloody Nabi Musa riot prompted the 1920 Palin Commission, which tried to find a peaceful venue for coexistence. No *modus vivendi* emerged and precious little genuine dialog between Arabs and Jews arose. The Arabs did not wish to participate in the Jewish economy or any political exchanges. Nor did they wish to accept autonomous or self-governing bodies, such as a proposed Legislative Council, if it bore the scent of binationalism or was packaged by the British authorities or was open to Jewish involvement—even proportionally minority Jewish representation. Typical was the Legislative Council proposal that would proportionally include eight elected Muslims, two Christians, and just two Jews. Zionist bodies agreed. Muslim organizations rejected the notion. When any Arab stepped forward to cooperate in any venture of conciliation, the Muslim community typically pressured or threatened him into immediate withdrawal. If elections were held, most Arabs refused to vote. If assurances were given that no political Arab rights would be compromised in any plan for binational coexistence, such assurances were scorned.[47]

"No" was the first word in the Arab political vocabulary and "maybe" did not mean "yes." Violence did not subside.

On March 28, 1921, after further Arab violent outbursts, Churchill gave notice that Britain would sever approximately 75 percent of western Palestine to create a new Arab state called Transjordan, later to be known as Jordan. Faisal's brother, Abdullah, was appointed as Emir of the Hashemite Kingdom. Churchill made clear that the mandate and indeed the Balfour Declaration enunciated two promises to two peoples: Arab and Jewish. Transjordan would become the Arab nation on some 75 percent of the land, and Jews would not be permitted to settle there.[48]

No matter. Weeks later, the Jaffa carnage of May 1921 broke out. Yet another inquiry was appointed; this one was the Haycraft Commission.[49]

In 1922, Churchill attempted to further publicly reassure the Arabs in unmistakable words. In an extensive memorandum that became known as its own white paper, Churchill declared, "Phrases have been used such as that Palestine is to become 'as Jewish as England is English.' His Majesty's Government regard any such expectation as impracticable and have no such aim in view. Nor have they at any time contemplated, as appears to be feared by the Arab Delegation, the disappearance or the subordination of the Arabic population, language, or culture in Palestine. They would draw attention to the fact that the terms of the Declaration referred to do not contemplate that Palestine as a whole should be converted into a Jewish National Home, but that such a Home should be founded in Palestine. In this connection it has been observed with satisfaction that at the meeting of the Zionist Congress, the supreme governing body of the Zionist Organization, held at Carlsbad in September, 1921, a resolution was passed expressing as the official statement of Zionist aims 'the determination of the Jewish people to live with the Arab people on terms of unity and mutual respect, and together with them, to make the common home into a flourishing community, the up-building of which may assure to each of the peoples an undisturbed national development.'"[50]

The fallout from uninterrupted violence, the post-Balfour uproar, and the two successive commissions progressively eroded British support for the Jewish National Home. Soon Jewish expansion was being curtailed in various parts of greater Palestine. Slowly, Jews were officially dissuaded or prohibited from buying land in certain areas. Moreover, Zionist entry into Palestine, once unrestricted, was curtailed following that 1922 Churchill white paper to match "the absorptive capacity" of the local economy.[51] Now the adversary in the minds of many Zionists was not only their Arab enemy but their British ally.

Britain's Mandate over Palestine was formally ratified by the League of Nations into the body of international law on July 24, 1922, with abundant safeguards for the local populations. Despite these safeguards written into international law, despite two Arab states created out of mandatory territories—one in Iraq and one in Jordan—despite a reduction of any possible Jewish home by 75 percent, despite limitations on Jewish immigration tied to economic growth, and despite property purchase curtailments, from the Arab perspective, even one more Jew on even one more dunam was one too many.

General Arab strikes were declared twice in 1925, once when Lord Balfour himself visited in March, and the second in November in sympathy with strikes against the equally detested French mandate in Syria. But a period of relative calm took hold for a few years, primarily because annual Jewish immigration began a serious decline. From 1925 to 1926, Jewish immigration dropped more than 60 percent, from an estimate of nearly 34,000 to an estimate of slightly more than 13,000 for the year; more importantly, an estimated 7,300 emigrated out of Palestine in 1926. The next year, 1927, the figure suffered an approximate 80 percent further free-fall to an estimate of slightly more than 2,700 newcomers; but the emigration level was almost twice the inflow, approximately 5,000 persons—so it produced a net loss. By 1928, the decline continued its downward spiral to its lowest level, estimated to be less than 2,200 for the year; and since an almost equal number left the country, the net numbers were essentially zero. For example, in March 1928, 200 Jews entered, but 261 exited.[52]

The radical and sustained drop from 1925 to 1928 was seen as sure progress by the Arabs of Palestine and a sure sign of Jewish containment. Several dynamics were among the causes of plummeting Jewish immigration from its 1925 peak to its 1928 nadir. More than just local politics, the immigration decrease also arose from world conditions—always the enzyme of Jewish immigration to Palestine. First, in some parts of Europe, Jewish living conditions improved somewhat as the advance of minority rights inched through the continent. Second, many of the most eager Jews had already immigrated to another popular refuge destination, the United States. Third, a severe currency collapse in Poland in 1925 following a period of hyperinflation there left many Polish Jews with worthless assets, making them unable to fund immigration and resettlement. Most immigrants were Polish, so this economic crisis had a decisive impact on the influx. Without economic means, Polish Jews simply stayed put in Poland.[53]

The external factors combined with facts on the ground in Palestine. In 1925, High Commissioner Herbert Samuel was replaced by Field-Marshal

Lord Plumer, seen by many as anti-Zionist. Samuel, an architect of the Jewish national home, was seen as a Zionist tool regardless of how he ruled for or against Jewish expansion in Palestine, for or against Arab empowerment or autonomy. Violence against Jews in Palestine was taking its toll. During those years, Tel Aviv had suffered an economic turndown. Net domestic product per capita in the Jewish community grew 16.2 in 1925 but cratered the next year to a negative 15.4 percent. Very few new jobs were available and a half million-dollar fund to relieve the unemployed was essentially depleted. What's more, in 1927, a magnitude 6.2 earthquake with its epicenter near Nablus crumbled hundreds of rudiment stone structures, reducing many of the area's iconic domed, terraced homes to sorrowful alluvial fans of rubble. The broad devastation killed more than 270 and injured more than 800, temporarily making Palestine a far less viable destination. By 1928, Jewish emigration levels out of Palestine nullified any population increase. Fed up with the mosquitoes, the violent attacks, and an earthquake, thousands just quit.[54]

But in the second half of 1929, more earthquakes shook, not just in Palestine but worldwide.

Perhaps it began when immigration into Palestine from Europe was visibly renewed. By March 1929, the turnaround was measurable. Reports asserted that in the month of March, for instance, 452 had immigrated to Palestine, 375 of whom were Jews. In April 1929, 417 entered, including 322 Jews, and only 70 Jews left Palestine. In Poland, the rise of anti-Semitism, including quotas on students in universities, was convincing many Polish Jews there that their future was bleak. For example, anti-Jewish mob action was erupting with increased frequency in Lemberg, also known as Lvov. The city was the third most populous Jewish center and previous harbinger of countrywide anti-Jewish unrest. In April 1929, several dozen Jews were stabbed in a fracas. On June 3, 1929, in another short-lived but telling disturbance, local Jewish newspaper offices were attacked, a student residence was invaded, synagogues were looted, and torahs were burned.[55]

Indeed, a renewed wave of anti-Semitism was gripping much of Europe and even the United States. It was significantly spurred on by Henry Ford's prolific international publication of *The Protocols of the Elders of Zion* as well as the rapid growth of the Nazi Party and all the anti-Jewish agitation that attended National Socialism. Even though the Nazis had lost seats in the previous election, *Brownshirts* continued their grass-roots rallies throughout Germany, demanding that Jews be expelled. On August 2, 1929, the Nazi annual rally in Nuremberg attracted a record 60,000. What's more, a new generation of doctrinaire Jew-hating Germans had now been established in the Hitler Youth.[56]

By summer, Palestine's Jewish economy had overcome its down years and had developed a sudden boom. All tallied, the Jewish economy could boast a $7.5 million investment, employing as many as 6,000 adults in some 600 commercial concerns of which 513 were industrial operations. That employment did not even include the 700 working at the burgeoning Palestine Electric Company, which supplied power to much of Palestine outside of Jerusalem. An international trade fair, the Palestine and Near East Exposition, was held in Tel Aviv to attract additional foreign trade. Net domestic product of the Jewish economy had boomed back to a 15 percent annual growth.[57]

Newly published estimates of the Jewish population in Palestine suggested that a near doubling had occurred within six years, from almost 84,000 counted in the 1922 census to an estimated 150,000 by August 1929. The Muslim population, despite its attempts at growth, remained stagnant during that time. Official estimates placed their number at 591,000, alongside a 73,000-strong Christian community. Hence, Jews comprised not only 100 percent of their own enclaves, they also constituted nearly 25 percent of the overall population. The demographic numerical superiority of Arabs was shrinking.[58]

In the fall of 1929, Jerusalem's flammable ingredients burned through the thin membrane separating them. Palestine combusted.

The most visible trigger this time was Jerusalem's Western Wall, Judaism's holy site, also known as the Wailing Wall or in Hebrew as the *Kotel*. The Wailing Wall, a majestic remnant of the Second Temple, is a massive array of sandstone blocks dappled with green foliage. It towers over all who approach it. For centuries, this exalted wall has been a place where Jews have sought to solemnly pray, in awe lay their hands upon its stone surface, and in hope wedge into the recesses small notes of supplication to God. This magnificent sacred wall also abuts the Noble Sanctuary, that is, the revered Islamic complex that includes the Dome of the Rock and Al Al-Aqsa mosque that was built upon the Temple site centuries after Herod. In Arabic, the wall is known as the al-Buraq Wall, named for Mohammad's winged steed al-Buraq. According to Islamic tradition, when Mohammad made his final journey atop his winged steed to "the further mosque," it was to this location, hence the name al-Al-Aqsa, which means "the furthest." While praying, the Prophet tied his winged horse to the wall, according to the tradition, thus the veneration by Muslims. For centuries, the rights of Jews to pray at the Wailing Wall were alternately granted, impeded, or otherwise regulated by Ottoman authorities in accordance with the Jews' *dhimmi* status as a subordinated people with a subordinated religion.[59]

During the mandate, Britain enforced the pre-mandatory Ottoman *status quo* regarding the Wall. That *status quo* embodied the legacy of prior Islamic edicts that generally prohibited Jews as dhimmis from making any improvements in their places of worship, and required Jews to pray only quietly so as not to be overheard, and to do so standing, not sitting, while near the Wall. One such edict cited by the Supreme Muslim Authority in 1928 and recognized by the British in Palestine was the Ottoman Firman of 1840, a ruling conveyed to the then-governor of the City of Jerusalem. The 1840 Firman merely reinforced earlier such decisions when it decreed, "There is no precedent for the Jews carrying out any such repairs in that area [the Western Wall] in the past; and whereas it has been established that it would be inadmissible under the Sharia Law (for them to do so); therefore the Jews must not be enabled to carry out the paving, and they must be cautioned against raising their voices and displaying their books (or utterances) and (informed) that all that may be permitted them is to pay visits to it as of old."[60]

A second recognized Ottoman ruling, this one from 1911 from the Administrative Council of the Liwa, declared: "the Sharia Court stated … that it is inadmissible by law in all respects that there should be placed chairs, screen[s], and similar articles."[61]

Based on the still-enforced dhimmi regulations, Jews in Palestine were not permitted to sit on benches at the Wailing Wall, not even the elderly, not even in the heat of the Jerusalem summer. Nor were they permitted to erect a partition between men and women. But Jews in their national homeland felt that after centuries of standing, they should be permitted to sit on benches if they chose to, and separate men and women in accordance with Orthodox tradition. Anywhere in the world, the decision to kneel, bow, genuflect, sit, or stand would be a matter of choice. But in Jerusalem, where every paving stone and crevice is a holy historic demarcation worth dying for, such a simple religious choice created an international incident.

In September 1928, on Yom Kippur, Jews brought their benches and sat while praying. They also erected a makeshift partition between men and women prayers called a *mechitza*, in accordance with Orthodox Jewish doctrine. Arab residents protested in anger that the Ottoman *status quo* prohibiting Jews from making further religious claims to the Wall had been breached by these benches and the *mechitza*. The British authorities agreed with the Muslim protest, and tried to stop Jews from sitting. In some instances, the police pulled chairs out from under Jewish worshippers. To underscore official Islamic control over the edifice, the British gave the Arabs formal permission to build a new mosque facility and minaret from one of the adjacent structures in the Noble Sanctuary. To show their utter dominance over Jewish observances, the Arabs then began louder calls to prayer, with the speaker volume turned way up, timed to disrupt Jewish prayer. Gongs and cymbals were clanged in a suddenly revived Sufi Islamic celebration known as *dhikr*. Mules were herded into the Jewish prayer section, sometimes depositing their dung. Bricks rained down from on high from time to time. Lest they inter-fere with Islamic rights to autonomously superintend the Noble Sanctuary area, the British remained detached. At the end of July 1929, after months of wrangling with international Jewish and Islamic protest over the Wall, Brit-ish authorities in Palestine gave the go-ahead for the new Arab construction to commence. The Zionist community in Palestine reacted in outrage and began protest marches. They insisted on their right to pray unimpeded and unmo-lested—and in a sitting position if desired, separating men and women if they chose.[62]

On August 15, 1929, during the fast of Tisha B'av, the solemn holiday that mourns the loss of the Temple to the Romans, thousands of observant Jews gathered at the Wall for their lamentations. Zionist activists also marched to the Wall waving blue and white starred Zionist flags and proclaiming "the Wall is ours." Rumors quickly spread through Arab neighborhoods like naph-tha fumes that the Jews intended to destroy the Noble Sanctuary and build their Third Temple.[63]

The next day, August 16, 1929, the city erupted.

Preprinted Arabic leaflets were circulated. They exhorted, "War, Jihad ... rebellion ... O Arab nation, the eyes of your brothers in Palestine are upon you ... rise up against the enemy who violated the honor of Islam and raped the women and murdered widows and babies." Thousands of shouting, enraged Arabs, daggers and swords at the ready, raced through the Old City via a new gate just created. They headed for the Wailing Wall.

"*Idhbah Al Yahood! Idhbah Al Yahood!* Slaughter the Jews. Slaughter the Jews." With knives and clubs, the mob attacked every Jew in sight, burnt Torah scrolls, and yanked supplication notes to God from the wall cracks and set them aflame.[64]

Attacks spread throughout the land over the next days. Jews were stabbed, shot at, beaten down with rocks, maimed, and killed in the Mea Shearim Quarter, in the Yemen Moshe district, and in various Jewish towns and sub-urbs. One by one, defenseless Jewish communities were looted and torched. Hartuv, a small Jewish village in the Judean Hills, was typical of the towns utterly laid waste: from hilltops miles away, a thick tilting column of black smoke against a clear sky could be seen rising from Hartuv's charred ruins.[65]

The chaos continued for days. With thousands of dagger and club wielding Arabs swarming throughout the city hunting Jews, wire services transmitted headlines such as "Thousands of Peasants Invaded Jerusalem and Raided all Parts of the City." In one instance, frenzied Arabs spotted a Jew and set upon him with their daggers. It was everything for policemen to finally extricate his lifeless body. In Motza, a village just outside Jerusalem, all but one hiding boy of the Makleff family was brutally murdered. By August 23, newspapers reported "The city is panic-stricken." Martial law was declared. Fifty British soldiers were rushed in from Egypt, and then another battalion joined them. Armored cars were brought in from Baghdad. British airplanes swept in to machine-gun Arab marauders. Flying low, the British pilots sprayed entire streets with aerial staccato, at first over the heads of rioters, and sometimes into the mobs to stop them.[66] But bullet volleys did little to deter them.

Violence continued to spread throughout Palestine. Jews fought back and retaliated with bricks and bars and whatever they could find. Then, the terror came to Hebron.

Hebron is the city of Abraham's tomb, where religious Jews had long lived, quietly studying at their yeshivas among their majority Arab neighbors. On August 23 and 24, 1929, Hebron became a bloody nightmare. The first strike on a Friday yielded only one victim to murder. That was enough. Arabs promised to return the next day. Defenseless Jews, nervous, fearful, tense, waiting, prayed that a detachment of a few dozen British police would protect them. Nearly the entire squad of police was Arab. But they were commanded by British police Chief Raymond Cafferata. He was determined to protect the town's Jews.[67]

Cafferata slept in his office all night waiting for the inevitable, a virtual outpost in a police station, with no word of reinforcements from the badly outmanned British forces. He could not stand alone against a horde, and many of his Arab policemen simply would not help. No matter, Cafferata loaded his weapons and just waited. By 2:30 p.m., Hebron's tense quiet was ended when an Arab boy riding a motorbike sputtered through the streets screaming a false report that the Jews were massacring thousands of Muslims in Jerusalem. No such thing was happening. But it was enough. In a mania, the Arabs rose up and attacked the Jews.[68]

A throng of armed Arabs waving axes ran after two Jewish boys, stoning one to death and stabbing another. Virtually alone and massively outnumbered, Cafferata fired his pistol at two of fleeing Arabs and then exhausted the rest of his bullets to disperse the mob. But then Cafferata fell off his horse, and could not hold back the attackers any further. Cafferata reloaded, fired, and reloaded again, wounding several in the mob. His Arab platoon largely stood by. Some of Cafferata's men did fire their rifles, but there were simply too many attackers. The mob broke through and screamed, "On to the ghetto, on to the ghetto."

House to house, they went, bursting into every room looking for hiding Jews. Religious books and scrolls were burned or torn to shreds. The defenseless Jews were variously beheaded, castrated, their breasts and fingers sliced off, and in some cases, their eyes plucked from their sockets. Infants and adults, men and women—it mattered not. The carnage went on for hours, with the Arab policemen standing down. Blood ran in streamlets down the narrow stone staircases outside the buildings. House to house, room by room, the savagery was repeated.[69]

One young boy, Yosef Lazarovski, later wrote of the horror: "I remember a brown-skinned Arab with a large mustache breaking through the door. He had a large knife and an axe that he swung through the doorjambs until he broke through. [He was] full of fury, screaming, '*Allah Akbar!*' and '*Idhbah al Yahood!*' ... My grandfather tried to hold my hand, then [he tried] to push me aside [and hide me], screaming, *Shema Yisrael* [the most solemn Jewish prayer] ... and then I remember another Arab ... with an axe that he brought down on my grandfather's neck."[70]

In the home of banker Eliezer Dan Slonim, where numerous families huddled in terror, the Arabs finally broke through. A yeshiva student quickly shoved one fifteen-year-old girl into a closet and held the door tight. Through the cracks, she saw her parents hacked to death. Her muffled screams were stifled by the student hiding with her. His hand was clamped so hard across her lips that her mouth ached for weeks. Twenty-two adults and children were gruesomely slaughtered there, including one six-year-old. Blood splatters reached to the rafters 12 feet up and pooled in the dips of the stone floor. A blood-soaked woman's undergarment was draped around a picture of Theodor Herzl.[71]

Not a single victim was simply killed. Each was mutilated and tortured in accordance with their identities, the specific information provided by local Arabs. The Jewish man who lent money to Arabs was sliced open and the IOUs burned in his body. The Jewish baker's head was tied to the stove and then baked. A Jewish scholar who had studied Koranic philosophy for years was seized, his cranium cut open, and his brain extracted. Another man was nailed to a door.[72]

At one point in the mayhem, an Arab in one household was preparing to behead a young child. The Arab had already swung once but the head was not yet severed. Shrieks pierced the street. A policeman who heard the screams ran up from a dark passage. Just as the killer was bringing his sword down for the final slice, the policeman broke in. The killer looked up. It was Cafferata, weapon now reloaded. He turned to Cafferata and swung his blade. But the lunge missed. The attacker was just inches from Cafferata's rifle barrel when Cafferata pulled the trigger and shot him in the groin. The Arab fell. As he dropped, Cafferata suddenly saw a cowering Jewish woman covered in blood. Standing over her with a dagger was yet another man. This one Cafferata knew, an Arab constable, Issa Sherif, of the Jaffa police station. Frantically, the Arab policeman fled into the next room and blockaded the door. He called out to Cafferata in Arabic, "Your Honor, I am a policeman!" Cafferata did not hesitate and burst in. He confronted the Arab constable—and fired.[73]

By the time reinforcements arrived, and the flames had been doused to a dark gray smolder, a total of sixty-seven Jews had either been murdered in the town or had died later of their wounds. Cafferata had almost single-handedly saved dozens. But many Arab families in Hebron also helped. They courageously hid their Jewish neighbors at great personal peril, vowing to protect them against marauders. This they did, history records, with stamina and bravery.[74]

More violence shook the country throughout the next 72 hours. Among the next massacres was the heinous killing of some 20 or more religious Jews in the Jewish holy city of Safed located in the north. Murdering and looting continued until finally suppressed by British troops.[75]

As August 1929 rumbled to a close, the blood-wet streets of Palestine descended into further acrimony. International investigations and protests echoed everywhere. Jews and Arabs gave contentious testimony and documentation going back centuries arguing whether Jews did or did not have the right to sit on benches while praying at the wall. Trials of some 195 Arabs and 34 Jews yielded death sentences for 17 Arabs and 2 Zionists who had violently retaliated. After commutation of most sentences to prison terms, 3 Arabs were hanged. Financial levies were assessed against 22 Arab communities. In the case of Hebron, the fine was 14,000 pounds. Compensation was also paid to individuals for destruction of property.[76]

London launched yet another sequence of inquiries and commissions, and these generated more white papers and reports. Accusations of cover-ups were leveled against the British as the mandatory government tried to quell a further Arab uprising and consequent armed Jewish retaliation. Militant right-wing Zionist organizations and mainstream Jewish defense units were tired of being on the defensive and ready to launch their own offensive measures. Arabs claimed that the Jews were exaggerating the mayhem, arguing that fewer beheadings had taken place than were alleged. At one point, a senior British official tried to minimize the havoc by concluding Jewish holy books were not actually burned—*only their pages*. Mutilations documented and photographed by first-responding police officials and journalists were later recanted and files sealed. London ultimately decided that peace could be kept only if Jewish emigration and land purchases were now further restricted.[77]

But the upheavals of fall 1929 were not yet finished, and October would be volcanic.

On October 3, 1929, German Foreign Minister Gustav Stresemann suddenly died of a stroke. Three years earlier, Stresemann, along with his French counterpart, Aristide Briand, had received the Nobel Peace Prize for his role in the multilateral negotiations that produced the so-called Locarno Treaties, intended to usher in an era of peace in Europe. Stresemann was also considered an architect of Germany's controversial war debt relief, a stalwart of German liberal foreign policy, and supporter for Jewish Palestine. His unexpected death left a prodigious vacuum in German politics and European diplomacy.[78]

Rushing into that vacuum was Hitler and his rabble-rousing Nazi Party. Despite electoral losses in the previous election, Hitler's appeal was rising among many in Germany, especially in the rural and non-cosmopolitan areas. Denied legitimacy in the traditional German press, Hitler expanded his own Nazi Party publications and widely disseminated anti-Semitic, anti-government flyers and pamphlets, again focusing on rural strongholds. Vituperative, hate-filled rallies from soapbox gatherings to great demonstrations of great attendance were staged throughout the country, day after day. One source estimated that the Nazis held as many as 7,000 local rallies, big and small, in October 1929 alone. These demonstrations were often in tandem with targeted violence against Jewish cemeteries and institutions. More than an ascendance just in Germany, Hitler's fascist movement spawned, inspired, or sponsored look-alikes or surrogates in many other countries, some wearing shirts of brown, some wearing black, some wearing silver. Moreover, the Nazis found common cause with, and in many ways emulated, Mussolini's *Fascisti*, the Italian movement that invented the very concept of fascism.[79]

Throughout 1929, Germany's economy teetered on the razor's edge of yet another disaster. Battered by a massive war debt imposed by the Versailles Treaty, mauled by the ravages of hyperinflation, beaten down by depressed farm prices and wages, Germany could bear little more. When the so-called Young Plan was developed by Washington to adjust Germany's reparations and structure a complex new bond program, it was hailed by Stresemann despite massive street protests by the Nazis. But by the first week of October, Stresemann had died.[80]

Then, everything completely collapsed.

On October 29, 1929, the world's economies imploded. Wall Street crashed. The Depression rose like a mushroom cloud with a blast radius and waves of fallout that were felt everywhere. Millions worldwide were immediately swept out of work and into endless breadlines as the global economy cratered. Millions of Germans were among the jobless, adding to that nation's decade of economic calamity. This socio-economic abyss was for Hitler a fertile field. He continued to hammer at his issues. He railed for rearmament and against the Jews who prevented it. He demanded restoration of Germany's territory and revenge against the Jews who had caused its dissection. He scorned the economy and the Jews who poisoned the monetary well. *Der Führer's* message was resonating with more and more men and women in Germany.

Indeed, the fascist cause and its race-based ideology were rippling through Europe, even England and the United States.

The Arabs had every reason to believe that world Jewry was about to be cracked and that Germany would lead the campaign.

But as Hitler's message of hate spilled across the borders to restive ethnic and nationalistic groups, into the radio broadcasts, newspapers, and newsreels of the day, the German Foreign Office tried to minimize the significance of the Nazi movement. Berlin staunchly proclaimed the Weimar commitment to democracy and its support of the Jewish people and their national home in Palestine.

In fact, during 1930, despite the worldwide Depression, the continuing rise of Nazism, Britain's retreat from the Balfour Declaration, and the death of Stresemann, the German Foreign Office took pains to reinforce its support for Jewish Palestine. For example, on February 20, 1930, in the wake of the horrors of Hebron, the Foreign Office helped sponsor a major *Pro-Palästina Komitee* conference in Hamburg for 1,500 Christian and Jewish notables under the chairmanship of Count von Bernstorff, former German ambassador to the Ottoman Empire, Mexico, and the United States. The elaborate occasion included a letter of encouragement from Albert Einstein, read aloud. Zionist leaders proclaimed their desire to live in peace with their neighbors. Germany issued reassurances that it fully backed a Jewish home in Palestine and stressed that it was German diplomats who had convinced the Ottoman regime to relent.[81]

A year later, despite the international torrents, there was still no change in Berlin's continuity of support. On January 16, 1931, the Foreign Office issued another letter to the *Pro-Palästina* Komitee: "The German government and the Foreign Office have repeatedly expressed their sympathy for the goals and efforts of your committee. My predecessor had indicated on several occasions, both verbally and in writing, that just as you, we view the work in Palestine as an excellent means for the economic and cultural development of the Orient, and the expansion of Germany's economic relations as well as and for the reconciliation of the people."[82]

In June 1931, seeking to avoid incitement of the Arabs, the British authorities issued a ruling enforcing the Turkish *status quo* proscribing the Jewish desire to sit at the wall or separate men and women. "To the Moslems belong the sole ownership of and the sole proprietary right to the Western Wall," declared the British in an official published ruling. "To the Moslems there also belongs the ownership of the Pavement in front of the Wall and of the adjacent so-called Moghrabi (Moroccan) Quarter opposite the Wall, inasmuch as the last-mentioned property was made Waqf [the reigning Islamic charitable trust] under Moslem Sharia Law, it being dedicated to charitable purposes.

Such appurtenances of worship and/or such other objects as the Jews may be entitled to place near the Wall either in conformity with the provisions of this present Verdict or by agreement come to between the Parties, shall under no circumstances be considered as, or have the effect of, establishing for them any sort of proprietary right to the Wall or to the adjacent Pavement. The Jews shall have free access to the Western Wall for the purpose of devotions at all times—subject to the explicit stipulations hereinafter to be mentioned ... The temporary instructions issued by the Palestine Administration at the end of September 1929, relative to 'appurtenances of worship' are to be made permanent, subject however to the one modification that it shall be permissible to place near the Wall the Cabinet or Ark containing the Scroll or Scrolls of the Law and the Table on which the Ark stands and the table on which the Scroll is laid when being read from, but only on the following occasions ... [to include] New Year's Day and on the Day of Atonement, and also on any other special 'holy days' that are recognized by the Government as such days on which it has been customary for the Ark containing the Scrolls of the Law to be brought to the Wall ... The temporarily enacted prohibitions against the bringing to the Wall of benches, carpets or mattings, chairs, curtains and screens ... are to be made absolute."[83]

In the aftermath of the 1929 riots and the British ruling, the Arabs of Palestine now ascended to the top of the Islamic world's consciousness. True, the British ruled that Muslim rule over the Western Wall was "absolute," but the ruling still insured that Jews had the official "right" to visit and even bring a table for their Torah scroll. Less than a one hundred percent verdict was unacceptable to the Arabs. Indeed, even a legal right to pray at the wall that was not subject to revocation was deemed a threat to Arab control. No longer spotlighted in the Muslim world only over the general issue of Zionism and Jewish settlement, Palestine's Arabs now also became a cause célèbre on the specific issue of whether Jews would be allow unfettered access to the Western Wall. To the Muslim world, efforts by Jews to sit at the Wall and bring in even a small partition between men and women were just the first inch of the conspiratorial mile in Zionism's ultimate plan to take control of and destroy Islam's holy sites.

Whereas Faisal sought to unify Mideast Arabs in a national movement, Palestinian Arabs sought to take the next step and unify the global Islamic community—energized by the struggle in Palestine. For generations an Islamic backwater, Jerusalem was now riding the crest of a religious tidal wave. It was the first successful effort.

In 1924, the new Turkey had abolished the Islamic caliphate, the seat of Islam jealously held by the sultans for centuries. Internecine and factional disputes erupted within the Islamic world as to where the new seat of Islam was to be located. Hussein of Mecca asserted his authority based on the holiest shrine in Islam and some recognized his primacy. But the majority of Muslims lived in British India, not the Arab Middle East. Indians wanted elections; and through their efforts, a Caliphate Congress was convened in Cairo in May 1926. To subvert attendance at the event and preserve Mecca's claim to the caliphate, the Saudi king invited leaders to a conference in Mecca during the season of the Hajj. Attendance was poor at the Cairo conference, and no new capital emerged.[84]

Just days after the September 1928 Yom Kippur incident in which Jews began their highly visible seated prayers and separation of the sexes, an emergency meeting of Muslims in the region was called. On November 1, 1928, representatives from across Palestine, Syria, Lebanon, and Transjordan assembled in Jerusalem to confront the new threat of Jews—sitting and separating without permission. The group agreed that the actual sitting position itself was not as important as the assumed "right to sit" without explicit Muslim consent.[85]

Now, with the intolerable 1931 British Wailing Wall decision in hand, Palestinian Arabs moved for an international Islamic congress to be convened in Jerusalem. This would bring global pressure onto London's rule. More than that, Palestine could become the new seat of religious authority and a shining center for cultural and academic institutions. Muslims worldwide, from India to Iraq, responded with enthusiasm and donations, as well as promises of attendance and communal support. On July 27, 1931, a World Islamic Congress in Jerusalem was announced. Invitations were sent to the heads of Muslim religious communities, political parties, and even the Muslim rulers so commonly detached from the common people. The date of the congress was carefully chosen—December 7, 1931, the anniversary of Mohammad's final flight from Mecca to al-Al-Aqsa in Jerusalem when he tethered his winged horse to the Wall.[86]

Many Muslim rulers and factional leaders protested the entire event. Turkey rejected the call and boycotted. But by December 7, 1931, approximately 150 delegates streamed in from 22 countries and regions, including Europe, to attend the ten-day affair. Many who could not attend sent letters of congratulations and endorsement. During their deliberations, congress delegates fumed first and foremost over the British espoused "Jewish right" to hold prayers at the Wall. Standing or sitting, any "right," minimal as it seemed, impermissibly violated Sharia and upturned a dhimmi class in their midst.[87]

December 17, 1931, the last day of the conclave, resolutions were heartily adopted. These included a solemn vow to repudiate the British decision on the Wailing Wall, defend the al-Buraq Wall against Jewish prayer and alleged hegemony, and outlaw further Arab land sales to Jews by such radical sanctions as denial of Islamic cemetery burial to violators. Threatening statements against the Jews were readily made available for the world to hear. Typical was this one given to the *New York Times*, invoking the specter of prior ghastly pogroms: "If the Jews continue their activities in Palestine, we shall be obliged to treat them in the way they know. We will only allow the Jews to stay in their homes and nothing else."[88]

The battle lines, already well-drawn, now saw forces on either side mobilizing as never before. But by the fall of 1932, all eyes turned to Germany. That country's national elections were scheduled for November 1932. Hitler was riding a wave of Depression-stoked outrage, thuggish intimidation tactics, and continuous propagandizing from street corners to stadiums. That crucial November 1932 election was indecisive. Hitler's party received only a third of the vote, about 12 million ballots. But that was enough to get him into the government. Would Hitler be included in the coalition? It was Hitler who refused to share power with the Socialists, who controlled some 20 percent of the vote, and the Communists, who controlled about 17 percent. Finally, in exasperation, on January 30, 1933, President Paul von Hindenburg exercised his emergency powers, appointing Adolf Hitler interim chancellor.[89]

Everything changed for everyone—for Germany, now propelled into uncertainty; for Europe, now slapped into astonishment; for the world, now holding its breath; for the Jews, now thrown into panic; and for the Arabs of Palestine, now thrown into hope as never before.

# **11**

# RISE OF THE MUFTI

T he Arab world and the larger global Islamic community were hardly monolithic. Rather they resembled a giant tree with a split trunk, great sprawling limbs and divergent branches. As Britain assumed its responsibility for Mandatory Palestine, that broad tree was badly splintered, fractured and, in some cases, withered. Palestine was located out on a political limb, removed from the mainstream. How did the fractious Arabs—each with their own colonial, tribal and dynastic wars to wage—come together over this territory heretofore forsaken by the Caliphate that ruled for half a millennium? Why did Muslims from many diverse countries rush towards tiny Palestine and Jerusalem to create an international anti-Zionist solidarity and a new Islamic center of gravity?

One man led the movement to repair and unify the contemporary Arab and Islamic family tree. He did so despite many disgruntled contenders to his leadership and many antagonists among his own people. He worked both sides of the Arab street and all corridors of the European halls of power. Cunning and politically astute, using different political voices for different political audiences, he was able to rise from a humble Ottoman soldier to the effective, albeit much-disputed, supreme head of the Arab and Muslim world in its battle against the Jews, Zionism, and Britain.

With a name spelled different ways and encompassing different honorifics at different times, the subject of many books and treatises, the intensely debated object of both scorn and admiration, the man, al-Hajj Muhammad Amin al-Husseini, was known everywhere simply as "the Grand Mufti of Jerusalem."

Who was he?

Husseini was the scion of a one of Palestine's most important families. Of the 16 or so prominent Arab families dwelling in Palestine for centuries, two powerful rival ruling factions arose: the Nashashibis and the Husseinis. The Husseinis were revered as descendants of Hussein, a son of Ali, the fourth caliph, who married Fatima, daughter of the prophet Muhammad. Factional detractors among the Palestinian clans disputed this noble lineage. Regardless, the family's prestige was felt throughout the Ottoman Mideast for centuries, especially in Palestine. Leading figures among the Husseinis were engaged in Palestinian commerce, including an olive oil soap factory. Through their ample connections to the Sultan's court in Istanbul, family members held numerous generation-to-generation administrative posts as well as seats in the legislature. In many Palestinian cities, Husseinis functioned as mayors.[1]

During the early twentieth century, at the advent of Arab nationalism, Husseinis were counted among the leaders of Arab secret societies such as the Green Flag Society, the Arab Brotherhood, and the Literary Club. During the pre-World War I years, Palestine was associated administratively with Egypt and/or Syria, so the Husseinis' sphere of recognition was hardly local. Not infrequently, when local farmers or peasants were overwhelmed by the Ottoman administrative morass, they sought assistance from the Husseinis as elders and as well-connected families. An October 1921 letter from Palestine High Commissioner Herbert Samuel to Winston Churchill makes clear that many considered the Husseinis "the oldest and most honorable family in Palestine."[2]

The Husseinis established their anti-Zionist credentials almost as soon as Herzl began his efforts during the final years of the nineteenth century. During the 1890s, in the Ottoman parliament and in Jerusalem's administrative bodies, family members agitated for laws forbidding Jewish emigration to Palestine from anywhere including other Arab lands. Elder Husseinis monitored land sales to ensure Jews did not purchase dunams in Palestine. British citizens were blocked from entering the port of Jaffa merely because they were Jewish. None of this anti-Zionist activism prevented Husseinis from harmonious coexistence with long-time Christian and Jewish families extant in Jerusalem, including doctors and merchants. For a time, a Jewish man managed part of the Husseini family's commercial enterprise. The Husseini public militancy on the issue did not preclude several prominent members of the Husseini family from selling parcels of land to Jews when the price was right.[3] But cordial concomitance with Jews rapidly curtailed once the Balfour Declaration was issued.

Perhaps most importantly, the Husseinis were known for their hold on key religious posts. As early as the seventeenth century, Husseini men had served as muftis of Jerusalem. In Islamic tradition, a mufti was the respected interpreter of Koranic law, as well as the sayings and ways of Muhammad. In many ways a mufti was also revered as the titular head of the community. The family's identification with the al-Aqsa mosque was a generation-to-generation constant.[4]

Amin Husseini, the charismatic man who became mufti during the Mandate, was born in the closing decade of the nineteenth century. Even his biographers quibble which birth year is correct, some suggesting it was 1893, others saying 1895 or even 1897. As a young man, the red-haired Amin Husseini was self-conscious, short, and frail. He spoke with a lisp. But he impressed others as highly intelligent and mature for his age. His father, Tamir, held the title of Grand Mufti until his death in 1908. Amin was too young to fill his father's shoes. Instead, the eldest brother, Kamil, assumed the important post. Kamil, meanwhile, sent teenaged Amin to Cairo to study at al-Azhar University.[5]

In Cairo, the young Amin met prominent Islamic reformers from many countries and became acquainted with the earliest champions of Arab nationalism. Soon, the youthful Amin became his own self-styled activist, recruiting other Palestinian students to agitate against Zionism. Amin reviled Zionism as the greatest threat to Arab nationalism—this, years before the Balfour Declaration was ever even framed.[6]

Events blocked the completion of Husseini's studies including the 1913 mandatory pilgrimage he undertook to Mecca, the Hajj. This status added "Hajj" to his name. Afterward, Amin went off to Istanbul to become an officer in the Ottoman army to sharpen his leadership skills. Harsh military training and deprivation toughened Husseini both physically and emotionally. During his soldiering years, he slept in dank clothes and bedbug-infested blankets. As disciplined as he was, however, the fervent Arab found he could not Turkify himself into a true Ottoman. His Turkish commanders discriminated against Arabs and gave them less food to eat. Amin could not join their wars. In fact, during World War I, he readily recruited local peasants for Faisal's Arab national uprising against the Turks. Amin helped rally more than 3,000 peasant volunteers from Jerusalem and Hebron to fight alongside Lawrence of Arabia. During those times, Amin professed allegiance to the British because he felt the path to the Arab national destiny passed not through Istanbul but through London.[7]

When Amin left the army, Husseini returned to Jerusalem and resumed his beloved campaign for Arab nationalism. He wrote mordant articles attacking Zionism. He rose locally as a thinker and activist on the topic. Amin was elected president of Jerusalem's Arab Club, whereupon he assumed virtual leadership of the anti-Zionist movement.[8]

When the British first occupied Jerusalem during World War I, they found

Husseinis prominent everywhere in the city. Kamil Husseini was Mufti. Mussa Husseini was mayor. Amin Husseini, although fully recognized by London as virulently anti-Zionist and an ardent foe of the Balfour Declaration, was a known popular supporter of the British military. Perceived as a key ally of London, British authorities awarded Kamil Husseini a medal, the Order of St. Michael C.M.G. and established him as president of the Sharia court.[9]

Quickly, as the ramifications of the Balfour Declaration became apparent in Palestine, Husseini soured on his transient alliance with the British. In 1918, Kamil walked out on a Jerusalem reception when local Zionist leaders began speaking of the bright binational future they envisioned. In the run-up to a celebration of the Balfour Declaration, Amin Husseini protested to his British contacts, but he was admonished not to obstruct the event. Defiant, Husseini began rallying fellow Arabs into more and varied anti-Zionist and nationalistic organizations, such as The Literary Society and the Youth People's Party. The twin themes of these overlapping groups were Arab national honor, and opposition to the Jewish influx.[10]

Thus, rejection of coexistence and Jewish emigration became more than an Arab discontent; it evolved into an organized cause célèbre. Arab or Islamic emigration from everywhere—India, Turkey, Morocco, Syria, Transjordan, Egypt—was considered ordinary and unremarkable by the Husseinis and their followers. Jewish émigrés from anywhere were demonized.

As the 1919 Paris peace process unfolded, with Arab promises discarded and Jewish promises fulfilled, the demarcation lines were becoming clearer. The umbrage of the Arabs from Damascus to Baghdad against the British and the French was palpable. But among the plumes of resentment that rose throughout the Mideast, Palestine's smolder was never out of sight and, indeed, for many Arabs became symbolic of their own local, regional, and Pan-Arab travail.

By 1920, the Husseinis had inspired Jerusalem Muslims to pray at the mosque for the Sultan of Turkey, that is, for a re-emergence of the caliphate. Carefully listening British authorities were completely befuddled by the Arab *volte face*, from staunch ally against the "terrible Turks" to wishful detached subjects of the Ottoman Empire hoping to see a *status quo ante*.[11] Under the Turks, their oppressors would at least be brother Muslims, not infidel Europeans and Jews.

The distance from prayer to violence was never a long one in Palestine. Riots would soon wrack Jerusalem. During the seething hours before the notorious April 1920 Nabi Musa pogroms, it was Amin Husseini and his cohorts who helped lead the crowd in syncopated jeers of Jew hatred, including *Filastin Bladna wa-l-Yahud Klabna!*, that is, "Palestine is our land, the Jews are our dogs!" His uncle, Mussa Husseini, the mayor of Jerusalem, joined the crowd-baiting.[12] This heinous five-day killing and looting spree was Amin Husseini's initiation into the realm of murder and massacre as a political tool. From that point, Amin Husseini became the visible leader of the churning Arab uprising against Zionism and British colonialism.

Husseini's method was not to raise his own axe, but to inspire the throng to raise their axes. A master of diplomatic understatement, double talk, double-speak, veiled threats, and talking diplomatically to authorities while fomenting the easily ignited rage of his followers, the prismatic Husseini deployed many faces, depending upon the setting. Nonetheless, the British police identified him easily as a ringleader of the pogrom of 1920. The military governor summarily fired Mayor Husseini, replacing him with an archrival from the Nashashibi clan. A court found Amin Husseini as well as a leading editor guilty of organizing and provoking the Nabi Musa bloodshed from the outset. But Husseini escaped arrest even before the expected judgment was rendered, fleeing by boat across the Dead Sea to Jordan, and from there to Damascus. In absentia, he was sentenced to 10 years in prison.[13]

While in Damascus during the latter days of April 1920, Husseini broadened his leadership, launching and leading yet more anti-Zionist societies, including one called the Arab Young Men's Society. Letters were written to Muslim leaders worldwide to rise up against the British and oppose Zionism. The group was planning to stage an invasion of northern Palestine from Syria, but after Feisal was defeated by the French, those plans faded. But Husseini was still a factor in Palestine's always tenuous peace. By September of 1920, British High Commissioner Samuel fully pardoned Husseini in an effort to restore equilibrium to the restive Arab community. Husseini triumphantly returned to Jerusalem. In December, 1920, the Third Arab Congress meeting in Haifa created yet another body, the Arab Executive Committee, to speak for all matters of nationalism. Deposed mayor Mussa Husseini was chosen to head up the Arab Executive, assisted by Amin Husseini. Among the measures decided was to internationalize the cause by producing Palestinian newspapers and distributing them free to Arab and Islamic communities in Europe.[14] The Husseinis were back in power in Palestine and telescoping their reach beyond the region.

During the first years of the British occupation, the post of Mufti of Jerusalem was held by Amin Husseini's brother, Kamil. On March 21, 1921, Kamil died and it was assumed Amin would simply inherit the position. But under a pre-existing 1910 Ottoman ruling, still in force, selecting the new Mufti required an election by an elite group of religious personalities. Six pious sheiks stood for the post, including several rival Nashashibis. The results exemplified the tribal divisions within Arab sentiment. Of the 62 votes cast, Amin Husseini polled fourth with just nine votes. Stunned, Husseini organized petition drives and posted flyers in the Old City protesting "Wake up Muslims, Jews interfered in the election of the Mufti." Arab communities across Palestine were duly agitated, dispatching angry protest communiqués to the government. Husseini warned the authorities that Muslim sensitivities were about to be stirred again. During this time, the other candidates, including the Nashashibis and the true vote-winner, Sheik Jar-Alla, remained quiet.[15]

With another round of explosive agitation looming, Husseini invited High Commissioner Samuel to a dinner and agreed to serve Britain obediently if only Samuel would intervene and simply appoint Amin to the position of Mufti. "May God lead us ... in the service of the country," Husseini wrote. Samuel undoubtedly thought Husseini was pledging fidelity to the British Mandate. Not so. Husseini was offering allegiance solely to Arab Palestine. Shortly thereafter, hopeful British officials convinced the Nashashibi mayor of Jerusalem to convince Sheik Jar-Alla, true winner of the Mufti election, to withdraw. Within hours of Sheik Jar-Alla's withdrawal on March 10, 1921, Samuel—the very incarnation of the British Jewish Zionist and Balfour-supporting High Commissioner—chose Husseini as titular head of the Palestinian Arabs.[16] From that moment on, Husseini would be known as the Mufti of Jerusalem. But more medallions were bestowed.

The British hoped that an extra epaulet would help Husseini pacify the many Arab communities who looked up to him. So they further aggrandized esteemed Husseini's title. He became the *Grand* Mufti of all of Palestine, not just any mufti as one might find in Damascus or Gaza, but now the Grand Mufti Hajj Muhammad Amin al-Husseini—boss mufti of Palestine. Samuel believed he was co-opting Husseini. But Husseini knew who was being co-opted—it was Samuel. Indeed, the new elevated Mufti did little to stop the periodic violence and, instead, spurred them on. Just a few months after his appointment, the May 1921 Jaffa riots broke out. But the Mufti was always in the background, and the British believed that having the Mufti on their side was a better fate than having him as their sworn enemy.

In furtherance of Samuel's program of co-option, yet another ruling body was invented, once again at Husseini's urging and once again as a British reaction to Arab unrest, hoping to mollify the populace. This newly minted entity was to be called the "Supreme Muslim Council." On August 24, 1921, Samuel summoned 56 leading sheiks and elders from across Palestine to Government House in Jerusalem. The various members of the council would have staffs and expenses paid for by the British government. In other words, now they were all put on the payroll. Husseini received an estimated £100,000 annually, which he was able to dispense as patronage to further secure his singular primacy. This funding created nothing less than the Mufti's personal gray government in Palestine. On December 20, 1921, the Supreme Muslim

Council was formally announced. Its constituent bodies would include the *Waqf*, the religious trust that held property deeds and sovereign management rights to the shrines of Islam. Samuel believed the Council would reign in the absence of an Ottoman Sultan and rule on all things Arab and Islamic in Palestine. This, he hoped, would persuade Arabs they had achieved a semblance of self-government under the Mandate. After a contentious leadership dispute with the Nashashibi clan, and with the backing of the British, Husseini was appointed president for life.[17]

Husseini's multiple British-bestowed cathedras only cemented in the minds of many Arabs that the new Mufti was the man who could stand up to the British and function as their ultimate leader. Less than a king, hardly a unanimous popular choice, disputed for sure by many of his coreligionists, in the context of Arab-British relations, the new Mufti was now the anointed one.

More than just a political leader, the Mufti used his position as the unofficial president of Palestine to launch Islamic projects, many of which were associated with or located within the Noble Sanctuary and al-Aqsa Mosque. In Jerusalem, he established an Islamic theological college, opened a library stocked with some 3,000 titles, and supervised religious schools. Husseini's local religious governance created global Islamic prestige and a global financial resource. This international reach allowed him to continually position the Palestine problem onto the world stage. Powering this newly found, worldwide stature was the Mufti's authority over the Wailing Wall, also known to Muslims as al-Buraq.[18]

The structures of the Noble Sanctuary were in severe disrepair, having suffered centuries of Ottoman neglect. From 1923, the Mufti's push to restore the dilapidated al-Aqsa mosque became a broadly-endorsed international campaign. Mufti deputations seeking money for the restoration were sent to Turkey, Syria, and Iraq. Using British governmental connections, especially Samuel, the Mufti made contact with General Edmund Allenby in Egypt to raise funds. Allenby connected Husseini to Egyptian King Fuad and happily purveyed the Mufti to the Cairo press. Samuel even wrote the King of England suggesting he contribute, an idea the monarch declined.[19] Samuel's advocacy was hardly based on architectonic enthusiasm for the mosque or benevolence toward Islam. Rather, it was based on India.

Seventy million Muslim Indians comprised much of the backbone of the British Empire, both in war and in peace. Muslim Indians in their festooned headgear, including the fabled Bengal Lancers, patrolled the most sensitive checkpoints and crossroads in both Iraq and Palestine.[20] None of this pragmatism escaped the Mufti, who keenly understood he could pressure on London from Jerusalem through New Delhi.

The Mufti's delegation to India met with particular success. Husseini was obligated to provide written assurances and personal promises in advance that his group would fund-raise only and not militate against British policy over Muslim populations on the sub-continent. This first trip to India was the beginning of Husseini's continuing sway with activist Indian Muslims. In fact, of the £104,956 raised for the al-Aqsa restoration project, £38,761 was contributed by King Hussein, and £16,478 was transferred by the Supreme Muslim Council—which, of course, involved fungible British government revenues. But three donation funds from India totaled £23,790. Hence, Indian monies exceeded Palestinian monies for the effort.[21] While in other countries, the Mufti was elevated as a valiant "defender of the holy places," the picture was different at home. Far and wide in Palestine, the newly empowered Mufti continued nailing down his power base using money, influence, and authority to become the strong man of Palestine. In Haifa, Jaffa, Jerusalem, and Nablus, Husseini's *Waqf* assumed control of several private schools, and the Mufti's men insured the pupils received a rigid dose of nationalism. The Mufti's emissaries visited small villages north and south to assert his authority. Not infrequently, this meant interfering in the established lines of tribal authority in a town or village. Money became a big issue. Husseini knew how to collect it, how to spend it, and how to wield it either as a weapon or as a reward. The large sums controlled by the Mufti that accrued from international givers and local sources were often usurped, spent, siphoned, and/or parlayed to the Mufti's advantage—and that made for disputes. Rival Arab families frequently wrote to foreign donors asking them to withhold their contributions because the money would be misspent or worse. These protestations were dismissed by the Mufti faction as complaints from "enemies."[22]

Despite the dismissive attitude of the Mufti and his camp, indignant locals constantly complained to the Jerusalem authorities to rein in their man. In 1925, some 1500 signatures on a petition were gathered from Nablus and 50 surrounding villages protesting the Supreme Muslim Council and the Mufti who led it. Arab newspapers sharply assailed Husseini's tactics. The Mufti was so bothered by one media attack, he sued renowned Palestinian poet Bulus Shihada, editor of *Mirat al-Sharq*, the newspaper considered at the forefront of the anti-Husseini factions. *Mirat al-Sharq* opposed the Mufti's autocratic ways and some of his anti-Jewish declarations, especially those that did not discriminate between traditional Palestinian Jews and Zionists. Husseini would not stand for the criticism and prevailed to a degree. The court awarded the Mufti £50 in damages.[23]

However, lawsuits and damage awards did not deter the opposition from rebelling against Husseini's tactics, behind which they sensed stood the British in dim light.

The British, for their part, cautiously stood by their man in the face of so

much opposition because they still believed, as one telling memo from acting district governor Harry Luke to High Commissioner Samuel declared,
"five-sevenths of the total population of the country stand with him."[24] More
than that, as rival political parties emerged to challenge electoral seats on
the Supreme Muslim Council, as protest petitions piled ever higher, as local
notable resentment swelled, the British saw their Caesar policy working:
*divide et impera*—divide and conquer.

By the summer of 1928, following years of internecine electoral disputes, popular protests, tribal quarrels, beckoned and resented government
meddling, and continuous challenges to Husseini's legitimacy, with his power
base shaken and Hussein's authority heading for excision, it was the Jews who
saved him. How? On Yom Kippur 1928, the Jews decided to sit down during
prayers at the Wailing Wall.

Now all eyes turned away from the petty distractions of pilfered tithe cof-
fers and hand-picked administrative intruders in the affairs of daily life. Arab
Palestine was hypnotized and unified by the affront to their religion that was
unfolding—or rather, that was sitting—at the Wailing Wall.

*     *     *     *

When the Jews had tried to sit on benches and separate men from women
with a portable partition on Yom Kippur, September 23, 1928, the Mufti
and his machinery began a nonstop protest movement against the perceived
encroachment. As the chief religious authority, it was Husseini who directed
that a muezzin, the man who calls Muslims to prayer from the minaret, position himself within earshot of the Wailing Wall pavement, and then dial the
volume up to rile Jews during prayer, this to prove Islamic dominance. At
the same time, it was Husseini who directed the revival of the cacophonous
*dhikr* ceremony, complete with repetitive shouts of *Allahu Akbar,* as well as
loud gongs and cymbals, once again, disrupting Jewish prayers with strategic
noise. The Mufti also was the one who permitted mules to trample through the
Jewish prayer area, dropping dung and creating the feel and smell of what one
Jerusalem newspaper termed "a latrine."[25]

Jews tried peaceful appeals to the Mufti. In October, the Va'ad Leumi,
the umbrella group for Zionist institutions in Palestine, published an open letter stating, "We herewith declare emphatically and sincerely that no Jew has
ever thought of encroaching upon the rights of Moslems over their own Holy
Places" but merely to pray. Knowing the Mufti's reputation for money, using
back channels, they offered cash—some called it a bribe, some called it traditional baksheesh. The Va'ad Leumi also suggested the city of Jerusalem formally appropriate the pavement abutting the Wall, making it public property

outside the purview of the Supreme Muslim Council. Zionists even offered to purchase the pavement outright. Meetings were called worldwide to protest the interference and beseech the Jewish right to pray without intrusion. None of these efforts proved fruitful.[26]

The Mufti's newspaper, *al-Jami'a al-Arabiyya* (*The Arab Union*), constantly agitated the view that the Jews were trying to dismantle and takeover the whole of the Noble Sanctuary. Sitting on benches and separating the genders was only the beginning, the newspaper claimed. Husseini created a militant *ad hoc* group known as the *Committee to Defend the Noble Buraq*, which dispatched members from village to village riling up the peasants, warning them that the Zionists were about to destroy or  convert the whole of the Noble Sanctuary. Not uncommonly, the words of reactive militant Zionists were quoted, misquoted, and skillfully excerpted for inflammatory flyers to create the impression that the total desecration of the sanctuary was imminent at the hands of Jews. The Mufti also began an accelerated construction program of his own that was generally thought to either lower part of the Wall, permitting the Mufti to enjoy a clearer view of the pavement from his offices, or transmogrify the area altogether with a new gateway. This construction plan, in turn, only further agitated militant Zionists. Then, in November of 1928, the Mufti convened a pan-Arab Muslim Conference for Jerusalem, which adopted resolutions that threatened "the growing agitation of Muslims" and forbid further land sales to Jews.[27]

For months, the Arab masses had been fed a steady diet of provocation by the forces of Husseini as well as Husseini himself. In the run-up to the massacres of August, 1929, the Arab press, heavily influenced by the Mufti and his agents, was filled with inflammatory messages, rumors, and warnings about a Jewish conspiracy. Throughout that August, the Mufti's agitators continued to fan out across Palestine to stoke local reaction. A leading, fast-moving rumor was that the Zionists were preparing a complete takeover of the Noble Sanctuary on Friday, August 23, 1929, and that the Mufti had summoned all good Muslims to rush to Jerusalem. By noon that day, August 23, that happened. Thousands of Arabs swarmed into Jerusalem armed with an assortment of deadly weapons, from swords to guns, and converged on the sanctuary courtyard. "*Sayf al-Din, al Hajj Amin,*" the throng rhythmically chanted. Translated, it means: The Sword of Religion, al-Hajj Amin.[28]

But after more than a year of pitched incitement by Husseini's machine, the Mufti suddenly conducted himself in the complete opposite fashion. Now he spoke only in pacifist terms, his words well heard and carefully documented by Mandate policemen in the crowd. Hence, while the Mufti's cohorts, then and there, in his presence, whipped the crowd into a frenzy, the Mufti could only be quoted as urging "calm and restraint." But as the throng

left the courtyard, they were not restrained. Instead, they pressed on to immediately commit murder and mayhem throughout Jerusalem.[29]

The next day, August 24, 1929, the Mufti issued a signed public appeal
to all Arabs to "arm yourselves with mercy, wisdom, and patience, for verily, God is with them who bear themselves in patience." The quoted record
in English was abundantly clear: his verbal statements and written promulgations preached "no violence." More than that, to show his reliability, the Mufti
urged the Palestine police to concentrate extra reinforcements in Jerusalem—
just in case.[30]

Where? In Jerusalem. Station the troops in Jerusalem.

What happened then? Scores of Jews were butchered that very day, not in
well-guarded Jerusalem where the police had been waiting, but in completely
outmanned Hebron to the south. In an organized pogrom, the Arabs descended
upon Hebron's defenseless Jewish ghetto and brutally killed or maimed all
they found as the scant British police unit waited for reinforcements.

In the official investigations, especially the Shaw Commission, the Mufti
was found to be blameless because his words and deeds on the two days in
question were not incriminating. For British eyes and ears, he had preached
peace and only peace. In fact, the Commission was compelled to conclude,
"The Mufti, both at noon on the 23rd of August and thereafter throughout the
period of the disturbances, exerted his influence in the direction of promoting
peace and restoring order." The Commission did qualify it could only base
its conclusion on the evidence it had—not what was done "out of view." In
that vein, no search of his offices was possible without desecrating the sanctity of the Noble Sanctuary. Acting district governor Luke penned in his diary
the curious observation that when he urged the Mufti to address the crowd to
restore calm, "He complied, but his arrival appeared to excite rather than to
calm the mob."[31]

High Commissioner John Chancellor had written to a family member just
days after the riots, "The rising which came like a bolt from the blue was evi-
dently carefully organized beforehand, and many leading Arabs must have
been aware of it. I believe Hajj Amin, the Grand Mufti, was largely responsible for it."[32]

When the Mufti's exoneration was discovered, charges of a whitewash
rang out everywhere. Zionists and Jewish groups decried the gullibility of the
Shaw Commission's findings. The inquiry, they claimed, had been duped by
the Mufti's doubletalk. Many agreed. Even British Prime Minister Ramsay
MacDonald rejected the report as "a bad report, an unfair report" compiled
from "insufficient evidence" that could be expected to "depress the Jews and
elate the Arabs."[33]

The Colonial Office was more specific in its rejection when a senior official wrote, "I think I may say, that it is our private opinion in the Office that the Mufti and some of his supporters were probably very much more responsible for some of the deplorable incidents which have occurred in Palestine than the majority of the Shaw Commission appear to think." The Shaw Commission's report was officially published over many British governmental objections. "I do not see that we can do otherwise," the Colonial Office stipulated, "since we have no definite facts supported by unimpeachable evidence ... and even if we had, I do not see what use we could make of it unless it was sufficient to enable us to take definite action against the Grand Mufti, which is obviously impossible. He is much too wily a bird to give us the chance."[34]

George Rendel, who sat on the Eastern Desk of the Foreign Office added, that the Mufti "seems to have been largely responsible for the outbreak of the disturbances" and urged his colleagues "to deal with him later on, as he deserves."[35]

Thus the Mufti was able to remain on the British payroll, stay blameless in the carnage he orchestrated, and continue to prove once again that he could say the right thing at the right time to the right person, yet superintend violent events with impunity.

The Shaw Commission Report, sympathetic to the Arab cause, was published on March 31, 1930. It was followed by two related inquiries in October. The Hope-Simpson Report was released on October 1, and on October 31, the Passfield White Paper was published. Together, the trio of papers virtually halted the forward motion of the Jewish national home by severely obstructing additional Jewish immigration and land sales to Jews. But shortly after these three reports were issued, London—at the highest levels—moved to completely negate their impact. British leaders were now on to Husseini and the manner in which British policy had been mooted and twisted back by continued calculated Arab violence.

British Prime Minister MacDonald took note of a vigorous public complaint campaign by Zionist leaders in Europe and the United States, which demanded adherence to the League of Nations Mandate despite the mob carnage. Weizmann met with MacDonald on May 12, 1930 and reminded him that Jews the world over "are anxious to see these words [the Balfour Declaration and the Mandate] confirmed by deeds." Pressure, public and private, was continuously exerted by both Jewish and Arab delegations contending in London during the spring and summer of 1930. The Arabs threatened more violence and demanded a complete cessation of the Mandate. Jewish arguments stressed prosperity in Palestine—an appealing notion during Britain's Depression, and a call for the rule of law, international and local. Eventually, the Jewish arguments were beginning to persevere with the Prime Minister's office. On November 6, 1930, just days after the Passfield White Paper was released, a bothered MacDonald responded to a lunch question about it, blurting, "There is no White Paper." He added with annoyance, "I understand there are errors in this White Paper."[36]

On November 14, 1930, MacDonald's office issued a communiqué, prior to a House of Commons debate on the subject, stating, "Doubts having been expressed as to the compatibility of some passages of the [Passfield] White Paper of October 21st with certain articles of the Palestine Mandate, and other passages having proved liable to misunderstanding, His Majesty's Government have invited representations of the Jewish Agency to confer with them on these matters." During that Parliamentary debate, the White Papers were roundly excoriated. For example, one of the White Papers complained of 7,000 Jews immigrating during a recent period. But, a member demanded to know why no mention was included about 14,000 Arabs from Syria entering the country during a similar period.[37]

MacDonald added this promise to the House debate: "The Government will carry out the Mandate in both its aspects and, in carrying out the Mandate, will lend every energy they have to enable the development of Palestine to be continued under conditions which will make harmony between Jew and Arab closer and closer so that the Arab may continue to enjoy the benefits he has already got from Jewish immigration and Jewish capital, and the Jew, the devoted Zionist, may see Palestine becoming more and more the complete embodiment of his ideal of a Jewish national home."[38]

A new pro-Zionist British policy was emerging. By late November 1930, a draft letter to Weizmann and the Zionist Organization was being circulated. On February 13, 1931, the long letter was delivered to Weizmann and read aloud to the House of Commons. It clarified that there was a need to "remove certain misconceptions and misunderstandings which have arisen … in the White Paper of October 1930." MacDonald's letter went on to laud Jewish emigration and the systematic improvement of Palestine. It made clear that "His Majesty's Government did not prescribe and did not contemplate any stoppage or prohibition of Jewish immigration, nor "imply a prohibition of acquisition of additional land by Jews." In unmistakable terms, the letter concluded that Britain "unequivocally affirmed that the obligations imposed … [and] its acceptance of the mandate are solemn international obligations from which there is not now, nor has there been at any time, any intention to depart."[39]

Zionists and Jews rejoiced. Arabs shook with anger and disbelief.

February 13, 1931, was a Friday. Coming on Friday the 13th, MacDonald's letter was forevermore dubbed by the Arab community as "the Black Letter" being issued on "a Black Friday." Days later, the Mufti's Arab Executive declared to all Arabs everywhere: "Let us leave this Government to flatter the

Jews as much as they desire and let us seek help from ourselves and the Arab and Islamic World ... Mr. MacDonald's new document has destroyed the last vestige of respect every Arab had cherished toward the British Government."[40]

On July 27, 1931, the Mufti announced a World Islamic Congress to be held in Jerusalem. He sent invitations to Muslims worldwide and, once again, the prime mover was Islamic outrage over the Jewish right to sit at the Wailing Wall. Arabs still fumed over Jews sitting on benches or partitioning the genders at the Wall. The lament: "The permission given to Jews to hold prayers and religious devotions in this place is inconsistent with Muslim Sharia Law." Some 150 delegates from 22 nations attended the Congress.[41] Now the Mufti's crusade was clearly international.

The opening session was held at the al-Aqsa Mosque. But with so many delegates from so many countries, the competing attendees wanted to cover a multitude of Islamic issues, including a takeover of the Hejaz Railway that ran from Damascus to Medina, financing of a new Islamic university, and other organizational issues. They disagreed on much. But they found unanimity in denouncing all manifestations of the Jewish presence in Palestine. Any who cooperated with the British, or any other non-Muslim regime in a Muslim land, was heretofore to be untouchable and killed as an apostate, the Congress resolved. Once dead, the ostracized could not even be buried in a Muslim cemetery. The resolution read: "The congress believes any Muslim who helps this authority, whatever his status, is an apostate."[42]

The purposes and the outcomes of the Congress, the British correctly understood, were tantamount to a declaration of war. What emerged from this event, and many other events taken together, culminated in the massive anger Arabs felt. It produced an Islamic fury toward the British and the Zionists. This fury was embodied by more than a single man—the Mufti. It was the well-populated movement he galvanized that rose up as a community of rejection and seething antagonism. Nor was this animus limited to Palestine. It was worldwide and entrenched. Even though there were many Arab and Islamic dissenters and abstainers from the cause, the official institutions and the majorities were now ready to do battle with the Jews and Britain on a wide array of fronts.

Finally, the Arabs and Muslims saw their best chance of permanently defeating the British and the Jews. On January 30, 1933, Hitler came to power.

CHAPTER 12

# THE ARABS REACH
# FOR THE REICH

s soon as Hitler came to power in January 1933, the Arabs of Palestine
and throughout the Middle East began reaching out to establish solidarity with the Reich. The Nazis were not interested. They considered
Semitic Arabs to be at the bottom of the racial ladder along with Jews. Moreover, Hitler at the time wanted to maintain good relations with England. *Der
Führer* believed the British Empire and its Anglo-Saxon character to be a significant and desirable branch of Aryan supremacy. Just as the Arabs failed to
grasp that Germany during Weimar days was pro-Zionist, they failed to grasp
that National Socialism reviled Arabs and was, for all the wrong reasons, as
pro-Zionist as prior German administrations.

Certainly, with the advent of Hitler, the Nazi Party came to Palestine. Yet
Arabs saw none of the brown shirt outbursts or swastika demonstrations in
Palestine that were common throughout Germany. Nazi strength and vitality in Palestine was anemic at best, and even fair-weather followers almost
always kept their ideology indoors.

German Palestinians numbered about 1800 souls during the Mandate, the
majority being devout Protestant Templars who observed their piety without
clergy. Traditional Lutherans and Catholics comprised the balance. Templars
and other Germans had lived in Palestine for decades, concentrated in several colonies, and had scrupulously kept out of the Arab-Jewish fracas. When
Hitler came to power in January 1933, the Nazis made a concerted effort to
bring all German citizens everywhere as well as all ethnic Germans of any

citizenry into the Party. The main Nazi organization of several devoted to this task was the AO or *Ausland-Organisation*, that is, the Overseas Organization. Certainly, the AO worked hard to bring Germans outside the country into the Nazi fold. However, Foreign National Socialist [NSDAP] units in the Mideast were under strict instructions from the AO to avoid displaying their swastikas in public or agitating against the local authorities—in this case, the British Mandate.[1]

Despite efforts after Hitler's ascent in 1933, German Palestinian Nazi membership could be counted on one hand. During the coming years, lackluster recruitment only produced an estimated 300 members, about a third of whom lived in the Jaffa colony alongside their Arab and Jewish neighbors. The second largest NSDAP cell numbered about 90 members in Haifa. But regardless of armbands worn in obligatory clubhouse meetings, German Palestinians by and large were never enthusiastic about the Nazi ideal. They preferred to peaceably coexist with Jews and Arabs, as well as with the British Mandate. Anti-Semitism went against their religious ideals. The community's true feeling was perhaps expressed best in an editorial in the German Palestinian newspaper *Die Warte des Tempels*, which stated early on, "We must never forget that we live in a non-German country in the midst of a non-German people, and that our task here in Palestine can never be a political one. It would also be wrong if those among us who more or less accept the ideas of National Socialism should come to scorn those who still have reservations." A later comment in the newspaper confessed, "One cannot reconcile the superiority of one race with one's belief in God the Father of all men."[2]

Arabs learned quickly they had to bypass overseas colonies of Germans in the Middle East and Palestine and instead directly approach the German government to entice a partnership with Nazis in their struggle against the Jews and Britain. But all such efforts were roundly rebuffed by Germany.

Grand Mufti Hajj Amin Husseini first visited the German consulate in Jerusalem on March 31, 1933, where he met with German Consul Heinrich Wolff. In a coded message to Berlin, Wolff reported, "The Mufti made expressly clear that Muslims within and without of Palestine salute the new government of Germany and hope for the spread of fascist anti-democratic governments elsewhere. Contemporary Jewish influence on economics and within politics is damaging everywhere and should be combated." To this end, Wolff's report continued, the Mufti was prepared to help join the boycott of Jewish businesses preached by the Nazis in Germany. The Mufti offered "to spread the word about a boycott through the use of special emissaries if necessary."[3]

Consul Wolff, however, had little patience for Arab approaches. As a member of the old guard, pre-Nazi Foreign Ministry, he was an active Zionist supporter with many Zionist contacts, both commercial and political. More-over, Wolff's wife was Jewish.[4] He did not recommend Berlin join forces with the Mufti.

Within a month, Consul Wolff found himself again conferring with the Mufti and a circle of leading local sheiks as well as an Indian Muslim activist. The occasion was a feast held at Nabi Musa in the desert. Quickly, even before cigarettes were exchanged, the Mufti again wanted to know about his earlier request to help Berlin in its anti-Jewish boycott. When Wolff questioned the wisdom of such a boycott, suggesting Jews had dramatically improved life in Palestine, the Mufti bristled, replying that the Arabs preferred all Jews out of Palestine. If Palestine needed modernizing, Husseini added, the Arabs would handle it by themselves.[5]

The official Supreme Muslim Council newspaper, *al-Jami'a al-Arabi-yya*, made the Palestinian Arab viewpoint abundantly clear. As Hitler came to power, it published an editorial extolling the Nazi campaign. "It is well known," the newspaper stated, "that Herr Hitler and his party are the most vio-lent adversaries of the Jews ... The Jews assume that Germany will become a center of hatred against the Jews, a phenomenon which is called *Anti-Semi-tism*. The Jews think that their life will become more miserable than in Czarist Russia. As far as the position of the Arabs ... because the Jews are our ene-mies our wish, and our hope, rests of course on Hitler according to this rule: the enemy of my enemy is my friend."[6]

Arab attempts to reach out to the Reich continued and now beyond Pal-estine. In fall 1933, Wolff learned of a request for Berlin to fund and equip an uprising in Syria against the French—an idea Wolff called preposterous and "childish." Emir Abdullah in Transjordan tried to meet with Wolff in mid-1934 in advance of sensitive discussions with the British in London. Wolff declined that meeting.[7]

Later Wolff did confer with Abdullah's aides, but again refused to do any-thing that would imply that Germany was coordinating with Arabs, especially against the British. Wolff's detailed report reveals his contempt. "As all such discussions begin," wrote Wolff, "so too did this one with assurances of the highest regard for the new Germany, and soon the discussion returned to the unambiguous question of whether Germany would be willing to support the Arab political aspirations in general, and specifically the Emir [of Transjor-dan]. When asked such questions I always reiterate that in the current eco-nomic and political situation, material support from Germany—and in the sense of the inquiry that means assistance with money, or materials such as weapons—it is inconceivable." Wolff continued that he tried to be vague and encouraging about Arab aspirations, and that "The response to such inter-twined declarations is generally responded to satisfactorily by Arab visitors by frequent iterations of the phrase, '*insha Allah*,' so that after a longer period of time the path for continuation of the conversation is cleared. So it was in this case as well." Holding nothing back, Wolff added, "I was able to point out that unlike my Italian or perhaps even also my French colleagues, I do not chase after the Arabs with seductive promises; rather, they came to me of their own will."[8]

Wolff mentioned that the Emir and his supporters were trying to "deal with the Arab opposition … with the Grand Mufti; he [Husseini] is now cracking down here." The German consul was quick to suggest, "Everyone who has the opportunity to observe Arab politics invariably becomes more skeptical with time. In this respect, just as the war-famed Lawrence said of them, the Arabs are brilliant 10-minute warriors, but when it requires perseverance, they rapidly go lame."[9]

Beyond Palestine, the situation was similar. In Baghdad, a Pan-Arab delegation approached the German ambassador seeking closer ties with Germany—it led to naught. In Cairo, an Arab activist visited a German diplomat "in order to express his sympathy for the new Germany," but the ambassador "refused to see the young man, and when the Arab persisted, the embassy reported it to Egyptian Department of Public Security. In Syria, a sheik delivered a letter to German diplomats written in French and addressed to "His Excellency the Reich's Chancellor of the German Reich, Who is zealously engaged on behalf of the homeland, Hitler! … I am ready to place 100 mounted horsemen at your disposal the moment I receive a wave to do so, in homage to your position and as a gesture of gratitude for your highly regarded deeds. We are always prepared to be of service at the first sign from you."[10]

At one point, Wolff in a note to Berlin mockingly scoffed, "As to the stance of the Arabs, one can only say that it is always the same thing. The gruel must be kept cooking, stirred to the right, then back to the left, and that is considered 'politics.'" Wolff appended this derision, "I am reminded of a discussion between the war-famed Lawrence [of Arabia]…in which Lawrence expressed himself thusly about the Arabs: 'I don't know how one can possibly take the Arabs seriously. I know them quite well. It isn't worth the effort.'"[11]

It wasn't just the old guard Weimar diplomats still stationed in embassies and consulates throughout the Mideast who were unwilling to engage the Arabs. Reich officials in Germany were in complete agreement. Berlin's stance was unequivocal. On weapons, the Foreign Office dispatched a clear policy: "Germany cannot support the Arabs with money or arms." A July 31, 1933 Foreign Office memorandum, distributed to German embassies in London, Cairo, Baghdad, Beirut, and Geneva, instructed diplomats to avoid Arab organizations, otherwise "members of the German Reich may otherwise come into suspicion of interfering in the political relationships of Palestine."[12]

With zero cooperation from the German government and no possibility of joining the Nazi Party, Arabs decided to form their own Fascist and Nazi parties. If they could not join them, they would imitate them. In April 1933, Joseph Francis, editor of *Falastin* and correspondent for three other Arab newspapers, approached German Consul Wolff in Jerusalem offering "the felicitations and admiration of the youth of Palestine." Francis requested German "guidance on how to create a Fascist Party of Palestine, with the goal of destroying the Jewish Communist movement which is devastating Palestine." Consul Wolff avoided any specific response. Francis came back in June 1933 and insisted that his request obtain a copy of Nazi Party bylaws be forwarded to senior Reich officials. If he didn't get a positive response, Francis suggested, he would contact Italian Fascists and use their bylaws—although he preferred the German bylaws.[13]

Wolff again refused to comply. In a memo headlined "Planned Establishment of a National Socialist Arab Party," Wolff told Berlin, "The slightest easily imaginable indiscretion could endanger or even lose me the necessary and requisite trust of the Mandate government." He added, "Promoting the activist Nationalist Arab tendencies would be seen as directly counter to their [the Mandate's] political objectives." The German Foreign Ministry in Berlin supported Wolff's refusal to cooperate. In a dispatch copied to several embassies, Berlin instructed, "All official German representatives will refrain from any foreign policy decisions behind the circles of acquaintance associated with Francis, for one because it is not clear what paths the planned movement intends to strike out upon."[14]

The same enthusiastic approach and stony response played out in other Arab capitals. In August 1933, the German envoy in Baghdad was contacted by the publisher of the newspaper *Istiqlal* as well as some Arab legislators. They "have informed me that they have been contemplating forming a National Socialist Party emulating that of Germany. They have asked me to provide them materials about the German National Socialist Party, and in particular the party planks and if possible the bylaws in either English or French." Activist Arab editor Amir Arslan, who headed up *La Nation Arabe*, circulated both in Geneva and in Syria, was repeatedly rebuffed in his efforts to schedule a meeting with Hitler or secure any assistance.[15]

Ultimately, Arabs did create numerous Nazi-style or Fascist parties without assistance. For example, in Lebanon, the Syrian National Socialist Party began in earnest in late 1933 just as Hitler was preparing for the crucial election that propelled him to power a few months later. Its founder, Antun Sa'adah, was broadly considered a Nazi ideologue. The Syrian National Socialist Party began as a secret society mixing populism, socialism, and fascism; the organization's moniker evolved through various permutations until it formally adopted the name Syrian National Socialist Party. Its members wore green shirts and its official banner was emblazoned with a giant red swirl version of the swastika that was never abandoned. In Cairo, the Young Egypt Society emerged as the local Nazi clone.[16] Most of these Arab National Socialist parties merely cherry-picked the appealing fragments of genuine Nazi ideology. The mutated credo that emerged combined pan-Arab Nationalistic fervor with Jew hatred and anti-colonial sentiment. But Arab national socialists never assimilated the racial aspects of Nazism that targeted them along with the rest of the *untermenschen*.

Failing to grasp the anti-Semitic fundamental of Nazism allowed Arab groups to celebrate the Hitler ethic not only in cloned organizations but also in music. The German anthem, *Deutschland über alles*, was mimicked in various Arab national songs. In Syria, for example, a nationalist party song, sung to the tune of *Deutschland über alles*, culminated with the Arabic phrase, "Syria, Syria above all."[17]

Among the first translations of Hitler's *Mein Kampf* was a serialized version that appeared in the newspaper *al-Alam al-Arab* beginning in October 1933. Others would quickly follow, such as the installment series in the Beirut newspaper *al-Nida*, that is, *The Call*, which circulated in Lebanon, Iraq, Transjordan, Palestine, and elsewhere in the Middle East. The Baghdad newspaper premiered their *Mein Kampf* series with the following introduction: "Hitlerism (*al-hitlariyya*) is a movement which preoccupies the world nowadays … The world and our country in particular should be aware of the fundamental aims of this movement. We cannot find anyone better qualified to explain them than its founder and herald, Adolf Hitler, the present leader of Germany. We are translating for our readers the book which he wrote … This book tells the wonderful story of the life of a great adventurer, the great German leader who rose from being a simple soldier to the leadership of a whole nation, one of the most culturally and scientifically developed nations in the world … We have endeavored to make this translation, which we now present to the reader, as close to the original as possible. We hope that it will find the reception it deserves."[18]

All Arab translations of *Mein Kampf* omitted the pivotal anti-Semitic nature of Hitler's screed. The German ambassador to Iraq was aware that the excerpts published in the Baghdad newspaper were popular but feared the Arab populace might become resentful if the true racial aspects were translated. In efforts to assist in a cleaned-up translation, the ambassador told the Ministry of Propaganda, "The legation should influence the translator to modify the treatment of the racial question in the book *Mein Kampf* to take into account the mentality and sensitivity of the racially conscious Arabs, without, however, distorting the original text. These questions should be addressed and cleared up before the relevant passages go to the press."[19]

Additionally, the ambassador reported to the German Foreign Office, "I have discussed the question of modifying those sections of the book that deal with the racial question and the mentality and sensitivity of racially conscious Arabs with Selim Hassoon, the publisher of the *al-'Alam al-'Arab*. He is willing to undertake all proposed modifications prior to printing the Arab translation. Therefore, I would like to propose the following modifications to the English edition of the book: instead of "anti-Semitic" on page 31 and 58: "anti-Jewish." The same alteration was suggested a reference to "anti-Semitism" on page 59.[20]

While Arabs were busy trying to become Nazis, events in Berlin were about to greatly magnify their problems in Palestine.

Several complicated economic dynamics came together in the first months of the Hitler regime that changed everything. Quickly, just weeks after *der Führer* came to power, the long-promised anti-Jewish program was put into law. The Nazis prepared to implement the Aryan paragraph of their platform with special decrees and legislation beginning April 7, 1933, that would sharply restrict or oust Jews from all facets of the German economy. Doctors, lawyers, accountants, professors, students, business executives, and many others would be forcibly dismissed from their positions once identified as Jewish or even part-Jewish.[21]

German Jewry was admittedly the most assimilated, established, and anti-Zionist Jewish population in Europe. Nearly all identified themselves as Germans first and Jewish a distant second. Of the approximately 550,000 Jews in Germany who were emancipated in 1871, by 1930, roughly 60,000 were either apostates, children raised without Jewish identity in a mixed marriage, or Jews who had simply drifted away. Even those consciously remaining within organized Jewish "communities" neglected their remnant Jewish identity. The Jews of twentieth-century Germany, like their Christian neighbors, embraced national identity far more than religious identity. In the minds of German Jews, they were "101 percent" German, first and foremost.[22]

Under the new Reich, all Germans with any trace of Jewish ancestry were about to be systematically pauperized. Germany had announced a comprehensive, interlocking sequence of census, registration, and data-mining programs that would identify every Jew. Unbeknownst to the average person, that special identification process would be designed and engineered by America's information powerhouse, IBM senior management in New York and Germany, including company president Thomas J. Watson. The company worked behind the scenes to bring Hitler's promises to life with great velocity and precision.[23]

The policy pogrom was the quietest form of the persecution. What began as a private campaign of violence against Jews was now, under Hitler, the unofficial policy of the day. Jews were murdered in their homes, daughters were raped before parents' eyes, rabbis were humiliated in the street, prominent leaders were found floating in the canals and rivers. As early as the first days after Hitler's surprise appointment as interim chancellor, the message was indeed clear to those who would pay attention: The Jews of Germany were facing an hourglass, and time was slipping away.[24] The Jews of the world and others of conscience, upon learning of Hitler's publicly announced plans and seeing the well-publicized mayhem on the ground, immediately recoiled in protest and anger. At a time when the world was suffering a debilitating Depression, at a time when Hitler's wherewithal depended upon providing jobs to millions of out-of-work Germans, at a time when the shredded Reich economy depended upon global exports to survive, the Jews of the world promised to fight Hitler with the one weapon Hitler feared: a Jewish boycott. Impervious to protest, steeled against diplomatic reproach, solipsistic in his own sense of a thousand-year destiny, Hitler did fear one thing: Jewish economic war. The entire Nazi belief system was built upon the fabricated phantasm that Jews operated an international monetary conspiracy capable of igniting wars, triggering depressions, and causing economic disaster.[25]

Indeed, a Jewish boycott had crumpled the defiance of Hitler's own personal hero, Henry Ford. The temperamental auto magnate had been forced to issue a retraction and apology for disseminating the fictitious *Protocols of the Elders of Zion* and circulating the virulently anti-Semitic *Dearborn Independent* during the 1920s. Yet Ford was the man the Nazi party and *der Führer* himself had lionized as the quintessential fighter of the so-called Jewish economic conspiracy. Hitler had once told reporters in Germany that "the struggle of international Jewish finance against Ford ... has only strengthened [Nazi] sympathies ... for Ford." In the first edition of *Mein Kampf* in 1925, Hitler had declared that "only a single great man, Ford," was able to stand up to Jewish economic power. Ford's unexpected surrender was so powerful a loss to Hitler's movement that the Nazis preferred to gloss over the retraction as a mere political expediency. The party continued printing *"The International Jew* by Heinrich Ford." Nonetheless, the tribute to Ford in *Mein Kampf* was changed in its second edition. The words "only a single great man, Ford," were replaced with the phrase "only a very few."[26]

Now, as Hitler's promises were about to be made real, Jewish groups abroad , especially in New York, organized a fast-moving, international coalition of labor unions, Catholic clerics, Protestant groups, political allies, and inter-faith protestors of all types to slap an ironclad boycott on any product or service of German origin. The diplomatic demands, protest marches, pickets, and front-page stories began quickly; and by mid-March 1933, the Jewish War Veterans—the men who had recently fought Germany in the trenches of

Europe during the last war—became the first to proclaim a public boycott. It was done in accordance with their charter: "To combat the sources of bigotry and darkness; wherever originating and whatever their target; to uphold the fair name of the Jew and fight his battle wherever unjustly assailed."[27]

History thus records that in an era distinguished by appeasement, the Jewish War Veterans (JWV) were the very first, anywhere in the world, to declare openly their organized resistance to the Nazi regime. They had fought Germany once and would fight again. This small association of ex-warriors, mostly men of little finesse and even less pretense, would not wait for the polished gentlemen of the main Jewish organizations for permission to fight back.

On March 13, 1933, hundreds of Jewish War Veterans strapped on their uniforms, shouldered their stars and stripes in carrier holsters, and hoisted hand-drawn placards to march in formation demanding a boycott of all things German. In a mile-long parade, cheered by thousands of bystanders ten deep and backed up onto the stoops, the JWV and cadres of local personalities, led by trombones and tubas, marched to City Hall in Manhattan protesting Hitler and vowing to fight back.[28]

Trombones and tubas were just the warning shots. The boycott idea and backlash spread across the world like fission. Protest and boycott committees formed in England, France, Czechoslovakia, and Poland as well as Latin America and Asia. Some joined to protest fascism, some to defend the Jews, some to stand up for civilization, and some just to steer lucrative German contracts in toys, pharmaceuticals, and steel to their countries during depression days. But every boycott placard, every radio report, and every picket sign sent a jolt through the Reich directly to the top.[29]

Boycotts are never measured in dollars and cents or reichsmarks and pfennigs. They are measured in ergs of fear.

Boycott fervor was spreading. In Warsaw, a coalition of political, commercial, and religious organizations began debating whether all of Poland should follow the lead of the Vilna Jews and the American Jewish War Veterans, who had already declared a boycott. Boycott movements were also fast developing in Lithuania, France, Holland, Great Britain, and in European circles in Egypt.[30]

Early results were beginning to show. German steamship lines in New York, which were valuable foreign-currency earners for the Reich, reported a rash of canceled bookings. One German vessel, the *Europa*, lost twenty-five passengers just before sailing; all of them transferred to the U.S. flagged *Manhattan*, citing their displeasure with the Hitler regime. British trade unionists and Labour party leaders began posting BOYCOTT GERMAN GOODS notices throughout London, especially the East End. One Jewish-owned firm immediately cancelled orders for £14,000 of German goods, and publicly resubmitted the orders to American suppliers.[31]

As the first anti-Nazi boycott rumblings were heard in Germany, Adolf Hitler was trying to emphasize Germany's desire for unhampered trade relations. In a major speech to the Reichstag on March 23, 1933, upon receiving his new dictatorial powers, *der Führer* declared: "We need contact with the outside world, and our foreign markets furnish a livelihood for millions of our fellow citizens." The German government followed up Hitler's speech with an immediate appeal to foreign correspondents whose newspapers were publicizing boycott activities. If the economic boycott against Germany were to be executed, "as is agitated by certain American circles," the Reich statement asked, how "is the question of private [international] debts to be regulated properly?"[32]

By the next day, March 24, Reich leaders realized that boycott agitation was accelerating, especially in Great Britain. Placards proclaiming BOYCOTT GERMAN GOODS spread infectiously throughout London, and now dangled in the windows of the most exclusive West End shops. Automobiles bedecked with boycott banners slowly cruised through the retail districts, alerting shoppers. Everywhere, store signs warned German salesmen not to enter. British Catholics had been urged by the Archbishop of Liverpool to join the protest. London's *Daily Herald* carried an interview with a prominent Jewish leader who admitted, "The [Jewish] leaders are hanging back," but the Jewish people are "forcing its leaders on." Already the boycott had damaged "hundreds of thousands of pounds worth of German trade."[33]

The volume of German goods sold abroad was already dangerously low. Germany simply could not stand further export reductions. By March 24, enough consular dispatches had been received in Berlin to paint a clear picture. The rudimentary boycott was indeed snowballing, apparently building to a climax, when it would be globally proclaimed by at least one of the major Jewish organizations, the American Jewish Congress. The American Jewish Congress, led by firebrand Dr. Stephen S. Wise, was the only representative Jewish organization in the country, boasting thousands of members. Many American Jewish Congress members were militant, working class, and Eastern European. Congress men and women had no use for the careful conference room diplomacy practiced by the two more established Jewish organizations, B'nai B'rith and the American Jewish Committee. Both the Committee and B'nai B'rith were heavily German Jewish, and fearful of provoking the Hitler regime against their relatives in the Reich. Rabbi Wise was a different breed—a passionate public speaker, a rabble-rouser, a man of the Jewish masses, and media savvy. With abundant political and interfaith connections, Wise intended to place German atrocities front and center.[34]

Step one would be a loud, vituperative million-man protest rally, epicentered at Madison Square Garden, to be coordinated with hundreds of simultaneous rallies throughout America and overseas. It would be a massive global reaction to Hitler's regime and its program of atrocities and Jewish persecution. The word *boycott* was on everyone's lips. Would it be hinted at, sporadic, or openly declared as an organized international campaign? Would a world movement emerge to make Germany crack that winter by crushing the Hitler re-employment scheme before it ever had a chance? The date of the meeting was March 27, 1933.[35]

Nazi leadership reacted to the planned March 27 Madison Square Garden event with paranoia and militancy. Hermann Goering, Prussian minister of the interior and president of the Reichstag, summoned the heads of Germany's three major Jewish organizations: Julius Brodnitz, chairman of the Central Verein, Dr. Max Naumann of the fiercely patriotic Union of National German Jews, and Heinrich Stahl, president of the Berlin Jewish Community. They were to appear in Goering's office at noon the next day, Saturday, March 25.[36]

The German Zionists had not been invited. Goering despised the Zionists, as did most Nazis. True, the National Socialists hoped to use Zionism to rid Germany—indeed Europe—of its Jews. But they also distrusted Zionism as one of the serpentine heads of "international Jewry." Zionism and the establishment of a Jewish State, in the Nazi view, were the ultimate goals of the Jewish conspiracy. Moreover, the Nazis knew that the German Zionist movement did not really represent German Jewry. Zionist groups themselves estimated their own strength at only one or two percent of the country's Jews.[37]

The Zionist concept was anathema to the overwhelming majority of Germany's Jews, who considered themselves assimilated, loyal Germans. Zionism was equally repugnant to orthodox German Jews, who spurned Jewish sovereignty in the Holy Land on religious grounds, believing that only the Jewish Messiah could reinstate the Kingdom of the Jews. In 1933, despite growth in Palestine, Zionism in Germany was a mere Jewish fringe movement.[38] So, of course they were excluded from the meeting.

Though not invited, the German Zionist Federation (ZVfD) did learn of the summit, just a few hours before the meeting. ZVfD official Martin Rosenbluth and Federation president Kurt Blumenfeld were mystified about the purpose of the conference, but both men concluded that German Zionism must be present. After frantic telephoning, a Reich contact succeeded in adding Blumenfeld's name to the invitation list.[39]

At about noon, March 25, the two Zionists entered the anteroom outside Goering's private office. The three other Jewish leaders were surprised to see them walk in. Brodnitz of the Centralverein, tried to be cordial and make small talk. But staunchly anti-Zionist Naumann of the Union of National

German Jews angrily lashed out at Rosenbluth. Why, demanded Naumann, should Zionists have any right to attend a meeting between the government and "the legitimate representatives of the German Jews?" Rosenbluth reacted with his own barbed rhetoric, and within moments, the two leaders were trading denigrations. The verbal fight ended only when a uniformed Goering aide entered the room.[40]

Hermann Goering was ready to see them, announced the aide, if they would follow him. All five Jewish leaders began walking into the inner office, but the aide stopped Rosenbluth, asserting that Blumenfeld was the only Zionist on the official list.[41]

As Naumann, Brodnitz, Stahl, and Blumenfeld entered the minister's office, they saw Goering standing in the middle of the room dressed in his Storm Trooper's uniform, thus making clear his dual capacity as government minister and Nazi party leader. In the beginning, decorum was observed. The uniformed aide formally introduced each Jewish leader by name and organization. But the formalities ended there. The men were not invited to be seated.[42]

It was plain that, unlike a few previous Jewish conferences in which Goering had politely apologized to Jewish leaders for transgressions of Nazi zealots, this would not be a friendly encounter. Goering immediately ripped into the Jewish leaders, accusing them of responsibility for the malicious and treasonable atrocity headlines in the English and American press. The Jewish leaders, trying to hold their ground, denied any knowledge of the newspaper articles.[43]

Goering theatrically snapped his fingers. The uniformed aide appeared. He was instructed to fetch the clippings. Once Goering had them in hand, he began reading them aloud, growing angrier with each paragraph. In a frenzied shout he warned, "Unless you put a stop to these libelous accusations immediately, I shall no longer be able to vouch for the safety of the German Jews!"[44]

The Jewish leaders attempted to downplay the newspaper accounts. But Goering would not hear any explanations. He ordered them to go to London immediately to convince the British Jews—and from there on to New York to tell the American Jews—that Jews in Germany were not experiencing physical mistreatment. He demanded they tell Jewish leaders that the newspaper stories were despicable lies.[45]

Goering then turned to his main worry, the upcoming day of protest and the giant Madison Square Garden rally. Goering cited the dangers of such a rally to Germany's position. With deadly seriousness, he gave the Jewish leaders his prime directive: "The most important thing is for you to make sure that the protest meeting called in New York by Dr. Stephen S. Wise is canceled. That assembly must not take place. Dr. Wise is one of our most dangerous and unscrupulous enemies."[46]

The three Jewish leaders in Goering's office, desperate to disown any supposed influence over Jewish actions in Great Britain or America, denied there would be any usefulness to their visiting London or New York. Speaking carefully, Brodnitz assured Goering that the Centralverein maintained absolutely no connections with overseas Jewish organizations. Brodnitz dared not mention that Centralverein vice-president Ernest Wallach was already in America trying to dissuade the American Jewish Congress. It was important for the German Jewish leaders to explicitly deny any relationship with Jews in other countries—if only to refute the Nazi accusation of an international Jewish conspiracy.[47]

But then Blumenfeld stepped forward on behalf of the Zionists, declaring that the German Zionist Federation was uniquely capable of conferring with Jewish leaders in other countries, since German Zionists were indeed affiliated with a worldwide organization.[48]

It was as though a giant bell had rung.

Once uttered, the words forever changed the relationship between the Nazis and the Zionists. It was suddenly clear that the Jewish group the Reich had been ignoring was, in fact, the one it should be negotiating with in its efforts to combat the Jewish presence in Germany. After all, both Nazis and Zionists agreed that Jews did not belong in Germany.

Blumenfeld quickly added that even if a Zionist representative did journey to London, there was no chance of exerting any influence over American or British Jewry unless the Zionists had permission to tell "the full truth."[49]

Goering exploded, shouting, "What is there to tell? You know perfectly well there has been no change in the situation of the Jews, and that nothing untoward has happened to them." Naumann bravely contradicted the shouting Goering, declaring that Goering "must not be well informed" if he was unaware of the radical change in the physical safety of Jews in Germany. The violence was everywhere for all to see, and Naumann boldly recited case after case of brutality against Jews, ranging from manhandlings to vicious beatings and deaths. He then produced a clipping of his own from a Nazi newspaper which included a photograph of Jews being forced to wash the streets in Chemnitz. Goering's tirade was abruptly halted by the clip. He passed over the Jewish evidence almost in embarrassment.[50]

Then, in a complete about-face, Goering declared he did not object to the facts being told to American and British Jewish organizations, as long as those foreign Jewish organizations would immediately call a halt to the "vicious atrocity propaganda." Tiring of the meeting, Goering demanded that whichever of them went to London was unimportant to him—so long as a delegation left Berlin by the next day and stopped Rabbi Wise's March 27 mass rally.[51]

An important, towering truth was emerging in Germany and perhaps elsewhere in Europe. The Zionists—men who had built their histories saving the remnant of decimated Jewish communities—saw something terrible coming. The establishment Jews of Germany refused to believe their entrenched position would be obliterated. But the Zionists were realists who recalled the precedents of a generation earlier when Herzl hurried directly to the greatest living enemy of Jews, Czar Nicholas, to negotiate their orderly exit after Kishinev. With Passover approaching, the Zionists were also mindful that the very first such negotiation was undertaken by Moses, who in his turn had gone to Pharaoh and demanded "Let my People Go."

That March 1933, multitudes of Jews in America, England and elsewhere, pre-occupied with the Hitler takeover, were also thinking of Passover—not of propositions but of plagues. Boycott fervor and anti-German protest was in the air. This was now a real live test of relief versus rescue in the heart of modern Europe with the Nazis holding the deciding vote over the fate of the Jews.

The two traditional major Jewish American organizations, that is, the American Jewish Committee and B'nai B'rith, were esteemed, if self-appointed, committees headed by polished leaders. But they were encumbered by relatives in Germany who stood squarely in the line of fire. These major Jewish groups were determined to pursue the path of appeasement with the Reich. They deluged the Jewish communal structure generally, the American Jewish Congress as an organization, and Rabbi Wise personally, demanding he cancel or moderate any Madison Square Center protest rally. Urgent messages alternately denying the Hitler program, pleading for restraint, and warning of Nazi retaliation against innocent German Jews burned across the telegraph and telephone lines. Messages piled high on Wise's desk. The Zionists joined their co-religionists in counseling against the rally, harder for Wise—one of the world's leading Zionist activists—to dismiss.[52]

But the passionate arguments against the rally did not work. Knowing how effective Jewish boycotts had been in the past—and with battle scars still fresh from persecution in Poland and Russia, the American Jewish Congress and Wise held their ground. Timidity was not in their vocabulary.[53]

Wise was a leader who thrived on controversy and the painful pursuit of his beliefs, no matter how bitter the consequences. He was a man who would sever a lifelong friendship because of a loose comment or cut himself off from his own people rather than retract a statement he believed to be true. And he was accustomed to rallying thousands in bitter, frequently violent battles to achieve a lasting principle.[54]

Yet, as the hour pulled closer for the Madison Square rally, even Wise experienced indecision. He weighed the moral imperative of standing up to Hitler against the risk of provoking the Nazis to unleash a countrywide pogrom that would leave Jews bloodied across Germany. Would the rally make a difference? Had the protest gone far enough—or was it only starting? Would delay merely provide the Third Reich with the breathing time it needed to organize its destruction of the Jews?[55]

Stephen S. Wise, who had stood alone on any issue, fought alone on any battle, could not make this decision alone.

On the morning of March 27, Rabbi Wise telephoned the one man in America whose judgment he valued perhaps more than his own—his dearest friend, Supreme Court Justice Louis Brandeis. Brandeis was also one of America's leading Zionist personages. The two men spoke briefly, and Wise put it to his friend simply. Do it or not? Brandeis answered, "Go ahead and make the protest as good as you can." Wise hung up. His decision was now final.[56]

*       *       *       *

Noon, March 27, 1933. Business in New York stopped.[57]

The rally didn't start until after 8:00 p.m., but by 2:30 p.m. on March 27, 1933, a crowd was already waiting outside Madison Square Garden. Once the doors were unlocked, a flow of people began. It continued for hours. By 5:30, traffic snarled as thousands more jammed the streets around Madison Square. People were backed all the way down the subway stairs. Six hundred policemen formed a blue-coat chain along the crosswalks just to allow pedestrians to pass.[58]

Suddenly, in the midst of the many, came a distant sound of drums and fifes that added a distinctly American excitement to the scene. Those people nearest the Garden probably could not see the approaching formation, even as the marching staccato became louder and closer. But then, off on a side street, a drum and bugle corps appeared, the Jewish War Veterans stepping proudly, with flying banners denouncing the Third Reich.[59]

By plan, the vets were to enter the Garden in a dramatic flourish. But as the streets became thicker, the marchers could not move. Up against barriers of mounted policemen, the veterans marched in place, waiting for an opening, their skirls and drumbeats continuing, a cadence for the entire crowd.[60]

Inevitably the streets became chaotic as protesters tried to force through the doors of the Garden. But the aisles and balconies and lobbies of Madison Square Garden were already filled.[61]

Orders went out. The doors were slammed shut with 20,000 inside. But the crowds outside demanded entry and the police started to react. Superior officers rushed in to calm the frenzy. Public loudspeakers were hastily mounted to control an estimated 35,000 anxious citizens crammed into the streets around the Garden. Pleas by police and protest marshals diverted some of the thousands to a second *ad hoc* rally at nearby Columbus Circle. It wasn't enough. More overflow rallies were frantically set up along the nearby intersections.[62]

New York had never seen anything like it.

Americans of all persuasions and descents seemed united against Adolf Hitler, and they wanted their country and the world to do something about it. Decades later, America and American Jewry would be falsely accused of apathy and inaction. But on March 27, 1933, the citizens of the United States were anything but apathetic.[63]

Fifty-five thousand were gathered in and around Madison Square Garden. Supportive rallies were at that moment waiting in Chicago, Washington, San Francisco, Houston, and about seventy other American cities. At each supportive rally, thousands huddled around loudspeakers waiting for the Garden event, which would be broadcast live via radio relay to 200 additional cities across the country. At least one million Jews were participating nationwide. Perhaps another million Americans of non-Jewish heritage stood with them.[64]

Hundreds of thousands more were waiting in Europe. American Jewish Congress president Bernard Deutsch had sent out last minute cables to Jewish protest leaders in Latvia, Czechoslovakia, and elsewhere throughout the Continent. Anti-Reich activists across the Atlantic had agreed to hold their protests in abeyance until signaled from New York. When the go-ahead was received, plans were speedily put into effect.[65]

Poland was typical. A national day of fasting was authorized by rabbinical bodies. The Warsaw Stock Exchange shut down early. Poland's government even released an order dissolving a large portion of the Polish Hitlerites. Anti-Hitler parades and meetings were granted approval, even as police banned counter demonstrations by Nazi sympathizers.[66]

In New York, inside the Garden itself, the guest speakers were delayed. People were shouting, feet were stamping, chairs were banging. The din was equaled outside, where loudspeakers pleaded for order as the program organizers tried to start.[67]

Abruptly, in the midst of the tumult, when it seemed the crowd would wait no longer, an 80-year-old Orthodox rabbi, M. S. Margolies, feebly approached the lectern and touched the microphone. The audience came to a sudden silence. The hush spread outside as people strained to hear. Rabbi Margolies chanted a plaintive Hebraic prayer of chilling power, his voice beseeching God in the name of humanity that the persecutions in Germany stop. By radio relay, the chant was heard around the world.[68]

Among the first to speak was Alfred E. Smith, former New York governor and popular Catholic figure. Smith, in his plain-folks style, declared that of all the times he had addressed the public in Madison Square Garden, no rally could give him greater satisfaction because the opportunity to stand up against bigotry was both a duty and a right. He admitted there had been great pressures to keep him from speaking: "I got all kinds of telegrams ... telling me there wasn't any reason for a meeting, that nothing had taken place [in Germany], that we wanted to avoid the possibility of hysteria at a time like this. Well, all I can say about that is ... drag it out into the open sunlight and give it the same treatment that we gave the Ku Klux Klan ... It don't make any difference to me whether it is a brown shirt or a night shirt." The crowd cheered its approval repeatedly as Smith used down-home lingo, puns, and sarcasm to ridicule *der Führer* and his Storm Troopers. But before Smith finished, he became stern and in sober tones warned the German nation not to descend into a barbaric war against the Jews.[69]

Catholic Bishop John J. Dunn of the Archdiocese of New York, because of State Department and American Jewish Committee assurances, had reneged on his promise to appear. But other clergymen, including Bishop Francis T. McConnell, refused to back down. Bishop McConnell warned, "People say, 'Why not let Germany run things to suit herself?' My friends, that is just the quickest way to plunge the world into war again. If there is no protest at all against so completely out-of-date a thing as the anti-Semitic movement ... [then] after a while ... the situation becomes intolerable and then we resort to force." He added that even if persecutions in Germany temporarily ceased, anti-Nazi rallies and protest actions must continue until the Nazis were out of power.[70]

The applause and cheers for Bishop McConnell's words were followed by a procession of politicians and clergymen, each likewise committing his supporters to the struggle against Hitlerism. Then the crowd heard from the most experienced economic battle group in America—organized labor.[71]

William Green, president of the American Federation of Labor, pledged the active involvement of 3 million American unionists. "I come tonight in the name of Labor," Green declared, "protesting in its sacred name against the atrocities ... perpetrated upon the Jewish population of Germany. I transmit to the ... German trade unions, the masses of the people, the hosts of labor in Germany, and to the Jewish people an expression of sympathy ... We pledge to them our moral and economic support ... [to] do all that lies within our power" to end "the campaign of persecution against the Jewish people in Germany."[72]

Labor's involvement could make any boycott almost totally effective, especially if longshoremen refused to offload German merchandise at the docks. So Green's words were powerful threats. "We will not remain passive and unconcerned when the relatives, families, and brethren of the Jewish members of our great organization are being persecuted and oppressed," Green promised.[73]

Other eminent figures continued to enthrall the rally, including crusading minister John Haynes Holmes, New York Senator Robert Wagner, *Der Tog* editor Samuel Margoshes, Joseph Tenenbaum of the American Jewish Congress, and Chaim Greenberg of the Labor Zionists. Many more wishing to address the meeting could not and sent telegrams instead: the Speaker of the U.S. House of Representatives, the Senate majority leader, the governors of Illinois, Oregon, and Iowa, as well as scores of civic, social, commercial, labor, fraternal, and religious organizations. All condemned the Third Reich in explicit language and expressed solidarity with the movement to overturn Hitler.[74]

The protest rally received such vocal support that the thousands ignored the nonappearance of the American Jewish Committee and B'nai B'rith. Nor did they notice the absence of any message from the one man the nation expected to sympathize: President Roosevelt.[75]

Then, with the audience primed and anxious, Rabbi Stephen S. Wise stepped forward to the most thunderous ovation he had ever received. After many attempts to speak, the crowd finally quieted, and Dr. Wise began. He surprised many by discarding some of the dramatic techniques he often employed. At first, he spoke in conciliatory tones, in the hopes of communicating with the people in Germany, "Not out of the bitterness of anger, but out of the ... spirit of compassion do we speak tonight ... We are not against Germany ... We are the friends of and believers in Germany—Germany at its highest, Germany at its truest, the German nation at its noblest."[76]

The other speakers had threatened and ridiculed the Nazis. Wise was showing the route away from conflict: cessation of anti-Jewish policy. He made it clear that even that demand was not an attempt to interfere with Germany's domestic affairs, but simply an insistence upon fundamental human rights or, as he called them, the "axioms of civilizations." At first, his manner was calm, steady.[77]

But then he began to build. "To those leaders of Germany who declare that the present situation in Germany is a local German question, we call attention to the words of Abraham Lincoln. Defenders of slavery urged and excused slavery on the ground that it was local. Lincoln's answer was slavery is local but freedom is national!" The crowd burst into excited approval. Wise kept building, as he demanded "the immediate cessation of anti-Semitic activities and propaganda in Germany, including an end to the racial discrimination against and economic exclusion of Jews from the life of Germany ... the human rights of Jews must be safeguarded ... Whatever be the threat of reprisal, none of these [demands] can be withdrawn or altered or moderated."[78]

Turning to Jewish leaders in Germany and their advocates in America,

Wise discounted their pleas for an end to the protest as "panic and terror" from those who had failed to fight Nazism before the NSDAP came to power.[79]

He vowed the anti-Hitler protest would escalate, even if pseudo-ameliorations appeared: "Even if life and human rights are to be safeguarded, there must not be a substitution of the status of helotry [serfdom] for violence. Such substitution will not satisfy us"—the throng interrupted with cheers of encouragement—"nor satisfy the aroused conscience of humankind." The crowd offered their own spontaneous punctuation as Wise declared, "Every form of economic discrimination is a form of violence. Every racial exclusion is violence. To say that there will be no pogroms is not enough. A dry and bloodless economic pogrom remains violence and force."[80]

Above the cheering, he warned the Third Reich, "And if things are to be worse because of our protest, if there are to be new penalties and new reprisals in Germany ... then humbly and sorrowfully we bow our heads in the presence of the tragic fate that threatens." But, "Hear the word of a great English statesman: 'Providence would deal good or ill fortune to nations according as they dealt well or ill by the Jews.' This is not a warning, but a prophecy!"[81]

Rabbi Stephen Wise paused to speak the final words of his oration. The crowd hushed. "To this mighty protest Germany cannot fail to give heed and to answer." Then his sweeping hand pointed dramatically to the members of the audience and in a firm voice said, "I ask *you* by rising to signify to us—and to all the world—that you agree with us in our stand to bring about justice ... from Germany to the Jew."[82]

In a thunderous motion, 20,000 Americans rose as one to their feet. The immense noise of the act and the rising voices created a sound that must have seemed like a massive sleeping animal suddenly awakening. That moment of solidarity was shared by the 20,000 in Madison Square Garden, the 35,000 more standing outside the Garden, a million others in supportive rallies in other cities, and millions more in their homes hearing the protest live on radio throughout America and in thirteen nations.[83]

The world was warned. Germany was on notice.

Rabbi Wise stood down from the podium, ready to accept whatever was Germany's response to his plea, challenge, and warning. Without question, the struggle against Hitler was now in the open.

*    *    *    *

Now, as the maelstrom of anti-Nazi protest confronted the realistic options on the ground for rescuing German Jews, several extraordinarily complex factors came together simultaneously in London, New York, Berlin, and Jerusalem. They all involved money.

First, unlike many, the Zionists believed the well-organized Nazis when they insisted they would dismantle, pauperize, and expel the Jewish community. By March 10, 1933, concentration camps, such as one at Dachau, had already been established for enemies of the state. These were no secret and the openings were accompanied by newsreel and headline fanfare. Hitler Youth were empowered to make Jews get on their hands and knees to wash the streets and pavements with toothbrushes and such incidents were publicized worldwide. Targeted vandalism, beatings, and murder of Jews were daily occurrences across Germany.[84] Members of the petrified Jewish establishment tried to hide their Jewish roots, convert to Christianity, or plead loyalty to the state, even a fascist state. None of it mattered. The pogrom-hardened Zionists understood this.

The rhythmic rallying call of the Nazis in their ever-present demonstrations was *Juden! Raus! Juden! Raus! Juden! Raus!* In English it meant *Jews! Out! Jews! Out! Jews! Out!*

Out. But to where?

The world was in a blistering Depression with millions out of work. Penniless German Jewish refugees were already flooding the train depots, steamship ports, and airplane terminals of the world. With currency restrictions, confiscatory Reich flight taxes, and Nazi prohibitions forbidding the removal of foreign currency or assets, German Jews in too many instances arrived in safe havens around the world clutching little more than their suitcases, twine-tied packs of their most treasured books, and the remnant shards of their pride. These refugees were not stereotypical unskilled Russian and Polish *shtetl* dwellers. Germany's fleeing Jews were among the country's elite, the finest musicians, attorneys, professors, and scientists. Yet, unless they were among the special few businessmen who could smuggle out significant assets, many German Jewish refugee men possessed only the suits on their backs, the women their finest travel dress, and the children a favorite doll. Refugee arrivals not only evoked compassion, but alarm for the economic burden they represented. In consequence, the gates of Jewish refuge would soon close in the United States, Europe, and elsewhere.

Nor did the Nazis want Jews relocating to New York, London, or Paris, or the other "centers of Jewish conspiracy" where they could join the chorus of anti-Reich protest and boycott. Berlin wanted her Jews expelled to far-off Palestine where they could be contained, that is, penned up. That policy was more than a political strategy; it was also a philosophical imperative. Nazis believed in the concept of *volk* or ethnic peoples, and a national racial hierarchy. Germany, in this mindset, ruled at the top. As for Jews, they belonged in Palestine first and foremost as that was their ancestral land.[85]

Palestine was rising as the top expulsion site—sort of a distant reservation where, in the Nazi view, Jews and their contamination could be quarantined—and dealt with later. The Palestine destination formed the second dynamic of an emerging reality.

The soon-to-be dwindling mass of a half million German Jews would literally need to be convinced it was time to quit Europe and transplant their middle class Jewish society to Palestine. The alternative was decimation. But Palestine lacked the infrastructure to abruptly absorb tens of thousands of Jews. Housing, roads, schools, and modern water facilities—where would that come from? Everything would need to be created out of dune, swamp, scrub, and rocky hillside. Moreover, few of Germany's middle class Jews could even guess how to adapt to the harsh desert conditions of Jewish Palestine, complete with its spartan utilitarian box housing. Money was needed. Where would that money come from, especially in a Depression—especially if German Jewry were prohibited from removing assets? Undeveloped Palestine comprised the third emerging dynamic.[86]

Further complicating the solution were British immigration barriers in place by 1933, allowing just enough laborers to enter to satisfy the work market. But middle class émigrés, such as those fleeing Germany, could not enter Palestine—that is, not without presenting proof of £1000 sterling, about $5,000, a so-called Capitalist certificate. Financial immigration restriction created the fourth dynamic.[87]

Complicating every layer of the equation was Palestine's Jewish economy, which depended upon the export of Jaffa oranges. Germany was the biggest customer. It could switch its imports to Valencia oranges from Fascist Spain in a flicker. Oranges—a mainstay of Jewish Palestine—comprised the fifth side of the prism.[88]

The antithetical threads came together. German Jewry was being scheduled for systematic persecution and pauperization, which required them to get out to anywhere, and Palestine was becoming the leading candidate. But the persecuted could not enter Palestine without the all-important Capitalist certificate. Yet, fleeing German Jews were not allowed to remove assets. Moreover, foreign currency was a precious commodity in the Reich, reserved for the regime's most prioritized transactions, such as the purchase of raw materials; obtaining foreign exchange required a special license from the Reich Foreign Currency Office. How could the Jews of Germany be brought to Palestine by means of a Capitalist certificate, bypassing the British currency requirement and saving them and their livelihoods?[89]

The answer lay within the nascent, still forming anti-Hitler boycott—or subversion of it.

The Nazis needed the boycott stopped before it started so they could restore their economy and grow employment. The Reich also wanted the Jews out of Germany, preferably into Palestine, an exodus that could not be accomplished without the refugees possessing £1000 in foreign currency, a Capitalist certificate. What's more, Nazis wanted to confiscate all Jewish assets. Two choices now loomed for Jewish leadership: see the Jews of Germany vanquished, their assets stolen, and their physical destiny delivered to brutality and perhaps concentration camps—or restart their lives in Palestine. The Zionists were the only ones who could make the arrangement, the only ones willing.

As Herzl before them, and Moses before him, the Zionist leadership in Germany, Palestine, and London negotiated with the Third Reich. The esoteric plan that emerged was so complicated that few would understand it. Under the program, Jews would liquidate their possessions in Germany placing the value in a blocked account or *sperrkonto*—this account covering everything from ordinary bank deposits to the liquidated value of homes and even personal possessions such as carpets. Those *sperrkonten* would reside in a newly formed German financial institution or clearinghouse called *Palästina Treuhandstelle zur Beratung deutscher Juden GmbH*, that is, the Palestine Trust Society for Advice to German Jews, Inc. This entity was called Paltreu for short—that is, the Palestine Trust. Sale revenues of German goods from automobiles to pipes to steel would be provided as an equivalent to the deposits. The Zionists would have to sell the goods throughout Palestine and the greater Middle East. Jews would be released from Germany in accordance with the volume of Nazi goods sold. The more goods sold, the more Jews could be released for Palestine. In essence, German Jewry was held hostage to the pace of merchandise sales. Proceeds of the sale of the goods would go into special numbered accounts at a new Zionist company called Ha'avara Ltd. located at the Anglo-Palestine Bank in Tel Aviv. The countervailing funds in Ha'avara Ltd. were to be allocated to the German immigrant, thus creating a personal cash asset of $5,000 or £1000 to meet the British financial requirement to enter Palestine. German Jews could not transfer all their assets, but rather a pittance—just enough to qualify for entry into Palestine. The entire project became known as *Ha'avara*. In English, *ha'avara* means transfer.[90]

Behold: the Transfer Agreement—the most controversial pact in the 5,000-year history of the Jewish people. Zionists could not rescue Jewish lives and assets from the Nazis by selling German goods, and at the same time batter the Reich into commercial destitution by a fierce, organized boycott. Without the boycott, no Transfer would have been approved by the Reich.

By means of the Transfer Agreement, the Nazis would successfully break the well-organized, Jewish-led anti-German boycott, arrange to confiscate the assets of German Jews in an orderly fashion, systematically force Jews out of the country and into Palestine, and in the process, expand the Reich's commercial vitality. For the Zionists, they would save Jews once again and build up Palestine sufficiently to receive the prodigious waves of Jewish refugees that many expected soon from across Europe, where the poison of Nazi hatred was rapidly spreading.

It was a deal with the devil made at the point of a gun. But the Zionists had faced down guns and swords before. That is what defined them as Zionists.

However, when news leaked out, the Jewish world—and indeed the entire Zionist movement—was ripped apart like a still beating chest torn open. Just when the Jewish masses and a broad non-sectarian coalition were coming together to do economic battle with the Reich, the Zionists had quietly negotiated a broad commercial pact that hinged on sales of those very same Nazi goods. Molten Jewish and Zionist acrimony erupted—party against party, faction against faction, brother against brother. Was this deal a betrayal or a pragmatic rescue? Wild accusations flew back and forth, and the brilliant head of the Jewish Agency's political department, who had engineered the complex agreement, Chaim Arlosoroff, was assassinated on the beach north of Tel Aviv just two days after returning from negotiations in Germany. Revisionist Zionists were tried and found guilty of the crime, a conviction they never agreed to accept.[91]

Despite continued uproar—muffled, mumbled, or, in many cases, shrieked—at meetings and on the front pages of Yiddish language newspapers, the Zionists continued their risky negotiation with Nazi currency officials during that summer of 1933.[92]

Finally, it all came to fruition on the afternoon of August 7, 1933. The Zionist delegation arrived at 76 Wilhelmstrasse in Berlin and announced their appointment to a lobby guard who was expecting them. He escorted the group to the Economics Ministry's conference room. One by one, they entered: Georg Landauer, director of the German Zionist Federation; E. S. Hoofien, director of the Anglo-Palestine Bank; Arthur Ruppin, Zionist Organization emigration specialist; and Moshe Mechnes, co-owner of Hanotaiah Ltd., one of the key orange exporting firms. Later they were joined by another Hanotaiah figure, Mr. Sam Cohen, a shadowy entrepreneur who had been instrumental in maneuvering between Reich and Zionist circles to achieve the agreement.[93]

Hans Hartenstein, director of the Foreign Currency Control Office, courteously greeted the Jewish leaders and did his utmost to make them feel welcome. The Reich and the Zionist delegation talked for some time. Money. Emigration. Boycott. Regulations. Timing. Public opinion. Boycott. Foreign exchange. Exports. Boycott. But there were contentious questions about just who in the Zionist establishment would actually control the transfer program. Would it be ordinary private sector merchants such, as Mr. Sam Cohen, or would it all be under official auspices of the Zionist organizations? Within the Zionist delegation there was a bitter rivalry and the Reich officials did not know who should be empowered to run the program. For the answer, they depended upon the recommendation of Consul Wolff in Jerusalem.[94]

At exactly 1:30 p.m., Jerusalem time, on August 7, 1933, Consul Wolff sent a telegram to the Foreign Ministry: "TO REICH ECONOMICS MINISTRY FOR THIS AFTERNOON'S MEETING ... A COMMITTEE FORMED SOME TIME AGO TO DEAL WITH TRADE WITH GERMANY AND CONSISTING OF PLANTERS, INDUSTRIAL WORKERS, IMPORTERS AND CONSUMERS, HAS TAKEN UP THE TRANSFER MATTER UNDER LEADERSHIP OF ANGLO-PALESTINE BANK. IT BELIEVES THAT IN VIEW OF ITS BROAD REPRESENTATION IT CAN ABSOLUTELY GUARANTEE THE IMPLEMENTATION OF THE TRANFER PLAN. A DELEGATION VISITED ME TODAY, STATING THAT HOOFIEN [of Anglo-Palestine Bank] HAS BEEN GIVEN UNLIMITED AND SOLE AUTHORITY FOR ... THE TRANSFER PLAN. AN OVERALL UMBRELLA ORGANIZATION IS BEING FORMED.[95]

At precisely 2:10 p.m. in the afternoon in Berlin, a messenger from Deutsche Reichspost walked into the Wilhelmstrasse offices of the Reich Foreign Ministry and handed them Consul Wolff's telegram. It was routed to the Palestine desk within the Eastern Department. In another part of the Wilhelmstrasse complex, the Hartenstein conference was nearing a frustrating end. About that time, the officer on the Palestine desk saw that Consul Wolff's telegram was actually intended for Hartenstein's meeting. He immediately telephoned the message over to Hartenstein's office. Hoofien, Landauer, Cohen, and the others had not yet left the conference room when the news was brought in. A moment of silence passed as the telegram's contents were noted. It is unknown whether Hartenstein read the words aloud, or whether he simply handed the handwritten note to them. But with Wolff's recommendation, the Transfer pact between the Third Reich and Zionist agencies was sealed.[96]

Three days later, on August 10, Hartenstein issued a decree authorizing Hoofien to create the twin transfer clearinghouses, one in Berlin and one in Tel Aviv. Several additional letters of confirmation and procedural refinement were exchanged between Hoofien and Hartenstein in the days immediately after that August 7 meeting. Those several letters were bureaucratically attached to official Reich Decree 54/33. Together, they became what would become known as the Transfer Agreement.[97]

Two transfer accounts were created. *Konto I* was for existing emigrants. They would deposit their marks into Paltreu's German-based blocked account. German exports would then be sold in Palestine, the proceeds being deposited in Ha'avara's balancing account. The transfer would indeed give the emigrants the cash they needed to restart their lives.[98]

*Konto II* was reserved for so-called potential emigrants or those wanting to invest in Palestine as a Jewish national home. German Jews could voluntarily deposit their marks into this second *konto*, but they could not be transferred until all the actual emigrant depositors of the first *konto* had been reimbursed. As such, these potential millions upon millions of frozen reichsmarks represented a long-term money pool the Zionists could utilize and collateralize for capital investments and development projects. Those who stayed behind would continually finance the expanding Jewish home for those who agreed to leave.[99]

After beseeching the supporters and allies of the Jews for decades, the Zionists realized that the moment of transfer would come not from friends but from foes, as Herzl had predicted. Forty years of struggle to create a Jewish State had come to a sudden and spectacular turning point. For some 40 years there had never been enough money, never enough land, never enough men. So long as those essential factors were lacking, the Jewish State was also never to be.

But in an office at Wilhelmstrasse on August 7, 1933, this all changed. A few men working with telegrams, letters of introduction, images, the power of prejudice and pretense, a few men who saw an opportunity for salvation within the abyss of Nazi injustice—those few men had simply arranged it.

Henceforth, when Jews would be threatened, as Jews always were, as Jews always would be, they would have a nation of their own to go home to. A nation no Jew would enter as a refugee or a stranger, a nation all Jews would enter as full citizens. The price of this new nation would be the abandonment of the war against Nazi Germany.

Whole branches of Judaism would wither, but the trunk would survive— these were Herzl's words. This one crucial and unparalleled time, the emergency would be used to secure a future, not ransom a past. From this crisis of humiliation, agony, and expulsion would come sanctuary, nationhood, and a new Jew, with a new home to call his own. These few men were willing to make those decisions.[100]

\*       \*       \*       \*

The Transfer Agreement saw many permutations, adjustments and expansions in the years following August 1933. Additional *Ha'avara*-style pacts, formal and informal, were sealed between the Zionists and the Reich-pressured governments in Poland, Czechoslovakia, Hungary, and other European countries where the life or death option for Jews became too crucial to ignore.[101]

As the years wore on, it became harder and harder to sell German goods because Germany's record of aggression and barbarism became globally apparent to anyone who read a newspaper, listened to a radio, or saw a newsreel. Although Zionists and other major Jewish leaders had prevailed upon Rabbi Wise and Jewish organizations to crack the well-organized boycott as first envisioned, a gamut of grass-roots groups worldwide never stopped picketing, protesting, and broadcasting their message: "For Humanity's Sake, Don't Buy German Goods."[102] The awesome appeal of the boycotter's valiant message was painfully subverted by a pragmatic Zionist movement that preferred to achieve victory by organized rescue and removal, not just by accruing impassioned calls of condemnation and tears over the mounting destruction of Jewish life and Jewish lives in Europe.

As for Wise, in a September 1933 press conference, he answered a testy question from a reporter, "When I was pressed to declare a boycott, my position was this: A boycott, yes, by all means, the stiffest, sternest kind of boycott against German wares, products, and goods. But there were ... considerations that moved me, and I am not in the least ashamed of having been governed by them." With his customary flair, Wise defiantly added, "Whether that was an error of judgment will be decided, not by you, ladies and gentlemen, but by the times that are to be."[103]

Quickly, German Jews became second-class citizens and eventually they could not be citizens at all. More concentration camps opened in Germany. In many German cities, torture rooms were operated by Nazi thugs. Brutality, street violence, and public humiliation spectacles became commonplace. Forced sale of Jewish homes and businesses became regular occurrences. Jews were not permitted to walk in many parks, not permitted to work in most jobs or professions, banned from many aspects of ordinary living, and subjected to vicious nonstop propaganda about their bacterial, subhuman nature. Prominent public signs warning "No Jews Allowed" were becoming more common in stores, museums, and entire neighborhoods. Jewish children were beaten and demoralized in school. Threats to life and limb were everywhere in Germany. In many instances, Jews were visited at night by Nazi cadres and told to leave the country or else. Suicides among Jews became epidemic.[104]

Nor was the anti-Jewish persecution limited to the Third Reich. After Hitler's influence began to poison Europe's political processes, Poland experienced a revival of anti-Semitic laws, as did other countries in Europe.[105]

Once again, Jews had to get out. Within one typical week in 1933, Paris suddenly found itself hosting hundreds of German Jewish refugees, straining its charitable organizations to the limit. It was the same in Czechoslovakia. Poland during that one-week period counted at least 3,000 fleeing German Jews, Switzerland saw at least 6,000 enter, and in Belgium, thousands of Jews

fled over the hills to freedom, many chased by the rifle fire of Reich border guards. Non-bordering European states such as Spain, Portugal, and even
England also felt the drama of escape as each new passenger ship yielded
more desperate disembarking German Jewish citizens.[106]

Soon, the doors of refuge began closing even tighter. The United States,
a traditional safe haven, was slamming its gate shut by virtue of a new quota-
based immigration law based on eugenic and racial formulae embodied in the
National Origins Act. Other countries, wracked by the Depression and unwilling to import yet another refugee crisis, followed suit. Later, Zionist Organization leader Chaim Weizmann would comment, "There are in this part of
the world [Europe] 6,000,000 people ... for whom the world is divided into
places where they cannot live and places where they cannot enter."[107]

But through the facility of the Ha'avara, Jews could enter one place—
Palestine. With the rise of Hitler, they came by the thousands—some legally
and counted, many illegally and not officially counted. In 1931, before the
Hitler threat matured, only an estimated 4,000 Jews arrived. But the next year,
1932, during the run-up to Hitler's ascendance, that number approximately
tripled and some say quadrupled to between an estimated 9,000 and 12,500
people, depending upon the source quoted; many were German Jews. During
1933, Hitler's first year in office, the number again either trebled or quadrupled, from an estimated 30,000 to an estimate of more than 37,000; an estimated 7,000 were German Jews. The next year, 1934, as Hitler's anti-Jewish
program bore new sting, and the *Ha'avara* ramped up, the estimated flow
increased to between 42,000 to 45,000, more than a fifth from Germany or
Austria.[108]

By 1935, after Hitler's Nuremberg Laws defined by percentage of blood-
line just who was a full-Jew, half-Jew, and even a sixteenth-Jew and, therefore, increasingly subjected to mandatory sterilization and other draconian
deprivations, the outflow into Palestine swelled to between an estimated
61,800 and 66,400; almost 15 percent from Germany and Austria. That year
alone, 1935, European Jews were entering Palestine at the rate of more than
5,000 per month. Indeed, in the four years since 1932, approximately 160,000
Jews had entered. Ultimately, an estimated 60,000 German Jews entered Palestine under *Ha'avara* during the 1930s.[109]

The reluctant *Ha'avara* refugees brought their German culture, in many
cases transplanting replicas of their homes back in the Third Reich. Most never
wanted to leave Germany and never wanted to enter Palestine. But when they
did, they brought a German fondness for music, for art, for spotless homes,
for cafes with Linzer tortes, for philosophy, for antiquities, for theater, for the
finer things that struggling Jewish Palestine had never stopped long enough to
develop. These enduring intangibles were transferred right along with durable

German motorcars, steel pipes, and radios. What's more, millions of dollars worth of assets—some $100 million, or about $1.7 billion in twenty-first century money—accompanied the refugees. True, the sums represented just a fraction of their original possessions, but it was enough—even after a hefty disagio—to purchase more and more land at the exorbitant prices many Arabs quietly agreed to settle for.[110]

Palestine became transformed in every way, and the accent was distinctly German.

Yes, the Mufti's lionized Hitler regime took the drastic action it had promised against the Jews. Their communities would be dismantled, their assets seized, and their expulsion organized. But in the process, Palestine would be flooded with more Jewish immigrants and economic wherewithal.

The more German Jews came in, the more they created an economic infrastructure and the economic absorptiveness to expand the so-called "Labor Schedule" for the ordinary working class Polish and Russian worker Zionists. Britain's "Labor Schedule" pegged the number of new Zionist immigrant workers admitted to Palestine based on the needs of the expanding economy. These Labor Schedule immigrants did not require £1000 for visas, only a certified job vacancy. Under Depression conditions, job growth was minimal. But with the impetus of Ha'avara, new jobs were created every day. Hence, not only did great numbers of middle-class Germans with some financial remnant enter to save themselves and restart their lives, they made it possible for a multitude of penniless or immigrants of modest means as well. This all created a robust, stratified Jewish social, civil, and economic society.[111] Clearly, a Jewish state was now in the making, right before the Mufti's eyes.

The whole prospect caused Consul Wolff to dispatch a snide letter to Berlin summarizing his view of the Arab enthusiasm for Hitler. "In their admiration of Germany, and the primitive nature of their political understanding," Wolff wrote, "they have not drawn the obvious conclusion of making Germany responsible for the increased Jewish immigration to Palestine!"[112]

Although some Arab leaders were painfully aware that Germany was solving its Jewish problem by resettling refugees in Palestine, the complex mechanics of the Ha'avara were by and large not openly aired within the Arab community. One leading pan-Arab editor and agitator, Amir Arslan, did quietly protest in October 1933, shortly after the Transfer Agreement had been finalized. "I am obliged in the name of all Arabs," wrote Arslan, "to ask you a rather serious if not grave question. It is concerning the Jewish Question. Hitler's Germany wants to eliminate the Jews ... However, there is another matter that concerns us directly and which we wish to bring to the attention of our German friends. One hears everywhere that Germany has promised the German Jews assistance in establishing themselves in Palestine. We do not understand this … The Jews will never forgive Germany for the politics which forced them to lose their predominance in your country. If there is any foundation to this news, Germany, having [already] done poorly with the Jews, will [also] lose all support in the Muslim world … As soon as they have a majority, it is over for the Arabs. Not only do we ask the German government not to aid Jews to immigrate to Palestine; we also ask not to permit our Palestine to become a Jewish state."[113]

But most other protests were muted as the anti-Zionist Arab circles still saw their best partner in the world to be the regime that wanted to destroy the Jews, the Third Reich, headed by Adolf Hitler.

Palestinian Arabs now broke into two factions. One was the so-called Opposition, primarily led by the Nashashibi clan, the Mufti's traditional rival. The Opposition group sought some accommodation with Jews, which meant lucrative land sales for Arabs willing to sell and join the move to modernity. The second faction was the rejectionist anti-Zionist view constantly fomented by the Mufti. During this time, Husseini continued to play the double game of igniting fires among the populace while speaking with passive discontent for outside observers. But ultimately, the Mufti's staunchly anti-Jewish faction overwhelmed any opposition.[114]

In the spring of 1936, as the European Jewish influx approached a tidal wave, the entire territory descended into a violent scorch. The moment of actuation came when the citrus harvest ended in early April 1936. Increasingly armed and violent Arab militants initiated a campaign of outright terrorism and ambushes. On April 15, 1936, Arab terrorists stopped a bus and pulled two Jews off—murdering them on the spot. No longer content to engage in mere self-defense, Zionist groups, especially the so-called *Irgun*, launched clear retaliation; they killed two Arabs. The cycle of Arab attacks and Zionist reprisal was now spinning out of control. On April 19, 1936, an Arab mob in Jaffa, incited with the usual false rumors of a Jewish massacre against Muslims, wantonly murdered Jews in Tel Aviv. By the next day, "national committees" had sprung up all across Arab Palestine from Jaffa to Haifa, almost in synchrony, as though planned well in advance.[115]

The palette of local and countrywide national committees began demanding a complete boycott of everything Jewish or British. They decreed a full work stoppage, cessation of all tax payments, and militant uprisings until the British completely terminated the Mandate and Jewish immigration. While the Mufti's colleagues agitated the community, the Mufti himself tried to remain outside the visible strike community. He was still the president for life of the Supreme Muslim Council, ordained by the British, and the recipient of large subventions from London. Openly advocating tax civil disobedience, tax refusal, a general strike, and sporadic violence would have cancelled his government privileges. Nonetheless, Husseini was convinced to imperil his British revenues and accept the presidency of yet another new Arab organization, this one known as the Arab Higher Command. This new consolidated body represented a coalition of all Palestinian Arab parties. It was a coalition of the eager and the reluctant within the Arab community. Obedience to the general strike was mandatory for all Arabs. Deviation was harshly repressed.[116]

Shopkeepers were obligated to shutter their doors and cease trading with Jews. The dictum was enforced with blood. Many of those Arabs dependent upon Jewish firms for employment lost their jobs as new immigrants happily took their place. Those who needed to purchase foodstuffs and other provisions from Jews, asked for deliveries at night to avoid detection. The general strike spread to other British and French dominated territories: Iraq on April 20, Trans-Jordan on April 23, and Lebanon on April 25. Solidarity demonstrations were staged in Syria and other Arab regions.[117]

The general strike was the smooth side of the revolt. Daily acts of Arab sabotage, ambush, and other violence against Jews and Jewish interests enveloped Palestine. April 20, a threshing floor at a Jewish enterprise was burned. Soon after, many other Jewish businesses were set aflame. Automobiles carrying Jews were attacked constantly with any weapon handy—nails, rifles, and now hand grenades.[118]

By May, a formal jihad was declared. Murders became more frequent. Jews were shot at point-blank range in the Old City, in the Edison film theater, and in other places where they had traditionally felt safe. Arab extremists also killed fellow Muslims who were simply working with Jews. An Arab vegetable vendor selling his goods in the Jewish market was murdered, as was an Arab watchman at a Jewish company. The terror campaign touched everyone. Riots against Jews ignited all over Palestine. In Haifa, 2,000 Arabs marched until they broke into rock throwing.[119]

At Nablus, an unruly throng assembled after midday prayers and promised a fight to the end. In Jaffa, protestors ran wild through the streets. Jewish buses were stoned everywhere. Bombs exploded with regularity across the country, including Jerusalem. On May 17, 1936, Jerusalem was besieged with riots. The results were disastrous. Due to the general strike, the thin Arab economy was almost exhausted.[120]

An international Arab response quickly became apparent as armed bands from Syria, Iraq, and Trans-Jordan established ambush and sabotage squads with their headquarters in the hills, where the British were loath to track them. A Court of the Revolt was established and *ad hoc* justice was dispensed, which often meant lashes or home demolitions for those out of step among the Arab populace. Suspected spies or collaborators were executed, sometimes by being beaten to death.[121]

British forces, no longer outmanned, finally had enough of Arab tactics and responded with iron repressive measures. A state of emergency was declared countrywide. The High Commissioner contemplated deporting the Mufti to help restore order but could not decide if Husseini's expulsion would help restore calm or further inflame the uprising. At the same time, London scheduled yet another investigation to produce yet another white paper. It would be known as the Peel Report, for its chairman, Earl Peel.[122]

As the recognized head of the Arab community, the Mufti was asked to testify. This also displayed London's commitment to evenhandedness in hearing the grievances of the two communities. When asked a question on the ability of Arabs to coexist with the growing Jewish population, now estimated to be 400,000, Husseini answered, "It is impossible to place two distinct peoples who differ from each other in every sphere of their life, in one and the same country. Such an impracticable attempt to try the impossible cannot hope for success, but must ultimately fail and result in doing harm to all."[123] Many thought his comment to be pivotal.

The Peel Commission agreed with the Mufti's declaration. In July 1937, after years of inextinguishable Arab violence, unstoppable Jewish immigration, and unbearable racial tension, the Peel Commission resolved in favor of partition, that is, creating two independent states, one Arab and one Jewish. The same approach had been used by the international community to separate an estimated million mainly-Christian Greeks and an estimated 500,000 mainly-Muslim Turks in Greek territories who were irreconcilable.[124] This same resolution could be applied to Palestine.

"The Jewish National Home is no longer an experiment," asserted Peel. "The growth of its population has been accompanied by political, social, and economic developments along the lines laid down at the outset. The chief novelty is the urban and industrial development. The contrast between the modern democratic and primarily European character of the National Home and that of the Arab world around it is striking. The temper of the Home is strongly nationalist. There can be no question of fusion or assimilation between Jewish and Arab cultures. The National Home cannot be half-national."[125]

The Mufti was openly blamed for much of the meltdown. "The functions which the Mufti has collected in his person," declared the Commission, "and his use of them have led to the development of an Arab *imperium in imperio* [an empire within an empire]. He [the Mufti] may be described as the head of a third parallel government."[126]

Peel made clear, "Arab nationalism is as intense a force as Jewish. The Arab leaders' demand for national self-government and the shutting down of the Jewish National Home has remained unchanged since 1929. Like Jewish nationalism, Arab nationalism is stimulated by the educational system and by the growth of the Youth Movement ... The gulf between the races is thus already wide and will continue to widen if the present Mandate is maintained."[127]

The Peel Report concluded that whatever administrative palliatives were set in motion in the realm of immigration, land, and education, "They cannot cure the trouble. The disease is so deep-rooted that, in the Commissioners' firm conviction, the only hope of a cure lies in a surgical operation ... 'The Jewish Problem' [created by the Third Reich] is not the least of the many problems which are disturbing international relations at this critical time and obstructing the path to peace and prosperity. If the Arabs at some sacrifice could help to solve that problem, they would earn the gratitude not of the Jews alone but of all the Western World. There was a time when Arab statesmen were willing to concede little Palestine to the Jews, provided that the rest of Arab Asia were free. That condition was not fulfilled then, but it is on the eve of fulfillment now. In less than three years' time, all the wide Arab area outside Palestine between the Mediterranean and the Indian Ocean will be independent [due to other national independence schemes], and, if Partition is adopted, the greater part of Palestine will be independent too ... Partition offers a possibility of finding a way through them, a possibility of obtaining a final solution of the problem which does justice to the rights and aspirations of both the Arabs and the Jews."[128]

But coexistence with the Jews was not an option for the now mainly radicalized Arab community in Palestine, nor for the Mufti. Despite the promise of a geographical bevy of Arab states now being rapidly inaugurated, Jewish independence was intolerable to the Arab Higher Committee. Bombings and assassinations by Arabs were multiplied, and, increasingly British policemen, especially Arab policemen were targeted. Those Arab elders who felt it possible that the two peoples in Palestine could separate peaceably were now being bullied, stabbed, shot, and dynamited by the followers of the Mufti, who himself always stayed aloof from the actual terror. London had long wanted to exile Husseini to a distant internment camp on the tiny Seychelles Islands in the Indian Ocean. But indecision had delayed any move.[129]

Finally, on September 26, 1937, the security situation was sliced open. Lewis Andrews, Acting District Galilee Commissioner, and his bodyguard were gunned down en route to a Nazareth church service. On October 1, 1937, the High Commissioner dissolved and/or made illegal the Arab Higher Committee and all the local "national committees" that comprised what became known as the Arab Revolt. Husseini was removed from his position as head of the Supreme Muslim Council—a British creation of convenience. Arrest warrants were issued for scores of known Arab agitators—including the Mufti.[130]

The British had tried to arrest Husseini before, since the onset of the Arab

Revolt in 1936. But the now-elusive Mufti always took refuge in the Noble Sanctuary and claimed the Islamic inviolability of its premises. Once, when he did leave for a meeting in June 1936, the police were waiting at the office building, but the Mufti disappeared out a back door. He and his large traveling party then slipped out of the country, driving to Damascus, where, on June 22, he checked into the Orient Palace Hotel. There he participated in numerous conferences with Palestinian agitators about merging the Syrian national bloc with the Palestinian Istiqlal resistance group. These meetings were attended not only by Syrians, but also by representatives from Saudi Arabia and Iraq.[131]

On July 3, the Mufti departed for the mountain village of Sofar in Lebanon, and then continued on to Beirut. Driving all day from Beirut, he suddenly reappeared in Palestine on July 4, 1937. Back in Jerusalem, the Mufti again hid within the protective grounds of the Dome of the Rock, where no Christian could enter. As Mufti and Chairman of the local Waqf religious trust, Husseini was custodian of the precious mosque complex—nearly untouchable. Nonetheless, the British were determined to arrest him. The new plan: dispatch Muslim officers from the Indian army to make the arrest.[132]

Again, Husseini was one step ahead. On October 12, 1937, he lowered himself down the outer wall of the Temple Mount complex to a waiting car, which drove him to the Jaffa port. There he boarded a boat for Lebanon, making good his escape. Once in Beirut, the French supposedly placed the Mufti under house arrest. But his "house arrest" was a pleasure. Husseini regularly regaled fellow nationalists and other leading Syrian personalities at festive dinner parties with his talk of a pan-Arab state stretching from Damascus to Jerusalem—all to the constant chagrin of the British. For two years, the Mufti was less a prisoner in Beirut than a *bon vivant*.[133]

At 6:00 a.m., September 1, 1939, Hitler launched his blitzkrieg against Poland, thus beginning World War II. This was the Mufti's moment. He seized it.

The French in Syria, eager to curry favor with Palestinian Arabs during the forthcoming struggle with Germany, continued to kowtow to the Mufti. When, just after war broke out, Husseini openly thanked various luminaries in the French government for gracious treatment during his visit, the highest authorities were quick to respond. For example, General Maxime Weygand, commander in chief of French forces in the eastern Mediterranean, effusively replied: "The letter in which Your Eminence has expressed to me his personal thanks, and that of the members of the Arab Higher Committee, for the hospitality extended to them by the French authorities ... has touched me deeply. I have been particularly moved," General Weygand added, "by the allusion which Your Eminence has made to the humanitarian spirit of France, which is one of the most noble traditions of my country. Your Eminence has been good enough also to assure me of the loyalty of the Arabs in Palestine; for this I express to you all my gratitude. I beg your Eminence to accept the assurance of my highest consideration."[134]

Now another tetrahedral dynamic was developing. The Third Reich was at war. Great Britain had become the enemy. Hitler intended to conquer and occupy much of Europe. That meant Palestine was no longer a territory for neutrality. It was a pressure point against Britain, and Berlin intended to press it, diverting military and political resources. What's more, the Reich policy of Jewish expulsions and transfers to Palestine had now gone so far as to create the potential of an actual Jewish state—the result of the Peel Partition Plan. In the Nazi mindset, this new Zionist State would create the ultimate accretion of Jewish conspiratorial power that would further attack Germany and advance world domination. Most importantly, the Arab world was sitting atop the one thing the British and French controlled, and the one thing the Nazis needed to fuel and lubricate their General Motors-manufactured Blitz troop transports, their Panzer tanks, and their vast military automotive fleets. The Arabs were sitting on top of the oil.

Germany now rapidly began changing its mind about the Arabs and found common ground in the old saying: "the enemy of my enemy is my friend."

As war burned across Europe, Husseini needed to say goodbye to his hosts in Lebanon. Hitler was fighting the two greatest nemeses of the Palestinian Arabs: the Jews and the British. Husseini had a critical role to play. The Mufti bribed the French chief of police with £500 to make sure gendarmes outside his house looked the other way. On the morning of either October 13 or 14, 1939, Husseini and his assistants donned the coverings of devout Muslim women and drove off unmolested. Only after Husseini failed to appear for his regular morning walk the next two days did guards admit that they saw the car depart—but presumed all within were women.[135]

The next day, the Mufti appeared at the epicenter of Britain's Mideast strategy and the font of its oil. Husseini was in Baghdad.[136]

# 13

# THE NAZI QUEST FOR OIL

**D**uring World War II, a confusing web of complex and contradictory political and economic relationships coursed from London to Berlin to Jerusalem and back, all involving oil, the Jews, and the Mideast. In 1941, the locus shifted to Iraq, as the forces of Arab nationalism joined Nazi aggression to confront the arch-importance of oil and the question of Jewish existence.

As a means of quelling the jihad against Britain, Mandate officials in London elevated Iraq to a kingdom in 1921 installing its old, reliable ally Faisal as king. Faisal was no Iraqi. But his credentials were good enough for London. The charismatic Hashemite son of Hussein from Arabia, Faisal fought alongside T.E. Lawrence in the war against the Turks, and led the unsuccessful struggle at the Paris Peace Conference to achieve the Arab Nation.

But Iraq was not quite a nation and Faisal was not quite a king when he and Great Britain signed the formal treaty of alliance on October 10, 1922. Although it was labeled a "treaty" as if between two governments and bore regal seals on its cover, the treaty was actually not with "the nation of Iraq," but with the king as an individual. That's because the new Iraq was nominally an independent kingdom, yet under international law it was still a mandated territory under the control and tutelage of the British. Moreover, King Faisal, although proclaimed a monarch, was required to take counsel and instructions from Britain's appointed resident, High Commissioner Sir Percy Cox.[1]

The 1922 bilateral friendship treaty, read like an earlier protectorate contract with the Sheikh of Kuwait except, in this case, it was not the nation being protected. After all, recalcitrant villages were still regularly being bombed by the RAF.[2] The real protectorates were British commercial interests—shipping, railroading, oil exploitation, and pipelines. They were being protected against Iraq itself.

Article VIII of the treaty guaranteed that no Iraqi land would be ceded or leased to any power other than Britain. Article IV assured that Faisal "agrees to be guided by the advice of His Britannic Majesty tendered through the High Commissioner on all important matters affecting the international and financial obligations of His Britannic Majesty for the whole period of the treaty." Article XI included an all-important nondiscrimination clause with a vital parenthetical: "There shall be no discrimination in Iraq against the nationals of any State" with whom England maintained diplomatic relations. The parenthetical added: "(including companies incorporated under the law of such State.)"[3] This last phrase was, in essence, sovereign sublimation of British oil companies and all foreign oil companies that London recognized. Oil companies ruled Iraq.

Iraq's vast oil resources, deemed among the most fabulous in the world, were mainly controlled by Iraq Petroleum Company, which was one of the many alter-egos of Britain's government-controlled oil cartel, the Anglo-Persian oil company. Its first major gusher shot black gold into the sky on October 1927. Its value was measured in billions of dollars; but the royalties paid to Iraq were always somehow less than promised and, at any rate, constituted a mere pittance of the true value. But those royalties—deflated or not—greatly enriched King Faisal's throne and the national treasury of Iraq.[4]

By the end of the 1920s, Iraq was placed on a multi-year path to full nationhood. Its mandate would be terminated and the country admitted into the League of Nations as a full voting member. But from London's point of view, Iraq was still a client state. England, in 1930, renegotiated its 1922 friendship treaty with what was now the almost sovereign nation of Iraq. The revised treaty guaranteed the British two air bases, along with military transit and basing rights in the event of war. Then, in 1932, by pre-agreement, the League of Nations ended Britain's mandate, and London sponsored Iraq's admission into the League as a full voting member.[5]

When the League of Nations originally granted the mandates for both Iraq and Palestine to Great Britain, oil was a leading consideration. Two pipelines were envisioned to carry Iraqi and Persian oil to the Mediterranean, traversing those territories. One, finally completed in mid-July 1934, traveled through Syria to meet the sea at Tripoli, Lebanon's trading port. The second, completed January 14, 1935, traveled from Kirkuk south to the Haifa coast in Palestine. The Kirkuk-Haifa line was opened to great fanfare with King Faisal presiding, along with many government officials and oil consortium executives in attendance, plus some 250 invited VIPs. That year, 1935, independent Persia changed its name to Iran. The Anglo-Persian Oil Company changed its name to Anglo-Iranian Oil Company. By this time, the Iraq Petroleum Company had formed hundreds of wholly-owned, interlocking subsidiaries throughout the Mideast and the world to drill for, refine, transport, and sell its petroleum.[6]

By the time World War II erupted on September 1, 1939, the strategic importance of Iraq, Iran and Palestine balanced atop a fulcrum of oil.

Hitler's plans were fueled by hate. But Hitler's tanks, trucks, automobiles, warships, submarines, and airplanes were fueled by octane. Moving parts in all German machinery, from mighty locomotives to hand-held Lugers, required lubricants. Germany's economic recovery was dependent upon great factories. Hitler's military campaigns deployed great armies and defenses. Foreign domination required an oppressive and far-flung administrative infrastructure. All of that required petroleum. Hitler needed oil. The more territory Hitler took, the more oil he needed to sustain his conquests.

In 1938, Reich consumption of petroleum products, from kerosene to aviation fuel, was estimated by some British experts at more than 6.5 million tons per year, growing exponentially as the Reich continued to mechanize, industrialize, rearm, and make ready for the war that everyone expected. Indeed, 1938 consumption grew by 1.2 million tons over the preceding year. Using synthetic processes and some local deposits, Germany produced only a few million tons of its total requirements. One report indicated that Germany produced as much as 100,000 barrels of oil per day from coal using the hydrogenation process. The rest was imported. One typical top-secret analysis, titled "The Oil Supply Problem in Germany," concluded, "In spite of her efforts, Germany was still dependent on imports for over 50 percent of her requirements." During the war, an almost weekly cascade of such British estimates varied in tons and percentages. However Nazi industrial secrecy fudged the numbers, British intelligence consistently concluded that Germany was overwhelmingly dependent on foreign oil. Moreover, the expanding Reich was carefully counting every barrel, because its shortfalls were several million tons per year.[7]

Where did Germany get its oil?

In 1939, Germany's oil industry was a maze of more than 70 refiners and distributors, most of them small, dominated by a half dozen or so giant firms. Several of these dominating companies were in the forefront of importation. Chief among them was a firm named Olex.[8]

Olex had long been a household name in Germany, with thousands of convenient gas stations across the country. Its name derived from its original 1904 telegraphic address, PETROLEXPORT; the middle four letters formed

OLEX. At the end of 1937, Olex's total of all petroleum products on hand, from motor fuel to diesel oil to lubricants, equaled 88,800 metric tons, valued at approximately 14 million reichsmarks. Just one year later, its total 1938 sales of all products topped 475,300 metric tons.[9]

But in addition to its domestic consumer business, Olex was a key importer of its oil. Where did Olex oil come from?

Its traditional, number one source was Romania. In 1937, Olex stocks in hand included some 6,100 metric tons of Romanian light benzine, 5,800 metric tons of Romanian middle benzine, 1,150 metric tons of Romanian heavy benzine, 387 metric tons of Romanian white spirit, plus Romanian tractor vapor oil and kerosene, all imported via river through Hamburg and Regensburg. A September 3, 1936, company memo examining imports spotlighted "the Romanian market, the chief source of Olex supplies."[10]

However, Olex also imported gas oil, diesel oil, and kerosene from Amsterdam. That Dutch oil was brought in through a seemingly unrelated company registered in the Netherlands. But in truth, the 1000 stock certificates controlling that Dutch company's ownership were held in two locations, 5 shares in its Dutch attorney's office and 995 shares in the Olex company safe in Berlin.[11]

Iran was also an important source for Olex because the company and Nazi Germany needed foreign currency. Much of the world would not accept any of the numerous species of reichsmarks, almost all unusable outside Germany, and many based on fraudulent values floated by the Hitler regime. The international anti-Nazi boycott dramatically reduced all Nazi exports, so Germany was earning precious little foreign currency and was rationing its monetary reserves. However, through complicated barters, Olex could earn some of the foreign currency it needed to purchase oil, bolster Reich reserves, and earn a profit. Boycott-breaking barters were terribly complicated, generally disguised, and involved several companies in different parts of the world swapping products at a discount in exchange for some foreign currency.[12]

In a typical Olex barter, the company would import Iranian oil and sell it to the German steel company, Ferrostahl, which would pay Olex in Germany with worthless reichsmarks spendable only in Germany. How would Olex find the British pounds to pay Iran? In one typical case, Ferrostahl purchased 15,000 tons of inferior Iranian champa rice at an inflated price in exchange for first-class construction and railroad steel that Iran paid for in British pounds sterling. The steel company would then turn over its British pounds to the Reichsbank, which would use it for general Nazi rearmament and other state purposes. Olex could then receive a portion of those British pounds to pay for the oil it purchased from Iran. An Olex review of the serpentine Ferrostahl barter concluded it was necessary for the Reich "because in this way Germany earns the right to some Iranian [foreign] currency." Without a cornucopia of intricate, multi-transactional barters, Germany could not import the tons of British-controlled Iranian oil it craved.[13]

Iranian barter deals like the Ferrostahl swap were common for Olex. A 1938 company balance sheet included separate entries for "barter transactions," which in that one reporting period totaled RM 150,000, yielding £12,000 in one category, and RM 171,000, fetching £12,457 in a second. So entrenched was Iran as a source of Olex's imports that when a German highway publication asked Olex for a pictorial, the oil company's advertising managers wrote, "Although we shall discuss in our article mainly our distribution facilities in Germany, we shall have to mention the Iranian origin of our motor fuel and give a short description of our production and refining activities in Iran and submit a few photos."[14]

Olex was a loyal vendor with the Third Reich, and highly visible. At first, Olex managers were worried about the ascent of Hitler. Depression-era sales had stagnated when they should have grown. But no sooner had *der Führer* assumed power than sales volume soared from slightly more than 200,000 long tons in 1932 to double that amount by the end of 1938. By 1939, Olex operated 7,000 gas stations throughout the country, sometimes adding as many as 1,000 per year as Hitler's forced economic recovery proliferated throughout the nation. During one three-month period of 1938, Olex ran seven advertisements at one-week intervals in more than 300 German newspapers, including Nazi party newspapers. Moreover, Olex printed all the newest road maps of Germany, which immediately incorporated the latest Nazified street names, such as Adolf Hitlerplatz and Adolf Hitlerstrasse. In this way, Olex became an important cog in the cultural apparatus of National Socialism.[15]

Who owned Olex? In truth, Olex was a wholly-owned subsidiary of Britain's Anglo-Iranian Oil Company, also known as Anglo-Persian Oil Company. In 1926, Anglo-Persian acquired 40 percent of the old-line Olex, increased its ownership to 75 percent in 1929, and then in 1931 bought out the remaining 25 percent from minority owner Deutsche Petroleum. Anglo-Persian called the new entity *Deutsche Benzin- und Petroleum*, or "BP." Throughout Great Britain, Anglo-Persian's green, three-pointed BP shield logo stood for British Petrol. Throughout the Reich, the identical shield stood for Benzin- und Petroleum. As a wholly owned subsidiary of Anglo-Persian, all of Olex's affairs were tightly controlled out of London.[16]

Anglo-Persian operated with several foreign oil partners, all of whom were also leading purveyors of Nazi oil. Standard Oil of New Jersey operated Deustche Amerikanische Petroleum Gesellschaft or DAPG. As one of Germany's top six firms, DAPG operated 17,500 gas stations in Germany. Shell operated 16,500. In fact, of Germany's approximate 64,000 gas stations in

1939, Shell, Standard, and BP operated 41,000. Olex also became a key supplier of Germany's growing aircraft industry and the Luftwaffe.[17]

When Olex purchased Iranian oil, in reality it was dealing with another
subsidiary of the same company, its own parent, Anglo-Iranian Oil Company—also called Anglo-Persian Oil Company. The so-called Iranian oil it
purchased was often Iranian in name only, since the twin oil fields of Naft
Khana and Naft i Shah straddled either side of the Iraqi-Iran border. The Iraqi
side was considered "transferred territory." British military planners at the
time declared they could consider "the two sections of Naft Khana/Naft i Shah
of the northern field as one unit." The transferred territories were, after all,
Iraqi land under the original 1901 Persian concession. But Iraqi oil processed
through the Iranian refinery at Abadan, across from Basra, now bore the stamp
of Iran.[18] Petroleum deposits, and the companies that tap them, do not recognize national borders because oil all runs underground. Oil knows no border.

Hence, with a clenched fist, England staunchly resisted the rise and rearmament of Hitler, while with its own imperial enterprise, Anglo-Iranian Oil
Company, partially government-owned and fully government-controlled
when it came to international matters, contributed mightily to the recovery
of the Third Reich and Hitler's preparations to wage war against nations and
ethnic groups. So did the other Anglo-Persian partners, Shell, Standard, and
France's Compagnie Française Des Petroles. Indeed, the Third Reich's massive consumption allowed Iraq's interlocked foreign oil companies to richly
compensate for the fallen Depression-era demand and profit stagnation the
rest of the world was suffering.

Once war began in 1939, Anglo-Iranian Oil Company and Olex followed
Nazi Germany across Europe. "It should be noted," recounted an Anglo-
Iranian internal review just after the war, "that Olex took advantage of the
expansion of Germany to extend their distributing network in Austria and into
Poland and Czechoslovakia." For example, in Yugoslavia, the company was
known as Olex Proizvodi, headquartered in Zagreb in Croatia.[19]

After Britain declared war on the Reich and its Axis partners, German
corporate "custodians" in Berlin designated Olex as enemy property, but
Reich economic officials did with Olex as they did with IBM, Ford, and General Motors. The companies were seized in name only, meaning that the funds
were merely sequestered in blocked *sperrkonten* accounts for collection later.
Such companies were left independent, and "in the case of Olex," Anglo-Iranian's internal review recounts, "the directors and managers were reappointed
by the Custodian as his advisors."[20] There was no change from one day to the
next at Olex. Anglo-Iranian's executives continued to run the company—only
the profits were temporarily frozen.

Ironically, the British also deemed Olex and its foreign operations as enemy activity. The Trading with the Enemy office in London sequestered what few accounts of Olex it could find in random bank accounts. For example, Olex Yugoslavia's minor assets in London were sequestered in Trading with the Enemy account Y 40720.[21]

Two other partners in Iraq's oil were also declared enemies. The first was the Compagnie Française des Petroles (CFP), because France had surrendered and transformed itself into a bifurcated national entity, half Nazi-occupied in the north, half Nazi collaborationist with a capital at Vichy in the south. However, by a special high-level British government decision, CFP was permitted to conduct its normal business, making investments in Iraq Petroleum Company oil ventures. CFP would merely contribute monies through the British custodian, who would forward the cash to the consortium working with Iraq Petroleum.[22] Thus, France's CFP was able to expand its Iraq-based oil empire during the war years.

But as the war progressed in late 1940, Hitler needed more and more oil. Reich purchases from Romania were not keeping up with the needs arising from German aggression. At the same time, the Allies wanted to deny Hitler the all-important fields in Romania by any means possible. Some even suggested defensively purchasing all Romania's output, just to keep petroleum out of Reich hands. Every other day, another British intelligence estimate forecast an ever-increasing Nazi shortfall, sometimes 1 million tons, sometimes more. No one knew the exact figures, but they knew that oil was powering the Nazi onslaught. Many analysts predicted Germany would invade Romania by spring 1940 to seize the Ploesti oil fields. As expected, in October 7, 1940, a division of Nazi troops were sent in to "guard" the Romanian oil fields.[23]

But even Romanian production was not enough to fuel what Hitler had in mind. At the end of 1940, *der Führer* issued secret Directive 21, authorizing Operation Barbarossa, the full-scale invasion of Russia, to commence in late spring 1941. The unprecedented offensive would require thousands of long-range bombers, 3 million soldiers, thousands of tanks and artillery pieces, and 600,000 motor vehicles—all in a coordinated three-pronged attack.[24] Barbarossa would drink a lot of petroleum.

The Allies were expecting the thrust into Russia because of decoded messages during the long run-up to the invasion. Given the Nazi rape of Poland, the conquest of much of Western Europe, the establishment of heinous concentration camps and horrid civilian ghettos across the continent, the Allied leadership was convinced that only a titanic effort could stop Hitler. Debate after debate yielded a common conclusion: only by drying up the Reich's oil supply could the Nazi war machine be halted.[25]

Typical was a mid-1940 British report by Lord Weir to Prime Minister

Neville Chamberlain, which asked, "Has this formidable enemy [the Third Reich] any real weakness on which we can concentrate?" Lord Weir then answered his own question: "I believe it has such a real weakness. Germany cannot deploy her great hitting strength for any sustained effort unless she can produce, take from storage or import vast quantities of petrol, diesel oil and lubricating oil. She is so committed to the internal combustion engine in every one of its applications—military and civil—that any dislocation of supply must limit and control her effort. No transport vehicle, no tank, no aeroplane, no submarine can function without fuel and lubricating oil. No great Army, Air Force or Navy, no amount of hard work or unity can find its effective expression without immense supplies of fuel. Germany lost the last war through lack of human fuel. This time, she should be made to lose it through lack of the fuel which goes into the fuel tanks." All attention now focused on where Hitler could find the extra fuel he needed. There was only one place: the gargantuan oil fields of Iraq and Iran. A 1941 War Cabinet strategy report concluded, "Oil is, of course, Germany's main economic objective both in Iraq and Iran (Persia). The oil production of Iraq (4 million tons a year) would be sufficient to solve Germany's oil problem, but there are many difficulties in the way of transporting it to Germany. The pipelines to Haifa and Tripoli must be under her control, and the sea routes in the Eastern Mediterranean must be open to her shipping."[27]

At the same time, British war planners understood that if Germany somehow did seize Iraq's oil fields, it would be cataclysmic. "The denial to us of the Iraq oil [and its pipelines]," the War Cabinet strategy report continued, "would be serious, as alternative sources of supply would involve the extra use of tankers, of which there is already a shortage." A Foreign Office report summarized the threat, "But for British control of oil production, Germany could buy all the oil which Iran could produce."[28]

Even more blunt was a focused report titled, "Note on Iraq as a Possible Source of Oil Supply to the Enemy." The report made clear that if Romanian oil was insufficient, the Nazis "must turn to the nearest source: Iraq." Focusing on the estimated billion-ton Kirkuk oil field, the report asserted that Iraq possessed enough petroleum "to supply the [British] Empire's oil requirements for half a century." Fortunately, the report explained, for 15 years, "relations between the concessionaire [the Iraq oil consortium] and the Government have been smoother than the relations of any other oil concessionaire with any other Government." The report continued, "Proof... can be cited [by] the fact that Iraq has leased to one set of interests the whole of its oil resources, a monopoly that no other country has emulated."[29]

Despite the smooth relations, the report emphasized that if the Third Reich somehow achieved a political foothold in Iraq—now an independent country—everything would change. The Mideast, the Gulf, and then the connection to India would come under Nazi domination. Germany would be unstoppable west to east. The report ended, "Conclusion: The Enemy could not be denied Iraq oil if he got there … Once there, the game is up, not only with Iraq oil, but with the whole of the Near East—and perhaps beyond."[30]

Enter the Mufti of Jerusalem.

*    *    *    *

Within weeks of the war's beginning, Husseini escaped his "house arrest" and dashed back to Baghdad. The Iraq he found in October 1939 had changed dramatically over recent years. In 1933, King Faisal had become ill. After tending to an outbreak of mass murder, rape, and looting by Kurdish tribesmen and Iraqi soldiers against Assyrian separatist villages, Faisal returned to Switzerland in September for medical treatment and died within days. He had, however, lived long enough to see Iraq gain its independence and enter the League of Nations as a full member.[31]

Faisal's 21-year-old son, Ghazi, succeeded him. Under King Ghazi, the nation quickly descended into a cavalcade of military coups, assassinations, tribal uprisings, military show trials, and political upheaval. New political parties and power bases emerged from communists, reformers, pan-Arabists, and ultra-nationalists. So volatile was the country that the London-based general manager of the Iraq Petroleum Company concluded in a November 11, 1937 meeting that he was unable to visit Baghdad to negotiate for additional oil development. Meeting minutes recorded: "It was considered that the political situation in Iraq at the moment was unsuitable for negotiations."[32]

Seven Sunni military men, all of them conspirators in previous coups and political murders, emerged as the strongmen of Iraq. The most powerful of these seven formed their own quadrumvirate, known as the "Golden Square" for the four corners of authority they possessed. Civilians governed only with their approval—tacit or explicit.[33]

In April 1939, King Ghazi died in a car crash. The nation went into mourning as great crowds lined up to see his funeral procession. Rumors that the British were responsible burned across Iraq, fanned by anti-British elements. Ghazi was succeeded by his son, Faisal II, a three-year-old toddler. A regent was needed to act for the boy king, so yet another Hashemite scion from the Arabian Peninsula, Prince al-Ilah, was recruited to fill the post. Prince al-Ilah was selected as regent to act in the boy king's stead precisely because he was staunchly pro-British. He, in turn, with London's approbation, established a new government led by Prime Minister Nuri al-Said, generally viewed as tolerant of the British presence in Iraq and tolerant of the Peel white paper calling for partition of Palestine. In fact, Nuri, years earlier, while serving as foreign minister, had been brought in by the British in Palestine to negotiate with the Mufti and the Arab Higher Committee to successfully end one paralyzing phase of the Arab Revolt of 1936.[34]

But the new seemingly pro-British rule of Prime Minister Nuri al-Said and Regent al-Ilah ran afoul of the fiercely nationalist and militantly anti-British "Golden Square" faction. At the outbreak of World War II, Nuri publicly proclaimed Iraq would honor its alliance with Great Britain. The prime minister went further and severed diplomatic relations with Germany, expelling its diplomats and interning German nationals. Against this fertile background of power imbalance and fast-moving events, the Mufti, in mid-October 1939, arrived in Baghdad. His entry was especially welcomed by the Golden Square because three of the four generals in the quadrumvirate had served with Husseini years earlier in the Turkish army. They had long ago become fast friends and comrades in the cause of Arab nationalism.[35]

The ground had been seeded for the Mufti's mission during his so-called house arrest in Beirut. In 1938, Husseini met secretly with Wilhelm Canaris, chief of Germany's *Abwehr*, or military intelligence. The *Abwehr* had sought to smuggle weapons into Palestine through Saudi Arabia to assist the Arab Revolt, but plans were aborted because Berlin feared the British would discover the source. In another meeting, this one in Damascus, Nazi diplomat and Arabist Fritz Grobba gave the Mufti's secretary £800 just to keep the financial connection with Berlin alive. Grobba had been watching developments in Iraq and had earlier reported to Berlin that Baghdad was now the most vociferous center of defiance against Peel's white paper. By 1939, Germany had finally concluded three minor arms sales with Baghdad, providing Iraq with numerous machine guns, 18 anti-aircraft pieces, and other equipment. Germany was known for pre-positioning military necessities in other countries through seemingly routine commercial transactions. Grobba and the *Abwehr* believed, as an intelligence colleague noted in his diary: "The Arab movement should be activated immediately."[36]

In early 1939, Hitler remained reluctant to meaningfully assist Arab national aspirations. *Der Führer's* mindset was still governed by a sham race theory that Arabs were just a second branch of the same decrepit eugenic line that created the hated Jews. In fact, Hitler personally named Operation Barbarossa for King Frederick Barbarossa, who in 1190 led the German Crusade against Islam in Palestine. But with a war raging, and the need for oil pivotal to every move, the Reich reversed its position on Arab national aspirations. Ironically, at the same time, Germany continued to oust Jews or convince its allies to do so across Europe; and those ousters often led to escape to Palestine via a variety of methods—legal and illegal.[37] As more European territory lost its Jews under German influence, Hitler achieved his racial goals and further aggravated the problem of the British in Palestine. But in the process, these continuing expulsions or refugee escapes only intensified the fury of the Arabs in Palestine.

But the Mufti did not care about the motivations of the Nazis, only whether the Reich could advance the aspirations of Arab Palestine. As for the Jewish refugees pouring into tiny Palestine, the Mufti fully expected they would be handled as Germany had treated Jews in Europe. The next step was to strengthen Germany and accelerate the Reich's victory. The life or death fate of the Jews, increasingly penned up in Palestine, would be decided later.

Upon entering Iraq in October 1939, Husseini immediately set about establishing a power base. The collaborationist Vichy police in Syria made things comfortable by hand-delivering the Mufti's motorcar and household goods from Beirut. In March 1940, two police inspectors traveled to Baghdad with Husseini's personal property as a sort of complimentary moving service. Their travel expense report, paid for by the Nazi collaborationist Vichy government, totaled 23,350 piastres for the 17 tins of automobile gasoline hauled along, plus food and lodging for two days in Baghdad, and an additional 100 piastres for the gasoline funnel they used to refill their vehicle from time to time.[38]

The Mufti began activating his campaign. Husseini wrote passionately to the powerful All-India Moslem League in Bombay seeking support for Palestine; he hoped to open yet another political front against Britain, this time in India. The Mufti also organized the Arab National Party to agitate for a Palestine without Jews. The new group included the foursome of the Golden Square, as well as leading government official, Rashid Ali Galiani, commonly called Rashid Ali. Golden Square officers were only too eager to join. Their bitterness with Britain was aggravated because London, short of equipment and fearing the very agitation that was then underway, had refused to sell the Iraqi military any quantity of arms. Months earlier, when the Iraq military had requested new equipment, London replied it could only spare four small howitzers and a few radio sets. Under the close hand of the Mufti, this new Arab National Party met in secret, its members used assumed names, and they swore allegiance on the Koran.[39]

As his first major plan of upheaval, the Mufti tried to spark a Palestine-style violent outbreak against Britons in Iraq. Everywhere, he and his followers sowed rumors about such an uprising in the spring or summer of 1940. To counteract the campaign, Nuri's government called for postal censorship. Plainclothes security police began arresting troublemakers in cafés. But the population grew more restive. Soon, with pressure mounting, Nuri resigned as prime minister, to be replaced by Rashid Ali, the Mufti's comrade in the fight against Zionism. Nuri stayed on as foreign minister, but the power had suddenly shifted demonstratively toward the Mufti and his cohorts in the Golden Square.[40]

Throughout May 1940, local establishment newspapers tried to calm the populace. One typical story in *Al Istiqlal*, on May 22, excoriated a "gang of the biased and wicked … engaged in the promotion of false rumors."[41]

Prime Minister Rashid Ali informed British representative C. J. Edmonds in Baghdad that the entire Anglo-Iraqi relationship was now completely tied to the events in Palestine. If London solved the Jewish question in Palestine, England would not need to divert resources from the global war with the Axis to defend Iraq and its oil fields against a German invasion. Edmonds and Rashid Ali debated Palestine back and forth, but it was as though they were not speaking the same language. Edmonds used political syllogisms and diplomatic verbiage. Rashid Ali insisted that no matter what rationales were invoked, everything in Iraq now was being driven by events in Palestine.[42]

Edmonds wrote that Rashid Ali then craftily declared, "This country would easily raise 100,000 men to take its part in the common defense. But as things were, he [Rashid Ali] could not be sure that the Iraq Army would [even] march to its appointed positions." In fact, if the army did deploy, said Rashid Ali, no one could guarantee they would not fall apart due to "internal trouble." Edmonds reported that Rashid Ali was explicit: "The situation could only be rendered sound by the solution of the Palestinian problem."[43] In others words, the Iraqis would let the Germans walk in, unopposed, and seize the oil wells unless Zionism was promptly thwarted in Palestine.

Startled, Edmonds retorted that he was profoundly shocked "that the Iraqi Army might not cooperate in the defense of their own country." Rashid Ali replied vaguely, but returned the discussion to negotiations with the Palestinians to undo the Peel white paper. When the meeting ended, Rashid Ali sharply reminded Edmonds, "the time was the present, and Baghdad the place; the Palestinian leaders were here and the Iraqi government, the honest broker, was willing and anxious."[44]

Soon, British diplomats in Iraq were sending home report after report warning that the Mufti was orchestrating a range of anti-British plots in Iraq, and the local situation was rapidly deteriorating. Typical was one diplomatic summary that belittled the new Iraqi "instinct to indulge in blackmail over Palestine." In July 1940, Rashid Ali's justice minister met secretly in Turkey with the Reich ambassador, Franz von Papen. The Mufti then sent his own secretary to talk to German foreign minister Joachim von Ribbentrop in Berlin. The Mufti's condition for an Arab rebellion in Iraq: a German declaration against the Zionist homeland and in favor of a pan-Arab state.[45]

The outlines of the demanded declaration were embodied in the Mufti's personal eight-point draft. It covered all the Islamic nations of the Arab realm: Syria, Lebanon, Kuwait, Egypt, Saudi Arabia, Sudan, Dubai, and Oman. All these countries were to be liberated from British protectorates, mandates, binding alliances, and other direct or indirect control. Key to the Mufti's draft declaration was point 7: "Germany and Italy recognize the illegality of the 'Jewish Home in Palestine.' They accord to Palestine and other Arab countries the right to resolve the problem of the Jewish elements in Palestine and other Arab countries in accordance with the interests of the Arabs, and by the same method that the question is now being settled in the Axis countries."[46]

To Nazi eyes, the phrase was perfect: "resolve the problem of the Jewish elements in Palestine and other Arab countries ... by the same method that the question is now being settled in the Axis countries." How was the Jewish problem being settled in the Axis countries of Greater Germany, Hungary, Romania, occupied Poland, and elsewhere? Identification, expulsion from the economy, confiscation of assets, enforced starvation, ghettoization, concentration in camps, and mass murder. The Mufti's offer was to extend Hitler's merciless international campaign of Jewish destruction into the Middle East.

The Mufti was not the only extremist courting the Third Reich. Other opportunist-minded Arabs beckoned as well, including Rashid Ali. Husseini and Rashid Ali now contended for control of precious Iraq. Yet, within their competition, each saw Berlin replacing London as the stage manager for nationalist aspirations in Palestine and across the Arab crescent. Just as had occurred 15 years earlier, promises and enticements now only escalated as the fabulous oil wealth and strategic location of Iraq became the prize.

The converse of the Lawrence of Arabia drama was now unfolding. The Arabs would again rise up for nationalism, but this time for German sponsors, not the British. In fact, Fritz Grobba, the central Nazi figure in rallying the Arab revolt, was openly nicknamed "German Lawrence." Grobba was actually born Arthur Borg. For affectation, he took his name, A. Borg, reversed the letters to read "groba" and added a second B for style to create "Grobba." His mysterious exploits and evolving alliances were covered in the newspapers. One *New York Times* article, headlined "'German Lawrence' Stirs Revolt," carried his photograph with the caption: "Dr. Fritz Grobba, whose exploits in the Arab world rival those of Britain's famous Lawrence."[47]

The *New York Times* article opened: "Behind the scenes of the war in Iraq, a German agent called Dr. Grobba has been playing an active part. Occasionally, his name has been mentioned in the dispatches, but it has never been disclosed who this man is, what he has done in the past, and what he is still doing. Officially, Dr. Grobba is the German envoy at the court of Ibn Saud, the ruler of Saudi Arabia. Previously, he was for many years the German envoy to Iran. But behind this official mission, something altogether different is concealed. In informed circles in Berlin, London, Cairo, Baghdad and Mecca, this man is called 'the German Lawrence.' It is true that he does not bear the slightest outward resemblance to his famous British predecessor of the [first] World War ... but so far as success is concerned, Grobba is not far behind the prototype."[48]

Although the Reich was obligated by oil and geography to cooperate with the Arabs, *der Führer* still viewed Arab nationalism as merely a means to an end, that is, as a stepping-stone to the Nazi conquest and domination of the entire Middle East. Grobba talked to Hitler about Iraq, and recalled, "When the deep split [rivalry] emerged in Berlin between Hajj Amin [Husseini] and Rashid Ali, I found myself facing a serious dilemma. Both sought from Hitler recognition as leader of the Arab world, and both put pressure on me to influence *der Führer* in this respect. Although Rashid Ali was the most prominent Arab politician who joined us against the democracies, we were aware that Hajj Amin [Husseini] enjoyed tremendous prestige in the Arab and Muslim world, as being fearless in the revolt against the British. When I tried to raise the issue of recognition in my talks with Hitler, *der Führer* put me off, arguing that the time had not yet come to install an Arab leader, and that the subject would be discussed when we conquered the Arab region."[49]

The Arabs carried no illusions about their status in Western eyes. Europe cared about them only as the people who walked the ground above the oil deposits. Beginning in July, the Iraqi catchphrase of the day became "absolute neutrality," that was an open codeword for disavowal of the Anglo-Iraq Treaty of Alliance, which called for mutual military assistance in times of war. But more than that, "absolute neutrality" advertised an Arab allegiance purchasable by either side—British or Nazi—for satisfaction of national desires.[50] Iraqis and Arabs everywhere called this moment a "golden opportunity."

*Al Istiqlal*, July 4, 1940: "Iraq's attitude of neutrality only safeguards her future and her integrity and the maintenance of her sovereignty." *Al Nasr*, August 6: "[Germany and Britain] each proclaim itself to be the sole champion of the Arabs and Arab ideals. But we may wonderingly ask whether any nation has ever served any cause but its own interests." *Al Yaum*, August 8: "The imperialistic powers are trying to make Iraq take sides, but such poisonous propaganda cannot grow in the soil of Iraq." *Al Istiqlal*, August 13: "Two peoples are fighting for world domination, each pretending to be fighting for the cause of civilization and the deliverance of small nations." *Basra Al Sijil*, September 2: "The real intentions of both sides are well-known by weak peoples, who realize that the present struggle is inspired by greed and the desire to subjugate peoples and rob them of their wealth."[51]

Often quoted by worried British officials was *Al Istiqlal*'s August 12 editorial: "The reason for this insistence [absolute neutrality] lies in the desire, on the one hand to avoid the danger of war, and on the other to exploit all opportunities which occur." The Mufti's forces in Iraq constantly preached Arab solidarity. *Al Rai al Am*, September 28: "The Arabs cannot turn this golden opportunity to profit, nor remove the yoke of imperialism, unless they organize themselves."[52]

By early October 1940, reports from Baghdad triggered serious alarms in Whitehall. Telegraph service between Iraq and Germany had been restored. Prime Minister Rashid Ali was openly cultivating diplomatic support from the Reich. Just a few months earlier, London had believed it could safely transport its Indian regiments north through Iraq, per its treaty rights, to confront an expected Nazi advance in Syria or to secure the oil fields. This was now in doubt. Their conclusions: "A) Active hostility on the part of the Iraqis might make it impossible to use the overland route for the passage of troops from Basra to Haifa or for the maintenance of our forces in the Middle East; B) Difficulties might be expected in the use of the Empire air route from Egypt to India, the Far East and Australia, which passes through Iraq; C) The Iraqis might cut off at [the] source the oil which was piped across the desert to Haifa. The hostility of Iraq might influence Iran, and so reduce the reliance to be placed on [the] Abadan [refinery] as a source of oil; D) If Iraq and Iran become subservient to the Axis powers, our enemies would be at the gates of India."[53]

Many in Whitehall now decided to either kidnap the Mufti and deport him to Cyprus or simply kill him—they weren't sure which. As for Rashid Ali, they wanted him "eliminated" as well. In a November 1, 1940, War Office review of the German push through the Balkans and into Syria, military planners wrote marginal notes with italics under the following statement: "A) Removal of present Iraqi Prime Minister: *We agree.* B) The elimination of the Mufti: *We do not agree that the assassination of the Mufti is unlikely to have ill effects. We agree, however, that it is essential to put an end to his current activities. "* Fully appreciating that thinly stretched British forces could not be diverted to Iraq, other planners wondered if the Iraqis could be bought off as in prior crises. "C) Financial and Economic Aid: *Since we are unable to spare troops for Iraq, or such war materiel as anti-aircraft guns, practically the only inducement for the Iraqis to behave in accordance with our wishes lies in the financial and economic sphere. "* But militant Iraqis weren't interested in stopping Nazism—just in furthering Palestine and Arab nationalism.[54]

Nuri, now waiting in the wings as foreign minister, agreed that drastic action was needed, and "evolved scheme after scheme for his [Rashid Ali's] elimination," as one British diplomat wrote, "but none progressed beyond its initial stages." In the end, London decided to ask the regent to exercise the powers of the king and simply fire Rashid Ali.[55]

Meanwhile, the Arab link to the Axis was growing closer. On January 20,

1941, the Mufti sent a long appeal to Adolf Hitler, using all the well-known anti-Semitic and trigger phrases of Nazi hate doctrine. "Your Excellence: England, that bitter and cunning enemy to the true freedom of the Arab nation, has never ceased to forge fetters to enslave and subjugate the Arab people, either in the name of a deceitful League of Nations, or by the expression of perfidious and hypocritical humanitarian feelings, but with the actual aim of effecting her imperialist machinations, which are camouflaged by principles of democracy and of deceitful internationalism." The Mufti's screed to Hitler detailed the Arab plight: "By geographical coincidence, the Arab people find themselves at the center of a land and sea crossroads which, according to the English, is the major intersection of the English Empire's 'transport lines'… the 'holy' British transport lines!"[56]

The Mufti then condemned Arab monarchs for giving England oil pipelines. "King Faisal the First," he wrote to Hitler, "agreed to a *modus vivendi*, and signed a treaty with England, and, despite the opposition of the majority of the Iraqi people, sold the relative independence of Iraq in return for oil concessions." Husseini's January 20, 1941 missive reviewed decades of international transgressions by the French in Syria and British in Palestine and Iraq, punctuating it with the resonant words, "This was done with the agreement of the Jews."[57]

Turning to Palestine, the Mufti made his most important point: "His Excellence is well aware of the problem faced by this country," he wrote, "which has also suffered from the deceitful actions of the English. They attempted to place an additional obstacle before the unity and independence of the Arab states by abandoning it to world Jewry, this dangerous enemy whose secret weapons—finance, corruption and intrigue—were aligned with British daggers … The Palestinian problem united all of the Arab states in a mutual hatred of the English and Jews. If mutual hatred is a prerequisite for national unity, it can be said that the problem of Palestine hastened this unity."[58]

Then came the Mufti's casbah-like offer of allegiance: "Freed from certain material impediments, the Arab peoples will be ready to serve the common enemy his just desserts, and to take their place enthusiastically alongside the Axis in order to fulfill their part in bringing about the well-deserved defeat of the Anglo-Jewish coalition … Allow me to add that the Arabs are willing to put all their weight behind the campaign, and to shed their blood in the holy war for their national rights and aspirations—on condition that certain interests of a moral and material order are assured." Husseini specifically focused on the Arab ability to disrupt "the transport lines of the [British] Empire and sever the contact between India and the Mediterranean region … through the Persian Gulf, and thus end the exploitation of the flow of oil for the benefit of England.[59]

"I close with wishes for long life and happiness for His Excellency," assured the Mufti, "and for a shining victory and prosperity for the great German people and for the Axis in the near future."[60]

In March 1941, Hitler replied through State Secretary Ernst von Weizacker. "*Der Führer* received your letter dated January 20," Weizacker's response began. "He took great interest in what you wrote him about the national struggle of the Arabs. He was pleased with the friendly words addressed to him in the name of Arab Nationalism." Now Hitler, through Weizacker, conveyed the words the Arabs wanted to hear. "Germany has never occupied any Arab countries and has no ambitions whatsoever in Arab lands. Our view is that Arabs, who possess an ancient culture and have proved their administrative, judiciary and military maturity, are capable of self-government. Germany recognizes the full independence of the Arab countries, or where this has not yet been attained, their right to it.[61]

"The Germans and the Arabs have common enemies in England and the Jews," the Reich letter continued, "and are united in the fight against them. Germany, traditionally friendly to the Arabs … is ready to cooperate with you and to give you all possible military and financial help required by your preparations to fight against the British for the realization of your people's aspirations. In order to enable the Arabs to begin the necessary preparations for their future war against the British, Germany is prepared to deliver to you immediately military material, if the means for transporting this material can be found." He added, "I request you keep the contents of this communication secret."[62]

Hitler's reply, however, fell short of the unequivocal statement of national recognition the Mufti was seeking, the type *der Führer* had extended to other ethnic groups in Europe to cement their support.

Although the language was still evolving, the Arab-Nazi axis was moving ahead. The Mufti's intrigues were hardly unknown to London intelligence. Whitehall most feared that Vichy Syria would allow the Germans to occupy and invade the Iraqi oil fields as part of a complete push past Russia and on to the east. Britain moved quickly now. London insisted that the regent dismiss Prime Minister Rashid Ali; and in doing so, stymie the Golden Square, the Mufti and the Nazi threat in one blow. The compliant regent was prepared to arrest Rashid Ali and his accomplices, but the Golden Square learned of his plans.[63]

On April 1, 1941, troops loyal to the Golden Square surrounded the palace, preparing to preemptively arrest the regent. The nervous regent donned a disguise, quietly slipped out to his aunt's house, and then stealthily made his way in a motorboat down the Tigris to Basra. There, he rendezvoused with a British gunboat. From Basra, the gunboat steamed to safety outside of Iraq.[64]

On April 3, 1941, with the regent gone, the Golden Square launched yet another *coup d'etat*, forming a new government under Rashid Ali and appointing trusted cronies to all the key positions, including the regency. Almost simultaneously, neighboring Syria, the anticipated gateway for the Nazi invasion, exploded with Reich propaganda, supported by Gestapo agents and specially trained Arab Nazis. The Arab Club, the National Youth Organization, and the Group of National Action all switched on a Nazi program. Their members all spoke fluent German. They distributed additional copies of the Arabic version of the Nazi Party's rabid newspaper, *Völkischer Beobachter*, and ensured that "the whole country is a hotbed of Nazi propaganda," as the *New York Times* reported. Soon, posters were popping up in the market. One featured a large swastika surrounded by the words "In Heaven, Allah is thy ruler. On Earth, Adolf Hitler will rule us."[65]

An anxious War Office sent a general to Baghdad to analyze the British mission's defensive position. If the Iraqis moved against British interests, diplomats, staff, and civilians in the oil industry across the country, along with their wives and children, would need evacuation from Baghdad and military protection. Code words were established: *sapphire* or *emerald* meant evacuate immediately to the British base at Habbaniya by any means possible. But the small contingent of British soldiers at Habbaniya would be hopelessly outnumbered. Sending additional weapons would not help, they concluded. The situation was dire; there were no armaments to spare. Nonetheless, 25 rifles and a few other small arms were dispatched.[66]

When calls for relief troops circulated, military commanders in the region confessed they were unable to assist. The commanding general cabled, "My forces are stretched to limit everywhere and I simply cannot afford to risk part of forces … at Basra."[67] With the British outmanned, with German troops preparing to enter via Vichy Syria to occupy the oil fields, and with the Iraqis willing to facilitate the Nazis, there seemed to be only one option remaining for the Allies.

Destroy the oil. Destroy it all.

\*       \*       \*       \*

No one was quite sure how to destroy an oil field. But the contingency had been considered as much as a year earlier. Some experts thought the fields could simply be dynamited. But they quickly concluded that an explosion would only bring more oil to the surface. Perhaps the field could be set ablaze, but then again the fire might burn for years, the experts worried. But if it worked, a new drill site into the vast oil layer of Kirkuk would reestablish the supply within months, even as another well burned. The wells could be plugged; but again, theorized the planners, new borings would remedy that.[68]

But more would be needed. The whole infrastructure would have to be blown up, that is, the storage tanks, pumping stations, pipelines, and refineries. Everything: from Kirkuk to Tripoli to Haifa. That was the only way to deny Iraq's oil to the Reich just as Barbarossa was about to launch.

As early as the summer of 1940, a secret memo was circulated to a trusted British manager of the Iraq Petroleum Company. "It is now advisable," the memo explained, "to consider what action the IPC should take in the way of preparations for demolition or putting plant[s] out of action, and/or prevent[ing] the possibility of supplies getting into enemy hands. It is suggested ... in the following order: 1) The destruction and elimination of stocks of Crude Oil from Tripoli. These stocks of crude oil today are approximately 113,300 tons. It is suggested that arrangements should now be made for the disposal of these stocks: by burning, or by opening the lines to allow the oil to discharge into the sea ... Consideration should be given to the immobilization of the field as a whole ... The IPC Management should now... draw up a line of attack... if, and when, it is necessary ... In the meantime, the IPC should give consideration to immediate action in the way of plugging up wells which are not required ... to keep Haifa Refinery going on a one million tons per annum basis; that is, only those wells that are in production should be left open and all others plugged off and even disconnected from the pipeline system. [In addition] stocks of crude oil at K1 and K3 [pumping facilities] should now be reduced to an absolute minimum."[69]

Some in the Ministry of Economic Warfare in London began to worry about just how many oil executives would be privy to the secret plans. In late June 1940, one planner wrote, "To this oil committee go quite a large number of persons, several of whom are in almost continual touch with representatives of the oil companies, many of which are international in character, and some of which must at the present time have in mind the future interest of their companies."[70]

By mid-July 1940, the War Cabinet concluded that to be effective, the pipelines running through Syria to Tripoli would have to be blown as well. "If the German war effort were to be turned eastwards," they decided, "it would be of the highest importance that the northern branch of the Iraq Pipeline should not remain intact. Even if the Kirkuk Oilfield in Iraq were put out of action, it would only be a few months before it could be brought back to production; only a relatively short part of the northern line runs through Iraq and this could be repaired by the time the field was able to produce. Destruction of the pumping stations and pipeline throughout Syria could cause a much greater delay before transport could be resumed."[71]

By November 1940, as the situation worsened, the generals wanted the demolition sequence solidified. "Plans already in preparation for the destruction of the Iraqi oil wells and the pipelines in Iraq, Syria and Palestine should be perfected," instructed one memo, "and brought to a state in which they could be operated without interference on a very short notice." The memo added, "It is important to keep these plans secret from the Iraqi Government."[72]

IPC general manager J. Skliros injected a dose of reality to the planners. During a December 18, conference on the question, Skliros explained that destroying Iraqi oil facilities would not be easy. In Palestine and Transjordan, he said, where British authorities reigned, the facilities could be junked at will, with troops overseeing the explosives. But in Iraq, Britain maintained a mere shadow military presence. "The Iraqi government probably suspected that such schemes were in mind," cautioned Skliros, "and, if occasion to put them into practice arose, the Iraqi Government would probably take measures to prevent the entry of British Military personnel into Iraq for the purpose, and the movements of Company personnel would probably be subject to surveillance."[73]

Skliros was correct. In the first days of April 1941, just after the Golden Square coup forced the regent to flee and then installed a tougher Rashid Ali government, Iraqi police units took up positions at Kirkuk and various pumping stations, as expected. Moreover, oil company personnel now came under intense suspicion and scrutiny.[74]

On April 18, 1941, Britain finally found a small contingent of troops to assist. They were suddenly airlifted and sealifted into Basra, ostensibly to transit through the country pursuant to treaty rights, but in fact to protect the oil fields and British civilians. As the naval ships approached, senior Iraqi officials were undecided whether they should challenge the landing or honor the treaty. Formal permission was granted just two hours before the seaborne troops actually arrived. The men were permitted to proceed to the British base at Habbaniya. But in view of the rapidly deteriorating position, more men would need to be mustered from Britain's overstretched forces.[75]

Ten days later, on April 28, the British Embassy advised the Iraqis that three more ships would be landing, this time carrying 2,000 men, only 400 of whom were actual combat troops. Within a few hours, the Golden Square issued a swift reply: They could not enter. The British, however, were determined, especially since an uprising against British civilians was rumored to erupt within a few days.[76]

The next day, April 29, evacuation orders were broadcast by the embassy. British women and children from all over Iraq were bused to the large base at Habbaniya. On April 30, Iraqi officials confronted the IPC's oilfields manager, demanding "a written guarantee that no wells or installations would be sabotaged." The statement was signed, and the installations were promptly taken over by Iraqi troops for good measure. In the meantime, a column of 9,000 Iraqi troops was ordered to proceed to the British base.[77]

The Habbaniya base, located almost midway between the Iraqi cities of Fallujah and Ramadi, sprawled across an eight-mile square. Its massive cantonment housed several thousand troops, 8,000 civilians, churches, shops, and barracks. Habbaniya was extremely habitable, but quite poorly defended. One British commander fondly remarked, "It is notorious that when the Germans occupy a new station, their first task is to build defenses around it, whereas the British in similar circumstances lay out cricket and football fields." Indeed, a quaint crossroads sign out front sported arrows with two air distances: London 3,287 miles to the west, Baghdad 55 miles to the east. The base, mainly the home of a military flying school, was hardly ready for combat.[78]

On April 30, 1941, an English-speaking Iraqi messenger delivered a demand to the base commandant that all British aircraft remain grounded and all troops remain confined to base. British commanders considered the note an "impertinent gesture." Planes were demonstratively sent aloft to photograph the enemy encampments. This revealed that Iraqis and several dozen howitzers were dug in just a half mile outside the perimeter and all across the high escarpments overlooking Habbaniya. Moreover, Golden Square forces had evacuated local tribesmen in surrounding hamlets to make way for a military action against the base. One British soldier who ventured out to collect mail was arrested by Iraqis.[79]

The night of May 1, 1941, British air commander Harry George Smart pondered his predicament. Habbaniya was vulnerable and British forces outnumbered. A telegram from Prime Minister Winston Churchill to Smart was explicit: "If you have to strike, strike hard."[80]

During the night of May 2, Iraqi advance troops penetrated to the base perimeter. At 5:00 a.m., Commander Smart decided this was a hostile and threatening act. He opened fire. Now the fight was on. Iraqi mortar shells began raining in on the base. The flight students scrambled to become instant combat pilots. Their orders: strafe and bomb Iraqi positions.[81]

One student, with only a few hours flying experience, jumped into an Airspeed Oxford twin prop trainer to ride as navigator for a sortie over Ramadi. At 2,000 feet, ground fire hit the plane, killing the pilot with a shot to the heart. The young lad pulled the pilot off the controls and attempted to land on his own. After three or four approaches, the student was finally able to put down safely.[82]

The students flew as many as 9 or 10 sorties each, round the clock, hitting every encampment and concentration of Iraqi troops. When the Iraqis tried to bring up a column from Fallujah, it became bottlenecked three miles from a bridge at a narrow bend in the road. At that choke point, the lane squeezed between palm groves elevated above irrigation ditches on either side. Hence, there was no possible way to turn around. British aircraft spotted the crawling line and attacked. First, they destroyed the lead vehicles, and then they hammered them over and over again with strafing runs and dive-bombing. Ammunition trucks exploded sending spirals of flame into the air. A convoy of troops in an assortment of vehicles all caught fire. A battery of mobile artillery along with every other type of mechanized vehicle was bombed into twisted, smoldering wreckage.[83]

A furious Mufti ordered that the precious British pipeline from Iraq to Haifa in Palestine be severed. He declared a jihad against the British. Rashid Ali sent an urgent appeal to Berlin for help.[84]

The German high command met on May 6, 1941 and decided to give all possible assistance to Iraq. Former ambassador to Baghdad Grobba was sent back to Baghdad under the code name "Franz Gehrke." Another diplomat, Rudolph Rahn was dispatched to coordinate weapon shipments. Rahn arrived in Beirut on May 10, 1941, where he met with French generals and was able to recruit the collusion of the Vichy French in Syria. The Nazi-allied French Army in Syria agreed to furnish French weapons and landing facilities for German aircraft at France's massive Rayak Airbase. By May 13, 1941, the first trainloads of weaponry pulled into the station yards at Mosul, in northern Iraq. Both Grobba and Rahn were then to rendezvous in Baghdad with the Mufti.[85]

At the same time, the Wehrmacht chief of air staff sent one of the Reich's top aviators, Major Axel von Blomberg, son of Hitler's first Field Marshal, to survey available landing strips so that the Luftwaffe could fly in and assist Rashid Ali. Two others pilots were ordered to help. Blomberg flew in circuitously by way of Athens and Damascus, landing in Mosul on May 11. There, he found two disused German Heinkel 111 bombers from the Iraqi air force. The next morning, Blomberg flew one of the Heinkels to Baghdad to meet with Rashid Ali. Flying low, the clearly marked German craft aroused celebratory fire from tribesmen. Several bullets pierced the cockpit, killing Blomberg. He was buried the next day, with Rashid Ali offering special condolences at the funeral.[86]

Blomberg's death did not pause the Nazi effort. Now, the Germans launched missions in earnest. A heavy-fighter unit and a bomber unit dispatched 16 more Heinkels and 10 Messerschmitt heavy fighters to aid in the attack on Habbaniya. This included aircraft stationed in occupied Rhodes awaiting orders to bomb the Suez Canal. Meanwhile, some two dozen German mechanics and airmen filtered into the country, along with Grobba and other Reich diplomats. The Luftwaffe began running strafing and bombing missions of their own against Habbaniya, as well as commando formations crossing the desert to aide the besieged camp. The Germans primarily used the Rayak airbase in Vichy Syria. But they set up a closer air and weapons base at Mosul, where large shipments had already been unloaded.[87]

With Germans running bombing missions and Habbaniya under continuous attack, the British turned off the oil spigot at Basra. The commander in chief in India sent a coded telegram to the War Office: "Iraqi troops have also occupied pumping station K1 and K2. Iraqi police have arrested engineer in charge of plant at H3." The telegram added. "All refineries and oil installations are in Iraqi hands and demolition now possible by air action."[88]

The students and instructors at Habbaniya were heroically flying day and night against both the small Iraqi air force and the German planes. Most enemy craft were destroyed on the ground, sometimes a dozen at a time. Churchill had already sent a foreboding cable to U.S. president Franklin D. Roosevelt, stating that if the Mideast fell to the Germans, victory against the Nazis would be a "hard, long and bleak proposition."[89] All understood that if Germany would secure Iraq's oil, she might proceed all the way to the East.

By May 15, 1941, urgent messages burned the telegraph wires as British commanders in the area informed London that land operations were now out of the question. One typical note declared: "In view changed situation Iraq, consider it will be impossible to destroy Kirkuk wells at short notice."[90]

Besieged and out of options, the British called an unlikely ally to save the day. London reached out for the *Irgun*, the extremist Zionist guerrilla force formed to defend kibbutzim and villages and retaliate for the constant Arab attacks. Irgun commander David Raziel, at that moment, was in a British prison in Palestine. Raziel was approached by British intelligence and asked if he would undertake a dangerous mission to destroy the oil refineries in Iraq, thereby denying the fuel to the Germans. The answer was yes, on one condition: Raziel wanted to kidnap the Mufti of Jerusalem and bring him back. Agreed.[91]

The next morning, May 17, 1941, Raziel and three comrades, along with a British officer, quietly entered the Tel Nof air base which was located south of Tel Aviv. There they climbed into an RAF plane, which flew them to Habbaniya. While in flight, however, the British high command in London decided that the destruction of Iraq's refineries should be delayed until the very last moment in the hope it would not be necessary. Rebuilding the pipelines would take years and place an enormous strain on British fuel needs for the rest of the war. Perhaps the Germans could be stopped after all. When Raziel landed in Iraq, he was given new orders: Undertake an intelligence mission preparatory to a British sweep into Fullajah as part of the final drive to retake Baghdad from Rashid Ali and the Golden Square.[92]

As Raziel was landing, a new Zionist military organization was being formed, again with the consent of the British. It would be known as the *Palmach*, or strike forces. Even before the units were properly assembled, their first mission would be an elite commando raid, made up of 23 volunteers and commanded by Zvi Spectre. British Major Anthony Palmer accompanied them. Their objective: Blow up the refineries in Tripoli that were providing fuel to the German airplanes bombing Iraq. Very late on the evening of May 18, 1941, a small British vessel, the *Sea Lion*, equipped with three oar-driven landing boats, departed Haifa for Vichy Lebanon. By this time, the British were bombing Tripoli, which placed Vichy defense forces around the Tripoli refinery on high alert. In the hours to come, the *Sea Lion* and all its men disappeared. *Palmach* commanders believed they were killed while approaching the refinery.[93]

Meanwhile back in Iraq, on May 17, Raziel, his three comrades, along with a British officer, set out by car from the Habbaniya base toward Fallujah. At the first river, they found a boat, only big enough for two. Raziel ordered his comrades to proceed, while he went back to the car with his fellow Irgunist and the British officer. Just then, from nowhere, a plane—no one knows if it was British or German—dived from on high, dropping a bomb. A direct hit. The car was destroyed and Raziel with it.[94]

That same day, RAF commanders notified the Air Ministry that the situation was becoming more precarious each day. Once German airpower had fully advanced from Syria into Iraq, the Luftwaffe would constitute a major threat to the refinery at Abadan in Iran at the waterway leading to the Persian Gulf, and also to the Suez Canal. By May 22, the RAF cabled back to London, "I submit that the time has come for taking action against the oil refinery at Alwand [about 100 miles northeast of Baghdad]" as well as four pumping stations. "Thus, we remove his [the enemy's] main attraction in that part of the world. The cable pleaded with the British high command to move quickly and remember that "the history of [such] demolitions is a history of 'too late.'"[95]

A few days later, around May 25, Hitler issued Order 30, declaring his support for Iraq. "The Arabian Freedom Movement in the Middle East," Hitler wrote, "is our natural ally against England. In this connection special importance is attached to the liberation of Iraq. It strengthens beyond the Iraq borders the forces in the Middle East hostile to England, disturbs English communications, and ties down English troops as well as English shipping space, at the cost of other theaters of war. I have therefore decided to move forward in the Middle East by supporting Iraq. Whether and how the English position between the Mediterranean and the Persian Gulf—in connection with an offensive against the Suez Canal—is to be later finally solved, is not up for decision until after Barbarossa."[96]

Hitler's directive established a new "Special Staff F" to coordinate with

Arab Nationalist movements everywhere, starting with Iraq. The directive outlined detailed assistance to Arab movements and Iraq—weapons, Luftwaffe aircraft disguised with Iraqi insignia, propaganda, and even the type of "tropical" uniforms military men were to wear. *Der Führer* specified that all such operations would be controlled and supervised by the top echelons of the Wehrmacht High Command and the Commander in Chief of the Luftwaffe.[97]

The Admiralty in London now gave the final order to destroy the refineries and pumping stations in Iraq at will. "If Germans occupy Iraq and Syria," the message read, "they cannot profit by the oil resources there for at least some time." But suddenly, the forces at Habbaniya were gaining the upper hand. Persistent bombing, Arab fighters abandoning their positions and equipment *en masse* to disappear into the populace, plus the sheer exhaustion of supplies had delivered what seemed like a victory to British forces.[98]

In the meantime, British land forces, including Jewish soldiers and the loyal regiments of the Arab Legion mustered in Palestine and Transjordan. Dubbed Habforce, its mechanized units, mobile guns and crack Gurka fighters streaked straight across the desert toward Habbaniya to relieve the beleaguered British. From there, they intended to tackle the Golden Square and take control of the oil. Like a cloud of armored dust, Habforce's steel-plated trucks, horse soldiers, and eager Sikh British contingents closed in. With no time to spare, Habforce, backed by a column of fighters supported by a squadron of British aircraft—called KingCol, broke through to Habbaniya, rescuing the base and its civilians.[99] Next stop: Baghdad.

Rumors of a massive armored British invasion sizzled through Baghdad like a fast-burning fuse. By May 28, Rashid Ali, in a state of panic, wired Germany. British tanks were nearing the city. The whole enterprise was failing.[100]

On May 29, 1941, the Mufti, Rashid Ali and several dozen confederates disappeared across the border into Iran. Reich bomber crews flew from Mosul back to Germany. Only two of the Heinkels had escaped destruction. Grobba and his staff departed Mosul by car. A mobile column of armored cars, backed up by howitzers and cavalry, gave chase; but by the time they reached Mosul, the culprits had escaped.[101]

May 30, the Arab Legion, led by Britain's legendary Major Henry Glubb, pushed past fatigued ground resistance and a steady barrage of German air attacks. Major Glubb reached Baghdad at about 4:00 a.m. to meet two Iraqi truce officers waving a white flag hanging from a pole. Since Rashid Ali, the Golden Square, and Grobba had fled to Iran or elsewhere, the mayor of Baghdad was the only authority figure left to come out and sign the cease-fire document.[102]

The coup and the threat were over, at least for now. The regent returned to Iraq.[103]

With Baghdad and Habbaniya in British hands, London rushed new superseding instructions about destroying the oil installations. "Scheme for the denial of the Iraq oil to the enemy... is quite clearly out of date," war planners in London stated. "If we regain control in Iraq, one of our first steps must be to secure the key points on the oil system with a view to their demolition [only] if we are compelled to withdraw subsequently." A new plan was devised: Operation Exporter. Exporter would leave the pipelines intact—if possible—and instead destroy the Lebanese oil infrastructure at Tripoli, now coming under full Nazi control. Orders from London specified, "Dangerous as it is to delay, I think we should not take immediate action against the Haifa pipelines or the installations which feed it until the success or failure of 'Exporter' becomes apparent." However, the note continued, local commanders must be prepared, "to ensure the destruction of the Iraq-Haifa pipeline system in the event of the failure of 'Exporter.'"[104]

The threat to Iraqi oil was not over. The Germans were still threatening a major new advance into Vichy Syria and Lebanon. Operation Exporter, conceived almost overnight, was the only Allied hope of denying the Reich an open door in Vichy Syria. An Australian strike force, augmented by Free French Forces, assembled to launch a sneak attack.[105]

Again, the British called upon the *Palmach*, this time to cross into Syria and pave the way for Exporter. *Palmach* commanders Moshe Dayan and Yitzhak Rabin were among the men who would lead the commando missions. Later these two would become among the greatest generals of the Jewish state. Dayan assembled a force of 30. The British required all of them to know Syrian territory intimately and speak perfect Arabic so they could enter disguised as Arabs. Dayan's commandos lied. None of them spoke Arabic. They didn't even have a map of Syria. But they had to go. Dayan hired a trusted Arabic guide. The group made ready.[106]

On the night of June 6, the *Palmach* commandos set off with a team of Australians to disrupt telegraph and telephone communications, eliminate key potential installations, and secure bridges together with other strategic points. By preemptively capturing or neutralizing resistance at the major crossing points, Exporter forces could race through Vichy Syria and Lebanon to secure the oil installations and airfields.[107]

Dayan's group was operating successfully at the Litani River. Suddenly, on the morning of June 8, 1941, having secured most of their objectives, Dayan's group came under French heavy machine-gun fire. He picked up a pair of binoculars to scout out the firing positions. An incoming bullet hit his binoculars, driving steel and glass deep into Dayan's left eye. The eye could not be saved, and Dayan would later don the eyepatch that for decades became the icon of defense for the Jewish people. Rabin, the youngest member of the squad, spent most of his time atop telephone poles cutting phone lines and did not sustain any injuries.[108] Both Rabin and Dayan went on to become commanders of the Jewish State's defense forces. Rabin would go on to become the state's prime minister.

The next day, June 9, 1941, Exporter launched a three-pronged assault—from Iraq, from Palestine, and from the sea. Their objective: seize Vichy Syria and Lebanon, thereby denying Germany the operating base and oil the Reich needed to dominate the Middle East. A British reporter embedded with the first troops punching in from Palestine sent back an eyewitness dispatch. Using just paper and pencil, he wrote, "I crossed from Palestine into Syria just before dawn this morning with Australian troops and am now speeding northward with our forces along the white cliffs toward Lebanon. Our advance into the French-mandated territories began under cover of darkness. Long lines of transports filled with grinning Diggers [Australians]... are now pushing forward at several points, accompanied by Bren gun carriers, guns and tanks. British troops, the Royal Air Force and the navy are cooperating. From dusk until midnight Sunday night our column had moved toward the frontier. While scouts crossed No-Man's Land, we waited under cover for the signal to advance ... French positions knew nothing."[109]

Within a matter of days, the Allied surprise attack, made up of Free French, Australian, and British forces, supported by *Palmach* scouts and commandos, overwhelmed tough Vichy forces in Syria and Lebanon.[110] The Allies dug in throughout Lebanon and Syria, stopping the Nazi advance in the Middle East. Hitler's Operation Barbarossa was launched against Russia on June 22, 1941, but Germany did so without Iraqi petroleum.

The oil installations were not destroyed, not in Iraq, not anywhere.

Now the Nazi-Arab alliance had come of age. What began as a reluctant propaganda and diplomatic ploy now fused into an earnest joint military effort. The Arabs—from Saudi Arabia to Syria to Iran to Palestine to Bosnia—would join the Nazi war against Europe and against the Jews. The time for telegrams was over. Now the killing would begin.

CHAPTER

# 14

# THE FARHUD

Violent dispossession. In Arabic, the word is *Farhud*. For decades after it occurred, many thought the nightmare was a sudden and unexpected convulsion. But in truth, the wild killing spree of June 1–2, 1941 was not unexpected. For years, the Jew-hatred, anti-British revolt, and Nazi agitation seethed just below the surface, like a smoking volcano waiting to erupt.

When the Allies granted Britain Iraq's mandate in 1920, Jews and Christians greatly expanded their middle class and establishment niches. Jews stepped into the vacuum created by the mass murder of about a million Armenians during the war. Much of that killing occurred in the provinces that would become Iraq. Because of their education, Jews were often given preference by mandate officials. Jewish professionals and clerical workers flocked to the new Allied-run bureaucracies. Jews served as lawyers, doctors, and judges. Jews dominated the cotton trade via their connections in Manchester and were pivotal in other imports and exports. Wealthy Jews operated nearly all the banks, continued as essential economic advisors to the Baghdad government, acted as money changers, and generally functioned as the bedrock of Iraq's entire financial apparatus. Independent Iraq's new monetary system was actually devised by Jewish financial experts. Jewish negotiators loyally extracted the highest possible royalties for Iraq's national treasury from Turkish Petroleum, an Anglo-Persian Oil Company affiliate. Several distinguished members of the Jewish community served in the Iraqi Chamber of Deputies and the Senate. Jews also became well known in the arts, letters, and music of the nation.[1]

By no means were all Iraqi Jews cosmopolitan Baghdadis. For many centuries, Jews lived in the north among the Kurds, mainly as simple farmers and herders, tending flocks and orchards and rejoicing at weddings with the same abundant food, dancing, and music as their neighbors. Rural Jews lived in Mosul, Kirkuk, Arbil, and other Kurdish areas along with the other Islamic and non-Islamic ethnic groups that created the Kurdish culture. In dress and manner, Kurdish Jews resembled their neighbors, and they adopted the national identity of their fellow Kurds in their struggle for independence. In the Shia south, Jews also blended in with their fellow citizens as simple peddlers and stall owners in the bazaar. They shared the same coffeehouses and were equally affected when British forces invaded during the Mesopotamian campaign.[2]

Various censuses measured the Jewish population of Iraq differently, depending on which disputed territories were included and the demographic ebb and flow of volatile Iraq. A 1906 Ottoman census counted 256,000 Jewish citizens. A Young Turk census in 1914 listed 187,000. As a result of emigration during the postwar upheaval years, Jewish numbers dropped, with the official 1920 census counting only 87,488. Slightly more than half of those lived in Baghdad, with the remainder split between Mosul in the north and Basra in the south.[3]

Naturally, Iraqi Jews often confronted persecution. This was especially so in the 1930s, after Nazi propaganda had begun to infect the thinking of many nations in Europe and especially the Middle East. Iraqi Jews were periodically expelled from some professions under *numerus clausus* quotas, just as they were in Germany. Although the Arab Revolt in Palestine caused uncomfortable reverberations for Jews throughout the Mideast, Iraq's Jews weathered the discrimination of the 1930s as they had for millennia. Iraqi Jews blamed their most recent troubles not on their domestic status as much as on the Zionist enterprise in Palestine, an enterprise they vocally rejected.[4]

Before 1941, Iraqi Jews simply did not identify with Zionism, not after 2,600 years of accepted life as Iraqis. They were, in fact, following the attitude adopted by most assimilated Jews settled in America, England, France, and Germany. Iraqi Jews, like most Jews in Arab lands, were genuinely anti-Zionist. Zionists understood this rejection and did not view the abundantly populated Arab countries next door as a source of immigration. During the 1920s and 1930s, no Zionist immigration representative was posted in Baghdad, and none was welcome.[5]

Iraqi Jewish journalist and parliamentarian Salman Shina, in speaking to top Zionist officials, ruled out Iraqi emigration in these words: "The Jews there live contented lives; they are involved in all branches of commerce and economy and, therefore, have no thought of emigrating."[6]

Menahem S. Daniel, an eminent leader of the Baghdad Jewish community, summed it up when he informed the Zionist Organization in London: "Any sympathy with the Zionist Movement is [seen by our neighbors as] nothing short of a betrayal of the Arab cause." Daniel reminded them, "Jews in this country hold indeed a conspicuous position. They form one-third of the population of the capital, hold the larger part of the commerce of the country and offer a higher standard of literacy than the Moslems ... [The Iraqi Jew] is, moreover, beginning to give the Moslem ... successful competition in government functions, which ... may well risk to embitter feelings against him. In this delicate situation, the Jew cannot maintain himself unless he gives proof of an unimpeachable loyalty to his country."[7]

Public denunciations by Iraqi Jews of a Jewish Palestine were common, as much to express their rejection as to preserve their status among militantly anti-Zionist neighbors. At the timeframe of the *Kristallnacht* riots in Germany, in November 1938, a leading Jewish attorney writing in the *Baghdad Times* declared: "The problem which the Balfour Declaration purported to solve is and remains a European problem, both by origin and present incidence." The chief rabbi of Iraq proclaimed, "Iraqi Jews will forever be against Zionism."[8]

But on June 1 and 2, 1941, more than two millennia of historic existence abruptly shattered like a fragile knee. Overnight, shocked Iraqi Jews could no longer stand on their ancient history and steadfast loyalty. Zionist visionaries had always been convinced that sooner or later anti-Jewish impulses would drive Jews from their countries, hence the need for a Jewish homeland. Iraqi Jews woke up on June 1 staunchly anti-Zionist. By the time they fell asleep on June 2, forlorn and traumatized, Zionism and Jewish Palestine had become an option—perhaps the only option.

*     *     *     *

The stage for the Iraqi tragedy was set almost as soon as Hitler came to power in 1933. While Iraqi Jews were thriving in the 1930s, things began happening all around the community that would soon destroy their world. Like most assimilated Jews, they ignored the warning signs and perceived the storm clouds too far over the horizon for concern. But in fact, they were always right around the corner.

Of course, the precedent for ethnic slaughter in Iraq existed in centuries of that nation's ingrained sectarian carnage. The twentieth century continued the grim tradition with the brutal extermination of more than a million Armenians by Arabs and Turks during World War I, many along the Baghdad-to-Berlin railway. Echoes of the Armenian mass murder undoubtedly were still fresh in the collective memory when the same heinous habit recurred during the Hitler years.

True, in 1932, Britain finally sponsored an independent Iraq for full membership in the League of Nations. A condition for admission to the League was acceptance by the Iraqi government of the league's Protection of Minorities Declaration. The Baghdad government signed the declaration. But no sooner was statehood granted, than state-sponsored violence against its own minorities was unleashed.[9]

In 1933, Iraq's armed forces brutally reacted to a nationalist surge by Assyrian Christians. Assyrians were one of the peoples that had dwelled in the region since the earliest days of ancient Mesopotamian civilization. In the first century of the Common Era, Assyrians widely adopted Christianity, forming one of the earliest Christian churches. After the Muslim Conquest, Christian Assyrians became a persecuted minority under both the Turks and mandate-era Iraqis. They energetically, but unsuccessfully, sought self-determination from the League of Nations and rebelled against Baghdad's authority.[10]

In August 1933, while King Faisal was in London, several thousand Iraqi troops were deployed to suppress an Assyrian insurrection. Under explicit orders, the soldiers mercilessly retaliated against all civilians in about 60 Assyrian villages. The Motor Machine Gun Unit systematically drove from village to village, dragging all the men out of their homes, lining them up in groups, and mercilessly machine-gunned them. About 500 to 1,000 were murdered in cold blood during this campaign. The corpses were piled into macabre heaps and then set on fire. To complete the vengeance, the army and Kurdish tribesmen thoroughly looted the villages, torched the homes, and destroyed the grain. This created hundreds of starving, homeless women and children. Some said the atrocities were too heinous for Faisal to bear and suggested that the emotional distress of the crisis actually hastened his death.[11] League declaration or not, independence in Iraq seemed a license to rise up against its minorities. Assyrians were first; Jews were next—this time with a Nazi accent.

Shortly after Iraq signed that 1932 declaration to protect all minorities, German Arab specialist Fritz Grobba arrived as Germany's *chargé d'affaires* in Baghdad. Soon after Hitler took power, Grobba acquired the Christian Iraqi newspaper, *al-Alem al Arabi*, converting it into a Nazi organ that published an Arabic translation of Hitler's *Mein Kampf* in installments. Once Hitler assumed office in 1933, Radio Berlin began beaming Arabic programs across the Middle East. The Nazi ideology of Jewish conspiracy and international manipulation were widely adopted in Iraqi society, especially within the framework of the Palestinian problem that dominated Iraqi politics.[12]

A confederate of Grobba and the Mufti of Jerusalem was Sami Shawkat, an Iraqi nationalist active in the Arab movement to adopt Nazism and Fascism. Shawkat's 1933 lecture to the student body of the Central Secondary School staunchly proclaimed the *au courant* Islamic Fascism and Arab Nationalism of the day: "The nation which does not excel in the Profession of Death with iron and fire will be forced to die under the hooves of the horses and under the boots of a foreign soldiery," proclaimed Shawkat. "He added, "Had Mussolini not tens of thousands of Black Shirts well versed in the Profession of Death? … Sixty years ago, Prussia used to dream of uniting the German people. What is there to prevent Iraq, who fulfilled her desire for independence ten years ago, from dreaming to unite all the Arab countries?"[13]

At first, Iraq's anti-Jewish actions were simple *numerus clausus* purges. In September 1934, a few dozen government clerks were ousted from their positions because they were Jewish. The next year, 1935, the Iraqi Ministry of Education adopted unwritten quotas for Jews seeking to attend institutions of higher education. In 1936, hundreds of Jews were dismissed from government service. Iraqi Jews saw these measures as fallout from the Arab Revolt in Palestine, not a manifestation of growing national hatred against their community. But over the next few years, the situation worsened as bombs and grenades were hurled at synagogues and Jewish schools. Even an appeal by King Ghazi in October 1936 did not stop the stream of murders and anti-Jewish incitement. Palestinian gangs mainly orchestrated the campaign, not infrequently buttressed by government officials such as the governor of Basra, who was a major fund-raiser for the anti-Zionist resistance in Palestine.[14]

As Arab Nationalism and Hitlerism fused, numerous Nazi-style youth clubs began springing up in Iraq, including one pivotal group known as *Futuwwa*. The name Futuwwa was reminiscent of a mystic, chivalrous, or perhaps cultic Islamic past. Its reincarnation in Baghdad in 1934 was nothing less than a clone of the Hitler Youth. One of its leaders was Shawkat, who by 1938 was appointed director-general of the Iraqi Ministry of Education, with authority over all schools and curricula. In that position, Shawkat required Futuwwa members to attend a candlelight Nazi Party rally in Nuremberg in 1938, at the invitation of Hitler Youth chief Baldur von Schirach. When the delegation came back from Germany, a common chant in Arabic was, "Long live Hitler, the killer of insects and Jews." In one instance, Jewish students were humiliated in front of the class by having their hair shorn.[15]

Another leader of Futuwwa was Yunus al-Sabawi, the man who translated *Mein Kampf* into Arabic. Military training was mandatory for Futuwwa. Col. Salah ad-Din as-Sabbagh, another member of the Nazi Arab vanguard, became Futuwwa's so-called "General Trainer." Sabbagh was known for his many publications extolling the Nazis and advocating destruction of the Jewish and British presence in Iraq and anything Zionist.[16] Nazi hate planks and Futuwwa doctrine became one and indivisible.

By now, the Mufti's circles and the transnational agitators of the Arab

Revolt in Palestine had thoroughly permeated Baghdad's ruling circles. For example, Taha al-Hashimi, Iraqi Chief of Staff, doubled as the head of the Committee for the Defense of Palestine. This committee brought together Fascist Arab newspaper editors and Syrian National Socialists to agitate against Britain, Jews and Zionism.[17] Propaganda and slanders against Iraqi Jews were now ceaseless.

Leading the charge of anti-Jewish agitation on behalf of Germany was Grobba, stressing to all that Jews in Iraq, despite their 2,600-year history there, were not true Iraqis, but a foul species apart. His anti-Jewish, anti-Zionist provocations were hardly secret and were covered in newspapers of the day from Palestine to Great Britain.

For example, in 1937, Grobba complained to Berlin that "Some 60–70 thousand Jews live in Baghdad at the moment. Eighty-five percent of the commerce is in their hands ... From the Zionist press in Palestine, which has now attacked me for the fourth time, one can deduce what the local Jews think of me. When a number of Jews were fired from the Ministry of the Post a number of years ago, an English-language Zionist newspaper, *The Palestine Post*, accused me of having been involved. When 12 Jews were killed over a period of two months before the [last] coup, the Tel Aviv Zionist newspaper *Ha'aretz* accused me of conducting National Socialist propaganda among the Iraqi authorities. After the coup, the Jewish reporters in Baghdad of the *Daily Express* and the *Daily Herald* published reports putting some of the blame for the coup on me, and accusing me of maintaining close ties with the conspirators." Grobba said he fought back against the headlines by disrupting the activities of the local *Ha'avara* office, which was selling German goods in Iraq via the Near and Middle East Commercial Corporation (NEMICO). Sales of Nazi goods via NEMICO only quickened the pace of transfers into Palestine. "Only after I had refused to cooperate with the local *Ha'avara* representative," bragged Grobba, "did the newspaper agree to amend the report and publish an apology. I have reported to the Foreign Ministry about all these matters."[18]

By June 6, 1939, Grobba wired another caustic report to Berlin, this one labeled "SECRET" and entitled: "The Jews—they are the origin of the propaganda against Germans and Italians in Iraq." In his report, Grobba predicted nothing less than a bloody massacre—using those very words: "The Jews were playing a dangerous game," railed Grobba. "They forget that this is not Germany, who indeed wants to remove them, yet treats them humanely, but Iraq, is an oriental land. If the Jews continue to make it difficult for Iraq with their deeds, a day will come when the anger of the masses will erupt, and the result will be: a massacre of Jews. When an oriental people's feelings erupt, all restraint disappears; they want to see blood." Grobba added a recent example, "Indeed, during the uprising [against the British] in 1920, six thousand Englishmen were killed by the Iraqi populace."[19]

Days later, on June 12, 1939, Grobba reported a pro-Hitler anti-British coup activity led by Nazified students. "An investigation revealed that the students belonged to a secret Nazi organization," he confirmed to the German Foreign Office. "The [Iraqi] government thus arrived at the conclusion that this anti-government position was the result of propaganda by German Nazi circles," he continued. "This activity (by the legation and the local Nazi organization) was carried out by German teachers ... As the director general of the Ministry of Education, Dr. Sami Shawkat, informed me in confidence, the suspicions of the government were reinforced by complaints made by Jewish students about the Nazi propaganda made by German teachers during class, and by the complaints made by other Jews who suspected this legation ... of supplying them with propaganda material." Grobba pointed out that Germany's fingerprints were now broadly apparent in the international Arab insurrections. "Further credence to the assessment that a German organization active throughout the Arab world was involved," he wrote, "was given by the fact that news of the murder of the British consul was made public on the same day in both Damascus and Beirut, and was broadcast that very evening on German radio, using a distinctly anti-British tone." Grobba closed his report with the assurance, "This report was prepared with the cooperation of the NSDAP [the Nazi Party] official in charge."[20]

To lure more Arabs to the Nazi cause, Grobba employed such tactics as dispensing lots of cash among politicians and deploying seductive German women among ranking members of the army. German radio broadcasting in Baghdad regularly reported fallacious reports about non-existent Jewish outrages in Palestine. Grobba, in conjunction with the Mufti, cultivated many Iraqis as surrogate Nazis.[21]

By the time the Golden Square began consolidating power in the spring of 1941, many in the Iraqi power structure simply assumed there would be a Nazi-style action against Jews. The question was merely when and how. Typical and telling was the incident involving a young Jewish Iraqi army officer, Shaul Sehayik. During the run-up to the 1941 coup, Sehayik was in charge of processing all orders submitted to military headquarters. Those orders were stamped in numerical sequence. One day, he noticed, that one order in the sequence was missing. Because Sehayik had keys to the commander's safe, he was able to satisfy his curiosity. When he looked, he discovered a document marked "Top Secret." Sehayik recalled his shock, "It ordered the battalion HQ to closely supervise the Jews ... since these were considered potentially disloyal elements, and also to prepare a list of all Jews ... in the province."[22]

On May 3, 1941, with the Golden Square coup in full swing and with

Sehayik no longer in the army, the Jewish ex-soldier visited a Baghdad coffee shop to discuss with a friend the impending confrontation with British. A number of men at nearby tables were "arguing vehemently about the war against the British." Sehayik later recalled, "In the heat of their debate, they began shouting their admiration of Hitler and the Germans and praised them for their mass murder of Jews. It would appear that they know more about this than we Jews did ourselves. One of them went so far as to say that they, the Iraqis, would have been able to annihilate the Jews more effectively than the Germans. His proposal was that the Jews be brought together in one place, doused with fuel and set afire alive. The enthusiastic youth concluded by stating that if he were able to put his hands on a Jew he would indeed burn him alive."[23]

On May 6, when British warplanes buzzed the capital, Iraqi Jews were accused of sending coded signals to the pilots. Many were accused and many were arrested. The next day, a fanatic crowd armed with knives broke into the local Jewish hospital, again accused Jews of infamy and then destroyed an x-ray machine, believing it was sending coded signals to the British. Police rescued the staff, but the hospital was closed and patients sent away. On May 8, Baghdad radio began repetitive messages: "After the victory over the British, revenge shall be taken on the 'internal enemy,' and we shall hand him over to your hands for destruction."[24]

But in those first days of May 1941, even as London pondered how it would protect Anglo-Persian's oil in Iraq, regain control of the airbase at Habbaniya, and relieve the besieged embassy staff in Baghdad, uppermost in Whitehall's strategy was to avoid any appearance of a British re-occupation of the country. In other words, what mattered most to the British was the oil and its strategic supply lines, not any civil, internal unrest or anti-Jewish violence in Baghdad.

On May 8, 1941 General Archibald Wavell, commander-in-chief of the Middle East theatre, expressed his reservation about a show of force in Iraq. He urged London "to avoid any action to suggest that we have any intention of infringing Iraqi independence or introducing British administration or control. This would unite the whole population behind Rashid Ali [and the Golden Square coup] and against us; and would not only involve us in most serious commitments in Iraq itself, but would have repercussions in Palestine Syria and Arab world generally." Just days later, Wavell reinforced his view, stating that the military's need for oil was paramount—and nothing more. "As long as the Iraqi administration meets our Military requirements it is not, repeat not, to be interfered with or superseded because it is inefficient in other directions," he said.[25]

In Basra, during mid-May 1941, as British troops loitered on the outskirts, anarchic bedlam exploded within the city limits. The British consul general wrote of the day, "the telephone rang without ceasing; and notables, professional men, and merchants begged that the British should take steps to prevent the looting, rape, and murder which was universally expected. I could only reply that the policy of His Majesty's Government was not to interfere in any way with the local administration or to occupy any quarter which was not essential to the safety of the troops; and that, therefore, the military could not intervene. The notables then took steps to recruit night watchmen, and many gave asylum in their own homes to Jews and other members of minorities who were in fear of their lives."[26]

On May 28, 1941, as Britain's Habforce relieved Habbaniya, and punched toward Baghdad, the Nazi-allied Golden Square and the Reich's wirepuller, Grobba, fled the capital. Before Rashid Ali departed, his circle set up a so-called Committee for Internal Security, seemingly led by the mayor together with senior army and police personalities. With Habforce's armored cars and Kingcol's machine-gunners poised near the city, the Committee opted for an armistice. On May 31, at 4:00 a.m., with the morning still more dark than dawn, the mayor emerged with a white flag and signed for the residue of authority in Iraq. The armistice was conceived as a face-saving measure for the Arabs that would preserve Britain's strategic access to the territory and oil. The key paragraph stipulated, "All facilities will be accorded immediately to the British military authorities for unimpeded through communication by rail, road, and river." At the same time, the agreement permitted the Iraqi military to retain all their weapons and return to normal.[27]

Most important was to preserve the fiction that Britain's invasion was just a temporary military relief mission, not a re-occupation. In fact, shortly after receiving the so-called armistice, recently-installed British Ambassador Kinahan Cornwallis asked British forces to studiously avoid using the term "occupation" in public, and to consider not publishing the actual document for fear "some of the terms might expose new Government to embarrassing criticism."[28]

The storyline of Britain's invasion fiction was that the rightful authority in Iraq was being restored to his office after an unpopular and illicit coup. In truth, the "legitimate authority" was London's handpicked Hashemite from the far-away Arabian Peninsula, Prince Abd al-Ilah, the puppet regent who would speak for the boy king the British wanted to sit on the puppet throne. Indeed, a British political adviser in Northern Iraq, W.A. Lyon bluntly characterized the British-installed regime as a "puppet" in his assessment to Ambassador Cornwallis.

London's intent was "that the British would control political appointments, kick out the rotten officials, appoint our friends, remedy the many injustices that have occurred, disarm or at least re-organize the Iraq Army," Lyon readily confirmed to Ambassador Cornwallis, adding, "They expected a puppet government and after all what else could they expect, since without British support they could only have a Nazi Government." Lyon acknowledged that the Iraqi populace "see the high places in government as well as many of the lower ones still occupied by traitors, they see that practically no disciplinary action has been taken, that the Iraq Army is filled with sullen and Pro Nazi Officers whose influence can thwart the police and successfully cow and estrange such other officers as would like to support us."[29]

There was no question in the British mind that the Iraqi army was a wild and rowdy force. "Another point of great importance," summarized Lyon, "is that the Iraq Army is still as a whole sullen, behaves churlishly in public and disregards the civil administration in the execution of its function. Those living in towns turn their radios on to Germany and encourage others to listen in defiance of instructions to the contrary. The army is completely useless as a force to defend or even assist in the defense of the country; and although I quite realize that a well paid force like this cannot be thrown onto the streets without creating an even greater evil, yet I find it hard to understand why the worst have not been court-martialled, and many lesser lights removed from the Army into a concentration camp ... In the event of future German pressure, the Iraq Army can only be regarded as a menace in its present state. The country is ruled by officials a large proportion of whom are disloyal and not afraid to show it."[30]

On June 1, with Habbaniya restored and the Golden Square coup plotters out of the country, the British puppet regent, Prince Abd al-Ilah, returned to Iraq. Lyon described his return in these words: "At the head of the State we have a Regent, admittedly weak in personality but not unfriendly. His weaknesses can be fortified . . . Government through the firm support and advice of the British Ambassador."[31]

However, during those few hours surrounding the regent's return, a power vacuum existed in the country. It resulted in a bloodbath on June 1–2 that became known as the Farhud.

*    *    *    *

The original plans for the anti-Jewish action of June 1 were intended to mimic Nazi extermination campaigns in Europe. Lists of Jews had already been compiled by the military using the familiar approach the Nazis and their allies employed in such countries as Poland and Romania during that same time frame. As early as May 30, Iraqi Nazi al-Sabawi, a member of the ad hoc Committee for Internal Security and now self-appointed governor of Baghdad, summoned the Baghdad Chief Rabbi Sassoon Kadoori. In a frightful conversation, al-Sabawi ordered Kadoori to instruct the Jewish community to lock themselves in their homes for a few days, stay off the telephones, cook enough food for a three-day journey, pack a single suitcase and prepare for transport to detention centers. This was eerily identical to the Nazi approach in Poland and elsewhere in East Europe. Unknown to Rabbi Kadoori was exactly how murderous the plans were. Radio broadcasts were scheduled for noon the next day, May 29, advising military and Iraqi Nazi gang units to exterminate Baghdadi Jews in their homes in a massive murderous pogrom. Jewish homes had already been marked in advanced with a blood-red mystic *hamsa* or palm print, to guide the killing. The victory broadcast text was already prepared, handwritten by al-Sabawi himself.[32]

Expecting certain destruction, even if he did not know the details, Kadoori gathered petrified senior members of the Jewish community together. They urged him to beg help from the only man with the compassion and power to save them, Baghdad mayor Arshad Umari. Designated the head of the Committee for Internal Security, it was Umari who had surrendered to the advancing British and signed the armistice with Habforce. The towering question now was who controlled the vacuum that was Baghdad—was it Umari the mayor or al-Sabawi the self-appointed governor? With the city reeling in chaos, Umari promptly agreed to see Rabbi Kadoori. Their meeting was one of high drama.[33]

Full-bearded Kadoori walked in to Umari's office and, in a fit of distress, threw his elaborate circular turban at the floor. To a Muslim such as Umari, this was a symbol of utter despair, surrender, and heartbreak. The mayor retrieved the turban from the floor and asked Kadoori what was wrong? Kadoori woefully told Umari what was happening and beseeched him, "Don't let them do this terrible thing." By meeting's end, Umari gave back the turban and assured Kadoori, "Please put it back on and go home. Tell your people not to worry."[34]

As noon May 29 drew near, many fearful Baghdadi Jews did not know if they would stay or be deported, live on, or be killed in their homes. Just before twelve, Umari confronted al-Sabawi, who was relieved of all power. One hundred dinars traveling cash was given to al-Sabawi, which augmented 15,960 dinars he had already pilfered from the Treasury. Cash in hand, al-Sabawi fled Iraq. His handwritten broadcast text was seized by the mayor. Umari took control of the city. At noon, the radio did not issue a call for the extermination of thousands of Iraqi Jews.[35]

Instead, the next day, on May 31, Iraq radio announced that order had been restored to Baghdad and that the regent was returning in the morning. Britain's plan was to be conspicuously absent during the regent's arrival. They remained encamped several miles from the city.[36]

Baghdad's Jews had every reason to celebrate. June 1 was the joyous holy day of Shavuot, commemorating when the Law was given to Jews as well as marking an agrarian festival. What's more, the return of the regent and the expulsion of the Nazified Golden Square meant peace and safety would be restored. Baghdad's Jews thought stability had returned to their 2,600-year existence in Iraq. They were so wrong. The heaving door of hatred was about to burst wide open.

At about 3:00 p.m., June 1, regent Prince Abd al-Ilah landed at the airport near Baghdad. He was making his way to the Palace from where he would speak for the boy king. A contingent of Baghdadi Jews, responding to radio calls and their ingrained respect for the establishment, went out to greet Prince Abd al-Ilah. It being a Jewish holiday, they were all dressed in their festive finest. As the group came to the al-Khurr bridge, they encountered a contingent of dejected soldiers returning from the dismal surrender to Habforce. The mere sight of these Jews was enough to enrage the soldiers.[37]

Suddenly, the Jews were viciously attacked with knives and axes. Several were hacked to death right then and there. The planned systematic extermination, now foiled, broke down into a spontaneous slaughter. Quickly, violence spread to the Al Rusafa district and beyond. Baghdad became a fast-moving hell. Frenzied mobs raced throughout the city and murdered Jews openly on the streets. Women were raped as their horrified families looked on. Infants were killed in front of their parents. Home and stores were emptied and then burned. Gunshots and screams electrified the city for hours upon hours. Beheadings, torsos sliced open, babies dismembered, horrid tortures, and mutilations were widespread. Severed limbs were waved here and there as trophies. One man remembered, "The mutilation of the bodies ... had distorted the victims' bodies and faces beyond recognition."[38]

Corpses and the injured littered the street helter-skelter. One woman shrieked in agony that her son had just been murdered; as she screamed, an Arab gunned his car and drove right over her. Two Jews were left dead in front of the cinema. Many were cut down in their yards while trying to flee their homes. An elderly rabbi, about a hundred years old, was killed, and a young man and a woman were dropped near him. One body lay unattended at the entrance to a police station. Many others were left bleeding in alleys where they had tried to outrun the killers. One minibus was captured, and about ten Jews were dragged out and slaughtered on the spot.[39]

As Baghdad burned, Jewish existence became smoke spires against the sky. Jewish shops and homes were looted and then torched. A synagogue was invaded, its Torahs defiled and then destroyed, and then burned in classic Nazi fashion. In some cases, a Jewish section would erupt with gunfire and chilling cries for help—and then fall ghoulishly silent. Then flames and smoke would rise. Yet British troops remained minutes away under orders not to move in.⁴⁰

Personal nightmares detonated through the city. For example, four Jews tried to flee the mayhem in a minibus. As the van turned down Ghazi Street, it suddenly ran into a mad mob of sword swinging Arabs. They surrounded the vehicle. Rioters pulled open the door and started beating passengers inside and then pulling them to the pavement. A Jewish man called Na'im escaped out a window. His son tried to crawl out the same window, but while the son's legs were still inside, the driver stepped on the gas and roared off. The Jewish man, Meir, was dragged out of the bus even as his brother tried to save him. Their brave friend Nahum escaped out the window, and tried to save Meir. Nahum's son Nissim tried to follow out the window, but his legs were still inside when the driver stepped on the gas and roared off. Both Meir and Nahum were never heard of again.⁴¹

But as the minibus on Ghazi Street zoomed off, fourteen-year-old Ovadia was left exposed. He turned to run. The mob gave chase, waving axes and swords. As fast as he could, Ovadia raced toward a police station some 100 meters away. Swinging their knives at his back, the Arabs were close behind. Finally, one came close and hit Ovadia between the legs, striking his testicles. Down Ovadia went as the mob descended. Fierce blows struck across his body, but Ovadia somehow stumbled away and continued running for his life. The police station was just over there. He ran. The screaming mob of 20 pursued. Finally, Ovadia reached the police station. An Arab policeman stepped outside, grabbed Ovadia's hand, and pulled his weapon. Pointing the barrel directly at the menacing crowd, the policeman said, "Don't worry, my son." Ovadia was the first to seek refuge in the police station, but soon about two dozen came in, many bleeding.⁴²

The streets were not safe for Jews. Their homes, already well-marked as Jewish residences, were even less safe. Gangs comprised of soldiers, police, and civilian looters invaded Jewish neighborhoods with impunity. Furniture was shoved up against the door as a barricade. As the invaders pushed at the doors, more and heavier furniture was shoved into place. The ceaseless battering and kicking eventually made progress, and inevitably, in house after house, the killers broke in. As the Arabs breached the entrances, many families would race to the roof, one step ahead. Only the looting and the distraction of seizing valuables after many saved many who fled with no time to spare.⁴³

Typical was the Muallem-Cohen house. Young Nezima was terrified. Her father had just returned from a brief morning foray to inspect a nearby synagogue. He was relating the terrible stories he had heard about daughters being raped and homes burned, when suddenly, shouting, armed men crashed through his own front gates. Quickly, Muallem-Cohen rushed his family to the stairs to escape to the roof. Up they scampered, first young Nezima, then her mother, and then her father. A shot—the senior Muallem-Cohen was dead. Mrs. Muallem-Cohen looked back in horror at her husband. Just then a policeman appeared. "They killed my husband," she shrieked. "How do *you* want to die?" he snapped back, and then cracked her skull with his gun.[44]

In the Dillal home on Ghazi Street, the looters, including uniformed Arab policemen, systematically carted away furnishings, carefully loading them into lorries. One policeman entered and from the door began cursing at the terrified family. Suddenly, he shot the mother in the head and she went down. At this, the daughter Bertin shrieked; he turned the weapon on Bertin, and shot her dead. When the horrified grandmother saw this and screamed, the policeman shot her as well. Then the aunt was also shot. Youngsters Rene and Hisquel escaped up to the roof. Rene hopped over the partition to safety, but Hisquel was only five and too young to vault over. A rioter caught up and lifted young Hisquel to the top of the partition and was about to slice him open with his sword, when Rene begged for her brother's life. Instead of swinging, the rioter picked Hisquel up and literally threw him over the roof partition. Rene caught him as the child landed, and he lived.[45]

Rooftops became life-savers for many victims. Fleeing Jews jumped from one roof to another to escape. In some cases planks were thrown across nearby roofs to allow families, include some of the less agile, to all get away. In some instances, parents and siblings threw children down from roofs to waiting blankets below. When there was no place beyond the roof, some Jews held off their attackers with boiling oil, stones, and whatever other makeshift defenses they could muster.[46]

In some cases, police units rolled up to a Jewish home in machine gun mounted vehicles. Without hesitation, those units would turn their weapon on the front door and start shooting. In one instance in the Abu Safayn neighborhood, when machine gun fire peppered a Jewish home, the man ran out with his family and tried to flee. Soldiers shouted to him down the roadway, "Stand still, you son of a Zionist dog." One member of the family kept running and would not look back, but after only about 20 steps, a soldier's bullet entered his back and exited his belly. The victim hit the ground as other soldiers closed in and took aim. Writhing in pain, the injured Jew began uttering the sacred Shema prayer beseeching the Lord. *Sh'ma Yisrael Adonai Eloheinu Adonai echad.* "Hear, Israel, the Lord is our God, the Lord is One." The others were about to shoot at close range when an Arab officer said, "This man is dying. Let him say his last prayers." Left for dead, the Jewish man later crawled away in an area where eight others lay dead or dying.[47]

Not even the sound of machine-gun fire brought British intervention.[48]

Women were defiled everywhere. Arabs broke into the girl's school and the students were raped—endlessly. Six Jewish girls were carted away to the Muslim village of Azaza fifteen kilometers north and located only later. One young girl was raped, and then her breasts slashed off—an all too typical crime that day. Young or old, Jewish females were set upon and mercilessly gang raped and often mutilated.[49]

Wounded Jews were as much at risk in the hospital. When injured Jews were taken to the hospital at Baghdad Medical College, the chief surgeon rushed to the operating room. But then reluctant Arab doctors and nurses in attendance declined to render aid. Eventually, they followed the doctor's adamant instruction and prepared for surgery. However, as the doctor scrubbed, soldiers in the hospital who were recovering from the Habbaniya campaign rose up angry at the sight of Jewish patients. Some soldiers, although wounded, tried to rape female Jewish patients right in the hospital. Suddenly, the surgeon stopped everyone in their tracks by barking into a megaphone that every soldier should return to his bed—or he would personally shoot them. Two guns clearly hung from his belt. He meant it. Everyone backed down. The tense situation in the operating room calmed. Still, for their own protection, Jews were soon transferred to other hospitals with more Jewish doctors.[50]

But stories of poisoned patients elsewhere quickly circulated. At Majidiyya government hospital, stories of poisoning were rampant. One nurse told a Jewish patient that dozens of patients had already been poisoned. "Be quiet and don't complain about any pain. Jews who complained and shouted ... get a shot of poison. Also don't take any medicine unless given to you by us, because the doctors give large doses of sleeping drugs that can kill you, or may kill you with injections. Even if the doctor is with us, don't accept any medicines from him unless we tell you not to be afraid. Then you can accept it."[51]

At one hospital, a large mob surrounded the entrance demanding to murder the Jewish medics and nurses. Hospital director Jamil Dallali begged the rowdy group to disperse. But the teeming crowd insisted on lynching the Jewish men and women staff members. When Dallali pleaded that nurses were all "servants of humanity," the mob demanded to have at least one male Jewish medic to satisfy them. Dallali agreed to hand the medic over, but instead called a loyal unit of the police. A detachment arrived just in time to rescue the hospital.[52]

In most cases, however, the regular police either openly joined the culprits in pillaging or declined to interfere with the pogrom. Mostly, they refused to follow standing orders to open fire on rioters. For example, an armored car appeared on Ghazi Street to quell the tumult. Policemen at first seemed to fire at the crowd, and the mob began to disperse. But in short order the hooligans realized the shooting was for show. It was only in the air. Soon, the mobs there descended upon nearby homes to loot and kill the Jewish inhabitants. Eventually, every time the police appeared, the mob applauded, cheered and wished them "long life." An official Iraqi government report on the riots concluded, "Killing and looting went on that entire night right before the eyes of the police. In addition to which, some individuals from the police ... took part in the looting, pillaging, and killing."[53]

Police refusal to fire upon rioters played out to an extreme. When senior police official figure Ali Khalid al-Hijazi saw soldiers and looters carrying looted furniture away, he asked the policemen on the scene why they were merely firing into the air. Officers replied that the Chief of Police "had given orders not to fire upon civilians." At that, al-Hijazi angrily rushed to Police General Headquarters, demanding that proper orders "to shoot" be issued to the police by the chief. But when al-Hijazi went back out to the streets, he only saw more policemen and youth gangs acting in concert to break down doors of Jewish homes and steal the contents. So al-Hijazi returned to Police Headquarters and again asked the Chief of Police to give the order for his men to fire directly upon the mobs. The Chief of Police explained that his men had run out of ammunition by shooting into the air. The assistant director general of the Interior Ministry, Mustafa al-Qarah Daghi was standing there and likewise demanded that police officials give the order to open fire at the killers. But a ranking police commander said he was not authorized to order direct fire upon civilians. Speaking for the Interior Ministry, al-Qarah Daghi snapped back that the situation did not require specific orders. The riot represented a grave emergency. Shoot! Back and forth, the officials insisting on receiving direct orders from ranking police superior or political leaders. But one by one, each of those individuals refused to issue such orders. As the minutes and hours wore on, youth gangs and soldiers continued their rampage of death and destruction literally unopposed.[54] Seeing no British coming to the rescue of the Jews only seemed to intensify the green light.

Finally, the Mayor, at wit's end telephoned the Regent himself, the supreme authority in the country and beseeched him to issue orders to open fire. That he did. As the order circulated, loyal units began opening fire, especially when rioters turned to Muslim neighborhoods to continue their pillage. As the units began shooting, rioters fled.[55]

The Farhud was not a one day event. It began on June 1, 1941 but no authority would suppress it; indeed, the police and army were active participants. No curfew was readily announced that first day because at first no one would sign a curfew order. The colonel functioning as director of operations agreed that a curfew was needed, but he refused to sign any such order. Up the chain of command went the request, all the way to the general, but no one would sign the order. Ultimately, the regent was contacted and he notified the general by telephone to issue a curfew. Even still, it was mere paper—no curfew was obeyed. In fact the violence only intensified the next day as Bedouins streamed across the bridge and joined with slum dwellers to plunder and maim.[56]

It was only on June 2, when British Ambassador Cornwallis reiterated an instruction to the regent not just to sit in the Palace but to actually form a government did the tumult settle down. Late that June 2 afternoon, Cornwallis wired a report to London, "I told the Regent both yesterday and this morning that the immediate formation of a Government was imperative." Referring to one of the handpicked British caretakers, Jamil Madfai, Cornwallis confessed that Madfai "refused to accept responsibility last night but this morning sent two emissaries to me and on my promising that I would give him my full support providing he carried out the treaty in the letter and spirit, he consented. I saw him later. He seems to have grown slow and rather senile so may prove a broken reed but he was the only available candidate with public support."[57]

Days later, when the regent eventually restored order, the British did enter the city. The oil was secure. The Jews of Baghdad were not.

By June 6, 1941, as news of the massacre began to circulate, the British-backed Iraqi authorities announced a special investigating commission. But Baghdadi Jews were continuously threatened to not cooperate with the panel or incriminate attackers lest another massacre be launched. "There has been no cessation in acts of intimidation by some officers and soldiers even up till now," the official inquiry concluded about a month later. "Many such instances have taken place recently, when officers and soldiers roaming the alleys of the Jewish Quarter threaten and intimidate anyone who might give damaging testimony against military men or civilians. A group of privates and corporals have begun frightening Jews with threats and are extorting money from them. For this reason, the Jews will continue to hold back from giving information concerning the killing and looting to any authority until the government takes the measures necessary to punish the perpetrators and to stop their torrent of threats. It is the opinion of this committee that the soldiers and officers—if at all possible—be sent to [detention] camps outside of town for the present in order to calm the Jews and make them safe from intimidation, so that they will come forward with information."[58]

In trying to determine the extent of the pogrom, the commission wrote, "As to the number of houses looted, no statistics have been made available by the police, even though this committee did request lists of the numbers of looted home and businesses from the various police stations, but received no reply. The committee concluded that the police did not undertake any accounting. The President of the Jewish Community claims that 586 shops and warehouses were sacked completely and that the value of what was taken came to a total of 271,301 dinars. He claims that 911 houses were looted in which were living 3,395 families, totaling 12,311 souls.[59]

In truth, no one will ever know many were murdered or maimed during those two dark days. The official statistics, based on intimidated and reluctant reports, listed about 110 Jews and Muslims dead, including 28 women. Hundreds were listed as injured. But Jewish leaders said the real numbers were far greater. One Iraq historian suggested as many as 600 were murdered during the overnight rampage. The Jewish Burial Society was afraid to bury the bodies. The corpses were ignominiously collected and entombed in a large, long, rounded mass grave that resembled a massive loaf of bread.[60]

P. M. Crosthwaite, who sat on the eastern desk of the Foreign Ministry in London, bluntly vented his outrage. "What the Baghdad populace need is a little rough handling," he wrote in a marginal note along a memo. "They do not get bombed, and their only reaction is to get cocky. It looks more than ever as if British troops were needed in Baghdad itself, and a roomy concentration camp opened for the reception of the most obstinate mischief-makers.[61]

Somerset de Chair, the Habforce intelligence officer, detailed a minute-by-minute account of the British push to secure Habbaniya. "Having fought our way, step by step, to the threshold of the city we must now cool our heels outside," wrote de Chair of the riot's outbreak. "It would, apparently, be lowering to the dignity of our ally, the Regent, if he were seen to be supported on arrival by British bayonets." Cynically, de Chair added, "So we waited and, as darkness settled like a mantle over the domes and minarets across the river, the shooting began. We did not hear it [eight miles away], but to the Brigadier's ears sleeping in the white colonial house of the British Embassy, came the growing crescendo of rifle and machine-gun fire. Baghdad was given up to the looters. All who cared to defend their own belongings were killed, while eight miles to the west waited the eager British force which could have prevented all this. Ah, yes, but the prestige of our Regent would have suffered."[62]

Sparing no criticism, de Chair concluded, "It was argued afterwards in the Chancery of Baghdad that the Iraqis would have gone on fighting rather than agree to an armistice on the basis of our immediate entry. Again, it was argued that our arrival would have precipitated street fighting with the brigade which we had pushed back into the town. Yet why, I asked, if they crumpled up on the outskirts, should they have stiffened in the middle?"[63]

The Farhud became a cherished event among Arabs in Baghdad, not a source of shame. Celebrated in song and slogans, Arab chants constantly warned that more was coming. One song opened with "How lovely if only a Farhud occurred every day." A common warning to the Jews of Iraq was this: "That was just a small festival. The time will come for the big one."[64]

The perpetrators the Farhud were not a gang, or a few errant officers. It was a mass movement unleashed, one that broadly adopted the Nazi desire to destroy the Jews. The Farhud was a turning point in Arab hatred for Jews. Now it was time for more Arabs across the Islamic world to join the war against the Jews. That they would do. Shoulder-to-shoulder with the murderous Nazis, from the battlefield to the concentration camp, from the propaganda offices, to the supply lines—Arabs would do their utmost to advance Hitler's war to exterminate the Jews, from Palestine to Poland.

*Farhud.* In Arabic, the word means violent dispossession. It was a word the Jews of Europe never knew. *Holocaust*, it was a word the Jews of Iraq never knew. But soon they would all know its meaning regardless of the language they spoke. After the events of June 1–2, 1941, both words came together.

CHAPTER

15

# THE ARAB-NAZI ALLIANCE

**O**ur hatred for the Jews dates from God's condemnation of them for their persecution and rejection of Isa [Jesus Christ], and their subsequent rejection later of His chosen Prophet [Mohammad]... Verily the word of God teaches us, and we implicitly believe this ... for a Muslim to kill a Jew ... ensures him an immediate entry into Heaven and into the august presence of God Almighty. What more then can a Muslim want in this hard world?

\*     \*     \*     \*

For the Nazis, their uneasy, contrived alliance with the Arabs and indeed with Islam was a political and military expediency, in many ways no different from the uncomfortable partnerships they had made with other ethnic groups across Europe, from the Cossacks to the Spanish. But for too many Arabs and too many within the wider Islamic world, the goals of Jewish expulsion, confiscation, and destruction were a natural. For the Arab national movement of the Hitler era, the Nazi notion that Jews were a vile filth to be cleansed from the earth was an ancient Koranic precept that survived, generation to generation, from the day Mohammad exterminated the Jews of Medina for not converting.

Hitler's initial prewar campaign to make Jews second-class citizens to be pent up in ghettos, subjected to restricted religious rights, extra taxes, and special confiscations, and compelled to wear yellow badges announcing their detestable presence, was but an unintended descendant of the very dhimmi statutes that had regulated Jewish existence in Muslim lands, on and off in

307

various permutations, sometimes pernicious and sometimes enlightened, during the 1,400-year reign of Islam. In other words, Hitler's approach appeared more than a millennium after the Muslim world had initiated the very same doctrine. What Islam decreed in the Pact of Umar in the seventh and eighth centuries, when it established the concept of dhimmitude, became a highly visible precedent for the Christian anti-Semites of the Middle Ages. That Christian anti-Semitic tradition was resurrected by the Third Reich. But the ideas were 1,400 years old.[1]

After the Peel Commission had raised the specter of two states for two peoples, Arabs everywhere showed their seething revulsion, not just as a matter of geopolitical stance, but as a religious precept. For example, in October 1937, King Abdul Aziz bin Abdul Rahman Al Saud—better known as ibn Saud—of Saudi Arabia summoned British diplomat Harold Dickson, who had been London's longtime representative in Kuwait but was by then inactive. During a 90-minute demarche, King Ibn Saud delivered the feelings of his people: a threat to the British for Dickson to convey and a presage of the emerging German alliance.[2]

"We are aware, O Dickson, that you are no longer a government official. But as you have held that high and honorable post under His Majesty's government for many years, we know also that you are trusted by your Government, and so not only do we make you doubly welcome, but we feel we can open our hearts to you, and we are glad that you have been able to visit us in our capital."[3]

"We are most anxious," the King continued, "that the British government should send us every eight months or so an experienced officer whom they trust, or equally well, an ex-official like yourself, who can listen personally to what we have on our minds, and what troubles our hearts, for times are deeply serious and full of danger these days. We feel that personal contact of such a nature will be far more efficacious than any amount of letter writing or telegraph representations. The latter ... nearly always fail to convey the full meaning of our thoughts and anxieties, and if anything, will tend rather to breed misunderstanding and misconception than remove same."[4]

Making sure the religious and cultural nuance of his message was completely understood, the King explained, "But such a person, if and when he is sent us, must be thoroughly conversant with our language (Arabic) and must understand the wider meaning of our beautiful tongue, which is so full of parable and expressive phrase. It is no use sending a man who has to listen to what we have to say through the medium of an interpreter. The person sent should know and understand our Arab psychology, be conversant if possible with our Arabian manners and customs, and above all should be acquainted with our Arab pride and our hopes, and have read something of God's Holy Word, as vouchsafed to us in our blessed Koran."[5]

With the pleasant preface out of the way, the King delivered the meat of the message. "O Dickson," the King continued, "when will your London government realize that we Arabs, by our very nature, can be bought body and soul by an act of kindness—and vice versa: become implacable enemies for all time of those who treat us harshly or deal unjustly with us?"[6]

"Today, we and our subjects are deeply troubled over this Palestine question," he complained, "and the cause of our disquiet and anxiety is the strange attitude of your British government, and the still more strange hypnotic influence which the Jews, a race accursed by God, according to His Holy Book, and destined to final destruction and eternal damnation hereafter, appear to wield over them and the English people generally."[7]

"God's Holy Book [the Koran] contains God's own word and divine ordinance, and we commend to His Majesty's government to read and carefully peruse that portion which deals with the Jews and especially what is to be their fate in the end. For God's words are unalterable and must be."[8]

"We Arabs believe implicitly in God's revealed word, and we know that God is faithful. We care for nothing else in this world but our belief in the One God, His Prophet, and our Honor. Everything else matters nothing at all—not even death. Nor are we afraid of hardship, hunger, lack of this world's goods, etc., and we are quite content to eat camel's meat and dates to the end of our days, provided we hold to the above three things," stipulated ibn Saud.[9]

"Our hatred for the Jews dates from God's condemnation of them for their persecution and rejection of Isa [Jesus Christ], and their subsequent rejection later of His chosen Prophet [Mohammad]. It is beyond our understanding how your government, representing the first Christian power in the world today, can wish to assist and reward these very same Jews who maltreated your Isa [Jesus]."[10]

The King continued, "We Arabs have been the traditional friends of Great Britain for many years, and I, Ibn Saud, in particular, have been your government's firm friend all my life. What madness then is this which is leading on your government to destroy this friendship of centuries, all for the sake of an accursed and stiff-necked race which has always bitten the hand of everyone who has helped it since the world began?"[11]

"It is far preferable from every point of view if Great Britain were to make Palestine a British possession and rule it for the next 100 years, rather than to partition it in the way they propose. Such partition cannot possibly solve the difficulty but must only perpetuate it and lead to war and misery. Some people seem to think that I, Ibn Saud, have an eye on Palestine myself and would like to benefit by the disturbed state of affairs existing there, to step in and offer to take it over myself. That certainly would be a solution, but God forbids that this should happen, for I have enough and to spare as it is."[12]

"Today," continued ibn Saud, "I am the Imam or the 'Spiritual Leader' as well as the Temporal Ruler of the greater part of Arabia. I also have not a little influence in all the great Muslim countries of the world. I am being placed in the most difficult and most invidious of all positions by the British government, my friends. On the one hand, I am being appealed to by means of myriads of letters and telegrams by day and night from all quarters of the Muslim world to step in and save Palestine for the Arabs. I am even urged by my own people of Najd, and all good Muslims in the outer world, to break with the English and save Palestine for its people by war. On the other hand, I see that it would be utterly futile to break with my old friends the English, for to do so would bring untold woe on the world and would be to play right into the hands of the Jews, the enemies of Arabia as well as of England."[13]

"I definitely shall not wage war against you English, and I have told my people this, because I am the only man among them who can see far ahead, and I know that by so doing I should lose the one potential ally I know I have. For are not Italy, Germany, and Turkey (especially the latter) like ravening wolves today seeking whom they may devour? They are all flirting with me at the present moment, but I know they will wish to devour me later. A friendly England will, I believe, always prevent them from accomplishing their ends. Hence, though as a Muslim I have no particular love for any Christian European nation, political interest demands that I keep in with the best of them, that is, England."[14]

Ibn Saud continued, "The difficulty is my Arabs and the Ikhwan tribes of Najd over this Palestine business. Their senses are only in their eyes, and they cannot see one cubit ahead. They even now blame me for wavering and obeying the orders of the English, and yet your government should remember that I am the Arabs' religious leader and so am the interpreter of the scriptures. God's word to them cannot be got 'round."[15]

Making himself crystal clear to the British, the King stated dramatically, "Verily the word of God teaches us, and we implicitly believe this, O Dickson, that for a Muslim to kill a Jew, or for him to be killed by a Jew, ensures him an immediate entry into Heaven and into the august presence of God Almighty. What more then can a Muslim want in this hard world, and that is what my people are repeatedly reminding me of?"[16]

Ibn Saud's caustic demarche went on. "The Jews are of course your enemies as well as ours," he declared, "though they are cleverly making use of you now. Later your government will see and feel their teeth. For the present they [the Jews] prefer biding their time. Perhaps your government does not know that the Jews contemplate as their final aim not only the seizure of all Palestine, but the land south of it as far as Medina. Eastward also they hope someday to extend to the Persian Gulf. They cozen certain imperialistic-minded Englishmen with stories of how a strong Jewish and pro-British state, stretching from the Mediterranean to the Persian Gulf, will safeguard England's communications with the East, saying that the Arabs are England's enemies and will always be so. At the same time, they play on the minds of the sentimental British masses, by telling them that the Old Testament prophets foretold how they, the Jews, would eventually return to their Promised Land, or again that they, the persecuted and wandering Bani Israel, should not be denied a small place in the world where to lay their weary heads. Now, O Dickson, would the people of Wales like it if you English suddenly gave the Jews their country? But no, it is easier to give away other people's countries— and not so dangerous."[17]

"That the Jews of Palestine are even now straining every nerve to cause a permanent split between the English people and the Arabs can be proved to the hilt by the recent murders of officials in Palestine. It is as clear as daylight to me that the Godless Arab gunmen, hired from abroad, who committed those vile deeds were hired and paid for by Jewish money. We state this to be an absolute fact, for did not the Grand Mufti of Jerusalem swear to us in the Haram [Noble sanctuary] of Mecca by the Holy Kaaba that he would never resort to any but constitutional methods in opposing the Zionist machinations in Palestine? And I believe him even today."[18]

"What we fear so greatly and what Great Britain must not allow to come to pass is the turning of the Arabs of Arabia and neighboring Arab countries into enemies of England. Once this happens then an irreparable crime will have been committed, for, as we said above, the Arabs will never forget an injury and will bide their opportunity to take revenge for 100 years if need be." Referring to the gathering storm clouds of a potential war with Germany, the King averred, "Enemies of England would not be slow to take advantage of this, and an England in difficulties, or engaged elsewhere in war, would then be the signal for the Arabs to act."[19]

"The very thought of the above happening is hateful to me. Yet, be assured, partition in Palestine will bring this about in spite of all your misdirected efforts. And, after all I cannot help you forever as I cannot live more than a few years more. I repeat then, that the only solution that I can see is for your government to rule Palestine herself. The Zionists of course will not like this, but their views should not be asked. The Arabs will agree to this solution, and those who do not must be made to agree by such people as myself."[20]

"The main thing at all costs," demanded the King, "is to prevent the Jews from having an independent state of their own, sliced out of Arab territory, with no one to guide their future acts and policy. For from such will come a perpetual struggle with the Arabs living round them. Firstly, because the Jews are determined to expand, will intrigue from the very beginning, and not rest until they have created discord between Great Britain and us Arabs, out of which they will hope to benefit. Secondly, they, having the money, will create a highly effective though perhaps small mechanized Army and Air Force, which they will assuredly use one day for aggressive purposes against the Arabs, seeing that their aim is the whole of Palestine, Transjordan, and their old stronghold Medina—the land they went to when driven out of Palestine and dispersed [from] after the Romans destroyed Jerusalem.[21]

"On top of this," the monarch insisted, "your government must at once restrict further immigration of Jews into Palestine, leaving alone all those already there but allowing no more to come in."[22]

King ibn Saud paused, for a breath and to allow his tense and forceful presentation to penetrate. Dickson tried to reply with an explanation of London's viewpoint. But the King dismissively cut him off. "By God, your government has no point of view except the willful committing of an injustice. Every God-fearing man, be he a Muslim or Christian, knows that it cannot be right to do a wrong, however cleverly the committing may be served up to the people. If I, an ignorant Bedouin Arab of Arabia can see, as clearly as I see the sun rise, that the proposed partition of Palestine is wicked and wrong in God's sight, surely the more clever Western politicians, if they fear God at all, can see this also. Thank God I believe in God and his Oneness, and I know that it is this very belief of mine that makes me see things as clearly as I do. I am firmly convinced that I am right, and that God has opened my eyes to the right, as I believe that God will punish me if I lie to him." The King concluded with a reference to Hitler. "Therefore there is no other side to this question except bargaining with Satan."[23]

These were the words of the King of Saudi Arabia about the Jews. Dickson duly delivered them to the British Foreign Office. Multitudes of Arabs and Muslims made good on the words of the King's final prophetic warning, "Therefore there is no other side to this question except bargaining with Satan."[24]

*   *   *   *

The incessant flow of contacts between Arabs and Nazis was so diverse and robust that the term "contacts" is inherently the wrong word. More than a mufti, this was a mass movement of partnership with the Third Reich. More than an avenue of cooperation, what unfolded was an alliance of war. From Arab kings and emirs, from emissaries to government officials, from organizational groups to ad hoc committees, from diplomats to potentates, from journalists to jihadists, from militants to muftis, Arabs fanned out across Europe and the Middle East to coordinate and coalesce with their chosen allies—the Axis. The locations included Berlin, Paris, Ankara, Rome, Jerusalem, Damascus, Beirut, and dozens of points in between. Sometimes the meetings were at the lowest operational level, and sometimes they were nothing less than summits between the Arab hierarchy and Hitler, Heinrich Himmler, and the other senior players orchestrating the crimes of the Third Reich. Often Mussolini and the Italian fascists were at the table, making the alliance not just one with Germany but one with the Axis. It would take a long bookshelf, thick with volumes, to catalog the breadth and scope of this partnership.

One feature characterized the confluence: a joint Nazi and Arab belief that Jewish people constituted a menace by their very existence on earth. Many of the meetings themselves were unsubtle and included Arab reminders that the Islamic mindset had been shaped for centuries by the original anti-Jewish extermination and expulsions waged by Mohammad and enshrined in the Koran. For the Arabs, the massacres at Mecca were not a forgotten chapter of ancient history, but rather grandiose epaulets of their current jihad. Frequently they invoked the memory to keep it fresh.

For example, in June 1939, just months before World War II broke out, Khalid al-Qarqani, a leading Saudi governmental minister and a personal envoy of King ibn Saud, met with Hitler in Berlin to coordinate a six-million-reichsmark weapons purchase. When Hitler railed that it was his intent to expel all the Jews from Germany, Qarqani repeated King ibn Saud's oft-expressed view that Mohammad had enforced the identical policy in Arabia centuries before.[25]

Hitler pandered to the Arab hatred. Just weeks before the Qarqani meeting, *der Führer* had broadcast the message: "What right has England to shoot down Arabs in Palestine solely because they support the cause of their homeland?" *Der Führer* repeated that theme a month later when he publicly rebutted criticism from President Franklin Roosevelt about territorial aggression. "The fact has obviously escaped Mr. Roosevelt's notice," barked Hitler, "that Palestine is at present occupied not by German troops but by the English; and that the country is having its liberty restricted by the most brutal resort to force, is being robbed of its independence, and is suffering the cruelest maltreatment for the benefit of Jewish interlopers. The Arabs living in that country ... voice a continuous appeal to the world, deploring the barbarous methods with which England is attempting to suppress a people which loves its freedom and is but defending it."[26]

For Muslims and Arabs, Hitler was clearly the deliverer, and his very persona was Islamicized. In the markets and in many public places through Arab cities, posters proclaimed, "In heaven, Allah is your master. On Earth, it is

Hitler." *Der Führer* was dubbed "Abu Ali" and was even provided a mythological Arab life. According to the popular reinvention, the German leader was in truth originally an Arab named Muhammad Haidar, born in a small Egyptian village, who had lived a devout Islamic life. Many Arab parents began naming their newborn children Adolf or Hitler, rivaling Mohammad in popularity. For example, the Tantawi family in Egypt named their infant son "Hitler." Hitler Tantawi grew up to be a leading general; he is readily identifiable as a key modern-day administrative official in Cairo who simply declined to change his name.[27] The Reich continued to capitalize on Arab sentiment. Arabic language broadcasts from Berlin's Zeesen shortwave transmitters deluged the capitals of the Arab world with thousands of hours of programming each month. Germany's *Voice of Free Arabism* and *Radio Berlin* offered activist religious as well as political programming. Typical was this refrain: "Oh, servants of God! Islam calls on Muslims, indeed it commands you to be brothers, to do good and avoid evil. It gives you these commandments because they are useful to you and are in your interest."[28]

The Arabs and the Nazis agreed on many aspects of the Jews. But Germany's concept of expulsion and sequestration to what Hitler called a "reservation" in Palestine was at odds with the Arabs' refusal to have Jews exist within their midst. What's more, as Hitler conquered additional territory in Europe through 1939 and 1940, the number of Jews who came under Nazi jurisdiction dramatically increased. In Germany, only some 550,000 Jews existed, but as Germany rolled into Austria, Czechoslovakia, France, Poland, and other countries, the Jewish population under Hitler's control swelled to millions. National Socialism vowed to make Europe *Judenrein*—Jew-free. If these millions of Jews could not live in Europe, and if they could not be exported to any refuge, and if they could not dwell in Palestine—then what?

By the summer of 1941, it had become obvious to the entire world that total extermination of the Jews now loomed as a clear option—and had been on the Nazi solution agenda for years.

The term *extermination* had become common parlance during World War I when referring to the systematic massacre of more than a million Armenians by Turkey, a mass murder that German diplomats, administrators, and military men were tangential to and very aware of. The very term extermination was commonly used by the League of Nations to justify dismantling the Ottoman Empire.[29]

In the run-up to World War II and in the conflict's first year, the notion of extermination— the German term *vernichtung* is unequivocal—was increasingly employed in the Reich media as a viable, if not demanded, solution to the "Jewish Problem." For example, rabid Hitler propagandist Julius Streicher, editor of the immensely popular and pornographic Nazi magazine

*Der Stürmer*, published some two dozen different articles from 1938 to 1941 preaching "extermination" of the full "root and branch" of the Jewish people. As early as September 1938, an article in *Der Stürmer* openly categorized the Jew as "a germ and a pest," not genuinely human. The eugenic concept of the Jews as bacteria was expressed in a passage that defined the Jew as "a parasite, an enemy, an evildoer, a disseminator of diseases who must be destroyed in the interest of mankind." Ironically, that sentiment coincided with the Koranic portrayal of Jews as subhuman filth and the de facto Muslim tradition of the day, in countries such as Iraq, where Jews were compelled to bring their own cups to coffeehouses and where the ground they stood on was commonly swept away after their departure. In another editorial, *Der Stürmer* warned that in fifty years, Jewish graves "will proclaim that this people of murderers and criminals has, after all, met its deserved fate." Streicher published one prewar article in May 1939 that pleaded for "a punitive expedition that will provide the same fate for them that every murderer and criminal must expect—death sentence and execution. The Jews in Russia must be killed. They must be exterminated root and branch." The notion of total extermination was so commonly articulated that an ordinary letter to the editor, printed in the February 1940 edition of *Der Stürmer,* compared Jews with "swarms of locusts which must be exterminated completely."[30]

By the late 1930s, the word extermination was routinely used worldwide to describe the Nazi threat against Jews. A *New York Times* feature on November 14, 1938, ominously asked, "Inasmuch as everything has been done to the Jews in Germany that can be done to a people short of physical extermination, there are arising some obvious speculations as to what these continued warnings may imply." The question was answered just days later on November 30, when *The New York Times* published an article headlined, "Jews in Germany Get Extermination Threat," quoting *Schwarze Korps*, the organ of Hitler's SS, as it advertised the potential for wholesale Jewish murder.[31]

On September 13, 1939, just after Germany launched the successful *Blitzkrieg* into Poland that ignited World War II, *The New York Times* reported the Reich's dilemma of having too many Jews under its control. The headline declared, "Nazis Hint Purge of Jews in Poland," with the subhead, "3,000,000 Population Involved." The article quoted the German government as declaring it wanted "removal of the Polish Jewish population from the European domain." *The Times* then added, "How ... the 'removal' of Jews from Poland [can be achieved] without their extermination ... is not explained."[32]

The Arabs had every reason to believe that their best hope for the extermination of the Jews before they could reach the shores of Palestine lay in the complete victory of the Nazis. The Arabs lacked the manpower, European-wide presence, and weaponry to wage the type of modern warfare that in 1941 raged across the Continent and the extended Middle East, a kind of "warfare" that so systematically identified, concentrated, and slaughtered the Jews. So as a movement, militant anti-Zionist Arab nationalists, collectively and individually, across a spectrum of countries and communal strata, elected to join the Axis. In some cases, they participated in the slaughter. But mostly, Arab Nazis were not able to personally load Jews onto trains, march Jews into gas chambers, or machine-gun them in ditches. Instead, this movement did all in its power to advance the cause of Nazi conquest and thereby facilitate Hitler's Final Solution. From Baghdad to Bosnia to Berlin, as saboteurs and spies, as paratroopers, artillerymen, and infantry, as propagandists and provocateurs, the Arab Nazi movement did its utmost to bring the Nazis ever closer to victory. The effort was not undertaken by a mere pack of renegade fanatics or a single militant political party, but a mass movement of many thousands of Arabs and Muslims, young and old, comprising whole divisions of Arab Nazis in a broad alliance with the one that King ibn Saud had so precisely and forcefully identified in his warning to London. Shoulder to shoulder in the town squares and the trenches, this alliance flexed and sacrificed to secure and protect the oil fields, fortify the battlefield flanks and fronts, distract and divert the Allies, carry the water, cheer the victories, and otherwise make common cause with the swastika as coequal with the crescent.

One cried in Arabic: *Allah Ma'ana! Allah Ma'ana!* One cried in German: *Gott mit uns! Gott mit uns!* It means the same thing in both languages: God is with us!

\*     \*     \*     \*

In many ways, the incomplete June 1–2, 1941, massacre that became known as the *Farhud* created a turning point for Arab Nazis. When a modicum of temporary order was restored to the streets of Baghdad, the Mufti of Jerusalem, deposed Golden Square coup leader Rashid Ali and a platoon of their cohorts fled north to Mosul and, from that region, into nearby Iran. In Iran, they found a hotbed of Nazi sympathizers and calculating German advisors ensconced throughout the government. Collectively, they posed a direct threat to Allied oil supplies from the abundant British-controlled oil deposits and to the transportation of vital war materiel across Iranian territory.

The ancient empire of Persia, which ruled so much of the world for so many centuries, the pioneer of proto-monotheism that gave rise to Zarathustra also known as Zoroaster, the dynasty that roared across continents with elephants and sky-darkening archer attacks, the mighty nation strong enough to conquer great lands and liberate whole peoples, was in the twentieth century helplessly trapped in a vise between two great powers. Growling on Persia's left flank was British oil imperialism, the force that descended from above to drill down below just to drink the subterranean thick and send it home in long, snake-like pipes and then across the seas in wide boats, all so wheels and cogs could move faster in fast-paced London. Mideast oil, the fireable fluid the West fought and died for, was epicentered here and embodied in the behemoth British imperialistic enterprise known as Anglo-Persian Oil Company. Snarling on Persia's right was Mother Russia, the sprawling Eurasian Soviet that had gobbled whole populations and regions to make them one with the fearsome Stalin cult of personality that combined state terror with gulags, soaring ballerinas, and evocative Tchaikovsky to rule the century as a cruel monster with a majestic velvet side. The Bolsheviks craved the whole of the Caspian Sea and the land of Baku in the Persia-bordering country of Azerbaijan, because the Russian appetite for caviar was insatiable, almost as insatiable as its thirst for the oil that made Baku famous for soaring fire pillars of petroleum decades before Persia knew its first gusher. Persia lay prone within the hegemonic grasp of Moscow and was incessantly pinched by its sphere of commercial, political, and social influence for the first decades of the twentieth century. Russia's political machinations in Persia played out in *agitato*.[33]

Squeezed between two vassalizing tectonic plates, one capitalist and one communist, one paternalistically colonial and the other brutish and ominous, with each seeking the prize of petroleum, the Persian Shah Reza Pahlavi saw the rise of Hitler's Germany and its commercial outreach as a escape route that would deliver his ancient kingdom to a modern new world. The Shah's push into modernity was more than just a commercial venture. He tried to remake Persian society. Honorary titles were largely abolished, and ancient Islamic veils and turbans were replaced by modern Western dress and plain brown, black, or grey caps. The police could enforce the new code with corporal punishment. Impoverished rural hamlets, hard-pressed for the money to purchase new western suits and dresses, often bought just one or two sets of clothes that anyone in the town could don for visits to official buildings.[34]

But the Shah's careful statecraft with Germany was largely overshadowed by the immense popularity of the Nazi regime within Persian society. The affinity was only natural. Like others in the extended Near East, ordinary Persians shared a collective memory of the Kaiser's triumphant visits and relished Germany's decades of friendship without apparent designs on Persian territory. The rise of Hitler struck a special chord with the country. Nazism's intense anti-Jewish philosophy resonated with a populace that deeply resented British arrogance in Persia and the growing Jewish presence in Palestine under seeming British auspices. As the Arabs mythologized Hitler, Persians also adopted a spiritual synchrony with Nazism. Many believed the Nazi swastika was derived from the bent cross Sanskrit good-luck symbol, the *svastika*, which occurs throughout Neolithic Indo-Iranian history. Variations of the symbol in its ancient Persian form can be found on stone objects and other artifacts across the region.[35]

Nazis and Persians shared a common ethnic identity—Aryan. In the case of the Persian people, the Aryans were their ancestral progenitors. The word "Iran" is nothing less than the linguistic equivalent of Aryan. In the case of Nazis, the term *Aryan* was transmogrified into a fictitious Nordic quality that soon became associated with the myth of Hitler's Nordic superiority and his bizarre notion of "the master race."[36]

Berlin also had its eyes on Persia's fabulous oil deposits, the same oil controlled by Britain and coveted by the Soviets. Tapping Persia's vast mineral wealth would permit the Third Reich to achieve the type of economic independence from the West that Nazis craved. What's more, Persia constituted a strategic land route from the Persian Gulf to Russia and India and Europe that would have to be controlled in the event of war. It was also a gateway to an invasion of Palestine.

Shortly after the Nazis seized power in 1933, Germany began luring Persia out of the British and Russian spheres and into the Reich's sphere. Berlin exploited the threads of ethnic coincidence to create a binding fabric between German Nazism and Persian popular sentiment that was tightly sewn beneath the burgeoning commercial relationship with the Shah's government. In July 1933, the Nazi Ministry of Propaganda began publishing in Persia the Farsi-language publication *Irane-e-Bastan—Ancient Iran*. Funding came principally from Siemens, the Nazi commercial conglomerate. The popular publication was brimming with cultural information glorifying the Persian past and the Nazi present.[37]

As Germany moved toward Persia in 1933, the Shah felt he could demand greater royalties from Anglo-Persian Oil Company—and London felt pressured to comply. The gargantuan oil concession was reduced from 500,000 square miles to just 100,000 square miles. The Shah at first believed he had achieved an improvement. But London cleverly arranged to parcel for itself the most petroliferous tracts of those remaining 100,000 square miles and then rigged per-barrel royalties to match artificially low prices the company created elsewhere in the world. Hence, Tehran did not increase its share of its own oil wealth. This only caused resentment against the British to further fester.[38]

At the same time, Russia propped up the economic errors of communism at Persia's expense. Moscow made Persia a convenient dumping ground for surplus goods manufactured by the Bolshevik workers' revolution. When it suited communist interests, Russia boycotted Persian wares and withheld its own goods from the Persian market. Moscow happily renounced claims on vast Russian loans and Russian-built highways, as well as commercial and telegraphic infrastructure in Persia. The Soviets claimed their actions were valued at some 582 million rubles. But critics in Persia scored the agreement to improve bilateral relations as little more than propagandistic efforts to "enslave Persia." In reality, secret protocols between the two countries conditioned Russian concessions on not permitting commercial rights to any other power, meaning Germany. Another secret annex provided automatic Soviet military rights on Persian land in the event any nation invaded Persia to reach Russia. Again, these provisions were aimed at Germany.[39]

Germany exploited Persian discontent to engineer a broad diplomatic and commercial alliance fortified by a popular wellspring of Nazi enthusiasm. The Reich's intent was solely to prepare for war. First, Berlin concluded a bilateral trade agreement with Tehran, structured like so many of Germany's other trade agreements, based not on money but barter. German technicians and advisors began pouring into Persia to build railroads and autobahns. At first blush, the Trans-Iranian Railway, an old Russian-inspired project overtaken in earnest by Reich engineers, seemed a benign modernization.[40]

But as Allied governments learned more about the train system, they discovered that the track gauge was narrower than all other neighboring countries, except Turkey, and consistent with the German Reichsbahn. Hence, the tracks could never connect to Russian railways. But Iran's railway could connect to Nazi rails. During the harsh Russian winter, when that country's waterways were frozen, the country would be cut off. Germany, however, would enjoy rapid movement of men and materials.[41]

During 1933 and 1934, German economic diplomats became increasingly influential in Tehran, and Nazi imagery became more commonplace in Tehran. The Aryan swastika saw a revival in the new Tehran architecture of the day. Then, in late January 1935, the Shah announced that as of March 22, the Iranian New Year, his nation would no longer be known as Persia, its famous name for centuries. Henceforth, the nation would be known by its ancient ethnic identity, Iran, that is, the land of the Aryans. Anglo-Persian Oil Company shortly afterward was compelled to change its name to Anglo-Iranian Oil Company to match.[42] Many thought the move was a direct salute to the Third Reich. But Tehran insisted it just preferred to be called by its ancient name. Either way, the solidarity with Nazi Germany was now becoming profound.

In October 1935, a special Payment and Clearing Agreement was signed by Berlin and Tehran that essentially elevated Nazi Germany to most-favored status pending expiration of prior most-favored trading agreements with Russia and Britain. In 1936, the Nazis decreed a special racial exemption for Iranians, identifying them as pure-blooded Aryans. In 1938, the Shah refused to renew Russia's most-favored trade agreement. German trade with Iran zoomed to more than 47 percent of imports, mainly at the expense of Russia whose imports fell to less than half of a single percentage point. Trade with Russia—once Tehran's single largest trading partner—essentially disappeared in favor of commerce with the Reich.[43]

Despite the increased trade with the Reich, by 1938 the Shah was beginning to see his dependence on Germany as almost out of control. Hitler was an immensely popular figure in Persia. Some ordinary Persians found it fashionable to sport Hitler mustaches. Iranian Nazi parties mimicked the Arab Nazi parties. Their arm bands brandished the Sumka cross with a slightly bent vertical. They pumped the Hitler salute palms open. Finally, the Shah banned the Nazi publication *Irane-e-Bastan* and declined an invitation from Hitler to visit him in Germany. But by now, the die seemed cast. Soon, it was rumored among diplomats that the Nazi-infected Iranian military planned to assassinate the Shah.[44]

In 1939, when war broke out, the Shah did what other Nazi-leaning British allies did. Tehran declared "neutrality." This in essence was a green light for Germany. Some 2,000 German advisors were swarming all over Iran's commercial, military, and governmental establishments. The Reich was diverting some 30 percent of all Iranian ore production. A terminal had been established at Semnan to transport 60 percent-pure iron ore, as well as high-quality nickel, copper, lead, and sulfur—all military necessities. By the time the war was in full swing, 103 of 109 Iranian locomotives were German or Austrian. Reich construction crews worked at a frantic pace on rail lines crisscrossing the vital routes of Iran.[45]

On June 22, 1941, three weeks after the *Farhud*, Operation Barbarossa was launched. The Nazis invaded Russia. Now the military value of Iran's vital supply lines and oil was clear. The Mufti of Jerusalem, the Golden Square, and German Gestapo agents had all congregated and stayed active in Iran since fleeing neighboring Iraq weeks earlier. Allied leaders now feared the Iranian army would go the way of Iraq's and join the Axis outright, especially with the Mufti exerting his leadership. If the Iranian military ousted the tenuous Shah and joined hands with Germany, Hitler would have unlimited oil for his blitzing army, the very oil that the Axis had wanted all along to deny to Britain and Russia.[46]

After Germany's June 1941 Russian invasion and the *Farhud*, Churchill and Stalin demanded the Shah immediately expel some 2,000 Nazi advisors and administrators from Iranian territory. Every one of them was suspected of being a spy or a Wehrmacht advance man. A major wartime intelligence operation had been established in Tabriz and in areas near Baku to report on Russian industrial operations that could be taken over. The Nazi media openly suggested creating German colonies in Iran. The joint demand for expulsion of its German advisors made on July 19, 1941, was ignored by Tehran.[47]

By August 16, 1941, Britain and Russia were again jointly demanding that the Shah expel all German advisors. Hitler sent the Shah a note demanding he hold firm while the Reich army proceeded against southern Russia. Intelligence suggested that a Golden Square-style coup was scheduled to oust the Shah sometime between August 22 and August 28. The clock was now ticking down to a new Islamic alliance with the Reich. This one would deliver Reich forces across the Caucasus Mountains and place them on a direct path to Palestine.[48]

The Mufti, long part of the Nazi intelligence apparatus, saw the war coming and to avoid capture by the British, made plans to move from Tehran to Turkey. But with Husseini a wanted man, the Turks denied him a visa. He asked Saudi Arabia, but the British presence there was still too great, and it was unclear how he could travel there in view of wartime conditions. He turned to Afghanistan and nervously awaited some word.[49]

The British columns that had rescued Habbaniya were now combined with other forces and cobbled together with British Indian units into a special rapid strike force. The Russians also assembled a rapid-deployment phalanx. At dawn on August 25, 1941, rushing at top speed in hopes of preventing another Axis coup, British and Russian forces invaded Iran. Oil facilities at Abadan operated by Anglo-Iranian Oil Company were seized by British Indian forces. Soviet bombers and ground forces attacked from the north. The Iranian military instantly collapsed. Allied units grabbed the key facilities of the Trans-Iranian Railway. By September 17, 1941, the Russian and British armies met up in Tehran. The Shah was arrested and exiled to South Africa. Thousands of Germans, Italians, Hungarians, and agents of other Axis members were quickly rounded up by the British and expelled. The Shah's son, also named Reza, was installed on the Peacock Throne on his promise to cooperate with Britain and Russia.[50]

The manhunt to find the Mufti now fanned out across Iran. First, the new Shah invited the Mufti for a friendly ministerial meeting with assurances he would be safe and unharmed. Hiding in the Japanese diplomatic compound, the Mufti sent some of his colleagues out first as a test. They were promptly arrested and sent to a detention camp in Rhodesia. By now, it was rumored that British generals had placed a £25,000 bounty on the Mufti's head—dead or alive. The Mufti slipped out of the Japanese legation and went into hiding in a private residence. Iranian police, now cooperating with the British, believed they had Husseini cornered. They were ready to swoop down—but he was gone.[51]

On September 23, 1941, a taxi driven by an Armenian inconspicuously wound its way through Russian territory en route to the Turkish border. The passenger appeared to be an ordinary businessman, wearing a suit, beardless, of little interest. Russian military checkpoint after checkpoint examined the businessman's papers and waved him through. The businessman was Husseini. He had left his wife and children behind. But to him, his mission was more important.[52]

British intelligence agents soon learned of the Mufti's escape—once again in disguise. They took Husseini's family into custody to hold as hostages, sequestered in a tiny jail cell. A British intelligence agent then took off in hot pursuit. Soon the Mufti learned that the British agent was not far behind. To stall the agent, the Mufti provoked some Russian soldiers into delaying the British agent when he arrived at the checkpoint. At one checkpoint, two Russians suddenly entered the taxi—but they only wanted to hitch a ride. Fine. They all rode together toward the Turkish border where a Japanese diplomat helped Husseini pass into Turkish territory. As he did, Husseini wept, knowing that his children and wife were now lost to him.[53]

No matter now. A new place for Husseini would be found in the war against the Jews. He would emerge from the backdrop and step into the foreground. In this vein, the Mufti knew he could not linger in Turkey, which was still allied with Britain in this war. He made plans to go directly to the Axis capitals of Rome and Berlin.[54]

Husseini's new mission was no longer just to provoke and incite. Now he would rise to a new role, to direct and demand that the Arab movements openly choose a side. He would rally them to openly don the Nazi uniform and jump aboard the Nazi troop transports and into the trenches to do Hitler's murderous bidding. The Mufti unambiguously declared his new mandamus for the Arab and Islamic worlds. He would not mince words. Husseini's new mantra for all, on his radio broadcasts and while recruiting Arab legions to join the Nazi military, was this: "Kill the Jews. Kill them wherever you find them. This pleases God, history, and religion. This serves your honor. God is with you!"[55]

*    *    *    *

Husseini's tortuous escape from Tehran brought him to a temporary respite in Rome. After conferring with Mussolini, the Mufti made his way to Berlin. He arrived there on November 6, 1941, where he was met by a coterie of senior Reich officials including Grobba, as well as Nazi propagandanists. Husseini was told that that his first major meeting would be with German Foreign Minister Joachim von Ribbentrop. When he met with the foreign minister, the Mufti made clear as he had so many times before that "the Arabs are natural friends of Germany, because both are engaged in the struggle against their three common enemies: the English, the Jews, and Bolshevism." A week later, Hitler agreed to a private audience.[56]

On November 28, 1941, *der Führer* welcomed the Mufti to their iconic meeting in Hitler's private offices. Newsreel cameras whirred as the Nazis propagandized to the world their solidarity with the Arab world. Husseini lavished praise on Hitler for his support of Arabs everywhere, especially Palestinian Arabs. The Mufti assured Hitler that Allah would deliver victory to the Reich because "the Almighty would never bestow victory upon an unjust cause."[57]

Husseini declared that the Arabs were devoted to "this battle for the independence and unity of Palestine, Syria, and Iraq." Arabs everywhere, Husseini promised Hitler, would organize acts of sabotage for the Reich and ignite local insurrections, as they had in Palestine, Iraq, and Iran. By this means, the Allies would be diverted from the main war, especially in the East.[58]

Hitler told the Mufti, "I am happy that you have escaped [from Iran] and that you are now with the Axis powers." During the exchange, *der Führer's* rhetoric was as replete with support for the Arab cause as the Mufti's was for Nazi Germany. The German leader assured, "I will keep up my fight until the complete destruction of the Judeo-Bolshevik rule."[59]

Clearly, the two leaders agreed on the principle of annihilating the "Jewish enemy." But what the Arab world craved, said Husseini, was a public proclamation by the Reich, recognizing the existence of the Arab Nation. *Der Führer* replied that now was not the right moment for such a public statement. Instead, Hitler offered private verbal assurances to the Mufti to "lock in the depths of his heart." When Reich tanks and divisions were able to cross the Caucasus Mountains, Hitler promised, the hour would come. At that point, Hitler would go public with the statement of support for the Arab Nation. That would be the moment for Nazi Germany to push all the way to Palestine, where its sole mission would be "the destruction of the Jewish element residing in the Arab sphere."[60]

In various meetings before the summit, it was explained to Husseini that it would take the Nazis three to six months, perhaps more, depending upon weather conditions, to push through the Caucasus. To the Mufti this meant that the German push to the East was the new imperative.[61] Once, Reich divisions were there, the final solution would come to Jewish Palestine.

Islamic forces throughout Europe and the Middle East were already rushing to join the Wehrmacht. Directive 32, in June 1941, had activated the "Arab National Movement" as official fighting forces of the Reich. From July, the 288th Training Battalion of Arabs began rigorous training both in Doeberitz, Germany, outside Berlin, and then the sunny Greek cape at Sunium to make them regular Nazi soldiers. Staff F, created by Hitler to coordinate Arab movements, took command of the units. Arab fighters would wear regular German military uniforms as Reich soldiers, but their armbands would read "Free Arabia." In many cases, their headgear would be the unmistakable fez and tassel, or a shortened cap-like version of it. The distinctive armbands and headgear did not change the fact that all the recruits saw themselves as "full-fledged members of the Axis" and made this clear to their instructors in Staff F.[62]

In time, the German-Arab battalions yielded parachute units, machine-gunners, and mortar platoons that could sweep through mountains and across large battle zones like a modern efficient fighting force, as well as elite sabotage squads that could stealthily disable oil facilities, bridges, and communications. Muslim volunteers streamed in from across the Islamic and Arab worlds in response to ceaseless radio and propaganda calls from the Mufti of Jerusalem and many other Arab agitations. "Kill the Jews," railed the Mufti. "Kill them wherever you find them. This pleases God, history, and religion. This serves your honor. God is with you!" Other times, he exhorted, "Kill the Jews before they kill you." In the marketplaces and mosques of the Muslim world, the flyers proclaimed, "In heaven, Allah is your master. On Earth it is Adolf Hitler." A special Arab Recruitment Center was established in Paris. But those Arabs and Muslims seeking to join the Nazis signed up wherever they could.[63]

So many volunteers answered the call that Staff F was able to organize the first wave of thousands of Muslims into four more battalions. Two mainly Tunisian battalions were established, along with one mainly Algerian battalion, and one mainly Moroccan battalion. Palestinians, Egyptians, Syrians, Iraqis, Transjordanians, Saudis, Libyans, Iranians, desert Bedouins, and others Muslims who volunteered were either formed into their own units or mixed into the larger battalions. A Staff F officer recorded, "Each battalion consisted of three infantry companies armed with carbines and light machine guns, and one heavy-weapons company equipped with mortars and heavy machine guns."[64]

The Wehrmacht used Arab Nazis as paratroopers, artillerymen, infantry, or special operations commandos wherever it needed them most. Among their first assignments—in Benghazi, Libya—they were airlifted and deployed as "a blocking force" attached to the army of Field Marshal Erwin Rommel, the Desert Fox. The North Africa campaign was crucial to the war and pitted the Allies against Hitler's vaunted *Afrika-Korps*, which was supported by Arab volunteers throughout the entire campaign. Arab units were also deployed in Sicily and Russia when additional manpower or firepower was required.[65]

Arabs served with distinction and impressed Nazi officers. One staff German officer wrote, "My Arabs never filched any of my personal belongings, though as a rule they stole like magpies. They liked to stuff themselves with good food; they liked to get drunk, to loot and rape; but they also knew how to die bravely, and they resisted pain remarkably well." When German soldiers were taken prisoner, the officer added, the Arabs frequently declined to melt away into the population and instead demanded to be taken away as POWs with their Wehrmacht comrades.[66]

However, all their diverse fighting units paled when compared to the record shown in Yugoslavia, where entire divisions of Muslims were raised to help Hitler achieve his Caucasus goal. There, in Yugoslavia, the record is one that has never stopped burning. For it was in Croatia that Muslims and Arabs came by the tens of thousands, under the leadership of the Mufti of Jerusalem and other regional Muslim personalities, to partner with the single most heinous name in the annals of the Holocaust, and indeed in the chronicle of World War II.

They partnered with the Ustasha.

*     *     *     *

Sometimes history must apologize to the future for recalling the gruesome realities of the past. The Holocaust is among the most horrid of historical events. But within the hierarchy of hell, the most ghastly niche is reserved for the fanatic Croatian nationalists known as the Ustasha. As the depraved and grisly details are recalled, history regrets its duty.

In a realm where the horrific is commonplace, the wartime history of Yugoslavia is the most disturbing of any in Europe. Yet, comparatively little is known or published about the bloody events that pitted Catholic Croats against Serbian Orthodox in a war of ethnic cleansing that assumed unspeakable dimensions of beastly violence. Many historians are hesitant to even describe the ethnic and nationalist rivalries, or the blood-curdling atrocities committed, because the documentation is so sparse, contradictory, confusing, and impenetrable, and is so intensely politicized. Shifting alliances, collaborations, and cross-killing among the rival groups occurred at a dizzying rate. One day, ethnic partners massacred a third group; and the next day, they turned their still sanguineous knives on each other. Much of the record and testimony is in Serbian or Croatian, making the killing chronology even more inaccessible. However, certain salient facts are known and now visible.

Yugoslavia was a creation of the post-World War I mapmakers, who, in successive diplomatic ventures, patched together a confederated kingdom comprised of what could be referred to as the realms of Serbia, Croatia, Macedonia, Kosovo, Bosnia-Herzegovina, Albania, and a number of other Balkan territories. Some referred to the composite kingdom as "the Versailles State," referring to the post-Paris Peace Conference process that evolved the transient nation that became Yugoslavia. In the madness that was Yugoslavia, creating generalities about which ethnic group committed which ethnic atrocity would be fruitless. They continually murdered each other. Each ethnic group was divided into factions, wracked by splinter groups within those factions and renegade blocs within those splinter groups—all of whom formed constantly morphing alliances and counter-alliances in a glissando of targeted three-way killing and ethnic cleansing. Estimates of the cross-carnage vary; but, certainly, many tens of thousands of Muslims and Catholic Croats were brutally murdered early on in World War II by Eastern Orthodox Serbians, especially the Serbian ultranationalists known as Chetniks. The Chetnik flag mimicked a Jolly Roger; it was emblazoned with a skull and crossbones against an ominous black background. They always made good on their diabolical mission of death and destruction. As many as a million Serbs were heinously mass murdered by the rival Catholic Croats, who, in their alliance with the Nazis, ultimately gained an upper hand in the reign of terror and death that gripped all of Yugoslavia.[67] Hence, the Croat alliance, backed by the Nazis, achieved mastery in the mass murder that ravaged the Balkans.

The only ethnic groups that did not wage campaigns of horrendous ethnic cleansing were the Gypsies and the Jews. Defenseless and powerless, Gypsies and Jews were caught in the whirlwind of human destruction in a way that pleased the Nazis and their anti-Jewish allies.

Axis forces from all sides invaded Yugoslavia on April 6, 1941. Italy seized the largely Muslim lands to the south, creating a Greater Albania client state. From the west, the Reich marched and parachuted into the main centers of Yugoslavia to secure land routes to the Mediterranean, which the German military demanded in their drive toward Greece. The Nazis set up a puppet Croatian government under the name "Independent State of Croatia" to rule over all the Croatian, Bosnian, and Serbian lands. In other words, the Croats, previously confined to their own areas, now had sway over the rival Serbs. That new Croatian puppet state's population has been estimated at approximately 6 million. Of this number, experts estimate Catholic Croats totaled approximately 3.3 million, while Orthodox Serbs amounted to some 2 million persons who existed alongside some 700,000 to a million Bosnian Muslims. The most extreme Bosnian Muslim nationalists were known as Bosniaks, and their fire burned for a Croatian national state at any cost.[68]

Ethnic Croats hated Serbians above all other groups and demanded they all either convert to Catholicism or be expelled or massacred. In fact, the Croatian credo was to exterminate a third of the Serbs, convert a third, and expel a third.[69] Serbs killed, and were killed, in great numbers.

Jews and Gypsies are estimated to have numbered more than 100,000 persons, depending upon the territory. Nearly all of them were butchered. The Jews and Gypsies, however, were mere corollary victims in a three-way orgy of death.[70]

In the Croatian maelstrom of ethnic and religious hatred, steered by Nazi mentors and puppet masters, Catholic Croats ironically decreed that all Muslims were Croats. This enabled the Catholic Croats to establish a majority in their enlarged territorial domain. That enlarged Independent State of Croatia was known in the dialect as Nezavisna Država Hrvatska, or the NDH. The NDH's all-controlling killing and terror militia was the Ustasha, the worst perpetrators of depraved killing in the Holocaust. The Independent State of Croatia was in fact a bi-ethnic murder regime sworn to exterminate the millions of Yugoslavians who were neither Catholic nor Muslim through their bi-ethnic killing machine, the Ustasha. Although Muslims were a minority in the NDH, the Bosniak Muslim faction and the Croatian Catholics jointly ruled and jointly murdered. The NDH's fascist extremist president was staunch Hitler ally and former Jesuit seminarian, Ante Pavelić. His official title was *Poglavnik,* a Croatian word that approximates *der Führer.* The vice president was Muslim Džafer-beg Kulenović, previously president of the Yugoslav Moslem Organization, a Bosniak nationalist organization.[71]

The Croatian Minister of Culture and Education was Mile Budak, a rabid Catholic Nazi who propagated the axiom of killing one-third, converting one-third and expelling one-third of all Serbs. Budak and other Catholic Croats believed that Muslims were actually descendants of the ancient Bogomil people who had inhabited the Croatian lands centuries earlier. As a leader in forging the Muslim-Catholic alliance, Budak enthusiastically proclaimed in 1941, "We Croats are happy and proud of our [Christian] faith, but we must be conscious of the fact that our Muslim brothers are the purest of Croats." He elaborated in a speech that the NDH was "Christian. [But] it is also a Muslim state where our people are of the Muslim religion." In July 1941, Budak openly declared that the new state must exterminate "foreign elements," that is Jews and Gypsies, as well as the larger enemy, Orthodox Serbs. Budak hid nothing about his plans. "The basis for the Ustasha movement is religion," announced Budak. "For minorities such as Serbs, Jews, and Gypsies, we have 3 million bullets."[72]

To cement the Muslim and Catholic killing coalition, NDH president Pavelić converted a local Zagreb museum to a huge and impressive mosque, adding surrounding minarets to its modern architecture, and naming the mosque after himself. Numerous NDH ministries were controlled or headed by Muslims. Pavelić even donned a Muslim fez to show his solidarity. Muslims were invited to join the barbaric Croatian Peasant Party and did so in significant numbers. When Muslims served in the Ustasha First Regiment, known as Black Legion, their black uniforms were the same as their Catholic co-kill-ers. Senior officers were dressed in identical garb. Ibrahim Pirić-Pjanić and Memesaga Dzubur led their own local Ustasha-affiliated contingents. Muslim Ustasha Muhamed Hadžiefendić led his own militia in Tuzla. Hadžiefendić's militia became so strong that Bosniaks wanted it to operate autonomously in Muslim areas of Bosnia.[73]

The Diet legislature, which passed a sequence of genocidal decrees, included 11 Muslims specifically appointed for that purpose. These decrees included outlawing Serbian and Jewish existence in Croatia, the looting of Serbian and Jewish property, and the systematic regimentation of Serbian and Jewish citizens into death camps and merciless killing fields. Catholic priests commonly operated the concentration camps, enforcing the most degrading of slaughter rituals. In Sarajevo, most of the looted and confiscated property of victims went to Muslims, who raced to grab Jewish and Serbian assets before their Catholic partners.[74]

Under Croatian decrees, Jews were compelled to wear yellow Star-of-David arm bands and back patches marked with a "Z" for *Zidov*, the Croa-tian word for Jew. Muslims plundered and decimated the Great Sephardic Synagogue in Sarajevo and the centuries-old synagogue in Dubrovnik. When Muslim families were moved out of their villages near the battle lines, the Ustasha evicted Jews from their homes so the Croatian Muslims could take their place. When Jews fled the November 1941 mass roundups in Sarajevo, preparatory to planned extermination, a number of them escaped only by dis-guising themselves under Muslim veils. At the same time, many of the Jews who did survive the Jew-hunts did so by appealing to merciful neighbors in the Muslim quarter that took them in and hid them until they could escape safely. Many Muslims in Sarajevo rejected the Bosniak Ustasha horror and tried—in vain—to protest to their coreligionists.[75]

Serbs suffered enormously. As Serbs were being forcibly converted to Catholicism, some 450 Serbian Orthodox churches were demolished and their religious icons defiled. Orthodox clergymen, from ordinary priests to the Met-ropolitan, were gruesomely tortured and their families shipped to concentra-tion camps where they were subjected to every inhumanity.[76]

NDH President Pavelić declared early on, "This is now the Ustasha and Independent State of Croatia. It must be cleansed of all Serbs and Jews. There is no room for any of them here. Not a stone upon a stone will remain of what once belonged to them." He later assured, "The Jews will be liquidated within a very short time." To this end, more than 20 Ustasha concentration camps were established for the killing process, manned by combined Catholic and Muslim forces. The most notorious of these camps was the hellish complex known as Jasenovac, considered by many to be more sadistic than Auschwitz by an immeasurable magnitude. Gas chambers were not needed. All death was personally inflicted.[77]

The Ustasha's barbaric methods for exterminating Jews and Serbs included sadistic group killing by cracking heads open with hammers until the cranial cavity was exposed. That was for adults. Children were commonly marched into the forest, where their heads were crushed with long mallets. Sometimes children were thrown live into flaming furnaces. Decapitation or dismemberment with giant lumber saws was frequent; Branko Jungic was one of many Serb villagers subjected to this monstrous murder technique. The terrifying photograph of his dismemberment became famous. Neck punctures with great iron bars were commonly accompanied by bowls carefully positioned to collect spurting blood, thus sparing uniforms the splatter. All too often, these Ustasha atrocities were not committed in fits of mad rage, but for sport, with the gleeful perpetrators smiling for the camera over the helpless victim waiting to be brutalized.[78]

Mass throat-slittings at great velocity were achieved with a small hand blade wrapped tight to the wrist and dubbed the "Serbcutter." They were specially designed and manufactured for the purpose. One night, guards at Jasenovac wagered amongst themselves to see who could cut the most throats with their Serbcutters. Guard Petar Brzica, a Franciscan priest, was determined to prove his skill, which he did by slicing the throats of an estimated 1,360 defenseless inmates. Guard Ante Zrinusic lost the bet by only cutting the throats of about 600 helpless prisoners. Guard Mile Friganović was close behind the winner, murdering only about 1,100 Serbs that night. But Friganović was also known for an unspeakable incident in which an old man was asked to shout a salute to Croat president Ante Pavelić. When the old man hesitated, Friganović systematically and gleefully cut off his ears first, then the nose and tongue, after which he gouged out his eyes, and then extracted the victim's heart—and only after all that did Friganović end it all by slitting the prisoner's throat. Friganović called the experience one of "ecstasy."[79]

Groups of shivering Jewish children were brought into a camp one day. For sport, one guard began spinning a child above his head as the other guards slashed at it with their bayonets. Eventually, the guard was left with nothing but the child's hand as a trophy. Other Ustasha trophies included eyeball collections, stored in wicker baskets for show and sometimes worn strung up in necklaces. NDH president Pavelić himself once showed a journalist a wicker basket filled with some 40 pounds of eyeballs. Pavelić joked that he could make an oyster stew with them.[80]

Women were carted away and raped endlessly until their captors were finished—at which time they were horribly mutilated for souvenir body parts. "A good Ustasha," Pavelić told his troops, "is he who can use his knife to cut a child from the womb of its mother."[81] The bi-ethnic Ustasha never disappointed their president.

Cruel and inhumane as the Nazis were, they retreated in wide-eyed astonishment when they learned of the joint Catholic-Muslim Ustasha atrocities. German General Edmund Glaise von Horstenau, the commanding officer of the region headquartered in Zagreb, reported back to Berlin, "According to reliable reports from countless German military and civil observers during the last few weeks, the Ustasha have gone raging mad." He added, "The Ustasha camps ... are the 'epitome of horror!'" In revulsion, Glaise von Horstenau wrote, "The most wicked [concentration camp] of all must be Jasenovac, where no ordinary mortal is allowed to peer in."[82]

Hermann Naubacher, Hitler's personal assistant for the Balkans, called the Ustasha exterminations "a crusade that belongs among the most brutal mass-murder undertakings in the entire history of the world." Naubacher somberly added, "According to the reports that have reached me, my estimate is that the number of those defenseless slaughtered is some three-quarters of a million."[83]

Ustasha horrors were always joint Muslim-Catholic endeavors; but Muslims, by virtue of their minority status, were frequently the junior partners in the carnage. Sometimes, however, they did their part in the ghastly acts to show they too could excel at bloodlust. Berberovic Hilmija, an Ustasha Muslim, swore in an affidavit exactly what he did at the city of Glina.

Hilmija's own words: "At the beginning of June [1941] my company was ordered to Glina to establish order and peace in that district and to collect all the arms and ammunition from the people ... On our arrival in Glina we searched the houses of that town and then went to the neighboring villages. When the searching was over, the Ustasha arrived from Zagreb and Petrinja and we were then ordered to round up from the villages all men from 20 to 45 years of age ... At the beginning we arrested only the men. We collected them from the villages and shut them in the court jail. There they remained several days, until the jails were filled, and they were then put to death. The killing was done in several ways. Some were locked up in the Orthodox Church in Glina, which could contain 1000 men. Then the company officer chose about fifteen men to do the killing. They were then sent into the church with knives."[84]

Hilmija explained, "During the butchering, sentries were placed before the church. This was necessary because some of the Orthodox Serbs climbed up the bell tower and jumped into the porch. All these were killed by the sentries in the porch. I was three times chosen to do the killing. Each time we were accompanied by some officers, Dobric Josip and Cvitkovic Mihailo, and some Ustasha officers. When we entered the church, the officers remained at the door and watched while we did the killing. Some we struck in the heart and some in the neck. Some we struck haphazard. During the killings there were no lights in the church, except that some soldiers were specially appointed to light our way with electric torches. It happened on several occasions that some Serb rushed us with his fists or kicked us in the stomach, but he was butchered immediately. There was always much noise during the killing. The Serbs used to shout 'Long live Serbia, long live the Serbs,' and 'Down with Pavelić,' and 'Down with the Ustasha,' and 'Down with the Croatian State,' etc."[85]

"The killing usually began at about ten o'clock in the evening and lasted until two o'clock in the morning, and the cries continued until the last Serb was killed. These killings in the church took place seven [or] eight times, and I took part in them three times. Every time, we were so bespattered with blood, our uniforms could not be cleaned. We therefore changed them in the store-house and washed them later. The church was washed after every killing, after the corpses were taken away in motor trucks. Usually they were thrown into the river Glina. Sometimes they were buried."[86]

Hilmija added, "Some Orthodox Serbs were taken from the jail to the river Glina and machine-gunned. Usually 300 or 400 persons were machine-gunned at a time. They were stood up in two ranks at the bank, tied arm to arm with ropes, and then shot with machine guns which were placed a few yards away. The machine-gunning was done by the Ustasha, while we stood guard around. The corpses of these persons were thrown into the Glina ..."[87]

"My company's task was to round up the Serbs in Glina and in the Glina district, but orders were also given that all Serbs in the districts of Topusko and Vrgin Most, as well as Glina, should be rounded up and killed. I do not know exactly how many Serbs were killed, but I have heard it said that about 120,000 Serbs from the abovementioned districts have been killed."[88]

In reviewing his confession, Hilmija declared, "I have nothing more to add. These notes have been read out to me, and all my statements have been correctly written down. I can read and write."[89]

Within six months of the Ustasha takeover, 15 combat battalions of militia and two service battalions of militia, totaling some 10,000 men, were terrorizing the enlarged Croatian territory. Meanwhile, some 32,000 men were serving in the Croatian regular army, supplemented by 10,000 in auxiliary units such as the Home Guard, Railroad Security, and various support and noncombat battalions.[90]

Quickly, those who escaped the murder machine slipped into the mountains and forests to form anti-Nazi partisan units allied under Communist leadership—sparked by Hitler's invasion of Russia, Operation Barbarossa. Known as The People's Liberation Front and led by Marshal Josip Broz Tito, partisan ranks were comprised of escaped Jews, Serbs, and even dissident

Muslims together with a combination of Croatians, Bosnians, Serbians, and many other groups. Eventually, wielding some 800,000 fighters in approximately 52 divisions, the Yugoslav partisan army became the strongest, best disciplined, and most effective resistance force of World War II. It was these partisans that pinned the Nazis down in the mud, gorges, and fields of the Balkans. Partisan warriors struck the Germans everywhere—at bridges and encampments and along mountain roads. Convoys were destroyed. Germany's forward progress was stalled. Employing both conventional and guerrilla warfare, the valiant Yugoslav partisan army fought nothing less than ferociously.[91] By 1942, the Nazis were hurting. Their thrust toward Russia and the Caucasus had been bogged down.

Berlin needed at least 20,000 Croatian fighters to assemble into new Waffen SS divisions. The Waffen SS were the vicious army of the Nazi Party, swearing allegiance directly to Adolf Hitler. Their missions were often the most militarily daunting and murderous. Their records matched their missions.[92]

Many of the Waffen SS divisions were comprised of foreign fighters.[93] However, it was everything the Croatian Ustasha forces could do to ethnically cleanse the NDH territory of millions of hated people and effectively murder their neighbors. The undisciplined, animalistic Ustasha battalions could not work in a formal combat environment under Wehrmacht command.

It was Himmler, a chief architect of the mass extermination of European Jewry, who decided that the answer lay in a special Waffen SS division of 10,000 Bosnian Muslim soldiers. After all, Himmler knew that Arab and Muslim volunteers were fiercely devoted to helping the Reich push into Russia past the Caucasus. That continuing thrust into Russia could not succeed without Yugoslavia's raw materials and supply lines. Nor could it be done with a persistent and fiery war on Operation Barbarossa's flank. Such a Balkan force of 10,000 would be vastly greater than the Ustasha and would require more Muslims than had ever been assembled.

The fragmented Muslim community was hardly unanimous in their support for the Ustasha or their methods. There was fear that once the Serbs were fully exterminated, the Muslims would be next. Moreover, the Bosniak extremist Muslims were more than willing to dispatch their own coreligionists to concentration camps and subject whole Muslim villages to internecine massacres if they strayed from the Croatian authoritarian line. Rape of Muslim women inflicted by unbridled, suddenly-empowered Ustasha men, was random but regular. As some Catholic elements of the splintered Ustasha began to suspect their Muslim cohorts of secret sympathies with the Communists, Catholics torched Muslim villages and launched wholesale slaughter of the residents. At one point, a number of Bosniak leaders approached Hitler to seek formal annexation into the Third Reich, thereby placing Muslims under formal Nazi protection. The eight-point Memorandum of the National Muslim Committee, written by a coalition of Muslim leaders led by Sarajevo Mayor Mustafa Softic, referred to Hitler as "our dear leader." It proclaimed, "Bosniak-Muslims are a part of the 300-million–[member] Islamic nation from the East, which can achieve its liberation only in the struggle against English imperialism, world Jewry, Free Masons, and Bolshevism, led by the German people under the leadership of its *Führer*." The appeal was rejected by Berlin.[94]

Historians estimate that as the NDH deepened its campaign of terror, perhaps only half of the Muslims in many areas actively supported the Ustasha regime.[95]

A number of leading imams issued *fatwas* of condemnation demanding Muslims— including their Bosniak coreligionists—not cooperate with Croatian nationalism. Moreover, by 1942, with Germany's Final Solution in full swing—both by mobile killing squads in the east, not far from the Balkan borders, and by gas, in such death camps as Auschwitz, many Nazi collaborators were pondering public forms of dissension, disapproval, and disobedience to use as a postwar alibi in case the Nazis failed and the Allies did as was eventually publicly announced in December 1942. That is when the Allies jointly and publicly declared war crimes trials would be conducted for the Nazis and all those who assisted in the extermination of the Jews.[96]

How could the Nazis raise an army of 10,000 Muslims under the wartime conditions of 1942? Himmler called in his partner in the extermination of the Jews. He brought the Mufti of Jerusalem to the Balkans. The Mufti successfully raised not just one division of Muslim fighters for the Wehrmacht, but three divisions; not just 10,000, but twice that number.[97]

\*        \*        \*        \*

By the time, the Reich decided to raise a Wehrmacht division in December 1942, Yugoslavia's Jews were almost all dead or dispatched to concentration camps. Belgrade was declared the first city in Europe to be *Judenrein*, that is, Jew-free. Those Jews who were not already hunted down and killed, or confined in hellish Croatian labor camps, were packed into trains and sent to Auschwitz. By December 1942, the Auschwitz death camp had been industrially mass murdering thousands of Jews daily in its Birkenau gas chambers. The Nazi killing process was now one that was out of the whispers. By December 1942, the Allies, through the newly formed United Nations, made their famous worldwide promulgation accusing the Nazis and their European allies of orchestrating the extermination of more than six million Jews—and promising war crime trials for all those directly or indirectly abetting that genocide. By December 1942, a Warsaw Jew named Natalia Zarembina had published a small book called *Auschwitz: The Camp of Death*, which clearly described incessant train unloading and the rapid gas chamber process. Zarembina's booklet grimly described the process: "A trip to Oswiecim, a flight of steps into the 'underground,' and death by gas." Published in eight languages during the coming two years, the Zarembina's booklet was mass distributed in English by the American Federation of Labor [AFL] and the Congress of Industrial Organizations [CIO].[98]

The new Balkan divisions were in the main not to be used against Yugoslavia's Jews. By late 1942, Bosnian Jews were mainly gone. Instead, these formations were to be whipped into disciplined military divisions, and deployed strictly to defeat the partisans and help speed the advance of the Third Reich, which would allow Hitler to apply the Final Solution to Jews as far the swastika could reach. Recruitment began in earnest in early 1943. Ustasha commanders enthusiastically responded to Berlin's call, assuming they could muster a blend of Catholic and Muslim soldiers from their ranks to create what they would name the "SS Ustasha Division." Quickly, both the Nazis and the Muslim leaders rejected this idea, preferring a pure Muslim division. Himmler resisted the Ustasha's suggestions of a mixed force, writing, "I still intend to form the division from Muslims." NDH's Muslim vice president Kulenović told Reich military recruiters, the situation had indeed changed since those first months of the Croatian state, asserting, "If this were 1941, not only 20,000, but 100,000 volunteers could have been procured." By 1943, so many large segments of the mainstream Bosnian Muslim community had been alienated by the Catholic-Bosniak movement within their midst, recruitment efforts "met with sound rejection by the Muslim population," as one German officer reported.[99]

In the recruitment, the plight of the Jews was never far from view. During one April 1943 recruitment visit to the scenic Croatian city of Slavonski Brod, the senior officers of the German-Muslim team were eerily reminded of Berlin's larger mission. Himmler's personal emissary, Serbian-born German officer Karl von Krempler and Muslim Ustasha commissioner for Eastern Herzegovina Alija Suljak witnessed a transport of Jews from Salonika, Greece passing through town, presumably en route to Auschwitz or one of the other death camps in occupied Poland. Some 98 percent of Salonika's estimated 50,000 Jews were destroyed after being systematically transported to murder camps in Eastern Europe. They traveled to their demise through routes such as those in the Balkans, and the Ustasha had a special Railroad Battalion to ensure smooth transit operation of the trains. One of the Jews who passed von Krempler and Suljak that day waved. The hapless Jew recognized von

Krempler, who had previously visited Greece, and von Krempler recognized him. As the transport passed north, von Krempler seemed to his colleagues to be briefly embarrassed by the wave.[100] No matter, the train continued on. So did von Krempler and Suljak. Each had his own destiny in the protracted nightmare of the Holocaust.

Despite efforts, von Krempler, Suljak and other recruiters could not raise volunteers in the numbers needed. For help, Himmler turned to the Mufti of Jerusalem, who at the time was ensconced in luxury in Germany. Enjoying a German Foreign Office salary of 90,000 reichmarks monthly, Husseini was also granted the use of five luxury homes and suites at the sumptuous Adlon Hotel in Berlin and at the Hotel Zittau near the Polish border. Husseini also had the use of the former Jewish Institute on Klopstockstrasse in Berlin. The Mufti had demanded he receive control of the formerly Jewish property, and German Foreign Minister von Ribbentrop finally granted that wish. In his role as honored Nazi collaborator, the Mufti enjoyed an elevated religious stature, rarefied and burnished by the Nazi hierarchy. Husseini was placed in charge of a newly created Islamic Central Institute as well as the Islamic Parish of Berlin. The Islamic Central Institute was opened with a gala ceremony attended by Propaganda Minister Paul Joseph Goebbels, symbolizing the senior Nazi attention devoted to the Mufti.[101]

It was from his well-feted existence and Nazified religious authority that the Mufti set about overruling the authority of the Bosnian imams and communal leadership that resisted the Ustasha and the new Waffen SS division recruitment campaign. On March 21, 1943, Husseini sent a public message to the Croatian and Bosnian Muslims. "The hearts of all Muslims must today go out," declared Husseini, "to our Islamic brothers in Bosnia, who are forced to endure a tragic fate. They are being persecuted by the Serbian and communist bandits [partisans], who receive support from England and the Soviet Union ... They are being murdered, their possessions are being robbed, and their villages are burned. England and its allies bear a great accountability before history for mishandling and murdering Europe's Muslims, just as they have done in the Arabic lands and in India."[102]

Within days, the Mufti hustled off to war-torn Croatia to raise a division of 10,000 men, to be known as the 13th Waffen SS Mountain Division Handschar, named for the emblematic Turkish *handschar* sword. The curved sword was pictured on the division's flag and other insignia. During the first two weeks of April 1943, the Mufti, accompanied by Nazi newspaper and newsreel reporters, toured the NDH to stir up enthusiasm for Handschar. Everywhere in Croatia, Husseini employed his Islamic authority to encourage Muslims to sign up. As he did, Husseini ostentatiously posed for the camera. He reviewed troops in formation, toyed with weaponry, shook hands warmly with local leaders, paternalistically congratulated volunteers, and did all in his power to build the division. Photographs of the smiling Mufti, proffering the Hitler salute, were plastered on the covers of Nazi publications and captured on film for newsreel exhibition.[103]

"The faithful recognized him as a true Muslim," reported a German Foreign Office official, adding, "he was honored as a descendant of the Prophets. Friends from his theological studies in Cairo and pilgrimage to Mecca welcomed him. He was presented gifts, old weapons, embroidery, and the like." As the Mufti maneuvered into the hearts of the populace, he shifted the perspective of the Bosnians to a new political center of gravity, from one-dimensional Croatian nationalism to broader solidarity with the Arabs in their struggle against Jews in far-off Palestine. "The Mufti was, in any case, quite reserved in regard to fighting Bolshevism," remembered a German observer. "His main enemies were the Jewish settlers in Palestine and the English. The visit [to Croatia] was a success, however, in that here was a high spiritual and political dignitary of Islam, known throughout the world, who was on the German side, appealing for a common front against common enemies."[104]

Husseini's inspirational words ignited fires within the minds of many Bosnians who heard his pleas. The Mufti's recruitment sermon in the main Sarajevo mosque was so forceful that members of the assembled faithful wept. "The entire Muslim world is united in the struggle against Britain and Soviet Russia," he cried to one group. "This I have assured the *Führer* ... The Muslim world stands united with Germany, which deserves and will achieve victory. The attitude of the Muslim world is clear. Those lands suffering under the British and Bolshevist yoke impatiently await the moment when the Axis will emerge victorious. We must dedicate ourselves to ... the complete destruction of the British Empire."[105]

By the time the Mufti completed his Croatian tour, about 8,000 Muslims had volunteered to join the Handschar division. They formed long lines at the ad hoc Wehrmacht offices. More than a few even deserted from the regular Croatian army in order to serve Germany. Standard Reich salaries were doled out to the volunteers. Since many of the Bosnian Muslims had multiple wives, recruits were asked to specify for German military paymasters which wife was to receive the payments and any other benefits. Still there weren't 10,000 recruits. So, even though the Mufti had insisted to Himmler that Handschar be an exclusively Muslim army, and Himmler agreed, local recruiters were compelled to accept some 2,600 Catholics to boost division strength to the operational minimum. Eventually, by relaxing recruitment ages and criteria and borrowing from other Croatian forces, thousands more Muslims were enrolled to the Handschar and corollary units. By summer 1943, Handschar was ready to take its place alongside other Waffen SS divisions.[106]

Handschar men trained at special camps set up in France, such as ones in Le Puy, Rodez, and Villefranche de Rouerguie. They were issued Wehrmacht fezzes emblazoned with the SS death head skull. At these camps, the men swore an oath: "I swear to *der Führer*, Adolf Hitler, as Supreme Commander of the German Armed Forces, loyalty and bravery. I vow to *der Führer*, and the superiors he designates, obedience until death. I swear to God the Almighty, that I will always be loyal to the Croatian State and its authorized representative, the Poglavnik [Croatian president Pavelić], that I will always protect the interests of the Croatian people and shall always respect the constitution and laws of the Croatian people."[107]

Muslims proved to be the most loyal of the division. A review of 155 deserters identified 121 Catholics and only 13 Muslims, the rest being Germans or Croatians of German descent. To maintain the Islamic fighting spirit, imams were assigned, one to each battalion as well as the regimental staff. The Wehrmacht developed its Imam Training Course, a three-week immersion into Nazi history and theory, conducted in a grand villa in Berlin. Among the leading Bosnian imams of the dozens trained were Imam Hussejin Dzozo, Imam Ahmed Skaka, and Imam Abdullah Muhasilović.[108]

Sometimes the Mufti visited to encourage the clerics in their war against Judaism and communism. On a typical visit in July 1943, the Mufti, dressed in his iconic black robe and round white turban, would stand at threshold of the villa steps overlooking the decorous slate patio where three rows of imams would stand at attention. With approving German officers and Nazis officials by his side, Husseini would charge the imams with their awesome duty. "This duty," the Mufti would typically exhort, "is the strengthening of the cooperation between the Muslims and their ally Germany." He added, "The active cooperation of the world's 400 million Muslims with their loyal friends, the Germans, can be of decisive influence upon the outcome of the war. You, my Bosnian Muslims, are the first Islamic division [and] serve as an example of the active collaboration." His instructions were sealed with the ever-present adage of Nazi-Muslim partnership: "My enemy's enemy is my friend."[109]

Himmler agreed wholeheartedly with the partnership. He declared, "Germany [and] the Reich have been friends of Islam for the past two centuries, owing not to expediency but to friendly conviction. We have the same goals." Ironically, the Mufti reportedly once asked his liaison officer, jokingly, "Wouldn't it be best if the Germans converted to Islam? The Muslims and Germans could then conquer the world!"[110]

The Handschar was authorized to function as a purely Islamic unit, eating only the foods permitted by sharia. Husseini told his Reich handlers that the Muslims would live off ordinary rations "exactly as the German soldiers [do], with the exception of pork and alcohol." Time was always set aside for daily prayers. It was not unusual to see an entire field of perfect rows with hundreds of Handschar warriors, kneeling foreheads to ground in traditional devotion.[111]

To guide Handschar fighters, the Mufti provided a foldout pamphlet titled in German *Islam und Judentum*—that is, *Islam and Judaism*. The pamphlet's text ended with this promise: "The Day of Judgment will come, when the Muslims will crush the Jews completely: And when every tree behind which a Jew hides will say: 'There is a Jew behind me, Kill him!'" That promise paraphrased the well-known Hadith verse from Book 41, Number 6985: "Abu Huraira reported Allah's Messenger as saying: The last hour would not come unless the Muslims will fight against the Jews, and the Muslims would kill them until the Jews would hide themselves behind a stone or a tree and a stone or a tree would say: 'Muslim, or the servant of Allah, there is a Jew behind me; come and kill him.'"[112]

Inspired by and burning for Germany's victorious push east, the Handschar fiercely fought the Croat partisans. Undertaking classic search and destroy, cleansing actions, sabotage, attack and counterattack, the well-armed Handschar battalions waged conventional and unconventional war against partisan positions, hideouts, and formations. For example, in March 1944, during Operation Signpost, Handschar was assigned to "cleanse" some 2,000 to 2,500 partisans from the swamp-laced Croatian forest lands of the Bosut area. Hundreds of battle-hardened Handschar troops were divided into three task forces, plus a blockade unit and various support contingents. Launching their assault before dawn, at four in the morning, at least five Handschar spearheads seized key positions in the area while the river Sava was blockaded. As the partisans were surrounded, big gun bombardment pounded those who retreated. It was a classic, polished, and well-planned military operation.[113]

Within 48 hours, Operation Signpost could claim victory. The Bosut area was under Nazi control. The partisans were routed, at least temporarily, and most had fled to safety through cracks in the perimeter. But German after-action reports noted that more than 500 partisan fighters were among the enemy dead, with 82 captured for interrogation. Quickly, Handschar distinguished itself as a reliable and fearsome SS division. In village fighting, the Bosnian Nazis were reported to have been savage. Reports reaching headquarters back in Berlin included one that claimed a Bosnian was seen "killing 17 of the enemy with his knife." In some cases, Handschar soldiers were said to be "cutting the hearts from their enemies." German generals could only wonder if these reports were true.[114]

In another well-staged battle, Operation Sava, Handschar regiments were assigned to cross and secure Bosnia's strategic Sava River at chokepoints. The soldiers were told by their German senior officer, "The *Führer* has provided you with his best weapons ... Each of you shall be standing in the place that you call home, as a soldier and a gentleman, standing firm as a defender of the idea of saving the culture of Europe—the idea of Adolf Hitler." As the men prepared to cross the river in a mighty military wave, their unit commanders each read a prepared message: "As we cross this river, we commemorate the great historic task that the leader of the new Europe, Adolf Hitler, has set for us—to liberate the long suffering Bosnian homeland and through this to form the bridge for the liberation of Muslim Albania. To our *Führer*, Adolf Hitler, who seeks the dawn of a just and free Europe: *Sieg Heil!*" As further inspiration, each soldier was given a personal memento, a photograph of Hitler. Within days, hundreds of partisan corpses littered the area. Victory could be claimed. The Sava River and its bridges were taken, ensuring for a while the vital movement of supplies for the Reich.[115]

Throughout April 1944, Handschar continued to wage fierce war against the partisans. In a number of other special operations, including Operation Easter Egg, the division mopped up, blocked, and destroyed partisan capability. Resistors continually reformed to strike again. So special "hunter teams" or *Jagdkommandos* were formed to stealthily seek out and crush remaining partisan groups. In one typical action on April 23, 1944, a "cleansing" operation was launched south of Bijelina against partisan bunkers. After fearsome hand-to-hand fighting, the Partisan body count exceeded 200, and 100 prisoners—mostly Italians and Jews—were taken.[116]

Although Handschar was mainly an anti-partisan force, when they did encounter Jews, the brutality exhibited shocked even the local villagers who were accustomed to Nazi atrocities. In one case, Hungarian Jewish slave laborers being guarded by Handschar were so viciously and mercilessly abused, local townspeople became outraged and wondered if they could help. But they could not. The maltreated Jews quickly became incapable of continuing in their work project. At that point, they were all marched away for mass shooting.[117]

The success of Handschar convinced the Germans that Muslim allegiance in the Balkans was enough to go beyond the one division. With Bosnia secure as an SS-dominated state that functionally subsumed the fragmented Croatian national authority, Berlin continued to look to more territory with its Islamic army in mind. Next destination for the next division: Albania.

\*      \*      \*      \*

Italy capitulated to the Allies in September 1943. As Mussolini's forces fell apart, so did the Italian sphere of influence in that part of the south Balkans called Greater Albania. To preserve German control over Albania, the SS command created a second Muslim division. As early as February 1944, German General Gottleib Berger, a main Nazi handler of the Handschar, wired back to Berlin an urgent need to create the Albanian force. His idea was to "pluck out" the Albanian Muslims from Handschar to create the nucleus of this second division. By April 1944, Himmler approved and ordered that the new force be assembled, starting with the Handschar's Albanian Battalion, which was detached and sent by train to join up with other units. This second military formation was known as the 21st Waffen SS Division Skanderbeg, named for the famous fifteenth century Albanian hero who fought for the Turks.[118]

To reach the goal of a second 10,000-man division, Himmler relied upon Albanian Minister of the Interior Xhafer Deva, the leading Albanian Muslim collaborator with the Reich. Nazi police units in Albania under the command of Josef Fitzthum—Himmler's SS plenipotentiary for Albania—worked directly with Deva, with the Albanian National Committee, and with the Albanian Nazi Party to assemble an initial roster of more than 11,000 names that could be called upon to fill Skanderbeg's ranks. Most were Muslim Kosovars from the Kosovo region augmented by Shqiptar fighters from southern Albania. The Kosovar units in particular operated under Deva's direct authority and were loyal to him.[119]

Slightly more than 9,000 of the proffered volunteers were deemed acceptable by the SS. Of this group, fewer than 6,500 were actually inducted into the 21st Waffen SS Division, thus giving Skanderbeg less than divisional strength. Its troops operated mainly in the Kosovo region, always distinctive for their SS issue skull-decorated fezzes. Despite Skanderbeg's lesser troop strength, its men were brutal in decimating Serb villages, having called for the utter extermination of the Serbian Christian population. Jews were luckier than the Serbs because many Albanian Muslims risked their lives and those of their families to shelter the small Jewish population of several hundred. Nonetheless, Skanderbeg units rounded up some 300 Jews in Priština and later managed to arrest other Jews in a sweep of "suspicious persons" who were later deported to certain death.[120]

The Mufti encouraged Albanians to collaborate as fervently as had the Bosnians. He worked with Bedri Pejani, Muslim leader of the Albanian National Committee, to formulate a plan for a pure Islamic state to reinforce the recruitment effort's appeal. Berlin, however, would not approve.[121]

Eventually, as the Nazi war effort began to deteriorate, Skanderbeg suffered from desertions and redistribution of many of its ranks into other German military units. But it was not the last Muslim division to be formed in the Balkans. The third division was Kama, the 23rd Waffen SS Mountain Division. Formed in September 1944, during the last nine months of the war, Kama took shape as an even smaller formation, with an estimated 2,600 Croatian and Bosnian Muslims. Berlin hoped to thrust these fierce fighters into neighboring Hungary to shore up action there. But as the Reich's war machine began to fall apart, eager Kama troops found battle opportunities wanting. Historians are divided over whether the Kama division ever saw action before the Reich retreated.[122]

The bloody Balkans was not the only region where Muslims and Arabs became part of the Hitler war machine. In North Africa, their role was salient in the Nazi campaign against Sephardic Jews.

*     *     *     *

Hitler's anti-Jewish war extended to the Jews of the Muslim world beyond Europe by virtue of Axis reach into the existing colonial and recently occupied lands of North Africa and the Middle East. As soon as France was bifurcated into an occupied northern Nazi zone and a Fascist regime in the south, the collaborationist French Vichy government imposed anti-Jewish legislation on its protectorates and colonies in Morocco, Algeria, Tunisia, and other French-dominated Arab lands. Italy extended anti-Jewish decrees into Libya. Germany's military presence in North Africa brought with it immediate implementation of Hitler's anti-Jewish statutes. As a result, the Jews of North Africa were subjected to the same public square humiliation, physical brutality, synagogue defilement, property seizures, forced labor camps, and even the Jewish star armbands that darkened Nazi Europe. In fact, the Reich's pioneer extermination expert, SS Colonel Walter Rauff, developer of the mobile gassing van, had been sent into Tunisia to rule over the terrified Jewish population there. Understandably, rumors of crematoria construction spread quickly.[123]

Overnight the Arab residents of Muslim North Africa became aware that their neighbors for centuries—the Jews—were now being marched toward a grim and ghastly fate. How did they react?

Many Arabs in the newly Nazified Muslim North African countries reached out with compassion to comfort and protect the afflicted Jews. Mirella Hassan recalled how her parents were helped with extra food, and "only this help given by these Tunisian Muslims, in their own way, what they could, a gesture often made with selfless friendship … enabled the saving of many lives." David Guez, from the town of Sfax in Tunisia, recalled, "Really, their behavior [Tunisian Arabs] was wonderful," he said. "I won't forget the Arab who helped me and allowed me to get an extra loaf of bread every day."[124] These Arabs were nothing less than good people acting boldly, even if quietly, under the hateful circumstances imposed from abroad, to assist their fellow man.

But many Arabs in the areas under the Nazi grip reacted with conspicuous silence or indifference, obediently going along with suddenly imposed bureaucratic anti-Jewish repression. Jews were systematically expelled from their professions, forbidden access to public places, and registered as enemies often with the prompt cooperation of the local Arab community. Many other Arabs reacted with opportunistic fervor at the dispossession of the Jews, selling Jews needed food and other goods at notoriously high prices and acquiring vanquished Jewish property at stunningly low prices. When Jews scrambled to temporary safety or succumbed to Axis power, some Arabs looted their possessions outright—often gruesomely. Necks of Jewish corpses were cut for necklaces. Fingers of Jewish corpses were chopped off for rings. Many Arabs reacted with glee as they gloated over their once well-regarded neighbors now abruptly marshaled into slave labor gangs, heinous punishment camps, and into the other recesses of Germany's well-honed hell transplanted to North Africa. Tunisian Jewish survivors typically recalled how Arabs jeered "take the shovel!" from the sidelines as Jewish residents were marched through town to brutal slave work sites.[125]

Mass atrocities by Arabs occurred in many cities. The scenic, coastal Tunisian town of Gabès was one of the worst. Gabès had enjoyed an intellectual and mercantile Jewish community going back to the twelfth century. But on May 20 1941, as the Mideast was convulsing with Nazi unrest in the days preceding the Farhud, a riot similar to the one in Iraq erupted in Gabès. The local synagogue was attacked and pillaged by a mob. As in Baghdad, Jews were brutalized in their homes. One woman was seized while she was cooking in her kitchen. The boiling pot of soup she was cooking was dumped onto her, after which she was tortured, then stoned, and then finally killed. In some cases, Arab neighbors who had enjoyed a meal together just hours or days earlier returned to loot and kill. Eight Jews were murdered during the Gabès mayhem.[126]

Certainly, the taskmasters and drivers of the North African Jewish nightmare were the French, Italian, and German thugs who were empowered with capricious life or death control over Moroccan, Libyan, Algerian, and Tunisian Jews. But everywhere, these European oppressors enjoyed abundant cadres of Arab enforcers, partners, and helpers, without which the machinery of anti-Jewish depravity could not have ground on so pervasively or cut so deeply. Elements of the local Arab communities commonly rose enthusiastically and mercilessly above and beyond the demands imposed upon them by the European bosses of terror. Through incessant local Arab collaboration in terror, the hell of Jewish life in Nazified North Africa became all the more hellish.[127]

Work, punishment, and concentration camps were erected throughout North Africa, often at mere points in the desert. In Tunisia, the names included

Ain-Zammit, Bizerte, Djeougar, and more than two dozen other camps. In Algeria, the names included Ain-Safra, Boussuet, Saida, and more than two dozen other camps. In Morocco, the names included Berguent, Casablanca, Missour, and more than two dozen other camps. How did the Axis suddenly erect and operate dozens of camps? They were mainly staffed with Arab guards and workers.[128]

Simply put, Arabs guards excelled at torture. Jewish prisoners were regularly whipped at the camps dotting the Sahara. Several of those Saharan camps, such as Berguent, were actually known as "punishment camps," precisely because they were operated mainly to inflict pain. One prisoner escaped from the large Vichy Algerian border-area camp at Colomb-Béchar, but Arab trackers on horseback hunted him down. When discovered, the hapless prisoner was tied to their horses and dragged all the way back to camp. That escapee was then tortured to death over a period of days at another nearby location. The Vichy Algerian desert edge concentration camp at Djenien Bou-Rezg was ruled by the sadistic Frenchman Lieutenant Pierre de Ricko; but among his brutal enforcers was an Arab policeman named Ali Guesni. The Arab overseer at the north Vichy Tunisian farm camp near Mateur became known for inflicting what one account stated was a "daily regimen of gratuitous pain and torture" upon the several dozen Jews laboring there.[129]

At the Vichy Algerian camp, Djelfa, which experienced a typhus outbreak from filthy water, the sadistic French commandant J. Caboche was fond of horsewhipping naked prisoners. Caboche's cruelty was aided by a devoted Arab assistant named Ahmed who made sure the abused prisoners also froze. The notorious camp at Djelfa became agony even before inmates arrived. The moment Jews disembarked at the train station, elite Spahi Algerian Arab horsemen took charge of them. The Arab officers mercilessly horsewhipped the Jews during the several-mile forced march through the desert from the depot to the camp.[130]

A common torture scrupulously supervised by Arab guards was confinement to the inhuman *tombeau*. The *tombeau* was a shallow tomb or grave. The depthless graves were just six feet long, twenty inches wide, and less than fourteen inches deep. Prisoners were required to dig their own *tombeaux*. As punishment for some imagined infraction, Jews were required to lie motionless in these graves for days and sometimes weeks at a time. *Tombeau* graves were arrayed in a neat row, just inches from each other. Arabs guarded them zealously. Sometimes a detachment of six Arab men watched the prisoners in two hour shifts. If the prone men flinched, even for a fly or a scorpion, the Arab guards crashed rifle butts into their skulls or threw stones at the man's face. It was not uncommon for the Jewish prisoners to lie in their own waste for days at a time while incarcerated in a *tombeau*. During the frigid desert nights, the immobilized men could easily freeze. Many did. One man suffered frostbite and both feet were amputated.[131]

A survivor recalled the inhumanity of Arab guards at one horrid camp. "For the slightest infraction of the rules," he said, "they would bury you in the sand up to your neck. And the Arabs would urinate on your head. And if you moved your head, they would take a big stone and smash your head. You weren't supposed to move."[132]

When camp survivor Harry Alexander was asked whether the Arabs were merely "following orders," under compulsion by superiors, his reply was this: "No, no, no! The cruelty and the barbaric manners of the guards, that came out by themselves. Nobody told them to beat us all the time ... Nobody told them to beat us up with chains and whips ... Nobody told them to tie us naked to a post and beat us, and to hang us by our arms and hose us down, to bury us in the sand so our heads should look up and bash our brains in and urinate on our heads. Nobody told them to do that ... No, they took this into their own hands and they enjoyed what they did. You could see it on their faces; they enjoyed it."[133]

The Arab interface with concentration camps went beyond the ad hoc brutality of North Africa and the unimaginable savagery of Yugoslavia. It extended to the very essence of the industrial Nazi camp system in Europe. No Arab muscle power was needed. Rather, the involvement with camps in the heart of Germany and Poland convinced Arab Nazis that they were on the winning side, and soon all Jews everywhere would be dead. The Arab Nazi goal was faster, faster, faster.

*       *       *       *

The Mufti of Jerusalem's was supremely aware of the Nazi's industrial solution to the Jewish problem. He relished it.

By mid-1941, the physical extermination of Jews in Europe was beginning—systematic mass murder. On or about July 31, 1941, Hermann Goering authorized SS-*Obergruppenführer* Reinhard Heydrich, Chief of the Reich Main Security Office (RSHA) to "make all necessary preparations" for a "total solution of the Jewish question" in all the territories under German occupation or influence, and to submit a "comprehensive draft" of a plan for the "final solution of the Jewish question."[134]

Heydrich's *Einsatzgruppen*, that is, mobile SS killing squads, were soon deployed in Eastern Europe to assemble and shoot groups of Jews—sometimes just a few dozen at a time, and sometimes tens of thousands in a day. Against walls in the villages, in the forests outside the city, at shooting pits just out of town, the heartless men of the *Einsatzgruppen* massacred every Jew they could find. Commonly, families were lined up into long, winding threads of terrified victims, stood up along an impromptu pit, and shot in the head or machine-gunned en masse. The corpses would fall into the blood-filled depth of bodies. Next group. Next group. Next group. For example, on October 2, 1941, *Einsatzgruppe* D reported in *Operational Situation Report USSR No.101*, 48 copies distributed, "Sonderkommando 4a in collaboration with *Einsatzgruppe* HQ and two Kommandos of police regiment South, executed 33,771 Jews in Kiev on September 29 and 30, 1941." The report added, The Kommandos continued the liberation of the area from Jews and Communist elements." In the period covered by the report, the towns of Nikolayev and Kherson in particular were freed of Jews ... From September 16 to 30, 22,467 Jews and Communists were executed. Total number 35,782." Approximately a million Jews were killed this way—no gas, just bullets.[135]

By the fall of 1941, numerous memoranda had been exchanged among senior Nazi officials confirming that the systematic extermination of Jews was proceeding in Europe, excepting those who could be temporarily spared for labor.[136]

Sometime near the end of 1941 or the beginning of 1942, the Mufti visited Nazi mass murder coordinator Adolf Eichmann and his assistant, Dieter Wisliceny, according to Wisliceny's testimony during war crime trials. Wisliceny testified, "Eichmann lectured to the Grand Mufti in his Map Room, where he had collected statistical accounts of the Jewish population of various European countries—he lectured in detail about the solution of the Jewish Question in Europe. The Grand Mufti, according to him, was most impressed and said to Eichmann that he had already asked Himmler and had in fact secured Himmler's consent on this point: that a representative of Eichmann should come to Jerusalem as his personal adviser when he, the Grand Mufti, would go back after the victory of the Axis Powers." The Mufti later wrote in his own hand in Arabic that Eichmann was "a rare diamond" and "the best redeemer for the Arabs."[137]

On January 20, 1942, a conference of ranking Nazi officials was convened at the Berlin suburb of Wannsee. The so-called Wannsee Conference set in motion the coordinated inter-departmental apparatus to work to death, or outright exterminate, all Jews who came within the grasp of the Third Reich or its allies.[138]

In March 1942, with Hitler's war of Jewish extermination raging in Europe, the Concentration Camp Inspectorate of the SS Economics Administration, responsible for all concentration camps of all types from Auschwitz to Zwickau, had just been installed in the T-Building at the Oranienburg portion of the Sachsenhausen camp, located some forty minutes outside of Berlin. The new administration represented a consolidation of other agencies in the Nazi administration's murder machine. Group D-II was responsible for the direct supervision of all the camps, from transit camps to labor camps to death factories. The complex utilized an array of custom-made IBM punch card machines, approved by the New York office of IBM, to keep track of exactly how many inmates were held at each of thousands of camps on a daily basis. By this means, the Reich could efficiently deploy Jews for slave labor across Europe until they were too weak to work and were liquidated, that is, murdered. The human numbers of the so-called "strength reports" went up and down daily as thousands died and were replaced with thousands more who were about to die.[139]

Shortly after the consolidated concentration camp administration, Group D-II, was installed at the Oranienburg portion of Sachsenhausen, the Mufti of Jerusalem and his entourage visited the camp. This was not the only camp the Mufti had visited. In fact, Arab delegations were so active in concentration camp site visits that the German Foreign Office began to express apprehension since the Mufti was known to loudly broadcast his desires that Jews be murdered as fast as possible. On July 17, 1942, the Mufti's long-time Nazi liaison, Grobba, wrote a secret report about this most recent visit. "I reported considerable concern," wrote Grobba, "about the participation of members of the entourage of Prime Minister Galiani [Rashid Ali, the ousted coup plotter who fled Iraq at the time of the Farhud] and of the Grand Mufti in SD [secret security police] courses and site visits to concentration camps." But, he added, "The visit by three assistants of the prime minister [Galiani] and one of the Grand Mufti at concentration camp Oranienburg had already taken place. The visit lasted about two hours with very satisfying results. The camp's commandant, an *Oberführer*, received the Arabs and made a presentation about the installation and the purpose of the camp, especially with regard to its educational value. Then took place the sighting of the line-up camp inmates; the Jews aroused particular interest among the Arabs." Grobba described the Mufti's tour of the barracks, stating, "It all made a very favorable impression on the Arabs." But, Grobba assured, "In the future, the concerns of the Foreign Office would be taken into consideration and future visits of concentration camps by Arabs would not take place."[140]

Some weeks after the Mufti's visit to Sachsenhausen, Wisliceny testified, "I was sent to Berlin in July or August 1942 in connection with the status of Jews from Slovakia ... I was talking to Eichmann in his office in Berlin when he said that on written order of Himmler, all Jews were to be exterminated. I requested to be shown the order. He took a file from the safe and showed me a top secret document with a red border, indicating immediate action. It was addressed jointly to the Chief of the Security Police and SD and to the Inspector of Concentration Camps. The letter read substantially as follows:

"The *Führer* has decided that the final solution of the Jewish question is to start immediately. I designate the Chief of the Security Police and SD and the Inspector of Concentration Camps as responsible for the execution of this order. The particulars of the program are to be agreed upon by the Chief of the Security Police and SD and the Inspector of Concentration Camps. I am to be informed currently as to the execution of this order." The order was signed in April of that year, said Wisliceny.[141]

Indeed, by May or April 1942, Rauff, the Reich's gas extermination expert stationed in Tunisia, had already reportedly flown to General Rommel's headquarters to plan extermination of the Jews of Cairo as soon as the *Afrika-Korps* captured Egypt.[142]

On October 4, 1943, Himmler—the Mufti's sponsor in Bosnia and the patron of the SS Handschar Division—delivered a tape-recorded speech to SS officers in Posen. "I want to also mention a very difficult subject ... before you, with complete candor. It should be discussed amongst us, yet nevertheless, we will never speak about it in public ... I am talking about the evacuation of the Jews, the extermination [*ausrottung*] of the Jewish people. It is one of those things that is easily said. 'The Jewish people are being exterminated,' every Party member will tell you, 'perfectly clear, it's part of our plans, we're eliminating the Jews, exterminating them, a small matter.'"[143]

Within a month, on November 3, 1943, the *Voice of Free Arabism* in Berlin broadcast a condemnation of the Zionist settlement in Palestine with an unmistakable appeal to mass murder Jews. "Should we not curse the time," asked the impassioned broadcast, "that has allowed this low race to realize their desires from such countries as Britain, America, and Russia? The Jews kindled this war in the interests of Zionism ... The world will never be at peace until the Jewish race is exterminated. Otherwise wars will always exist. The Jews are the germs, which have caused all the trouble in the world."[144]

At the same time, the Mufti, speaking at the Islamic Central Institute in Berlin, rendered yet another blistering, venom-filled sermon about Jews that equaled, if it did not exceed, anything in the Nazi vocabulary. Jews, Husseini preached, were "parasites among the nations, sucking their blood, embezzling their property, corrupting their morals, while still demanding the same rights as the native populations." Once again, invoking the ever-present theme of Mohammad's original extermination of the Jews, Husseini reminded the Muslim masses of the Koranic verse, "You will find that those who are most hostile to the believers [Muslims] are the Jews." Husseini added, "They had even tried to poison the revered Prophets ... They were hostile to them and schemed against them more than 1,300 years ago and had never ceased spinning webs of intrigue against the Arabs and Muslims."

The Mufti demanded that all Muslims unite against the notion of Jews in Palestine. He urged all Muslims to work for "the expulsion of all the Jews from all Arab and Muslim countries. This is the only remedy. It is what the Prophet did 13 centuries ago." He publicly declared that Muslims everywhere should follow the example of the Germans, who had found a "definitive solution to the Jewish problem." This, he preached, was the basis "of common interest of both nations, of their unified stance toward a common enemy in a battle."[145]

Most importantly, the Mufti wanted to ensure that no Jews escaped from the jaws of Hitler's extermination program in Europe. By mid-1943, Jews vulnerable to extermination had become a commodity of exchange. They could be sold for extravagant sums of ransom money, bartered for goods, exchanged in prisoner swaps and even ostentatiously rescued by Nazi perpetrators and their cohorts to create alibis or cover stories in the event of an Allied victory and consequent war crime trials.[146] Such deals, whether negotiated through *ad hoc* emergency committees, governmental units, or the International Red Cross, howsoever squeamishly obtained, could have saved many thousands of lives. Yet, in several well-known cases, the Mufti vetoed the barters, rescues or transports of Jewish children and others to Palestine, ensuring they would be mass murdered by the swiftly moving Nazi murder machine. Indeed, by mid-1943, Himmler had already confirmed to the Mufti that approximately 3 million Jews had already been liquidated.[147] But even one survivor was too many for Husseini.

For example, the British House of Commons in early spring 1943 let it be known that negotiations were underway to permit 4,000 Jewish children and approximately 500 adults to exit Bulgaria—and what was expected to be certain death—to safety in Palestine. On May 6, 1943, the Mufti began a campaign to halt any evacuation. He wrote to the Bulgarian foreign minister, "The Jews, once they have emigrated, could without let or hindrance contact their *Rassengenossen* (members of their race) in the rest of the world and inflict more injury on the country they had left than before. They would be given the opportunity of settling in Palestine or any other country in the Middle East, where they would get themselves organized and continue to pursue their iniquitous practices to an even greater extent."[148]

The Mufti's alternative suggestion was this: "Therefore, I permit myself to draw your attention to the fact that it is very proper and more useful to prevent the Jews from leaving your country and to send them to a place where they will be under strict supervision, such as Poland, for example. Thus, one will be protected from the danger they represent, and you will render a great service to the Arab people, who will appreciate your action, and thus the friendly relations with your people will become yet closer."[149]

One letter was not enough, lest the 4,000 children be saved. Husseini complained in a May 12, 1943 letter to the Italian Embassy, seeking its intervention. The next day, May 13, 1943, Husseini delivered a similar letter to German Foreign Minister Ribbentrop, especially since the governments of Romania and Hungary were planning similar transports of children to safety. The Mufti made clear to Ribbentrop that the Arabs were "deeply hurt" by such a betrayal and, again, insisted the Jews be sent to Poland where they could be under "surveillance" or "under control." By now, it was clear to all that a demand to send Jews to Poland was nothing less than a demand to send them to a death camp.[150]

Every time a variant of the proposed Bulgarian transport became known, the Mufti demanded it be halted. Foreign Office Counselor Wilhelm Melchers, who regularly worked with Husseini, wrote of the Bulgarian child rescue effort, "The Mufti kept cropping up all over the place and lodging protests: in the Minister's office, in the Undersecretary of State's waiting room and in other government departments: for example, the Home Office, the Press Office, the broadcasting service, and also the SS ... At the AA it was a foregone conclusion that steps would be taken—specifically by the Mufti—in protest of any activity concerning the Balkan Jews ... The Mufti was a sworn enemy of the Jews and made no secret of the fact that he would rather see them all killed."[151]

Husseini launched similar anti-rescue agitation weeks later, in June 1943. While in Rome, the Mufti learned of plans to rescue 900 Hungarian children accompanied by 100 adults. On June 28, 1943, Husseini dispatched an urgent message to the Hungarian Foreign Minister. Writing in French, Husseini stated, "You no doubt know of the struggle between the Arabs and Jews of Palestine, what it has been and what it is, a long and bloody fight, brought about by the desire of the Jews to create a national home, a Jewish State in the Near East, with the help and protection of England and the United States. In fact, behind it lies the hope which the Jews have never relinquished, namely, the domination of the whole world through this important, strategic center, Palestine. In effect, their program has, among other purposes, always aimed at the encouragement of Jewish emigration to Palestine and the other countries of the Near East. However, the war, as well as the understanding that the members of the Three-Power Pact have of the responsibility of the Jews for its outbreak—and finally their evil intentions toward these countries which protected them until now—all these are reasons for placing them under such vigilant control as will definitely stop their emigration to Palestine or elsewhere.[152]

"Lately I have been informed of the uninterrupted efforts made by the English and the Jews to obtain permission for the Jews living in your country to leave for Palestine via Bulgaria and Turkey. I have also learned that these negotiations were successful, since some of the Jews of Hungary have had the satisfaction of emigrating to Palestine via Bulgaria and Turkey and that a group of these Jews arrived in Palestine towards the end of last March. The Jewish Agency, which supervises the execution of the Jewish program, has published a bulletin that contains important information on the current negotiations between the English government and the governments of other interested states to send the Jews of Balkan countries to Palestine. The Jewish Agency quotes, among other things, its receipt of a sufficient number of immigration certificates for 900 Jewish children to be transported from Hungary, accompanied by 100 adults."[153]

The Mufti demanded the child transport be stopped. "To authorize these Jews to leave your country," he continued, "under the above circumstances and in this way, would by no means solve the Jewish problem and would certainly not protect your country against their evil influence—far from it!—for this escape would make it possible for them to communicate and combine freely with their radical brethren in enemy countries in order to strengthen their position and to exert a more dangerous influence on the outcome of the war, especially since, as a consequence of their long stay in your country, they are necessarily in a position to know many of your secrets and also about your war effort. All this comes on top of the terrible damage done to the friendly Arab nation, which has taken its place at your side in this war and which cherishes for your country the most sincere feelings and the very best wishes."[154]

Once again, Husseini wanted the Jews shipped to lethal Poland. "This is the reason," he insisted, "why I ask your Excellency to permit me to draw your attention to the necessity of preventing the Jews from leaving your country for Palestine; and if there are reasons which make their removal necessary, it would be indispensable and infinitely preferable to send them to other countries where they would find themselves under active control, for example, in Poland, in order thereby to protect oneself from their menace and avoid the consequent damage."[155]

When 1,800 children and 200 adults were to be rescued from Romania, once again the Mufti demanded the release be stopped. Where did he want Romania to send the children? Once again, specified Husseini, to Poland.[156]

Many of the transfers were indeed blocked. Many more were undoubtedly never finalized. How many deaths did the Mufti facilitate? There is no way to know. But looking back, the Mufti wrote in his diary, "My letters [to the European governments] had positive and useful results for the Palestinian problem."[157]

Fearing he could not stop thousands of Jews from fleeing Europe or being rescued, with an ultimate destination of the only country that would take them, Palestine, the Mufti and his cohorts set about to extend the extermination of the Jews into the Holy Land itself. Husseini lobbied the German

Luftwaffe to bomb Tel Aviv and Jerusalem. He was particularly hopeful that a bombing run on November 2, 1943 could be made on Jerusalem, which was the scene of an international Zionist conference that included an observance of the November 2, 1917 Balfour Declaration. Luftwaffe generals were unable to identify the specific building of the conference and could not assure they would even come close to hitting a purely Jewish target other than a public building. Hence, Berlin rejected the idea as too costly and too ambiguous a military use for their bombers. Every time the German high command rejected a bombing mission, the Mufti would suggest it again and again. "An air attack on Tel Aviv," wrote a Nazi officer, "the citadel of Palestinian Jewry and immigration, has in the past six months been suggested repeatedly by the Arab side, and particularly by the Grand Mufti." The memo went on to confirm that his suggestions were always rejected. Even though such an attack, given the inaccuracy of bombing, would have guaranteed many Arab deaths, the Mufti continued to suggest it.[158]

Nor was aerial bombing the only avenue considered for extermination of Jews in Palestine. A plan was formulated to dispatch Rauff, the poison gas specialist, with a specially tasked *Einsatzgruppe* into Palestine right after what the Germans and the Mufti thought would be their ultimate victory in North Africa. In July 1942, a new killing unit was contemplated, *Einsatzkommando Egypt*. Orders stated, that "the deployment of the SS Commando with the Panzer Army Africa will be handled as follows ... It is authorized, in the framework of its writ, and on its own responsibility, to undertake executive measures against the civilian population." Seven SS officers and a compliment of 17 non-commissioned officers believed they could organize a vast local Arab army to help them systematically eradicate the Jews of Palestine. Nazi flags emblazoned with large swastikas and the German word *Palästina* had already been designed and produced. But the unlikely plot never advanced because Rommel's army was defeated in North Africa, causing Rauff to be redirected to his terror campaign in Tunisia. Nor could the Germans and their collaborators, Arab or otherwise, have achieved the type of *Einsatzgruppe* success they had in Eastern Europe where Jews meekly walked in line to the shooting pits, defenseless and terrified.[159]

Zionist Jews in Palestine would never march to a pit, stand up against a wall, or willingly cooperate with their executioners. Hitler's Holocaust and decades of combating Arab violence had made a new post-European Jew that believed in the maxim "never again" before this phrase came into common parlance.

Six million Jews were killed in Europe, North Africa, and the Middle East in plain sight of the world with the knowledge, encouragement, and collusion of Arab and Muslim armies, Arab and Muslim leaders, and a vast cross-section of ordinary collaborators. From the fertile crescent of the Middle East to the hot sands of North Africa to the muddy and mountainous battlefields of Europe, Hitler's Holocaust was advanced, accelerated and made more efficient by the open, eager, and enthusiastic help he received from the Islamic world.

Why did Hitler fail to kill more Jews and wipe out Jewish Palestine? Four reasons: Operation Torch, in 1942, which landed the Allies at North Africa; the Normandy Invasion, in 1944, that breached Nazi Europe to the west; the irrepressive Russian counter-offensive to the East, beginning in 1942; and the valiant, indomitable, courageous, sacrificing, determined, and unrelenting will to fight back manifested by partisans, ghetto resistors, forest fighters, and decent people of every religion and every caste in every country who refused to succumb to the legacy of hate and a future of extermination. Their heroism has been alternately recorded in glory in film, song, and fanfare, yet for many is held quietly as a scared history, to be shared only in precious moments of private recollection.

Hitler's war against the Jews in Europe came to a colossal, toppling demise on May 5, 1945, when the Third Reich finally cracked. The war against the Jews stopped—in Europe. But it continued throughout the Arab world in the Mideast as the forces of hatred refused to subside. It still burned fiercely in Arab capitals as a million Jews in Muslim lands were targeted for persecution, expropriation, and expulsion during the several years after the 1948 birth of the State of Israel. The Farhud was not a beginning, not an ending. It may not even be a midpoint.

# AFTER THE HOLOCAUST

Hitler's defeat in May 1945 did not bring the Arab world squarely into the Allied fold. Many Nazis melted away from the Reich, smuggled out by such organizations as the infamous Odessa group and the lesser-known Catholic lay network Intermarium, as well as the CIA and KGB.[1] They ensured the continuation of the Nazi legacy in the postwar Arab world.

Egypt was a prime destination for German Nazi relocation in the Arab world. Dr. Aribert Heim was notoriously known as "Dr. Death" for his grotesque pseudo-medical experiments on Jewish prisoners in the Sachsenhausen, Buchenwald, and Mauthausen concentration camps. He was fond of surgical procedures including organ removals without anesthesia, injecting gasoline into prisoners to observe the manner of death, and decapitating Jews with healthy teeth so he could cook the skulls clean to make desk decorations. Dr. Heim converted to Islam and became "Uncle Tarek" Hussein Farid in Cairo, Egypt, where he lived a happy life as a medical doctor for the Egyptian police.[2]

Two of Goebbels's Nazi propagandists, Alfred Zingler and Dr. Johann von Leers, became Mahmoud Saleh and Omar Amin respectively, working in the Egyptian Information Department. In 1955, Zingler and von Leers helped establish the virulently anti-Semitic Institute for the Study of Zionism in Cairo. Hans Appler, another Goebbels propagandist, became Saleh Shafar who, in 1955, became an expert for an Egyptian unit specializing in anti-Jewish and anti-Zionist hate propaganda. Erich Altern, a Gestapo agent, Himmler coordinator in Poland, and expert in Jewish affairs became Ali Bella, working as a military instructor in training camps for Palestinian terrorists. A German newspaper estimated there were fully 2,000 Nazis working openly and under state protection in Egypt.[3]

Franz Bartel, an assistant Gestapo chief in Katowice, Poland, became El Hussein and a member of Egypt's Ministry of Information. Hans Becher, a Gestapo agent in Vienna, became a police instructor in Cairo. Wilhelm Boerner, a brutal Mauthausen guard, became Ali Ben Keshir, working in the Egyptian Interior Ministry and as an instructor for a Palestinian terrorist group.[4]

Egyptian society was so enamored with the Nazi war against the Jews that a young army officer felt compelled to write a postwar letter to Hitler via the Cairo weekly, *Al Musawwar*, as though Hitler were still alive. "My dear Hitler," the officer wrote. "I congratulate you from the bottom of my heart. Even if you appear to have been defeated, in reality you are the victor. You succeeded in creating dissensions between Churchill, the old man, and his allies, the Sons of Satan ... Germany will be reborn in spite of the Western and Eastern powers ... The West, as well as the East, will pay for her rehabilitation—whether they like it or not. Both sides will invest a great deal of money and effort in Germany in order to have her on their side, which is of great benefit to Germany ... As for the past, I think you made mistakes, like too many battlefronts and the shortsightedness of [Foreign Minister Joachim von] Ribbentrop vis-a vis the experienced British diplomacy ... We will not be surprised if you appear again in Germany or if a new Hitler rises up in your wake." The letter was signed "with affection" by Col. Anwar Sadat, later president of Egypt and the first Arab leader to sign a peace treaty with Israel.[5]

But Egypt was hardly alone in reinventing the Nazi war against the Jews. German Nazis also took up postwar positions of influence in Syria, Lebanon, and Iran. But Iraq, long a Nazi Arab stronghold, was arguably among the most agitated in the Arab world.

Many Iraqis seemed driven more by their obsession with Jewish Palestine and perpetuating Nazi precepts and anti-Jewish campaign than by a desire to rebuild their country or strengthen their democracy. At war's end, in mid-1945, hundreds of thousands of dispossessed European survivors emerged from their ghettos, concentration camps, and forests, desperate to enter Jewish Palestine to restart their lives. However, rather than stirring humanitarian notes in Iraq, the European Jewish plight only heightened hatred against Arab Jews, especially in Iraq. Many mainstream Arabs resented and belittled the Holocaust as nothing more than another ploy for expanding Jewish Palestine's population. This view was little more than a continuation of the Mufti's own wartime preaching.

Everything escalated fiercely in February 1947, when the United Nations agreed to vote on the question of Palestine's partition. The 1937 Peel

Commission's recommendation for partition had now evolved from a white piece of paper into a binding international ballot among the world's governments. The possibility of a legitimized and recognized Jewish State in the midst of Arab lands in Palestine was more than unthinkable. The Palestine conflict still dominated and defined the Iraqi national agenda, paralyzing Iraqi action on its other vital needs, such as the economy, infrastructure, health services, and education. The country's newspapers warned that if "the Zionist entity" came into nationhood, no Iraqi government could control the Arab Street in Baghdad. Uniformly, the Arab regimes, including the Baghdad government, officially threatened that if the UN dared vote yes to partition, the Arabs would exact reprisals against the 700,000 Jews who dwelled in countries throughout the Middle East.[6]

Violence against Iraqi Jews intensified in the months leading up to the vote. For example, on May 9, 1947, a Baghdad mob killed a hapless Jewish man after hysterical accusations of giving poisoned candy to Arab children. In the Jewish quarter of Fallujah, homes were ransacked and local Jews were compelled to move in with friends and relatives in Baghdad. Large Jewish "donations" were regularly extorted and sent to Palestinian Arabs. The names of the "donors" were read on the radio to encourage more of the same. Yet the Jews still deluded themselves that as loyal Iraqis, they belonged in the nation where they had dwelled for 2,600 years. This hardship would pass, they believed. But the Jewish Agency emissary in Iraq, encouraging relocation to the Jewish State, reported back to Jerusalem: "No attention is paid [by the Jews] to the frightful manifestations of hostility around them, which place all Jews on the verge of a volcano about to erupt."[7]

On November 29, 1947, the UN voted 33 yes, 13 no, with 10 abstentions, to create two states: one Palestinian Arab, the other Jewish.[8]

Once the UN vote registered, a new anti-Jewish campaign exploded in Iraq. This time, it was not just pogroms but systematic pauperization, taking a cue from the confiscatory techniques developed by the Nazis. Jews were charged with trumped-up offenses and fined exorbitant amounts. All the while, mob chants of "death to the Jews" became ever more commonplace.[9]

Israel was set to declare its independence on May 14, 1948. In April 1948, Iraq shut down the Kirkuk-Haifa oil pipeline, thereby slashing its own income from oil royalties. Production at the Kirkuk field was immediately cut by 25 percent, from 4.3 million tons annually to 3.1 million tons. Moreover, the pipeline closure convulsed the delicate negotiations between the Baghdad regime and the British Petroleum-controlled Iraq Petroleum Company [IPC] over a number of vital issues, such as calculation of royalties in gold as compared to pounds sterling, which had recently declined in value. By necessity, the question of hiring Iraqis as key company officers, and even a much-needed

£3 million IPC loan to the Iraq government were also sent to the back burner.[10] In Iraq's view, business and the national economy were overshadowed by the need to confront Israel.

The day after Israel declared its independence on May 15, 1948, the new nation was invaded from all sides by armies contributed by most of the Arab states. It was not termed a war of liberation by the Arab leadership but a war of utter extermination. "This will be a war of extermination and a momentous massacre, which will be spoken of like the Mongolian massacres," promised Azzam Pasha, Secretary-General of the Arab League. Iraq's military forces saw very limited action. But martial law was imposed by Baghdad, so the dismal battle news was censored. The Arab armies, although more numerous, and rich in death rhetoric, were poorly organized, disunified, and militarily unprepared. Israel was not defeated. The UN negotiated and implemented an armistice with Egypt, Transjordan, Syria, and Lebanon. Only Iraq refused to sign, continuing its state of war and demanding what it called "a second round," or another chance to fight. Ironically, as a result of the war, Israel now controlled even more of the land of Palestine.[11] It was very convenient to once again blame Iraq's Jews and Zionist gangs for this latest military disaster.

On July 19, 1948, Iraq amended penal code Law 51 against anarchy, immorality, and communism, adding the word "Zionism." Zionism itself now became a crime, punishable by up to seven years in prison. Every Jew was thought to be a Zionist, thereby criminalizing every Jew. Only two Muslim witnesses were needed to denounce a Jew, with virtually no avenue of appeal. In urban sweeps, thousands of Jewish homes were searched for secret caches of money thought destined for Israel. Frequently this necessitated demolishing walls as part of the search. One man was sentenced to five years' hard labor for merely possessing a scrap of paper with an Old Testament Hebrew inscription; the paper was presumed to be a coded Zionist message. Hundreds of Jews were now arrested, forced to confess under torture, punished financially, and sentenced to long jail terms.[12]

The greatest shock to the Jewish community occurred when the single wealthiest Jew in Iraq, Ford automobile importer Shafiq Ades, was accused of sending cars to Israel. Ades was tried by a military tribunal, quickly found guilty, fined $20 million and handed a death sentence. His entire estate was liquidated. A few days later, on September 23, 1948, Ades was publicly hanged in Basra. His body was allowed to languish in the square for hours, to be abused by the celebrating crowds.[13]

Many more arrests, executions, and confiscations followed. In October, all Jews—an estimated 1,500—were summarily dismissed from their government positions. This satisfied those with animus against the Jews, but crippled such key infrastructure departments as the Irrigation Department, the

Basra port, the Telephone and Telegraph Office, and the Railways Administration. For example, about 25 percent of the Basra port staff suddenly became unavailable. Some 350 Jewish workers were dismissed from the Railway Administration alone; there was no one to replace them and no personnel to train replacements, so workers were imported from Pakistan. The Jewish banks, key to foreign commerce, lost their licenses to import money.[14]

Soon, the familiar sequence of Nazi-style pauperization began. Once a prosperous, generously spending community, the Iraqi Jews stopped purchasing and general spending, from the bazaars to the restaurants. Jewish businesses were boycotted; their owners were arrested; funds dried up. Many Jewish firms went out of business and their Arab employees soon became ex-employees, which only further punished the weakened consumer economy. Many purged Jewish government employees, highly skilled and formerly well paid, were now destitute and reduced to selling matches on the streets to avoid being arrested for vagrancy. Jewish home values dropped by 80 percent. What's more, the national treasury was crippled as a result of a 50 percent drop in oil revenues due to the Haifa line shutdown and the considerable military expenditures for the unproductive venture against Israel in the 1948 war.[15]

The once genteel and gracious life of Jews in Iraq was about to terminate. The Zionists had seen the process during prior years in Germany, Austria, Poland, Holland, Hungary, and elsewhere. Now it was time for the Zionist underground to step up its activities. They had been smuggling Jews out of Iraq for years, generally through Transjordan and Lebanon. But the war for Israeli independence had obstructed those westward routes. The refugee caravans now looked east to Iran. The first 26 persons were smuggled through in November 1948, even though Islamic Iran had not recognized Israel. But now, the transit operation would not be limited to dozens but to thousands. A little bribery helped immensely; $450,000 was given, mainly to the Iranian prime minister, but some to other government officials and media sources. Bribes in hand, Iran's prime minister announced that his country would open its doors as a grand humanitarian gesture in keeping with its 6,000-year tradition of tolerance. Iraqi Jews in large numbers were now permitted to transit via Iran, eventually 1,000 per month.[16]

With the escapees went their money and some possessions; in other words, it was a flight of capital as well as people. This further battered Iraq's national economy. A debate gripped Iraq. Should the Jews be expelled? Expelling Jews to Israel would only provide more manpower to the Jewish State. On the other hand, every Jew was considered a spy and an enemy; why keep them in the country? Should all their economic holdings be seized? That would only glut the market with cheap land, homes, and possessions, especially since Jews were already sacrificing their assets at just 5 and 10 percent of their worth—anything to extract some value and flee. One refugee recalled, "When the Jews left, they sold their possessions for pennies. A rug worth 2,000 to 3,000 dinars sold for 20 to 30 dinars."[17]

Moreover, the rapid subtraction of Jews from the financial, administrative, retail, and export sectors was devastating. One day, they were just gone. Unlike Germany, a nation of 60 million where non-Jews had rushed in to fill the professional and commercial vacuum, within the small Iraqi population, in many cases, there was no one to replace the Jews—certainly not overnight.

An estimated 130,000 Jews lived in the Iraq of 1949, with about 90,000 residing in Baghdad. The Baghdad Chamber of Commerce listed 2,430 member companies. A third were Jewish; and, in fact, a third of the chamber's board and almost all of its employees were Jewish. Jewish firms transacted 45 percent of the exports and nearly 75 percent of the imports. A quarter of all Iraqi Jews worked in transportation, such as the railways and port administration. The controller of the budget was Jewish. A key director of the Iraqi National Bank was Jewish. The Currency Office board members were all Jewish. The Foreign Currency Committee was about 95 percent Jewish. Over the centuries, Jews had become essential to the economy.[18]

On March 3, 1950, to halt the uncontrolled flight of assets and people, Iraqi Prime Minister Tawfig as-Suwaydi engineered the passage of an amendment to Law 1, the Denaturalization Act. The amendment authorized revocation of citizenship to any Jew who willingly left the country. The new measure mimicked similar legislation in Nazi Germany. Upon exit, Jewish assets were frozen but were still available to the emigrants for use within Iraq. Once Jews registered to emigrate, the decision was permanent, and they were required to leave within 15 days. The window would not be wide. The amendment to Law 1 would expire in one year.[19]

The doors swung open, albeit only briefly. Iraqi officials guesstimated that 7,000 to 10,000 of the most undesirable Jews, mainly those already pauperized, would be the only ones to leave. The wealthier Jews, officials were convinced, would never abandon their lives. The state thought it could declare "good riddance" to just a fraction of its Jewish citizens and maintain the remainder.[20] They were wrong.

The exit doors became floodgates. Thousands immediately registered to leave. Household by household, Jewish families finally—almost unanimously—realized that their precious 2,600-year existence in Iraq was over. In wave after wave, groups of refugees left the country via the overland route. Soon, large overcrowded refugee camps sprang up in Iran to accommodate the exodus.[21]

Quickly it became clear that the land route was now insufficient for such a volume. Israel's Mossad Le-Aliya, the clandestine group invented during the Hitler era to smuggle Jews to safety, knew an airlift was needed to rescue as many Jews as possible before Iraq changed its mind. The Mossad called in its most reliable partner for airlifting Jews: Alaska Airlines. Its president, James Wooten, had been instrumental in rescuing the Jews of Yemen just after the state was born. El Al, Wooten, and Alaska formed a new airline with a new identity called Near East Air Transport (NEAT). Israeli ownership was hidden, so NEAT appeared to be strictly an Alaska Airlines venture.[22]

Israel's original passenger projections vastly exceeded anything that the stunned Iraqi government officials had contemplated. Israel envisioned flying out about half the Iraqi Jewish population—40,000 the first year, and more thereafter, for a total of 60,000. Flights would operate through Nicosia, Cyprus, or possibly direct to Tel Aviv if the fact of Israel-bound flights could be kept secret. NEAT needed an Iraqi partner to secure charter rights in Iraq. The perfect partner was the well-established Iraq Tours, based in Baghdad. Who was the chairman of Iraq Tours? It was Iraq Prime Minister Tawfig as-Suwaydi, the man who had engineered Law 1, the Denaturalization Act.[23]

On May 19, 1950, the first 175 Jews were airlifted out of Iraq in two C-54 Skymasters.[24] Israel at first called the rescue Operation Ali Baba, but it later became known by the original code name, Operation Ezra and Nehemiah, for the prophets who had led the Jews of Babylon out of exile back to Israel millennia before.

Within days of the airlift's inauguration, some 30,000 Jews had registered at their synagogues and were therefore required to leave within 15 days. But only 7,000 of those first registrants had completed the lengthy and redundant bureaucratic process of obtaining all the right forms, from all the right people, with all the right stamps, in all the right order. Once at the airport, departing Jews were abused and humiliated. Rings were pulled from their hands and linings were torn from their hats as officials looked for valuables during a thorough search. Their papers were slowly re-registered and re-stamped, and only then were they finally approved for takeoff—generally, an additional six-hour ordeal.[25] There weren't enough hours in the day, seats on the small two-engine aircraft, or planes in the tiny NEAT fleet to possibly transfer the thousands who were now stateless in their own country, penniless amid all the wealth they had left behind, and reviled in the nation they had loved for two millennia.

The Iraqi government, furious over the mass departure, made it clear: These Jews were now stateless refugees, devoid of legal rights in Iraq and essentially all Zionist criminals. Many were now homeless and sleeping on the streets. Baghdad's government announced that if these Jews were not removed—and swiftly—the government was prepared to move them into concentration camps.[26] The very phrase "concentration camp," coming on the heels of the Holocaust, was chilling.

More planes were needed. More firms were needed. The British wanted their national airlines, BOAC and BEA, to participate in the lucrative airlift. The Iraqis also wanted their national airline, Iraqi Airways, to join the project. So Iraqi Airways was given the ground maintenance contract, 30 dinars for every flight. British planes were used, but with a 7.7 percent fee to Iraqi Airways. Who was the director-general of Iraqi Airways? It was Sabah Said, the son of the re-ascended Iraqi Prime Minister, Nuri Said; the prime minister's son received an additional 5.5 percent "special fee."[27] However, Israel's fragile infrastructure was now so strained it could barely accept any more Iraqi refugees. Scores of thousands of refugees were also streaming in from war-ravaged Eastern Europe as well as other Arab nations. Tiny Israel did not know whether it had enough tents, let alone housing units. The Jewish State tried to negotiate for fewer refugees per month.[28]

Nuri Said now realized that his 120,000 captive Jews constituted more than just undesirables. These Jews could be turned into a demographic weapon against Israel. In March 1951, Nuri engineered yet another statute, this one, Law 5, permanently freezing all the assets of the Jews who were denaturalized by the previous law. Technically, those seizures were deemed a mere "freezing" of accounts, not a legal confiscation; so under international law, the assets could never be claimed. Law 5 was concocted in secret; leading government officials only learned about it just before the vote. As the measure was being ratified, Baghdad's telephones went dead so desperate Jews would not learn of the new law and use precious moments to transfer or save their property. To make sure Jews could not touch their funds, the government ordered the banks closed for three days.[29]

Now, 120,000 Jews would arrive in Israel penniless with no hope of later calling on their former wealth. Concomitantly, Nuri demanded that Israel absorb 10,000 refugees per month, every month—this to intensify the strain on Israel's resources. Exacerbating the crisis, Nuri ruled that as of May 31, 1951, no more exit visas would be issued. If Israel would not accept these stateless enemies now, the concentration camps would be readied. Indeed, the Iraqi parliament had already discussed establishing such camps. Nuri clearly expected the Jewish State to crack beneath the weight of the humanitarian effort. Numbers negotiation commenced between Iraqi and Israeli go-betweens. However, Nuri was adamant that the Jews must transfer en masse, not according to Israel's capacity to accept them, but according to Iraq's roiling impatience to expel them. Otherwise, camps. It would be Germany all over again.[30]

Jewish Agency emissaries in the field confirmed the dire conditions of refugees who would now arrive with nothing. "The number of destitute people is growing," reported one agent. "After the passing of this law, we are liable to reach a situation where 80 percent are penniless and unable to [even] cover the cost of their emigration ... In Basra, the situation is very bad. The immigrants leaving on the next three aircraft are all poor. They have sold their blankets in return for food."[31]

Israeli foreign minister Moshe Sharett vociferously condemned Iraq's extortion and state-sponsored theft. Estimates of the value of Iraqi Jewry's blocked assets ranged from 6 million to 12 million dinars or, at its highest valuation, some $300 million in twenty-first-century money. Sharett swore that Israel "considers this act of robbery by force of law to be the continuation of the evil oppression which Iraq has always practiced against defenseless minorities ... We have a reckoning to conduct with the Arab world as to the compensation due to Arabs who left Israeli territory and abandoned their property there because of the war of the Arab world against our state. The act perpetrated by the Iraqi kingdom against the property of Jews that have not transgressed against Iraqi law, and have not undermined her status or plotted against her, forces us to combine the two accounts. Hence," Sharett declared, "the government has decided to inform the appropriate UN institution and I proclaim this publicly, that the value of the Jewish property frozen in Iraq will be taken into account by us in calculating the sum of the compensation we have agreed to pay to Arabs who abandoned property in Israel."[32]

Israel had no choice but to absorb all 120,000 Iraqi Jews. The flights increased, day and night, using twin engines, four engines, any craft available, through Nicosia or direct to Tel Aviv—as many as possible, as fast as possible. In some months, as many as 15,000 people were flown. The daily spectacle in Baghdad of forlorn Jews being hustled into truck after truck, clutching nothing but a bag and their clothes, was a cause for great jubilation on the streets of Baghdad. The crowds gleefully stoned the trucks that delivered the refugees to the airport. The Jews were mocked every step of the way.[33]

Between January 1950 and December 1951, Israel airlifted, bussed, or otherwise smuggled out 119,788 Iraqi Jews—all but a few thousand.[34] Within those two years, Iraq—to its national detriment—had excised one of its most commercially, industrially, and intellectually viable groups, a group that for 2,600 years had loyally seen the three provinces of Mesopotamia as their chosen place on earth. This dispossessed group, who arrived in Israel with nothing but their memories, rose to become some of the Jewish State's most productive citizens.

Indeed, hundreds of thousands of Arab Jews from across the Moslem world, expelled to Israel during those first years, transformed the Jewish State from a European haven to a true Mideast country, now also vastly populated with citizens of Arab countries—citizens who by religion were Jewish. They cherish their forgotten multimillennial legacy of greatness in Babylon. They shudder for their forgotten role in the Holocaust. They tremble for a posterity that may not remember either.

# LESSONS OF
# THE FARHUD

## by Samuel Edelman

The first time I had heard term "Farhud" was in the early summer of 2003. I was in Northern Iraq for three weeks to interview Kurdish survivors of chemical warfare in anticipation of future trials, having been invited by the Kurdish UN Mission. I had been teaching college courses about Saddam Hussein's genocidal attacks on the Kurds of northern Iraq for years.

While in Iraq, my *peshmergah* guard and driver took me to the synagogue in Sulimaniyah and a place where Jewish silversmiths once plied their trade. While we took a break for sweetened tea in a little café, he explained that his grandfather, now in his 90s, had been born Jewish and wanted to tell me some family stories. One of the stories was about the massacre of Jews in Baghdad in 1941. He called the event *the Farhud*. I was stunned to learn of the violence. He also told me of many in the Kurdish community, both Jews and Muslims, who had helped rescue and protect Jews from Baghdad and other places.

Since then, I have been able to meet with a few survivors of the Farhud in the Baghdadi Jewish communities in Los Angeles and Israel. I joined Edwin Black and a number of Holocaust scholars in pressuring the United States Holocaust Memorial Museum to allow their displays and website to reflect information about the impact of the Holocaust in North Africa and the Middle East. We also joined historians worldwide who made the same argument to Yad Vashem, Israel's Holocaust Memorial. We were ultimately successful with Yad Vashem. But it was not enough. A vast misunderstanding still remains that the Holocaust was a purely European tragedy. Edwin Black's work in this book helps to end that misunderstanding. Sadly, many in the Muslim world in North Africa, Syria, Iraq, and Iran embraced Nazi ideology and anti-Semitism as if it were their own. In doing so, they facilitated and, in many cases, inflicted mass murder.

Black's chapters on the National Socialists in the Middle East and on the Grand Mufti of Jerusalem and their twin influences on the political and religious ideology from WWII onward is an exploration of the depth and breadth of the underpinnings of the very fabric of the Arab world view as it regards mass murder of Jews. These twin influences became central to the development of the Muslim Brotherhood in Egypt and the Ba'ath Parties of both Syria and Iraq, following the teachings of Michel Aflaq and Sayyid Qutb, both of whom incorporated Nazi ideology into their writings. Saddam Hussein himself was strongly influenced by the Mufti and Hitler. Ba'ath Party ideology combined fascism, socialism, and Muslim religious theology with the fictitious *Protocols of the Elders of Zion* into a witch's brew of hate still spewed today by Hamas (included in its charter), Hezbollah, the Muslim Brotherhood, and al-Qaeda.

It is now clear. First, came the Arabs massacres of Jews in Hebron and elsewhere in mandatory Palestine during the 1920s and 1930s. Then, in the 1940s, the focus changed to Baghdad, culminating in the Farhud. Then, the mass killing by Arabs continued into North Africa, the Balkans, and the rest of Nazi-occupied Europe. These massacres were the direct actions of Arab policies determined to carry out Nazi anti-Jewish activities as a central part of the Arab political and social worldview. That worldview was expressed by the Grand Mufti as the Arab desire to rid the Middle East in general, and Palestine specifically, of all Jews. As Black demonstrates, the Mufti was so committed to his worldview that he enthusiastically joined the Nazi mass extermination effort to personally recruit Arabs in the nightmare of Nazi-occupied Yugoslavia. Hebron and the Farhud were the Mufti's training ground, preceding his eventual open support for the mass killing of Jews in Europe.

The greatest irony is the contemporary application of the label "Nazi" to Israel by many in the Arab world and elsewhere when it was the very selfsame Arab world that embraced and carried out Nazi policies against the Jews of Iraq and mandate-era Palestine. Black's work gives the lie to the allegation continually made by anti-Israel propagandists that Arabs had nothing to do with the mass murder of Jews in Europe so why must they pay the penalty of having a Jewish entity (Israel) in their midst. Black's writing documents the very core of the Arab embrace of Nazi ideology in the very center of the Arab world that led to the mass murder of thousands of Jews and eventually the exile of more than 800,000 to one million Jews from Arab and Iranian lands after the State of Israel was born in 1948. Jewish communities that had existed for many centuries were completely destroyed in only a few short years.

What began in Palestine and Baghdad in the 1930s and 40s still plays out in much of the twenty-first century Arab world. This process of demonization, delegitimization, and double standard was evident in the 1930s and 40s in British-controlled Iraq and Palestine. Ironically, the twenty-first century world we inherited arose from the forces of British and French colonialism, the Arab embrace of Nazi ideology and imagery, and the greed and bigotry that Edwin Black has uncovered in his exploration of the Farhud and its origins. That is why our understanding of what Edwin Black has written in *The Farhud* is so very important. The chief lesson of the book teaches how critical it is that we believe that people really mean what they say—and say what they mean. Time and again, people and governments did not believe the Nazis would do what they promised or that the Grand Mufti and his cohorts would not do what they swore to do. It was a major error to ignore what Hitler and the Mufti said in public, just as we are in error if we ignore the words of twenty-first century hatemongers who preach the making of another Farhud.

*Samuel Edelman is emeritus Professor of Communication Studies and Jewish Studies at California State University, Chico, and currently the executive director of Scholars for Peace in the Middle East.*

# NOTES

## Abbreviations

| | |
|---|---|
| AA/PA | Auswärtiges Amt / Politische Amt (Germany) |
| AJA | American Jewish Archives |
| AJC | American Jewish Congress (U.S.) |
| ADM | Admiralty - National Archives (UK) |
| AIR | Air Ministry - National Archives (UK) |
| *AJS Review* | *Association for Jewish Studies Review* |
| BL | British Library Archives (UK) |
| BNA | National Archives (UK) |
| BP | British Petroleum Company Archives |
| *BoB* | *Banking on Bagdad* by Edwin Black |
| BSOAS | *Bulletin of the School of Oriental and African Studies* |
| BT | Board of Trade - National Archives (UK) |
| CAB | Cabinet Office - National Archives (UK) |
| *Chi Trib* | *Chicago Tribune* |
| CNN | Cable News Network |
| CO | Colonial Office - National Archives (UK) |
| CZA | Central Zionist Archives |
| DGFP | Documents in German Foreign Policy |
| FO | Foreign Office - National Archives (UK) |
| FRUS | Foreign Relations of the United States |
| IPC | Iraq Petroleum Company |
| ISA | Israel State Archives |
| *JDB* | *Jewish Daily Bulletin* |
| JJAC | Justice for Jews from Arab Countries (Urman Collection) |
| *JQR* | *The Jewish Quarterly Review* |
| *JTA* | *Jewish Telegraphic Agency* |
| *LA Times* | *Los Angeles Times* |
| L/MIL | British Library Archives - Military (UK) |
| L/PS | British Library Archives - Political and Secret (UK) |
| *LBIY* | *Leo Baeck Institute Yearbook* |
| LoN | League of Nations |
| *MG* | *Manchester Guardian* |
| MFA | Ministry of Foreign Affairs (Israel) |
| MIL/L | British Library Archives - Military (UK) |
| NA | National Archives (US) |
| NARA | National Archives and Records Administration (US) |
| *NYT* | *New York Times* |

| NY Trib | New York Tribune |
|---|---|
| PA/AA | Politische Amt/ Auswärtiges Amt (Germany) |
| PBS | Public Broadcasting System |
| POWE | Ministry of Fuel and Power - National Archives (UK) |
| PREM | Prime Minister's Office - National Archives (UK) |
| PS/L | British Library Archives - Political and Secret (UK) |
| RAF | Royal Air Force (UK) |
| RG | Record Group (U.S. National Archives and Records Administration) |
| T | Treasury - National Archives (UK) |
| USHMM | U.S. Holocaust Memorial Museum |
| WP | Washington Post |
| WSJ | Wall Street Journal |
| WO | War Office - National Archives (UK) |
| YVA | Yad Vashem Archives |

## Chapter 2: 2,600 Years of Iraqi Jewry

1. See Map, "The Near East 3200–1600 BC," Postgate, J. N., *Early Mesopotamia: Society and Economy at the Dawn of History* (London, UK: Routledge, 1994), 2.

2. See generally Stillman, Norman A., *The Jews of Arab Lands* (Philadelphia: The Jewish Publication Society of America, 1979).

3. See Serjeant, R.B., "The 'Sunnah Jāmi'ah,' Pacts with the Yathrib Jews, and the Tahrīm of Yathrib: Analysis and Translation of the Documents Comprised in the So-called 'Constitution of Medina,'" *Bulletin of the School of Oriental and African Studies (BSOAS), University of London*, vol. 41 (1978), 1–42. Sonn, Tamara, *A Brief History of Islam* (Malden, MA: Blackwell, 2004), 7. See Author's email exchange with Lawrence Schiffman, Feb 2010.

4. See Stillman, 1–10

5. See generally Koran. See *Encyclopedia Judaica*, s.v., "Muhammad."

6. *Encyclopedia Judaica*, s.v., "Muhammad."

7. See Koran 42:52. See Koran 33:40. See Stillman 1–10. See Sonn, 1–5.

8. Goitein, S. D. & O. Grabar, *The Encyclopaedia of Islam*, s.v., "al-Kuds." El-Khatib, Abdallah, "Jerusalem in the Qur'an," *British Journal of Middle Eastern Studies*, vol. 28 (2001), 25–53. See "Which way is Jerusalem? Which way is Mecca?," The Baha'i Faith Index, www.bahaindex.com.

9. See generally Denny, Frederick M., "Components of Religion: The Case of Islam," *OAH Magazine of History*, vol. 6 (1992), 23–28.

10. Stillman, 9–10.

11. Stillman, 13. See Bauer, Susan Wise, *The History of the Medieval World: from the Conversion of Constantine to the First Crusade* (New York; London: W. W. Norton, 2010), 294f.

12. Stillman, 13.

13. Stillman, 14.

14. Ibn-Hisham, *Sīrah an-Nabawiyyah*, vol. 2 (Cairo, 1955), 233–245 as cited by Stillman, 14.

15. Ibn-Hisham, 233–245,as cited by Stillman.

16. Stillman, 18–19.

17. See generally Black, Edwin, *Banking on Baghdad (BoB): Inside Iraq's 7,000-Year History of War, Profit, and Conflict* (Washington, DC: Dialog Press, 2008), chaps. 1–4.

18, Koran 2:61. Koran 4:46. Koran 4:160.

19, Koran 2:61. See Stillman, 150.

20, Koran 4:46.

21, Koran 4:160.

22, Koran 5:51.

23, Koran 9:30.

24, Hadith, Book 41, no. 6983.

25, Hadith, Book 41, no. 6984.

26, Hadith, Book 41, no. 6985.

27, Ramadan, Tariq, *In the Footsteps of the Prophet: Lessons from the Life of Muhammad* (New York: Oxford University Press, 2007), iv. "History of Iran: Sassanid Empire," The Iran Chamber Society, www.iranchamber.com/history/sassanids/sassanids.php.

28. See Iran Chamber Society.

29. Bauer, 28–30.

30. Bauer, 28–30. See map, "The Conquests of Muhammad and Abu Bakr," Bauer, 295 and map, "Byzantium, the Arabs, and the Bulgars," Bauer, 323.

31. Bauer, 28–30. Al-Tabari, *History of the World* (Albany: State University of New York Press, 1985), 2053, quoted by Lewis, *Islam: From the Prophet Muhammad*, 228.

32. Glubb, Sir John, *The Empire of the Arabs* (Englewood Cliffs, NJ: Prentice-Hall, 1963), 24–26. See map, "Operations in Syria & Palestine, 634–635," Glubb, 25. See Iran Chamber Society.

33. Crone, Patricia, "The Rise of Islam in the World," in Francis Robinson, ed., *The Cambridge Illustrated History of the Islamic World* (Cambridge, UK: Cambridge University Press, 1996), 11.

34. See map, "The Conquests of Muhammad and Abu Bakr," Bauer, 259.

35. Butzer, Karl W., "Environmental Change in the Near East and Human Impact on the Land," in Jack M. Sasson, ed., *Civilizations of the Ancient Near East* (New York: Scribner, 1995), 123, 127. Nissen, Hans J., Peter Damerow, and Robert K. Englund, *Archaic Bookkeeping: Early Writing and Techniques of Economic Administration in the Ancient Near East*, Paul Larsen, trans. (Chicago: University of Chicago Press, 1993), 8. See also Finkelstein, J. J., "Mesopotamia," *Journal of Near Eastern Studies*, vol. 21 (1962), 73–92. Nissen, "Ancient Western Asia before the Age of Empires," in Sasson, 795. See "The Halaf Period (6500–5500 B.C.)," Metropolitan Museum of Art, www.metmuseum.org/toah/hd/half/hd_half.htm.

36. Nissen, "Ancient Western Asia before the Age of Empires," in Sasson, 795. *Encyclopedia Judaica*, s.v., "Jericho." See Yener, K. Aslihan, "The Archaeometry of Silver in Anatolia: The Bolkardag Mining District," *American Journal of Archaeology*, vol. 90 (1986), 469–472. See "The Halaf Period (6500–5500 B.C.)." See "The Ubaid Period (5500–4000 B.C.)," www.metmuseum.org/toah/hd/ubai/hd_ubai.htm.

37. "On Part of Mesopotamia between Sheriat-el-Beytha, on the Tigris, to Tel Ibrahim," *Proceedings of the Royal Geographical Society of London*, vol. 11 (1866–1867), 157.

38. Nissen, "Ancient Western Asia before the Age of Empires," 795–796.

39. Roux, George, *Ancient Iraq* (New York: Penguin Books, 1992), 12–13. Postgate, 15–19, 157. Englund, Robert K., lecture, University of Connecticut, April 2004, 1, 9. Author's e-mail and telephone corresp. with Robert K. Englund.

40. Astour, Michael, "Overland Trade Routes in Ancient Western Asia," in Sasson, 1401–1420.

41. Nissen, *Archaic Bookkeeping*, 14–15, 70–71. Schmandt-Besserat, Denise, *Before Writing* (Austin, TX: University of Texas Press, 1992), 176–178. Sasson, "Timeline of Ancient Near Eastern Civilizations." Author's e-mail and telephone corresp. with J. N. Postgate, Robert K. Englund, and Denise Schmandt-Besserat, May 2004.

42. Schmandt-Besserat, "Accounting with Tokens in the Ancient Near East," *Numerals Project*. See Englund, Robert K., "Proto-Cuneiform Account Books and Journals," in M. Hudson and C. Wunsch, eds., *Creating Economic Order: Record-keeping, Standardization and the Development of Accounting in the Ancient Near East* (Bethesda, MD: CDL Press, 2004), 24, 25, 26. Author's e-mail and telephone corresp. with Hans J. Nissen, Englund, Schmandt-Besserat, and Avi Winitzer, May 2004. Melville, Duncan J., "Tokens: The Origin of Mathematics," http://web.stlawu.edu. Schmandt-Besserat, *Before Writing*, 108–110, 126–127. See Englund, "Proto-Cuneiform."

43. Nissen, *Archaic Bookkeeping*, 118–119. Schmandt-Besserat, *Before Writing*, 198–199. Englund, Robert K., "Texts from the Late Uruk Period," in *Mesopotamien: Späturuk- und Frühdynastische Zeit*, Waefler and Attinger, eds. (Oxford: Oxford University Press, 1998), ii–iv. Author's e-mail and telephone corresp. with Hans J. Nissen and J. N. Postgate.

44. Roux, 356–358, 360, 361. See Postgate, 66–67. See Allen, G. Donald, "Babylonian Mathematics," www.math.tamu.edu.

45. "Laws of Hammurabi," in Roth, Martha T., ed., *Law Collections from Mesopotamia*

*and Asia Minor* (Atlanta: Scholars Press, 1997), 73, 80–81. See Roth, 71–142. See Greengus, Samuel, "Legal and Social Institutions of Ancient Mesopotamia," in Sasson, *Civilizations*, 472. See also Meek, Theophile J., trans., "The Code of Hammurabi," in *Ancient Near Eastern Texts Relating to the Old Testament*, James B. Pritchard, ed. (Princeton, NJ: Princeton University Press, 1950), 163–180. See also Horne, Charles F., "The Code of Hammurabi: Introduction," and "Code of Hammurabi," L. W. King, trans., *Avalon Project*, www.law.yale.edu. See photo, Stele of Hammurabi, Sb 8, www.louvre.fr. See "Laws of Eshnunna," Roth. See generally Yaron, Reuven, *The Laws of Eshnunna* (Jerusalem: Magnes Press, Hebrew University, 1988). Author's e-mail and telephone corresp. with Martha T. Roth, Avi Winitzer.

46. See Roux, 357–371.

47. See "Timeline, Prehistory," Roux, 501–502. See figure, "The Temple at Eridu," Postgate, 25. See Postgate, 110. See Nissen, *Archaic Bookkeeping*. See Johnson, Denise, "Art 101, Ancient Near Eastern Art Part I, Lecture 5," www.msjc.edu. See Genesis 11:1–6.

48. Roux, 179, 184–185, 389–396.

49. See "The Treaty Between Hattusilis and Ramesses II," www.bakeru.edu. See "Peace Treaty between Ramses II and Hattuili III, Hittite Version," http://nefertiti.iwebland.com.

50. Roux, 319–323, 325.

51. Roux, 333, 334–335. See "The Taylor Prism," Museum No. ME 91032, British Museum (BM), www.britishmuseum.org. See Crown, Allen D., "Redating the Schism between the Judaeans and the Samaritans," *The Jewish Quarterly Review (JQR), New Series*, vol. 82 (1999), 17–50.

52. II Kings 24:14–15. See Jeremiah 52:15, 27–30. See Map, "Nebuchadnezzar's Campaigns against Judah," NIV Study Bible, 566–567. See also Roux, 377–379.

53. Roux, 386–387. See "Cyrus Cylinder" and photo of Cyrus Cylinder, Museum No. ME 90920, www.britishmuseum.org.

54. See Weissbach, F. H., trans., "Cyrus," Pritchard, J. B., ed., *Ancient Near Eastern Texts Relating to the Old Testament* (Princeton, NJ: Princeton University, 1969), 315–316. See Lendering, Joanna, "Cyrus Takes Babylon," www.livius.org.

55. Ezra 1:1–4.

56. See Timeline, "Achaemenian and Hellenistic Periods," Roux, 515.

57. Genesis 12:2. See Joshua 24:2. *Encyclopedia Judaica*, s.v., "Terah."

58. Genesis 15:5. Genesis 17:4–5.

59. Genesis 21:8–18.

60. Pasachoff, Naomi E. & Robert J. Littman, *A Concise History of the Jewish People* (Lanham, MD: Rowman & Littlefield, 2005), 67.

61. Morony, Michael G. *Iraq after the Muslim Conquest* (Princeton: Princeton University Press, 1984), chaps 10–12.

62. See Gil, Moshe & David Strassler, *Jews in Islamic Countries in the Middle Ages* (Leiden; Boston: Brill, 2004), 491.

63. Morony, 310–311.

64. Linfield, H. S., "The Relation of Jewish to Babylonian Law," *The American Journal of Semitic Languages and Literatures*, vol. 36 (1919), 40–66.

65. Hachlili, Rachel, *Ancient Jewish Art and Archaeology in the Land of Israel* (Leiden: Brill, 1988), 87. See also Author's notes on visit to Capernaum.

66. Goode, Alexander D., "The Exilarchate in the Eastern Caliphate, 637–1258," *JQR*, vol. 31 (1940), 149–169. Morony, 316–319, 321.

67. Goode, 149–169.

68. Morony, 307. Gil & Strassler, 507.

69. See Gil & Strassler. See Cohen, Mark R., "On the Origins of the Office of Head of the Jews in the Fatimid Empire," *Association for Jewish Studies (AJS) Review*, vol. 4 (1979), 27–42. Morony, 321–325.

70. Cohen, 27–42.

71. See Morony, 277–279, 358–372, 372–379.

72. See Morony, chap. 11.

73. Rosenthal, F., "Aramaic Studies During the Past Thirty Years," *Journal of Near Eastern Studies*, vol. 37 (1978), 81–82. Glubb, 26. See map, "Arab Invasion of Persia," Glubb, 27. See

Hitti, Phillip K., *History of the Arabs: From the Earliest Times to the Present* (Hampshire, UK: Palgrave Macmillan, 2002), 123, 156–157. See generally Black, *BoB*.

74. See Morony, chaps. 10–12.

75. See Black, *BoB*, 34–35.

76. Koran 9:29.

77. Koran 9:29, Abdullah Yusufali, trans., www.sacred-texts.org.

78. Pickthall, Mohammed Marmaduke, *The Meaning of the Glorious Qur'ān* (Hyderabad-Deccan: Government Central Press, 1938), 9:29, www.sacred-texts.org.

79. Koran 9:29, M.H. Shakir, trans., (Elmhurst, NY: Tahrike Tarsile Qur'an, 1938), 10ᵗʰ ed.

80. See Stillman. See *Islam and the Arab World*, Bernard L. Lewis, ed. (London: Alfred A. Knopf, 1976). Marcus, Jacob Rader and Saperstein, Marc, *The Jew in The Medieval World: A Source Book, 315–1791* (Cincinnati: Hebrew Union College Press, 1999), 13–15.

81. Lewis, *Jews*, 15. Stillman 167–168, 251. See Rizq Allāh Ghanīmah, Yūsuf, *A Nostalgic Trip into the History of the Jews of Iraq*, Reading A Dallal, trans., Sheila Dallal, ed. Lanham, MD: University Press of America, 1998., 123. See also Marcus & Saperstein, 14.

82. Stillman, 35–39. Morony, 320–321.

83. Stillman, 35–37. See Beth Hatefutsot, s.v. "The Jewish Community of Baghdad," www.bh.org.il.

84. See Morony, chap. 11.

85. Stillman, 33–36.

86. Stillman, 35–39.

87. See Ye'or, Bat, *The Dhimmi: Jews and Christians under Islam*, David Maisel, Paul Fenton, and David Littman, trans. (Cranbury, NJ: Fairleigh Dickinson University Press/Associated University Presses; London: AUP, 1985, 6ᵗʰ printing, 2003).

88. See Irwin, Robert, "The Emergence of the Islamic World System, 1000–1500," Francis Robinson, ed., *The Cambridge Illustrated History of the Islamic World* (Cambridge, UK: Cambridge University Press, 1996), 45, 46. See Phillips, E. D., *The Mongols* (New York: Frederick A. Praeger, 1969), 58, 60. See Saunders, J. J., *The History of the Mongol Conquests* (Philadelphia: University of Pennsylvania Press, 1971), 55. See Morgan, David, *The Mongols* (Oxford: Basil Blackwell, 1986), 68.

89. See Curtin, Jeremiah, *The Mongols: A History*. (Cambridge, MA: Da Capo Press, 2003), 101. See Phillips, 60. See Saunders, 104.

90. Spuler, Bertold, *History of the Mongols, Based on Eastern and Western Accounts of the Thirteenth and Fourteenth Centuries*, Helga and Stuart Drummond, trans. (Berkeley: University of California Press), 1972, 84. Carpini, Fr. Giovanni DiPlano, *The Story of the Mongols Whom We Call the Tartars*, Erik Hildinger, trans. (Boston: Branden Publishing, 1996), 71, 75, 125. See Chambers, James, *The Devil's Horsemen: The Mongol Invasion of Europe* (New York: Atheneum, 1985), 54, 62–63. Nicolle, David, *The Mongol Warlords: Genghis Khan, Kublai Khan, Hulegu, Tamerlane* (Poole, UK: Firebird Books, 1990), 28. See Morgan, xii–xiii. See Phillips, 50–51.

91. See Chambers, 64, 65. See Nicolle, 32, 35. See Carpini, 76.

92. See Saunders, 56. See Phillips, 41. See Irwin, 47. See Ratchnevksy, Paul, *Genghis Khan: His Life and Legacy*, Thomas Nivison Haining, ed. and trans. (Oxford: Blackwell, 1991), 151, 152, 158. Saunders, 65, 216f.

93. Phillips, 60, 61.

94. Phillips, 61.

95. Ratchnevksy, 130.

96. Irwin, 47.

97. Carpini, 78. See Saunders, 56. Hitti, 414.

98. Hitti, 482. See Hitti, 482n5. See Curtin, 122, 125.

99. See Irwin, 47–48.

100. See Schurmann, H. F., "Mongolian Tributary Practices of the Thirteenth Century," *Harvard Journal of Asiatic Studies*, vol. 19 (1956), 304–389. See Waugh, Daniel C., "The Pax Mongolica," www.silk-road.com.

101. See Curtin 184–185. See Chambers, 142, 143.

102. See Nowell, Charles E., "The Old Man of the Mountain," *Speculum: A Journal of*

*Mediaeval Studies*, vol. 22 (1947), 497–501, 504. See Lockhart, Lawrence, "Hasan-i-Sabah and the Assassins," *Bulletin of the School of Oriental Studies, University of London*, vol. 5 (1930), 677–682, 685–688. See Irwin, 48. See Morgan, 146–148. See Saunders, 109. See Chambers, 142.

103. See Nowell, 514. Phillips, 88–89. Morgan, 148, 149.

104. See Saunders, 108. See Phillips, 88. See Allsen, Thomas T., *Mongol Imperialism: The Policies of the Grand Qan Möngke in China, Russia, and the Islamic Lands, 1251–1259* (Berkeley: University of California Press, 1987), 202, 203. See Allsen, *Culture and Conquest in Mongol Eurasia* (Cambridge, UK: Cambridge University Press, 2001). 19.

105. Saunders, 108. Ratchnevsky, 159. See Morgan, 158. See Phillips, 34, 35.

106. See Saunders, 107, 108, 109.

107. See Curtin, 247. See Nicolle, 109.

108. See Curtin, 247–248.

109. Curtin, 248.

110. See Phillips, 90. See Black, *BoB*, 44–48.

111. See Phillips, 90. See Curtin 252–254.

112. See Nicolle, 132.

113. See Morgan, 152. See Chambers, 145. See Curtin, 254. See Phillips, 90.

114. See Saunders, 110, 112. See Morgan, 151.

115. Savory, Roger M., "Land of the Lion and the Sun," as cited by Lewis, *Islam*, 246. See Morgan, 151. See Curtin, 253.

116. See Saunders, 113. See Curtin, 260.

117. See Curtin, 252, 253. See Saunders, 111–112.

118. Stillman, 34–35.

119. Stillman, 34–35.

120. See Morgan, 152. Saunders, 177–178.

121. Stillman, chap. 4. Rizq Allāh Ghanīmah, Yūsuf, *A Nostalgic Trip into the History of the Jews of Iraq*, Reading A Dallal, trans., Sheila Dallal, ed. (Lanham, MD: University Press of America, 1998), 123–125.

122. Morgan, 200–201. See photo, "Portrait Head of Timur," Nicolle, 144. Nicolle, 145, 152, 153. Hitti, 699.

123. Saunders, 173–174. Hitti, 699.

124. Nicolle, 157–158. See Morgan, 93. See Ghanīmah, 123–125. See Beth Hatefutsot, s.v. "The Jewish Community of Baghdad," www.bh.org.il.

125. Hookham, Hilda, *Tamburlaine the Conqueror* (London: Hodder & Stoughton, 1962), 150–151. Nicolle, 161. Hitti, 699, 701. See Ghanīmah, 123.

126. Nicolle, 166, 167, 169. Hookham, 3. Manz, Beatrice Forbes, *The Rise and Rule of Tamerlane* (Cambridge UK: Cambridge University Press, 1989), 73.

127. Hookham, 114, 115. Irwin, 56.

128. Nicolle, 168. Saunders, 177–178. See Ghanīmah, 123–125.

129. Beth Hatefutsot, s.v. "The Jewish Community of Baghdad," www.bh.org.il.

130. Koprülü, M. Fuad, *The Origins of the Ottoman Empire*, Gary Leiser, ed. and trans. (New York: State University of New York Press, 1992), 43, 44. Imber, Colin, *The Ottoman Empire, 1300–1650: The Structure of Power* (New York: Palgrave MacMillan, 2002), 5. Shaw, Stanford J., *The History of the Ottoman Empire and Modern Turkey*, vol. 1: *Empire of the Gazis—The Rise and Decline of the Ottoman Empire, 1280–1808* (Cambridge, UK: Cambridge University Press, 1976), 4, 5.

131. Inalcik, Halil, *The Ottoman Empire: The Classical Age 1300–1600*, Norman Itzkowitz and Colin Imber, trans. (London: Wiedenfeld & Nicolson, 1973), 4. Koprülü, 3, 43, 45–47. Shaw, *Empire of the Gazis*, 9, 10–11. Imber, 120, 121. Hitti, 716.

132. Imber, 8–10. Shaw, *Empire of the Gazis*, 12–16.

133. Imber, 28–29. Shaw, *Empire of the Gazis*, 56–57. *Science Daily Encyclopedia*, s.v., "Constantinople."

134. See Lewis, Bernard, *Cultures in Conflict: Christians, Muslims, and Jews in the Age of Discovery* (New York, Oxford University Press, 1996), 3–25. Imber, 121. Inalcik, 14. Shaw, Stanford J., and Ezel Kural Shaw, *The History of the Ottoman Empire and Modern Turkey*, vol.

2: *Reform, Revolution, and Republic: The Rise of Modern Turkey, 1808–1975* (Cambridge, UK: Cambridge University Press, 1977), 15.

135. Lewis, *Cultures*, 39n13. Henriques, H.S.Q., "The Jew in History," *Westminster Review*, vol. 160 (1903), 66.

136. Lewis, Bernard, *The Jews of Islam* (Princeton: Princeton University Press, 1987), 126.

137. Lewis, *Cultures*, 23. Lewis, *Jews of Islam*, 131–132, 133. See Black, *BoB*, 82.

138. See Black, *BoB*, 58–59. Lewis, *Jews of Islam*, 123.

139. Imber, 178–180. Inalcik, 106.

140. Hitti, 737. Imber, 180–181.

141. See Bent, J. Theodore, "The English in the Levant," *English Historical Review*, vol. 5 (1890), 661. Inalcik, 140–141.

142. Inalcik, 144–145, 150–151, 154–155. Shaw, *Empire of the Gazis*, 156–160.

143. Inalcik, 128. Imber, 192–193. See Beth Hatefutsot, s.v. "The Jewish Community of Baghdad," www.bh.org.il.

144. Simon, Reeva S., Michael M. Laskier, & Sara Reguer, eds., *The Jews of the Middle East and North Africa in Modern Times* (NY: Columbia University Press), 351–352. Abdullah, Thabit A.J., *Merchants, Mamluks, and Murder: The Political Economy of Trade in Eighteenth-Century Basra* (Albany: SUNY Press, 2001), 108.

145. See Longrigg, 166–170. Palmer, 50. Cole and Momen, "Mafia," 122.

146. "Memorandum by Mr. Kennedy on the Jews of Meshed," enclosure to confidential letter, Sir H. Drummond Wolff to Marquis of Salisbury, Apr 6, 1890: BNA FO511. Levin, Itamar, *Locked Doors: The Seizure of Jewish Property in Arab Countries*, Rachel Neiman, trans. (Westport, CT: Praeger, 2001), 2–3.

147. Sultan Abdulmecit I, "A Firman Addressed to the Chief Judge at Constantinople," Nov 6, 1840 (12 Ramadan 1256), BNA FO78/416, as quoted by Stillman, 401–402.

148. Nuri as-Said, "Lectures on the Arab Revolt," May 1947, quoted by Basri, Meer, "Iraqi Jews Fought with the Arabs for Independence in the First World War," *The Scribe: Journal of Babylonian Jewry*, nos. 72, 23, www.dangoor.com.

149. Sir A. Nicolson, "Note on the Future Status and Administration of Basrah," Feb 2, 1915: BNA FO800/377. Levin, 3. Gat, Moshe, *The Jewish Exodus from Iraq, 1948–1951* (London: Frank Cass, 1997), 12–13.

150. Gat, *The Exodus*, 10.

151. Shaw, *Empire of the Gazis*, 241. Levin, 7–8.

## Chapter 3: Oil Lust

1. d'Errico, Francesco, "The Invisible Frontier: A Multiple Species Model for the Origin of Behavioral Modernity," *Evolutionary Anthropology*, vol. 12 (2003), 193. Longrigg, Stephen H., *Oil in the Middle East: Its Discovery and Development* (London: Oxford University Press, 1968), 10–11. Giddens, Paul H., *The Birth of the Oil Industry* (New York: Macmillan, 1938), 11. Rister, Carl Coke, "The Oilman's Frontier," *Mississippi Valley Historical Review*, vol. 37, no. 1. (Jun 1950), 4–5.

2. Roux, George, *Ancient Iraq* (New York: Penguin Books, 1992), 151–152, 163. Exodus 2:2–3. Ellis, Edward S., and Charles F. Horne, "Biography of King Sargon of Akkad," *The Story of The Greatest Nations and the World's Famous Events*, vol. 1 (New York: Auxiliary Educational League, 1921).

3. See Longrigg, *Oil*, 10.

4. Xenophon, *Cyropaedia*, Henry G. Dakyns, trans., F. M. Stawell, ed. (Champaign, IL: The Gutenberg Project, 2002), bk. 7, chap. 5. Hitti, Philip K., *History of the Arabs* (New York: Palgrave Macmillan, 2002), 202. Longrigg, *Oil*, 11.

5. Miller, E. Willard, "The Industrial Development of the Allegheny Valley of Western Pennsylvania," *Economic Geography*, vol. 19 (1943), 401. See Scoville, Warren C., "Growth of the American Glass Industry to 1880–Continued," *Journal of Political Economy*, vol. 52 (1944), 345. Giddens, 19–20.

6. Giddens, 2–3, 14. Longrigg, *Oil*, 11.

7. Rezneck, Samuel, "Energy: Coal and Oil in the American Economy," *Journal of*

*Economic History*, vol. 7 supp. (1947), 63. See Darrah, William Culp, *Pithole: The Vanished City* (Gettysburg, PA: William C. Darrah, 1972), 2. See Tarbell, Ida M., *The History of the Standard Oil Company*, vol. 1 (Gloucester, MA: Peter Smith, 1963), 5. See Giddens, 14, 58–59. Miller, 402. See Darrah, 2–3. Miller, 394. Tarbell, vol. 1, 10, 12. See photo, The Drake Oil Well in 1859—The First Oil Well, Tarbell, vol. 1, 10f.

8. Tarbell, vol. 1, 12–20, 30–34. Rezneck, 64, 65. Giddens, 30. Miller, 394–395.

9. See Tarbell, vol. 1, 30–33. Miller, 391.

10. Darrah, 3. Giddens, 83, 86, 87, 114. See "Table of Yearly and Monthly Average Price of Refined," Tarbell, vol. 1, 384–385.

11. Lloyd, H. D., "Story of a Great Monopoly," *Atlantic Monthly*, vol. 47 (Mar 1881), 317–334. Giddens, 100. Rezneck, 64. Tarbell, vol. 2, 395. See Giddens, 101–113. See report, "Yearly Production of Crude Petroleum of the Principal Oil Producing Countries Since 1900," ca. Jan 1918: BNA CAB21/119.

12. Montague, Gilbert Holland, "The Rise and Supremacy of the Standard Oil Company," *Quarterly Journal of Economics*, vol. 16 (1902), 267. Rezneck, 65. See Giddens, 101–113.

13. Darrah, 32, 38, 40–42, 60–61, 77, 231, 232. See Montague, 266. See Tarbell, vol. 1, 24–25. See photo, "Holmden Street, Pithole, August, 1895," Giddens, 136f. See Giddens, 139–140.

14. See generally Black, Edwin, *Banking on Baghdad (BoB): Inside Iraq's 7,000-Year History of War, Profit, and Conflict* (Washington, DC: Dialog Press, 2007), chap. 6.

15. See Earle, Edward Meade, *Turkey, the Great Powers, and the Baghdad Railway: A Study in Imperialism* (NY: Macmillan, 1923), vii, 4–5, 6–7. See Chesney, Colonel W. Ainsworth, "A General Statement of the Labours and Proceedings of the Expedition to the Euphrates, under the Command of Colonel Chesney, Royal Artillery, F.R.S.," *Journal of the Royal Geographical Society of London*, vol. 7 (1837), 411–439.

16. Bright, Arthur A., Jr., *The Electric-Lamp Industry: Technological Change and Economic Development from 1800 to 1947* (New York: Macmillan, 1949), 70–71, 71n3. Rezneck, 64.

17. Longrigg, *Origins*, 9. Ferrier, 18–19.

18. See Faroqhi, Suraiya, *Subjects of the Sultans: Culture and Daily Life in the Ottoman Empire* (London: I.B. Tauris Publishers, 2000), 167. See Panzac, Daniel, "International and Domestic Maritime Trade in the Ottoman Empire during the 18th Century," *International Journal of Middle East Studies*, vol. 24 (1992), 189–206.

19. Palmer, Alan, *The Decline and Fall of the Ottoman Empire* (New York: M. Evans & Co., 1992), 128. Lord Kinross, *The Ottoman Centuries: The Rise and Fall of the Turkish Empire* (New York: William Morrow & Co., 1977), 509. Quataert, Donald, *The Ottoman Empire, 1700–1922* (Cambridge, UK: Cambridge University Press, 2000), 71–72. See Anderson, Olive, "II: Great Britain and the Beginnings of the Ottoman Public Debt, 1854–55," *Historical Journal*, vol. 7 (1964), 47–51. See Longrigg, *Four Centuries*, 277–278.

20. Black, *BoB*, 88–91.

21. Livingston, A.A., "Some Early Italian Parallels to the Locution of the Sick Man of the East," *PMLA*, vol. 25 (1910), 460. Palmer, Alan, *The Banner of Battle: The Story of the Crimean War* (London: Weidenfield & Nicolson, 1987), 14. Black, *BoB*, 88–91.

22. Livingston, 460. Black, *BoB*, 88–91.

23. Black, *BoB*, 88–91.

24. Livingston, 459–460, 460n. Palmer, *Decline*, 118.

25. Schonfield, Hugh. *The Suez Canal in Peace and War, 1869–1969.* (Coral Gables, FL: University of Miami Press, 1969), 37. See "The Suez Canal, an Achievement of Enthusiasm and Diplomacy," *Bulletin of the Business Historical Society*, vol. 3, no. 4. (Jun 1929), 1–8.

26. Sumida, Jon Tetsuro, "British Naval Administration and Policy in the Age of Fisher," *The Journal of Military History*, vol. 54, no. 1 (Jan 1990), 3–4. See Jones, Archer, and Andrew J. Keogh, "The Dreadnought Revolution: Another Look," *Military Affairs*, vol. 49 (1985), 124–131. Ferrier, R. W., *The History of the British Petroleum Company*, vol. 1: *The Developing Years, 1901–1932* (Cambridge, UK: Cambridge University Press, 1982), 10. See photo, "Coaling Ship, 1910," Ritchie, Berry, *Portrait in Oil: An Illustrated History of BP* (London: James & James Publishers Ltd., 1995), 28. Miller, Geoffrey, *Straits: British Policy towards the Ottoman Empire and the Origins of the Dardanelles Campaign* (Hull, UK: University of Hull, 1997), 424.

27. Lord Kinross, *The Ottoman Centuries: The Rise and Fall of the Turkish Empire* (New York: William Morrow & Co., 1977), 565–566. Longrigg, *Origins*, 17. Letter, Arminius Vambery to Thomas Sanderson, Nov 28, 1898: BNA FO800/33, as cited by Miller, 8. See photo, "State Visit to Jerusalem of Wilhelm II of Germany in 1898," Matson Collection, LC-DIG-matpc-04610, www.loc.gov. See photo, "The Jaffa Gate," *Encyclopedia Judaica*, 1,427.

28. "The Baghdad Railroad Convention, 5 March 1903," Cd. 5635 (1911), 37–48, reproduced in J. C. Hurewitz, ed., *Diplomacy in the Near And Middle East*, vol. 1, *1535–1914* (Gerrards Cross, UK: Archive Editions, 1987), 252–263. Longrigg, *Oil*, 27. Longrigg, *Origins*, 35. Kent, Marian, *Oil and Empire: British Policy and Mesopotamian Oil, 1900–1920* (London: Macmillan Press Ltd., 1976), 16.

29. Rohrbach, Paul, *Bagdadbahn* (Berlin: Wiegandt & Grieben, 1911), quoted by Schonfield, Hugh, *The Suez Canal in Peace and War, 1869–1969* (Coral Gables, FL: University of Miami Press, 1969), 62–63.

30. Rohrbach, 43–44, quoted by Kent, *Oil*, 16.

31. Black, *BoB*, 118–119.

32. "Agreement by the Shaikh of Kuwait Regarding the Non-reception of Foreign Representatives and the Non-cession of Territory to Foreign Powers or Subjects, 23rd January 1899," *The Road to Independence*, Al-Diwan Al-Amiri, www.da.gov.kw/eng/. "Exclusive Agreement: The Kuwayti Shaykh and Britain, 23 January 1899," reproduced in Hurewitz, vol. 1, 218–219. Tetreault, Mary Ann, "Autonomy, Necessity, and the Small State: Ruling Kuwait in the Twentieth Century," *International Organization*, vol. 45 (1991), 570–575. See Rush, Alan deLacy, ed., *Records of Kuwait, 1899–1961*, vol. 1 (London: Archive International, 1989), 149, as cited by Tetreault, 575. See Longrigg, *Oil*, 26.

33. "The Baghdad Railroad Convention, 5 March 1903." See Longrigg, *Oil*, 27. See generally Earle, Edward Mead, *Turkey, the Great Powers, and the Baghdad Railway: A Study in Imperialism* (New York: Macmillan Company, 1923).

34. Jack, Marian, "The Purchase of the British Government's Shares in the British Petroleum Company 1912–1914," *Past and Present*, no. 39 (Apr 1968), 140, 140n1, 141. "Summary of Investigations of the Committee Dealing with the Supply of Oil Fuel for His Majesty's Ships with Notes on Subsequent Action," Contract Department, Admiralty, Sep 1907: May Ms, NMM MAY 6, as cited by Miller, 424. Miller, 424.

35. Black, *BoB*, 121. See Black, *BoB*, chap. 7.

36. Miller, 28–29.

37. "Memorandum of Association of the Anglo-Persian Oil Company, Limited" Apr 14, 1909: BP 90423. Ferrier, 67, 86–88. Miller, 425. Ritchie, 19.

38. Black, *BoB*, chap. 8.

39. Longrigg, *Origins*, 46–47.

40. "Sultan Must Quit," *NYT*, Apr 20, 1909, 1. "Abdul Awaits Fate; Young Turks Have Not Told What They Will Do," *NYT*, Apr 21, 1909, 1. McCullagh, Frances, "Sultan Beaten; Capital Falls; 6,000 Are Slain," *NYT*, Apr 25, 1909. Shaw and Shaw, 279–280. See Longrigg, *Origins*, 47.

41. See Longrigg, *Origins*, 47.

42. "Abdul Hamid Deposed," *NYT*, Apr 28, 1909, 8. McCullagh, Frances, "Abdul Hamid is Deposed; Mehmed V Rules," *NYT*, Apr 28, 1909, 1. "Deposition of Sultan Abdul Hamid and Accession to the Throne of Mohammed V," paraphrase of telegram, Ambassador Leishman to Secretary of State, Apr 27 1909: File no. 10044/167, *FRUS* 1909, 581. Letter, Ambassador H. Kiazim to Secretary of State, Apr 27, 1909: File no. 10044/174, *FRUS* 1909, 581.

43. "Sultan to Pay Young Turks' Bills," *NYT*, Apr 27, 1909, 2. "Abdul Not to Be Tried," *NYT*, Apr 29, 1909, 1. "250 Mutiny Leaders Executed in Turkey," *NYT*, Apr 30, 1909, 1. "Young Turks Suspend Siege in Honor of New Sultan," *NYT*, Apr 29, 1909, 2. Longrigg, *Oil*, 28–29.

44. "Oilfields in Mesopotamia," confidential summary of correspondence, Dec 1911–Jan 1912, Jan 26, 1926: BNA FO371/1487 no. 911. Memo, Apr 6, 1912: BNA FO371/1487 no. 911. Letter, Gerard Lowther to Edward Grey, Oct 13, 1912: BNA FO371/1487 no. 911. Kent, *Oil*, 22–23. See Longrigg, *Origins*, 66–67, 68–75.

45. Black, *BoB*, 133.

46. Winston Churchill, "Oil Fuel Supply for His Majesty's Navy," report, Jun 16, 1913:

BNA CAB/115/39. Adm. Fisher to Winston Churchill, Dec 10, 1911, *WSC Comp.*, vol. 2, pt. iii, 1926–1927, as cited by Miller, 425. Ferrier, 13, 163. See letter, W. S. Churchill to Lord Fisher, Jun 11, 1912, quoted by Churchill, Randolph S., *Winston S. Churchill*, vol. 2, *1904–1914, Young Statesman* (Boston: Houghton Mifflin, 1967), 590.

47. Ferrier, 132–134, 135, 139–140, 148–149, 162–163. See photos, "SS *Anatolia*, First Vessel Alongside Abadan, 1909." "Laying the Pipeline, 1910," Ferrier, 131, 133. Ritchie, 22–24, 25. See photo, "A Group of Bahktiari," Ritchie, 22.

48. Churchill, W., "Oil Fuel Supply for His Majesty's Navy." Ferrier, 163.

49. Letter, Winston Churchill to John Fisher, Jun 11, 1912, reproduced in Churchill, Randolph, 590–591.

50. Ferrier, 150. Ritchie, 25. Admiralty memo on adequacy of supplies of oil, Mar 18, 1913: BNA ADM116/1209, vol. 3, 44–45.

51. Louis Mallet, memo, Nov 15, 1912: BNA FO371/1486 no. 48688. Questions to Greenway, "First Report."

52. Louis Mallet, minute sheet, Nov 1912: BNA FO371/1486 no. 55654, quoted by Jack, 147.

53. Confidential letter, Louis Mallet to Charles Greenway, Feb 5, 1913: BNA FO371/1760 no. 2463. See confidential letter, Foreign Office to India Office, Feb 5, 1913: BNA FO371/1760 no. 2463.

54. Louis Mallet, memo, Nov 6, 1912: BNA FO371/1486 no. 47846. Jack, 142n9.

55. Questions to Greenway, "First Report."

56. Admiralty memo on adequacy of supplies of oil, Mar 18, 1913. See "For British Navy's Oil," *NYT*, Jun 17, 1914, 4.

57. "Admiralty memorandum as to the adequacy of supplies of oil," Mar 18, 1913: BNA ADM116/1209, vol. 3.

58. Dumas, diary entry, Jan 7, 1913: IWM PP/MCR/96, as cited by Miller, 428.

59. Winston Churchill, secret Admiralty memo, Jun 16, 1913: BNA CAB37/115.

60. "Protocol Relating to the Delimitation of the Turco-Persian Boundary Signed at Constantinople on November 4th (17th), 1913," *League of Nations Official Journal.* See Barstow, "Points Discussed at the Conference," Apr 9, 1919: BNA T1/12544/18025 no. 1920.

61. Edward Grey, "Turkish Petroleum Concessions," memo, Apr 20, 1914: BNA FO195/2456 no. 64, 368. See "Minute re—Civil List Firmans," May 27, 1914: BNA FO195/2456 no. 64, 454.

62. Letter, Anglo-Persian Oil Company to the Treasury, May 20, 1914, reproduced in Ferrier, R.W., *The History of the British Petroleum Company*, Vol. 1: *The Developing Years, 1901–1932* (Cambridge, UK: Cambridge University Press, 1982), app. 6.1, 644–645. "An Agreement, Made the Twentieth Day of May 1914," May 20, 1914: BP 99693. Jack, Marian, "The Purchase of the British Government's Shares in the British Petroleum Company 1912–1914," *Past and Present*, no. 39 (Apr 1968), 161–162.

63. See telegram, Eyre Crowe to Gerard Lowther, enclosure no. 1, Feb 24, 1913: BNA FO424/237 no. 237, 119, as cited by Haddad, Mahmoud, "Iraq Before World War I: A Case of Anti-European Arab Ottomanism," in Rashid Khalid et al., eds., *The Origins of Arab Nationalism* (New York: Columbia University Press, 1991), 134. Longrigg, *Origins*, 82, 83. Kent, *Oil*, 109. Grey, Edward, "Turkish Petroleum Concessions," memo, Apr 20, 1914: BNA FO195/2456 no. 64, 368.

64. Churchill, minute sheet, Jun 9, 1914: BNA CAB 37/120 1914 no. 68. Miller, Geoffrey, *Straits: British Policy Towards the Ottoman Empire and the Origins of the Dardanelles Campaign* (Hull, UK: The University of Hull, 1997), 460–461. "The Naval Oil Agreement; Protest by Traders," *Times*, Jun 10, 1914: BNA T1/11953 no. 119238. See "Orders of the Day: Anglo-Persian Oil Company (APOC), Acquisition of Capital," Jun 17, 1914: BNA T1/11953 no. 119238, cols. 1123–1124.

65. George Lloyd, "Parliamentary debate on APOC's acquisition of capital," Jun 17, 1914, *Parliamentary Debates*, vol. 63 (1914), cols. 1156, 1159.

66. George Lloyd, "Parliamentary debate," Jun 17, 1914, col. 1155.

67. Arthur Ponsonby, "Parliamentary debate," Jun 17, 1914, col. 1174.

68. Ponsonby, "Parliamentary debate," Jun 17, 1914, col. 1178.

69. "Parliamentary debate," Jun 17, 1914, col. 1250. Letter, Charles Greenway to John Cargill, Jun 19, 1914: BP 78/63/4, as cited by Ferrier, 199.

70. "The Navy and Persian Oil," editorial, *Times*, Jun 18, 1914, 9.

71. See Earle, Edward Meade, "The Turkish Petroleum Company—A Study in Oleaginous Diplomacy," *Political Science Quarterly*, vol. 39 (1924), 270. See Kent, 238n57.

72. Letter, Grand Vizier of Turkey to British Ambassador, Jun 28, 1914, quoted in "History of the IPC and Mr. Gulbenkian's Part in Its Foundation," Apr 1944: BP 27508, 8–9.

73. Jevtic, Borijove, "Assassination of Archduke Franz Ferdinand," *WWI Document Archive*, wwi.lib.byu.edu/index.php/The_Assassination_of_Archduke_Franz_Ferdinand.

74. "Memoir of Count Franz von Harrach, ca. Jun 1914," Michael Duffy, ed., *firstworldwar.com*, www.firstworldwar.com. Jevtic, "Assassination."

75. "Archduke Ignored Warning," Jun 28, 1914, *NYT*, 1. "Bravery of Archduke," Jun 28, 1914, *NYT*, 1. "Exchanged Dying Words," *NYT*, Jun 29, 1914, 2. Shackelford, Michael, "Assassination of Archduke Franz Ferdinand," ca. Dec 2003, *WWI Document Archive*, wwi.lib.byu.edu/index.php/Sarajevo_Article.

## Chapter 4: Britain and the Taking of Mesopotamia

1. "Casualty Record of Belligerents," *NYT*, Jan 19, 1919, 39. "Military Casualties of World War One," Michael Duffy, ed., *firstworldwar.com*. BBC News, "The War to End All Wars," http://news.bbc.co.uk. "Timeline: 1914–1918—Casualty Figures," *Trenches on the Web: An Internet History of the Great War*, The Great War Society, eds., www.worldwar1.com. See "The Cost of War," *WP*, Nov 27, 1916, 4. See "Primary Documents: D. F. Houston on U. S. War Readiness, 1917," *firstworldwar.com*.

2. "The Battle of the Somme, 1916," *firstworldwar.com*. "The Battle of Verdun, 1916," *firstworldwar.com*. "The Gallipoli Front—An Overview," *firstworldwar.com*. BBC History, "Battle of the Somme: 1 July–13 November 1916," Mar 2002, www.bbc.co.uk. BBC History, "Daily Mirror Headlines, Published 31 July 1916," Jan 2002, www.bbc.co.uk. "At Verdun," *NYT*, May 3, 1916, 12. See "Allied Efforts on the Somme Called 'Gallipoli on the Continent,'" *WP*, Dec 10, 1916, 5. See "How the Battle Was Won," *NYT*, Dec 17, 1916, 2. "Timeline: 1914–1918—Casualty Figures." "Military Casualties of World War One."

3. Buchanan, Sir George, *The Tragedy of Mesopotamia* (London: William Blackwood & Sons, 1938), 4–5. See map, Buchanan, 287ff. Moberly, Brigadier General F. J., *History of the Great War: The Campaign in Mesopotamia, 1914–1918*, vols. 1–3 (London: H. M. Stationery Office, 1925), 78–81. Letter, Anglo-Persian Oil Company to Sir John Bradbury, Jul 30, 1914: BNA T1/11952/20174/1916 pt 1 no. 119238. Letter, John Bradbury, Nov 27, 1914: BNA T1/11952/20174/1916 pt 1 no. 119238. H. M. Treasury resolution, Nov 27, 1914: BNA T1/11952/20174/1916 pt 1 no. 119238.

4. Moberly, vol. 1, 104. See Buchanan, 4.

5. Moberly, vol. 1, 127–128, 130–131. Buchanan, 4–5. Wilson, Sir Arnold T., *Loyalties: Mesopotamia, 1914–1917: A Personal Record* (London: Oxford University Press, 1930), 10–11.

6. Barrow, Sir Edmund, "Military Situation in the Middle East," Jan 25, 1915: BNA CAB37/123/5. Miller, Geoffrey, *Straits: British Policy Towards the Ottoman Empire and the Origins of the Dardanelles Campaign* (Hull, UK: University of Hull, 1997), 463. See table, "World Production of Petroleum, 1913–1920," Kent, Marian, *Oil and Empire: British Policy and Mesopotamian Oil, 1900–1920* (London: Macmillan Press Ltd., 1976), 202–203.

7. Letter, Hardinge to H. M. the King-Emperor, Oct 8, 1915: Hardinge ms, vol. 105, pt 2, as cited by Kent, 119.

8. See Dawn, C. Ernest, "The Origins of Arab Nationalism," in Rashid Khalidi et al., eds., *The Origins of Arab Nationalism* (New York: Columbia University Press, 1991), 3–23.

9. See Tauber, 1–10, 57.

10. See Shaw, Stanford J., and Ezel Kural Shaw, *The History of the Ottoman Empire and Modern Turkey*, vol. 2: *Reform, Revolution, and Republic: The Rise of Modern Turkey, 1808–1975* (Cambridge, UK: Cambridge University Press, 1977), 302–303, 304, 309–310. Antonius, 102. 104–105, 106–107. See Tauber, 2–3.

11. Kedourie, Elie, "The End of the Ottoman Empire," *Journal of Contemporary History*, vol. 3, no. 4. (Oct 1968), 20. Wilson, *1914–1917*, 22.

12. "Report on the Conditions for Trade in Mesopotamia," ca. Aug 1919: BL L/PS/10/386. Driver, G. R., "The Religion of the Kurds," *Bulletin of the School of Oriental Studies, University of London*, vol. 2 (1922), 197, 210.

13. See Black, Edwin, *Banking on Baghdad (BoB): Inside Iraq's 7,000-Year History of War, Profit, and Conflict* (Washington, DC: Dialog Press, 2007), 175–178, 180. See generally Black, *BoB*, chap. 10.

14. al-Fatat, "Resolution," as quoted by Tauber, 57. Tauber, 57.

15. "Introduction," "The Hashemites," "The Hashemite Family Tree," official website of King Hussein, www.kinghussein.gov.jo. "New Caliph of Islam Is in Power," *WP*, Jun 25, 1916, ES1. See Marquise de Fontenoy, "Turks Long Hated by the Arabians," *WP*, Dec 29, 1914, 6.

16. Secret letter, Lord Kitchener to Sir Edward Grey, Feb 6, 1914: BNA FO6672/6672/14/44 no. 22 as quoted in "British Imperial Connexions to the Arab National Movement." See Introduction to "The Husayn-McMahon Correspondence," Hurewitz, 13. See de Fontenoy.

17. Letter, Sir Louis Mallet to Sir Edward Grey, Mar 18, 1914: BNA FO13871/4688/14/44 no. 103, as quoted in "British Imperial Connexions to the Arab National Movement."

18. See Ireland, Phillip Willard, *Iraq: A Study in Political Development* (New York: Macmillan Company, 1938), 67n5. See Friedman, Isaiah, "The McMahon-Hussein Correspondence and the Question of Palestine," *Journal of Contemporary History*, vol. 5 (1970), 83.

19. See *Correspondence between Sir Henry McMahon and The Sherif Hussein of Mecca, July 1915–March 1916 (With a Map)*, Cmd. 5957, Miscellaneous No. 3 (London: HM Stationery Office, 1939), 2–18, esp. letters 4–8. See also Antonius, 164–183.

20. Letter, Lord Kitchener to Sharif Hussein, Oct 31, 1914: Israel State Archives 65/2847a: 1, as quoted by Tauber, 69.

21. Antonius, 157–158. See map, "The Eastern Arab World," Antonius, 160f.

22. Antonius, 159. See "Memorandum on Proposed Agreement with the French," enclosure to secret letter, Capt. W. R. Hall to Sir Arthur Nicolson, Jan 12, 1916: BNA FO 371/2767.

23. Letter, Hussein to McMahon, Sep 9, 1915 (letter 3), *McMahon-Hussein Correspondence*.

24. Letter, Sir Henry McMahon to Sherif Hussein, Oct 24, 1915 (letter 4), *McMahon-Hussein Correspondence*.

25. Letter, Sherif Hussein to Sir H. McMahon, Nov 5, 1915 (27th Zil Hijja 1333) (letter 5), *McMahon-Hussein Correspondence*.

26. Letter, Hussein to McMahon, Nov 5, 1915 (letter 5), *McMahon-Hussein Correspondence*.

27. See Toynbee, Arnold, "The McMahon-Hussein Correspondence: Comments and a Reply," *Journal of Contemporary History*, vol. 5 (1970), 186. Antonius, 169.

28. Busch, Briton Cooper, *Britain, India, and the Arabs, 1914–1921* (Berkeley, CA: University of California Press, 1971), 60. Tauber, 65. See Tauber, 88–89, 90–91. See Moberly, vol. 1, 156.

29. See Tauber, 82, 251. Sa'id, *al-Thawra*, vol. 1, 156, as quoted by Tauber, 251.

30. Clark, Arthur Tillotson, *To Baghdad with the British* (New York: D. Appleton & Co., 1918), 1–2. See Liukkonnen, Petri, "Who's Who: T. E. Lawrence," *firstworldwar.com*

31. Private telegram, Sir Percy Cox to the Viceroy, Nov 23, 1914, as quoted by Moberly, vol. 1, 133. Moberly, vol. 1, 133–134.

32. Private telegram, Sir Percy Cox to the Viceroy, Nov 23, 1914 as quoted by Moberly, vol. 1, 133–134. Letter, Fisher to Asquith, Nov 5, 1915: Asquith ms., 15/124, as quoted by Kent, 123.

33. Wilson, *1914–1917*, 80–83.

34. Moberly, vol. 2, 63–64, 64n. See "The Present and Prospective Situation in Syria and Mesopotamia," in Moberly, vol. 2, 467–468, 472–474. See generally Townsend, Charles Vere Ferrers, *My Campaign*, vol. 1 (New York: James A. McCann Company, 1920), 249–276, 277–302, 303–332. See "The Battle of Ctesiphon, 1915," Michael Duffy, ed., *firstworldwar.com*. See "Blunder Made in Mesopotamia Campaign Vigorously Assailed in House of Lords," *WP*, Sep 17, 1916, ES1.

35. Moberly, vol. 2, 282, 439–453, 455, 456–457. Townsend, vol. 2, 95–96, 155–157, 171–172, 203, 205–206, 208–209, 214. Wilson, *1914–1917*, 93–94. Clark, 78–79, 82.

36. Townshend, vol. 2, 235–237. Moberly, vol. 2, 459, 460n. Wilson, *1914–1917*, 99.

37. Wilson, *1914–1917*, 99–100.

38. Wilson, *1914–1917*, 99–100.

39. Moberly, vol. 2, 461–463. Wilson, *1914–1917*, 130 133, 134–138.

40. See photos, British Troops Moving through a Baghdad Street, Indian Troops Entering Baghdad through a Heavy Dust Storm, Clark, 200f. See "Turkish Armies May Be Surrounded," *NYT*, Mar 18, 1917, XXI. See Wilson, *1914–1917*, 231–234.

41. Moberly, vol. 2, 465.

42. Proclamation, delivered by Gen. Stanley Maude to the people of Baghdad, Mar 19, 1917, reproduced in Moberly, vol. 3, 404–405 and Buchanan, Sir George, *The Tragedy of Mesopotamia* (London: William Blackwood & Sons, 1938), 169–172.

## Chapter 5 : Return to Zion

1. See Nti, Kwaku, "Action and Reaction: An Overview of the Ding Dong Relationship between the Colonial Government and the People of Cape Coast," *Nordic Journal of African Studies*, vol. 11 (2002), 4–5.

2. Faroqhi, Suraiya, *The Ottoman Empire: A Short History*, Shelly Frisch, trans. (Princeton: Markus Wiener, 2009) 172. See Knight, Edward Frederick, *The Awakening of Turkey: A History of the Turkish Revolution* (Philadelphia: J.B. Lippincott, 1909), 75–76. See "Balkan Problems," *The Nation*, vol. 52 (Feb 19, 1891), 152–153.

3. See Black, *BoB*, 174–175, 176.

4. Ruppin, Arthur, *The Jews of To-day*, Margery Bentwith, trans. (NY: Henry Holt & Co., 1913), 25, 47–50. See Schreckenberg, Heinz, *The Jews in Christian Art: An Illustrated History* (NY: Continuum, 1996), 14–15. See generally Black, Edwin, *The Transfer Agreement* (Washington, DC: Dialog Press, 2009). See Weider, Ben, "Napoleon and the Jews," *The Napoleon Series*, www.napoleon-series.org. See Nordau, Max Simon & Gustav Gottheil, *Zionism and Anti-Semitism* (New York: Fox, Duffield & Co., 1905), 68.

5. Halphen, Achille-Edmond, ed., *Recueil des Lois: décrets, ordonnances, avis du conseil d'état, arrêtés et règlements concernant les israélites depuis la Révolution de 1789* (Paris: Bureaux des archives israélites), 229. Mendes-Flohr, Paul R. & Jehuda Reinharz, eds., *The Jew in the Modern World: A Documentary History* (Oxford: Oxford University Press, 1980), 118. See Sorkin, David, "The Genesis of the Ideology of Emancipation, 1806-1840," *Leo Baeck Institute Yearbook (LBIY)*, vol. 32 (1987), 14.

6. Sachar, Howard M., *A History of Israel: From the Rise of Zionism to Our Time* (New York: Alfred A. Knopf, 2007), 3–4. See generally *Transactions of the Parisian Sanhedrim: or, Acts of the Assembly of Israelitish Deputies of France and Italy, Convoked at Paris by an Imperial and Royal Decree, Dated May 30, 1806*, Diogene Tama, trans. (London, 1807). See Barnavi, Eli & Miriam Eliav-Feldon, eds., Florence Brutton, trans., *A Historical Atlas of the Jewish People: from the Time of the Patriarchs to the Present* (NY: Schocken Books, 2002), 158–159. See Weider, "Napoleon and the Jews." See *Encyclopedia Judaica (EJ)*, s.v. "Sanhedrin, French."

7. "Jewish Modern and Contemporary Periods (ca.1700–1917)," Jewish Virtual Library, www.jewishvirtuallibrary.org/jsource/History/modtimeline.html. Henriques, U.R.Q., "The Jewish Emancipation Controversy in Nineteenth-Century Britain," *Past & Present*, no. 40 (1968), 126–146. "The Hatti Şerif of Gülhane, 3 November 1839," 46th US Cong, spec sess (March 1881), Senate, Exec Docs, vol. 3, 106–108 as reproduced in J. C. Hurewitz, ed., *Diplomacy in the Near and Middle East*, vol. 1, 1535–1914 (Gerrards Cross, UK: Archive Editions, 1987), 113–116. See Weiker, Walter F., "The Ottoman Bureaucracy: Modernization and Reform," *Administrative Science Quarterly*, vol. 13 (1968), 454. Barnavi & Eliav-Feldon, 158–159.

8. See Ruppin, chaps. 1–11. See Cohon, Samuel S., "The Mission of Reform Judaism," *The Journal of Religion*, vol. 2 (1922), 27–43. See Schoolman, Leonard A., *Reform Judaism and Zionism: One Perspective* (NY: Union of American Hebrew Congregations, 1983).

9. See Ruppin, 135–136.

10. Sachar, 22–23

11. Sachar, 23, 24. See Sachar, 24.

12. Angell, James B., "The Turkish Capitulations," *The American Historical Review*, vol. 6 (1901), 254–259. Thayer, Lucius Ellsworth, "The Capitulations of the Ottoman Empire and the

Question of their Abrogation as it Affects the United States," *The American Journal of International Law*, vol. 17 (1923), 207–233.

13. Angell, 254–259.

14. Stillman, Norman A., *The Jews of Arab Lands in Modern Times* (Philadelphia; New York: The Jewish Publication Society, 1991), 10. Sachar, 24.

15. Sachar, 23, 24.

16. Merriam-Webster Dictionary Online, s.v. "pogrom."

17. Cohn Jr., Samuel K., "The Black Death and the Burning of Jews," *Past & Present*, vol. 196 (2007), 3–36.

18. Klier, John D., "The Pogrom Paradigm in Russian History," in John Doyle Klier & Shlomo Lambroza, eds., *Pogroms: Anti-Jewish Violence in Modern Russian History* (Cambridge: Cambridge University Press, 1992), 15–22. Aronson, I. Michael, "The Anti-Jewish Pogroms in Russia, 1881," in Klier & Lambroza, 39. Klier, "Russian Jewry on the Eve of the Pogroms" in Klier & Lambroza, 5. Orbach, Alexander, "The Russian Jewish Community, 1881–1903," in Klier & Lambroza, 138–139. Ruppin, 36. "The May Laws," as reproduced in Mendes-Flohr & Reinharz, 380. "Russia's Jewish Problem," *The New York Times* (*NYT*), Feb 3, 1895, 23.

19. Shilo, Margalit, "The Immigration Policy of the Zionist Institutions 1882–1914," *Middle Eastern Studies*, vol. 30 (1994), 600–601. See Nini, Yehuda, *The Jews of the Yemen, 1800–1914*, H. Galai, trans. (Chur; Philadelphia: Harwood Academic Publishers, 1991), 173–186. Mandel, Neville J., "Ottoman Policy and Restrictions on Jewish Settlement in Palestine: 1881–1908: Part I," *Middle Eastern Studies*, vol. 10 (1974), 312–332. "Zionist Movement Aimed At," *NYT*, Dec 31, 1898, 6. Sachar, 25–27.

20. Sachar, 24–30. See Shilo, "The Immigration Policy," 600–601. See Nini, 173–196.

21. Herzl, Theodor, *A Jewish State: An Attempt at a Modern Solution of the Jewish Question*, Jacob de Haas, ed.; Sylvia D'Avigdor, trans. (NY: Federation of American Zionists, 1917, 3rd ed.), 2.

22. See generally Herzl, de Hass, & D'Avgidor.

23. Knee, Stuart E., "Jewish Non-Zionism in America and Palestine Commitment 1917–1941," *Jewish Social Studies*, vol. 39 (1977), 209–226. Black, *Transfer*, 168. See Reinharz, Jehuda, *Fatherland or Promised Land: The Dilemma of the German Jew, 1893–1914* (Ann Arbor: U Michigan, 1975), 172–174. See Dalin, David G., "Cyrus Adler, Non-Zionism, and the Zionist Movement: A Study in Contradictions," *AJS Review*, vol. 10 (1985), 55–87. See Sachar, 43.

24. Weinryb, Bernard D., "East European Immigration to the United States," *JQR*, vol. 45 1955), 512–515. Gartner, Lloyd P., "Notes on the Statistics of Jewish Immigration to England 1870–1914," *Jewish Social Studies*, vol. 22 (1960), 97–102. See generally Gartner, Lloyd P., "Jewish Migrants En Route from Europe to North America: Traditions and Realities," *Jewish History*, vol. 1 (1986), 49–66.

25. See Daniels, Roger, "Immigration in the Gilded Age: Change or Continuity?," *OAH Magazine of History*, vol. 13 (1999), 22. See Alroey, Gur, "Demographers in the Service of the Nation: Liebmann Hersch, Jacob Lestschinsky, and the Early Study of Jewish Migration," *Jewish History*, vol. 20 (2006), 266, 271, 272. See Gartner, "Jewish Migrants," 49, 55. See Weinryb, 515, 520. See Gartner, "Notes," 98. See Ruppin, 40.

26. See Black, *Transfer*, 5.

27. Timeline, Herzl, de Haas, & D'Avgidor, vi. Black, *Transfer*, 75. Oke, Mim Kemal, "The Ottoman Empire, Zionism, and the Question of Palestine (1880–1908)," *International Journal of Middle East Studies*, vol. 14 (1982), 329–341.

28. See Sachar, 47. See Woods, H. Charles, "The Baghdad Railway and Its Tributaries," *The Geographical Journal*, vol. 50 (1917), pp. 38–39. See Farrington, Anthony, "The Beginnings of the English East India Company," *Trading Places: The East India Company and Asia*, www.fathom.com/course/21701760/.

29. Herzl, de Haas, & D'Avgidor, 12. See Oke, "The Ottoman Empire," 329–341.

30. Sachar, 43. See Bodenheimer, M.I., *Prelude to Israel: The Memoirs of M.I. Bodenheimer*, Henriette Hannah Bodenheimer, ed.; Israel Cohen, trans. (NY: Yoseloff: 1963), 89. Herzl, Theodor, *The Complete Diaries*, vol. 1, June 19, 1896.

31. "Emperor William in Turkey," *NYT*, Oct 20, 1898, 7. "The Kaiser in Turkey," *NYT*, Oct

22, 1898, 7. "The Kaiser in Jerusalem," *NYT*, Nov 27, 1898, 19. Photos, Kaiser Visits Jerusalem and Kaiser William in Jerusalem, Author's Collection. Sachar, 47–48. See "Holy Places Vandalized," *NYT*, Oct 23, 1898, 7. See Black, *BoB*, 117.

32. Röhl, John C.G., "Herzl and Kaiser Wilhelm II," in Ritchie Robertson & Edward Timms, eds., *Theodor Herzl and the Origins of Zionism* (Edinburgh: Edinburgh University Press, 1997), 34–35. Sachar, 48, 50.

33. Sachar, 48. Stewart, 21.

34. Grant, Jonathan, "The Sword of the Sultan: Ottoman Arms Imports, 1854–1914," *The Journal of Military History*, vol. 66, (2002), 23–24. "German Enterprise in the East," *The Times*, Oct 28, 1898, 5. Herzl, *Diaries*, vol. 3, Jan 3, 1901.

35. Weisgal, Meyer W., ed., *Theodor Herzl: A Memorial* (NY: New Palestine, 1929), 10. de Haas, Jacob, *Theodor Herzl: A Biographical Sketch*, vol. 1 (Chicago; New York: The Leonard Co., 1927), 148. Bodenheimer, 88–89.

36. Sachar, 49. See Sachar, 50. Herzl, *Diaries*, vol. 3, Aug 22, 1899; May 19, 1901.

37. See Chiswick, Barry R., "Soviet Jews in the United States: An Analysis of Their Linguistic and Economic Adjustment," *International Migration Review*, vol. 27 (1993), 262. Judge, Edward H., *Easter in Kishinev: Anatomy of a Pogrom* (NY: NYU Press, 1992), 8–11. See generally Black, *Transfer*, chap. 7.

38. Bein, Alex, *Theodor Herzl: A Biography* (Philadelphia: The Jewish Publication Society of America, 1940), 352. Sachar, 50.

39. de Haas, *Herzl*, vol. 2, 13–15.

40. de Haas, *Herzl*, vol. 2, 13–15.

41. de Haas, *Herzl*, vol. 2, 13–15.

42. See Ünal, Hasan, "Britain and Ottoman Domestic Politics: From the Young Turk Revolution to the Counter-Revolution, 1908–9," *Middle Eastern Studies*, vol. 37 (Apr 2001), 1–22. de Haas, *Herzl*, vol. 2, 13–15.

43. Sachar, 50. Herzl, *Diaries*, vol. 3, May 19, 1901, May 21, 1901.

44. Sachar, 50. de Haas, *Herzl*, vol. 1, 359.

45. Oke, "The Ottoman Empire," 335–336. de Haas, *Herzl*, vol. 1, 367–368. de Haas, *Herzl*, vol. 2, 44–45, 47.

46. Mandel, "Ottoman policy," 312–332. de Hass, *Herzl*, vol. 2, 48–49.

47. Sachar, 52. Bein, 415.

48. "The Anti-Semitic Disturbances in Galicia," *The Times*, Jun 18, 1898, 7. "Religious Kidnapping in Galicia," *The Times*, May 22, 1900, 7. "The Jewish Question in Rumania," *The Times*, Oct 9, 1902, 11. "Heavy Immigration of Jews," *Washington Post* (*WP*), Mar 11, 1900, 5. See "Aliens on our Shores," *WP*, Sep 28, 1900, 8. Vital, David, *The Origins of Zionism* (Oxford: Clarendon Press, 1975), 40–41. de Haas, Herzl, vol. 1, 319. See generally Judge, chap 2.

49. Moruzzi, Norma Claire, "Strange Bedfellows: The Question of Lawrence Oliphant's Christian Zionism," *Modern Judaism*, vol. 26 (2006), 55–73. See Sachar, 28. See Mandel, "Ottoman Policy," 312–313. Goldman, Shalom, *Zeal for Zion: Christians, Jews, and the Idea of the Promised Land* (Chapel Hill: University of North Carolina Press, 2009), 7–8, 15–16. See Goldman, 4–14. Hechler, Rev. William, "The Restoration of the Jews to Palestine," broadside, ca. 1884, as reproduced in Goldman, 21. *EJ*, s.v. "Oliphant, Laurence."

50. See Gartner, "Notes," 97–102. See National Archives UK, "Events of 1901: Moving to Britain," www.nationalarchives.gov.uk/pathways/census/events/britain4.htm.

51. "Paupers Sent To England," *NYT*, Oct 19, 1902, 4. See "East End Problems in London and New York," *NYT*, May 26, 1902, 6. Fraenkel, Josef, "Theodor Herzl and the Royal Commission on Alien Immigration," *Canadian Jewish Chronicle*, Apr 6, 1956, 4. See also Pannick, David, QC, "A Century ago Immigration Control Was an Alien Concept; How It Has Changed," *The Times*, Jun 28, 2005. de Hass, *Herzl*, vol. 2, 68.

52. Bein, 388–389. de Hass, *Herzl*, vol. 2, 67. Herzl, *Diaries*, vol. 4, Jul 5, 1902.

53. See Vital, David, *Zionism: The Formative Years* (Oxford: Clarendon Press, 1982), 135–136. de Haas, *Herzl*, vol. 2, 68.

54. Herzl, de Haas, & D'Avgidor, 12.

55. Vital, *Zionism*, 140. Bein, 388, 390–391. See de Hass, *Herzl*, vol. 2, 103–104. See Herzl, *Diaries*, vol. 3, Nov 7, 1889.

56. de Haas, *Herzl*, vol. 2, 67. Bein, 392–394.

57. See Oke, 334. See generally Black, *BoB*, chap. 6.

58. Photo, Joseph Chamberlain in 1894, in Garvin, J.L., *The Life of Joseph Chamberlain*, vol. 3, *Empire and World Policy* (London: Macmillan, 1934), ii. Garvin, 3, 5, 27. Garvin, J.L. & Julian Amery, *The Life of Joseph Chamberlain*, vol. 4, *At the Height of his Power* (London: Macmillan, 1951), 256–257, 259–261. "Mr. Chamberlain on the Australian Colonies," *Times*, Nov 12, 1895, 6. Sachar, 53–54. Vital, *Zionism*, 145–147. de Haas, *Herzl*, vol. 2, 103–104. Herzl, *Diaries*, vol. 4, Oct 23, 1902.

59. Garvin & Amery, vol. 4, 263. Bein, 418. Herzl, *Diaries*, vol. 4, Oct 23, 1902; Apr 24, 1903.

60. Vital, *Zionism*, 146–154. "Snapshots of the Expedition that Investigated El Arisch," de Haas, *Herzl*, vol. 2, 120. Herzl, *Diaries*, vol. 4, Oct 24, 1902.

61. Farwell, Byron, *The Great Boer War* (London: Allen Lane, 1977), 392–393, 397. Krebs, Paula M., "'The Last of the Gentlemen's Wars': Women in the Boer War Concentration Camp Controversy," *History Workshop*, no. 33 (Spring 1992), 39. See Krebs, 41. Garvin & Amery, vol. 4, 28–29, 36–37, 78. Photo, Lizzie van Zyl, Author's Collection.

62. "British Generals Attacked," *NYT*, May 24, 1902, 9. "Says The Boer War Will End This Week," *NYT*, May 29, 1902, 8. "The Future of South Africa," *NYT*, Jun 2, 1902, 8. Farwell, 192, 240–241. Matrix Evans, Martin, *Encyclopedia of the Boer War* (Santa Barbara; Denver; Oxford: ABC-CLIO, 2000), 57–58. See "Gen. Botha First Premier," *NYT*, May 22, 1910, c2.

63. Mwakikagile, Godfrey, *Africa and the West* (Huntington, NY: Nova Science Publishers, 2000), 86. Garvin & Amery, vol. 4, 287, 289–291. Vital, *Zionism*, 155–156. "Topics of the Day in the British Capital," *NYT*, Nov 2, 1902, 4.

64. Mwakikagile, 86. Garvin, vol. 3, 19. Vital, *Zionism*, 156–157.

65. Mwakikagile, 86. Garvin & Amery, vol. 4, 262–263.

66. Vital, *Zionism*, 159n73. See "Mr. Chamberlain's Tour," *The Manchester Guardian* (*MG*), Feb 25, 1903, 5. "Welcome to Chamberlain," *NYT*, Mar 15, 1903, 4. Herzl, Diaries, vol. 4, Apr 24, 1903.

67. Vital, *Zionism*, 158–159.

68. Davitt, Michael, *Within the Pale: The True Story of Anti-Semitic Persecutions in Russia* (NY: A.S. Barnes, 1903), 56, 99–100, 124, 191–196. Judge, 18, 20, 21, 36–37, 40–42. Lambroza, Shlomo, "The Pogroms of 1903–1906," in Klier & Lambroza, 196–197, 204. Schoenberg, Philip Ernest, "The American Reaction to The Kishinev Pogrom Of 1903," *American Jewish Historical Quarterly*, vol. 63 (1974), 262. "Accusations which Led to Kishineff Massacre," *NYT*, Jul 16, 1903, 7. See "How Jewish Riots Started," *NYT*, Jul 4, 1903, 7. See Vital, *Zionism*, 239, 241.

69. Lambroza, "The Pogroms," in Klier & Lambroza, 198–199, 201. Davitt, 56, 99–100, 124, 191–196. Judge, 18, 20, 21, 36–37, 40–42. "How Jewish Riots Started," *NYT*, Jul 4, 1903, 7. "Minister Plehve's Part in Kishineff Massacre," *NYT*, May 31, 1903, 5. Cahan, Abraham, "Jewish Massacres and the Revolutionary Movement in Russia," *North American Review*, 53. Penkower, Monty Noam, "The Kishinev Pogrom of 1903: A Turning Point in Jewish History," *Modern Judaism*, vol. 24 (2004), 187. See Vital, *Zionism*, 239, 241. See "Russian Police View of Kishineff Horrors," *NYT*, Jun 6, 1903, 3.

70. Penkower, 190. "Massacre of Jews," *MG*, May 12, 1903, 7. Judge, 49–51, 61. See Davitt, 124. Davitt, 166–167. "An Eye-Witness's Letter," *NYT*, May 14, 1903, 5.

71. Dekel, Mikhal, "'From the Mouth of the Raped Woman Rivka Schiff,' Kishinev, 1903," *Women's Studies Quarterly*, vol. 36 (2008), 199–200. "More Details of the Kishineff Atrocities," *NYT*, May 15, 1903, 16. Penkower, 187.

72. Davitt, 123, 135–136, 172–173. Judge, 37, 52, 55–56. Lambroza, "The Pogroms," in Klier & Lambroza, 201–203. Penkower, 188. "An Eye-Witness's Letter," *NYT*, May 14, 1903, 5. Vital, 240. See "Kishineff Jews Were Disarmed By Soldiers," *NYT*, Jun 6, 1903. 3.

73. "The Anti-Semitic Outrages At Kishineff," *The Times*, May 18, 1903, 10. "Minister Plehve's Part in Kishineff Massacre," *NYT*, May 31, 1903, 5. "Minister Plehve's Guilt," *NYT*, Jun 22, 1903, 1. "Further Accusation against de Plehve," *NYT*, Jun 6, 1903, 3. See "Massacres In Russia," *NYT*, May 14, 1903, 8. "Responsible for Kishineff Horror," *NYT*, May 18, 1903, 1. "The Kishineff Outbreak," *NYT*, May 11, 1903, 3. Judge, 53–61.

74. "More Details of Massacre," *NYT*, May 17, 1903, 1. See "The Anti-Semitic Riots At

Kishineff," *The Times*, May 12, 1903, 5D. Judge, 71–75. Lambroza, "The Pogroms," in Klier & Lambroza, 200. Davitt, 108–109.

75. "Attacks on Jews," *MG*, Apr 24, 1903, 9. "Jewish Massacre Denounced," *NYT*, Apr 28, 1903, 6. "Massacre of Jews," *MG*, May 12, 1903, 7. See "Police Connived At Kishineff Massacre," *NYT*, May 20, 1903, 3. "Hebrews Slain in Racial Riot," *The Atlanta Constitution*, Apr 24, 1903, 4. "Russians Murder 25 Jews," *Chicago Daily Tribune*, Apr 24, 1903, 5. "More Details of Massacre." Dekel, 201.

76. Garner, James Wilford, "Record of Political Events," *Political Science Quarterly*, vol. 18 (1903), 724. "Chinese Help for Jews," *NYT*, May 12, 1903, 3. "Russia's Attitude on the Kishineff Massacre," *NYT*, Jun 11, 1903, 9. "Russian Versions of Outrages on Jews," *NYT*, May 18, 1903, 2. "Kishineff Incident Closed, Mr. Hay Says," *NYT*, Jul 18, 1903, 7. "Big Plan to Aid Jews," *Chicago Tribune*, May 24, 1903, 4. "Salvation Army Plan," *NYT*, May 24, 1903, 12. Adler, Cyrus, ed., *The Voice of America on Kishineff* (Philadelphia: Jewish Publication Society of America, 1904), xi–xii, 476–480. Dekel, 201. Schoenberg, 265, 266. Judge, 85, 87–88, 89–90. See generally Adler, *The Voice*. See "Gorki Denounces The 'Cultivated' Russians," NYT, May 23, 1903, 3. See "Jews in Romania and Poland Alarmed," *NYT*, May 21, 1903, 2." See "Letter from Count Tolstoi," *NYT*, May 22, 1903, 2. See Library of Congress Exhibition, "From Haven to Home: 350 Years of Jewish Life in America," www.loc.gov/exhibits/haventohome/haven-home.html.

77. "Cure for Russian Outrages," *NYT*, Jun 8, 1903, 7. "Expulsion Ordered of Kishineff Refugees," *NYT*, Jul 19, 1903, 4. "London Horrified By Kishineff Revelations," *NYT*, May 19, 1903, 1. "Jews Taking Up Arms," *WP*, May 22, 1903, 3. "Roumanian Jews in Peril," *NYT*, Jun 10, 1903, 5. "Russian Jews Massacred," *NYT*, Aug 28, 1904, 1. "The Kishineff Outrages," *The Times*, Jun 22, 1903, 7. Photos, Kishinev pogrom, 1903, Dorot Jewish Division, New York Public Library, http://legacy.www.nypl.org/research/chss/jws/russian1.html. See Untitled Article datelined Gomel, *NYT*, Sep 24, 1903, 1. Adler, *The Voice*, 331–334. See also photo, "Figure 40: Five of the 49 Victims of the Kishinev Pogroms in 1903," Author's Collection.

78. Vital, *Zionism*, 159, 160–162, 278. Bein, 445–446. Herzl, *Diaries*, vol. 4. May 19, 1903.

79. Vital, *Zionism*, 160–162, 269. Herzl, *Diaries*, May 23, 1903.

80. de Hass, *Herzl*, vol. 2, 133, 145.

81. Vital, *Zionism*, 246–247, 248. "Czar May Help Zionists," *Chicago Tribune*, Aug 26, 1903, 2. de Hass, *Herzl*, vol. 2, 133, 143, 147–148. Herzl, *Diaries*, vol. 4, Jul 8, 1903.

82. Vital, *Zionism*, 249. Judge, 93. de Hass, *Herzl*, vol. 2, 144. Herzl, *Diaries*, vol. 4, Aug 10, 1903. See "Czar May Help Zionists."

83. Vital *Zionism*, 249n40, 254. de Hass, *Herzl*, vol. 2, 145, 148–149. "Russia Covertly against Zionism," *NYT*, Sep 2, 1903, 1. "Czar May Help Zionists."

84. de Hass, *Herzl*, vol. 2, 145–146.

85. Vital, *Zionism*, 252–255. de Hass, *Herzl*, vol. 2, 150–156.

86. Vital, *Zionism*, 260–264. de Hass, *Herzl*, vol. 2, 150, 151–152, 153, 154.

87. Vital, *Zionism*, 260–264. de Hass, *Herzl*, vol. 2, 155, 156.

88 "Czar May Help Zionists." "Russia to Aid Jews," *WP*, Aug 26, 1903, 1. Vital, 251–252.

89. Vital, 258, 270. See "Would Buy Palestine," *NY Tribune*, Aug 8, 1903, 3. See Vital, 125–126.

90. "Jewish State for Jews," *NYT*, Aug 24, 1903, 5. de Hass, *Herzl*, vol. 2, 158–162.

91. Zolotkoff, Leon, "For A New Zion in East Africa," *Chicago Tribune*, Sep 13, 1903, 2. "Zionist Delegates Welcomed Home," *NYT*, Oct 4, 1903, 9. de Hass, *Herzl*, vol. 2, 162–168.

92. Zolotkoff. Vital, 280, 304. de Hass, *Herzl*, vol. 2, 167, 174, 176–177.

93. de Hass, *Herzl*, vol. 2, 186.

94. Vital, 308, 309–311, 313–315, 318–319. de Hass, *Herzl*, vol. 2, 184–185, 214, 215, 233, 236–237. See generally de Hass, *Herzl*, vol. 2, chap. xix.

95. "Dr. Theodor Herzl Dead," *NYT*, Jul 4, 1904, 5. de Haas, *Herzl*, vol. 2, 243–245, 249.

## Chapter 6: The Zionist Moment

1. Keogh, Dermot, *Jews in Twentieth-Century Ireland: Refugees, Anti-Semitism, and the Holocaust* (Cork: Cork University Press, 1988), 26–51. "Topics of the Times," *NYT*, Apr 12,

1904, 8. "Anti-Jewish Riots in Russia," *Manchester* Guardian (*MG*), Sep 23, 1904, 4. "Fear of Second Kishenef," *WP*, Apr 9, 1904, 9. Untitled article from St. Petersburg, *NYT*, Nov 4, 1904, 2. "Path of Revolution," *MG*, Nov 4, 1905, 9. "When Blood Flowed Like Water at Odessa," *NYT*, Nov 26, 19005. See Vital, David, *Zionism: The Formative Years* (Oxford: Clarendon Press, 1982), 309–310. Lambroza, "The Pogroms of 1903–1906," in Klier & Lambroza, 215–218, 223, 230–231, 232–233. Photo, Child Victims of the Ekaterinoslav Pogrom of 1905, in Lambroza, "Pogroms," 229. See Weinberg Robert, "The Pogrom of 1905 in Odessa: A Case Study," in Klier & Lambroza, 248–281.

2. Sachar, Howard M., *A History of Israel: From the Rise of Zionism to Our Time* (New York: Alfred A. Knopf, 2002), 59–63. Weizmann, Chaim, *The Letters and Papers of Chaim Weizmann, Series B*, vol. 1, Barnet Litvinoff, ed. (New Brunswick: Rutgers Press, 1986), 64–66.

3. Weizmann, Chaim, *Trial and Error* (New York: Harper & Brothers, 1949), 4–28. *EJ*, s.v. "Chaim Weizmann."

4. Rose, Norman, *Chaim Weizmann: A Biography* (New York: Viking, 1986), 8, 26, 32–44. See also Manchester University Centre for Jewish Studies, *Manchester and Zionism*, exhibition, www.mucjs.org/EXHIBITION/INDEXPAGE.HTML.

5. Merkley, Paul, *The Politics of Christian Zionism, 1891–1948* (London; Portland, OR: Frank Cass, 1988), 45–46. Rose, 27.

6. Shimoni, Gideon, *The Zionist Ideology* (Hanover, NH: Brandeis Press, 1995), 115. Rose, 96–103.

7. Young, Kenneth, *Arthur James Balfour: The Happy Life of the Politician, Prime Minister, Statesman, and Philosopher, 1848–1930* (London: G. Bell & Sons, 1963), 256–266, 259, 386–387, 388. Weizmann, *Trial*, 106–107. *EJ*, s.v. "Chaim Weizmann."

8. Speech, Arthur James Balfour to the House of Lords, Jun 21, 1922, quoted in MacArthur, Brian, ed., *The Penguin Book of Twentieth-Century Speeches* (London; New York: Penguin, 2000), 91–94.

9. See Friedman, Isaiah, "The Response to the Balfour Declaration," *Jewish Social Studies*, vol. 35 (1973), 105–124. Young, 255–258. See Vereté, Mayir, "The Balfour Declaration and Its Makers," *Middle Eastern Studies*, vol. 6 (1970), 48–76.

10. Lambroza, Shlomo, "Pogroms," in Klier & Lambroza, 192–193, 220–221. Vital, 167, 168–169.

11. Sherman, A.J., "German-Jewish Bankers in World Politics: The Financing of the Russo-Japanese War," *Leo Baeck Institute Yearbook*, vol. 28 (1968), 68 as cited by Lambroza, "Pogroms," in Klier & Lambroza, 214–215. Aronsfeld, C.C., "Jewish Bankers and the Tsar," *Jewish Social Studies*, vol. 35 (1973), 101–102. "Mr. Schiff's View," *WSJ*, Aug 31, 1905, 2. Black, *Transfer*, 30. Vital, 166–169. See "Czar Grants Some Liberty," *NYT*, Dec 15, 1904, 1. See "Russia Granted A Parliament," *Chi Trib*, Aug 19, 1905, 1.

12. Gillon, D.Z., "The Antecedents of the Balfour Declaration," *Middle Eastern Studies*, vol. 5, (1969), 134. Amery, L.S., "Notes on Possible Terms of Peace," memo, Mar 11, 1917, BNA CA24/10 as cited by Gillon, 134.

13. See Black, *BoB*, 127, 129.

14. Black, *BoB*, 169.

15. Black, *BoB*, 184–185.

16. See Ireland, Phillip Willard, *Iraq: A Study in Political Development* (New York: Macmillan Company, 1938), 67n5. See Friedman, Isaiah, "The McMahon-Hussein Correspondence and the Question of Palestine," *Journal of Contemporary History*, vol. 5 (1970), 83.

17. See *McMahon-Hussein Correspondence*, 2–18, esp. letters 4–8. See also Antonius, George, *The Arab Awakening: The Story of the Arab National Movement* (NY: Capricorn Books, 1965), 164–183.

18. Letter, Lord Kitchener to Sharif Hussein, Oct 31, 1914: Israel State Archives 65/2847a: 1, quoted by Tauber, Eliezer, *The Arab Movements in World War I* (London: Frank Cass, 1993), 69.

19. Antonius, 157–158. See map, "The Eastern Arab World," Antonius, 160f.

20. Antonius, 159. See "Memorandum on Proposed Agreement with the French," enclosure to secret letter, Capt. W. R. Hall to Sir Arthur Nicolson, Jan 12, 1916: BNA FO 371/2767.

21. See Tauber, 71–73. See Kitchener to Grey, Feb 6, 1914. See Friedman, Isaiah, "The

McMahon-Hussein Correspondence and the Question of Palestine," *Journal of Contemporary History*, vol. 5 (1970), 84–87.

22. Letter, Sherif Hussein to Sir Henry McMahon, Jul 14, 1915 (letter 1), *McMahon-Hussein Correspondence*, 3–4.

23. Letter, Sir Henry McMahon to Sherif Hussein, Aug 30, 1915 (letter 2), *McMahon-Hussein Correspondence*, 4–5.

24. Letter, Sherif Hussein to Sir H. McMahon, Sep 9, 1915 (29th Shawal 1333) (letter 3), *McMahon-Hussein Correspondence*, 5–7.

25. Letter, Hussein to McMahon, Sep 9, 1915 (letter 3).

26. Letter, Sir Henry McMahon to Sherif Hussein, Oct 24, 1915 (letter 4), *McMahon-Hussein Correspondence*, 7–9.

27. "Tripartite (Sykes-Picot) Agreement for the Partition of the Ottoman Empire: Britain, France and Russia," reproduced in J.C. Hurewitz, ed., *Diplomacy in the Near and Middle East*, vol. 2 (Gerrards Cross, UK: Archive Editions, 1987), 18–22. Ireland, Philip Willard, *Iraq: A Study in Political Development* (New York: Macmillan, 1938), 68–70. See letter, Sir M. Sykes to Foreign Office, Jan 16, 1916: BNA FO371/2767 no. 11844. See "Negotiations with Arabs," memo, Jan 21, 1916: BNA FO371/2767 no. 14106.

28. Letter, Sir T. Holderness to Sir A. Nicolson, Jan 13, 1916: BNA FO371/2767 no. 8117. Sir A. Hirtzel, "Enclosure in Note 1," Jan 13, 1916: BNA FO371/2767 no. 8117.

29. Telegram, Crewe to Hardinge, Nov 12, 1914: *India Sec. War*, May 1915, as cited by Busch, Briton Cooper, *Britain, India, and the Arabs* (Berkeley, CA: University of California Press, 1971), 63.

30. Secret telegram to Sir George Buchanan, Mar 16, 1915: BNA FO371/2627 no. 51288.

31. Kent, Marian, *Oil and Empire: British Policy and Mesopotamian Oil 1900–1920* (London: Macmillan Press, 1976), 121–122.

32. Duffy, ed., "The Defense of the Suez Canal," *firstworldwar.com*, www.firstworldwar.com/battles/suez.htm.

33. Horne, Charles F., ed., *Source Records of the Great War*, vol. 5 (National Alumni, 1923), as cited by Michael Duffy, ed., "Sir Edmund Allenby on the Fall of Jerusalem, 9 December 1917," *firstworldwar.com*, www.firstworldwar.com/source/jerusalem_allenby1.htm. "The Third Battle of Gaza, 1917," *firstworldwar.com*, www.firstworldwar.com/battles/gaza3.htm. See "The Defense of the Suez Canal."

34. "Victory Parade of General Allenby after occupied Jerusalem," digitized newsreel, Israel State Archives, www.youtube.com/watch?v=kD55ZhUsCc4. "Sir Edmund Allenby on the Fall of Jerusalem, 9 December 1917." "Jerusalem Falls to British Army," *NYT*, Dec 11, 1917, 1. "Jerusalem and Bagdad," Dec 11, 1917, *NYT*, 14.

35. Wasserstein, Bernard, "Herbert Samuel and the Palestine Problem," *The English Historical Review*, vol. 91 (1976), 753–775. Gillon, 149n1. Weizmann, *Trial*, 150. See Young, 389. Sachar, *History*, 99. See generally Sachar, 90–122.

36. Young, 388–390. Weizmann, *Trial*, 152.

37. "The Armenian Atrocities," *NYT*, Jan 2, 1895, 5. "The Worst Was Not Told," *NYT*, Jan 14, 1895, 3. Morgenthau, Henry, *Ambassador Morgenthau's Story* (Garden City, NY: Doubleday, Page & Co., 1918), 276–277. See "Tales of Horror Retold," *NYT*, May 20, 1895, 3.

38. Photo, Adana Massacres, April 1909, in Balakian, Peter, *The Burning Tigris: The Armenian Genocide and America's Response* (New York: HarperCollins, 2003), 236ff. Balakian, 145–152. "Moslem Massacres Take 5,000 Lives," *NYT*, Apr 21, 1909, 2.

39. "Greatest Horrors in History Mark Massacres in Armenia, Declares an Official Report," *WP*, Oct 4, 1915, 5. "Turks Are Evicting Native Christians," *NYT*, Jul 12, 1915, 4. Telegram, Henry Morgenthau to Secretary of State, Jul 16, 1915: NA RG59 867.4016/76, as reproduced in Balakian, 236ff.

40. Telegram, Henry Morgenthau to Secretary of State. "Armenians Are Sent To Perish in Desert," *NYT*, Aug 18, 1915, 5. "Answer Morgenthau by Hanging Armenians," *NYT*, Sep 16, 1915, 1. "Bryce Asks Us to Aid Armenia," *NYT*, Sep 21, 1915, 3. "800,000 Armenians Counted Destroyed," *NYT*, Oct 7, 1915, 3.

41. "Greatest Horrors in History Mark Massacres in Armenia." See "*New York Times* headlines of 1915," Balakian, 236ff.

42. Engle, Anita, *The Nili Spies* (London: Hogarth, 1959), 99. Verrier, Anthony, ed., *Agents of Empire: Anglo-Zionist Intelligence Operations 1915–1919* (London; Washington, DC: Brassey's), 12, 206–207. See Verrier, 17. See generally Engle, *Nili*. See generally Verrier, Part 2.

43. Engle, *Nili*, 100–101.

44. Guttmann, Oscar, *The Manufacture of Explosives*, vol. 2 (London, Whittaker and Co., 1895), 258–262. "Israel: After a Small Pause," *Time*, Oct 11, 1948, www.time.com. See Guenther, John, "Chaim Weizmann, Zionist Leader," *Life*, Jun 12, 1939, 59–62. See "Chaim Weizmann of Israel is Dead," *NYT*, Nov 9, 1952, 1, 90. Young, 353. Weizmann, *Trial*, 170–175.

45. "Israel: After a Small Pause." "Chaim Weizmann, Zionist Leader," 61. "Chaim Weizmann of Israel is Dead." Weizmann, *Trial*, 170–175. Rose, 152–158.

46. Gilner, Elias, *War and Hope: A History of the Jewish Legion* (NY: Herzl Press, 1969), 30, 35–41. Sugarman, Martin, "The Zion Muleteers of Gallipoli," *Jewish Virtual Library*, www.jewishvirtuallibrary.org/jsource/History/gallipoli.html. "Zionist Refugees Brave at Gallipoli," *NYT*, Apr 16, 1916, 5. "First Jewish Corps in a Christian Army," *WP*, Nov 27, 1915, 1. Bloom, Cecil, "Colonel Patterson, Soldier and Zionist," *Jewish Historical Studies*, vol. 31 (1998–1990), 231–232. See "Says Turks Desire to Destroy Zionism," *NYT*, Oct 8, 1915, 2.

47. Sugarman. Gilner, 48.

48. Sugarman. Gilner, 42.

49. Sugarman. Gilner, 42. Bloom, 234.

50. See "Turks at Dardanelles Cut Off by The Allies," *NYT*, Aug 22, 1915, 3. Sugarman. Gilner, 49–51.

51. Sugarman. Gilner, 58–59. Bloom, 233.

52. Sugarman.

53. Sugarman. "Zionist Refugees Brave at Gallipoli." See generally Bloom, "Colonel Patterson," 231–246. See "With the Zionists in Gallipoli," *NYT*, Jun 18, 1916, BR247.

54. "J. Patterson Dies; Led Jewish Legion," *NYT*, Jun 20, 1947, 20. See "With the Zionists in Gallipoli." *NYT*. Sugarman. See generally Bloom, 231–246.

55. Young, 390–392. Reinharz, Jehuda, "The Balfour Declaration and Its Maker: A Reassessment," *The Journal of Modern History*, vol. 64 (1992), 458, 460.

56. Rosen, Jacob, "Captain Reginald Hall and the Balfour Declaration," *Middle Eastern Studies*, vol. 24 (1988), 57–58, 60. Beesley, Patrick, *Room 40: British Naval Intelligence 1914–1918* (London: Oxford University Press, 1984), 130–131. Jones, R.V., "Alfred Ewing and 'Room 40,'" *Notes and Records of the Royal Society of London*, vol. 34 (1979), 86–87. See Beesley, 132.

57. National Archives, "Teaching with Documents: The Zimmermann Telegram," www.archives.gov/education/lessons/zimmermann/.

58. "Teaching with Documents: The Zimmermann Telegram." "Washington Exposes Plot," *NYT*, Mar 1, 1917, 1. "Zimmermann Defends Act," *NYT*, Mar 4, 1917, 1. See "German Plans Known Long," *Chi Trib*, Apr 1, 1917, 4. See "Lansing Assails Zimmermann's Plot Defence," *NY Trib*, Apr 1, 1917, 2. "Berlin Fears U.S. Learned of More Plots," *NY Trib*, Apr 2, 1917, 1. "Zimmermann Says Again Neutral Ships Will Be Sunk," *NYT*, Mar 1, 1917, 1. See "Mexican Complications," *NYT*, Jan 1, 1917, 8. See "Rush Troops to Laredo," *WP*, Jan 1, 1917, 1. See "May Withdraw Border Troops," *LA Times*, Jan 2, 1917, 12. See "100,000 Germans are in Mexico," *NYT*, Mar 1, 1917, 2.

59. Schapiro, Leonard, *The Russian Revolutions of 1917* (New York: Basic Books, 1984), 74. See generally Service, Robert, *The Russian Revolution* (Hampshire, UK: Macmillan, 1991). See generally Service, Robert, *A History of Twentieth Century Russia* (Cambridge, MA: Harvard Press, 1998).

60. "Turks Still Flee before the British," *NYT*, Mar 1, 1917, 5. "Turkish Defeat Becomes a Rout," *NYT*, Mar 2, 1917. "British in Bagdad, London Believes," *NYT*, Mar 10, 1917. Strong Forces of Arabs, United to Fight Turks, Enable British Army to Advance toward Bagdad," *WP*, Mar 10, 1917. "British Capture Ancient City of Bagdad," *Chi Trib*, Mar 12, 1917, 1. "The Fall of Bagdad," *Chi Trib*, Mar 12, 1917, 2. "British Forces Drive the Turks from Bagdad," Mar 12, 1917, 1. Candler, Edmund, "British Welcome in Bagdad," *MG*, Mar 16, 1917, 6.

61. Horne, ed., vol. 5, as cited in "U.S. Declaration of War with Germany, 2 April 1917," *firstworldwar.com*, www.firstworldwar.com/source/usawardeclaration.htm. See "Comment of Today's Newspapers on the President's Address," *NYT*, Apr 3, 1917, 2.

62. "U.S. Declaration of War with Germany." "President's Proclamation of a State of War,"

*WP*, Apr 7, 1917, 1. See "England Is Denounced by Russian Socialists as Foe of Revolutionists' Plan," *WP*, Apr 15, 1917. 12. See "Russia Stronger with Freedom," *NYT*, Apr 20, 1917, 2. See Young, 402–403.

63. Weizmann, *Trial*, 206–207.

64. Weizmann, *Trial*, 57–58, 193–194.

65. Reinharz, "Balfour," 463–464. See generally Reinharz, "Balfour," 455–499. Weizmann, *Trial*, 206–207. See Gillon, 133–134.

66. "'Must Fight Only to Save Russia' Kerensky Declares," *WP*, Oct 22, 1917, 1. "Petrograd Council Demands Early Peace," *NYT*, Oct 25, 1917, 2. See Young, 388–389. See generally Reinharz, "Balfour," 455–499.

67. Weizmann, *Trial*, 206–207.

68. Rabinowitz, Ezekiel, *Justice Louis D. Brandeis: The Zionist Chapter of his Life* (New York: Philosophical Library, 1968), 71–72. Weizmann, *Trial*, 206–207.

69. Wiseman, Sir William, "Notes of an Interview with the President at the White House, October 16, 1918," Edward M. House Papers, Yale University Library as cited by Nelson, Keith, *Victors Divided: America and the Allies in Germany, 1918–1923* (Berkeley: UC Press, 1975), 270n59. Weizmann, *Trial*, 206–207.

70. Weizmann, *Trial*, 206–207.

71. Weizmann, *Trial*, 208.

72. Letter, Balfour to Lord Rothschild, Nov 2, 1917, reproduced in Israel Ministry of Foreign Affairs, "The Balfour Declaration," www.mfa.gov.il/MFA/Peace%20Process/Guide%20to%20the%20Peace%20Process/The%20Balfour%20Declaration.

73. "Russia Signs a Peace Treaty," *NYT*, Mar 4, 1918, 10. "Terms of Peace That Russia Signed, Involving Disarmament of Nation," *NYT*, Mar 6, 1918, 2.

74. Falls, Cyril, *Armageddon: 1918* (Philadelphia: J.B. Lippincott, 1964), 21–23, 26–27. Rickard, J., "Battle of Megiddo, 19–25 September 1918," *Military History Encyclopedia on the Web*, www.historyofwar.org/articles/battles_megiddo1918.html. See generally Falls.

75. Falls, 23–24, 36. Map, "Megiddo, 1918, Zero Hour, Sept. 18," Falls, ii. Rickard.

76. Falls, 106–110. Rickard. See Falls, 90–92.

77. Falls, 50–52. Rickard.

78. Falls, chap. 4. Rickard.

79. "British Drive Turks 19 Miles; Capture 3,000," *Chi Trib*, Sep 21, 1918, 2. Massey, W.T., "Turks Outwitted by Gen. Allenby," *NYT*, Sep 23, 1918, 1. Ottoman Resistance West of Jordan Blotted Out," *WP*, Sep 23, 1918, 1, 2. "40,000 Turks in Trap; 2 Armies Are Wiped Out," *Chi Trib*, Sep 24, 1918, 3. Falls, chaps. 8, 9. Rickard.

## Chapter 7: Creating Iraq

1. See Ferrier, R.W., *The History of the British Petroleum Company*, vol. 1: *The Developing Years, 1901–1932* (Cambridge, UK:Cambridge University Press, 1982), 42–73. See Black, *BoB*, 119–120.

2. See Ferrier, 42–73. See Black, *BoB*, 119–120.

3. Letter, C. Greenway to Foreign Office (FO), Feb 24, 1916: BNA T1/11952/20174/1916 pt. 1 no. 119238. See confidential letter, de Bunsen to Secretary of the Treasury, Mar 2, 1916: BNA T1/11952/20174/1916 pt. 1 no. 119238.

4. de Bunsen to Secretary of the Treasury. Kent, Marian, *Oil and Empire: British Policy and Mesopotamian Oil 1900–1920* (London: Macmillan Press Ltd., 1976), 129–130.

5. Letter, A. Hirtzel to Under Secretary of State, Apr 1, 1916: BNA FO371/2768 no. 62655.

6. Gulbenkian, C. S., "Memoirs of Calouste Sarkis Gulbenkian with Particular Relation to the Origins and Foundation of the Iraq Petroleum Company Limited," Sep 16, 1945: NA RG59 890.G.6363/3-148, 17.

7. Gulbenkian, "Memoirs," 18.

8. "Tripartite (Sykes-Picot) Agreement for the Partition of the Ottoman Empire: Britain, France and Russia," quoted in J. C. Hurewitz, ed., *Diplomacy in the Near and Middle East*, vol. 2 (Gerrards Cross, UK: Archive Editions, 1987), 19. Longrigg, Stephen H., *The Origins*

*and Early History of the Iraq Petroleum Company, Known from 1912 to 1929 as the Turkish Petroleum Company* (BP Archives, 1968), 55, 88. Gulbenkian, "Memoirs," 23.

9. Letter, W. Graham Greene to Under Secretary of State, Apr 14, 1916: BNA T1/11952/20174/1916 pt. 1 no. 19238. See "H. M. Petroleum Executive," memo, Mar 18, 1918: BNA T1/12144/11109. See telegram, Walter Long to Sir Frederick Black, Mar 14, 1918: BNA T1/12144/11109. Ferrier, 214.

10. Greene to Under Secretary of State. See Kent, 132–139.

11. Ferrier, 218. Letter, C. Greenway to Inchcape, Apr 11, 1917: BNA T1/12054 no. 119238.

12. Ferrier, 218–219. See "Summary of Profits for 18 Months Ended 31st March, 1918, Anglo Persian Oil Company," Dec 17, 1918: BNA T1/12342/26812. Greenway, "Memorandum re: Purchase of British Petroleum Company and Allied Concerns," May 31, 1917: BNA T1/12054 no. 119238. "Finance Arrangements for Purchase of British Petroleum Co. & O.," ca. May 1917: BNA T1/12054 no. 119238.

13. "Oil Interests in Which the Anglo Persian Oil Company Are Concerned Outside of the Area Covered by Their Persian Concern," memorandum, ca. Apr 1918: BNA T1/12366/35297/1919 no. 14799.

14. Letter, L. D. Wakely to the Under Secretary of State, Dec 18, 1919: BNA T1/12544/18025/1920 no. 55286.

15. Letter, C. Greenway to the Secretary of the Treasury, Aug 2, 1918: BNA T1/12366/35297/1919.

16. Greenway to Secretary of the Treasury.

17. Admiral Sir E. J. W. Slade, "The Petroleum Situation in the British Empire," Jul 29, 1918: BNA CAB21/119 no. 5264, 1–6.

18. Slade, 6. See letter, M. P. A. Hankey to Prime Minister, Aug 1, 1918: BNA CAB21/119.

19. Maj. Gen. F. H. Sykes, "Notes by the Chief of the Air Staff on Admiralty Memorandum No. G.T./5267 dated 30th July 1918," Aug 9, 1918: BNA CAB21/119. Letter, M. P. A. Hankey to Sir Eric Geddes, Jul 30, 1918: BNA CAB21/119.

20. Townshend, Maj. Gen. Charles Vere Ferrers, *My Campaign* (New York: James A. McCann, 1920), 246–275, 280–282.

21. Wilson, Lt. Col. Sir Arnold T., *Mesopotamia 1917–1920: A Clash of Loyalties* (London: Oxford University Press, 1931), 16. Hankey to Prime Minister, Aug 1, 1918.

22. Wilson, *1917–1920*, 18.

23. Wilson, *1917–1920*, 17–19.

24. Wilson, *1917–1920*, 16, 19–20.

25. Wilson, *1917–1920*, 17, 19–21.

26. Wilson, *1917–1920*, 18–21.

27. Wilson, *1917–1920*, 21, 22–23.

## Chapter 8: Peace and Petroleum

1. See Buchanan, Sir George, *The Tragedy of Mesopotamia* (London: William Blackwood and Sons, Ltd., 1938), 266–267.

2. Letter, Brig. Gen. Macdonough to Sir Arthur Nicolson, Jan 7, 1916, as cited by Efraim Karsh & Inari Karsh, *Empires of the Sand: The Struggle for Mastery in the Middle East, 1789–1923* (Cambridge, MA: Harvard University Press, 1999), 225.

3. Wilson, Woodrow, "Fourteen Points Speech," address to Congress, Jan 18, 1918.

4. Wilson, "Fourteen Points Speech."

5. See Tripp, Charles, *A History of Iraq* (Cambridge, UK: Cambridge University Press, 2000), 34–36. See Black, *The Transfer Agreement* (Washington D.C.: Dialog Press, 2009), 72–76. See Dawn, C. Ernest, "The Origins of Arab Nationalism," in Rashid Khalidi et al., eds., *The Origins of Arab Nationalism* (New York: Columbia University Press, 1991), 3–23. See Sowards, Steven W., "Lecture 13: Serbian Nationalism from the 'Nacertanije' to the Yugoslav Kingdom," Michigan State University Library, http://staff.lib.msu.edu/sowards/balkan/lect13.htm. See "League of Nations: Armenia: Correspondence between the President of the Armenian Delegation and the Secretary General," Aug 25, 1921: LoN Archive A. 20, 1921 VII.

6. "Laws of War: Laws and Customs of War on Land (Hague II)," Jul 29, 1899, Section III, LoN Archive. "Laws of War: Laws and Customs of War on Land (Hague IV)," Oct 18, 1907, Section III, LoN Archive. Ireland, Philip Willard, *Iraq: A Study in Political Development* (NY: Macmillan Company, 1938), 80–85.

7. Paris, Timothy J., "British Middle East Policy-Making after the First World War: The Lawrentian and Wilsonian Schools," *Historical Journal*, vol. 41 (1998), 773–774, 779–782. Marlowe, J., *Late Victorian: The Life of Sir Arnold Talbot Wilson* (London: Cresset Publishers, 1967), 13. Letter, A. P. Waterfield to Barstow, Apr 9, 1919: BNA T1/112544/18025/1920. Letter, Col. A. T. Wilson to Sir A. Hirtzel, Mar 5, 1920: BL Wilson papers, Add. mss 52455C, as cited by Paris, 779.

8. Paris, 773–774, 779–782. Marlowe, J., *Late Victorian: The Life of Sir Arnold Talbot Wilson* (London: Cresset Publishers, 1967), 13. Letter, A. P. Waterfield to Barstow, Apr 9, 1919: BNA T1/112544/18025/1920. Letter, Col. A. T. Wilson to Sir A. Hirtzel, Mar 5, 1920: BL Wilson papers, Add. mss 52455C, as cited by Paris, 779.

9. Private letter, Capt. A. T. Wilson to Col. C. E. Yate, Nov 28, 1914: BNA FO371/2482 no. 12124. See also "Govt's Future Action in Mesopotamia," minute sheet, Jan 28, 1915: BNA FO371/2482 no. 12124. See also letter, Col. Yate to Edward Grey, Jan 28, 1915: BNA FO371/2482 no. 12124.

10. Minutes, Nov 6, 1915: BL L/PS/10/524, as cited by Paris, 779. Paris, 779. Also see Wilson, Sir Arnold T., *A Clash of Loyalties: Mesopotamia, 1917–1920: A Personal Record* (London: Oxford University Press, 1931), v.

11. Busch, Briton Cooper, *Britain, India, and the Arabs* (Berkeley, CA: University of California Press, 1971), 22–24. Ireland, 96–97.

12. Ireland, 81–82, 87–89. Wilson, Lt. Col. Sir Arnold T., *Loyalties: Mesopotamia 1914–1917* (London: Oxford University Press, 1930), 283–284, 321–322. Letter and attached note, J. S Grosland to Craig, Sep 25, 1916: BNA T1/12047/14548 no. 19238. See also Wilson, *1914–1917*, 88.

13. Ireland, 72.

14. Ireland, 81–84.

15. Ireland, 86–87.

16. Ireland, 81. Wilson, *1914–1917*, 66–67.

17. Wilson, *1914–1917*, 290. Ireland, 74–75.

18. "Note on the Future Status and Administration of Basrah," Feb 24, 1915: BNA FO800/377. "The Prospects of British Trade in Mesopotamia and the Persian Gulf," 1919: BL L/PS/RS/386, 41–44. See Buchanan, Sir George, *The Tragedy of Mesopotamia* (London: William Blackwood and Sons Ltd., 1938), 276. Wilson, *1914–1917*, 196–198.

19. "Note on the Future Status and Administration of Basrah." "The Prospects of British Trade in Mesopotamia and the Persian Gulf," 41–44.

20. Buchanan, 5–7, 134–138. Wilson, *1914–1917*, 196–198. See telegrams, Feb 1920: BNA T1/12544/18025/1920.

21. "The Prospects of British Trade in Mesopotamia and the Persian Gulf," 41–44. "Note on the Future Status and Administration of Basrah," 2, 7.

22. "The Prospects of British Trade in Mesopotamia and the Persian Gulf," 42. Buchanan, 248–250.

23. "Baghdad Trade and Politics," *Times*, Jun 11, 1910, 7–8, as cited by Haddad, Mahmoud, "Iraq Before World War I: A Case of Anti-European Arab Ottomanism," in Khalidi et al., eds., *The Origins of Arab Nationalism* (New York: Columbia University Press, 1991), 126. Willcocks, Sir William, *Sixty Years in the East* (London: 1935), 72, as cited by Haddad, 126.

24. Tripp, 36–37. Ireland, 111–113. "Report on the Conditions for Trade in Mesopotamia Prepared in the Office of the Civil Commissioner in Baghdad," memo, ca. Aug 1919: BL L/PS/10/386. See also "Second Additional Note on the Situation in Kurdistan," memo, Jan 10, 1920: BL L/PS/10/782.

25. Ireland, 74–77.

26. Wilson, 79.

27. Ireland, 94–95. Wilson, 77–79.

28. Ireland, 94–95.

29. Tauber, Eliezer, *The Arab Movements in World War I* (London: Frank Cass and Co., 1993), 32. Ireland, 76–77. Wilson, 73, 377.

30. Tauber, 32–33. Wilson, 74–75.

31. Tauber, 33. Wilson, 75. Letter, Gertrude Bell to Lowthian Bell, May 4, 1918: Gertrude Bell Letters. Letter, Gertrude Bell to Lowthian Bell, Sep 13, 1918: Gertrude Bell Letters.

32. Wilson, 75–76.

33. Wilson, 76.

34. Letter, Lord Eustace Percy to Sir George Clerk, Jun 5, 1919: BNA FO368/2095 no. 85781. Letter, Crowe to Curzon, Oct 10, 1919: Lloyd George mss, F/33/2/66, as cited by Kent, Marian, *Oil and Empire: British Policy and Mesopotamian Oil 1900–1920* (London: Macmillan Press Ltd., 1976), 141.

35. Letter, French Minister to Secretary of State for Foreign Affairs (trans.), Jan 6, 1919: BNA FO368/2095 no. 3251. See "Agreement for Participation of French and British Interests in World Oil Production," minute sheet, Jan 8, 1919: BNA FO368/2095 no. 3251. "Statement of D'Arcy Exploration Company's Claim to Mesopotamian Oil Concession," Nov 12, 1918: BP 100687.

36. Letter, French Minister to Secretary of State for Foreign Affairs." See "Agreement for Participation of French and British Interests in World Oil Production," minute sheet, Jan 8, 1919: BNA FO368/2095 no. 3251. "Statement of D'Arcy Exploration Company's Claim to Mesopotamian Oil Concession," Nov 12, 1918: BP 100687.

37. Letter, M. Hankey to Stanley Baldwin, Dec 13, 1918: BNA T1/12442/54465/1919 no. 171.

38. Hankey to Baldwin. Letter, Stanley Baldwin to A. H. Stanley, Dec 21, 1918: BNA BT15/76 no. 119238. See handwritten notes, Dec 21, 1918: BNA T1/12442/54465/1919.

39. Hankey to Baldwin. Baldwin to Stanley. Handwritten notes of Dec 21, 1918.

40. "Agreement for Participation of French and British Interests in World Oil Production."

41. Letter, Clemenceau to President du Conseil, Ministre de la Guerre, and Commissaire General aux Essences & Combustibles, Paris, Jan 30, 1919: BNA FO368/2242 no. 21777.

42. Kent 140–144. Hankey to Baldwin. Baldwin to Stanley. Handwritten notes of Dec 21, 1918.

43. Longrigg, Stephen H., *The Origins and Early History of the Iraq Petroleum Company, Known from 1912 to 1929 as the Turkish Petroleum Company* (BP Archives, 1968), 98–99.

44. Kent, 143–146.

45. Kent, 145.

46. Curzon to Balfour, dispatch 1837, Apr 2, 1919: BNA FO608/231 no. 2642.

47. Longrigg, 97–98. See also Gulbenkian, C. S., "Memoirs of Calouste Sarkis Gulbenkian with Particular Relation to the Origins and Foundation of the Iraq Petroleum Company Limited," Sep 16, 1945: NA RG59 890.G.6363/3-148, 20–24.

48. Longrigg, 92, 272–274.

49. Longrigg, 94–96. See Kent, 178–181. Earle, Edward Mead, "The Turkish Petroleum Company—A Study in Oleaginous Diplomacy," *Political Science Quarterly*, vol. 39, (1924), 273. See "The Royal Dutch Shell Groups," memo, Oct 4, 1919: BNA T1/12351/30112.

50. Kent, 178.

51. Kent, 178.

52. Kent, 179. See "The Royal Dutch Shell Groups."

53. Kent, 179–180. "The Royal Dutch Shell Groups."

54. Earle, 273.

55. "B. 322. Mesopotamia Oil Policy," memo, Apr 10, 1919: BNA T1/122544/18025/1920.

56. "B. 322. Mesopotamia Oil Policy." Waterfield to Barstow. Office of the Civil Commissioner to the Under Secretary of State for India, Apr 20, 1920: BNA T1/122544/18025/1920. "Anglo-Persian Oil Co., Ltd. Baghdad," memorandum, Jul 30, 1919: BNA T1/122544/18025/1920. "Minutes of an Inter-Departmental Meeting held at the India Office, on Monday, 27th October 1919, to consider Colonel Wilson's proposals regarding the disposal of the Fleet and Oil Barges in Mesopotamia," memorandum, Nov 1, 1919: BNA T1/122544/18025/1920. Letter, L. D. Wakely to the India Office, Nov 19, 1919: BNA T1/122544/18025/1920. See draft letter to the Anglo-Persian Oil Company, Limited, ca. Apr 1919: BNA T1/122544/18025/1920.

57. Longrigg, 94. See also Kent, 152.

58. Kent, 172.

59. Kent, 172.

60. Kent, 172–174. See also Longrigg, 272–274.

61. "Covenant of the League of Nations," Article 22.

62. "Covenant of the League of Nations," Article 22.

63. Ferrier, R. W., *The History of the British Petroleum Company* (Cambridge, UK: Cambridge University Press, 1982), 357. Kent, 148.

64. "The Menace of Foreign State Monopolies to the American Petroleum Industry," memorandum, ca. Sep 1919: NA RG59/250/23/25/3 box 7236. Curzon to Cambon, Jul 27, 1919: BNA FO368/2095. Letter, French Chargé d'affaires to Curzon, Aug 12/13, 1919: BNA FO368/2095 no. 115404.

65. Longrigg, 272–274.

66. Longrigg, 274.

67. Kent, 149–155.

## Chapter 9: Jihad

1. See generally Wheatcroft, Andrew, *The Ottomans: Dissolving Images* (London: Viking, 1995), chaps. 7 and 8 ("The Lustful Turk" and "The Terrible Turk").

2. "The Bulgarian Atrocities," *NYT*, Jul 29, 1876, 2. "The Barbarities in Bulgaria," *NYT*, Aug 29, 1876, 1. "Despatch from Mr. Henry Wood, Correspondent of the American 'United Press' at Constantinople; Published in the American Press, 14th August 1915," in Arnold J. Toynbee, ed., *The Treatment of Armenians in the Ottoman Empire* (London: Hodder & Stoughton, 1916), 2–3.

3. Holcomb, Willard, "Abdul a Great Ruler," *WP*, Apr 28, 1909, 2. See "The War on the Danube," *NYT*, Sep 6, 1876, 1. Palmer, Alan, *The Decline and Fall of the Ottoman Empire* (New York: M. Evans & Co., 1992), 146.

4. Morgenthau, Henry, *Ambassador Morgenthau's Story* (Garden City, NY: Doubleday, Page & Co., 1918), 337–338, 339. See Varzhabedian, D. K., "Armenians in Turkey," *WP*, Jan 7, 1895, 2. See poster, "You Won't Let Me Stave, Will You?," reproduced in Balakian, Peter, *The Burning Tigris: The Armenian Genocide and America's Response* (New York: HarperCollins Publishers, 2003), 236ff.

5. Morgenthau, 333–334.

6. Fox, Albert, "Ratification Refused; 49 To 35, Senate Vote; Pact Sent To Wilson," *WP*, Mar 20, 1920, 1. Gerard, James, "The Mandate for Armenia," *NYT*, Jun 1, 1919, 38. "Why America Should Accept Mandate for Armenia," *NYT*, Jul 6, 1919, 44.

7. "The Balfour Declaration," Nov 2, 1917, reproduced in J. C. Hurewitz, ed., *Diplomacy in the Near And Middle East*, vol. 2 (New York: Van Nostrand Company, 1956), 26.

8. "The Balfour Declaration."

9. See "Resolution of the General Syrian Congress, 2 July 1919," reproduced in Hurewitz, vol. 2, 62–64.

10. "Anglo–French Declaration, 7 November 1918," reproduced in Hurewitz, vol. 2, 30. See introduction, "British and Anglo–French Statements to the Arabs, January–November 1918," reproduced in Hurewitz, vol. 2, 28–29.

11. "Anglo–French Declaration, 7 November 1918."

12. Tanenbaum, Jan Karl, "France and the Arab Middle East, 1914–1920," *Transactions of the American Philosophical Society*, vol. 68, pt. 7 (1978), 21, 34, 35. Quai d'Orsay memo, "Note sur la Syrie," Feb 14, 1919: Archives du Ministère des Affaires Etrangères (AAE), série: Levant S-L-C, vol. 10, fol. 46, quoted by Tanenbaum, 27.

13. "Amir Faysal's Memorandum to the Supreme Council at the Paris Peace Conference, 1 January 1919," reproduced in Hurewitz, vol. 2, 38–39.

14. "Amir Faysal's Memorandum to the Supreme Council."

15. "Amir Faysal's Memorandum to the Supreme Council."

16. "Amir Faysal's Memorandum to the Supreme Council."

17. "Amir Faysal's Memorandum to the Supreme Council."

18. Weizmann, Chaim, *Trial And Error: The Autobiography of Chaim Weizmann* (New York: Harper & Brothers, 1949), 234–235. "The Faisal-Weizmann Agreement, January 1919," reproduced in George Antonius, *The Arab Awakening: The Story of the Arab National Movement* (New York: Capricorn Books, 1965), 437–439.

19. "The Faisal-Weizmann Agreement."

20. Letter, Clemenceau to Faisal, Apr 17, 1919: AAE, série: Levant, Arabie-Hedjaz, vol. 4, fol. 85, and "Declaration," Apr 17, 1919: AAE, série: Levant, Arabie-Hedjaz, vol. 4 fols. 36–37, as cited by Tanenbaum, 30. Tanenbaum, 29, 30, 31. See letter, Phillip Hitti to the editor, *NYT*, Feb 3, 1919, 32. Generally see Longrigg, Stephen, *Syria and Lebanon under French Mandate* (London: Oxford University Press, 1958).

21. Letter, Faisal to Clemenceau, Apr 20, 1919: AAE, série: Levant S-L-C, vol. 12, fols. 133–134, quoted by Tanenbaum, 30.

22. "Resolution of the General Syrian Congress at Damascus, 2 July 1919." Tanenbaum, 27–31. Antonius, 297. See letter, Hitti to editor.

23. de Caix, memo, "Esquisse de l'organisation de la Syrie sous le mandat français," Jul 17, 1920: AAE série: Levant S-L-C, vol. 31, fol. 28, quoted by Tanenbaum, 36. Tanenbaum, 31, 36. Longrigg, *Lebanon and Syria*, 75–77, 78, 79, 82.

24. "The Provisional Agreement of January 6, 1920," AAE, série: Levant: 1918-1920, Arabie, vol. 8, fols. 83–86 quoted by Tanenbaum, 44–45. Tanenbaum, 35–36. Longrigg, *Lebanon and Syria*, 82. "Henri Gouraud," *firstworldwar.com*, www.firstworldwar.com/bio/gouraud.htm. "General Gouraud on the Second Battle of the Marne, 16 July 1918," *firstworldwar.com*, www.firstworldwar.com/source/marne2_gouraud.htm.

25. Tanenbaum, 37.

26. Encrypted telegram, Egyptian G. H. Q. to War Office, Mar 12, 1920: BL L/MIL/5/799. Tanenbaum, 37–38. Antonius, 304.

27. Letter, Alexandre Millerand to Paul Cambon, Mar 13, 1920: AAE, série: Levant S-L-C, vol. 25, fol. 5, quoted by Tanenbaum, 38. Letter, Lord Curzon to General Allenby, quoted in letter, Cambon to Millerand, Mar 13, 1920: AAE, série: Levant S-L-C, vol. 24, fol. 55, quoted by Tanenbaum, 38.

28. Letter, Curzon to Allenby, quoted by Tanenbaum, 38. Tanenbaum, 38.

29. Elkis, Abram, "Former Envoys' Remedies for Evil of Turkish Rule," *WP*, Mar 21, 1920, 64.

30. "Imperialism in Turkey," *WP*, Apr 1, 1920, 6.

31. "San Remo Meeting to Take Up Turkey," *NYT*, Apr 3, 1920, 3. "The Carving of Turkey," *WP*, Apr 18, 1920, 24. See James, Edwin, "Asks British Denial of Turkish Treaty," *NYT*, May 8, 1920, 3. See Secretary of State for India, "Note on the Causes of the Outbreak in Mesopotamia," secret note, ca. Aug 1922: BL L/MIL/5/799. See "Chronology, 1920," League of Nations Photo Archive.

32. "The Mandate for Syria and Lebanon, 24 July 1922," reproduced in Longrigg, *Lebanon and Syria*, 376–380. "The Mandate for Palestine, 24 July 1922," reproduced in Hurewitz, vol. 2, 107–111. See "Treaty of Alliance: Great Britain and Iraq, 10 October 1922," reproduced in Hurewitz, vol. 2, 111–114. See letter, John Davis to Earl Curzon, May 12, 1920: BNA BT15/16/119238.

33. Wolff, Stefan, "Long-Term Consequences of Forced Population Transfers: Institutionalized Ethnic Cleansing as the Road to New (In)-Stability? A European Perspective," in Vardy, Steven Bela, T. Hunt, Tooley, & Agnes Huszar Vardy, eds., *Ethnic Cleansing in Twentieth-Century Europe* (Boulder, CO: East European Monographs, 2003), 773–786. See De Zayas, A., "International Law and Mass Population Transfers," *Harvard International Law Journal*, vol. 207 (1975).

34. Wolff. "Massacre by Ukrainians," *NYT*, Sep 21, 1920, 13. Kenez, Peter, "Pogroms and White Ideology," in Klier & Lambroza, 294, 295. See "Red Cross Report on Bolshevist Barbarities in Kiev," *NYT*, Sep 20, 1920, XX2. "Jews Burned Alive in a Synagogue," *MG*, Sep 22, 1920. See "Suffering of Jews after War Related," *NYT*, Aug 15, 1920, 12. See "Aid for Ukrainian Jews," *NYT*, Nov 8, 1920, 29. See De Zayas. See also Bernstein, Herman, "Blunders Through Which Allies Have Aided Bolsheviki," *NYT*, Aug 29, 1920, XX1. See also "FRANCE: Petlura Trial," *Time*, Nov 7, 1927, www.time.com.

35. "Draft Agreement Concerning Petroleum," confidential attachment to letter, John Davis to Secretary of State, May 7, 1920: NA RG59 800.6363/113.

36. "Memorandum of Agreement between M. Phillipe Berthelot, Directeur des Affaires politiques et commerciales au Ministère des Affaires Etrangères, and Professor Sir John Cadman, KCMG, Director in Charge of His Majesty's Petroleum Department," Apr 24, 1920: BP IPC 168-F4: FO Agreement Correspondence Oct 1912–Oct 1927.

37. "Memorandum of Agreement."

38. "Memorandum of Agreement."

39. "Memorandum of Agreement." Letter, Secretary–General of the Hedjaz Delegation to Secretary-General of the Council of the League of Nations, May 8, 1920: LoN K1 1/4284/4284. Kent, Marian, *Oil and Empire: British Policy and Mesopotamian Oil 1900–1920* (London: Macmillan Press Ltd., 1976), 155. See telegram, Department of State to American Embassy, London, May 10, 1920: NA RG59 800.6363/111a.

40. Letter, Secretary-General of the Hedjaz Delegation to Secretary–General of the Council of the League of Nations.

41. Letter, Secretary-General of the Hedjaz Delegation to Secretary–General of the Council of the League of Nations.

42. "Riots in Jerusalem," *NYT*, Apr 8, 1920, 15. See Longrigg, *Syria and Lebanon*, 96–97. See "Note on the Causes of the Outbreak in Mesopotamia." See letter, Millerand to Gouraud, May 11, 1920: AAE, série: Levant S-L-C, vol. 27, fol. 240, quoted by Tanenbaum, 39–40. See Lawrence, T. E., "A Report on Mesopotamia," *Sunday Times*, Aug 22, 1920. See telegram to Wilson, Apr 7, 1919: BNA AIR2/122.

43. See letter, Hardinge to Allenby, Jul 16, 1920, quoted by Tanenbaum, 39. Letter, Curzon to Millerand, May 18, 1920: AAE, série: Levant S-L-C, vol. 28, fol. 35, quoted by Tanenbaum, 40. "Proposition d'une reunion de conference pour redaction d'instructions au general Gouraud," May 19, 1920: AAE, série: Levant S-L-C, vol. 28, fols. 76–77, quoted by Tanenbaum, 40. Tanenbaum, 39–40.

44. Letters, Millerand to Gouraud, July 23 and 24, 1920: AAE, série: Levant S-L-C, vol. 31, fols. 117 and 164, quoted by Tanenbaum, 41. Longrigg, *Syria and Lebanon*, 101–102.

45. "French Begin War on Feisal in Syria; Columns Moving on Aleppo and Damascus," *NYT*, Jul 17, 1920, 1. "Syria Arms For War," *WP*, Jul 19, 1920, 1. "Feisal Mobilizes Against French in Syria; Gouraud Reported Ready to Move Today," *NYT*, 12. James, Edwin, "French Rout Emir; Enter Damascus," *NYT*, Jul 26, 1920, 1. Longrigg, *Syria and Lebanon*, 102–103.

46. "Anglo-French Oil Agreement Is Out," *NYT*, Jul 24, 1920, 7.

47. "Ten Thousand Jews Thank Great Britain," *NYT*, Jul 13, 1920, 12. See "Zionists Elect Brandeis," *WP*, Jul 24, 1920, 4. See photo, The London Zionist Conference, Jewish Agency for Israel, www.jafi.org.il. See "The Foundation Fund," *Zionist Bulletin*, Jul 26, 1920, 8 reproduced in "The London Zionist Conference 1920 and the Foundation of Keren Hayesod," The Jewish Agency for Israel.

48. Antonius, 312.

49. "Chart Showing Approximate Area Effected by One H. P. Machine Carrying 10–9.45 Gas Bombs," attachment to memo, C. A. S. to R. Brooke-Popham, Dec 13, 1919: BNA AIR2/122.

50. "Churchill Proposes to Guard Mesopotamia by Air Patrol," *NYT*, Mar 23, 1920, 1. "Report on Air Squadrons in Middle East," Nov 4, 1919: BNA AIR2/122. See memo, War Office, Apr 14, 1919: BNA AIR2/122.

51. Secret memo to Air Ministry, Apr 19, 1919: BNA AIR2/122.

52. "Weapons of War: Poison Gas," May 2002, First World War Online. War Department, "General Orders, No. 62," Jun 28, 1918: U. S. Army Center for Military History. See Black, *War against the Weak: Eugenics and America's Campaign to Create a Master Race* (Washington, DC: Dialog Press, 2009), 258.

53. Note to the Flying Office Directorate, Air Board, May 2, 1919: BNA AIR2/122.

54. Churchill, minutes, May 12, 1919, reproduced in Gilbert, Martin, *Winston S. Churchill, Companion* to vol. 4 (London: Heinemann: 1977), 649.

55. Churchill, minutes, May 12, 1919.

56. Memo, R. M. Groves, May 19, 1919: BNA AIR2/122. R. M. Groves, War Office minute sheet B9967, May 24, 1919: BNA AIR2/122.

57. Brooke-Popham, note, Jun 16, 1919: BNA AIR2/122.

58. Brooke-Popham, minute sheet 16A, Jun 16, 1919: BNA AIR2/122

59. Brooke-Popham, memo, Jun 30, 1919: BNA AIR2/122.

60. Brooke-Popham, memo, Jun 30, 1919. "Chart Showing Approximate Area Effected by One H. P. Machine Carrying 10–9.45 Gas Bombs."

61. Tauber, Eliezar, "The Struggle for Dayr al-Zur: The Determination of Borders between Syria and Iraq," *International Journal of Middle East Studies*, vol. 23 (1991), 367. Wilson, Sir Arthur T., *A Clash of Loyalties: Mesopotamia, 1917–1920: A Personal Record* (London: Oxford University Press, 1931), 231.

62. Wilson, 232. Tauber, 367.

63. "British Air Service Plan," *WP*, Dec 15, 1919, 4. Wilson, 234. Meilinger, Philip, "Trenchard and 'Morale Bombing': The Evolution of Royal Air Force Doctrine before World War II," *Journal of Military History*, vol. 60 (1996), 251.

64. Secret telegram to War Office, Apr 6, 1920: BL L/MIL/5/798.

65. Wilson, 249.

66. "Note on the Causes of the Outbreak in Mesopotamia." Telegram, Wilson to Secretary of State for India, May 8, 1920, reproduced in "Note on the Causes of the Outbreak in Mesopotamia."

67. Telegram, Wilson to Secretary of State for India, May 8, 1920.

68. Vinogradov, Amal, "The 1920 Revolt in Iraq Reconsidered: The Role of Tribes in National Politics," *International Journal of Middle East Studies*, vol 3 (1972), 135. Wilson, 253–254.

69. Vinogradov, 134–135. Wilson, 253.

70. Vinogradov, 135. Wilson, 255.

71. Vinogradov, 135–136.

72. Ireland, Phillip Willard, *Iraq: A Study in Political Development* (New York: Macmillan Company, 1938), 238–239. Wilson, 273.

73. Wilson, 274.

74. Ireland, 262.

75. Ireland, 259.

76. "Lost 161 in Mesopotamia," *NYT*, Jul 20, 1920, 9. Ireland, 266, 267. Wilson, 277, 278.

77. "Lost 161 in Mesopotamia." Wilson, 278–279, 279n. Ireland, 266, 267–268, 269.

78. Ireland, 268. "French Rout Emir; Enter Damascus."

79. Churchill, "Situation in Mesopotamia, 20th August 1920," secret Cabinet memo, Aug 20, 1920: BL L/MIL/5/799. Wilson, 272, 282, 293.

80. Churchill, "Situation in Mesopotamia, 2nd September 1920," secret Cabinet memo, Aug 2, 1920: BL L/MIL/5/800. Wilson, 294.

81. Ireland, 270–271. Wilson, 292.

82. Wilson, 298. Despatch from High Commissioner, Baghdad, Oct 4, 1920: BL L/MIL/5/800.

83. Wilson, 298. Ireland, 272n3.

84. Secret telegram from Civil Commissioner, Baghdad, Aug 6, 1920: BL L/MIL/5/799.

85. Wilson, 270–271, 277.

86. Wilson, 271.

87. Churchill, "Recent Events in Mesopotamia," secret Cabinet memo, Sep 30, 1920: BL L/MIL/5/800.

88. "Churchill Proposes to Guard Mesopotamia by Air Patrol." Secret telegram from War Office, Oct 5, 1920: BL L/MIL/5/800.

89. "Situation in Mesopotamia, 2nd September 1920." Secret telegram, General Officer Commanding (GOCM), Mesopotamia to War Office, Aug 28, 1920, reproduced in "Situation in Mesopotamia, 2nd September 1920." Secret memo, GOCM to War Office, Sep 30, 1920: BL L/MIL/5/800. Vinogradov, 137.

90. Secret telegram, GOCM, Mesopotamia to War Office, Aug 28, 1920, reproduced in "Situation in Mesopotamia, 2nd September 1920." See Secret telegram, GOCM to War Office, Sep 28, 1920: BL L/MIL/5/800. Secret telegram, War Office to GOCM, Oct 5, 1920: BL L/MIL/5/800.

91. Churchill, "Air Staff Memorandum on the Air Force as an Alleged Cause of the Loss of Popularity of the Mesopotamia Civil Administration," Aug 27, 1920: BL L/MIL/5/800. Meilinger, 244.

92. Meilinger, 244. See "Sir Arthur 'Bomber' Harris (1892-1984)," BBC History, www. bbc.co.uk.

93. Vinogradov, 137, 138–139.

94. Vinogradov, 138.

95. Wilson, 321. Ireland, 277–278, 286–287, 326, 335. See "Churchill's Speech Displeases Paris," *NYT*, Jun 16, 1921, 3.

96. Fraser, Lovat, "The War-Mongers," *Daily Mail*, July 12, 1920, quoted by Busch, Briton Cooper, *Britain, India, and the Arabs, 1914–1921* (Berkeley, CA: University of California Press, 1971), 409. Antonius, 315. Ireland, 273. See secret telegram, War Office to G. H. Q. Mesopotamia, Sep 8, 1920: BL L/MIL/5/800.

97. Dobbs, Sir Henry, "Britain's Work in Iraq and Prospects of the New State," address to the Royal Empire Society, Feb 1933, quoted by Buchanan, Sir George, *The Tragedy of Mesopotamia* (London: William Blackwood & Sons, 1938), 285.

98. Buchanan, 285–286.

99. Ferrier, 308–309.

100. *Iraq: Treaty with King Feisal*, Cmd. 1757 (1922). "British Conclude Alliance with Irak," *NYT*, Oct 12, 1922, 5.

101. Secret telegrams to War Office, Aug 22, 1920, Aug 24, 1920, Aug 26, 1920, and Aug 26, 1920, reproduced in Churchill, "Situation in Mesopotamia," secret cabinet memo, Sep 2, 1920: BL L/MIL/5/800.

102. *Iraq: Treaty with King Feisal*. "British Conclude Alliance With Irak."

103. See letter to Mead Taylor, Apr 26, 1924: BNA BT15/27/119238.

104. Wilson, Woodrow, "Fourteen Points Speech," address to Congress, Jan 18, 1918. Letter, Bainbridge Colby to Earl Curzon, Nov 20, 1920: NA RG59 800.6363/196A, *FRUS* 1920, 669, 670.

105. Turkish Petroleum Company, *Limited Convention with The Government of Iraq*, Mar 14, 1925: BNA CO730/158/9/119238. "The Omens from Lausanne," *WP*, Jan 25, 1923, 6. See Black, *BoB*, chap. 15.

## Chapter 10: Germany and the Middle East

1. Simon, Reeva S., *Iraq Between the Two World Wars: The Militarist Origins of Tyranny* (NY: Columbia University Press, 2004), 5, 7–11, 13, 14–16. See Simon, 2–3. Grant, Jonathan, "The Sword of the Sultan: Ottoman Arms Imports, 1854–1914," *The Journal of Military History*, vol. 66 (2002), 16, 22–24, 27. Wild, Stefan, "National Socialism in the Arab Near East between 1933 and 1939," *Die Welt des Islams*, new ser., bd. 25 (1985), 128–130. "The Terms of Peace," *NY Trib*, Jan 28, 1878, 4. "Peace at Last," *NY Trib*, Feb 4 1878, 1. See "Germany and Turkey," *MG*, Feb 20, 1882, 8. See "German Enterprise in the East," *Times*, Oct 28, 1898, 75. See Grant, "Sword," 14.

2. Wild, 129–130. Simon, 30, 31. See generally Fichte, Johann Gottlieb, *Addresses to the German Nation*, R.F. Jones & G.H. Turnbull, trans. (Chicago; London: Open Court Publishing, 1922). See generally Engelbrecht, Helmuth Carol, *Johann Gottlieb Fichte: a Study of his Political Writings with Special Reference to his Nationalism* (NY: Columbia University Press, 1968).

3. The Baghdad Railroad Convention, 5 March 1903, Cmd. 5635 (1911), 37–48 reproduced in J. C. Hurewitz, ed., *Diplomacy in the Near and Middle East*, vol. 1, 1535–1914 (Gerrards Cross, UK: Archive Editions, 1987), 252–263. Longrigg, Stephen H., *Oil in the Middle East: Its Discovery and Development* (London: Oxford University Press, 1968), 27. Longrigg, Stephen H., *The Origins and Early History of the Iraq Petroleum Company, Known from 1912 to 1929 as the Turkish Petroleum Company* (BP Archives, 1968), 35. Kent, Marian, *Oil and Empire: British Policy and Mesopotamian Oil, 1900–1920* (London: Macmillan, 1976), 16. Rohrbach, Paul, *Bagdadbahn* (Berlin: Wiegandt & Grieben, 1911), quoted by Schonfield, Hugh, *The Suez Canal*

*in Peace and War, 1869–1969* (Coral Gables, FL: University of Miami Press, 1969), 62–63. Rohrbach, 43–44, quoted by Kent, *Oil*, 16. Black, *BoB*, 118.

4. "Kaiser William's Tour," *NY Trib*, Sep 12, 1898, 3. "Emperor William's Royal Pilgrimage Arrives at Jaffa, *Chi Trib*, Oct 28, 1898, 1. "The Kaiser in Palestine," *MG*, Nov 2, 1898, 6. See "Emperor William to Return," Nov 1, 1898, 1.

5. "The Kaiser at Jerusalem," *NYT*, Oct 31, 1898, 7. "The Kaiser's Tour in Palestine," *MG*, Nov 4, 1898, 5. "The Kaiser at Beyrout," *NY* Trib, Nov 6, 1898, 7. "The Kaiser in Jerusalem," *NYT*, Nov 27, 1898, 19. Avitzur, Shmuel, "The Power Plant on Two Rivers," *Israel Ministry of Foreign Affairs Newsletter*, May 22, 2003. See "Sees Armed Alliance between Germany and Turkey in the East," *Chi Trib*, Nov 6, 1898, 13. See "Germany and Turkey: Alleged Agreement between the Two Countries," *Chi Trib*, Nov 6, 1898, 13. See "Topics of the Times," *NYT*, Dec 4, 1898, 18.

6. "Agreement by the Shaikh of Kuwait Regarding the Non-reception of Foreign Representatives and the Non-cession of Territory to Foreign Powers or Subjects, 23rd January 1899," *The Road to Independence*, Al-Diwan Al-Amiri, www.da.gov.kw/eng/. "Exclusive Agreement: The Kuwayti Shaykh and Britain, 23 January 1899," reproduced in Hurewitz, vol. 1, 218–219. Tetreault, Mary Ann, "Autonomy, Necessity, and the Small State: Ruling Kuwait in the Twentieth Century," *International Organization*, vol. 45 (1991), 570–575. See Rush, Alan deLacy, ed., *Records of Kuwait, 1899–1961*, vol. 1 (London: Archive International, 1989), 149, as cited by Tetreault, 575. See Longrigg, *Oil*, 26.

7. Lawrence, T.E., *Seven Pillars of Wisdom* (London: Wordsworth Editions, 1997), 60. Trumpener, Ulrich, "Liman von Sanders and the German-Ottoman Alliance," *Journal of Contemporary History*, vol. 1 (1966), 179–180. "New German Head for Turks," *NYT*, Aug 12, 1915, 2. Suny, Ronald Grigor, "The Holocaust before the Holocaust: Reflections on the Armenian Genocide," in Hans-Lukas Keiser & Dominik J. Schaller, eds., *Der Völkermord den Armeniern und die Shoa / The Armenian Genocide and the Holocaust* (Zürich: Chronos, 2002), 89–90. Bloxham, Donald, "Power Politics, Prejudice, Protest, and Propaganda: a Reassessment of the German Role in the Armenian Genocide," in Keiser & Schaller, 223," Wild, 129–130. See generally Bloxham, "Power Politics," in Keiser & Schaller, 213–237. See Kiernan, Ben, *Blood and Soil: A World History of Genocide and Extermination from Sparta to Darfur* (New Haven: Yale University Press, 2007), chap. 10. See Trumpener, 181.

8. Yazbak, Mahmoud, "Templars as Proto-Zionists? The 'German Colony' in Late Ottoman Haifa," *Journal of Palestine Studies*, vol. 28 (1999), 40–54., Nicosia, Francis R.J., "Weimar Germany and the Palestine Question," *LBIY*, vol. 24 (1979), 322.

9. Friedman, Isaiah, "The Response to the Balfour Declaration," *Jewish Social Studies*, vol. 35 (1973), 105–124. Friedman, "The Austro-Hungarian Government and Zionism: 1897–1918 (Continued)," *Jewish Social Studies*, vol. 27 (1965), 236–237. Friedman, *The Question of Palestine: British-Jewish-Arab Relations, 1914–1918*, (London: Routledge, 1973), 296, 298–299. Nicosia, "Jewish Affairs and German Foreign Policy during the Weimar Republic," *LBIY*, vol. 33 (1988), 262–263, 263n6.

10. Szajkowski, Zosa, "The German Ordinance of November 1916 on the Organization of Jewish Communities in Poland," *Proceedings of the American Academy for Jewish Research*, vol. 34 (1966), 111–112. Nicosia, "Jewish Affairs, Weimar," 261, 266, 276n43, 278n49.

11. Nicosia, "Jewish Affairs, Weimar," 276, 277, 277n45–46.

12. PA: Pol Abt III, Innere Verwaltung 14-Palästina, Aufzeichnung, 23rd Sep 1920. 8: PA: Pol Abt III, Politik 16-Palästina, Jahresbericht über die Verhältnisse der deutch-evangelischen Gemeinde zu Jerusalem 1922/1923, III 0 3167/23, 10th Oct 1923. PA: Pol Abt III, Innere Verwaltung 14-Palästina, Aufzeichnung der Pol. III, 10th Sep 1920. Pol Abt III, Politik 6-Palästina, DK/Triest an AA/Berlin, No, 2452, 26th Jul 1921. PA: Pol Abt III, Innere Verwaltung 14-Palästina, Aufzeichnung der Pol III, 10th Nov 1920. PA: Pol Abt. III, Politik 10-Palästina, Bd. 1, Aufzeichnung Sobernheims, III 0 493, 11th Sep 1924. Nicosia, "Weimar Germany," 323–324, 323n5–7, 324n8–11.

13. Nicosia, "Jewish Affairs, Weimar," 296n22.

14. Aschheim, Steven E., *Brothers and Strangers: The East European Jew in German and German Jewish Consciousness, 1800–1923* (Madison: University of Wisconsin Press, 1982), 238–240, 242–245. Hagen, William H., "Murder in the East: German-Jewish Liberal Reactions

to Anti-Jewish Violence in Poland and Other East European Lands, 1918–1920," *Central European History*, vol. 34 (2001), 3–5. See generally Hagen, 1–30. Black, *Nazi Nexus: America's Corporate Connections to Hitler's Holocaust* (Washington, DC: Dialog Press, 2009), chap. 1.
15. Black, *Nazi Nexus*, 2–3, 6–7, 8, 9, 10. Black, *Transfer*, 26. Judge, *Easter in Kishinev*, 32. See Black, *Nazi Nexus*, 5. See Black, *Transfer*, 27.
16. Hitler, Adolf, *Mein Kampf*, Ralph Manheim, trans. (Boston: Houghton Mifflin, 1946), 307–308, quoted in Joly, Maurice, *The Dialogue in Hell Between Machiavelli and Montesquieu*, John S. Waggoner, trans. (Lanham, MD: Lexington Books, 2003), 366n6. "Berlin Hears Ford Is Backing Hitler," *NYT*, Dec 20, 1922, 2. "Police Find Bomb in P.O. Building in Philadelphia," *NY Trib*, Jan 1, 1919, 4. See "Police Here Ready for Reds," *NY Trib*, May 1, 1920, 1. See "Berger Defends Red Flag; Says He's Not a 'Red,'" *Chi Trib*, Jan 1, 1919, 15. See "U. S. Hunts Bombers," *Chi Trib*, Jan 1, 1919, 1. See "Bolshevik Plot Is Seen Behind Bomb Outrages," *NY Trib*, Jan 1, 1919, 1.
17. Black, *Nazi Nexus*, chap. 3. See generally Black, *War against the Weak*.
18. Black, *Transfer*, chap. 7.
19. Black, *Transfer*, chap. 7, 169, 172.
20. Black, *Transfer*, 167–168.
21. Black, *Transfer*, 167–169, 173–177.
22. PA/Bonn: Pol. Abt. III, Jüd. Politische Angelegenheiten, Allgemeines, Bd. 7, "Bericht über eine in London stattgehabte Sitzung des Zentralkomitees für das Judäistische Institut an der Universität Jerusalem," zu III 0 1585, 1. Juli 1925. Vital, *Zionism*, 424. Nicosia, "Weimar Germany," 321. Nicosia, "Jewish Affairs, Weimar," 278.
23. Nicosia, "Weimar Germany," 326–327, 328. Nicosia, "Jewish Affairs, Weimar," 279. "Germany Elected Member of League and of its Council," *WP*, Sep 9, 1926.
24. Photo, "Foundation Meeting of the Pro-Palästina Komitee on 15th December 1926," Nicosia, "Weimar Germany," 328f. Nicosia, "Weimar Germany," 329–331, 330n30.
25. PA: Pol. Abt. III, Politik 2-Palästina, Aufzeichnung von Schuberts, 2nd September 1920. PA: Pol.Abt.III, Politik 6-Palästina, Bd.1, DB/London an AA/Berlin, K.Nr. 69, 1.Sept.21., 4. Black, *Transfer*, 6. Nicosia, "Weimar Germany," 325–326, 335–336.
26. Gilbert, Martin, *The Routledge Atlas of the Arab-Israeli Conflict*, 7th ed., (New York: Routledge, 2002), 11. Gilbert, *Churchill and the Jews: A Lifelong Friendship* (New York: Henry Holt, 2007), 58–62. Williams, T. Walter, "Palestine is Still a Land of Problems," *NYT*, Jul 10, 1921, 27. "Upholds Palestine Plan," *NYT*, Apr 1, 1921, 2. "Promises The Arabs Rights in Palestine," *NYT*, Apr 2, 1921, 2.
27. Gilbert, *Churchill*, 58.
28. Gilbert, *Churchill*, 60. See "Promises The Arabs Rights in Palestine."
29. Zerubavel, Yael, "The Politics of Interpretation: Tel Hai in Israel's Collective Memory," *AJS Review*, vol. 16 (1991), 133, 135. Sachar, 123–124.
30. "188 Casualties in Jerusalem from Conflict on Easter Day," *NYT*, Apr 6, 1920, 15. "Racial Disorders in Jerusalem," *MG*, Apr 6, 1920, 6. "Riots in Jerusalem," *NYT*, Apr 8, 1920, 15. "Fresh Street Fighting in Jerusalem," *MG*, Apr 8, 1920, 6. "Military in Control in Jerusalem," *MG*, Apr 9, 1920, 7. Segev, Tom, *One Palestine, Complete: Jews and Arabs under the British Mandate*, Haim Watzman, trans. (New York: Henry Holt, 2000), 127–129. Sachar, 123–124.
31. "188 Casualties in Jerusalem." "Racial Disorders in Jerusalem" "Riots in Jerusalem." Segev & Watzman, 127–129. Sachar, 123–124.
32. Sachar, 213–214.
33. "Scores are Killed in Palestine Riots," *NYT*, May 4, 1921, 7. *Palestine, Disturbances in May, 1921: Reports of the Commission of Inquiry with Correspondence Relating Thereto* (London: HM Stationery Office, 1921), 5–6, 44–45.
34. Gilbert, *Routledge Atlas*, 11. Walter, "Palestine is Still a Land of Problems."
35. PA/Bonn: Pol. Abt. III, Jüd. Politische Angelegenheiten, Allgemeines, Bd. 2, Aufzeichnung Sobernheims, 4. Oktober 1921., 1.
36. PA/Bonn: Pol. Abt. III, Jüd. Politische Angelegenheiten, Allgemeines, Bd. 2, Aufzeichnung Sobernheims, 4. Oktober 1921., 1.
37. PA/Bonn: Pol. Abt. III, Jüd. Politische Angelegenheiten, Allgemeines, Bd. 2, Aufzeichnung Sobernheims, 4. Oktober 1921., 5.

38. PA/Bonn: Pol. Abt. Ill, Jüd. Politische Angelegenheiten, Allgemeines, Bd. 2, Aufzeich-nung Sobernheims, 4. Oktober 1921., 1.

39. Nicosia, "Weimar Germany," 339n72.

40. PA: Pol. Abt. III, Politik 2 (Iran), Bd. 1, AA/Berlin an die Deutsche Vertretung in Tehe-ran, IV, Ps 1102, Nr. 288, 11. Dez. 1921. Nicosia, "'Drang nach Osten' Continued? Germany and Afghanistan during the Weimar Republic," Journal Contemporary History, vol 32 (1997), 242. Nicosia, "Arab Nationalism and National Socialist Germany, 1933–1939: Ideological and Strategic Incompatibility," International Journal of Middle East Studies, vol. 12, (1980), 4–5.

41. Shaw, J. V. W., ed., A Survey of Palestine, Prepared in December 1945 and January 1946 for the information of the Anglo-American Committee of Inquiry, vols. 1–3 (Jerusalem: Government Printer, 1946–1947),185. A Survey, 21, 23, 185. "Poles Prefer Palestine," NYT, Aug 24, 1925, 12. See "138,066 in Palestine," NYT, Mar 14, 1926, 31.

42. A Survey, 21, 23. 185. "Poles Prefer Palestine." See "138,066 in Palestine."

43. A Survey, 21, 23. 185. "Poles Prefer Palestine." See "138,066 in Palestine."

44. See Caplan, Neil, "Arab-Jewish Contacts in Palestine after the First World War," Jour-nal of Contemporary History, vol. 12 (1977), 635–668.

45. Levy, Joseph M., "Juggling of Facts on Arabs Charged," NYT, Dec 12, 1929, 8. A Sur-vey, 244, 245.

46. See generally A Survey.

47. Enquiry into Rioting in Jerusalem in April 1920, BNA FO 371/5121 E 9373, E 9373. See Palestine: Disturbances in May, 1921, Reports of the Commission of Inquiry with Corre-spondence Relating Thereto, Cmd. 1540 (London: HM Stationery Office, 1921). See Avneri, Aryeh L., The Claim of Dispossession: Jewish Land-settlement and the Arabs, 1878–1948 (New Brunswick, NJ: Transaction Publishers, 1984), chaps. 6, 7. See generally See Caplan, "Arab-Jewish Contacts."

48. Tessler, Mark, A History of the Israeli-Palestinian Conflict (Bloomington, IN: Indiana University Press, 1994), 164. Gil-Har, Yitzhak, "British Commitments to the Arabs and Their Application to the Palestine-Trans-Jordan Boundary: The Issue of the Semakh Triangle," Mid-dle Eastern Studies, vol. 29 (1993), 690–701. Gil-Har, "Boundaries Delimitation: Palestine and Trans-Jordan," Middle Eastern Studies, vol. 36 (2000), 68–81. "The Making of Transjordan," History, The Hashemite Kingdom of Jordan, www.kinghussein.gov.jo/his_transjordan.html. Palestine: Correspondence with the Palestine Arab Delegation and the Zionist Organisation, Cmd. 1700 (London, HM Stationery Office, 1922).

49. Palestine: Disturbances in May.

50. Palestine: Correspondence with the Palestine Arab Delegation and the Zionist Organisation.

51. Palestine: Correspondence with the Palestine Arab Delegation and the Zionist Organisation.

52. Table, "Jewish Immigration to Palestine, 1922–1929," Smith, Barbara Jean, The Roots of Separatism in Palestine: British Economic Policy, 1920–1929 (Syracuse, NY: Syracuse Uni-versity Press 1993), 65. A Survey, 23, 185. See "Poles Prefer Palestine," NYT, Aug 24, 1925, 12.

53. Table, "Jewish Immigration to Palestine, 1922–1929," Smith, 65. Landau, Zbigniew & Jerzy Tomaszewski, The Polish Economy in the Twentieth Century, vol. 1985, pt. 2, Wojciech Roszkowski, trans, (London: Croon Helm, 1985), 60–63. Segev & Watzman, 225. Table, "Coun-try of Origin," A Survey, 186.

54. "Palestine's High Commissioner," NYT, May 23, 1925, 14. See "New Men Indicate New British Policy," NYT, Jun 7, 1925, E13. "20,000 Here Protest the Arab Outrages," NYT, Aug 30, 1929, 5. Halevi, Nadav, "The Political Economy of Absorptive Capacity: Growth and Cycles in Jewish Palestine under the British Mandate," Middle Eastern Studies, vol. 19 (1983), 462–463, "Labor Row in Palestine," NYT, Dec 18, 1927, E8. See three photographs, Nablus 1927 Earthquake, Author's Collection. Al-Dabbeek, Jalal & Radwan El-Kelani, "Local Site Effects in Palestinian Cit-ies: A Preliminary Study Based on Nablus Earthquake of July 11, 1927 and the earthquake of Febru-ary 11, 2004," presented to First International Conference of Applied Geophysics for Engineering, October 13–15, 2004, Università di Messina. Wachs, D. & D. Levitte, "Damage Caused by Land-slides During the Earthquakes of 1837 and 1927 in the Galilee Region," HYDRO/5/78-Jerusalem-June 1927, Ministry of Energy and Infrastructure. Segev & Watzman, 225.

55. "Palestine Immigration," *NYT*, Jun 2, 1929, N6. "Palestine Gained in March," *NYT*, Jun 2, 1929, E8. Central Conference of American Rabbis, *Year Book of the Central Conference of American Rabbis*, vol. 39 (1929), 234. "36 Students Stabbed," *NYT*, Apr 25, 1929, 6. "A Record of Pogroms in Poland," *NYT*, Jun 1, 1919, 43. Polonski, Anthony, "Lemberg: a Failed Pogrom," in Yisrael, Gutman, Ezra Mendelsohn, Jehuda Reinharz, & Chone Shmeruk, eds., *The Jews of Poland between Two World Wars* (Hanover, NH: University Press of New England, 1991), 109–125. See Hope Simpson, Sir John, *Palestine: Report on Immigration, Land Settlement and Development*, Cmd. 3686–3687, (London, HM Stationery Office, 1930), chap. 10. See Author's Corresp. with Antony Polonski.

56. Fulda, Bernhard, *Press and Politics in the Weimar Republic* (New York: Oxford University Press, 2009), 146. Rosenhaft, Eve, *Beating the Fascists: the German Communists and Political Violence, 1929–1933* (Cambridge: Cambridge University Press, 1983), 63. Ailsby, Christopher, *The Third Reich Day by Day* (St Paul: MBI, 2001), 29. Black, *Nazi Nexus*, 8–10. See Hamilton, Richard F., "Hitler's Electoral Support: Recent Findings and Theoretical Implications," *Canadian Journal of Sociology*, vol. 11 (1986), 3. See generally Kater, Michael H., *Hitler Youth* (Cambridge, MA: Harvard University Press, 2004).

57. Halevi, "The Political Economy." 462. "Palestine Industry Up," *NYT*, Jun 2, 1929, E3. Avitzur, "The Power Plant on Two Rivers."

58. Metzer, Jacob, "Jewish Immigration to Palestine in the Long 1920s: An Exploratory Examination," *Journal of Israeli History*, vol. 27 (2008), 221–225. "150,000 Jews in Palestine, 2,000 of them Americans," *NYT*, Aug 30, 1929, 1. A *Survey*, 185.

59. *Report of the Commission appointed by His Majesty's Government in the United Kingdom of Great Britain and Northern Ireland, with the approval of the Council of the League of Nations, to determine the rights and claims of Moslems and Jews in connection with the Western or Wailing Wall at Jerusalem* (London: HM Stationery Office, 1931), chaps. III, IV, V.

60. *Western or Wailing Wall Commission Report*, chaps. III, IV, V.

61. *Western or Wailing Wall Commission Report*, chap. III.

62. "Wailing Wall Permit Stirs Palestine Jews," *NYT*, Aug 1, 1929, 8. Mattar, Philip, "The Role of the Mufti of Jerusalem in the Political Struggle over the Western Wall, 1928–29," *Middle Eastern Studies*, vol. 19 (1983), 105–106, 109, 110–111, 113. Wasserstein, Bernard, *The British in Palestine: The Mandatory Government and the Arab-Jewish Conflict 1917–1929* (Oxford: Basil Blackwell, 1991), 42. Porath, Yehoshua, *The Emergence of the Palestinian-Arab National Movement, 1918–1929* (London: Frank Cass, 1974), 266–267. "Palestine Presses Trials for Riots," *NYT*, Sep 24, 1929, 6. See Mattar, "Role of the Mufti," 107. See "Wailing Wall Plea Vain," *NYT*, Aug 7, 1929, 6. See "Jews Allege Arabs Desecrate Wall," *NYT*, Aug 25, 1929, 5. See generally *Western or Wailing Wall Commission Report*.

63. Krämer, Gudrun, *A History of Palestine, from the Ottoman Conquest to the Present* (Princeton: Princeton University Press, 2008), 230–234. "10,000 Jews Guarded at the Wailing Wall," *NYT*, Aug 16, 1929, 2. "Arab Mob Invades Wailing Wall Lane," *NYT*, Aug 17, 1929, 16. Mattar, "Role of the Mufti," 113.

64. "Arrest Ten Arabs for Attack on Jews," *NYT*, Aug 18, 1929, 24. "Arabs Opened Attack after Noon Prayers," *NYT*, Aug 25, 1929, 5. See Levy, Joseph M., "Palestine Death Toll Mounts Hourly, with Fifteen Americans among Slain," *NYT*, Aug 27, 1929, 1. See generally Wasserstein. *Records of the Hebron Pogrom*, Hebron Archives, Hebron Heritage Museum.

65. Photo, "The Jewish colony of Artuf, or Hartuv, set on fire during the riots of 1929 in Palestine, when 133 Jews and 116 Palestinians were killed in week-long massacres and disturbances," Library of Congress Photographs and Prints. "47 Dead in Jerusalem Riot; Attacks by Arabs Spread; British Troops Rush to City," *NYT*, Aug 25, 1929, 1, 5. "Arabs Opened Attack after Noon Prayers." Mattar, "Role of the Mufti," 115–116.

66. Hertzog, Chaim & Shlomo Gazit, *The Arab-Israeli Wars: War and Peace* (NY: Vintage Books, 2005), 58. "Planes Use Machine Guns on Arabs in Palestine; Armored Cars Fire into Mobs on City Streets," *NYT*, Aug 26, 1929, 1. "47 Dead in Jerusalem Riot." See Levy, Joseph M., "12 Americans Killed by Arabs in Hebron as British Troops Reach Jerusalem; Armed Moslems Threaten New Attack," *NYT*, Aug 26, 1929, 1, 6. Greenwald, Toby Klein, *The Story of Hebron: Seventy-Five Years from Tarpat* (Hebron: Jewish Action, 2004), 2.

67. Levy, Joseph M., "Troops Seize Arab Chiefs at Gates of Jerusalem; Move to Take

City Foiled," *NYT*, Aug 30, 1929, 1, 4. See "12 Americans Killed by Arabs." Mattar, "Role of the Mufti," 116. Greenwald, 4. Segev, 318–319. Segev, 318–319. Author's Hebron Massacre Collection.

68. "Troops Seize Arab Chiefs." "12 Americans Killed by Arabs." Segev, 321.

69. See Zeevi, Rehavam, "The Hebron Pogrom of 24 August 1929," in Michal Rachel Suissa, ed., *Hebron: Rebirth from Ruins* (Hebron: Jewish Community of Hebron, 2009), 39–61. Segev, 323, 324. Author's Hebron Massacre Collection.

70. Greenwald, 7. *Records of the Hebron Pogrom.* Author's Hebron Massacre Collection. See generally Wasserstein.

71. Greenwald, 5, 6–7. *Records of the Hebron Pogrom.* Author's Hebron Massacre Collection. See generally Wasserstein.

72. "Troops Seize Arab Chiefs."

73. Morris, Benny, *Righteous Victims: A History of the Zionist-Arab Conflict, 1881–2001* (NY: Vintage Books, 2001), 114. Segev, 322–323. Author's Hebron Massacre Collection.

74. Greenwald, 7, 8. Segev, 325–326. Author's Hebron Massacre Collection.

75. "Arabs Burn City of Safed; 22 Killed, Scores Wounded; Syrians Invade from North," *NYT*, Aug 31, 1929, 1, 4. Greenwald, 8. Morris, 115. Author's Hebron Massacre Collection.

76. *Report of the Commission on the Palestine Disturbances of August, 1929*, Cmd. 3530 (London, HM Stationery Office, 1930). Kolinsky, Martin, "Premeditation in the Palestine Disturbances of August 1929?," *Middle Eastern Studies*, vol. 26 (1990), 30–31. "The Palestine Report," *NYT*, Apr 2, 1930, 23. Author's Hebron Massacre Collection.

77. Levy, Joseph M., "British Cease Raids on Moslem Towns," *NYT*, Sep 6, 1929, 6. *Report of the Palestine Disturbances Commission.* "The Palestine Report." See generally Wasserstein. *Records of the Hebron Pogrom.*

78. "Dr. Stresemann Dies Suddenly in Berlin; Long in Ill Health," Oct 3, 1929, 1. "World Statesmen Get Nobel Prizes," *NYT*, Dec 11, 1926, 5. "Stresemann Urges Speed on Debt Plan," *NYT*, Jul 9, 1929, 8. "Germans Protest Plan," *NYT*, Aug 24, 1929, 4.

79. Fulda, 146. Black, *Transfer*, 260–262.

80. Fulda, 146. "All Germany Plans to Protest Treaty," *NYT*, Jun 27, 1929, 12. "Germans Protest Plan," *NYT*, Aug 24, 1929, 4. "Stresemann Urges Speed on Debt Plan." See Woolf, S.J., "Stresemann, Voice of the New Germany," *NYT*, Aug 4, 1929, SM2. See "Young Plan Approved by the German Cabinet," *NYT*, Sep 4, 1929, 14.

81. "Says Germany Backs Palestine Movement," *NYT*, Feb 21, 1930, 6. Nicosia, "Weimar Germany," 330–331, 340.

82. PA: Pol. Abt. III, Politik 2a-Palästina, Bd. 2, AA/Berlin an das Pro-Palästina Komitee, III 0 161, 16th January 1931.

83. *The Palestine (Western or Wailing Wall) Order in Council, 1931, Made on 19 May 1931*, (London: HM Stationery Office, 1936). Mattar, "Role of the Mufti," 108.

84. Hosein, Imran N., *The Caliphate, The Hejaz, and The Saudi-Wahhabi Nation-State* (Bay Shore, NY: Masjid Darul Qur'an, 1996), 54–67.

85. Jbara, Taysir, *Al-Hājj Muhammad Amīn al-Husaynī, Mufti of Jerusalem: The Palestine Years, 1921–1937* (NY: New York University Press, 1982), 82.

86. Jbara, *The Palestine Years*, 150–151.

87. Jbara, *The Palestine Years*, chap. 4.

88. Levy, Joseph M., "Moslem Threatens Jews in Palestine," *NYT*, Dec 14, 1931, 4.

89. Black, *Transfer*, 3.

## Chapter 11: Rise of the Mufti

1. See letter, Herbert Samuel to Winston Churchill, Oct 27, 1921: BNA T1/161/146 no. 119238. Mattar, Philip, *The Mufti of Jerusalem: Al-Hajj Amin Al-Husayni and the Palestinian National Movement* (New York: Columbia University Press, 1988), 6–7. Jbara, Taysir, *Al-Hājj Muhammad Amīn al-Husaynī, Mufti of Jerusalem: The Palestine Years, 1921–1937* (NY: NYU Press, 1982), 1–8.

2. Jbara, 13. See letter, Herbert Samuel to Winston Churchill, Oct 27, 1921.

3. Stein, Kenneth W., *The Land Question in Palestine, 1917-1939* (Chapel Hill, NC:

University of North Carolina Press, 1984), 233. Segev, *One Palestine, Complete*, 275. Mattar 7–8.

4. Mattar, *Mufti*, 6–7.

5. Mattar, *Mufti*, 7–8. Jbara, *The Palestine Years*, 16–17, 19.

6. Jbara, Taysir, *Palestinian Leader Hajj Amin Al-Husayni, Mufti of Jerusalem* (Princeton: The Kingston Press, 1985), 14.

7. Jbara, *The Palestine Years*, 1, 22–24, 28–30.

8. Jbara, *The Palestine Years*, 34-5, 37. See Black, *BoB*, 295.

9. Jbara, *The Palestine Years*, 31.

10. BNA FO 371/5121/E9379/85/44, June 1918 as cited by Jbara, *Palestinian Leader*, 33. Jbara, *Palestinian Leader*, 27–28, 33, 35. Muslih, Muhammad Y., *The Origins of Palestinian Nationalism* (NY: Columbia University Press, 1988), 170.

11. Jbara, *The Palestine Years*, 40–41.

12. Krämer, *A History of Palestine*, 207-210. Jbara, *The Palestine Years*, 43–44, 55–58.

13. Bentwich, Norman & Helen Bentwich, *Mandate Memories* (London: Hogarth Press, 1965), 189, as cited by Jbara, *The Palestine Years*, 46n55. Jbara, *The Palestine Years*, 38, 46–48.

14. Kupferschmidt, Uri M., *The Supreme Muslim Council: Islam under the British Mandate for Palestine* (Leiden: Brill, 1987), 21. Jbara, *The Palestine Years*, 49. Black, *BoB*, 295–296.

15. Jbara, *The Palestine Years*, 58–59. Porath, Yehoshua, *The Emergence of the Palestinian-Arab National Movement, 1918–1929* (London: Frank Cass, 1974), 189–190. See Porath, *Emergence*, 191.

16. Jbara, *The Palestine Years*, 59–60.

17. Kupferschmidt, 17–19. Jbara, *Palestinian Leader*, 41, 46–49, 66–69. See Wasserstein, "Herbert Samuel and the Palestine Problem," *The English Historical Review*, vol. 91 (1976), 773–774. See generally *Palestine, Disturbances in May, 1921: Reports of the Commission of Inquiry with Correspondence Relating Thereto*, Cmd. 1540 (London: HM Stationery Office, 1921).

18. Jbara, *The Palestine Years*, 68–72. Jbara, *Palestinian Leader*, 49–50.

19. Jbara, *The Palestine Years*, 81–85.

20. Jbara, *The Palestine Years*, 84–86. See Khalidi, Omar, "Indian Muslims and Palestinian Awqaf," *Jerusalem Quarterly*, no. 40 (2009–2010), 52, 55. Photo, Indian Army Lancers in Palestine, Author's Collection.

21. Jbara, *The Palestine Years*, 85–88.

22. Jankowski, James P. & Israel Gershoni, eds., *Rethinking Nationalism in the Arab Middle East* (NY: Columbia University Press, 1997), 321n52. Jbara, *The Palestine Years*, 68–72, 70–73, 88. Jbara, *Palestinian Leader*, 50–52. Muslih, 243. Porath, *Emergence*, 203–204. See Porath, *Emergence*, 193–194.

23. Jbara, *Palestinian Leader*, 50–52. Porath, *Emergence*, 218, 226.

24. BNA CO733/172/1/67296, From Harry Luke to the High Commissioner, Jan 14, 1929. Jbara, *The Palestine Years*, 79.

25. Mattar, "Role of the Mufti," 105–106, 111. See "Jews Allege Arabs Desecrate Wall," *NYT*, Aug 25, 1929, 5.

26. BNA CO 733/160/57540/11, Va'ad Le'umi letter of 10 Oct 1928, quoted by Mattar, "Role of the Mufti," 107. Wasserstein, *British in Palestine*, 229. Mattar, "Role of the Mufti," 107, 109–110.

27. Wasserstein, *British in Palestine*, 228–229. Mattar, "Role of the Mufti," 107, 109–110. See Porath, 253–254, 266–267.

28. Porath, *Emergence*, 266–267. Mattar, "Role of the Mufti," 114. See Kolinsky, Martin, "Premeditation in the Palestine Disturbances of August 1929?," *Middle Eastern Studies*, vol. 26 (1990), 23. See Porath, *Emergence*, 265–266.

29. Wasserstein, 236–237. Mattar, "Role of the Mufti," 114–115. "Arrest Ten Arabs for Attack on Jews," *NYT*, Aug 18, 1929, 24. "47 Dead in Jerusalem Riot; Attacks by Arabs Spread; British Troops Rush to City," *NYT*, Aug 25, 1929, 1. "Arabs Opened Attack after Noon Prayers," *NYT*, Aug 25, 1929, 5. See Levy, Joseph M., "Palestine Death Toll Mounts Hourly, with Fifteen Americans among Slain," *NYT*, Aug 27, 1929, 1.

30. Mattar, "Role of the Mufti," 115.

31. Kolinsky, 23, 24, 33n29.

32. Stein, Kenneth, "A Reply to Philip Mattar," *International Journal of Middle East Studies*, vol. 25 (1993), 184–185.

33. Ofer, Pinhas, "The Commission on the Palestine Disturbances of August 1929: Appointment, Terms of Reference, Procedure, and Report," *Middle Eastern Studies*, vol. 21 (1985), 354, 356. See Ofer, 360n62.

34. Ofer, 356, 357. See Ofer, 360n62.

35. Ofer in 360n62. Minute of 12 Sept. 1929 to telegram from the Secretary of State for the Colonies to the High Commissioner of Palestine 7 Sept. 1929: BNA FO 371/13753. E4617/4198/65 as cited by Ofer, 360n62.

36. "Goalen, Paul, "MacDonald's 'Black Letter,'" *Journal of Interdisciplinary Studies in History and Archaeology*, vol. 1 (2004) 90–91, 95–97. See Weizmann, Chaim, *Letters and Papers of Chaim Weizmann*, vol. 14, C. Dresner, ed. (Jerusalem: Israel University Press, 1978), 290.

37. Goalen, 97–98.

38. Goalen, 98–99

39. "Text of Premier's Letter on Palestine," *NYT*, Feb 14, 1931, 8. Goalen, 99–100.

40. Porath, *The Palestinian Arab National Movement: from Riots to Rebellion, 1929–1939*, vol. 2 (London: Frank Cass), 33–34. Goalen, 100–101.

41. Jbara, *Palestinian Leader*, 150–151, 160–162. Kupferschmidt, chap. 9.

42. Kupferschmidt, 207–214, 244–245. See Kupferschmidt, 220. Jbara, *Palestinian Leader*, 160–162.

## Chapter 12: The Arabs Reach for the Reich

1. Nicosia, "Jewish Affairs, Weimar," 261, 262, 263. Nicosia, "Zionism in National Socialist Policy in Germany, 1933–39", *Journal of Modern History*, vol. 50 (1978), D1253–D1282. Schmidt, H. D., "The Nazi Party in Palestine and the Levant 1932–39", *International Affairs*, vol. 28, (1952), 461–463, 464, 466. See "The Gestapo: a History of Horror", Jacques Delarue (Barnsley, 2008), 90. See also Speer, Albert, *Inside the Third Reich: Memoirs* (NY: Simon & Schuster, 1970), 96.

2. "NSDAP-Landesgruppe/Palästina, 1934–1939; Mitgliedstand vom April, 1937." Nicosia, "National Socialism and the Demise of the German-Christian Communities in Palestine during the Nineteen Thirties", 241–243.

3. Auswärtiges Amt: "Telegramm (Geh.Ch.V.) Jerusalem, den 31, März 1933, 20, 35 Uhr Ankunft, den 31, März 1933, 23,15 Uhr Nr. 5, vom 31.3." signed by Wolff.

4. PA: Pol.Abt.III, Politik 2-Palästina, Bd. 1, DGK/Jerusalem an AA/Berlin, Telegramm Nr. 5, 31 März 33. See also: PA: Pol.Abt.III, Politik 2-Palästina, Bd. 1, DGK/Jerusalem an AA/Berlin, Nr. Polit. 3/33, 20.März 33. Nicosia, ⬜Arab Nationalism,⬜ 353. Black, *Transfer*, 161–163.

5. PA: Abt.IV-Kultur, Minderheiten Nr.14, Bd.1, DGK/Jerusalem an AA/Berlin, Nr. Polit. 24/33, 20.Apr.33. Nicosia, "Arab Nationalism," 353n9.

6. Wild, Stefan, "National Socialism in the Arab Near East Between 1933 and 1939", *Die Welt des Islams*, New Ser. Bd. 25 (1985), 142n55.

7. AA: August 25, 1933, signed by Wolff, File No. 111/33. PA: Pol.Abt.III, Politik I, Nr.3, Bd.i, DGK/Jerusalem an AA/Berlin, Nr. Polit. 55/34, 7.June.34. Nicosia, "Arab Nationalism," 354, 355. Wild, "National Socialism," 134. AA, Letter from the prince Rahhal Scheiban to Hitler 7 July 1934, L319297.

8. PA: Pol.Abt.III, Politik I, Nr.3, Bd.i, DGK/Jerusalem an AA/Berlin, Nr.Polit.55/34, 7.June.34.

9. PA: Pol.Abt.III, Politik I, Nr.3, Bd.i, DGK/Jerusalem an AA/Berlin, Nr.Polit.55/34, 7.June.34.

10. AA: Abt.III 0, Letter from Bagdad, den 2. February 1935, signed Grobba, L355621. AA: Letter from the prince Rahhal Scheiban to Hitler 7 July 1934, L319297. Wild, "National Socialism," 134n27.

11. AA, August 25, 1933, signed Wolff, File No.111/33.

12. 21 PA: Geheim Akten 1920-1936, Syrien-Pol.2, Aufzeichnung Prufers, III o 4210, 7.Nov.34. 22 BA: R43/II-1420, Vermerk, Rk.9952, 10.Nov.34.AA: Jerusalem to Berlin, July 31, 1933, IIIO 2362, L319098 and L015481, R78325 zu III O 2362. Nicosia, "Arab Nationalism," 354n21–22.

13. AA: Jaffa to Jerusalem, April 13, 1933, signed Joseph Francis, L015432. AA: III O 22362-33, from Jaffa, June 23, 1933, signed Joseph Francis, L319091. June 27, 1933, Filing No. 74/33.

14. Wolff memo: June 27, 1933, Filing No. 74/33. Berlin memo: AA, Jerusalem to Berlin, July 31, 1933, IIIO 2362, L319098 and L015481. (R78325 zu III O 2362).

15. AA: Bagdad to Berlin, Aug 10, 1933, signed Grobba, D3799. Arslan: PA; Pol.Abt.III, Judische Angelegenheiten, Jud.Pol.1, Bd.13, AA/Berlin an DK/Genf, III O/3856, 26 Okt.33; 21 PA: Geheim Akten 1920-1936, Syrien-Pol.2, Aufzeichnung Prufers, III O 4210, 7.Nov.34; 22 BA: R43/II-1420, Vermerk, Rk.9952, 10.Nov.34. Nicosia, "National Socialism," 354n20–22.

16. Gershoni & Jankowski, *Confronting Fascism in Egypt: Dictatorship versus Democracy in the 1930s* (Stanford: Stanford University Press, 2010), 139–140. Lewis, *Semites and anti-Semites: An Inquiry into Conflict and Prejudice* (NY: W.W. Norton, 1999), 149. Wild, "National Socialism," 130, 132, 133–135, 148–149, 150–151. See generally Wild, "National Socialism." See swastika variant, Syrian Social Nationalist Party website, www.ssnp.net [Oct 1, 2010].

17. Wild, "National Socialism," 132n21. Gershoni & Jankowsi, *Confronting Fascism*, 140. Lewis, *Semites and anti-Semites*, 148–149.

18. Wild, "National Socialism," 147–148, 150–151.

19. Wild, "National Socialism," 153n92. Wild, "National Socialism in the Arab Near East Between 1933 and 1939," in Shmuel Moreh & Zvi Yehuda, eds., *Al-Farhūd: The 1941 Pogrom in Iraq* (Jerusalem: Hebrew University Press, 2010), 52n93 ("National Socialism II"). Wild, "National Socialism I," 139–147. Wild, "National Socialism I," 147–170.

20. Wild, "National Socialism II," 53. Wild, "National Socialism I,"154n94.

21. Black, *IBM*, 54.

22. Black, *IBM*, 54.

23. Black, *IBM*, 54.

24. See generally Black, *Transfer*.

25. See generally Black, *Transfer*, chap. 3.

26. Black, *Transfer*, 27–30.

27. Transcript of Interview of Morris Mendelsohn by Moshe Gottlieb, July 20, 1965, Author's Collection. See Black, *Transfer*, 11, 33.

28. Black, *Transfer*, 20, Photos, Black, *Transfer*, 213ff.

29. Black, *Transfer*, 113, 129–130, 179–180, 180–182, 188.

30. Black, *Transfer*, 34.

31. Nazi Attacks Stir British Catholics," *NYT*, Mar 24, 1933, 3. Black, *Transfer*, 33–34, 34n4.

32. "Speech of Hitler in Reichstag on His Policies for Germany," *NYT*, Mar 24, 1933, 2. Black, *Transfer*, 34.

33. "Move for Boycott Gaining in London," *NYT*, Mar 25, 1933, 10. Nazi Attacks Stir British Catholics." Black, *Transfer*, 34.

34. Black, *Transfer*, 7–11.

35. See generally Black, *Transfer*, chap 5.

36. Black, *Transfer*, 34.

37. Black, *Transfer*, 34–35.

38. Black, *Transfer*, 35.

39. Black, *Transfer*, 35.

40. Black, *Transfer*, 35.

41. Black, *Transfer*, 35.

42. Black, *Transfer*, 35.

43. Black, *Transfer*, 35–36.

44. Black, *Transfer*, 36.

45. Black, *Transfer*, 36.

46. Black, *Transfer*, 36.

47. Black, *Transfer*, 36.

48. Black, *Transfer*, 36.

49. Black, *Transfer*, 36.

50. Black, *Transfer*, 36–37.

51. Black, *Transfer*, 37.

52. Black, *Transfer*, 37–41.

53. Black, *Transfer*, 38–41.

54. Black, *Transfer*, 38, 40, 41.

55. Black, *Transfer*, 41.

56. Black, *Transfer*, 41. Letter, S. Wise to L.D. Brandeis, Sept. 19, 1933, Brandeis Papers Microfilm Archive at AJA.

57. "35,000 Jam Streets outside the Garden," *NYT*, Mar 28, 1933, 1, 13. Black, *Transfer*, 41–42.

58. "35,000 Jam Streets outside the Garden." Black, *Transfer*, 41–42.

59. "35,000 Jam Streets outside the Garden." Black, *Transfer*, 42.

60. "35,000 Jam Streets outside the Garden." Black, *Transfer*, 42.

61. "35,000 Jam Streets outside the Garden." Black, *Transfer*, 42.

62. "55,000 Here Stage Protest on Hitler Attacks on Jews; Nazis Order a New Boycott," *NYT*, Mar 28, 1933, 1. "35,000 Jam Streets outside the Garden." Black, *Transfer*, 42.

63. Black, *Transfer*, 42.

64. "250,000 Jews Here to Protest Today," *NYT*, Mar 27, 1933. "Chicago Jews Demand U.S. Act to Curb Nazis," *Chi Trib*, Chicago Daily Tribune, Mar 28, 1933. "55,000 Here Stage Protest on Hitler Attacks on Jews." Black, *Transfer*, 42.

65. Black, *Transfer*, 42.

66. Wise, Stephen, *Challenging Years: The Autobiography of Stephen Wise* (New York: Putnam, 1949), 250. "Jews Fast in Poland," *NYT*, Mar 28, 1933, 13. Black, *Transfer*, 42.

67. Black, *Transfer*, 43.

68. Black, *Transfer*, 43. "55,000 Here Stage Protest."

69. Black, *Transfer*, 43. "Smith Calls for a World-Wide Fight on Religious Bigotry," *NYT*, Mar 28, 1933, 13.

70. Black, *Transfer*, 43. "55,000 Here Stage Protest."

71. Black, *Transfer*, 43.

72. Black, *Transfer*, 43–44. "250,000 Jews Here to Protest."

73. Black, *Transfer*, 44. "55,000 Here Stage Protest."

74. "Leaders of Nation Send in Protest," *NYT*, Mar 28, 1933, 13. Black, *Transfer*, 44.

75. Black, *Transfer*, 44.

76. Black, *Transfer*, 44n13. "'We Ask Only for the Right,' Says Wise," *NYT*, Mar 28, 1933, 12. Letter, S. Wise to J. Mack, March 29, 1933, quoted in Carl Hermann Voss, ed., *Stephen S. Wise: Servant of the People*, (Philadelphia: Jewish Publication Society, 1969), 181–182. See Author's Interview with Rabbi David Polish, Oct 18, 1981. See Author's Interview with Justine Wise Polier, Oct 21, 1981.

77. Black, *Transfer*, 44. "'We Ask Only for the Right.'" See letter, S. Wise to J. Mack, Mar 29, 1933.

78. Black, *Transfer*, 44–45. "'We Ask Only for the Right.'" See Author's Interview with Justine Wise Polier.

79. Black, *Transfer*, 45. "'We Ask Only for the Right.'"

80. Black, *Transfer*, 45. "'We Ask Only for the Right.'"

81. Black, *Transfer*, 45. "'We Ask Only for the Right.'"

82. Black, *Transfer*, 45. "'We Ask Only for the Right.'"

83. Black, *Transfer*, 45. "250,000 Jews Here to Protest." "50,000 Here Stage Protest."

84. Black, *Transfer*, 71. See generally Black, *Transfer*.

85. Letter, Wolff to RFM, June 15, 1933, NAT-120 roll 4954, L368939 et seq. Nicosia, "Germany and the Palestine Question, 1933–1939," 87–88, 88n2. Marcus, Ernst, "The German Foreign Office and the Palestine Question in the Period 1933–1939," in *Yad Vashem Studies on the European Jewish Catastrophe and Resistance*, vol. 2 (Jerusalem: Yad Vashem), 181, 183–184. See *Jewish Daily Bulletin* (*JDB*), Jul 5, 1933, 4. "German Zionist Paper Banned After

Answering Attack By Rosenberg," *JDB*, Aug 21, 1933. See generally Black, *Transfer*, chaps. 1, 2.

86. See Black, *Transfer*, 6, 121, 136.

87. Black, *Transfer*, 141, 373.

88. Black, *Transfer*, 320. "Nazis Report Deal with Palestine," *NYT*, Aug 29, 1933, 4.

89. Black, *Transfer*, 141, 373.

90. Black, *Transfer*, 249. "The Ministry of Economics to the Foreign Ministry," and enclosure, "The Minister of Economics to Herr S. Hoofien," Aug. 10, 1933, *DGFP*, 735–736. See circular no. 54/33, Ministry of Economics, Aug. 28, 1933, in "Financial Arrangements Between German Government and Certain Organizations in Palestine for the Promotion of the Emigration of German Jews to Palestine," Sep. 14, 1933: BNA FO 371/16757-1527. See Michaelis, Dolf, "The Economic and Political Development of the Emigration and Transfer Question in National-Socialist Germany," in Werner Feilchenfeld, Dolf Michaelis, & Ludwig Pinner, eds., *Haavara-Transfer Nach Palestina Und Einwanderung Deutscher Juden, 1933-1939* (Tubingen: Mohr Verlag, 1972), 27. See also Feilchenfeld, Werner, *Five Years of Jewish Immigration from Germany and the Haavara-Transfer, 1933–1938* (Tel Aviv: Haavara Ltd., n.d.), 5, 16–18.

91. Black, *Transfer*, 72, 146–153, 162, 172, 258, 294, 296, 172.

92. Black, *Transfer*, chaps. 8, 10, 15, 31.

93. Black, *Transfer*, 246–247. "Ministry of Economics to the Foreign Ministry," Aug. 10, 1933, and enclosure, "The Minister of Economics to Herr S, Hoofien," *DGFP, 1918-1945*, ser. C 1, (London, HM Stationery Office, 1957), 732-736. Also see Photo, Sam Cohen, Author's Collection. See handwritten notes, E. S. Hoofien, .n.d., CZA A-95/19. Alex Bein, ed., *Arthur Ruppin: Memoirs, Diaries, Letters* (London, Weidenfeld and Nicolson, 1971), 264. See minutes, Political Committee of the 18th ZC, 5th meeting, Aug. 29, 1933: CZA Z4/232/4, 30. See letter, Sam Cohen to Dr. Eberl, Aug. 1, 1933: NA T-120 roll 4954, L369093/5.

94. Black, *Transfer*, 247–248.

95. Black, *Transfer*, 248.

96. Black, *Transfer*, 247.

97. Black, *Transfer*, 249.

98. Black, *Transfer*, 249.

99. Black, *Transfer*, 249.

100. Black, *Transfer*, 250.

101. Black, *Transfer*, 376.

102. Black, *Transfer*, 47.

103. Black, *Transfer*, 368.

104. "More Suicides," *Jewish Chronicle (JC)*, May 19, 1933, 14. Black, *Transfer*, 107. See generally Black, *Transfer*.

105. Black, *Transfer*, chap. 28.

106. Black, *Transfer*, 712. "Refugee Jews Tax Paris Charity Funds," *NYT*, April 3, 1933. "20 German Refugees Smuggle Themselves into Belgium," *JDB*, April 6, 1933. "German Ban Halts Tide of Refugees," *NYT*, April 6, 1933. "3,000 Jewish Refugees Cross Swiss Border," *JDB*, April 7, 1933. "Jewish Refugees in Holland," *JC*, April 7, 1933. "10,000 Jews Flee Nazi Persecution," *NYT*, April 15, 1933. "Sir John Simon Replies," *JC*, April 21, 1933.

107. Weizmann, Chaim, *The Letters and Papers of Chaim Weizmann: December 1931–April 1952*", Ser. B, vol. 2, Barnet Litvinoff, ed. (New Brunswick, NJ: Transaction Publishers, 1984), 108. See also Black, *War*, chap. 14.

108. Bauer, Yehuda, *My Brother's Keeper: A History of the American Jewish Joint Distribution Committee 1929–1939*, Michael Palomino, transcription & subtitles (Philadelphia, Jewish Publication Society of America, 2007), 163. Feilchenfeld, Michaelis, & Pinner, 90. Porath, Yehoshua, *The Palestinian Arab National Movement: from Riots to Rebellion, 1929–1939*, vol. 2 (London: Frank Cass, 1977), 39. See Porath, *Riots to Rebellion*, chap. 4.

109. *A Survey of Palestine*, 185. Porath, *Emergence*, 39

110. Black, *Transfer*, xiii, 379. See also Black, *BoB*, 297.

111. See Black, *Transfer*," 91.

112. AA, Jerusalem to Berlin, Jan. 15, 1934, signed Wolff, Copy III O 278, L319215

113. Letter to Geneva Consulate-General: Oct 3, 1933, signed Chékib Arslan, L332906. Also

see attachment: AA: Berlin to Geneva, Oct. 26, 1933, signed Prüfer, III O 3856, L332804

114. Porath, *Riots to Rebellion*, 164–165, 169, 193, 193n261–263. Jbara, *The Palestine Years*, 208.

115. Porath, *Riots to Rebellion*, 162, 163–164. Jbara, *The Palestine Years*, 207–208.

116. Porath, *Riots to Rebellion*, chap. 7. Jbara, *The Palestine Years*, chap. 8.

117. Porath, *Riots to Rebellion*, 162–163, 175, See Porath, Porath, *Riots to Rebellion*, chap. 7. Jbara, *The Palestine Years*, chap. 8. Jbara, *Palestinian Leader*, 142–143.

118. See Levy, Joseph M, "11 Killed, 50 Hurt in Palestine Riots," *NYT*, Apr 20, 1936, 1. 7. See Levy, "Deaths Rise to 20 in Palestine Riots," *NYT*, Apr 21, 1936, 12. Porath, *Riots to Rebellion*, 178–179.

119. Black, *BoB*, 298–299, 299n15.

120. Black, *BoB*, 298–299, 299n15.

121. Porath, *Riots to Rebellion*, 188–190.

122. Porath, *Riots to Rebellion*, 195n273. Black, *BoB*, 299. Jbara, *Palestinian Leader*, 143–144, 144n21–22, 154–168.

123. Transcript of Testimony taken on January 12, 1937, from Hajj Amin al-Husayni, *Report of the Palestine Royal Commission*, Cmd. 5479 (London: HM Stationery Office, 1937) (*Peel Commission Report*). Jbara, *Palestinian Leader*, 156–157.

124. Beeley, Brian W., "The Greek-Turkish Boundary: Conflict at the Interface," *Transactions of the Institute of British Geographers*, New Ser., vol. 3 (1978), 351–366. *Peel Commission Report*.

125. *Peel Commission Report*.

126. Black, *BoB*, 29917. *Peel Commission Report*.

127. *Peel Commission Report*.

128. *Peel Commission Report*.

129. Black, *BoB*, 299. Porath, *Riots to Rebellion*, 234.

130. Porath, *Riots to Rebellion*, 235n20.

131. Porath, *Riots to Rebellion*, 236–241

132. Donald Mallett, secret minutes, Feb. 27, 1946, BNA FO 371/27078. British Consul to High Commissioner for Palestine, Jul. 5, 1937. Mattar, *Mufti*, 28–29, 82, 83. Jbara, *Palestinian Leader*, 61–63, 64–65. Black, *BoB*, 299–300.

133. Black, *BoB*, 300. Porath, *Riots to Rebellion*, 236–237.

134. Black, *BoB*, 300–301.

135. Black, *BoB*, 301.

136. Black, *BoB*, 301.

## Chapter 13: The Nazi Quest for Oil

1. *Iraq: Treaty with King Feisal*, Cmd. 1757 (London: HM Stationery Office, 1922). "British Conclude Alliance with Irak," *NYT*, Oct 12, 1922, 5.

2. Secret telegrams to War Office, Aug 22, 1920, Aug 24, 1920, Aug 26, 1920, and Aug 26, 1920, as reproduced in Churchill, "Situation in Mesopotamia," secret cabinet memo, Sep 2, 1920: BL L/MIL/5/800.

3. *Iraq: Treaty with King Feisal*. "British Conclude Alliance With Irak."

4. See Black, *BoB*, chap. 15. See photos, Baba Gurgur No. 1 Well—Oil Gushing through Side of Arbor Head and A River of Oil Flowing from Baba Gurgur No. 1 Well, in Bamberg, James, *The History of the British Petroleum Company*, vol. 2: *The Anglo-Iranian Years, 1928–1954* (Cambridge, UK: Cambridge University Press, 1994), 160.

5. Great Britain, *Treaty of Preferential Alliance: The United Kingdom and Iraq*, Jun 30, 1930, *Parliamentary Papers 1931*, Treaty Series No. 15, Cmd. 3797, reproduced in J. C. Hurewitz, ed., *Diplomacy in the Near And Middle East*, vol. 2 (New York: Van Nostrand, 1956), 178–181. Introduction to *Treaty of Preferential Alliance*, Hurewitz, 178. Ireland, Phillip Willard, *Iraq: A Study in Political Development* (New York: Macmillan Company, 1938), 413–415, 417–418.

6. Confidential letter, Sir F. Humphreys to Sir John Simon, Jan 28, 1935: BL L/PS/12/2882 v 17. Roach, E. Keith, "Pipe Line across a Desert Will Link East with West," *NYT*, Apr 15,

1934, XXVII. "First Iraq Oil at Mediterranean Port," *WSJ*, Jul 18, 1934, 1. See letter, Emir Abdullah to Sir John Cadman Pasha (trans.), Jan 24, 1935: BP IPC 100-P26: See letter, Sir John Cadman to Emir Abdullah, Jan 25, 1935: BP IPC 100-P26: Political, Transjordan, 1934–39. See confidential letter, High Commissioner for Palestine to H. M. Principal Secretary of State for the Colonies, Feb 15, 1935: BL L/PS/12/2882 v 17. Bamberg, *History of BPC*, vol. 2, xxvii.

7. "Plan W.A. 6, Appendix A: The Oil Supply Problem in Germany," July 1939: BNA AIR9/122 no. 119738. See "Analysis of German Petroleum Economy," ca. 1939: BNA AIR9/122 no. 119738. "Second Report of the Sub-Committee on the German Oil Position," ca. 1941: BNA CAB77/13. Carmical, J.H., "Oil is not lacking in First War Year," *NYT*, Sep 8, 1940, 65.

8. "Oil Allocation and Distribution for Civilian Consumption in Germany," Jul 1944: BP 16548.

9. British Petroleum, "Report on Germany," Jan 1, 1947: BP 69501. "Valuation of Stock End-In-Hand at December 31st, 1937."

10. "Oil Allocation and Distribution for Civilian Consumption in Germany." Olex, "Valuation of Stock End-In-Hand at December 31st, 1937": BP 92868. Letter, W. B. Blackwood to F. G. C. Morris, Sep 3, 1936: BP 72201.

11. Olex, "Shares in and Advances to or from Subsidiary Companies at 31st December 1936": BP 90518.

12. Letter, F. C. Starling to A. C. Hearn, Aug 5, 1936: BP 68318. Olex, "Memorandum: Proposed Barter Transaction: Germany," Feb 6, 1936: BP 68318. Blackwood to Morris, Sep 3, 1936. Generally see Black, *Transfer Agreement*.

13. See letter, R. Blackwood to F. G. C. Morris, May 12, 1936: BP 72201. Starling to Hearn. "Proposed Barter Transaction: Germany." Olex-BP, "Anglo-Iranian Oil Company Ltd, London, Claims at 31st December 1936," Mar 15, 1937: BP 90518.

14. Olex, "Anglo-Iranian Oil Company Ltd., London: Claims at 31st December 1938": BP 90492. Letter, "Olex" Deutsche Benzin- Und Petroleum Gesellschaft mit beschrankter Häftung to Anglo-Iranian Oil Co. Ltd., Continental Distribution Department, Oct 28, 1936: BP 64902.

15. See photo, "Pump Installation in Germany, 1926," Ferrier, R.W., *The History of the British Petroleum Company* (Cambridge, UK: Cambridge University Press, 1982), 490. See photo, "'Olex' BP Service Station in Germany, Mid-1930s," Bamberg, *History of BPC*, vol. 2, 135. Bamberg, *History of BPC*, vol. 2, 132–133. "Oil Allocation and Distribution for Civilian Consumption in Germany." Memo, N. B. Fuller to Capt. W. J. A. Brown, Jul 7, 1928: BP 64902. "Draft of a Letter to the Automobile Association," Jun 2, 1936: BP 64902. See Ferrier, 489.

16. Olex, "Tale of the Family Tree," ca. 1950: BP 90030. See "Trade Mark Registration Certificate No. 499538," Jan 27, 1938: BP 97583. See letter, L. Lefroy to F. Mann, Jul 26, 1937: BP 67857. See letter, M. R. Bridgeman to F. G. C. Morris, Jul 25, 1938: BP 67857. See letter, F. G. C. Morris to L. M. Lefroy, Jul 27, 1938: BP 67857.

17. "Standard Oil Co. (N.J.): II," *Fortune*, vol. 21, (1940). "Oil Allocation and Distribution for Civilian Consumption in Germany." See letter, W. B. Blackwood to F. G. C. Morris, Dec 29, 1936: BP 72201. See letter, W. B. Blackwood to F. G. C. Morris, May 31, 1937: BP 72201. See "Trade Mark Registration Certificate No. 511307," May 5, 1939: BP 97574. See "Trade Mark Registration Certificate No. 508749," Mar 13 1939: BP 97585. See "Trade Mark Registration Certificate No. 434021," Mar 10, 1930: BP 97599.

18. Bamberg, 63–64. "Secret: An Appreciation of the Oil Position in Iran and Iraq," Oct 4, 1941: BNA POWE33/1085 no. 119945.

19. "Report on Germany."

20. "Report on Germany." See generally Black, *IBM*.

21. "Particulars from Custodian of Enemy Property Records," ca. 1941: BNA BT271/592 no. 119571.

22. "Record of a Meeting Held in the Petroleum Department on Monday 29th July 1940, at 4:30 P.M. to Consider the Position of French Interests in the Iraq Petroleum Company," Jul 19, 1940: BNA FO371/24561 no. 119238.

23. "Report by the Petroleum Department: The Levant Plan," ca. 1940: BNA CAB77/12 no. 358. "Lord Weir's Note of 1st April, 1940": BNA PREM1/434 no. 119738. War Cabinet, "Lord Hankey's Committee on Preventing Oil From Reaching Germany," Jul 14, 1940: BNA CAB77/12 no. 310. See Pilot Officer M. A. ap Rhys Price, "Bombing the Enemy's Fuel

Supplies," secret report, Jan 27, 1940: BNA AIR9/122 no. 119738. See "R.A.F. Pours Bombs on Reich to Forestall Invasion Attempt," *WP*, Jun 21, 1941, 1.

24. Gilbert, Martin, *The Second World War: A Complete History* (New York: Henry Holt & Co., 1989), 144–147. See generally Mineau, André, *Operation Barbarossa: Ideology and Ethics against Human Dignity* (Amsterdam: Rodopi, 2004).

25. "Lord Weir's Note of 1st April, 1940." "Bad Faith Charged," *NYT*, Jun 22, 1941, 1.

26. "Lord Weir's Note of 1st April, 1940."

27. War Cabinet Joint Planning Staff, "Future Strategy Review," Jun 1941: BNA CAB84/31 no. 119945.

28. "Future Strategy Review." "German Activities in Oil Producing Countries of Middle East," secret minute sheet, Dec 11, 1940: BNA FO371/24549. "Extract from D.O. (41) 39th Meeting" Jun 5, 1941: BNA AIR8/497 no. 119945.

29. "Note on Iraq as a Possible Source of Oil Supply to the Enemy," ca. 1940, BP IPC 255: Protective Measures.

30. "Note on Iraq as a Possible Source of Oil Supply to the Enemy."

31. "Feisal of Iraq Dies Suddenly in Berne," *NYT*, Sep 9, 1933, 1, 3. Tripp, Charles, *A History of Iraq* (Cambridge, UK: Cambridge University Press, 2000), 80.

32. "Ghazi Is Proclaimed King," *NYT*, Sep 9, 1933, 3. See Khadduri, Majid, *Independent Iraq: A Study in Iraqi Politics Since 1932* (London: Oxford University Press, 1951), 47–53, chaps. 4–8. "Extract from Minutes of Group Meeting Held 17/11/37," Nov 11, 1937: BP IPC 100-45: Pipeline Survey.

33. Tripp, 81, 94–98. Warner, Geoffrey, *Iraq and Syria, 1941* (Newark, DE: University of Delaware Press, 1974), 35.

34. Tripp, 98–99. Mattar, 89. Warner, 35. Khadduri, 137–139, 140–142.

35. Warner, 35. Tripp, 98–99. Air Commodore F. W. Walker, "A Review of the Battle of Habbaniya, May 1941," ca. June 1941: BNA AIR8/549 no. 119909, 1.

36. See generally Black, *IBM*.

37. See Black, *War*, 261–277, 279–318. See Black, *IBM*, 93–96. See generally Black, *Transfer*, 371–380, chap. 7. See generally Avriel, Ehud *Open the Gates: Dramatic Personal Story of "Illegal" Immigration to Israel* (Worthington, UK: Littlehampton Book Services, 1975).

38. "Vichy Police Chief Aided Mufti in Syria," ca. June 1940: BNA FO371/61926 no. 119288.

39. Letter, War Office to D. J. M. D. Scott, Nov 24, 1939: BNA FO371/23207 no. 119238. "The Mufti's Bid for Indian Moslem Aid," copy of letter, Mufti to President of All-India Muslim League, Bombay, Mar 2, 1940 (22 Moharrem 1359): BNA FO371/61926 no. 119288. Elpeleg, Zvi, The Grand Mufti: Haj Amin Al-Hussaini, Founder of the Palestinian National Movement, David Harvey, trans., Shmuel Himelstain, ed. (London: Frank Cass, 1993), 58.

40. Sir Basil Newton to Lord Halifax, Jun 10, 1940: BNA FO371/24561 no. 119238. Khadduri, 154–155.

41. "Enclosure in Baghdad Despatch No. 238 of 28.5.40: Extracts from the Local Press," May 28, 1940: BNA FO371/24561 no. 119238.

42. Letter, C. J. Edmonds to Sir Basil Newton, May 19, 1940: BNA FO371/24561 no. 119238.

43. Edmonds to Newton.

44. Edmonds to Newton.

45. "A Review of the Battle of Habbaniya, May 1941." Letter, Sir Basil Newton to Viscount Halifax, May 20, 1940: BNA FO371/24561 no. 119238. Letter, C. J. Edmonds to Sir Basil Newton, Jul 1, 1920, enclosure in Baghdad Despatch No. 315: BNA FO371/24561 no. 119238. See confidential letter, Sir Basil Newton to Mr. Eden, Feb 25, 1941: BNA FO371/27100 no. 119904. Mufti al-Amin, "Proposed Draft of an Official Declaration by Germany and Italy with Respect to the Arab Countries," ca. 1940: BNA FO371/61926 no. 119288. Elpeleg, 59. Khadduri, 195.

46. "Proposed Draft of an Official Declaration by Germany and Italy with Respect to the Arab Countries."

47. Pol, Heinz, "'German Lawrence' Stirs Revolt," *NYT*, May 18, 1941, E5.

48. "'German Lawrence' Stirs Revolt."

49. Epleleg, 68.

50. See letter, Sir Basil Newton to Viscount Halifax, Oct 9, 1940: BNA FO371/24561 no. 119238.

51. Newton to Halifax, Oct 9, 1940.

52. Newton to Halifax, Oct 9, 1940.

53. Newton to Eden, Feb 25, 1941. War Office, "Iraq: February 1940 to August 1941 and May 1941 to January 1942," ca. Feb 1942: BNA WO32/11437 no. 120130.

54. "Comments on Paragraphs 9–13 of Chiefs of Staff Report of November 1st on an Enemy Advance through the Balkans and Syria to the Middle East," Nov 5, 1940: BNA FO371/24549. Elpeleg, 59–60.

55. Confidential letter, Sir Basil Newton to Mr. Eden, Jan 17, 1941: BNA FO371/27100 no. 119904.

56. Letter, Mufti Hussein al-Amin to Adolf Hitler, Jan 20, 1941, as translated and reproduced in Elpeleg, 202–205.

57. Mufti to Hitler.

58. Mufti to Hitler.

59. Mufti to Hitler.

60. Mufti to Hitler.

61. Secret letter, Ernst Friherr von Wiesacker to Mufti Hussein al-Amin, Mar 1941: BNA FO371/61926 no. 119288.

62. Von Wiesacker to Mufti.

63. "Pro-Axis Leader Ousts the Premier in Iraq," NYT, Apr 5, 1941, 2. "Iraqi Coup Denounced," NYT, Apr 8, 1941, 7. Khadduri, 180–183. See "Accused of Plot, Regent Quits Iraq," NYT, Apr 9, 1941, 12.

64. "Pro-Axis Leader Ousts the Premier in Iraq," NYT, Apr 5, 1941, 2. "Iraqi Coup Denounced." Khadduri, 180–183. See "Accused of Plot, Regent Quits Iraq."

65. "New Regent Is Elected," NYT, Apr 12, 1941, 5. Khadduri, 182. Geyder, G. E. R., "Syrians Say Nazis Keep Unrest Alive," NYT, Apr 5, 1941, 2. Letter to Mr. J. Skliros, Apr 5, 1941, and enclosure: letter of resignation, Taha al-Hashimi to H. R. H. The Regent, Apr 1, 1941: BP IPC 99-M4C: Misc. Correspondence. See "Uprising in Levant Fought by French," NYT, Mar 27, 1941, 1, 2.

66. See secret telegram, Baghdad to Foreign Office, Apr 5, 1941: BNA CAB84/28 no. 119909. "Defence of British Embassy and American Legation, Baghdad," memo, Apr 11, 1941: BNA AIR23/5925 no. 119909. "Kirkuk," memo, Apr 13, 1941: BNA AIR23/5925 no. 119909.

67. Telegram, General Wavell to C. I. G. S., May 3, 1941 as quoted in "Iraq: February 1940 to August 1941 and May 1941 to January 1942."

68. See secret telegram, Baghdad to Foreign Office, Apr 5, 1941: BNA CAB84/28 no. 119909. "Defence of British Embassy and American Legation, Baghdad," memo, Apr 11, 1941: BNA AIR23/5925 no. 119909. "Kirkuk," memo, Apr 13, 1941: BNA AIR23/5925 no. 119909. War Cabinet Chiefs of Staff (COS) Committee, "Iraq Oil: Note by the Secretary," May 30, 1941: BNA AIR8/497 no. 119945. Major D. Morton, "Iraq Oil: Memorandum by Major Morton," Jun 4, 1941: BNA AIR8/497 no. 119945. See telegram, Commander in Chief, Baghdad to War Office, Apr 15, 1941: BNA CAB85/29 no. 119909.

69. Iraq Petroleum Company, memo, Jul 1, 1940.

70. Most secret and personal letter, Noel Hall to Commodore J. C. Slessor, Jun 26, 1940: BNA AIR9/122 no. 119738.

71. "Note to Petroleum Department: Syria."

72. Dudley Pound, memo, Nov 17, 1940: BNA FO371/24549.

73. "Aide Memoire on Meeting Held at the Petroleum Department on 18th December, 1940."

74. Secret letter, J. Skliros to M. R. Bridgeman, Apr 10, 1941: BP IPC 255: Protective Measures.

75. "British Army Lands in Iraq to Guard Prized Oil Fields," NYT, Apr 20, 1941, 1. Secret letter, British Consulate, Basra, to Sir K. Cornwallis, Jul 16, 1941: BNA FO371/27079.

76. Letter, Sir K. Cornwallis to Anthony Eden, Jun 6, 1941: BNA FO371/27077 no. 20157. "A Review of the Battle of Habbaniya, May 1941."

77. Letter, J. Skliros to M. R. Bridgeman, Mar 3, 1942. "Note, Strictly Private and

Confidential," Jun 9, 1941: BNA FO371/27078. Halder, Generaloberst Franz, *German Use of Arab Nationalist Movements in World War II* (1956), as cited in Historical Division, *Supplement Guide to Foreign Military Studies, 1945–1954* (Washington, DC: National Archives, 1959).

78. Walker, 1–2. De Chair, Somerset, *The Golden Carpet* (New York: Harcourt, Brace & Co., 1945), 79. Glubb, Sir John, *The Story of the Arab Legion* (London: Hodder & Stoughton, 1948), 277–278.

79. Walker, 3.

80. Churchill to AOC, May 2, 1941, quoted in "Diary of Events Immediately Preceding the Outbreak of Hostilities," *RAF History*, www.raf.mod.uk/history_old/prevents.html.

81. Walker, 4. Glubb, 278. Letter to Anthony Eden, Jun 6, 1941: BNA FO371/27077 no. 120157.

82. Walker, 4–5. "Airspeed Oxford Mk I Military Trainer Aircraft," *Military Aircraft*, www.military-aircraft.org.uk/trainers/airspeed-oxford-i.htm.

83. Walker, 5. Porch, Douglas, "The Other 'Gulf War'—The British Invasion of Iraq in 1941," *The Center for Contemporary Conflict*, www.ccc.nps.navy.mil. See generally Lyman, Robert, *First Victory: Britain's Forgotten Struggle in the Middle East, 1941* (London: Constable & Robinson, 2006).

84. Lyman, *Iraq 1941: The Battles for Basra, Habbaniya, Fallujah and Baghdad* (Osprey, 2006), 43.

85. See Lyman, *Iraq 1941*, 52.

86. "Sonderkommando JUNCK," ca. Sep 8, 1952: BNA AIR20/9945 no. 119738. "Reported Killed," *NYT*, May 18, 1941, 4. Gilbert, *The Second World War*, 182. Lyman, *Iraq 1941*, 63, 65.

87. "Sonderkommando JUNCK." Secret telegram from Sir K. Cornwallis, "List of Germans who arrived in Iraq from 2nd May, 1941," Jun 26, 1941: BNA FO371/27077 no. 120157. Secret telegram, A. H. Q. Iraq to R. A. F., May 14, 1941: BNA AIR8/549 no. 119909. Sulzberger, C. L., "Nazis At Air Bases," *NYT*, May 15, 1941, 1. Sulzberger, C. L., "Syrian Bases Bombed," *NYT*, May 18, 1941, 1. Brock, Ray, "Nazis Tell of Plan to Take Near East," *NYT*, May 13, 1941, 3. See "Attack is Expected Soon," *NYT*, May 1, 1941, 3. See Hullen, Bertram D., "Nazi Drive for All Africa Seen; Suez and Dakar Held in Peril," *NYT*, May 1, 1941, 1. See James, Edwin L., "Britain Facing a Crisis in the Mediterranean," *NYT*, May 4, 1941, E3. See "British," *NYT*, May 4, 1941, 47. See Baldwin, Hanson W., "Middle East Campaign Fought for Big Stakes," *NYT*, May 4, 1941, E5.

88. Telegram, Commander in Chief, Middle East, to War Office, May 3, 1941: BNA AIR8/497.

89. Personal telegram, W. S. Churchill to F. D. Roosevelt, May 4, 1941, quoted by Gilbert, Martin, *Winston S. Churchill*, Vol. 6, *Finest Hour, 1939–1941* (Boston: Houghton Mifflin, 1983), 1078–1079. Walker, 5–6. Shirer, William, *Rise and Fall of the Third Reich* (New York: Simon & Shuster, 1981), 829.

90. See Commander in Chief to War Office, May 3, 1941.

91. Lapidot, Yehuda, *The History of the Irgun*, Chaya Galai, trans., The Irgun Site, www.etzel.org.il/english/. Elpeleg, 60. Bell, J. Bowyer, *Terror Out of Zion: The Fight for Israeli Independence* (New Brunswick, NJ: Transaction Publishers, 1996), 55.

92. Lapidot.

93. Dayan, Moshe, *Moshe Dayan: Story of My Life* (New York: William Morrow, 1976), 63–64. *Encyclopedia Judaica*, s.v. "Palmach."

94. Lapidot. Boyer, 55–56. Elpeleg, 60.

95. Telegram, Major-General Sir H. L. Ismay to War Cabinet, May 22, 1941: BNA AIR8/497.

96. Adolf Hitler, "Order No. 30: Middle East," May 23, 1941: BNA FO371/61926 no. 110288.

97. Adolf Hitler, "Order No. 30: Middle East," May 23, 1941.

98. "A Review of the Battle of Habbaniya, May 1941," 11. "Glubb's Arabs to Parade," *NYT*, Jun 4, 1941, 3. "Mosul is Occupied by British Troops," *NYT*, Jun 5, 1941, 4. "German Flight Reported," *NYT*, Jun 1, 1941, 3. Telegram, Commander in Chief, Iraq, to Foreign Office, May 31, 1941: BNA FO371/27073 no. 120157. Most secret telegram, Assistant Secretary for War to First Sea Lord, May 24, 1941: BNA AIR8/497. Secret telegram, Sir K. Cornwallis to General, Basra, May 30, 1941: BNA AIR8/549 no. 119909.

99. "A Review of the Battle of Habbaniya, May 1941," 11. "Glubb's Arabs to Parade." "Mosul is Occupied by British Troops." "German Flight Reported." Telegram, Commander in Chief, Iraq, to Foreign Office, May 31, 1941. Most secret telegram, Assistant Secretary for War to First Sea Lord. Secret telegram, Sir K. Cornwallis to General, Basra, May 30, 1941. "Despatch on Operations in Iraq, East Syria, And Iran, from 10th April, 1941 to 12th January, 1942," *London Gazette*, Aug 13, 1946, 4093–4101.

100. Lyman, *Iraq 1941*, 83–84.

101. Lyman, *Iraq 1941*, 84. "A Review of the Battle of Habbaniya, May 1941," 11. "Glubb's Arabs to Parade." "Mosul is Occupied by British Troops." "German Flight Reported." Telegram, Commander in Chief, Iraq, to Foreign Office, May 31, 1941. Most secret telegram, Assistant Secretary for War to First Sea Lord, May 24, 1941. Secret telegram, Sir K. Cornwallis to General, Basra, May 30, 1941. "Despatch on Operations in Iraq," 4095.

102. Lyman, "*Iraq 1941*, 84–85. "A Review of the Battle of Habbaniya, May 1941," 11. "Glubb's Arabs to Parade," *NYT*, Jun 4, 1941, 3. "Mosul is Occupied by British Troops," *NYT*, Jun 5, 1941, 4. "German Flight Reported," *NYT*, Jun 1, 1941, 3. Telegram, Commander in Chief, Iraq, to Foreign Office, May 31, 1941. Most secret telegram, Assistant Secretary for War to First Sea Lord, May 24, 1941: BNA AIR8/497. Secret telegram, Sir K. Cornwallis to General, Basra, May 30, 1941: BNA AIR8/549 no. 119909.

103. "Sonderkommando JUNCK." "German Flight Reported." Telegram, Sir K. Cornwallis to Foreign Office, May 31, 1941: BNA FO371/27073 no. 120157. "Armistice Ends Revolt in Iraq; Arab Chief Flees," *NYT*, Jun 1, 1941, 1. Anderson, David, "War in Iraq Ends; Regent in Baghdad," *NYT*, Jun 1, 1941, 1, 3. Telegram, D. Knabenshue to Secretary of State, Jun 1, 1941: NA RG59 740.0011 European War 1939/11558: Telegram, *FRUS*, 1941, 511.

104. "Extract from minutes of Chief of Staff Meeting held on 31st May, 1941," secret, May 31, 1941: BNA AIR8/497 no. 119945.

105. "Long Allied Columns Drive North in Syria," *NYT*, Jun 9, 1941, 4. Connell, John, *Wavell: Scholar and Soldier to June 1941* (London: Collins, 1964), 490–492.

106. Dayan, 66–68. Teveth, Shabtai, *Moshe Dayan: The Soldier, The Man, The Legend*, Leah and David Zinder, trans. (Boston: Houghton Mifflin, 1973), 116–117.

107. Dayan, 66–68. Teveth, 116–117.

108. Slater, Robert, *Rabin of Israel* (New York: St. Martin's Press, 1993), 46. Teveth, 123–124.

109. "Long Allied Columns Drive North in Syria." "Advance Towards Capitals," *NYT*, Jun 9, 1941, 1. MacRae, James, "Airfields Blasted," *NYT*, Jun 9, 1941, 1. See Connell, 490–492.

110. Anderson, David, "War in Iraq Ends; Regent in Baghdad," *NYT*, Jun 1, 1941, 1, 3. "Bad Faith Charged," *NYT*, Jun 22, 1941, 1.

## Chapter 14: The Farhud

1. Sir A. Nicolson, "Note on the Future Status and Administration of Basrah," Feb 2, 1915: BNA FO800/377. Levin, Itamar, *Locked Doors: The Seizure of Jewish Property in Arab Countries*, Rachel Neiman, trans. (Westport, CT: Praeger, 2001), 3. Gat, Moshe, *The Jewish Exodus from Iraq, 1948–1951* (London: Frank Cass, 1997), 12–13.

2. Gat, 10.

3. Shaw, Stanford J., & Ezel Kural Shaw, *The History of the Ottoman Empire and Modern Turkey*, vol. 2: *Reform, Revolution, and Republic: The Rise of Modern Turkey, 1808–1975* (Cambridge, UK: Cambridge University Press, 1977), 241. Levin, 7–8.

4. Gat, 18–19.

5. Gat, 16. See Black, *Transfer*, 71–82.

6. Gat, 16.

7. Letter, Menahem S. Daniel to Zionist Organization, Sep 8, 1922: Central Zionist Archive (CZA) Z4/2101.

8. "Rabbi Attacks Zionism," *NYT*, Apr 9, 1947, 8. Gat, 19.

9. See Letter, Abdullah ibn al-Hussein to Secretary of State for the British Colonies, Jul 11, 1940: FO371/24549. See Ireland, Phillip Willard, *Iraq: A Study in Political Development* (New York: Macmillan Company, 1938), 418.

10. Khadduri, Majid, *Independent Iraq: A Study in Iraqi Politics Since 1932* (London:

Oxford University Press, 1951), 44–46. Phares, Walid, "Middle East Christians," in Malka Hillel Shulewitz, ed., *The Forgotten Millions: The Modern Jewish Exodus from Arab Lands* (London: Cassel, 1999), 20. See Stafford, R. S., "Iraq and the Problem of the Assyrians," *International Affairs*, vol. 13, (1934), 165–166.

11. Stafford, 174–177.

12. De Luca, Anthony, "'Der Grossmufti' in Berlin: The Politics of Collaboration," *International Journal of Middle East Studies*, vol. 10, (1979), 127. Gat, 18.

13. Shawkat, Sami, "The Profession of Death," in Sylvia G. Haim, ed., *Arab Nationalism: An Anthology* (Berkeley; Los Angeles: University of California Press, 1962), 97–99. Wild, Stefan, "National Socialism II," 35–36.

14. "The Jews in Iraq: Government Officials Take Part in Incitements," *Jewish Telegraphic Agency* (*JTA*), Oct 26, 1936: BNA FO954/12. Gat, 18.

15. Elliot, Matthew, *Independent Iraq: the Monarchy and British influence, 1941–58* (London: I.B. Tauris, 1996), 46. Cohen, Hayyim J., "The Anti-Jewish 'Farhūd' in Baghdad, 1941," *Middle Eastern Studies*, vol. 3 (1966), 6. Wild, "National Socialism II," in Moreh, Shmuel & Zvi Yehuda, eds., *Al-Farhūd: The 1941 Pogrom in Iraq* (Jerusalem, Magnes Press, 2010), 34–36. See also Bashkin, Orit, *The Other Iraq: Pluralism and Culture in Hashemite Iraq* (Stanford University Press, 2009).

16. See Berg, Nancy E., *Exile from Exile: Israeli Writers from Iraq* (Albany: SUNY Press), 21–22. Moreh & Yehuda, xiii–ix. Kazzaz, Nissim, "The Communists in Iraq and Rashid 'Ali al-Kaylani's Revolt," in Moreh & Yehuda, 176–177n28. Cohen, "Anti-Jewish 'Farhūd,'", 7.

17. Moreh, "The Role of Palestinian Incitement and the Attitude of Arab Intellectuals to the Farhūd, 127. Cohen, "Anti-Jewish 'Farhūd,'", 6.

18. Letter from Grobba in Baghdad, June 19, 1937, Yad Vashem Archive (YVA): JM 3234, quoted in Yehuda, "Selected Documents on the Pogrom (Farhūd)," in Moreh & Yehuda, 252–253. See Black, *Transfer*, 373.

19. Letter from Grobba in Baghdad, June 6, 1939, marked "Secret!", YVA: JM 2495, quoted in Yehuda, "Selected Documents," 253–254.

20. Letter from Grobba in Baghdad, June 12, 1939, marked "Secret!", YVA: JM 3234, quoted in Yehuda, "Selected Documents," 253–254.

21. "The Report of the Iraqi Commission of Inquiry on the Farhūd," quoted in Stillman, *The Jews of Arab Lands in Modern Times* (Philadelphia: Jewish Publication Society, 1991), 413–414.

22. Testimony given by Dr. Shaul Sehayik on 25 September 1990: Zvi Yehuda Archive, quoted in Yehuda, "Selected Documents," in Moreh & Yehuda, 256.

23. Testimony by Dr. Saul Sehayik.

24. Diary of Abraham Twena (Baghdad Jew), May 6–8, 1941, quoted in Kedourie, Elie, "The Sack of Basra and the *Farhud* in Baghdad," in Kedourie, *Arab Political Memoirs and Other Stories* (London: Frank Cass, 1974), 307. Kedourie, "The Sack," 314n64.

25. Wavell to WO, May 8, 1941, quoted in Kedourie, "The Sack," 286. Copy of Wavell's telegram, May 11, 1941:FO371/27069, 2180/1/93, quoted in Kedourie, "The Sack," 287.

26. Kedourie, "The Sack," 290–291.

27. Kedourie, "The Sack," 297.

28. FO371/27074, 2803/1/93, quoted in Kedourie, "The Sack," 295. Kedourie, "The Sack," 295.

29. Letter from the Political Adviser, Northern Area to Sir K. Cornwallis, Kirkuk, 1 September 1941:FO624/60, Part II, quoted in Kedourie, "The Sack," 309–312.

30. Letter from the Political Adviser.

31. Letter from the Political Adviser.

32. Letter from Shim'on Hajj Moshe, July 7, 1941: Zvi Yehuda Archive, quoted in Yehuda, "Selected Documents," in Moreh & Yehuda, 304–308. See Black, *IBM*, 55, 59, 134, 203. Ioanid, Radu, "The Holocaust in Romania: The Iasi Pogrom of June 1941," *Contemporary European History*, vol. 2 (1993), 119–148. "Report of the Iraqi Commission of Inquiry," 415. Shamash, Violette, *Memories of Eden: A Journey through Jewish Baghdad*, Mira Rocca & Tony Rocca, eds. (Surrey, UK: Forum, 2008), 195. Moreh, "The Pogrom of June 1941 in the Literature of Iraqi Jews in Israel," in Moreh & Yehuda, 32. Yehuda, "Selected Documents," in Moreh & Yehuda, 57–58.

33. Shamash, 196.
34. Shamash, 196. Photo, Rabbi Sasōn Khdūrī, in Moreh & Yehuda, 156.
35. "Report of the Iraqi Commission of Inquiry," 412–413. Shamash, 196.
36. Testimony of Dr. Nissim Kazzaz, 1990: Zvi Yehuda Archive, quoted in Yehuda, "Selected Documents," in Moreh & Yehuda, 271–273.
37. Testimony of Nissim Kazzaz. Testimony of Ovadia Gourji, Attorney-at-law, 1990: Zvi Yehuda Archive, quoted in Yehuda, "Selected Documents," 274–276. Testimony of anonymous Jewish chauffeur, 1 July 1941:CZA S25/5289. Testimony of Ya'qūb, son of Siōn Dillāl, 29 May 1997: ZYPA, quoted in Yehuda, "Selected Documents," 278–279. Testimony of Anonymous witness, 29 July 1941:CZA S25/5289, quoted in Yehuda, "Selected Documents," 279–283. Testimony of Anonymous witness, 2 August 1941: CZA S25/5290, quoted in Yehuda, "Selected Documents," 283–284. Testimony of Anonymous witness, 16 July 1941: CZA S25/5289, quoted in Yehuda, "Selected Documents," 284–286. Black, BoB, 332.
38. Testimony of Nissim Kazzaz. Testimony of anonymous Jewish chauffeur. Letter from Shim'on Hajj Moshe. Cornwallis to Eden, Jul 11, 1941. Habousha, Hayim V., "The Farhud," lecture, Midrash ben Ish Hai, www.midrash.org/articles/farhud/index.html. Itamar, Locked Doors, 6. See de Chair, Somerset, The Golden Carpet (New York: Harcourt, Brace, & Co., 1945), 127.
39. "Report of the Iraqi Commission of Inquiry," 406. Testimony of Ovadia Gourji, Attorney-at-law. Testimony of Ya'qūb, son of Siōn Dillāl. Testimony of Anonymous witness, 14 July 1941: CZA S25/5289, quoted in Yehuda, "Selected Documents," 286–288.
40. Testimony of Ya'qūb, son of Siōn Dillāl. Testimony of Anonymous witness, 29 July 1941. Testimony of Anonymous witness, 16 July 1941. Cohen, 11–12.
41. Salim Fattal, In the Alleys of Baghdad (Jerusalem: Carmel, 2004), 102–105. Cf. Kazzaz Nissim, Warrior and Scholar: Memoirs / Sayfa ve-Safra, Zichronot (Jerusalem: Association of Jewish Academics from Iraq & Ruven Mass Ltd., 2010), 80–87. Testimony of Dr. Nissim Kazzaz. Testimony of Ovadia Gourji, Attorney-at-law.
42. Testimony of Ovadia Gourji, Attorney-at-law.
43. Shamash, 206.
44. Levin, 5–6.
45. Testimony of Ya'qūb, son of Siōn Dillāl.
46. Shamash, 206. Testimony of Anonymous witness, 16 July 1941.
47. "Report of the Iraqi Commission of Inquiry," 406. Testimony of Anonymous witness, 29 July 1941.
48. See generally de Chair.
49. Testimony of Anonymous witness, 14 July 1941. Testimony of Yehuda (Gourji) Barshan, 1990: Zvi Yehuda Archive, quoted in Yehuda, "Selected Documents," 290–292.
50. Telegram, Sir K. Cornwallis to Foreign Office, 29th July 1941: BNA FO/371/27028, quoted in Yehuda, Selected Documents," 317–318.
51. Testimony of Wife of the merchant Hisqēl 'Abūdī, 17 July 1941: CZA S25/5289, quoted in Yehuda, "Selected Documents," 296. Testimony of Anonymous witness, 29 July 1941.
52. "Report of the Iraqi Commission of Inquiry," 406.
53. "Report of the Iraqi Commission of Inquiry," 406.
54. "Report of the Iraqi Commission of Inquiry," 406–408.
55. "Report of the Iraqi Commission of Inquiry," 406–410.
56. Kedourie, "The Sack," 298, 301. Black, BoB, 333–334. Habousha, "The Farhud." See Levin, 6.
57. Kedourie, "The Sack," 303–304.
58. "Report of the Iraqi Commission of Inquiry," 416.
59. "Report of the Iraqi Commission of Inquiry," 410.
60. "Report of the Iraqi Commission of Inquiry," 410. Photo, Mass Grave of the Farhūd Victims, 1945, Author's Collection. Testimony of Moïse Itah, 20 July 1941:CZA S25/5289, quoted in Yehuda, 299–304. Testimony of Anonymous witness, 2 August 1941. Kedourie, "The Sack," 298.
61. Minute by P.M. Crosthwaithe, 7 Feb 1940, quoted in Kedourie, "The Sack," 301.
62. de Chair, Somerset, The Golden Carpet (New York: Harcourt, Brace, & Co., 1945), 127–128.

63. de Chair, 128.

64. Testimony of Anonymous witness, 29 July 1941. Moreh, "Role of Palestinian Incitement," 130.

## Chapter 15: The Arab-Nazi Alliance

1. See generally Almog, Shmuel, ed., *Antisemitism through the Ages* (New York: Pergamon Press, 1988). See generally Chazan, Robert, *Medieval Stereotypes and Modern Antisemitism* (Berkeley; Los Angeles: University of California Press, 1997).

2. Letter, H.R.P Dickson to George Rendell: BNA FO371/20822 E7201/22/31. Dickson, Harold Richard Patrick, *Kuwait and Her Neighbours* (London: Allen & Unwin, 1956), 388–393.

3. Dickson to Rendell. Dickson, 388–393.

4. Dickson to Rendell. Dickson, 388–393.

5. Dickson to Rendell. Dickson, 388–393.

6. Dickson to Rendell. Dickson, 388–393.

7. Dickson to Rendell. Dickson, 388–393.

8. Dickson to Rendell. Dickson, 388–393.

9. Dickson to Rendell. Dickson, 388–393.

10. Dickson to Rendell. Dickson, 388–393.

11. Dickson to Rendell. Dickson, 388–393.

12. Dickson to Rendell. Dickson, 388–393.

13. Dickson to Rendell. Dickson, 388–393.

14. Dickson to Rendell. Dickson, 388–393.

15. Dickson to Rendell. Dickson, 388–393.

16. Dickson to Rendell. Dickson, 388–393.

17. Dickson to Rendell. Dickson, 388–393.

18. Dickson to Rendell. Dickson, 388–393.

19. Dickson to Rendell. Dickson, 388–393.

20. Dickson to Rendell. Dickson, 388–393.

21. Dickson to Rendell. Dickson, 388–393.

22. Dickson to Rendell. Dickson, 388–393.

23. Dickson to Rendell. Dickson, 388–393.

24. Dickson to Rendell. Dickson, 388–393.

25. *Documents on German Foreign Policy, 1918–1945*, Ser. D, IV (Washington, DC: Government Printing Office), 743–744. Melka, R., "Nazi Germany and the Palestine Question," *Journal of Middle Eastern Studies*, vol. 5, (1969), 225–226, 226n4.

26. Melka, 227.

27. Patterson, David, *A Genealogy of Evil: Anti-Semitism from Nazism to Islamic Jihad* (New York: Cambridge University Press, 2010), 98. Wild, Stefan, "National Socialism in the Arab Near East between 1933 and 1939," *Die Welt des Islams*, New Ser., Bd. 25 (1985), 128. See Mohsen, Omar, "Take a Bite out of Crime," *Egypt Today*, Dec 2004, www.egypttoday. com/article.aspx?ArticleID=2978. Black, *BoB*, 319.

28. Herf, Jeffrey, *Nazi Propaganda for the Arab World* (New Haven, CT: Yale University Press, 2009), 37–38, 47.

29. "Greatest Horrors in History Mark Massacres in Armenia, Declares an Official Report," *WP*, Oct 4, 1915, 5. "Turks Are Evicting Native Christians," *NYT*, Jul 12, 1915, 4. "Armenians Are Sent To Perish in Desert," *NYT*, Aug 18, 1915, 5. "Answer Morgenthau by Hanging Armenians," *NYT*, Sep 16, 1915, 1. "Bryce Asks Us to Aid Armenia," *NYT*, Sep 21, 1915, 3. "800,000 Armenians Counted Destroyed," *NYT*, Oct 7, 1915, 3. See "*New York Times* headlines of 1915," Balakian, Peter, *The Burning Tigris: The Armenian Genocide and America's Response* (New York: HarperCollins, 2003), 236ff.

30. "Judgment: Streicher," in *Trial of the Major War Criminals before the International Military Tribunal, Nuremberg, 14 November 1945–1 October 1946* (Nuremburg: International Military Tribunal, 1947), reproduced in http://avalon.law.yale.edu/imt/judstrei.asp. Author's corresp. with Shmuel Moreh, Sep 2010. Shaul, Anwar, *The Story of My Life in Mesopotamia (Memoirs)* (Jerusalem: Association of Jewish Academics from Iraq, 1980), 27.

31. "Extremists Sway Nazis and Jews are Menaced with More Drastic Rule," *NYT*, Nov 14, 1938, 1, 6. "Jews in Germany Get Extermination Threat," *NYT*, Nov 30, 1938, 14.

32. "Nazis Hint 'Purge' of Jews in Poland," *NYT*, Sep 13, 1939, 5.

33. Wohl, Paul, "Iran: How Nazis Gained Control," *Christian Science Monitor*, Sep. 19, 1941, 6. See generally Black, *BoB*.

34. "Iran to End Feudal Titles," *NYT*, Aug 10, 1935, 10. See Paine, Chris & Erica Schoenberger, "Iranian Nationalism and the Great Powers: 1872–1954," *MERIP Reports*, no. 37 (1975), 15. Wohl, "Iran."

35. *Holocaust Encyclopedia*, s.v. "History of the Swastika," United States Holocaust Memorial Museum (USHMM), www.ushmm.org/wlc/en/article.php?ModuleId=10007453. See generally Wilson, Thomas, *The Swastika: the Earliest known Symbol & its Migrations; with Observations* (Washington, DC: Smithsonian Institution, Government Printing Office, 1896).

36. "Persia Described as Land of Aryans," letter, G. Djalal, Minister of Persia to the Editor, *NYT*, Jan 20, 1935, E5. Breasted, James Henry, *Ancient Times: A History of the Early World; An Introduction to the Study of Ancient History and the Career of Early Man* (Boston: Athenæum Press, 1916), 176–179. See "Persia Changes Its Name; To Be 'Iran' from Mar. 22," *NYT*, Jan 1, 1935, 1. See generally Poliakov, Leon, *The Aryan Myth: A History of Racist and Nationalist Ideas in Europe* (NY: Basic Books, 1974).

37. Rezun, Miron, *The Soviet Union and Iran: Soviet Policy in Iran from the Beginnings of the Pahlavi Dynasty to the Soviet Invasion in 1941* (Leiden: Sijthoff & Noordhoff, 1981), 319, 319n24. See "Iran-e Bastan Weekly (Ancient Iran)," *International Institute of Social History*, www.iisg.nl/meca/irane-bastan.php.

38. Paine & Schoenberger, "Iranian Nationalism," 13–14. See Bamberg, J.H., *The History of the British Petroleum Company*, vol. 2, *The Anglo-Iranian Years, 1928–1954* (Cambridge, UK: Cambridge University Press, 1994), 233–236.

39. Volodarskiĭ, Mikhail I., *The Soviet Union and its Southern Neighbours: Iran and Afghanistan, 1917–1933* (Portland, OR: Frank Cass, 1994), 50–51. Manzhulo, A.N., ed., *The USSR and International Economic Relations* (London: Central Books, 1987), 34. Paine & Schoenberger, "Iranian Nationalism," 15. See Duranty, Walter, "Big Gain in Output on Soviet Program," *NYT*, Mar 10, 1930, 7. See Denny, Harold, "Germans in Iran Worry Russians," *NYT*, Jun 26, 1938, 23.

40. Wohl, "Iran." Paine & Schoenberger, "Iranian Nationalism," 15. See Denny, "Germans in Iran Worry Russians."

41. Wohl, "Iran."

42. Rezun, *The Iranian Crisis of 1941* (Köln; Wien: Böhlau Verlag, 1982), 29. "Persia to be called 'Iran,'" *Times*, Jan 29, 1935, 11. "Iran or Persia?," *Times*, Jan 30, 1935, 13. "Iran or Persia," letter, Hussein 'Ala, Persian Minister in London to the Editor, *Times*, Jan 31, 1935, 10. "Persia Changes its Name." Black, *BoB*, 294. Paine & Schoenberger, "Iranian Nationalism," 15. See Rezun, *Iranian Crisis*, 319. See Denny, "Germans in Iran Worry Russians."

43. Ramazani, Rouhollah K., *The Foreign Policy of Iran: A Developing Nation in World Affairs, 1500–1941* (Charlottesville, VA: University Press of Virginia, 1966), 283. Rezun, *Iranian Crisis*, 28.

44. Rezun, *The Soviet Union and Iran*, 267. Rezun, *Iranian Crisis*, chap. 3. Picture of SUMKA flag, Author's Collection.

45. "Iran to Remain Neutral," *NYT*, Jun 27, 1941, 2. Brock, Ray, "Berlin Said to Threaten Rupture with Iran if Germans are Ousted," *NYT*, 3. "The Germans in Iran," *MG*, Aug 18, 1941, 5. Wohl, "Iran." Paine & Schoenberger, "Iranian Nationalism," 16. See "Iran at the Crossroads," *NYT*, Aug 19, 1941, 20.

46. Rezun, *The Soviet Union and Iran*, 354, 367. Rezun, *Iranian Crisis*, chap. 2.

47. Rosenblatt, Naomi R., "Oil and the Eastern Front: US Foreign and Military Policy in Iran, 1941–1945," Penn Humanities Forum Mellon Undergraduate Research Fellowship Final Paper, April 2009, 2–5, Bill, James A., *The Eagle and the Lion: The Tragedy of American-Iranian Relations* (New Haven, CT: Yale University Press, 1998), 18, as cited by Rosenblatt, 3. "Iran Refuses to Oust Nazis," *NYT*, Jul 30, 1941, 7. Wohl, "Iran."

48. Rezun, *The Soviet Union and Iran*, 267.

49. Mattar, Philip, *The Mufti of Jerusalem: Al-Hajj Amin Al-Husayni and the Palestinian National Movement* (New York: Columbia University Press, 1988), 96.

50. "Iran Is the Old Meeting Place of Britain and Russia," *NYT*, Aug 25, 1941, 14. "March Into Iran," *NYT*, Aug 26, 1941, C18. See "Iranians Expect Showdown," *NYT*, Aug 23, 1941, 3. See Beaumont, Joan, "Great Britain and the Rights of Neutral Countries: The Case of Iran, 1941," *Journal of Contemporary History*, vol. 16 (1981), 213–228.

51. Mattar, *Mufti*, 96–97.

52. Mattar, *Mufti*, 97.

53. Mattar, *Mufti*, 97.

54. Mattar, *Mufti*, 97, 102.

55. Mufti's broadcast of Mar 1, 1944, quoted in Gensicke, Klaus, *The Mufti of Jerusalem and the Nazis: The Berlin Years*, Alexander Fraser Gunn, trans. (Portland, OR: Vallentine Mitchell, 2010), 117.

56. Gensicke, 58, 60, 62–63.

57. Gensicke, 66.

58. Gensicke, 66–67.

59. Gensicke, 67. "The Mufti's Diary on his Meeting with Hitler," reproduced in Joseph B. Schechtman, *The Mufti and the Fuehrer: The Rise and Fall of Haj Amin el-Husseini* (New York: Yoseloff, 1965), 306–308.

60. Gensicke, 66–67. Herf, *Nazi Propaganda*, 77–78.

61. Herf, *Nazi Propaganda*, 77–78. Gensicke, 67.

62. Halder, Generaloberst Franz, "German Exploitation of Arab Nationalist Movements," MS P-207, in *Foreign Military Studies, 1945–1954* (Washington, DC: National Archives, 1959), 8–11.

63. Gensicke, 117. Herf, *Nazi Propaganda*, 88.

64. Halder, 11, 19.

65. Halder, 10.

66. Halder, 16.

67. Lemkin, Raphaël, *Axis Rule in Occupied Europe: Laws of Occupation, Analysis of Government, Proposals for Redress* (Washington, DC: Carnegie Endowment for International Peace, 1944), chap. 26. Gumz, Jonathan, "German Counterinsurgency Policy in Independent Croatia," *The Historian*, vol. 61 (1998), 33–50. Images of Chetnik (Četnik) Flag, Author's Collection. Denich, Bette, "Dismembering Yugoslavia: Nationalist Ideologies and the Symbolic Revival of Genocide," *American Ethnologist*, vol. 21 (1994), 374. See Denich, "Dismembering," 367–390. Jelinek, Yeshayahu A., "Bosnia-Herzegovina at War: Relations between Moslems And Non-Moslems," *Holocaust and Genocide Studies*, vol. 5 (1990), 289.

68. "Croat 'State' Wins Axis Recognition," *NYT*, Apr 16, 1941, 5. *Holocaust Encyclopedia*, s.v. "Jasenovac," www.ushmm.org/wlc/en/article.php?ModuleId=10005449. *Holocaust Encyclopedia*, s.v. "Axis Invasion of Yugoslavia," www.ushmm.org/wlc/en/article.php?ModuleId=10005456. Lepre, George, *Himmler's Bosnian Division: The Waffen-SS Handschar Division 1943–1945* (Atglen, PA: Schiffer Military History, 1997), 14. Trifković, Srdjan, "Rivalry between Germany and Italy in Croatia, 1942–1943," *The Historical Journal*, vol. 36 (1993), 880, 890. Jelinek, "Bosnia-Herzegovina," 281. See "Balkans Aflame," *NYT*, Apr 6, 1941, E1. See "Yugoslav Envoy Denounces Nazis," *NYT*, Apr 11, 1941, 12. See Matthews, Herbert, "Anxious Italy Eyes Events in Albania," *NYT*, Apr 8, 1941, 4. See "Opposition Indicated," *NYT*, Apr 19, 1941, 3.

69. Savich, Carl, "The Black Legion: A History of the 1ˢᵗ Ustasha Regiment," *Serbianna*, www.serbianna.com/columns/savich/049.shtml. Gumz, 33. See "Croats Worry Vatican," *NYT*, Apr 18, 1941, 6. See Tomasevich, Jozo, *War and Revolution in Yugoslavia, 1941–1945: Occupation and Collaboration* (Stanford, CA: Stanford University Press, 2001), 379, 381. See Trifković, "Rivalry," 880.

70. Brock, Ray, "Nazis Held Ready to Crush Serb Guerrillas and Jews," *NYT*, May 11, 1941, 1. *Holocaust Encyclopedia*, s.v. "Jasenovac." See Brock, "Nazis Execute 80,000 Serbs, Turkey Hears; Guerrillas Continue to Harry Conqueror," *NYT*, Jul 23, 1941, 3. See Tomasevich, *Occupation and Collaboration*, 380. See generally Pedaliu, Effie G.H., "Britain and the 'Hand-over' of Italian War-Criminals to Yugoslavia, 1945–48," *Journal of Contemporary History*, vol. 39 (2004), 503–529. See generally Walston, James, "History and Memory of the Italian Concentration Camps," *The Historical Journal*, vol. 40 (1997), 169–183.

71. Tomasevich, *Occupation and Collaboration*, 53, 380–381. Trifković, 880, 890. Savich, "Black Legion." Jelinek, "Bosnia-Herzegovina," 278–279, 284. See Jelinek, "Bosnia-Herzegovina," 280. Gensicke, 130.

72. Carmichael, Cathie, *Ethnic Cleansing in the Balkans: Nationalism and the Destruction of Tradition* (New York: Routledge, 2002), 36. Savich, "The Holocaust in Bosnia-Hercegovina, 1941–1945, *Serbianna*, www.serbianna.com/columns/savich/006.shtml. Jelinek, "Bosnia-Herzegovina," 278. Savich, "Black Legion." Gensicke, 130.

73. Tomasevich, *Occupation and Collaboration*, 496. Jelinck, "Bosnia-Herzegovina," 280, 286. *Hrvatski List* (Osjek), 22 July 1941, as cited by Jelinek, "Bosnia-Herzegovina," 281n19. Carmichael, 36. Trifković. 880. Lepre, 16. Donia, Robert J., *Sarajevo: A Biography* (Ann Arbor: University of Michigan Press, 2006), 173. See photo, Zagreb Mosque, Author's Collection. See photos, "Axis History Factbook: Gallery: Ustasha (Croatia)," *Axis History Factbook*, www.axishistory.com/index.php?id=7917. See video, "NDH Kula Fazlagic," Mar 2008, Author's Yugoslavia Period Film and Video Collection.

74. Donia, *Sarajevo*, 174–176. Tomasevich, *Occupation and Collaboration*, 378–379. Jelinek, "Bosnia-Herzegovina," 280–281, 286–288. Savich, "Black Legion."

75. Donia, *Sarajevo*, 174–176, 178. Savich, "Black Legion." Savich, "Holocaust." See Donia, *Sarajevo*, 179–180. Jelinek, "Bosnia-Herzegovina," 288.

76. Trifković, 880. Savich, "Holocaust." Donia, *Sarajevo*, 174–176.

77. Savich, "Holocaust." Savich, "Black Legion." Jelinek, "Bosnia-Herzegovina," 283.

78. Photo, Execution of Branko Jungic, Author's Collection. Photos, Young Ustasha Holding a Man's Head wearing a Serb Cap with Royalist Insignia; Young Ustashas Show Off a Serb's Decapitated Head after the Massacre of Drakulić, 7 Feb 1942, in Rivelli, Marco Aurelio, *Le Génocide Occulté: État Indépendant de Croatie, 1941–1945* (Lausanne: Editions L'Age d'Homme: 1998), XI. Pâris, Edmond, *Genocide in Satellite Croatia, 1941–1945: A Record of Racial and Religious Persecutions and Massacres* (Chicago: American Institute for Balkan Affairs, 1961), 132. See Fisk, Robert, "'Cleansing' Bosnia at a Camp Called Jasenovac," *The Independent*, Aug 15, 1922, www.independent.co.uk.

79. Schindley, Wanda B., "Hidden History: The Horror of Jasenovac," in Krstić, Dušan & Goran Marić, eds., *Jasenovac—Donja Gradina: The Industry of Death, 1941–1945* (Belgrade: Svetlopisno odeljenje, 2005), www.jerusalim.org/cd/index_en.html. See *Jasenovac*, Gustav Gavrin & Kosta Hlavaty, dirs., (The Film Company of Democratic Federative Yugoslavia, Regional Board for Croatia, 1945), MPG, in Krstić & Marić. Photos, Ustasha Serbcutter; Ustasha Victims, Author's Collection.

80. Bailey, Ronald H., *Partisans and Guerrillas* (London: Time-Life, 2000), 87. Tribovich, Marco, "First International Conference Documents Jasenovac Holocaust," Serb National Federation Archives.

81. Bailey, 87. See "Depositions of Serbian Women Given to the State Commission for War Crimes," UN Security Council Document A/47/813; S/24991, 18 Dec 1992.

82. Jelinek, "Bosnia-Herzegovina," 281. Savich, "Black Legion." Trifković, 880–881. Lisciotto, Carmelo, "The Jasenovac Extermination Camp: 'Terror in Croatia,'" *Holocaust Research Project*, www.holocaustresearchproject.org/othercamps/jasenovac.html. Letter: Glaise von Horstenau on the Ustase Concentration Camps, quoted in Krstić & Marić.

83. Kostić, Lazo M., *The Holocaust in the Independent State of Croatia: An Account Based on German, Italian, and the Other Sources* (Chicago: Liberty, 1981), 3. Naubacher, Hermann, *Sonderaufrag Sudost 1940–1945: Bericht eines fliegenden Diplomaten* (Gottingen, 1956), quoted in "Jasenovac: Proceedings of the First International Conference and Exhibit on the Jasenovac Concentration Camps," Oct 29–31, 1997, Kingsborough Community College of the City University of New York.

84. Affidavit, "Berberovic Hilmija," quoted in Ruth Mitchell, *The Serbs Choose War* (Garden City, NY: Doubleday, 1943), 258–260.

85. Affidavit, "Berberovic Hilmija."

86. Affidavit, "Berberovic Hilmija."

87. Affidavit, "Berberovic Hilmija."

88. Affidavit, "Berberovic Hilmija."

89. Affidavit, "Berberovic Hilmija."

90. Savich, "Black Legion."

91. Savich, "Black Legion." Donia, *Sarajevo*, 180–186. Fisk, Robert, "'Cleansing' Bosnia." See Batinić, Jelena, "Gender, Revolution, and War: The Mobilization of Women in The Yugoslav Partisan Resistance during World War II," Ph D diss., Stanford University, 2009. See Tomasevich, *Occupation and Collaboration*, 93.

92. Stein, George H., *The Waffen SS: Hitler's Elite Guard at War, 1939–1945* (Ithaca, NY: Cornell University Press, 1966).

93. Stein, *Waffen SS*, chap. 4. See Stein, *Waffen SS*, chap. 5.

94. Savich, "Bosnia and the Kama Division," *Serbianna*. Jelinek, "Bosnia-Herzegovina," 282. Lepre, 15, 17. Tomasevitch, *Occupation and Collaboration*, 496–497.

95. Jelinek, "Bosnia-Herzegovina," 279, 281–283.

96. "War-Guilt Court Reported on Way," *NYT*, Dec 29, 1942, 3. See "Rules out 'Superior Orders,'" *NYT*, Feb 19, 1943, 10. See Jelinek, "Bosnia-Herzegovina," 282, 286. See Lopasic, Alexander, "Bosnian Muslims: A Search for Identity," *Bulletin (British Society for Middle Eastern Studies)*, vol. 8, (1981), 121–122.

97. Savich, "Kosovo during World War II, 1941–1945 and Genocide in Kosovo: The Skenderbeg SS Division," *Serbianna*, www.serbianna.com/columns/savich/004.shtml. Lepre, 35.

98. Zarembina, Natalia, *Oswiecim, Camp of Death*, Polish Labor Federation, trans. (New York: Poland Fights, 1944), 33–34. Black, *IBM*, 376–377. See generally Lebeli, Jennie, *Until The "Final Solution:" The Jews in Belgrade, 1521–1942* (Bergenfield, NJ: Avotaynu, 2007). See "Czechs Accuse Nazis of 50,000 Executions," *NYT*, Jul 24, 1943, 3. See "Czechs Report Massacre: Claim the Nazis Killed 7,000 in Prison Gas Chambers," *NYT*, Jun 20, 1944, 5.

99. Lepre, 21–22, 23, 27. See Gensicke, 131.

100. Savich, "The Bosnian Muslim Role in the Ustasha and Nazi Genocide," *Serbianna*, http://serbianna.com/blogs/savich/?p=60. Lepre, 24, 28. *Holocaust Encyclopedia*, s.v. "Salonika," www.ushmm.org/wlc/en/article.php?ModuleId=10005422. Simon, Reeva S. et al. eds., *The Jews of the Middle East and North Africa in Modern Times* (New York: Columbia University Press, 2003), 301–302.

101. Schechtman, *Mufti*, 143. Gensicke, 107–108, 166.

102. Savich, "Bosnia and Kama." Savich, "Holocaust." Lepre, 31–32. Jelinek, "Bosnia-Herzegovina," 281–282.

103. Lepre, 31–33. Gensicke, 132–133. Photo, Mufti Inspecting Bosnian Waffen SS Troops, Author's Collection. Photo, Grand Mufti of Jerusalem Greeting Bosnian Muslim Recruit," reproduced in Savich, "Bosnia and Kama."

104. Lepre, 32–33. Savich, "Bosnia and Kama."

105. Lepre, 33. Gensicke, 132.

106. Lepre, 29, 34, 35, 38, 49–50. See Savich, "Holocaust."

107. Lepre, 46–48, 54–55. Stein, *Waffen SS*, 181–182. Photo, SS Untersturmfuehrer Alfred Berger of the Kama/Handzar/Batschka Nazi SS Divisions, reproduced in Savich, "Bosnia and Kama."

108. Savich, "Bosina and Kama." Stein, *Waffen SS*, 181–182. Lepre, 60, 71–75.

109. Lepre, 71–75, 77. Photo, Bosnische SS-Freiwillige beim Gebet (Bosnian SS Volunteers at Prayer), Bild 146-1977-137-20, Nov 1943: Bundesarchiv. Photo, The Mufti Addresses the Imams at Babelsberg, July 1943, reproduced in Lepre, 77.

110. Lepre, 125, 183. Savich, "Bosnia and Kama." Savich, "Holocaust."

111. Lepre, 24–25, 79–80. Savich, "Bosnia and Kama." Savich, "Holocaust." Gensicke, 139. Photo, Bosnische SS-Freiwillige beim Gebet.

112. Photo, Handschar Troops Reading *Islam und Judentum*, Bild 101III-Mielke-036-23, Summer 1943: Bundesarchiv. Savich, "Sarajevo Synagogue Destroyed by Bosnian Muslims." *Serbianna*, http://serbianna.com/blogs/savich/?p=308. Shay, Shaul, *Islamic Terror and the Balkans* (New Brunswick, NJ: Transaction Publishers, 2009), 33. Hadith, Book 41, no. 6985. See Savich, "Holocaust." See Savich, "Bosnia and Kama."

113. "Savich, "Islam Under the Swastika: The Grand Mufti and the Nazi Protectorate of Bosnia-Hercegovina, 1941–1945," *Serbianna*, www.serbianna.com/columns/savich/022.shtml. See Muñoz, Antonio J., *The East Came West: Muslim, Hindu, and Buddhist Volunteers in the German Armed Forces, 1941–1945* (Bayside, NY: Axis Europa, 2001), 267. Lepre, 145–151.

114. Lepre, 150–151. Savich, "Islam under the Swastika."

115. Lepre, 151. Savich, "Islam under the Swastika."

116. Lepre, 165, 168–169. See Muñoz, 267.

117. Goldsworthy, Terry, *Valhalla's Warriors: A History of the Waffen-SS on the Eastern Front, 1941–1945* (Indianapolis, Dog Ear Publishing, 2007), 110.

118. Bracker, Milton, "Gen. Eisenhower Announces Armistice," *NYT*, Sep 9, 1943, 1, 3. Savich, "Kosovo and Genocide." "21. Waffen-Gebirgs-Division der SS Skanderbeg," *Axis History Factbook*, www.axishistory.com/index.php?id=1927. Hilberg, Raul, *The Destruction of the European Jews*, Vol. 2 (New Haven, CT: Yale University Press, 2003), 751. Shay, *Islamic Terror*, 33–34. Tomasevich, *Occupation and Collaboration*, 149–150. Lepre, 165. Goldsworthy, 110. Stein, *Waffen SS*, 185. See Sulzberger, C.L., "Albania Prepares for Post-war Day," *NYT*, Mar 4, 1943, 9. See Bracker, "Dawn is Zero Hour," *NYT*, Sep 3, 1943, 1. See "Italy Invaded," *NYT*, Sep 3, 1943, 18. See "Yugoslavs Request Allies' Aid in Italy," *NYT*, Sep 6, 1943, 5. See "Bars Italian Surrender," *NYT*, Sep 7, 1943, 8.

119. See generally Fischer, Berndt Jürgen, *Albania at War, 1936–1945* (West Lafayette, IN: Purdue University Press, 1999). Savich, "Bosnia and Kama." Savich, "Kosovo and Genocide." Tomasevich, *Occupation and Collaboration*, 149–150.

120. Savich, "Kosovo and Genocide." Savich, "Kosovo and the Holocaust: Falsifying History," *Serbianna*, www.serbianna.com/columns/savich/060.shtml. Hilberg, 450–451. Goldsworth, 110.

121. Savich, "Kosovo and Genocide." Savich, "Kosovo and the Holocaust."

122. Stein, *Waffen SS*, 185. Savich, "Bosnia and Kama."

123. "Death of the Third Republic," *NYT*, Jul 10, 1940, 18. "Deposition of SS Obersturmfuehrer Walter Rauff," *The Nizkor Project*, www2.ca.nizkor.org/ftp.cgi/people/r/rauff.walter/Rauff-deposition-translation. Black, *IBM*, 292. Satloff, Robert, *Among the Righteous: Lost Stories from the Holocausts Long Reach into Arab Lands* (New York: Public Affairs, 2006), 42, 45, 48, 54–55. See Letter, SS-Obersturmbannführer Walter Rauff to Criminal Technical Institute, Reich Criminal Police Office, Mar 26, 1942, quoted in "Letter Requesting 'Special Vans' at Mauthausen," *Jewish Virtual Library Holocaust Sources*, www.jewishvirtuallibrary.org/jsource/Holocaust/Rauffletter032642.html. See generally Marrus, Michael Robert, and Robert O. Paxton, *Vichy France and The Jews* (Stanford: Stanford University Press, 1996). See generally Satloff, *Among the Righteous*, chap. 2.

124. Satloff, *Among the Righteous*, 34, 100–101.

125. Satloff, *Among the Righteous*, 73–77.

126. Satloff, *Among the Righteous*, 85–86.

127. Satloff, *Among the Righteous*, 79, 86–97.

128. Bundesministerium der Finanzen, "Prison Camps as Recognized under the Article 2 Agreement with the Jewish Claims Conference," 3 December 2009. Satloff, *Among the Righteous*, 75, 79, 80–82, 86.

129. Satloff, *Among the Righteous*, 62–64, 80. Map, Slave Labour Camps of the Sahara, 1941–1942, Gilbert, *The Routledge Atlas of the Holocaust* (London, Routledge, 2002), 56, reproduced in Satloff, *Among the Righteous*, 62.

130. Oliel, Jacob. *Les Camps de Vichy: Maghreb-Saraha, 1939–1945* (Montréal: Éditions du Lys, 2005), 105. Annet Michel, "Camp at Djelfa (Alger)," *French Internment Camps in 1939–1944*, www.apra.asso.fr/Camps/En/Camp-Djelfa.html. Satloff, *Among the Righteous*, 80, 105.

131. Satloff, *Among the Righteous*, 69–70, 81–82.

132. Transcript of Oral History, Harry Alexander, Feb 11, 1992, quoted in Satloff, *Among the Righteous*, 82–83.

133. Transcript of Oral History, Harry Alexander.

134. Browning, Christopher R., & Jürgen Matthäus, *The Origins of the Final Solution: The Evolution of Nazi Jewish Policy, September 1939–March 1942* (Lincoln: University of Nebraska Press, 2004), 314–315.

135. "Einsatzgruppen Operational Situation Report USSR No. 101, October 2, 1941." quoted in *Nizkor*, www.nizkor.org/hweb/orgs/german/einsatzgruppen/osr/osr-101.html. Langerbein, Helmut, *Hitler's Death Squads: The Logic of Mass Murder* (College Station: Texas A&M University Press, 2004), 15, 196n1.

136. Einsatzgruppe A, General Report up to October 15, 1941: Nuremburg Document L-180. Order, Reichskommisar for Ostland to Hoeherer SS- und Polizeifuehrer in Riga; Generalkommissare in Reval, Riga, Kovno, Minsk, December 2, 1941: Nuremburg Document PS-3664. See generally Arad, Yitzhak, *The Holocaust in the Soviet Union* (Jerusalem: Yad Vashem, 2009).

137. Gensicke, 128. Transcript, Trial of Adolf Eichmann, Session 74, part 1, 28 Sivan 5721 (12 June 1961), reproduced in *Nizkor*, www.nizkor.org/hweb/people/e/eichmann-adolf/transcripts/Sessions/Session-074-01.html.

138. Bigart, Homer, "Eichmann Testifies He Felt Like Pilate," *NYT*, Jun 27, 1961, 1, 2. Gerlach, Christian, "The Wannsee Conference, the Fate of German Jews, and Hitler's Decision in Principle to Exterminate All European Jews," *The Journal of Modern History*, vol. 70 (1998), 759–812. See also "Eichmann Visits Auschwitz," reproduced in *The Nizkor Project*, www.nizkor.org/ftp.cgi/ftp.py?people/e/eichmann.adolf/eichmann.003.

139. Black, *IBM*, 352–354. *USA v. Pohl et al.*: The Indictment, reproduced in "The Pohl Case," http://avalon.law.yale.edu/imt/indict4.asp.

140. F. Grobba to Pol. VII, 17 July 1942, IfZ, Nbg. Dok., NG-5446. Gensicke, 119.

141. "Affidavit of Dieter Wisliceny," reproduced in *Nazi Conspiracy and Aggression,* vol. VIII (Washington, DC: USGPO, 1946), 606–619.

142. Schwanitz, Wolfgang G., "Amin al-Husaini and the Holocaust: What Did the Grand Mufti Know?," *World Politics Review*, May 8, 2008, www.worldpoliticsreview.com/articles/2082/amin-al-husaini-and-the-holocaust-what-did-the-grand-mufti-know.

143. Transcript of speech, Heinrich Himmler to SS Gruppenführers, Oct 4, 1943, Posen, reproduced in *The Nizkor Project*, www.nizkor.org/hweb/people/h/himmler-heinrich/posen/oct-04-43/.

144. Gensicke, 109–110. Herf, *Nazi Propaganda*, 184–185.

145. Gensicke, 109–110. Herf, *Nazi Propaganda*, 184–185, 187.

146. See generally Bauer, Yehuda, *Jews for Sale? Nazi-Jewish Negotiations, 1933–1945* (New Haven: Yale University Press, 1994).

147. Gensicke, 123, 127.

148. Gensicke, 117–120.

149. Transcript, Trial of Adolf Eichmann, Session 62, part 1, 17 Sivan 5721 (1 June 1961), reproduced in *Nizkor*, http://www.nizkor.org/hweb/people/e/eichmann-adolf/transcripts/Sessions/Session-062-01.html.

150. Gensicke, 120.

151. Gensicke, 122.

152. Transcript, Trial of Adolf Eichmann, session 16, 10 Iyar 5721 (26 April 1961), reproduced in *Nizkor*, www.nizkor.org/hweb/people/e/eichmann-adolf/transcripts/Sessions/Session-016-01.html. Letter, Haj Amin al-Husseini to Minister of Foreign Affairs for Hungary, Jun 28, 1943, quoted in Nation Associates, *The Arab Higher Committee: Its Origins, Personnel and Purposes* (New York: Nation Associates, 1947). Mattar, *Mufti*, 105. De Luca, Anthony R., "'Der Grossmufti' in Berlin: The Politics of Collaboration," *International Journal of Middle East Studies*, vol. 10 (1979), 136. Elpeleg, Zvi, *The Grand Mufti: Haj Amin Al-Hussaini, Founder of the Palestinian National Movement*, David Harvey, trans., Shmuel Himelstein, ed. (London: Frank Cass, 1993), 69–70. Black, *BoB*, 352.

153. Transcript, Trial of Eichmann, Session 16. Letter, Husseni to Minister of Foreign Affairs. Mattar, *Mufti*, 105. DeLuca, "'Der Grossmufti,'" 136. Elpeleg, 69–70. Black, *BoB*, 352.

154. Transcript, Trial of Eichmann, Session 16. Letter, Husseni to Minister of Foreign Affairs. Mattar, *Mufti*, 105. DeLuca, "'Der Grossmufti,'" 136. Elpeleg, 69–70. Black, *BoB*, 352.

155. Transcript, Trial of Eichmann, Session 16. Letter, Husseni to Minister of Foreign Affairs. Mattar, *Mufti*, 105. DeLuca, "'Der Grossmufti,'" 136. Elpeleg, 69–70. Black, *BoB*, 352.

156. Mattar, *Mufti*, 105. Gensicke, 126.

157. Elpeleg, 73.

158. "Document Tells Of Mufti Plot to Bomb Jerusalem," *WP*, Jan 24, 1947, 4. Gensicke, 158, 160–161.

159. Mallman, Klaus-Michael and Cüppers, Martin, "Elimination of the Jewish National Home in Palestine: The Einsatzkommando of the Panzer Army Africa, 1942," in *Yad Vashem*

*Studies*, vol. 37, part 1, (Jerusalem, Yad Vashem, 2005), 113, 124. Breitman, Richard, *U.S. Intelligence and the Nazis* (Cambridge University Press, New York, 2005), 154. Schwanitz, "Amin al-Husaini and the Holocaust." See "Mufti Denies Charges," *NYT*, May 13, 1947, 17.

## Epilog: After the Holocaust

1. Simpson, Christopher, *Blowback* (New York: Weidenfeld & Nicolson, 1988), 89, 177–185, 192.

2. Mekhennet, Souad & Nicholas Kulish, "Uncovering Lost Path of the Most Wanted Nazi," *NYT*, February 4, 2009, A1. See Patterson, David, *A Genealogy of Evil: Anti-Semitism from Nazism to Islamic Jihad* (New York: Cambridge University Press, 2010), 93–95.

3. Ye'or, Bat, *Eurabia: The Euro-Arab Axis* (Cranbury, NJ: Associated University Presses, 2005), 42. *Frankfurter Illustrierte*, Aug 25, 1957, as cited by Ye'or, 42n9.

4. Laskier, Michael M., "Egyptian Jewry under the Nasser Regime," *Middle Eastern Studies*, vol. 31 (1995), 585. "Nazis in Cairo," *Patterns of Prejudice*, vol. 1, no. 2 (Mar/Apr 1967), 6–8. Schoeman, Roy H., *Salvation Is from the Jews: The Role of Judaism in Salvation History* (San Francisco: Ignatius Press, 2003), 264–265. See Patterson, 93–95.

5. Bostom, Andrew G., *The Legacy of Islamic Antisemitism* (Amherst, NY: Prometheus Books, 2008), 155. Letter, Anwar Sadat to Hitler, *al-Musawwar*, No. 1510 (Sep. 18, 1953), quoted by Bostom, 155.

6. World Jewish Congress, "The Treatment of Jews in Egypt and Iraq," white paper, ca. 1948, 20: AJC WP1948.B140.31.

7. "The Treatment of Jews in Egypt and Iraq," 20. Gat, Moshe, *The Jewish Exodus from Iraq, 1948–1951* (London: Frank Cass, 1997), 29.

8. "United Nations General Assembly Resolution 181," Nov 29, 1947, reproduced in *Avalon Project*, www.yale.edu/lawweb/avalon/un/res181.htm.

9. Gat, 29–30.

10. Bamberg, J.H., *The History of the British Petroleum Company*, vol. 2: *The Anglo-Iranian Years, 1928–1954* (Cambridge, UK: Cambridge University Press, 1994), 338–339.

11. Letter, H.Y. Orgel to *NYT*, Aug 28, 1958, 26. Sachar, Howard M., *A History of Israel: From the Rise of Zionism to Our Time* (New York: Alfred A. Knopf, 2007), 333. Tripp, Charles, "Iraq and the 1948 War: Mirror of Iraq's Disorder," in Eugene L. Rogan & Avi Shlaim, eds., *The War for Palestine* (New York: Cambridge University Press, 2001), 125, 139.

12. "Law No. (11) of 1948, Amending Law No. (51) of 1938, Supplemental to the Baghdad Penal Code," *Iraq Government Gazette*, Nov 14, 1948: JJAC 1948/1. World Jewish Congress, "Memorandum on the Treatment of the Jewish Population in Iraq," Oct 22, 1949: AJC UNF48–49.B139.8. Gat, 36.

13. "Iraq Hangs Wealthy Jew for Arms Aid to Zionists," *NYT*, Sep 24, 1948, 8. "Wealthy Jew Hanged for Treason in Iraq," *WP*, Sep 25, 1948, 3. "Iraq Merchant to Die for Aid to Palestine," *NYT*, Sep 14, 1948, 17. "Memorandum on the Treatment of the Jewish Population in Iraq."

14. *Redifot Yehudim be-Iraq*, Nov 15, 1949: Israel State Archives (ISA) RG93, box 90, fol. 1. Mack to Bevin, "Annual Review for 1948," Jan 17, 1941: BNA FO371/75125/E773/1011/93. Mack to Bevin, "Notes on Position of Jews in Iraq," Mar 3, 1949: BNA FO371/75182. Gat, 37. Levin, Itamar, *Locked Doors: The Seizure of Jewish Property in Arab Countries*, Rachel Neiman, trans. (Westport, CT: Praeger, 2001), 38, Tripp, 141–142.

15. "Some Editorial Comment on the Irak Bill by the Baghdad Paper, *Al Shaab*," Mar 3, 1950: JJAC 1950/4. "Report of Interview with 'Mr. S.,' Recently Come from Iraq," Jan 13, 1950: JJAC 1950/2. Baghdad to Foreign Office, Apr 1, 1950: FO371/EQ1571/17, as cited by Gat, 92. Gat, 32. Schechtman, Joseph B., "The Repatriation of Iraqi Jewry," *Jewish Social Studies*, vol. 25 (1953), 160.

16. Kadmon to Mossad, Oct 19, 1948: Hagana Archives (HA), as cited by Gat, 42–43. "On the Immigration of the Jews from Iraq," ca. Jan 1950: ISA RG130, box 2563, fol. 8. Basra to State Department (SD), Mar 14, 1950: NA RG59 887.411/3-1450. Gat, 42–44, 71–72. Schechtman, "Repatriation," 157. See Levin, 27. See confidential memo, Basra to SD, Feb 8, 1950, Feb 15, 1950, Mar 1, 1950, Mar 8, 1950: NA RG59, S250, R41, C10, S7, Box 5488. See secret telegram, Baghdad to Secretary of State, Mar 18, 1950: NA RG59 887.411/3-1850.

17. Schechtman, "Repatriation," 159. Levin, 44.

18. "Comment on Charges of Economic Discrimination against Jewish Community in Iraq," enclosure to despatch no. 432, Baghdad to SD, Nov 28, 1949: NA RG59 890G.4016/11-2849. Gat, 74. Levin, 7. Author's email exchange with Moshe Gat, Sep 2010.

19. Parliament of Iraq, "Iraqi Law No. 1 for 1950," Mar 9, 1950: JJAC 1950/1. See "Debate on the Jewish Emigration Bill in the Irak Chamber of Deputies," *Al-Shaab*, Mar 3, 1950. "Iraq House Adopts Bill to Permit Jews to Leave," *NYT*, Mar 4, 1950, 8. Ross, Albion, "Jews Leaving Iraq in a Steady Flow," *NYT*, Jan 24, 1950, 11. Telegram, Baghdad to Secretary of State, Mar 6, 1950: NA RG59 887.411/3-650. Confidential telegram, Baghdad to Secretary of State, Mar 11, 1950: NA RG59 887.411/3-1150.

20. Letters, Baghdad to Foreign Office, Mar 7, 1950 and Mar 21, 1950: BNA FO371/82478. Letter, Baghdad to Foreign Office, Apr 1, 1950: BNA FO371/82478.

21. Teheran to Israeli Government, Mar 19, 1950: CZA S/41/256II, as cited by Gat, 83. Yerahmiel to Zerubavel, Mar 18, 1950: CZA S/20/539II, as cited by Gat, 83. Gat, 83. See confidential despatch, Basra to SD, Mar 15, 1950: NA RG59 887.411/3-1550.

22. Michael to Kadmon, Mar 15, 1950: HA, as cited by Gat, 88. Mack to Bevin, Mar 21, 1950: FO371/EA1571/9 as cited by Gat, 88. Gat, 88. "Jewish Drive Here Brings in $5,925,000," *NYT*, Mar 8, 1950, 14. "Air-Sea Migration of 90,000 Planned," *NYT*, Mar 18, 1950, 6. Confidential telegram, Tehran to Secretary of State, Mar 23, 1950: NA RG59 887.411/3-2150.

23. "Iraqi Jews Flown by Lift to Israel," *NYT*, May 22, 1950, 5. Schechtman, "Repatriation," 161. Gat, 92. See restricted despatch, Basra to SD, Mar 28, 1950: NA RG59 887.411/3-2850. See confidential telegram, Baghdad to Secretary of State, Apr 12, 1950: NA RG59 887.411/4-1250.

24. "Iraqi Refugees Fly to Israel," *NYT*, May 20, 1950, 6. Schechtman, "Repatriation," 164. Gat, 101.

25. See Wilson, Earl, "Travel Bar by Baghdad Explained in Tel Aviv," *WP*, Aug 31, 1951, B11. See Schechtman, "Repatriation," 163. Gat, 105, 107.

26. "Iraqis Fix Deadline for Jewish Exodus," *NYT*, Jan 20, 1951, 4. Middle East Department to Evron, ca. Mar 1951: ISA RG 136, box 2387, fol. 4. Schechtman, "Repatriation," 163.

27. Cable, Duron and Dror to Mossad, May 7, 1950: HA 14/429: May–Jun 1950. Gat, 106, 128–129, 138–139.

28. "Israel in Dilemma over Immigration," *NYT*, Mar 6, 1950, 7. "Camp Life in Israel 'Shocks' Morgenthau," *NYT*, Jan 20, 1950, 5. See "Immigrants Entering Israel From 1950 to May 1951 According to Immigration Ministry Data," Jun 20, 1951: ISA RG 130, box 2387, fol. 4.

29. Parliament of Iraq, "Law for the Control and Administration of Property of Jews Who Have Forfeited Iraqi Nationality," *Iraq Government Gazette*, Mar 10, 1951/2 Jamadi al-Akhara 1368: JJAC 1951/4. "Resumé of Iraqi Law No. 5 for 1951," Mar 10, 1951: JJAC 1950/1. "Iraq Acts against Jews," *NYT*, Mar 11, 1951, 23. Levin, 46. Note, Mar 17, 1951: HA 14/435.

30. "Israel in Dilemma Over Immigration." "Iraqis Fix Deadline for Jewish Exodus." See memo, Mar 17, 1951, HA 14/435 no. 66. Gat, 131, 152, 155. "Editorial Regarding Immigration of Jews from Iraq," despatch, Jerusalem to SD, Mar 27, 1950: NA RG59 887.411/3-2750.

31. Berman to Mossad, Mar 17, 1951: HA, as quoted by Gat, 151.

32. Sharett, Moshe, address to Knesset, Mar 19, 1951, quoted by Schechtman, "Repatriation," 170. "Iraqi Action Brings Israeli Retaliation," *NYT*, Mar 20, 1951.

33. Levin, 46. Schechtman, "Repatriation," 164.

34. Gat, 158. See Parsons, Arch, Jr., "Israel to Restrict '52 Immigration," *WP*, Dec 23, 1951, B2.

# MAJOR SOURCES

## Archives

Original papers and documents were accessed at several dozen archival repositories, record collections, and unprocessed files in England, the United States, Germany, and Israel. The challenging range of repositories spanned the gamut from governmental, military, and organizational archives to corporate and private files. Most of the repositories utilized are listed below, but space precludes a complete roster.

**Germany**
Auswärtiges Amt / Politische Amt (AA/PA)    Berlin
Berlin Documentation Center    Berlin
Bundesarchiv    Berlin
Institut für Zeitgeschichte    Munich
Prussian State Archives (PSA)    Berlin

**Israel**
Archives of Dr. Zvi Yehuda    Jerusalem
Central Zionist Archives (CZA)    Jerusalem
Government Press Office Photo Archive    Jerusalem
Hagana Archives    Tel Aviv
Hebron Archives, Hebron Heritage Museum    Hebron
Israel State Archives (ISA)    Jerusalem
Weizmann Archives (WA)    Rehovet
Yad Vashem Archives (YVA)    Jerusalem

**Poland**
Auschwitz Museum Archives    Oswiecim

**United Kingdom**
Anglo-Iranian Oil Company (AIOC) files    Coventry
Anglo-Persian Oil Company (APOC) files    Coventry
Board of Deputies of British Jews (BDBJ)    London
British Library (BL)    London
British Petroleum Company (BP) files    Coventry
Gertrude Bell Papers    New Castle
Iraq Petroleum Company (IPC) files    Coventry
Modern Records Centre, Warwick University    Coventry
National Archives (British) (BNA)    Kew
Turkish Petroleum Company (TPC) files    Coventry

**United States**
American Jewish Archives (AJA)    Cincinnati

American Jewish Congress Archives (AJC)    New York
American Jewish Committee Archives (AJCmA)    New York
Columbia University Library Lehman Suite    New York
Iraq Foundation Archives    Washington, DC
League of Nations (LoN) Archive, Harvard University    Cambridge
Museum of the Oriental Institute Photo Archive    Chicago
National Archives (NA)    College Park
Rockefeller Family Archives (RF)    Sleepy Hollow
Urman Collection, Justice for Jews from Arab Countries (JJAC)    West Orange
YIVO    New York

# Libraries

Libraries are crucial to research because each library maintains its own unique and often precious collection of obscure literature and local materials, including personal memoirs of diplomats and military men. In addition, many libraries maintain manuscript collections of original papers or organizational files. Most of the libraries accessed are listed below, but space precludes a complete roster.

**France**
Bibliothèque Nationale de France (BF)    Paris

**Germany**
Berlin State Library    Berlin
Bibliothek der Friedrich-Naumann-Stiftung (BFN)    Königswinter
Library of Contemporary History (LCH)    Stuttgart
Universitätsbibliothek (UBB)    Bonn

**Israel**
al-Aqsa Mosque Library
National Library of Israel    Jerusalem
Tel Aviv University Central Library    Tel Aviv

**United Kingdom**
British Library    London
Camden Library, Holborn Branch    London
Camden Library, Swiss Cottage Branch    London
Charing Cross Library, Westminster    London
University of Warwick Library    Coventry
Wiener Library    London

**United States**
Alvin Sherman Library, Nova Southeastern University    Fort Lauderdale
Asher Library, Spertus Institute of Jewish Studies    Chicago
Blaustein Library, American Jewish Committee    New York
Center for Muslim-Jewish Engagement, Univ. of Southern California    Los Angeles
Columbia University Library    New York
Emerson Library, Webster University    St. Louis
Fenwick Library, George Mason University    Fairfax
Gelman Library, George Washington University    Washington, DC
Genesee County District Library    Flint, MI
Hoover Institution on War, Revolution, and Peace    Stanford
Johnson Center Library, George Mason University    Fairfax
Klau Library, Hebrew Union College    Cincinnati
Lamont, Harvard University    Cambridge
Lauinger Memorial Library, Georgetown University    Washington, DC
Library of Congress    Washington, DC
Library of the Simon Wiesenthal Center    Los Angeles
Meriam Library, California State University    Chico
Monterey Institute of International Studies Library    Monterey

Montgomery County Public Libraries    Rockville
Montgomery College Library    Rockville
New York Public Library, Dorot Jewish Division    New York
New York Public Library, General Research Division    New York
New York Public Library, Main Branch    New York
New York Public Library, Science, Industry, and Business Library    New York
Ostrow Library    Bel-Air
Perkins Library, Duke University    Durham
University of Kansas Library    Lawrence
University of Michigan    Flint, MI
U.S. Holocaust Memorial Museum Library    Washington, DC

## Electronic Sources

Electronic and digital sources were used extensively. Modern research cannot be efficiently undertaken without the use of Internet search engines as well as institutional databases. However, while Internet research is essential to historical investigation, the caveat remains that the web is profoundly unreliable, including some web sites operated by respected academic entities. At the same time, I found certain official organizational and governmental sites important, as were a very limited number of private research sites. Hence, while I consulted and searched through hundreds, perhaps thousands of web sites, only a precious few of the most reliable are listed below. On the other hand, the digital databases of documents and publications that I used were pivotal to my work.

**Digital Archives, Libraries, and Databases:**
JSTOR, The Scholarly Journal Archive
Lexis-Nexis
Michigan elibrary, Mel.org, Lansing MI
MUSE
ProQuest Historical Newspapers:
  *Atlanta Constitution*
  *Chicago Tribune*
  *Los Angeles Times*
  *Manchester Guardian*
  *New York Times*
  *New York Tribune*
  *Wall Street Journal*
  *Washington Post*
*The Times* Digital Archive
WorldCat/OCLC

**Web sites**
Avalon Law Project, Yale University Law School, http://avalon.law.yale.edu/
Axis History Factbook, www.axishistory.com
The Baha'i Faith Index, www.bahaindex.com.
Baker College, www.bakeru.edu
Beit Hatfutsot, the Museum of the Jewish People, www.bh.org.il
BBC News, news.bbc.co.uk
Bible History Online, www.hp.uab.edu
British Library, www.bl.uk
The British Museum, www.britishmuseum.org
Columbia University, Fathom Archive, www.fathom.com
French Internment Camps in 1939–1944, www.apra.asso.fr/Camps/En/Accueil-Camps.html
The Gertrude Bell Papers, www.gerty.ncl.ac.uk
The Hashemite Kingdom of Jordan, www.kinghussein.gov.jo
The Holocaust Resource, www.nizkor.org
Holocaust Research Project, www.holocaustresearchproject.org
Indiana University, www.indiana.edu
International Institute of Social History, www.iisg.nl
Internet Sacred Text Archive, www.sacred-texts.org

The Iran Chamber Society, www.iranchamber.com
The Irgun Site, www.etzel.org.il/english/
Israel Ministry of Foreign Affairs, www.mfa.gov.il/MFA
United States Holocaust Memorial Museum, www.ushmm.org
The Jewish Agency for Israel, www.jafi.org.il
The Jewish Virtual Library, www.jewishvirtuallibrary.org
The Knesset, www.knesset.gov.il
The League of Nations Photo Archive, University of Indiana, www.indiana.edu/~league/
Library of Congress, www.loc.gov
Livius: Articles on Ancient History, www.livius.org
Louvre Museum, www.louvre.fr
Manchester University Centre for Jewish Studies, www.mucjs.org
Metropolitan Museum of Art, www.metmuseum.org
Michigan eLibrary, www.mel.org
Michigan State University, www.lib.msu.edu
Midrash ben Ish Hai, www.midrash.org
Military Aircraft, www.military-aircraft.org.uk
Military Legal Resources, www.loc.gov/rr/frd/Military_Law/NT_major-war-criminals.html
Military History Encyclopedia on the Web, www.historyofwar.org
Mt. San Jacinto College, www.msjc.edu.
The Napoleon Series, www.napoleon-series.org
National Archives and Records Administration, www.archives.gov
New York Public Library, http://legacy.www.nypl.org/research/
PBS: Frontline, www.pbs.org/wgbh/pages/frontline/
National Archives (UK) Public Records Office, www.nationalarchives.gov.uk
The Royal Air Force, www.raf.mod.uk
St. Lawrence University, http://web.stlawu.edu
Serbianna, www.serbianna.com
*The Scribe: Journal of Babylonian Jewry,* www.dangoor.com
The Silk Road Foundation, www.silk-road.com
State of Kuwait (official website), Al-Diwan Al-Amiri, www.da.gov.kw/eng/
Syrian Social Nationalist Party, www.ssnp.net
Texas A&M, Department of Mathematics, www.math.tamu.edu
*Time,* www.time.com
Trenches on the Web: An Internet History of the Great War, www.worldwar1.com
U.S. Army Center for Military History, www.army.mil/cmh-pg/
United States Holocaust Memorial Museum, www.ushmm.org
The World War I Document Archive, www.lib.byu.edu/~rdh/wwi/
*WorldWarOne.com,* www.worldwarone.com

## Printed and Published Materials

A vast array of printed and published materials was utilized—from diplomatic papers to books, from periodicals to period materials and photographs. Space prohibits a complete list, and the listings here approximate about half of the materials consulted.

### Published Diplomatic Papers
Documents in British Foreign Policy (DBFP)
Documents in German Foreign Policy (DGFP)
Foreign Relations of the United States (FRUS)
*British & Foreign State Papers.* Vol. 105 (1912). Edited by Edward C. Blech and Harry I Sherwood. London: H. M. Stationery Office, 1915.
*A Select Chronology and Background Documents Relating to the Middle East.* Committee on Foreign Relations, U. S. Senate. Washington, DC: U.S. Government Printing Office, 1969.
Covenant of the League of Nations. League of Nations (LoN).
*Records of the Hashemite Dynasties: A Twentieth Century Documentary History.* Slough, UK: Archive Editions, 1995.
*Records of Iraq, 1914–1966.* Slough, UK: Archive Editions, 2001.

*British Documents on the Origins of the War, 1898–1914.* London: H. M. Stationery Office, 1926–1938.
*Diplomacy in the Near And Middle East.* Vols. I–III. Edited by J. C. Hurewitz. New York: Van Nostrand, 1956. Also Gerrards Cross, UK: Archive Editions, 1987.
*Foreign Military Studies, 1945–1954.* German Exploitation of Arab Nationalist Movements, MS P-207. Washington, DC: National Archives, 1959.
*Nazi Conspiracy and Aggression.* Washington, DC: US Government Printing Office, 1946.
*Political Diaries of the Arab World: Iraq, vol. 6: 1932–1947.* Edited by Robert L. Jarman. Slough, UK: Archive Editions, 1998.
*Trial of the Major War Criminals before the International Military Tribunal, Nuremberg, 14 November 1945–1 October 1946.* Nuremburg: International Military Tribunal, 1947.

### Command Papers, Great Britain

*Correspondence between Sir Henry McMahon and The Sherif Hussein of Mecca, July 1915–March 1916.* (With a map.) Cmd. 5957, Misc. No. 3. London: H. M. Stationery Office, 1939.
*Iraq: Treaty with King Feisal.* Cmd. 1757. London: H.M. Stationery Office, 1922.
*Palestine: Correspondence with the Palestine Arab Delegation and the Zionist Organisation.* Cmd. 1700. London: H.M. Stationery Office, 1922.
*Palestine, Disturbances in May, 1921: Reports of the Commission of Inquiry with Correspondence Relating Thereto.* London: H.M. Stationery Office, 1921.
*Palestine: Report on Immigration, Land Settlement and Development.* Cmd. 3686–3687. London: H.M. Stationery Office, 1930. [Hope Simpson, Sir John]
*The Palestine Western (or Wailing) Wall, Order in Council, 1931: Made on 19 May 1931.* London: H.M. Stationery Office, 1936.
*Report of the Commission appointed by His Majesty's Government in the United Kingdom of Great Britain and Northern Ireland, with the approval of the Council of the League of Nations, to determine the rights and claims of Moslems and Jews in connection with the Western or Wailing Wall at Jerusalem.* London: H.M. Stationery Office, 1931.
*Report of the Commission on the Palestine Disturbances of August, 1929.* Cmd. 3530. London: H.M. Stationery Office, 1930.
*Report of the Palestine Royal Commission.* Cmd. 5479. (Peel Commission Report.) London: H.M. Stationery Office, 1937.

### Books

Adler, Cyrus, ed. *The Voice of America on Kishineff.* Philadelphia: Jewish Publication Society of America, 1904.
Abdullah, Thabit A. J. *Merchants, Mamluks, and Murder: The Political Economy of Trade in Eighteenth-Century Basra.* Albany: SUNY Press, 2001.
Ailsby, Christopher. *The Third Reich Day by Day.* St Paul: MBI, 2001.
Ali, Abdullah Yusuf, trans. *The Meaning of the Glorious Qur'n.* Cairo: Dar Al-Kitab Al-Masri, 1934.
Al-Tabari. *History of the World.* Albany, NY: State University of New York Press, 1985.
Allsen, Thomas T. *Culture and Conquest in Mongol Eurasia.* Cambridge, UK: Cambridge University Press, 2001.
Allsen, Thomas T. *Mongol Imperialism: The Policies of the Grand Qan Möngke in China, Russia, and the Islamic Lands, 1251–1259.* Berkeley, CA: University of California Press, 1987.
Almog, Shmuel, ed. *Antisemitism Through the Ages.* New York: Pergamon Press, 1988.
Antonius, George. *The Arab Awakening: The Story of the Arab National Movement.* New York: G. P. Putnam's Sons, 1946. Reprint, New York: Capricorn Books, 1965.
Arad, Yitzhak. *The Holocaust in the Soviet Union.* Jerusalem: Yad Vashem, 2009
Aschheim, Steven E. *Brothers and Strangers: The East European Jew in German and German Jewish Consciousness, 1800–1923.* Madison: University of Wisconsin Press, 1982.
Avneri, Aryeh L. *The Claim of Dispossession: Jewish Land-settlement and the Arabs, 1878–1948.* New Brunswick, NJ: Transaction Publishers, 1984.
Avriel, Ehud. *Open the Gates: Dramatic Personal Story of "Illegal" Immigration to Israel.* Worthington, UK: Littlehampton Book Services, 1975.
Bailey, Ronald H. *Partisans and Guerrillas.* London: Time-Life, 2000.
Balakian, Peter. *The Burning Tigris: The Armenian Genocide and America's Response.* New York: HarperCollins, 2003.
Baldwin, Neil. *Henry Ford and the Jews: The Mass Production of Hate.* New York: PublicAffairs, 2003.

Bamberg, James. *The History of the British Petroleum Company, Vol. 2: The Anglo-Iranian Years, 1928–1954.* Cambridge, UK: Cambridge University Press, 1994.

Barnavi, Eli, and Miriam Eliav-Feldon, eds. *A Historical Atlas of the Jewish People: from the Time of the Patriarchs to the Present.* Translated by Florence Brutton. NY: Schocken Books, 2002.

Bashkin, Orit. *The Other Iraq: Pluralism and Culture in Hashemite Iraq.* Stanford University Press, 2009.

Bauer, Josef, Robert K Englund, and Manfred Krebernik. *Mesopotamien: Späturuk- und Frühdynastische Zeit.* Edited by Pascal Attinger, Markus Waefler, and Walther Sallaberger. Oxford: Oxford University Press, 1998.

Bauer, Susan Wise. *The History of the Medieval World: from the Conversion of Constantine to the First Crusade.* New York: W. W. Norton, 2010.

Bauer, Yehuda. *Jews for Sale? Nazi-Jewish Negotiations, 1933–1945.* New Haven: Yale University Press, 1994.

Bauer, Yehuda. *My Brother's Keeper: A History of the American Jewish Joint Distribution Committee 1929–1939.* Transcription and subtitles by Michael Palomino. Philadelphia: Jewish Publication Society of America, 2007.

Beesley, Patrick. *Room 40: British Naval Intelligence 1914–1918.* London: Oxford University Press, 1984.

Bein, Alex. *Theodor Herzl: A Biography.* Philadelphia: The Jewish Publication Society of America, 1940.

Bein, Alex, ed. *Arthur Ruppin: Memoirs, Diaries, Letters.* London: Weidenfeld & Nicolson, 1971.

Bell, J. Bowyer. *Terror Out of Zion: The Fight for Israeli Independence.* New Brunswick, NJ: Transaction Publishers, 1996.

Berg, Nancy E. *Exile from Exile: Israeli Writers from Iraq.* Albany: State University of New York Press, 2010.

Bill, James A. *The Eagle and the Lion: The Tragedy of American-Iranian Relations.* New Haven, CT: Yale University Press, 1998.

Black, Edwin. *Banking on Baghdad: Inside Iraq's 7,000-Year History of War, Profit, and Conflict.* Washington, DC: Dialog Press, 2008.

Black, Edwin. *IBM and the Holocaust: The Strategic Alliance between Nazi Germany and America's Most Powerful Corporation.* Washington, DC: Dialog Press, 2008.

Black, Edwin. *Internal Combustion: How Corporations and Governments Addicted the World to Oil and Derailed the Alternatives.* Washington, DC: Dialog Press, 2008.

Black, Edwin. *Nazi Nexus.* Washington, DC: Dialog Press, 2009.

Black, Edwin. *The Plan: How to Rescue Society the Day the Oil Stops—or the Day Before.* Washington, DC: Dialog Press, 2008.

Black, Edwin. *The Transfer Agreement: The Dramatic Story of the Pact between the Third Reich and Jewish Palestine.* Washington, DC: Dialog Press, 2009.

Black, Edwin. *War Against the Weak: Eugenics and America's Campaign to Create a Master Race.* Washington, DC: Dialog Press, 2008.

Bodenheimer, M. I. (Max Isidor). *Prelude to Israel: The Memoirs of M.I. Bodenheimer.* Edited by Henriette Hannah Bodenheimer. Translated by Israel Cohen. New York: T. Yoseloff, 1963.

Bostom, Andrew G. *The Legacy of Islamic Antisemitism.* Amherst, NY: Prometheus Books, 2008.

Bostom, Andrew G. *The Legacy of Jihad.* Amherst, NY: Prometheus Books, 2008.

Breasted, James Henry. *Ancient Times, A History of the Early World: An Introduction to the Study of Ancient History and the Career of Early Man.* Boston: Athenæum Press, 1916.

Breitman, Richard. *U.S. Intelligence and the Nazis.* Cambridge University Press, New York, 2005.

Bright Jr., Arthur A. *The Electric-Lamp Industry: Technological Change and Economic Development from 1800 to 1947.* New York: Macmillan, 1949.

Browning, Christopher R., and Jürgen Matthäus. *The Origins of the Final Solution: The Evolution of Nazi Jewish Policy, September 1939–March 1942.* Lincoln: University of Nebraska Press, 2004.

Buchanan, Sir George. *The Tragedy of Mesopotamia.* London: William Blackwood and Sons, 1938. Reprint, New York: AMS Press, 1974.

Busch, Briton Cooper. *Britain, India, and the Arabs, 1914–1921.* Berkeley, CA: University of California Press, 1971.

Carmichael, Cathie. *Ethnic Cleansing in the Balkans: Nationalism and the Destruction of Tradition.* New York: Routledge, 2002.

Carpini, Fr. Giovanni di Plano. *The Story of the Mongols Whom We Call the Tartars (Historia Mongalorum quos nos Tartaros Appellamus).* Translated by Erik Hildinger. Rome: 1252. Reprint, Boston: Branden Publishing, 1996.

Chambers, James. *The Devil's Horsemen: The Mongol Invasion of Europe.* New York: Atheneum, 1985.

Chazan, Robert. *Medieval Stereotypes and Modern Antisemitism.* Berkeley: University of California Press, 1997.

Churchill, Randolph S. *Winston S. Churchill, Vol. 2: Young Statesman, 1900–1914* and companion volume. Boston: Houghton Mifflin, 1967.

Clark, Arthur Tillotson. *To Baghdad with the British.* New York: D. Appleton, 1918.

Connell, John. *Wavell: Scholar and Soldier, to June 1941.* London: Collins, 1964.

Curtin, Jeremiah. *The Mongols: A History.* Boston: Little, Brown, and Company, 1908. Reprint, Cambridge, MA: Da Capo Press, 2003.

Darrah, William C. *Pithole, The Vanished City: A Story of the Early Days of the Petroleum Industry.* Gettysburg, PA: William C. Darrah, 1972.

Davitt, Michael. *Within the Pale: The True Story of Anti-Semitic Persecutions in Russia.* New York: A.S. Barnes, 1903.

Dayan, Moshe. *Moshe Dayan: Story of My Life.* New York: William Morrow, 1976.

de Chair, Somerset. *The Golden Carpet.* New York: Harcourt, Brace, 1945.

de Haas, Jacob. *Theodor Herzl: A Biographical Study.* Vols. 1 and 2. Chicago, New York: The Leonard Co., 1927.

de Lacy Rush, Alan, ed. *Records of Kuwait 1899–1961, Vol. 1: Internal Affairs I.* London: Archive International, 1989.

Delarue, Jacques. *The Gestapo: A History of Horror.* Translated by Mervin Savill. New York: Skyhorse Publishing, 2008.

Dickson, Harold Richard Patrick. *Kuwait and Her Neighbours.* London: Allen and Unwin, 1956.

Donia, Robert J. *Sarajevo: A Biography.* Ann Arbor: University of Michigan Press, 2006.

Earle, Edward Mead. *Turkey, the Great Powers, and the Baghdad Railway: A Study in Imperialism.* New York: Macmillan, 1923.

Elliot, Matthew. *Independent Iraq: the Monarchy and British influence, 1941–58.* London: I. B. Tauris, 1996.

Ellis, Edward S., and Charles F. Horne. *The Story of The Greatest Nations and the World's Famous Events, Vol. 1.* New York: Auxiliary Educational League, 1921.

Elpeleg, Zvi. *The Grand Mufti: Haj Amin Al-Hussaini, Founder of the Palestinian National Movement.* Edited by Shmuel Himelstein. Translated by David Harvey. London: Frank Cass, 1993.

Engelbrecht, Helmuth Carol. *Johann Gottlieb Fichte: A Study of His Political Writings with Special Reference to His Nationalism.* New York: Columbia University Press, 1968.

Engle, Anita. *The Nili Spies.* London: Hogarth, 1959.

Falls, Cyril. *Armageddon: 1918.* Philadelphia: J. B. Lippincott, 1964.

Faroqhi, Suraiya. *The Ottoman Empire: A Short History.* Translated by Shelly Frisch. Princeton, Markus Weiner, 2009.

Faroqhi, Suraiya. *Subjects of the Sultans: Culture and Daily Life in the Ottoman Empire.* London: I. B. Tauris, 2000.

Farrington, Anthony. *Trading Places: The East India Company and Asia 1600–1834.* London: British Library, 2002.

Farwell, Byron. *The Great Boer War.* London: Allen Lane, 1977.

Fattal, Salim. *In the Alleys of Baghdad.* Jerusalem: Carmel, 2004.

Feilchenfeld, Werner. *Five Years of Jewish Immigration from Germany and the Haavara-Transfer, 1933–1938.* Tel Aviv: Haavara Ltd., 1972.

Feilchenfeld, Werner, Dolf Michaelis, and Ludwig Pinner, eds. *Haavara-Transfer Nach Palästina Und Einwanderung Deutscher Juden, 1933-1939.* Tübingen: Mohr Verlag, 1972.

Ferrier, Ronald W. *The History of the British Petroleum Company, Vol. 1: The Developing Years, 1901–1932.* Cambridge, UK: Cambridge University Press, 1982.

Ferrier, Ronald W., and J. H. Bamberg. *The History of the British Petroleum Company, Vol. 2: The Anglo-Iranian Years, 1928–1954.* Cambridge, UK: Cambridge University Press, 1994.

Fichte, Johann Gottlieb. *Addresses to the German Nation.* Translated by R. F. Jones and G. H. Turnbull. Chicago: Open Court Publishing, 1922.

Fischer, Berndt Jürgen. *Albania at War, 1936–1945.* West Lafayette, IN: Purdue University Press, 1999.

Friedman, Isaiah. *The Question of Palestine: British-Jewish-Arab Relations, 1914–1918.* London: Routledge, 1973.

Friedman, Isaiah, ed. *Germany, Turkey, and Zionism, 1914-1918.* New York: Garland, 1987.

Fulda, Bernhard. *Press and Politics in the Weimar Republic.* New York: Oxford University Press, 2009.

Garvin, J. L. *The Life of Joseph Chamberlain, Vol. 3: Empire and World Policy.* London: Macmillan, 1934.

Garvin, J. L., and Julian Amery. *The Life of Joseph Chamberlain, Vol. 4: At the Height of his Power.* London: Macmillan, 1951.

Gat, Moshe. *The Jewish Exodus From Iraq, 1948–1951.* London: Frank Cass, 1997.

Gensicke, Klaus. *The Mufti of Jerusalem and the Nazis: The Berlin Years.* Translated by Alexander Fraser Gunn. Portland, OR: Vallentine Mitchell, 2010.

Gershoni, Israel, and James Jankowski. *Confronting Fascism in Egypt: Dictatorship versus Democracy in the 1930s.* Stanford: Stanford University Press, 2010.

Ghanīmah, Yūsuf Rizq Allāh. *A Nostalgic Trip into the History of the Jews of Iraq.* Translation, Introduction, and Update by Reading A. Dallal. Edited by Sheila Dallal. Lanham, MD: University Press of America, 1998.

Giddens, Paul H. *The Birth of the Oil Industry.* New York: Macmillan, 1938.

Gil, Moshe. *Jews in Islamic Countries in the Middle Ages.* [Series: *Études sur le Judaïsme Médiéval,* 28.] Translated by David Strassler. Leiden: Brill, 2004.

Gilbert, Martin. *Churchill and the Jews: A Lifelong Friendship.* New York: Henry Holt, 2007.

Gilbert, Martin. *In Ishmael's House: A History of Jews in Muslim Lands.* New Haven: Yale University Press, 2010.

Gilbert, Martin. *The Routledge Atlas of the Arab-Israeli Conflict.* New York: Routledge, 2002.

Gilbert, Martin. *The Routledge Atlas of the Holocaust.* London, Routledge, 2002.

Gilbert, Martin. *The Second World War: A Complete History.* New York: Henry Holt and Company, 1989.

Gilbert, Martin. *Winston S. Churchill, Vol. 4: The Stricken World, 1917–1922* and companion volume. London: Heinemann, 1977.

Gilbert, Martin. *Winston S. Churchill, Vol. 6: Finest Hour, 1939–1941* and companion volume. Boston: Houghton Mifflin Company, 1983.

Gilner, Elias. *War and Hope: A History of the Jewish Legion.* New York: Herzl Press, 1969.

Glubb, Sir John. *The Empire of the Arabs.* Englewood Cliffs, NJ: Prentice-Hall, 1963.

Glubb, Sir John. *The Story of the Arab Legion.* London: Hodder and Stoughton, 1948.

Goldman, Shalom. *Zeal for Zion: Christians, Jews, and the Idea of the Promised Land.* Chapel Hill: University of North Carolina Press, 2009.

Goldsworthy, Terry. *Valhalla's Warriors: A History of the Waffen-SS on the Eastern Front, 1941–1945.* Indianapolis, Dog Ear Publishing, 2007.

Greenwald, Toby Klein. *The Story of Hebron: Seventy-Five Years from Tarpat.* Hebron, Israel: Jewish Action, 2004.

Gutman, Yisrael, Ezra Mendelsohn, Jehuda Reinharz, and Chone Shmeruk, eds. *The Jews of Poland Between Two World Wars.* Hanover, NH: University Press of New England, 1991.

Guttmann, Oscar. *The Manufacture of Explosives.* Vol. 2. London, Whittaker and Co., 1895.

Hachlili, Rachel. *Ancient Jewish Art and Archaeology in the Land of Israel.* Leiden: Brill, 1988.

Haim, Sylvia G. ed., *Arab Nationalism: An Anthology.* Los Angeles: University of California Press, 1962.

Halphen, Achille-Edmond. *Recueil des Lois: décrets, ordonnances, avis du conseil d'état, arrêtés et règlements concernant les israélites depuis la Révolution de 1789.* Paris: Bureaux des archives israélites, 1851.

Herf, Jeffrey. *Nazi Propaganda for the Arab World.* New Haven, CT: Yale University Press, 2009.

Hertzog, Chaim, and Shlomo Gazit. *The Arab-Israeli Wars: War and Peace.* New York: Vintage Books, 2005.

Herzl, Theodor. *A Jewish State: An Attempt at a Modern Solution of the Jewish Question.* Edited by Jacob de Hass. Translated by Sylvia D'Avigdor. New York: Federation of American Zionists, 1917.

Herzl, Theodor. *The Complete Diaries.* Vols. 1–5. Edited by Raphael Patai. Translated by Harry Zohn. New York: The Herzl Press, 1960.

Hilberg, Raul. *The Destruction of the European Jews,* Vol. 2. New Haven, CT: Yale University Press, 2003.

Hitti, Philip K. *History of the Arabs: From the Earliest Times to the Present.* London: Macmillan, 1937. Reprint, New York: Palgrave Macmillan, 2002.

Hookham, Hilda. *Tamburlaine the Conqueror.* London: Hodder and Stoughton, 1962.

Hosein, Imran N. *The Caliphate, The Hejaz, and The Saudi-Wahhabi Nation-State.* Bay Shore, New York: Masjid Darul Qur'an, 1996.

Hovannisian, Richard G., ed. *Remembrance and Denial: The Case of the Armenian Genocide.* Detroit, MI: Wayne State University Press, 1998.

Hudson, Michael, and Cornelia Wunsch, eds. *Creating Economic Order: Record-keeping, Standardization, and the Development of Accounting in the Ancient Near East.* Bethesda, MD: CDL Press, 2004.

Imber, Colin. *The Ottoman Empire, 1300–1650: The Structure of Power.* New York: Palgrave MacMillan, 2002.

Inalcik, Halil. *The Ottoman Empire: The Classical Age, 1300–1600.* Translated by Norman Itzkowits and Colin Imber. London: Wiedenfeld and Nicolson, 1973.

Ireland, Phillip Willard. *Iraq: A Study in Political Development.* New York: Macmillan, 1938.

Jankowski, James P., and Israel Gershoni, eds. *Rethinking Nationalism in the Arab Middle East.* New York: Columbia University Press, 1997.

Jbara, Taysir. *Al-Ḥājj Muhammad Amīn al-Husaynī, Mufti of Jerusalem: The Palestine Years, 1921–1937.* [Book print of Jbara's PhD dissertation.] New York: New York University, 1982.

Jbara, Taysir. *Palestinian Leader Hajj Amīn Al-Husaynī, Mufti of Jerusalem.* Princeton: The Kingston Press, 1985.

Joly, Maurice. *The Dialogue in Hell between Machiavelli and Montesquieu.* Translated by John S. Waggoner. Lanham, MD: Lexington Books, 2003.

Judge, Edward H. *Easter in Kishinev: Anatomy of a Pogrom.* New York: NYU Press, 1992.

Karsh, Efraim, and Inari Karsh. *Empires of the Sand: The Struggle for Mastery in the Middle East, 1789–1923.* Cambridge, MA: Harvard University Press, 1999.

Kater, Michael H. *Hitler Youth.* Cambridge, MA: Harvard University Press, 2004.

Kazzaz, Nissim. *Sayfa ve-Safra, Zichronot / Warrior and Scholar Memoirs.* [In Hebrew.] Jerusalem: Association of Jewish Academics from Iraq and Ruven Mass Ltd., 2010.

Kedourie, Elie. *Arab Political Memoirs and Other Stories.* London: Frank Cass, 1974.

Keiser, Hans-Lukas, and Dominik J. Schaller, eds. *Der Völkermord den Armeniern und die Shoa* or *The Armenian Genocide and the Holocaust.* [In German and English.] Zürich: Chronos, 2002.

Kent, Marian. *Oil and Empire: British Policy and Mesopotamian Oil, 1900–1920.* London: Macmillan, 1976.

Keogh, Dermot. *Jews in Twentieth-Century Ireland: Refugees, Anti-Semitism, and the Holocaust.* Cork: Cork University Press, 1988.

Khadduri, Majid. *Independent Iraq: A Study in Iraqi Politics Since 1932.* London: Oxford University Press, 1951.

Khalid, Rashid, Lisa Anderson, Muhammed Muslih, and Reeva S. Simon, eds. *The Origins of Arab Nationalism.* New York: Columbia University Press, 1991.

Kiernan, Ben. *Blood and Soil: A World History of Genocide and Extermination from Sparta to Darfur.* New Haven: Yale University Press, 2007.

Kinross, Lord J. P. D. B. *The Ottoman Centuries: The Rise and Fall of the Turkish Empire.* New York: William Morrow, 1977.

Klier, John Doyle, and Shlomo Lambroza eds. *Pogroms: Anti-Jewish Violence in Modern Russian History.* Cambridge: Cambridge University Press, 1992.

Knight, Edward Frederick. *The Awakening of Turkey: A History of the Turkish Revolution.* Philadelphia: J. B. Lippincott, 1909.

Koprülü, M. Fuad. *The Origins of the Ottoman Empire.* Edited and translated by Gary Leiser. New York: State University of New York Press, 1992.

Kostić, Lazo M. *The Holocaust in the Independent State of Croatia: An Account Based on German, Italian, and the Other Sources.* Chicago: Liberty, 1981.

Krämer, Gudrun. *A History of Palestine, from the Ottoman Conquest to the Founding of the State of Israel.* Translated by Graham Harman and Gudrun Krämer. Princeton: Princeton University Press, 2008.

Krstić, Dušan, and Goran Marić, eds. *Jasenovac—Donja Gradina: The Industry of Death, 1941–1945.* Belgrade: Svetlopisno odeljenje, 2005.

Kupferschmidt, Uri M. *The Supreme Muslim Council: Islam under the British Mandate for Palestine.* Leiden: Brill, 1987.

Lacqueur, Walter. *A History of Zionism: From the French Revolution to the Establishment of the State of Israel.* eBook. New York: Schocken Books: 2009.

Landau, Zbigniew, and Jerzy Tomaszewski. *The Polish Economy in the Twentieth Century.* Translated by Wojciech Roszkowski. London: Croon Helm, 1985.

Langerbein, Helmut. *Hitler's Death Squads: The Logic of Mass Murder* (College Station, TX : Texas A&M University Press, 2004.

Lawrence, T. E. *Seven Pillars of Wisdom.* London: Wordsworth Editions, 1997.

Lebeli, Jennie. *Until The "Final Solution:" The Jews in Belgrade, 1521–1942* (Bergenfield, NJ: Avotaynu, 2007).

Lemkin, Raphaël. *Axis Rule in Occupied Europe: Laws of Occupation, Analysis of Government, Proposals for Redress.* Washington, DC: Carnegie Endowment for International Peace, 1944.

Levin, Itamar. *Locked Doors: The Seizure of Jewish Property in Arab Countries.* Translated by Rachel Neiman. Westport, CT: Praeger, 2001.

Lepre, George. *Himmler's Bosnian Division: The Waffen-SS Handschar Division 1943–1945.* Atglen, PA: Schiffer Military History, 1997.

Lewis, Bernard. *Cultures in Conflict: Christians, Muslims, and Jews in the Age of Discovery.* New York: Oxford University Press, 1996.

Lewis, Bernard, ed. *Islam and the Arab World.* London: Alfred A. Knopf, 1976.

Lewis, Bernard, ed. and trans. *Islam from the Prophet Mohammed to the Capture of Constantinople, Vol. 1: Politics and War.* New York: Oxford University Press, 1987.

Lewis, Bernard. *The Jews of Islam.* Princeton: Princeton University Press, 1987.

Lewis, Bernard. *Semites and Anti-Semites: An Inquiry into Conflict and Prejudice.* New York: W. W. Norton, 1999.

Longrigg, Stephen. *Four Centuries of Modern Iraq.* Oxford: Clarendon Press, 1925. Reprint, Farnborough, UK: Gregg International Publishers, 1968.

Longrigg, Stephen. *Oil in the Middle East: Its Discovery and Development.* London: Oxford University Press, 1968.

Longrigg, Stephen. *Syria and Lebanon under French Mandate.* London: Oxford University Press, 1958.

Lyman, Robert. *First Victory: Britain's Forgotten Struggle in the Middle East, 1941.* London: Constable and Robinson, 2006.

Lyman, Robert. *Iraq 1941: The Battles for Basra, Habbaniya, Fallujah, and Baghdad.* Oxford: Osprey, 2006.

MacArthur, Brian, ed. *The Penguin Book of Twentieth-Century Speeches.* London and New York: Penguin, 2000.

Manz, Beatrice Forbes. *The Rise and Rule of Tamerlane.* Cambridge UK: Cambridge University Press, 1989.

Manzhulo, A.N., ed. *The USSR and International Economic Relations.* London: Central Books, 1987.

Marcus, Jacob Rader, and Marc Saperstein. *The Jew in the Medieval World: A Source Book, 315–1791.* Cincinnati: Hebrew Union College Press, 1999.

Marlowe, John. *Late Victorian: The Life of Sir Arnold Talbot Wilson.* London: Cresset Press, 1967.

Marrus, Michael Robert, and Robert O. Paxton. *Vichy France and The Jews.* Stanford: Stanford University Press, 1996.

Masters, Bruce. *Christians and Jews in the Ottoman Arab World: The Roots of Sectarianism.* Cambridge: Cambridge University Press, 2001.

Marix Evans, Martin. *Encyclopedia of the Boer War.* Oxford: ABC-CLIO, 2000.

Mattar, Philip. *The Mufti of Jerusalem: Al-Hajj Amin al-Husayni and the Palestinian National Movement.* New York: Columbia University Press, 1988.

Mendes-Flohr, Paul R., and Jehuda Reinharz, eds. *The Jew in the Modern World: A Documentary History.* Oxford: Oxford University Press, 1980.

Merkley, Paul. *The Politics of Christian Zionism, 1891–1948.* London: Frank Cass, 1988.

Miller, Geoffrey. *Straits: British Policy towards the Ottoman Empire and the Origins of the Dardanelles Campaign.* Hull, UK: University of Hull, 1997.

Mineau, André. *Operation Barbarossa: Ideology and Ethics against Human Dignity.* Amsterdam: Rodopi, 2004.

Mitchell, Ruth. *The Serbs Choose War.* Garden City, NY: Doubleday, 1943.

Moberly, Brigadier General F. J. *History of the Great War: The Campaign in Mesopotamia, 1914–1918.* Vols. I–III. London: H. M. Stationery Office, 1925.

Moreh, Shmuel, and Zvi Yehuda, eds. *Al-Farhūd: The 1941 Pogrom in Iraq.* Jerusalem: Hebrew University Magnes Press, 2010.

Morgan, David. *The Mongols.* Oxford, UK: Basil Blackwell, 1986.

Morgenthau, Henry. *Ambassador Morgenthau's Story.* Garden City, NY: Doubleday, Page and Co., 1918.

Morony, Michael G. *Iraq after the Muslim Conquest*. Princeton: Princeton University Press, 1984.

Morris, Benny. *Righteous Victims: A History of the Zionist-Arab Conflict, 1881–2001*. New York: Vintage Books, 2001.

Muñoz, Antonio J. *The East Came West: Muslim, Hindu, and Buddhist Volunteers in the German Armed Forces, 1941–1945*. Bayside, NY: Axis Europa, 2001.

Muslih, Muhammad Y. *The Origins of Palestinian Nationalism*. New York: Columbia University Press, 1988.

Mwakikagile, Godfrey. *Africa and the West*. Huntington, NY: Nova Science Publishers, 2000.

Nelson, Keith. *Victors Divided: America and the Allies in Germany, 1918–1923*. Berkeley: UC Press, 1975.

Nicolle, David. *The Mongol Warlords: Genghis Khan, Kublai Khan, Hulegu, Tamerlane*. Poole, UK: Firebird Books, 1990.

Nini, Yehuda. *The Jews of the Yemen, 1800–1914*. Translated by H. Galai. Chur, Switzerland: Harwood Academic Publishers, 1991.

Nissen, Hans J., Peter Damerow, and Robert K. Englund. *Archaic Bookkeeping: Early Writing and Techniques of Economic Administration in the Ancient Near East*. Translated by Paul A. Larsen. Chicago: University of Chicago Press, 1993.

*NIV Exhaustive Concordance*. Grand Rapids, MI: Zondervan, 1990.

*NIV Study Bible*, 10th Anniversary Edition. Grand Rapids, MI: Zondervan, 1995.

Nordau, Max Simon, and Gustav Gottheil. *Zionism and Anti-Semitism*. New York: Fox, Duffield and Co., 1905.

Oliel, Jacob. *Les Camps de Vichy: Maghreb-Saraha, 1939–1945*. Montréal: Éditions du Lys, 2005.

Palmer, Alan. *The Banner of Battle: The Story of the Crimean War*. London: Weidenfeld and Nicolson, 1987.

Palmer, Alan. *The Decline and Fall of the Ottoman Empire*. New York: M. Evans and Co., 1992.

Pasachoff, Naomi E., and Robert J. Littman. *A Concise History of the Jewish People*. Lanham, MD: Rowman and Littlefield, 2005.

Patterson, David. *A Genealogy of Evil: Anti-Semitism from Nazism to Islamic Jihad*. New York: Cambridge University Press, 2010.

Phillips, E. D. *The Mongols*. New York: Praeger, 1969.

Poliakov, Leon. *The Aryan Myth: A History of Racist and Nationalist Ideas in Europe*. New York: Basic Books, 1974.

Porath, Yehoshua. *The Emergence of the Palestinian-Arab National Movement, 1918–1929*. London: Frank Cass, 1974.

Porath, Yehoshua. *The Palestinian Arab National Movement: From Riots to Rebellion, 1929–1939*. (Vol. 2.) London: Frank Cass, 1977.

Postgate, J. N. *Early Mesopotamia: Society and Economy at the Dawn of History*. London: Routledge, 1994.

Pritchard, J. B., ed. *Ancient Near Eastern Texts Relating to the Old Testament*. Princeton, NJ: Princeton University Press, 1969.

Quataert, Donald. *The Ottoman Empire, 1700–1922*. Cambridge, UK: Cambridge University Press, 2000.

Rabinowitz, Ezekiel. *Justice Louis D. Brandeis: The Zionist Chapter of His Life*. New York: Philosophical Library, 1968.

Ramadan, Tariq. *In the Footsteps of the Prophet: Lessons from the Life of Muhammad*. New York: Oxford University Press, 2007.

Ramazani, Rouhollah K. *The Foreign Policy of Iran: A Developing Nation in World Affairs, 1500–1941*. Charlottesville, VA: University Press of Virginia, 1966.

Ratchnevsky, Paul. *Genghis Khan, His Life and Legacy*. Edited and translated by Thomas Nivison Haining. Oxford, UK: Basil Blackwell, 1991.

Reinharz, Jehuda. *Fatherland or Promised Land: The Dilemma of the German Jew, 1893–1914*. Ann Arbor: University of Michigan, 1975.

Rejwan, Nissim. *The Many Faces of Islam: Perspectives on a Resurgent Civilization*. Gainesville, FL: University Press of Florida, 2000.

Rejwan, Nissim. *The Last Jews in Baghdad: Remembering a Lost Homeland*. Austin: University of Texas Press.

Rezun, Miron. *The Iranian Crisis of 1941—The Actors: Britain, Germany, and the Soviet Union*. Köln; Wien: Böhlau Verlag, 1982.

Rezun, Miron. *The Soviet Union and Iran: Soviet Policy in Iran from the Beginnings of the Pahlavi Dynasty to the Soviet Invasion in 1941*. Leiden: Sijthoff and Noordhoff, 1981.

Ritchie, Berry. *Portrait in Oil: An Illustrated History of BP*. London: James and James, 1995.

Rivelli, Marco Aurelio, *Le Génocide Occulté: État Indépendant de Croatie, 1941–1945*. [In French.] Lausanne: Editions L'Age d'Homme: 1998.

Rizq Allāh Ghanīmah, Yūsuf. *A Nostalgic Trip into the History of the Jews of Iraq*. Translation, Introduction, and Update by Reading A Dallal. Edited by Sheila Dallal. Lanham, MD: University Press of America, 1998.

Robinson, Francis, ed. *The Cambridge Illustrated History of the Islamic World*. Cambridge, UK: Cambridge University Press, 1996.

Robertson, Ritchie, and Edward Timms, eds. *Theodor Herzl and the Origins of Zionism*. Edinburgh: Edinburgh University Press, 1997.

Rogan, Eugene L., and Avi Shlaim, eds. *The War for Palestine*. New York: Cambridge University Press, 2001.

Rose, Norman. *Chaim Weizmann: A Biography*. New York: Viking, 1986.

Rosenhaft, Eve. *Beating the Fascists: The German Communists and Political Violence, 1929–1933*. Cambridge: Cambridge University Press, 1983.

Roth, Martha T. *Law Collections from Mesopotamia and Asia Minor*. Atlanta, GA: Scholars Press, 1997.

Roux, Georges. *Ancient Iraq*. New York: Penguin Putnam, 1992.

Ruppin, Arthur. *The Jews of To-day*. Translated by Margery Bentwith. New York: Henry Holt and Co., 1913.

Sachar, Howard M. *A History of Israel: From the Rise of Zionism to Our Time*. New York: Alfred A. Knopf, 2007.

Sasson, Jack M., ed. *Civilizations of the Ancient Near East*. New York: Scribner, 1995.

Satloff, Robert. *Among the Righteous: Lost Stories from the Holocausts Long Reach into Arab Lands*. New York: Public Affairs, 2006.

Saunders, J. J. *The History of the Mongol Conquests*. Philadelphia, PA: University of Pennsylvania Press, 1971.

Schapiro, Leonard. *The Russian Revolutions of 1917*. New York: Basic Books, 1984.

Schechtman, Joseph B. *The Mufti and the Fuehrer: The Rise and Fall of Haj Amin el-Husseini*. New York: Thomas Yoseloff, 1965.

Schmandt-Besserat, Denise. *Before Writing*. Austin, TX: University of Texas Press, 1992.

Schwanitz, Wolfgang. *Germany and the Middle East, 1871–1945*. Princeton: Markus Weiner, 2004.

Schoeman, Roy H. *Salvation Is From the Jews: The Role of Judaism in Salvation History*. San Francisco: Ignatius Press, 2003.

Schonfield, Hugh. *The Suez Canal in Peace and War, 1869–1969*. Coral Gables, FL: University of Miami Press, 1969.

Schoolman, Leonard A. *Reform Judaism and Zionism: One Perspective*. New York: Union of American Hebrew Congregations, 1983.

Schreckenberg, Heinz. *The Jews in Christian Art: An Illustrated History*. New York: Continuum, 1996.

Segev, Tom. *One Palestine, Complete: Jews and Arabs under the British Mandate*. Translated by Haim Watzman,. New York: Henry Holt, 2000.

Service, Robert. *A History of Twentieth Century Russia*. Cambridge, MA: Harvard Press, 1998.

Service, Robert. *The Russian Revolution*. Hampshire, UK: Macmillan, 1991.

Shamash, Violette. *Memories of Eden: A Journey through Jewish Baghdad*. Edited by Mira Rocca and Tony Rocca. Surrey, UK: Forum, 2008.

Shaul, Anwar. *The Story of My Life in Mesopotamia (Memoirs)*. Jerusalem: Association of Jewish Academics from Iraq, 1980.

Shaw, J. V. W. ed. *A Survey of Palestine, Prepared in December 1945 and January 1946 for the Information of the Anglo-American Committee of Inquiry*. Vols. 1–3. Jerusalem: Government Printer, 1946–1947.

Shaw, Stanford J., and Ezel Kural Shaw. *The History of the Ottoman Empire and Modern Turkey, Vol. II: Reform, Revolution, and Republic—The Rise of Modern Turkey, 1808–1975*. Cambridge, UK: Cambridge University Press, 1977.

Shay, Shaul. *Islamic Terror and the Balkans*. New Brunswick, NJ: Transaction Publishers, 2009.

Shimoni, Gideon. *The Zionist Ideology*. Hanover, NH: Brandeis Press, 1995.

Shirer, William. *Rise and Fall of the Third Reich*. New York: Simon and Shuster, 1981.

Shulewitz, Malka Hillel, ed. *The Forgotten Millions: The Modern Jewish Exodus from Arab Lands*. London: Cassel, 1999.

Simon, Reeva S. *Iraq Between the Two World Wars: The Militarist Origins of Tyranny*. New York: Columbia University Press, 2004.

Simon, Reeva S., Michael M. Laskier, and Sara Reguer, eds. *The Jews of the Middle East and North Africa in Modern Times*. New York: Columbia University Press, 2003.

Simpson, Christopher. *Blowback.* New York: Weidenfeld and Nicolson, 1988.

Slater, Robert. *Rabin of Israel.* New York: St. Martin's Press, 1993.

Smith, Barbara Jean. *The Roots of Separatism in Palestine: British Economic Policy, 1920–1929.* Syracuse, NY: Syracuse University Press, 1993.

Sonn, Tamara. *A Brief History of Islam.* Malden, MA: Blackwell, 2004.

Speer, Albert. *Inside the Third Reich: Memoirs.* New York: Simon & Schuster, 1970.

Spuler, Bertold. *History of the Mongols, Based on Eastern and Western Accounts of the Thirteenth and Fourteenth Centuries.* Translated by Helga and Stuart Drummond. Berkeley, CA: University of California Press, 1972.

Stein, Kenneth W. *The Land Question in Palestine, 1917–1939.* Chapel Hill, NC: University of North Carolina Press, 1984.

Stein, George H. *The Waffen SS: Hitler's Elite Guard at War, 1939–1945.* Ithaca, NY: Cornell University Press, 1966.

Stillman, Norman A. *The Jews of Arab Lands: A History and Source Book.* Philadelphia, PA: Jewish Publication Society of America, 1979.

Stillman, Norman A. *The Jews of Arab Lands in Modern Times.* Philadelphia; New York: The Jewish Publication Society, 1991.

Suissa, Michal Rachel, ed. *Hebron: Rebirth from Ruins.* Hebron: Jewish Community of Hebron, 2009.

*The Swastika: The Earliest Known Symbol and its Migrations, with Observations.* Washington, DC: Smithsonian Institution, Government Printing Office, 1896.

Tama, Diogene, trans. *Transactions of the Parisian Sanhedrin: or, Acts of the Assembly of Israelitish Deputies of France and Italy, Convoked at Paris by an Imperial and Royal Decree Dated May 30, 1806.* London: 1807.

Tarbell, Ida M. *The History of the Standard Oil Company.* New York: Macmillan, 1904. Reprint, Gloucester, MA: Peter Smith, 1963.

Tauber, Eliezer. *The Arab Movements in World War I.* London: Frank Cass, 1993.

Tessler, Mark. *A History of the Israeli-Palestinian Conflict.* Bloomington, IN: Indiana University Press, 1994.

Teveth, Shabtai. *Moshe Dayan: The Soldier, the Man, the Legend.* Translated by Leah and David Zinder. Boston: Houghton Mifflin, 1973.

Tomasevich, Jozo. *War and Revolution in Yugoslavia, 1941–1945: Occupation and Collaboration.* Stanford: Stanford University Press, 2001.

Townshend, Maj. Gen. Charles Vere Ferrers. *My Campaign.* Vols. I and II. New York: The James A. McCann Company, 1920.

Toynbee, Arnold, J., ed. *The Treatment of Armenians in the Ottoman Empire.* London: Hodder and Stoughton, 1916.

Tripp, Charles. *A History of Iraq.* Cambridge, UK: Cambridge University Press, 2000.

Vardy, Steven Bela, T. Hunt Tooley, and Agnes Huszar Vardy, eds. *Ethnic Cleansing in Twentieth-Century Europe.* Boulder, CO: East European Monographs, 2003.

Verrier, Anthony, ed. *Agents of Empire: Anglo-Zionist Intelligence Operations 1915–1919.* London: Brassey's, 1995.

Vital, David. *The Origins of Zionism.* Oxford: Clarendon Press, 1975.

Vital, David. *Zionism: The Formative Years.* Oxford: Clarendon Press, 1982.

Volodarskiĭ, Mikhail I. *The Soviet Union and Its Southern Neighbours: Iran and Afghanistan, 1917–1933.* Portland, OR: Frank Cass, 1994.

Voss, Carl Hermann, ed. *Stephen S. Wise: Servant of the People.* Philadelphia: Jewish Publication Society of America, 1969.

Warner, Geoffrey. *Iraq and Syria, 1941.* Newark, DE: University of Delaware Press, 1974.

Wasserstein, Bernard. *The British in Palestine: The Mandatory Government and the Arab-Jewish Conflict, 1917–1929.* Oxford: Basil Blackwell, 1991.

Weisgal, Meyer W., ed. *Theodor Herzl: A Memorial.* New York: New Palestine, 1929.

Weizmann, Chaim. *Trial and Error: The Autobiography of Chaim Weizmann.* New York: Harper and Brothers, 1949.

Weizmann, Chaim. *Letters and Papers of Chaim Weizmann: December 1931–April 1952, Series B.* Vol. 2. Edited by Barnet Litvinoff. New Brunswick, NJ: Transaction Books, 1984.

Weizmann, Chaim. *Letters and Papers of Chaim Weizmann.* Vol. 14. Edited by C. Dresner. Jerusalem: Israel University Press, 1978.

Wheatcroft, Andrew. *The Ottomans: Dissolving Images.* London: Viking, 1995.

Wilson, Lt. Col. Sir Arnold T. *Loyalties, Mesopotamia, 1914–1917: A Personal and Historical Record*. London: Oxford University Press, 1930.

Wilson, Lt. Col. Sir Arnold T. *Mesopotamia 1917–1920, A Clash of Loyalties: A Personal and Historical Record*. London: Oxford University Press, 1931.

Wise, Stephen. *Challenging Years: The Autobiography of Stephen Wise*. New York: Putnam, 1949.

Xenophon. *Cyropaedia*. Translated by H. G. Dakyns. [eBook, www.gutenberg.net.] Champaign, IL: Gutenberg Project, 2002.

Yad Vashem Studies on the European Jewish Catastrophe and Resistance. Jerusalem: Yad Vashem, 1958.

Yaron, Reuven. *The Laws of Eshnunna*. Jerusalem, Israel: Magnes Press, Hebrew University, 1969.

Ye'or, Bat. *The Dhimmi: Jews and Christians under Islam*. Translated by David Maisel, Paul Fenton, and David Littman. Cranbury, NJ: Fairleigh Dickinson University Press, 2003.

Ye'or, Bat. *Eurabia: The Euro-Arab Axis*. Cranbury, NJ: Associated University Presses, 2005.

Young, Kenneth. *Arthur James Balfour: The Happy Life of the Politician, Prime Minister, Statesman, and Philosopher, 1848–1930*. London: G. Bell and Sons, 1963.

Zarembina, Natalia. *Oswiecim, Camp of Death*. Translated by the Polish Labor Federation. New York: Poland Fights, 1944.

**Journals and Periodicals:**

*Administrative Science Quarterly*
*American Ethnologist*
*American Historical Review*
*American Jewish Historical Quarterly*
*American Journal of Archaeology*
*The American Journal of International Law*
*The American Journal of Semitic Languages and Literatures*
*Annals of the American Academy of Political and Social Science*
*Association for Jewish Studies Review (AJS Review)*
*The Atlanta Constitution*
*The Atlantic Monthly*
*British Journal of Middle Eastern Studies*
*Bulletin (British Society for Middle Eastern Studies)*
*Bulletin of the Business Historical Society*
*Bulletin of the School of Oriental Studies, University of London*
*Bulletin of the School of Oriental and African Studies (BSOAS), University of London*
*Business History Review*
*Canadian Jewish Chronicle*
*Canadian Journal of Sociology*
*Central European History*
*Christian Science Monitor*
*Economic Geography*
*The Economic History Review*
*Egypt Today*
*The English Historical Review*
*Evolutionary Anthropology*
*Fortune*
*The Geographical Journal*
*Harvard International Law Journal*
*Harvard Journal of Asiatic Studies*
*The Historian*
*The Historical Journal*
*The Historical Review*
*History Workshop*
*Holocaust and Genocide Studies*
*The Independent*
*Insight: News and Views for the Process, Power and Offshore Industries*
*International Affairs*
*International Journal of Middle East Studies*
*International Migration Review*
*International Organization*

*Israel Ministry of Foreign Affairs Newsletter*
*Jerusalem Studies in Arabic and Islam*
*Jewish Historical Studies*
*Jewish History*
*Jewish Quarterly*
*The Jewish Quarterly Review (JQR), New Series*
*Jewish Social Studies*
*Jewish Telegraphic Agency (JTA)*
*Journal of the American Oriental Society*
*Journal of Contemporary History*
*The Journal of Economic History*
*Journal of Field Archaeology*
*Journal of Interdisciplinary Studies in History and Archaeology*
*Journal of Israeli History*
*The Journal of Military History*
*The Journal of Modern History*
*Journal of Near Eastern Studies*
*Journal of Palestine Studies*
*The Journal of Political Economy*
*The Journal of Religion*
*Journal of the Royal Geographical Society of London*
*Journal of World Prehistory*
*League of Nations Official Journal*
*Leo Baeck Institute Yearbook (LBIY)*
*The Manchester Guardian (MG)*
*MERIP Reports*
*Middle Eastern Studies*
*Military Affairs*
*The Mississippi Valley Historical Review*
*Modern Judaism*
*The Nation*
*The New York Times*
*New York Tribune (NY Tribune)*
*Nordic Journal of African Studies*
*Notes and Records of the Royal Society of London*
*OAH Magazine of History*
*Past and Present*
*Patterns of Prejudice*
*PMLA*
*Political Science Quarterly*
*Proceedings of the American Academy for Jewish Research*
*Proceedings of the Royal Geographical Society of London*
*The Quarterly Journal of Economics*
*The Scientific Monthly*
*Slavic Review*
*Smithsonian Magazine*
*Speculum: A Journal of Mediaeval Studies*
*Time*
*Transactions of the American Philosophical Society*
*Transactions of the Institute of British Geographers, New Series*
*Die Welt des Islams*
*The Westminster Review*
*Wiener Library Bulletin*
*Year Book of the Central Conference of American Rabbis*

**Newspapers, Magazines, Wire Services and Other Media**
*al-'Alam al-'Arab (Jeruslem)*
*al-Alem al-Arabi (Baghdad)*
ABC News

British Broadcasting Corporation (BBC)
Cable News Network (CNN)
CBS News
*The Chicago Tribune (Chi Trib)*
*al-Difa*
*Filastine*
*The Guardian*
*al-Jami'ah al-Arabiah*
*al-Jami'a al-Islamiah*
*The Jerusalem Post*
*Jewish Chronicle*
*Jewish Daily Bulletin (JDB)*
*Life*
*London Gazette*
*Los Angeles Times (LA Times)*
*The Manchester Guardian (MG)*
*The Nation*
*The New York Times (NYT)*
*The New York Tribune (NY Trib)*
*North American Review*
*The Palestine Post*
Public Broadcasting System (PBS)
*al-Sirat al-Mustaqim*
Sky News
*Sunday Times*
*Time*
*The Times (London)*
*The Wall Street Journal (WSJ)*
*The Washington Post (WP)*
*Women's Studies Quarterly*

## Secondary Sources

**Papers, Lectures, and Conference Proceedings**

Dabbeek, Jalal, and Radwan El-Kelani. "Local Site Effects in Palestinian Cities: A Preliminary Study Based on Nablus Earthquake of July 11, 1927 and the Earthquake of February 11, 2004." First International Conference of Applied Geophysics for Engineering. Messina, ME, Italy: Università di Messina: October 13–15, 2004.
Englund, Robert K. Lecture. Connecticut: University of Connecticut, April 2004.
"Jasenovac: Proceedings of the First International Conference and Exhibit on the Jasenovac Concentration Camps," Oct 29–31, 1997, Kingsborough Community College of the City University of New York.
Rosenblatt, Naomi R. "Oil and the Eastern Front: U.S. Foreign and Military Policy in Iran, 1941–1945." Penn Humanities Forum, Mellon Undergraduate Research Fellowship: Final Paper, April 2009

**Unpublished Manuscripts**

Allen, G. Donald. "Babylonian Mathematics."
Batinić, Jelena. "Gender, Revolution, and War: The Mobilization of Women in The Yugoslav Partisan Resistance during World War II." Ph D diss., Stanford University, 2009.
Church, Matthew. "The Imperial Attachment to the Suez Canal from 1914 to 1945."
Englund, Robert K. "Proto-Cuneiform Account-Books and Journals." April 2004.
Kanwar, Ranvir Singh. "States, Firms and Oil: British Policy, 1939–54." Ph D diss., University of Warwick, 2000.
Longrigg, Stephen H. *The Origins and Early History of the Iraq Petroleum Company, Known from 1912 to 1929 as the Turkish Petroleum Company.* BP Archives, 1968.

# INDEX

437

Made in the USA
Middletown, DE
21 September 2018